MW00558839

The Death of a Prophet

DIVINATIONS: REREADING
LATE ANCIENT RELIGION

Series Editors
Daniel Boyarin, Virginia Burrus, Derek Krueger

A complete list of books in the series
is available from the publisher.

The Death of a Prophet

The End of Muhammad's Life and the Beginnings of Islam

Stephen J. Shoemaker

PENN

UNIVERSITY OF PENNSYLVANIA PRESS

PHILADELPHIA

Copyright © 2012 University of Pennsylvania Press

All rights reserved. Except for brief quotations used for purposes of review or scholarly citation, none of this book may be reproduced in any form by any means without written permission from the publisher.

Published by
University of Pennsylvania Press
Philadelphia, Pennsylvania 19104-4112
www.upenn.edu/pennpress

Printed in the United States of America on acid-free paper

2 4 6 8 10 9 7 5 3 1

Library of Congress Cataloging-in-Publication Data
Shoemaker, Stephen J., 1968–
The death of a prophet : the end of Muhammad's life and the beginnings of Islam / Stephen J. Shoemaker. — 1st ed.
p. cm. — (Divinations : rereading late ancient religion)
Includes bibliographical references and index.
ISBN 978-0-8122-4356-7 (hardcover : alk. paper)
1. Islam—History. 2. Islam—Historiography.
3. Muhammad, Prophet, d. 632. I. Title.
BP55.S46 2002
297.6'35—dc23

2011016426

For Melissa

CONTENTS

INTRODUCTION

The publication of Patricia Crone and Michael Cook's controversial study *Hagarism* in 1977 unquestionably marks a watershed in the study of religious culture in the early medieval Near East, even if its significance has occasionally been underestimated by other specialists in this field.[1] In particular, this relatively slim volume highlighted the potential importance of non-Islamic literature for knowledge of religious (and secular) history in the seventh and eighth centuries, a so-called dark age for which sources are often sparse and spotty.[2] Perhaps more importantly, however, this study proposed a radical new model for understanding both the formation of the Islamic tradition and the general religious landscape of the early medieval Near East. Together with the contemporary works of John Wansbrough, *Hagarism* articulated an innovative reinterpretation of formative Islam as a faith intimately intertwined with the religious traditions of Mediterranean late antiquity and in need of extensive study in the context of this religiously complex and intercultural milieu.[3]

There are, it must be admitted, some considerable and undeniable flaws in *Hagarism*'s reinterpretation of formative Islam, as even its most sympathetic readers have often acknowledged. Most significantly, *Hagarism* has been rightly criticized for its occasionally uncritical use of non-Islamic sources in reconstructing the origins of Islam.[4] Wansbrough, for instance, asks rather pointedly of Crone and Cook's reconstruction: "Can a vocabulary of motives be freely extrapolated from a discrete collection of literary stereotypes composed by alien and mostly hostile observers, and thereupon employed to describe, even interpret, not merely the overt behavior but also the intellectual and spiritual development of helpless and mostly innocent actors?"[5] Undoubtedly, Wansbrough's question is intended as rhetorical and meant to impugn the value of non-Islamic sources for understanding earliest Islam. Nonetheless, I think that the most honest and accurate answer to this question is in fact, possibly. While such information perhaps cannot be freely extracted from these sources, when analyzed with some care they may potentially yield historically valuable information concerning the beginnings of Islam

The imperfections of *Hagarism* should not lead us to discount completely the important insights that both this study and its approach have to offer.[6] While some scholars have somewhat unfairly dismissed *Hagarism* and its approach as either hopelessly colonialist or methodologically flawed,[7] there is still much to gain from this seminal book. Wansbrough's more considered rejection of *Hagarism* reflects his concern for the overwhelming and historically distorting impact of "salvation history," that is, theologized, sacred history, on both the Islamic and non-Islamic sources, and in light of this he essentially committed himself to an historical agnosticism regarding the origins of Islam.[8] Yet such resignation is not our only option. Admittedly, both Wansbrough and Robert Hoyland after him have correctly noted that non-Muslim sources alone "cannot provide a complete and coherent account of the history of Early Islam," as was essentially proposed in *Hagarism*.[9] But this recognition does not somehow make non-Islamic witnesses to the religious history of the seventh and eighth centuries any less valuable as a whole than the early Islamic sources, and on particular points they may possibly report more reliably than the Islamic tradition, as this study will argue. Almost all the documentary resources for understanding the formative period of Islam, including even the Qur'ān, are highly problematic from a religious historian's viewpoint: these sources are frequently overwhelmed and controlled by a master narrative of sacred history, as well as being influenced by the social, political, and theological concerns of the particular groups that produced them. But such conditions do not present an altogether uncommon or impossible circumstance.

There are ways of extracting historically credible data from such "contaminated" repositories. We must deploy methods capable of identifying different types of bias and excavating information from these sources, along the lines of those techniques used to reconstruct the historical Jesus from the highly theologized narratives of the Christian gospels. This endeavor will not yield, to be sure, history "wie es eigentlich gewesen," but this was always a hyper-modern fantasy in any case.[10] Instead, we will be able to reconstruct a narrative (or quite possibly several narratives) of Islamic origins that possesses a degree of probability derived from the particular methodological principles used to assess the relative reliability of various testimonies concerning the formation of Islam. *Hagarism* opened the door to this new approach, and in its wake we must critically assess the strikingly dissimilar descriptions of earliest Islam often found in the non-Islamic sources of the seventh and eighth centuries and in the more traditional Islamic accounts from the later eighth and ninth centuries. While a great deal of investigation still remains to be done along these lines, the past two decades have already seen some excellent work in this area, much of it inspired by the initial insights of Crone and Cook.[11]

Rather than pursuing one of the many new issues that undoubtedly await exploration, the present study will return to what was surely one of *Hagarism*'s most startling revelations: its identification of widespread reports from seventh- and eighth-century writers that Muhammad was still alive and leading the Islamic community as his followers began their invasion of the Roman Near East. This indication is strikingly at odds with the traditional account of Muhammad's death before the Near Eastern conquest at Medina in 632, first recorded in the earliest Islamic biographies of the mid-eighth and ninth centuries. With so many unanswered questions still to pursue, one might rightly question the return to an issue raised now already over thirty years ago. There are, however, several reasons for doing so. In the first place, Crone and Cook merely note the existence of this discrepancy in the sources, gathering many of the most significant references together in an endnote. Instead of carefully evaluating the historical significance of these witnesses both individually and collectively, they conclude their list of references with only the remark: "The convergence is impressive."[12] Indeed it is, but can we say something more than this? Might a critical analysis of the sources give us some sense of how much historical weight they can bear, both individually and collectively? Is it possible that, even if Muhammad did not in fact lead the Islamic conquest of Palestine, this tradition might reveal something about the nature of formative Islam?

In all fairness, we are presently much better equipped to pose such questions, in large part due to the excellent work of Hoyland, most notably in his *Seeing Islam as Others Saw It*. Not only has Hoyland produced an outstanding catalogue of the many references to early Islam made in non-Islamic sources,[13] but he takes the project that was begun in *Hagarism* an important step forward by proposing a basic methodology for evaluating the significance of these sources, as well as providing examples of its application. In essence, Hoyland proposes that we should ask three basic questions of each potential witness to assess its historical worth: What is the source of its observation(s) about early Islam? What is the character of the observation? And what is the subject of the observation? The first question rather straightforwardly asks us to consider the reliability of each author's source: Was he himself an eyewitness to what he reports? Did she hear it from those who were eyewitnesses? Or is it merely hearsay or gossip?[14] Clearly there is a descending scale of reliability as one moves down this list. In addition, Hoyland suggests that we consider the nature of the observation itself: does the source report a "simple observation of fact," or does the information in question serve some sort of apologetic agenda or "totalizing explanation"?[15] "Simple observations," Hoyland suggests, will likely have a much higher degree of historical veracity. Somewhat related to this is the third principle, which questions the nature of the matter that the non-Islamic source describes: Is it something that an outsider would likely have accurate knowledge of? That is, does the statement reflect something that would be readily observable by a non-Muslim, or even better, is it something that would have directly affected non-Muslims? In such cases, the witness of non-Muslim writers is more likely to transmit reliable information. When the same writers comment on aspects of Islamic belief and intra-communal life, however, we must adopt a more skeptical approach to their reports.[16]

These are sound principles for assessing the relative worth of the various non-Islamic witnesses to the earliest history of Islam, to which I would add one further: the criterion of multiple, independent attestation, one of the oldest and most fundamental principles of modern biblical criticism and particularly important for studies of the historical Jesus.[17] As biblical scholars have long recognized, a higher degree of historical probability inheres in observations attested by several independent sources, since this pattern makes it highly unlikely that a particular writer has invented a given report. When a particular tradition from the non-Islamic sources meets all of these criteria, there is a significant probability that such a report reflects genuine information about the formative period of Islam. While it cannot be said with any certainty that these witnesses disclose what really happened, such reports present high-quality information that derives from the period in question. Nevertheless, despite their exceptional value, these testimonies should not simply be taken at face value, and they need to be compared critically with related traditions from the earliest Islamic sources.

When there is sharp disagreement with the canonical narratives of Islamic origins, as is the case with the circumstances of Muhammad's death, one must also subject the relevant Islamic sources to a similar scrutiny, in order to determine if the difference reflects the influence of later theological, political, literary, or other interests within the Islamic tradition. This process will involve bringing the full toolkit of historical criticism to bear on the traditions of the Qur'ān and the earliest narratives of Islamic origins, including elements of form criticism, tradition criticism, *Tendenz* criticism, and, whenever possible, source criticism and redaction criticism. Likewise, in such circumstances it will be important to look for any anomalies within the Islamic tradition that might corroborate the reports of the non-Islamic sources. Here the criterion of embarrassment or dissimilarity (that is, dissimilarity from the later tradition) is particularly valuable. According to this cornerstone of historical Jesus studies, material sharply at odds with the received tradition is unlikely to have been invented by the later community; such divergences from established belief and practice are instead likely remnants of an older formation, preserved in spite of their deviance on account of their antiquity.[18] When a number of witnesses converge to reveal the same discordant theme, there is a high probability that this material reflects a particularly early tradition that has been effaced from the canonical sources. Moreover, if evidence from the non-Islamic sources exhibits coherence with such anomalies in the early Islamic sources, then there is an even greater likelihood that this represents a primitive aspect of the Islamic faith that was either altered or abandoned by the later tradition.

Hoyland has recently questioned the value of this criterion of dissimilarity or embarrassment for the reconstruction of early Islam, characterizing such reasoning as "highly dubious."[19] As evidence against the value of this principle, Hoyland refers to John Burton's explanation of the Satanic Verses episode from Muhammad's early biographies: while scholars have overwhelmingly looked to this embarrassing moment from Muhammad's career as almost certainly genuine, since "it is unthinkable that the story could have been invented by Muslims,"[20] Burton suggests that the story was indeed invented to show "that Qur'anic verses could be divinely withdrawn without verbal replacement."[21] Nevertheless, Burton's rather complicated argument has not gained much traction, and his proposal that the entire story was invented simply to provide justification for a particular form of Qur'ānic abrogation is not very persuasive and certainly does not afford sufficient grounds for abolishing this core principle of historical and textual analysis.[22] Hoyland further remarks that the reasoning behind this criterion "implies that our modern views on what is favourable or not coincide with those of early Muslims." Yet Burton's alternative merely replaces this modern viewpoint with the arcane world of early Qur'ānic exegesis, and one must admit that it is certainly no less problematic to view the origins of Islam through the lens of the medieval Islamic tradition and its interpretive categories. In this regard, Gerald Hawting's analysis of the Satanic Verses tradition offers a far more compelling interpretation than Burton's, while also preserving the value of the criterion of dissimilarity.[23] Arguing on the basis of the Qur'ān, Hawting persuasively identifies angelic intercession rather than idolatry as the main issue here, establishing a credible context for this episode within the religious milieu reflected in the Qur'ān. Likewise, Hawting makes equally clear the improbability that the story is a later fabrication based on the Qur'ān, as well as explaining its suppression in many sources as a result of the Islamic tradition's association of Muhammad's opponents with polytheism and idolatry.[24]

Admittedly, Hoyland's caution that one must be careful about assuming that modern ideas of tension or contradiction within the Islamic tradition coincide with those of early Muslims is an important point. Such concerns certainly warrant constant and careful consideration, but they need not paralyze historical analysis: reconstruction of the past always involves viewing its events through the lens of the present, no matter which methods or criteria the historian applies.[25] No (post)modern historian can escape the limitations of her social and intellectual context, and as salubrious as Hoyland's warning is to historians in general, it seems there is no alternative "view from nowhere" that does not bring contemporary concerns and perspectives to the analysis of the past. If we are to abandon the toolkit of modern historical study simply because of its own historical contingencies, then we presumably must resign ourselves either to a radical historical agnosticism or to the indigenous critique of the Islamic tradition itself. Moreover, the application of this criterion of historical analysis is not simply a matter of judging a tradition "either false or authentic," as Hoyland somewhat incorrectly draws the dichotomy in his critique, but instead this method affords principles for identifying a probability that certain material is unlikely to have originated in specific historical circumstances. In the case of traditions that are strongly divergent from the beliefs and practices of second- and third-century Islam or its canonical memory of origins, one must admit that these are less likely to have been invented by the later community than traditions undergirding the classical Islam of the ʿAbbāsid era. While Hoyland's implicit critique of modern historiography's claim to divide truth from fiction is welcome, his rejection of this method of analysis for its failure to yield such objective results is not fully persuasive.

On the basis of these methodological principles, the present study will argue that the witness of certain non-Islamic sources that Muhammad survived to lead the invasion of Palestine preserves what is quite possibly a genuine early Islamic tradition, despite the fact that several recent articles would suggest otherwise. For instance, Hoyland, who generally advocates the value of non-Islamic sources for reconstructing early Islamic history, has somewhat surprisingly taken the opposing view. In his study of Muhammad's life as reported in Christian writings, Hoyland initially notes the clear witness of these sources to Muhammad's sustained vitality but then rather strangely concludes that these sources are collectively mistaken in their notice of a later date for Muhammad's death. Without much explanation at all, he declares the accuracy of the traditional Islamic sources on this matter, despite the fact that his own criteria could seem to favor the reliability of the Christian sources in this case.[26] To my knowledge the only other study to address the relationship between the various Christian accounts of the Arab conquests and the Islamic biographies of Muhammad specifically and in any detail is an article entitled "La 'Sira' du Prophète Mahomet et les conquêtes des arabes dans le Proche-Orient d'après les sources syriaques," an article published in the proceedings from a conference on the life of Muhammad some thirty years ago. Unfortunately, its author, Bertold Spuler, not only disregards some of the most important sources, but he rather astonishingly asserts the fundamental harmony of all the sources and completely overlooks their differences concerning Muhammad's involvement in the Palestinian campaign.[27] Finally, we may add to this a report in the popular media that Crone and Cook have allegedly "backed away from" their earlier views concerning the date of Muhammad's death as expressed in *Hagarism*, although I have not yet found any evidence of such a retraction in print.[28] In fact, to the contrary, Cook has maintained the significance of the non-Islamic sources on this point, writing in the same year as the article in question that "non-Muslim sources written in the following decades [after 632] give only very scrappy information and are subject to problems of their own. One point of interest is that they suggest that Muhammad was still alive when the Muslim expansion outside Arabia began."[29] Even more recently, Crone has similarly written that these sources "convey the impression that he was actually leading the invasions. Mohammad's death is normally placed in 632, but the possibility that it should be placed two or three years later cannot be completely excluded."[30]

In light of the rather negative assessment that this report of Muhammad's vitality during the Palestinian invasion has received in recent publications, it seems necessary to revisit the question of Muhammad's death, not so much with the goal of determining when he really died, but with an eye toward whether these non-Islamic sources may in fact preserve an early tradition that was subsequently revised as Islam's self-image and self-understanding were transformed. This book seeks to determine if Muhammad's leadership during the invasion of Palestine is something that might have comported with the beliefs of the earliest Muslims, insofar as they can be known, and, likewise, if are there reasons to suspect that there might have been cause to re-remember the end of his life differently at a later point. The larger purpose of this investigation thus lies not in the possibility of adjusting the date of Muhammad's death by a few years. Instead, this difference in the early sources affords an important opening through which to explore the nature of primitive Islam more broadly. Likewise, this study aims to demonstrate the potential value of non-Islamic sources for reconstructing the history of formative Islam, when these sources are used in a methodologically critical manner and in conjunction with, rather than isolation from, Islamic sources. While others have already made similar demonstrations, including Lawrence Conrad and Hoyland in particular,[31] in view of the generally negative reception of *Hagarism* and its approach within Islamic studies as a whole, it would appear that this point bears repeating.

A related goal of the study is to work toward narrowing the divide that exists between the study of religion and culture in Mediterranean late antiquity and the investigation of Islamic origins, an objective that it shares with much recent scholarship on late antiquity and early Islam.[32] In both its methods and its conclusions, this monograph presents a case for interpreting the beginnings of Islam more within the context of the broader late ancient world, rather than according to the more traditional view of Islam's formation in the relative isolation of the Ḥijāz. By interpreting the rise of Islam in continuity with, rather than separation from, the world of Mediterranean late antiquity, we are sure to gain new perspectives on both.[33] Moreover, this study aims to demonstrate the value of studying Islamic origins using the same methods and perspectives that have long been utilized in the investigation of early Christianity and early Judaism. The hermeneutics of suspicion have profoundly affected the modern study of formative Christianity and Judaism, but this skeptical approach has yet to significantly affect the comparatively more sanguine attitudes often displayed by scholars of early Islam. Accordingly this book is aimed not only at scholars of early Islam but also at scholars of the New Testament and early Christianity. It is hoped that by attempting to bridge the disciplines of Christian and Islamic origins methodologically this study might generate further comparative discussion among experts in both fields.

This investigation thus will adopt the more skeptical approach to the sources that is characteristic of the historical-critical study of early Christianity and the historical figure of Jesus. It expects of early Islamic traditions that they meet the same rigorous criteria that scholars of formative Christianity have applied in judging the historicity of traditions contained in early Christian literature. Although this study will treat traditional narratives of Islamic origins with a great deal of suspicion, this will not exceed the skepticism that scholars of religious history bring to bear on similar narratives of Christian origins. It is very important to stress this methodological consistency, particularly in light of the fact that the *sīra* traditions and their historicity have lately become a sensitive issue in contemporary Islam. While the medieval Islamic tradition was itself rather circumspect regarding the historical authenticity of these traditions, in more recent years, largely in response to the historical-critical study of these traditions in the West, the *sīra* traditions have become in the Islamic world "almost a holy writ, whose reliability was accepted almost without asking questions."[34] The result is a deep and widening gap between Western and Islamic interpretation of both the *sīra* traditions and the *ḥadīth* more generally: the methodological skepticism that guides much modern scholarship on these topics is often rejected out of hand by traditional Islamic scholarship and occasionally seen as an attack on Islam itself.

This divide between modern secular and traditional Islamic scholarship over the historical reliability of the *sīra* and *ḥadīth* presents an important context for understanding both the nature and intensions of this investigation into early Islamic history. This study and the methods that it employs are in no way aimed at casting doubt on the religious truth of the Islamic tradition. Instead, this book explores a particular aspect of formative Islam from a point of view outside the Islamic tradition, with explicit commitments to the principles of modern, secular historical criticism and the hermeneutics of suspicion rather than fidelity to the traditions and values of the Islamic faith. When approached from this secular perspective, with its specific concerns and commitments, the formative period of Islam will rather obviously look quite different than it does from within the *umma*. It is important to recognize, however, that both perspectives on Islamic origins are certainly valid, and within their own contexts and communities they are rightly understood to disclose truth. One approach interprets early Islam from the outside, confessing the skepticism of the secular academy, while the other presents a sacred history of formative Islam, a narrative that both shapes and is shaped by the Islamic faith and its community.

Neither perspective then can claim to represent an unbiased account of Islamic origins that somehow is obvious to any objective observer: both understandings are fully intelligible only within the particular interpretive communities that produce them. Moreover, one perspective does not necessarily invalidate the other, and the conclusions of traditional Islamic and modern secular scholarship can both rightly claim to be valid within their own cultural and intellectual contexts. In fact, it is quite possible for an individual to approach a particular issue simultaneously from both a secular point of view and a confessional one, as numerous Western scholars have demonstrated.[35] What must be conceded on all sides, however, is that truth depends on the context of an interpretive community, be it religious or secular, and there is no objective truth that will appear as such to every individual and in every cultural context. This approach then does not negate the truth of Islamic accounts of formative Islam: they are in fact true for those whose worldview has been and continues to be shaped most fundamentally by the Islamic tradition. Likewise, those outside the Islamic faith community will not necessarily find Islam's representation of its own early history to be true in the same way that Muslims do.[36] In similar fashion, however, secular knowledge must also recognize the situatedness of its own truth claims: it may only claim to be objective perhaps in the somewhat limited sense that it approaches Islam, for instance, from the outside and thus as an object of study.[37]

Finally, if some readers may perhaps think it entirely implausible that the Islamic tradition has incorrectly preserved something as significant as the time and place of its founder's death, a quick glance at formative Christianity is instructive. Undoubtedly many scholars of early Islam will want to persist in maintaining the accuracy of the traditional Islamic accounts of Muhammad's death and burial, regarding the deviant reports considered in this study as simply misinformed errors coming from those outside of the Islamic community. Yet it is not at all clear why the traditional Islamic narratives of Muhammad's death should warrant such implicit confidence, particularly in the face of this alternative early tradition. The simple fact that the Islamic accounts were produced by insiders in no way guarantees the accuracy of their information, any more so than one would presume that the Christian gospels accurately record the life and death of Jesus on the basis of their production by insiders. Indeed, to the contrary, it is for this very reason that New Testament scholars are generally suspicious of the gospel accounts, seeking to test them whenever possible by quality evidence drawn from external sources. This sharp contrast with the study of early Islam is seen quite clearly in F. E. Peters's recent comparative study, *Jesus and Muhammad*, where the discussion of Jesus begins with evidence from the "pagan" and

Jewish sources, while evidence from non-Islamic sources for the beginnings of Islam is rather strangely ignored.[38]

The earliest extant gospels were written between forty and seventy years after the death of Jesus, based in part on earlier literary sources that had begun to form perhaps some twenty years after his death, a considerably smaller interval than the time elapsed between Muhammad's death and his earliest biographies. Yet despite the fact that Jesus' biography took written form more quickly than did Muhammad's, the gospels have significant disagreements in chronology, including perhaps most famously the differences between the synoptic and Johannine gospels regarding the length of Jesus' ministry. Likewise, the date of Jesus' death, for instance, can only be known approximately: 28–33 CE.[39] Yet perhaps more comparable with the tradition of Muhammad's death in Medina are actually the accounts of Jesus' birth. These reveal that only half a century after Jesus' death, the early Christians had created a historically improbable tradition of his birth in Bethlehem to serve the needs of Christian salvation history.[40] Still more apt is the comparison of Islam's apostle with early Christian traditions about its apostles. Take, for example, the apostle Peter, whose death and burial are located in Rome by multiple, independent reports written just over a century after the fact: there is even an early tomb identified as the site of this burial. Yet there is considerable debate as to whether Peter was ever even in Rome, and the most recent analysis argues rather persuasively that in fact he was not.[41] Likewise, traditions from the second century identify Ephesus as the apostle John's final resting place, some of which are allegedly based on oral transmission spanning only two generations. Yet the strong consensus of New Testament scholarship rejects the accuracy of these reports.[42] If then early Christian traditions concerning Jesus and the apostles could be subject to such manipulation over the course of just a century or even less, how much more so might one expect to find similar developments in the early Islamic biographies of Muhammad, whose contents are widely regarded as highly stylized and untrustworthy.

Such adjustments to a religious tradition's memory of its early history are in fact not at all unusual and need not be judged as either deceptive or the product of some insidious conspiracy (as some scholars of early Islam have wanted to insist). To the contrary, it is quite common to find that a religious community has revised certain important aspects of its formative history to comport with its most cherished theological principles, as the Christian Nativity traditions bear witness. Often such revisions serve to extend and intensify the interpretive power and cohesion of a religion's core narrative by incorporating various important religious symbols and practices into the story of its origins. The early Christian gospel writers, like Muhammad's early biographers presumably, simply were not interested in writing an objective description of past events in the fashion that modern history values. Their narratives urgently seek to communicate the truth about Jesus Christ and the meaning of his life, death, and resurrection: to expect a dispassionate inventory of events would be both anachronistic and absurd. Moreover, the pious fictions of early Christian literature would be wrongly condemned as frauds or deceptions: to the contrary, they undoubtedly were efforts to proclaim the truth, as seen by the authors and their communities, with perfect clarity.[43] One would only expect that similar impulses and developments are to be found in the nascent Islamic tradition, and as I will argue, the early Islamic traditions of the end of Muhammad's life (much like the Christian Nativity traditions) appear to have adapted the arc of his biography to fit the needs of early Islamic identity and salvation history nearly a century after his death. Consequently, our knowledge of exactly when Muhammad died is not nearly as certain as much previous scholarship has assumed, and it seems we must accordingly adjust our historical estimate for the end of his life to sometime more approximately within the period 632–35 CE.

The first chapter of this study examines the various sources from the seventh and eighth centuries that attest to Muhammad's survival and leadership at the time of the initial assault on the Roman Near East, circa 634–65. Although later sources, particularly from the Christian tradition, continue to repeat this tradition, this chapter focuses on witnesses from the first century and a half after Muhammad's death. Sources from this period hold special value as potential bearers of early traditions that may subsequently have been displaced once the canonical narratives of Islamic origins came to be established during the later eighth century.[44] At that time, Ibn Isḥāq's officially sanctioned biography of Muhammad, as well as the teachings of other contemporary Medinan traditionists, began to be widely known. From this point onward, the life of Muhammad as remembered by Muslims and non-Muslims alike was largely governed by the contents of these canonical biographies. Early evidence of their influence outside of the Islamic tradition can be seen already in the early ninth-century *Chronicle* of Theophanes, which, owing to direct influence from Islamic sources, is the first non-Islamic source to "correctly" relate Muhammad's decease prior to the invasion of Palestine. The fact that later Christian sources, and in particular the Western Christian accounts of Muhammad's death surveyed by Etan Kohlberg, should largely adhere to the traditional Islamic chronology is merely testimony to the ascendency and authority of these canonical biographies within the Islamic tradition of the second and later centuries.[45]

Eleven different sources from this period, including even one from the Islamic tradition itself, indicate Muhammad's continued survival at the beginnings of Near Eastern conquests. Each of these documents is first evaluated individually to assess the quality of its testimony. Then, the chapter considers the collective value of these reports, reaching the conclusion that they convincingly bear witness to an early tradition that Muhammad was still alive and leading the Islamic community as his followers invaded Roman Syria and Palestine. This tradition, it would appear, reached each of the various religious communities of the early Islamic empire by the beginning of the second century AH, and it is not contradicted by the more traditional chronology of Muhammad's decease until after the composition of Ibn Isḥāq's influential biography of Muhammad around 750 CE. As such, this divergent tradition regarding the end of Muhammad's life merits serious historical consideration.

The following chapter turns to the traditional Islamic account of Muhammad's death and burial, focusing especially on Ibn Isḥāq's biography, the earliest surviving Islamic narrative of Muhammad's life and the beginnings of Islam. Here the details of Muhammad's sudden illness, his demise, and his interment as recorded in this collection are first described and then compared with other early biographical sources, in order to determine which traditions might possibly derive from earlier authorities. The results of this endeavor, however, prove rather meager, and most of the material concerning Muhammad's death and burial in Ibn Isḥāq's biography cannot be assigned to any earlier figure. While a limited number of traditions can be attributed to Ibn Isḥāq's teacher, al-Zuhrī (d. 742 CE), these reveal only Muhammad's sudden illness and death in an urban context, surrounded by his wives and in the vicinity of a place of prayer where his followers regularly gathered to worship. The location of Muhammad's death and burial in Medina and the chronology of these events relative to the Near Eastern conquests, however, cannot be ascribed with any assurance to al-Zuhrī. Ibn Isḥāq's biography remains the earliest witness to these traditions, and while one certainly cannot entirely exclude the possibility that he had received this information from al-Zuhrī or some other early authority, there is no evidence for this hypothesis.

This chapter continues to consider the issue of chronology within the early biographies of Muhammad more generally, observing that modern scholarship judges the traditional chronology of Muhammad's life to be among the most artificial and unreliable elements of these narratives, apparently devised by his biographers only near the end of the first Islamic century. Moreover, a handful of sources from the early Islamic tradition indicate either a period of seven or thirteen years for Muhammad's Medinan period (instead of ten years) or a date for the *hijra* of 624/25 (instead of 621/22): these variants reveal a significant pattern consistent with the possible revision of an earlier tradition of Muhammad's death in order to place these events prior to the invasion of Palestine. Finally, Chapter 2 examines several anomalous reports from Ibn Isḥāq's biography that could suggest traces of an older tradition associating Muhammad with the assault on Palestine. On the whole, these features of Muhammad's earliest biographies invite a possibility that the traditional memory of Muhammad's death in the Ḥijāz prior to the invasion of the Near East is a relatively recent development.

Nevertheless such significant revisions to the ending of Muhammad's life in early Islamic memory would seem to require some sort of substantial catalyst. Several broad literary tendencies of the early biographical traditions could seem to favor these changes, including particularly the strong influence of certain biblical typologies on the structure of the narrative. Nevertheless, while these tendencies may have contributed to such a reconfiguration of Muhammad's biography, they do not in themselves seem sufficient to have generated this change. The second half of this monograph accordingly identifies evidence of significant ideological shifts in early Islamic eschatology, confessional identity, and sacred geography that profoundly transformed the nature of Muhammad's original religious movement. These dramatic changes not only provide a context that can account for the existence of an early tradition associating Muhammad with the invasion of Palestine, but they also present circumstances that would explain a need to sever his connection with the Near Eastern conquest and instead to memorialize the death of Islam's founding prophet in the Ḥijāz.

Chapter 3 argues that Muhammad was an eschatological prophet who together with his earliest followers expected to witness the imminent end of the world in the divine judgment of the Hour, seemingly within his own lifetime. Much twentieth-century scholarship, particularly in English, has sought to minimize this aspect of earliest Islam, identifying Muhammad instead as a social-reforming prophet of ethical monotheism. But the evidence of the Qur'ān and certain early apocalyptic (or more precisely, eschatological) *ḥadīth* clearly show that Muhammad and the early members of his religious movement believed that they would soon see the end of history.[46] Moreover, it seems rather likely that the eschatological fervor shared by Muhammad and his earliest followers was a driving force behind the Islamic conquest of the Near East: their anticipation of the Hour was, it would appear, closely linked with the restoration of Abraham's descendants to the Promised Land. Yet when Muhammad died before the *eschaton*'s arrival and the Hour continued to be delayed, the early Muslims had to radically reorient their religious vision. The Hour was thus increasingly deferred into the distant future, and in less than a century Islam swiftly transformed itself from a religion expecting the end of the world to a religion that aimed to rule the world. In the course of such a profound transition, one would imagine that more than just the eschatological timetable was revised, and as the fourth chapter demonstrates, there were related changes in the nature of the early Islamic community's confessional boundaries and the location of its sacred geography.

The final chapter looks first at the seemingly nonsectarian nature of the early Islamic community.[47] Numerous signs point to the existence of a primitive, inter-confessional "community of the Believers" that welcomed Jews and apparently even Christians to full membership, so long as they subscribed to a simple profession of faith in "God and the last day." Muhammad does not appear to have been understood at this stage as a prophet of unique stature but was viewed instead as an eschatological herald who had been sent to warn the descendants of Abraham before the final judgment of the Hour. Unsurprisingly, the eschatological hopes of these early Believers looked to Jerusalem and Palestine, the Promised Land of their common inheritance, as the sacred landscape within which God would soon realize the climax of history. Although Muhammad's religious movement may perhaps have originated somewhere in the Ḥijāz, it seems clear that the western coast of Arabia was not originally its holy land. Jerusalem, and not Mecca and Medina, appears to have stood at the center of early Islam's sacred map, which is only to be expected if Islam began, as seems likely, as an eschatological faith grounded in a shared Abrahamic identity. Only as Islam progressively transformed itself over the course of the seventh century from an inter-confessional Abrahamic eschatological movement into the distinctively Arab faith of an empire defined by Muhammad's unique prophetic message did its sacred geography change accordingly. During this period, the Ḥijāzī cities of Mecca and Medina gradually emerged at the center of a new sacred geography more suited to the sectarian, Arabian faith of classical Islam. This struggle to redefine the Islamic holy land reached its climax in the events of the Second Civil War, a conflict that seems to have been partly grounded in competing ideas of sacred geography and whose outcome appears to have largely settled the matter in favor of the Ḥijāz.

These changing circumstances can persuasively explain the existence of an early tradition of Muhammad's leadership during his followers' invasion of Palestine as well as its eventual replacement. One would expect that a religious movement driven by an urgent eschatology focused on Jerusalem, which earliest Islam appears to have been, would have originally wanted to remember its founding prophet as leading the faithful into the Promised Land to meet the Final Judgment. Even if Muhammad never actually made it to the Holy Land, one can well imagine that his early followers would have come to remember their early history as such. Yet once the focus of Islamic devotion turned to Mecca and Medina, a new memory of Muhammad's quietus would be required, one that joined the fulfillment of his career to the newly consecrated landscape of the Ḥijāz: just such an account one finds in the canonical Islamic narratives of Muhammad's death.

The similarity of this hypothesis to the solution proposed by the authors of *Hagarism* certainly should not be missed. As the eschatological hopes of the early Believers went unfulfilled, Jerusalem and the Holy Land lost much of their significance, eventually to be replaced by the sacred cities of Mecca and Medina. Consequently, Crone and Cook conclude that "the Prophet was disengaged from the original Palestinian venture by a chronological revision whereby he died two years before the invasion began."[48] While certain other facets of *Hagarism*'s reconstruction of Islamic origins may now seem somewhat dubious, such as its proposal concerning an early Islamic messianism, the identification of earliest Islam as an eschatological movement focused on Jerusalem and the Holy Land remains persuasive and has been validated by much subsequent research. As this study argues, the reports indicating Muhammad's leadership during the Near Eastern conquests first identified by *Hagarism* most likely reflect an early Islamic tradition that was eventually abandoned: the information is attested by a wide range of high-quality sources, and the tradition's early acceptance as well as its eventual rejection both comport with certain major changes in the development of primitive Islam.

Finally, while some scholars of Islam might protest that such an approach merely perpetuates the sins of earlier Orientalist scholarship, I would argue that such accusations are neither very helpful nor warranted. To be sure, the manner in which we choose to represent other cultures, and particularly those cultures that have been victims of Western colonization and aggression, demands serious and constant reflection.[49] Out of such concerns, many scholars from both the Islamic world and the West have proposed that the academic study of Islam must accordingly respect Islamic truth claims regarding Islam's most authoritative traditions, the Qur'ān and the Sunna, and refrain from subjecting them to historical criticism. To do otherwise, some would maintain, is to commit what essentially amounts to an act of intellectual colonialism.[50] Although I deeply sympathize with the concerns that give rise to this position, it simply does not present an adequate solution in my view, at least not from the vantage of the academic discipline of religious studies.[51] Insofar as the approach taken in this study merely applies methods and perspectives of analysis to formative Islam that have now for well over a century been utilized in the study of Jewish and Christian origins, one must recognize just how "othering" it is to insist that Islam—and it alone—should be shielded from similar study. One thereby runs the risk of presenting the Islamic tradition in comparison as something fragile and pristine, whose unique perspective is somehow harmed by the application of modern criticism. Thus, while the broader political context identified by Edward Said as well as many others certainly cannot be simply ignored, I would argue that it is at the same time essential, for both intellectual and pedagogical reasons, to conduct investigations into the earliest history of Islam, as Chase Robinson recommends, "committed to the idea that the history made by Muslims is comparable to that made by non-Muslims."[52]

CHAPTER I

"A Prophet Has Appeared, Coming with the Saracens"

Muhammad's Leadership during the Conquest of Palestine According to Seventh- and Eighth-Century Sources

At least eleven sources from the seventh and eighth centuries indicate in varied fashion that Muhammad was still alive at the time of the Palestinian conquest, leading his followers into the Holy Land some two to three years after he is supposed to have died in Medina according to traditional Islamic accounts. As will be seen, not all of these witnesses attest to Muhammad's leadership with the same detail: some are quite specific in describing his involvement in the campaign itself, while others merely note his continued leadership of the "Saracens" at this time. When taken collectively, however, their witness to a tradition that Muhammad was alive at the time of the Near Eastern conquests and continuing to lead his followers seems unmistakable. The unanimity of these sources, as well as the failure of any source to contradict this tradition prior to the emergence of the first Islamic biographies of Muhammad beginning in the mid-eighth century, speaks highly in their favor. In fact, no source outside the Islamic tradition "accurately" reports Muhammad's death in Medina before the invasion of Palestine until the early ninth-century *Chronicle* of Theophanes, a text that shows evidence of direct influence from the early Islamic historical tradition on this point as well as others.

It would appear that this tradition of Muhammad's continued vitality and leadership during the campaign in Palestine circulated widely in the seventh-

and eighth-century Near East. Although the majority of the relevant sources are of Christian origin, collectively they reflect the religious diversity of the early medieval Near East, including witnesses from each of the major Christian communities as well as a Jewish, a Samaritan, and even an Islamic witness to this discordant tradition. This confessional diversity is particularly significant, insofar as it demonstrates the relative independence of these accounts and the diffusion of this information across both geographic distance and sectarian boundaries. Indeed, the multiple independent attestation of this tradition in a variety of different sources demands that we take seriously the possibility that these eleven sources bear witness to a very early tradition about Muhammad. Presumably, it was a tradition coming from the early Muslims themselves, since it seems highly improbable that all of these sources would have so consistently stumbled into the exact same error concerning the end of Muhammad's life. If this deviant report arose simply through misunderstanding, one would accordingly expect that at least some sources would have managed to understand these events "correctly." At the very least, this evidence seems to indicate that a tradition of Muhammad's death at Medina before the invasion of Palestine had not yet become clearly established prior to the beginnings of the second Islamic century.

It should again be made clear from the outset, however, that the existence of this tradition invites much more than an opportunity simply to extend the longevity of Muhammad by a mere two or three years, and the discrepancy of the source materials on this point instead calls for some sort of explanation. Why are there very different memories concerning Muhammad's relation to the expansion of his religious movement outside of Arabia and his followers' invasion of Roman territory in Syro-Palestine? Admittedly, one cannot entirely exclude the possibility that the difference is simply the result of a collective misunderstanding, but as this chapter will argue, the nature of the sources in question renders this solution improbable. The fact that no source, Islamic or non-Islamic, from the first Islamic century locates Muhammad's death before the Near Eastern invasions indicates that it is not simply a matter of having guessed incorrectly. Possibly the esteem expressed for Muhammad by members of this new religious movement may have led each of these non-Islamic writers to the false assumption that he remained in charge for a few years longer than had actually been the case. Such a scenario is certainly not inconceivable, but it would imply that a profound and prolonged ignorance regarding the basic "facts" about Islam's founding prophet remained pervasive in the various non-Islamic religious communities of the seventh and early eighth centuries. Indeed, if the earliest Muslims had clearly recalled from the start that Muhammad died two years before their invasion of Syria and Palestine, it is hard to imagine that not a single one of the early non-Islamic sources (not to mention the letter of ʿUmar) would manage to get this right. Alternatively, as this study proposes, dramatic changes in the faith of the early Muslims may have given rise to these divergent traditions and could potentially explain the eventual displacement of one tradition by the other. Indeed, as will be seen in chapters to come, there appears to have been some effort initially to deny the reality of Muhammad's death within the earliest community. Likewise, there is considerable evidence to suggest that primitive Islam transformed rapidly from a non-confessional monotheist faith with an extremely short eschatological timeline into an imperial religion grounded in a distinctively Arabian and Arab identity. Such changes, as we will see, provide a credible context for the apparent shift in early memories about the end of Muhammad's life.

Doctrina Iacobi nuper Baptizati (July 634 CE)

The earliest extant text to mention Muhammad is the Greek account of a dialogue that purportedly took place in July 634 in Roman North Africa, in the context of the empire's forced conversion of North African Jews in 632. The text, entitled *Doctrina Iacobi nuper Baptizati*, was most likely written very soon after the events that it describes, as seems to be required by its concern to address the specific issue of the forced baptism of 632, as well as by references to contemporary political events that suggest a time just after the first Arab attacks on the Roman Empire.[1] The text identifies its author as Joseph, one of the participants in the dialogue, but its central character is Jacob, a Jewish merchant from Palestine who had recently been coerced into baptism while on an ill-timed business trip to Africa. As the text begins, Jacob addresses the other Jews who have been forcibly baptized and explains that he has come to see the truth of Christianity through a miraculous vision and careful study of the scriptures. After extensive instruction and dialogue with his audience, he successfully persuades these newly baptized Jews to commit with their hearts to the faith that they have received through compulsion. Several days later, and approximately midway through the text, a new character appears: Justus, the unbaptized cousin of one of Jacob's pupils, who has recently arrived from Palestine. Justus is upset that his cousin and so many other Jews have accepted their Christian baptism, and he is persuaded to debate the issue with Jacob before the group. Unsurprisingly, given that this is a Christian text, the story ends with Justus's conversion. Yet despite this rather clichéd conclusion, the text is a rich source for understanding the history of the eastern Mediterranean world during the crucial period just after the Persian occupation and at the beginnings of the Islamic conquest.

Among other things, this remarkable text is one of our most important resources for understanding relations between the Jewish and Christian communities in the Byzantine provinces, since, unlike so many other early Byzantine writings on Jews and Judaism, the *Doctrina Iacobi* is regarded as a particularly reliable and accurate source. Anti-Jewish polemics were especially popular during the early Byzantine period, and for the most part this literary tradition is replete with stereotypes and rhetoric, bearing a complicated and very tenuous link with the historical realities of the day. Although these texts usually give the appearance of being directed at converting the Jews, this cannot have been the actual cause for their production, since they frequently misrepresent or misunderstand Judaism so badly that they would have little hope of effectively reaching this audience. These texts are instead best understood as insider literature, intended to reassure the Christian faithful of the truth of their faith by demonstrating (in Christian terms) the superiority of Christianity to Judaism, which was Christianity's main religious rival in the pre-Islamic Near East.[2]

Nevertheless, the *Doctrina Iacobi* defies most of the literary conventions—and conventional interpretations—of the *adversus Iudaios* genre: it is, as David Olster explains, "the exception that proves the rule."[3] The *Doctrina Iacobi* is distinguished from its kin most especially by the accuracy with which it portrays Judaism and Jewish life in the late ancient Mediterranean. Whereas most anti-Jewish literature from this period presents a highly stereotyped construct that is rhetorically designed to demonstrate the superiority of Christianity, the *Doctrina Iacobi* presents a highly detailed and realistic depiction of late ancient Judaism. It is in fact so accurate and nuanced that Olster concludes not only that the *Doctrina Iacobi* was most likely written with a Jewish audience in mind, but also that its author was almost certainly a converted Jew; otherwise, it is difficult to conceive how the text could have such depth of insight into seventh-century Jewish life.[4] Moreover, the *Doctrina Iacobi*'s author displays considerable knowledge of Palestinian geography, as well as of the contemporary situation in North Africa, lending credibility to the text's genesis among a group of Palestinian Jews who found themselves in Roman Africa at this inopportune time.[5] In addition, the text details the business dealings of both Jacob and Justus, and even the circumstances of its own production, creating a high level of verisimilitude.[6] Even if the latter elements are merely in place to enhance "the reality effect" of the story, the author's descriptions of contemporary social and political life are astonishingly accurate when compared with other sources.[7] The *Doctrina Iacobi* stands out within its genre for its careful and accurate representation of such historical details and, more remarkably, for the thorough and thoughtful contextualization of its dialogue within this broader historical setting.[8]

An important part of this backdrop is the appearance of a new prophet in Palestine, who, although he is unnamed, is unquestionably to be identified with Muhammad. The passage in question follows Justus's conversion, and, like the rest of the dialogue, it is remarkable for its attention to certain details:

> Justus answered and said, "Indeed you speak the truth, and this is the great salvation: to believe in Christ. For I confess to you, master Jacob, the complete truth. My brother Abraham wrote to me that a false prophet has appeared. Abraham writes, 'When [Sergius][9] the *candidatus* was killed by the Saracens, I was in Caesarea, and I went by ship to Sykamina. And they were saying, "The *candidatus* has been killed," and we Jews were overjoyed. And they were saying, "A prophet has appeared, coming with the Saracens [ὁ προφήτης ἀνεφάνη ἐρχόμενος μετὰ τῶν Σαρακηνῶν], and he is preaching the arrival of the anointed one who is to come, the Messiah." And when I arrived in Sykamina, I visited an old man who was learned in the scriptures, and I said to him, "What can you tell me about the prophet who has appeared with the Saracens?" And he said to me, groaning loudly, "He is false, for prophets do not come with a sword and a war-chariot. Truly the things set in motion today are deeds of anarchy, and I fear that somehow the first Christ that came, whom the Christians worship, was the one sent by God, and instead of him we will receive the Antichrist.[10] Truly, Isaiah said that we Jews will have a deceived and hardened heart until the entire earth is destroyed. But go, master Abraham, and find out about this prophet who has appeared." And when I, Abraham, investigated thoroughly, I heard from those who had met him [Καὶ περιεργασάμενος ἐγω Ἀβραάμης ἤκουσα ἀπὸ τῶν συντυχόντων αὐτῷ] that one will find no truth in the so-called prophet, only the shedding of human blood. In fact, he says that he

> has the keys of paradise, which is impossible.' These things my brother Abraham has written from the East."[11]

What can one make of this passage, which mixes vivid historical detail with obvious polemic? Is its indication that Muhammad was still alive and leading the invading Arabs as they entered Palestine of any historical significance or has the author (or one of his sources) simply made a mistake? To a certain extent, this judgment will depend on whether other independent witnesses also credibly describe Muhammad as alive at the time of the invasion of Palestine, and as this chapter will demonstrate, a number of such sources exist. In its own right, however, the *Doctrina Iacobi* is a historical source of particularly high quality that was written very close to the events that it describes. Since the *Doctrina Iacobi* has repeatedly shown itself to be a reliable source with regard to various other matters, perhaps one should initially give its near contemporary report of Muhammad's involvement in the conquest of Palestine at least the benefit of the doubt.

For example, comparison with other historical texts confirms the accuracy of the *Doctrina Iacobi*'s reference to a *candidatus* Sergius of Caesarea who was killed by the Arabs. Two other sources report the death of Sergius the *candidatus* in combat with the Arabs: the *Syriac Common Source*, a now lost chronicle from the mid-eighth century discussed below, and a Syriac chronicle from the year 640.[12] In the *Doctrina Iacobi* we seem to have an almost contemporary witness to Sergius's defeat by the Arab army as described in these later sources.[13] While this by no means ensures that the passage is accurate in all of its other details, the verification of this point by independent sources is a testimony in favor of its general reliability as a historical source. Likewise, the *Doctrina Iacobi*'s report that Muhammad claimed to possess the "keys of paradise" seems to reflect a very early Islamic tradition that was later abandoned. Not only do other Byzantine sources repeat this tradition, but certain Islamic sources preserve it as well, although the latter attempt to soften the audacity of Muhammad's claim by reducing it to a metaphor.[14] Perhaps even more important, however, is the high level of conformity between the *Doctrina Iacobi* and other witnesses to the social, political, and religious events of the early 630s noted already above. As Olster's persuasive analysis of this text demonstrates, the *Doctrina Iacobi*'s accurate representation of its historical circumstances is precisely what makes it so remarkably different from other anti-Jewish writings of the same period. Thus, while one certainly cannot assume that this source is reliable in every detail, we nevertheless may take some confidence in the fact that the *Doctrina Iacobi* has been shown to be generally trustworthy through comparison with other sources from the period. The fact that it was probably written so close to the time it describes only adds to its credibility.

Particularly significant in this report is the *Doctrina Iacobi*'s notice that this prophet who arrived in Palestine with a Saracen army was "preaching the arrival of the anointed one who is to come, the Messiah." As Crone and Cook observe, this earliest witness to Muhammad's religious message from outside of the Islamic tradition portrays him as preaching Jewish messianism. Although Cook and Crone initially characterize this idea as "hardly a familiar one," thanks in large part to their own work, it has become much less unfamiliar.[15] Most importantly, the seventh-century Jewish apocalypse preserved in the *Secrets of Rabbi Shimʿōn* (discussed below) confirms that there were in fact Jews who understood Muhammad and his message as the fulfillment of Jewish messianic expectations. Theophanes' *Chronicle* echoes this information at a greater distance, and the report in Sebeos's Armenian *History* of Arab and Jewish unity during the assault on Palestine, discussed in the final chapter, may also point indirectly to such beliefs.[16] Moreover, the Qurʾān itself would appear to substantiate these reports: as discussed below in Chapter 3, the Qurʾān's unmistakable eschatological urgency reveals that Muhammad and his early followers believed themselves to have been living in the final moments of history, just before the impending judgment and destruction that would soon arrive with the Hour. In Jewish ears, this forecast of the *eschaton*'s proximate arrival would inevitably awaken expectation of the messiah's advent, which was expected to precede the Final Judgment. As will be seen in the final chapter, substantial evidence signals the presence of a significant Jewish element among Muhammad's earliest followers, and undoubtedly these Jewish "Believers" would have understood his eschatological preaching through the lens of their own traditions. Thus, while Fred Donner is certainly correct to note that the early Islamic sources do not reveal any clear belief in a coming messianic figure, as both he and Suliman Bashear rightly conclude, the Jewish members of the early community of the Believers undoubtedly would have interpreted Muhammad's eschatological message according to their own messianic expectations.[17]

Hoyland's criteria ask that we push beyond these conclusions, however, and scrutinize the source's source, as it were. In this regard the situation is less than ideal, but it is much better than it might be. In the best possible case, we would have the statement of an eyewitness (or better still, eyewitnesses). In the *Doctrina Iacobi*, we find instead what essentially amounts to third-hand testimony, although the account is allegedly based on reports from eyewitnesses. Jacob, the author, heard this report of the Arab invasion of Palestine from Abraham's letter, which Abraham's brother Justus read aloud in his presence. Abraham, who was living in Palestine, identifies the source of his information in interviews that he had personally conducted with "those who had met him [that is, Muhammad]." Despite these intervening steps, we may take some measure of confidence in Jacob's report: according to this genealogy, it derives from the testimony of multiple eyewitnesses and was then quickly committed to writing before reaching Jacob. Moreover, the report's close proximity to the actual events themselves stands further in its favor: mere months seem to have transpired since the invasion. On the whole, these circumstances present a much more credible line of transmission than the pedigrees that accompany the earliest Islamic traditions about Muhammad and the conquest. As will be seen in the following chapter, their chains of transmission (*isnāds*) are notoriously unreliable and often highly artificial, purporting to document transmission over multiple generations. By comparison, the transmission of Jacob's report is both immediate and relatively uncomplicated.

Admittedly, there are elements of polemic in this passage, including especially the diatribe against Muhammad as a false prophet. But by and large the details are descriptive and often can be confirmed by other sources, as seen in the case of Sergius the *candidatus* and the report that Muhammad claimed to hold the keys to paradise: although the latter is potentially polemical, as noted above, later Byzantine and Islamic sources corroborate this characterization. Even the allegation that Muhammad was preaching the advent of the messiah seems to be more or less accurate, reflecting a Jewish understanding of his eschatological message that is evident in other early sources. In similar fashion, the *Doctrina Iacobi*'s indication that Muhammad was still alive and coming with the Arabs during the Palestinian campaigns of 634 seems to be a descriptive, non-polemical observation that is confirmed by a number of other sources. It is, moreover, information that could have been known to Abraham's informants, "who had met him," as he reports, and potentially to others as well who had experienced the Arab invasion of Roman Palestine.

More importantly, there is no obvious apologetic or polemical reason for the *Doctrina Iacobi*'s author (or his sources) to have invented Muhammad's leadership during the campaign in order to serve a broader ideological purpose.[18] Hoyland suggests, somewhat half-heartedly it seems, that the widespread Christian reports of Muhammad's participation in the conquest of Palestine may stem from an effort "to emphasize his un-prophetlike behavior."[19] This would certainly fit with the *Doctrina Iacobi*'s polemic against Muhammad as a false prophet, since, as the "old man" says, "prophets do not come with a sword and a war-chariot." Nevertheless, as Hoyland himself concedes within the very same sentence, "the essence of [this representation] is already encountered in the very foundation document of the Muslim community, the so-called Constitution of Medina, which unites believers under the 'protection of God' to fight on his behalf."[20] Moreover, as Hoyland notes elsewhere, the Qur'ān itself attests that "coming with sword and chariot" was an integral part of Muhammad's message: "That religion and conquest went hand in hand in Muḥammad's preaching is clear from many passages in the Qur'an which command: 'Fight those who do not believe in God and the Last Day . . . until they pay tribute' (ix.29) and the like."[21] It is thus highly unlikely that the *Doctrina Iacobi*, along with the various other non-Islamic sources that will be examined, has falsely represented Muhammad as alive at the time of the Islamic invasion of Palestine in order to discredit him by portraying him as a prophet who preached a message of conquest. The Islamic sources themselves preserve this image of Muhammad rather well, and there would have been little need for these authors to invent data in order to emphasize a point that otherwise emerges quite clearly from both the Qur'ān and the early Islamic tradition. On the whole then, the *Doctrina Iacobi* generally fares well in regard to Hoyland's criteria and should accordingly be taken seriously in its report of a tradition that as late as 634 Muhammad came to Palestine "*with* the Saracens."[22]

Of course, one cannot completely exclude the possibility that the sources behind *Doctrina Iacobi* may have simply misunderstood Muhammad's relation to the invasion of Palestine. Perhaps Muslim confessions of Muhammad as a religious prophet whose teachings they followed were mistakenly understood as indications that he was a still-living military and political leader of the Muslims. Since Muhammad was a bellicose prophet who had preached *jihād*, it is possible that the conquered peoples of Palestine and the Near East merely assumed that he was leading the *jihād* that subdued their territory and brought it under the dominion of his religious movement. Nonetheless, as will be seen in the remainder of this chapter, the wide range of sources conveying this tradition strongly suggests that such a misunderstanding is unlikely to be the origin of this difference between the Islamic and non-Islamic sources. If such confusion were the cause of Muhammad's representation as still living at the beginning of the Palestinian campaign, then one must assume that a large number of independent sources have somehow separately made the same mistake. While this certainly is not impossible, it becomes increasingly improbable with each source, and the broad geographic spread of this tradition across the various religious communities of the early Islamic world instead suggests more probably a primitive tradition that underlies these reports. Likewise, the fact that no source "correctly" locates Muhammad's death before the Palestinian invasion or otherwise clearly separates him from these events before the emergence of his official Islamic biography in the middle of the eighth century is a strong indication that this association of Muhammad with the conquest of Palestine reflects an early tradition that circulated widely among the different religious groups of the Mediterranean world in the seventh and eighth centuries. There are, as will be seen in chapters to follow, other more likely explanations for the discrepancy between these early sources and the later Islamic tradition on this issue. Consequently, even if Muhammad did not in fact survive to personally lead the invasion of Palestine, as the *Doctrina Iacobi* reports, the convergence of so many sources on this point seems to reveal what is likely an early tradition, presumably coming from within Islam itself, that Muhammad led his followers into the Abrahamic land of promise. There they seem to have anticipated that he would guide them to meet the *eschaton*'s impending arrival, signaled here by Jewish expectations of the messiah's appearance.

The Apocalypse of Rabbi Shimʿōn b. Yoḥai (635–45?)

As Crone and Cook are quick to note in *Hagarism*, certain medieval Jewish apocalyptic traditions ascribed to Rabbi Shimʿōn b. Yoḥai form an important compliment to the *Doctrina Iacobi*'s witness, particularly in providing further evidence of a messianic understanding of the Islamic conquests among many contemporary Jews.[23] Nevertheless, Crone and Cook fail to note the parallel indication by these Jewish visionary texts that Muhammad led his followers in the invasion of Palestine, an oversight owing itself most likely to their dependence on Bernard Lewis's translation of a key passage in 1950.[24] While Lewis's translation is certainly not incorrect, it is problematic inasmuch as it obscures certain grammatical ambiguities that are essential for the present question of Muhammad's relation to the invasion of Palestine. As will be seen, the full complement of witnesses to these Rabbi Shimʿōn b. Yoḥai traditions indicates that this early Jewish vision of the Islamic conquests identified Muhammad as the leader of the Ishmaelite army that was believed to be the agent of Israel's divine deliverance from Roman oppression in Palestine.

Several closely related apocalyptic texts describe Rabbi Shimʿōn's visions of the Islamic conquests, each giving a slightly different version of events that seems to depend on an earlier common source. The earliest of these works, and also the most important, is *The Secrets of Rabbi Shimʿōn b. Yoḥai*, an apocalypse written sometime around the middle of the eighth century whose visions cover the period between the Islamic conquests and the ʿAbbāsid revolution. As *The Secrets* begins, Rabbi Shimʿōn reflects on the "Kenite" of Numbers 24:21, which is revealed to him as a prediction concerning the Ishmaelites and their coming dominion over the land of Israel.[25] When he cries aloud with frustration, asking if the Jews had not yet suffered enough oppression at the hands of Edom (that is, Rome), the angel Metatron comes to him and reassures him that God will use the Ishmaelites to free the Jews from Byzantine oppression. "Do not be afraid, mortal, for the Holy One, blessed be He, is bringing about the kingdom of Ishmael only for the purpose of delivering you from that wicked one (that is, Edom [Rome]). In accordance with His will He shall raise up over them a prophet. And he will conquer the land for them [והוא מעמיר עליהם נביא כרצונו ויכבוש להם את הארץ], and they shall come and restore it with grandeur. Great enmity will exist between them and the children of Esau."[26] The revelation continues as Metatron responds to Rabbi Shimʿōn's questions by equating Israel's liberation through this Ishmaelite prophet to the messianic deliverance foretold by Isaiah's vision of the two riders (Isa. 21:6–7).[27] This identification of Muhammad as the fulfillment of Jewish messianic hopes is remarkable, and it offers important corroboration of the *Doctrina Iacobi*'s report that the Saracen prophet was "preaching the arrival of the anointed one who is to come, the Messiah." Predictions concerning the various Umayyad rulers then follow, including a prophecy that Muhammad's successor, apparently the caliph ʿUmar, would restore worship to the Temple Mount.[28] The apocalypse then concludes with the ʿAbbāsid revolution, which is identified as the beginnings of an eschatological confrontation between Israel and Byzantium that will result in a two-thousand year messianic reign, followed by the Final Judgment.[29]

In view of this rather positive assessment of Muhammad's prophetic mission and the early years of Islamic rule, numerous scholars have observed that *The Secrets of Rabbi Shimʿōn* almost certainly depends on a much earlier source for its description of these events.[30] It is hard to imagine that a Jewish author of the mid-eighth century would have written so glowingly of the advent of Islam, painting Muhammad and his followers in such messianic hues over a century later. Moreover, as Crone and Cook rightly observe, "the messiah belongs at the end of an apocalypse and not in the middle" as one finds in *The Secrets*, an anomaly that also seems to indicate the inclusion of older material.[31] On the whole, the character of this section of the apocalypse strongly suggests that *The Secrets* here has incorporated some very lightly edited traditions from an older Jewish apocalypse that was roughly contemporary with the events of the conquests themselves, possibly written in the first decade after the Arab invasions. Moreover, this lost apocalypse appears to relate the perspective of a Jewish group either within the early Islamic movement or closely allied with it. We have long known from the Islamic tradition itself that in the early stages Jewish groups were welcomed into Muhammad's new religious community while maintaining their Jewish identity. Yet according to Muhammad's early biographers, this was a brief experiment limited to certain Jewish tribes of Medina that was quickly abandoned after it failed. There is increasing evidence, however, that for the first several decades Muhammad's followers comprised an inter-confessional, eschatological religious movement focused on Jerusalem and the Holy Land that welcomed Jews and other monotheists within the community, as will be seen further in the final chapter. The older apocalypse of Rabbi Shim'ōn echoed in this more recent text almost certainly derives from this milieu: otherwise, it is difficult to understand its proclamation of the invading Arabs as divinely appointed "messianic" deliverers who would restore worship to the Temple Mount.

It is of special note that this seventh-century apocalypse of Rabbi Shim'ōn appears to have described this Ishmaelite "messiah," unmistakably here Muhammad, as leading this conquest of the Holy Land and liberating it from the Romans. Yet Lewis translates the crucial passage, cited above, as follows: "He raises up over them a Prophet according to His will and will conquer the land for them and they will come and restore it in greatness."[32] Lewis's translation determines God, "the Holy One," as the actor who will conquer the land for the Ishmaelites. The Hebrew, however, is in fact ambiguous on this point. The verb in question is an imperfect third-person singular (יכבוש), and thus its subject is potentially either God or the prophet that God will raise up. Lewis has determined to understand God as the one who will conquer the land, and while this certainly is a possibility, it seems more likely that the prophet is in fact intended: God will raise up the prophet, but it is the prophet who will lead the conquest of the land. No doubt Lewis was inspired to translate the passage as he did by the Islamic historical tradition, which relates Muhammad's death in Medina prior to the invasion of Palestine. Writing in 1950, Lewis was presumably unaware of this counter-tradition that Muhammad led his followers in the initial assault on Palestine; consequently, he not unreasonably assumed that *The Secrets* and its source envisioned God, rather than Muhammad, as subduing the land, since according to the received Islamic tradition Muhammad was already dead by this time. Nevertheless, in view of the new sources that have now come to light, one must seriously consider the possibility that, as the text seems to suggest, it is the prophet who conquers the land. Inasmuch as God raised up this Ishmaelite prophet for the purpose of delivering the Jews from the Romans, it seems implicit that the prophet was to achieve this divine mission by leading the conquest of the land himself.

Indeed, the reading that it is the prophet, rather than God, who conquers the land seems highly preferable here, as is confirmed by the other witnesses to this seventh-century Jewish apocalypse, all of which preserve a memory of the Ishmaelite prophet, rather than God, as the one who conquers the land. For example, a fragment preserving the opening section of *The Secrets of Rabbi Shimʿōn* survives among the Cairo Geniza texts, and according to this version, "He raises over them a crazy prophet, possessed by a spirit, and he conquers the land for them [והוא מעמיר עליהם נביא שוטה ואיש הרוח והוא מכבש לפניהם את הארץ] and they come and seize dominion in greatness and there will be great enmity between them and the sons of Esau."[33] Here Lewis translates the passage so that the prophet ("he" instead of "He") is identified as conquering Palestine, which seems to be indicated by the context: surely God would not conquer the land for this crazy, possessed prophet and his followers. The same reading is also confirmed by another manuscript in Munich, which preserves a version very similar to that of the Geniza fragment.[34] Thus these other manuscript witnesses to *The Secrets* clearly relate this prophecy as describing the conquest of the land by an Ishmaelite prophet, whom the circumstances clearly identify as Muhammad.

Other closely related sources convey a similar understanding of Muhammad's role in the conquest of Palestine, namely, the *Ten Kings Midrash* and *The Prayer of Rabbi Shimʿōn b. Yoḥai*, both of which seem to have drawn independently on the now lost seventh-century apocalypse of Rabbi Shimʿōn.[35] Judging from the historical figures identified in the *Ten Kings Midrash*, it is roughly contemporary with *The Secrets of Rabbi Shimʿōn*, placing its composition sometime not long after the reign of al-Walīd II (d. 744).[36] And while the *Ten Kings Midrash* appears to have also made direct use of this older apocalypse of Rabbi Shimʿōn b. Yoḥai, there is no mention in the *Ten Kings Midrash* of God raising up an Ishmaelite prophet, and the original Ishmaelite "messianism" of this source has been slightly rearranged. Nevertheless, the relevant section concludes with the following prediction concerning Muhammad. "At the beginning of his dominion, when he goes forth, he will seek to do harm to Israel, but great men of Israel will join with him and give him a wife from among them, and there will be peace between him and Israel. He will conquer all the kingdom and come to Jerusalem and bow down there and make war with the Edomites and they will flee before him and he will seize the kingship by force and then he will die."[37] The indication that Muhammad led the conquest of Palestine and would die only afterward is unambiguously clear here, confirming what we have seen in the *Doctrina Iacobi* and *The Secrets of Rabbi Shimʿōn*, but the notice that he would actually come to Jerusalem to "bow down there" is otherwise unprecedented to my knowledge. Nevertheless, this feature would appear to comport with the exalted status of Jerusalem in earliest Islam, as is further discussed in the final chapter.

Likewise, *The Prayer of Rabbi Shimʿōn b. Yoḥai*, a more recent text dating from the time of the First Crusade, also describes Muhammad as leading the invasion of Palestine. Although *The Prayer of Rabbi Shimʿōn* has transformed the relevant prophecy so that it relates to the events of the Crusades, its words clearly echo both the Cairo and Munich versions of *The Secrets*, noting that "a crazy man possessed by a spirit arises and speaks lies about the Holy One, blessed be He, and he conquers the land, and there is enmity between them and the sons of Esau."[38] While the Ishmaelite prophet is here portrayed in strongly negative terms, this leader, originally Muhammad one must assume, is said to conquer the land. Thus, despite the change of historical context, *The Prayer of Rabbi Shimʿōn* has reused this older tradition of the Ishmaelite prophet's conquest of Palestine, applying it unchanged to the new circumstances presented by the Crusades.

The persistence of this particular theme, Muhammad's conquest of the land, across all of these sources, despite their heavy revisions to this prophecy, rather strongly suggests that this was an original feature of the earlier seventh-century apocalypse on which they have all drawn. Although each has altered the originally positive, messianic assessment of Muhammad and his religious movement that was present in their now lost source, their convergence in reporting Muhammad's leadership of the Arab invasion of Palestine seems to confirm that this feature was a primitive element of this near contemporary apocalyptic vision of the Islamic conquests. Thus, this complex of texts bears witness to a tradition of Muhammad's continued vitality and leadership during the invasion of Palestine within the context of Jewish messianic expectations, seemingly recorded, like the *Doctrina Iacobi*, close to the time of the Arab conquests themselves. It is an impressive convergence on this point, which appears to reflect a very early memory from the Palestinian Jewish community of Muhammad's leadership during the invasion of Palestine.

It is somewhat difficult to assess the quality of this witness according to Hoyland's criteria, particularly in light of its apocalyptic genre. On the one hand, the source of its information is identified as the angel Metatron, and it presents the Ishmaelite prophet's invasion of Palestine within a totalizing narrative of Israel's deliverance at the hands of this prophet and his followers. On the other hand, it would appear that this notice, despite its obvious literary conventions, originated within a context that was either very close to or perhaps even inside the primitive Islamic community itself. The early Jewish apocalyptic vision of the Islamic conquest that has been collectively adopted by these later texts clearly seems to have anticipated Jewish redemption through the invading Ishmaelites and their prophet. The seventh-century Jewish group that produced the original apocalypse of Rabbi Shimʿōn at a time close to the events of the Arab conquest themselves appears to have placed its faith in the "Islamic" prophet and the early caliphs as deliverers raised up by God. In its acceptance of Muhammad's divine guidance, the apocalypse thus seems to reflect a viewpoint that in some sense is that of an insider.

While this perspective is perhaps difficult to comprehend in light of the confessional boundaries that have long since separated Islam and Judaism, recent research into Islamic origins has revealed that such divisions were likely not as important during Islam's first decades. The apocalypse of Rabbi Shimʿōn is itself important evidence of the early Islamic community's openness to other monotheist confessions, and it would seem that it preserves the visionary hopes of a Jewish group that joined cause with the invading Arabs and the message of their prophet, whom they saw as their liberator. There are in fact strong indications that Islam's sacred geography originally focused not on Mecca and the Ḥijāz, but instead on Jerusalem and Palestine, which Muhammad's earliest followers seem to have regarded as the promised land of their inheritance, a holy land rightfully belonging to Abraham's descendants, Jews and Arabs alike. The Islamic invasion of the Holy Land thus seems to have been conceived at least in part as the liberation of the Abrahamic patrimony from Roman rule and oppression, an undertaking that would have aligned the Arab cause with Jewish apocalyptic hopes.

Consequently, one would imagine that this apocalypse of Rabbi Shimʿōn reflects the perspective of a Jewish group that was sympathetic to, if not even allied with, the invading Arabs and their prophet. Its prediction that this prophet would lead the conquest of the Holy Land thus seems to reflect the perspective of contemporary eyewitnesses who themselves had some experience of the invasion and early Islamic rule over Jerusalem. Whatever the precise nature of the community behind this text may have been, it clearly describes the invading Arabs and their prophet in positive terms, as divinely appointed agents of deliverance. The sharp dissonance of this favorable assessment of Muhammad and his devotees with later Jewish attitudes toward Islam speaks not only to the antiquity of the source itself; this quality also diminishes the possibility that Muhammad's participation in the conquests was contrived to serve some polemical purpose. To the contrary, it is extremely difficult to envision a later Jewish redactor inventing the idea of Muhammad's divinely appointed liberation of the Holy Land. It is instead much easier to understand such sentiments as reflecting the impressions of contemporary Jews whose apocalyptic expectations aligned them, at least for a time, with the invading Muslims and their prophet.

The *Khuzistan Chronicle* (ca. 660 CE)

Further evidence of Muhammad's leadership during the conquest of Palestine occurs in a brief, anonymous Syriac chronicle that was probably composed in the Khuzistan region of southwestern Iran, where most of its events take place. The *Khuzistan Chronicle*, as this text is often called,[39] is generally dated to around 660 on the basis of its contents, including most notably the fact that it makes no clear reference to any event after 652.[40] The chronicle's account of the Islamic conquests is somewhat unusual in that it describes the events of the conquests twice and in two very different contexts. The chronicle first gives a rather general notice of the conquests according to its chronological sequence, and then near its conclusion, the author returns to a discussion of the Islamic invasions outside of the broader chronology and in more detail, focusing especially on Islamic military activity in Khuzistan. This doublet reflects a rather peculiar feature of the chronicle's general organization. Most of the chronicle adheres to a strict chronological order in relating events, marking time according to the succession of both the Persian emperors and the leaders of the East Syrian (that is, "Nestorian") church. But following accounts of the reigns of Emperor Yazdgerd III (632–52) and Patriarch Maremmeh (646–49), the work suddenly alters its structure. The chronicle's final entries include, in order, "an account of the miraculous conversion of some Turks by Elias of Merv (d. after 659), a list of towns founded by Seleucus, Semiramis and Ninus son of Belus, a portrayal of the Arab conquests (630s-40s), and a short survey of Arabian geography."[41] This sudden departure from chronological sequence has led many interpreters to suggest that these final sections are the work of another author, who has appended this material, including the second description of the Islamic conquests, to an earlier chronicle that originally concluded with Patriarch Maremmeh's death.[42] Other factors, however, suggest that both sections are in fact the work of the same author, and as Hoyland has proposed, "it may be, then, that the disjuncture is not an indication of a change in author, but of a change of focus and/or source."[43] It seems plausible that upon reaching the end of his historical narrative, the chronicler turned in his conclusion to focus on topics of special significance for mid-seventh-century Khuzistan and East Arabia. This shift of focus presumably reflects the author's interest in his own milieu, and consequently, there is a very real possibility that the information in this section is based on eyewitness reports or even the author's own personal knowledge.

In this final section, the chronicle's second account of the Islamic conquest narrates the Arab invasion of northern Khuzistan, focusing especially on the capture of the cities Shush and Shushtar. The account is so rich in detail that it almost certainly derives from eyewitness reports,[44] but inasmuch as it describes the conquest of Mesopotamia instead of Palestine and does not identify Muhammad as leading the invasion, this vivid account is unfortunately irrelevant to the matter at hand. The chronicle's initial notice of the Islamic conquests, however, which appears according to chronological sequence, is more valuable in this regard. Here the chronicler describes the initial Arab assaults against both Persia and the Byzantines in Syro-Palestine, reporting these events as follows:

> And Yazdgerd, who was from the royal lineage, was crowned king in the city of Estakhr, and under him the Persian Empire came to an end. And he went forth and came to Māḥōzē and appointed one named Rustam as the leader of the army. Then God raised up against them the sons of Ishmael like sand on the seashore. And

> their leader was Muhammad [ܘܡܕܒܪܢܗܘܢ ܐܝܬܘܗܝ ܗܘܐ ܡܚܡܕ], and neither city walls nor gates, neither armor nor shields stood before them. And they took control of the entire land of the Persians. Yazdgerd sent countless troops against them, but the Arabs destroyed them all and even killed Rustam. Yazdgerd shut himself within the walls of Māḥōzē and in the end made his escape through flight. He went to the lands of the Huzaye and the Mrwnaye,[45] and there he ended his life. And the Arabs took control of Māḥōzē and all the land. They also went to the land of the Byzantines, plundering and laying waste to the entire region of Syria. Heraclius, the Byzantine king, sent armies against them, but the Arabs killed more than one-hundred thousand of them.[46]

The structure of this passage seems to indicate Muhammad's leadership of the Arabs during their initial attacks against the Persians and the Romans. After first naming the Persian "king," Yazdgerd, and then identifying the leader of the Persian army in Rustam, the chronicler describes the Arab invasion of Persia, designating Muhammad as the Arab leader in this specific context. Muhammad's positioning alongside of these other leaders in the conflict, including Heraclius, strongly suggests Muhammad's participation in the initial phase of the Near Eastern conquest.

Unfortunately, we know very little regarding the sources from which the author obtained his information that Muhammad was leading the Muslims at the time of the conquests. The chronicler identifies his sources rather generally as the ecclesiastical and secular histories from the period between the death of Hormizd son of Khosro and the end of the Persian Empire.[47] But since the *Khuzistan Chronicle* was composed so soon after the events of the Islamic conquests, it is certainly possible that its author relied on reports of eyewitnesses rather than written sources for knowledge of the Islamic invasion, particularly since he appears to have relied on eyewitness testimony for his description of Khuzistan's conquest. In any case, the author himself was most likely not an eyewitness to the Palestinian campaign or to Muhammad's role therein: how he came by the information that Muhammad was leading this powerful army is not known. But in the *Khuzistan Chronicle*'s favor are the facts that its author seems to have taken a special interest in recording the events of the Islamic conquest, and that he had access to eyewitness testimonies (or perhaps even personal experience?) for at least some of his information. As for the character of the observation, it is not polemical, nor does the notice of Muhammad's leadership during the conquests serve any sort of grand narrative within the chronicle; here the chronicle makes descriptive observations about events that took place less than thirty years prior. Thus the *Khuzistan Chronicle* forms an additional witness to a tradition of Muhammad's continued leadership of the Muslims as they began their conquest of Rome and Persia, in a source written outside the boundaries of Rome, at the heart of the recently fallen Persian Empire.

Jacob of Edessa, *Chronological Charts* (691/92 CE)

Jacob of Edessa was a prolific author of the later seventh century, of whom it has been said that his importance in Syriac Christian culture is equivalent to that of Jerome in Western Christendom.[48] Jacob's contributions to the medieval West Syrian (that is, "miaphysite") church are extensive. In his day he was particularly renowned, or perhaps more accurately, notorious, for his work in canon law: in addition to producing a number of important works on the subject, he famously burned a copy of the ecclesiastical regulations while bishop of Edessa to protest the laxity of their observance in the church, after which he (perhaps wisely) withdrew to a monastery. Jacob was also instrumental in standardizing aspects of Syriac grammar, and the West Syrian tradition of indicating vocalization was his invention. Like Jerome, he labored to produce a more accurate version of the biblical text, and he wrote numerous biblical commentaries in addition to various theological and philosophical works. In his youth Jacob had gone to Alexandria to undertake advanced study of Greek, which enabled him to translate, among other things, the works of Severus of Antioch from Greek into Syriac and the *Categories* of Aristotle. He also authored a number of liturgical texts, and his extensive correspondence with people across Syria also survives.[49] But our primary concern in the present context is Jacob's *Chronicle*, or his *Chronological Charts* as the text is perhaps more accurately named: these present a somewhat complicated, but nevertheless important, witness to the tradition of Muhammad's leadership during the invasion of Palestine.

Jacob's *Chronological Charts* were prepared with the intent of covering the interval from the end of Eusebius's *Church History* up until the end of the seventh century by presenting "in brief the events of the time and the years of empires . . . placed facing each other so that it might be for those coming to it [to see] who were at a certain time the kings, generals, scholars, writers."[50]

Unfortunately, much of this chronicle is lost: only a series of extracts has survived, preserved in a single manuscript from the tenth or eleventh century. Among the missing sections is Jacob's record of events from 631 until 692, the year that he composed the chronicle. Ordinarily, this would considerably limit the text's value for assessing the date of Muhammad's death, since it breaks off just before the traditional date of his death in 632. Nevertheless, in this case we are the beneficiaries of a rare and fortunate error in Jacob's chronology. According to Jacob's charts, in 620/21 "the first king of the Arabs, Muhammad, began to reign for seven years."[51] Seven years later, the chart records in 627/28 the beginning of Abū Bakr's reign as the second king of the Arabs, which lasted for two years and seven months.[52] This of course places Muhammad's death in 627/28, four to five years before the traditional date. Jacob's lapse in chronology here is surprising, given the fact that Jacob's chronicle is otherwise highly regarded for its accuracy.[53] Nonetheless, a list of caliphs compiled between 705 and 715 gives the same dates for Muhammad's reign, perhaps having followed Jacob's charts, as does the *Hispanic Chronicle of 754*, discussed below.[54]

At first glance, one would hardly think that Jacob's report could strengthen an argument for extending the time of Muhammad's death beyond its traditional date, since according to Jacob, it occurred even earlier. No doubt this is why Cook, Crone, and Hoyland do not include this witness among the Christian sources identifying Muhammad as still alive during the campaign in Palestine. While Jacob may have had erroneous knowledge of the length of Muhammad's reign, he nevertheless is in complete harmony with these other sources in recording the onset of the Islamic conquest of Palestine while Muhammad was still alive and leader of the Muslims. Beginning with Muhammad's reign, Jacob's chronological charts are ordered into four columns that count the years of the various Roman, Persian, and Islamic leaders, alongside a count of the years since Jacob's charts began in the twentieth year of Constantine's reign. On both sides of these charts are comments noting important historical events that coincide with the regnal years tabulated in the charts. Beside the year 625/26, on the left side of the chart, Jacob records that "the Arabs began to make raids in the land of Palestine."[55] The sentence begins next to 625/26 and ends on the following line, beside the year 626/27, but it is clear that this comment identifies the beginning of the Islamic campaign in Palestine with the fifth year of Muhammad's reign, two years before his death.

Conceivably, one could interpret this notice as possibly referring to the first minor skirmish between a small Muslim force and an army of Arab tribes allied with the Byzantines at Mu'ta in 629, if one were determined to bring this report more in line with the traditional chronology. But this solution does not seem very likely, at least according to the traditional understanding of this early confrontation between Muhammad's followers and the "Romans."[56] Although Mu'ta was technically in *Palestina tertia*, about twenty-five miles south of the province of Arabia in what is today Jordan, it was certainly very much on the margins of the Byzantine Empire. There is no evidence of any Roman troops at Mu'ta during the sixth and seventh centuries, and the forces that actually would have engaged the Muslims were from a variety of Arab confederates. The battle itself was rather minor: it consisted of a single engagement in which the Muslims were soundly defeated. A small skirmish on the fringes of the empire between Christian and Muslim Arabs at a minor outpost hardly seems worthy of Jacob's notice of Islamic raids in Palestine. Perhaps more importantly, the conflict at Mu'ta is unattested in the Syriac historical tradition, or in any Syriac text at all to my knowledge. The sole reference to the battle of Mu'ta outside of the Islamic historical tradition is the Greek *Chronicle* of Theophanes, written in the early ninth century, and Theophanes almost certainly relied on Islamic sources for his account of this battle.[57]

By contrast, the initial phase of the Islamic conquest of Palestine sounds very much like the "raids" that Jacob envisions. In 633–34, the Islamic army moved into southern Palestine, in the province of *Palestina prima*, and made a number of smaller engagements, mostly with local garrison forces in the countryside. But initially there were no major confrontations with the Byzantine army, and the towns and cities remained under Byzantine control.[58] These circumstances more credibly reflect the events that Jacob describes as "raids" in Palestine, two years, according to his count, before Abū Bakr succeeded Muhammad as the leader of the Muslims after the latter's death. Therefore, even though Jacob is mistaken in the length he assigns to Muhammad's reign, his chronicle provides yet another witness to the tradition that Muhammad was still alive as the conquest of Palestine began. We do not know the source of Jacob's information in this instance, although we can assume that an individual in Jacob's position would have had access to a number of different sources, both written and oral. His general reliability in sifting through these sources makes Jacob's error concerning the precise date and number of years that Muhammad ruled quite surprising. There are moreover no signs of any apologetic agenda or totalizing explanation in the terse outlines of these charts, which rather dryly signal the beginnings of the Palestinian conquest before Muhammad's death.

The *History of the Patriarchs of Alexandria*: The Life of Patriarch Benjamin (before 717 CE)

The *History of the Patriarchs of Alexandria* is a rather complex text that was first compiled in late antiquity, but over the centuries it has continually been augmented, revised, and updated as new patriarchs have sat on the throne of St. Mark: the most recent update was added in 1942.[59] Most of the material covering the first millennium was originally composed in Coptic, and in the tenth century this was all translated into Arabic, which has been the language of composition ever since. Through a careful analysis of editorial notes scattered throughout the earliest extant versions of this text, David Johnson has been able to identify various redactional layers from the first thousand years of its history.[60] The earliest portion of the text derives from a Coptic *History of the Church* that today is known only in fragments. This first segment covers the period from the founding of the Egyptian church up to the reign of Dioscorus (first century–451).[61] This section is followed by a second redactional unit that was composed by a certain George the Archdeacon, who narrates the interval between Patriarch Cyril (d. 444) and the reign of the caliph Sulaymān (715–17).[62]

As a part of his contribution to the *History of the Patriarchs of Alexandria*, George the Archdeacon includes a life of Patriarch Benjamin (626–65), during whose lengthy reign the Muslims conquered Egypt along with the rest of the Byzantine Near East. George begins his account of the Islamic conquests with a dream of Heraclius, which warned him, "Truly, a circumcised nation will come upon you, and they will defeat you, and they will take possession of the land."[63] Mistakenly thinking that the dream warned against the Jews, Heraclius ordered all the Jews and Samaritans in the Roman Empire to be baptized. The narrative then explains his mistake with the following account of the rise of Islam:

> And after a few days, there arose a man among the Arabs, from the southern regions, from Mecca and its vicinity, named Muhammad. And he restored the worshippers of idols to knowledge of the one God, so that they said that Muhammad is his messenger. And his nation was circumcised in the flesh, not in the law, and they prayed toward the south, orienting themselves toward a place they call the Kaʿba. And he took possession of [وملك] Damascus and Syria, and he crossed the Jordan and damned it up.[64] And the Lord abandoned

> the army of the Romans before him, because of their corrupt faith and the excommunication that was brought against them and because of the Council of Chalcedon by the ancient fathers.[65]

This passage identifies Muhammad as leading the conquest of "Damascus and Syria," crossing over the river Jordan with his followers and into Palestine, where the Roman armies fell before him. We do not know the source of the information, since the various biographies that comprise the *History of the Patriarchs* generally draw on earlier, individual *vitae* while adding some supplementary material.[66] In view of this fact, it is quite likely that this report of Muhammad's involvement in the conquests antedates George the Archdeacon's addition to the *History of the Patriarchs of Alexandria*: George probably has taken this information from an earlier *vita* of Benjamin. Muhammad's capture of Damascus and Syria and his crossing into Palestine are reported here in a direct, matter-of-fact manner that is in no way polemical. While there are references to broader historical narratives, particularly the Council of Chalcedon (which is unsurprisingly condemned), there is no trace of any anti-Islamic or apologetic agenda in this account of the rise of Islam.

The *Spanish Eastern Source* (ca. 741 CE)

During the earliest years of Islamic rule in Spain, two Latin chronicles, the *Byzantine-Arab Chronicle of 741* and the *Hispanic Chronicle of 754*, were written almost simultaneously. Surprisingly, these are the only surviving Latin historical works composed during the many centuries of Islamic dominion in southern Spain. Although there are considerable differences between the two chronicles, some of which we will note, both have drawn on a common source for most of their information regarding the history of Islam.[67] Inasmuch as the information that concerns us derives from this shared source, we will consider these two related chronicles together in order to ascertain the witness of their earlier source regarding Muhammad's role in the conquest of Palestine. The precise nature of this source, however, remains something of a mystery.

The *Spanish Eastern Source*, as we will name this shared document, is perhaps most surprising for its rather favorable treatment of Muhammad and the early Islamic caliphs. This comes through most clearly in the *Byzantine-Arab Chronicle of 741*, which, although it shows signs of having abbreviated the *Spanish Eastern Source*, does not add any sort of polemic to its source's consistently positive descriptions of the Islamic leaders. This is in contrast to the *Hispanic Chronicle of 754*, which "often adds a pejorative remark or omits the notice altogether if it is too positive, as with that on Muhammad."[68] The *Spanish Eastern Source*'s positive representation of Islam led one early interpreter to suppose that its author must have been a Spanish Christian who had converted to Islam, but for numerous reasons, this hypothesis seems unlikely.[69] Roger Collins suggests instead that the author was a Christian writing in Spain or North Africa, and that the rather favorable treatment of the Islamic leaders was a necessary condition of writing under Islamic rule. Since the *Spanish Eastern Source* generally avoids religious topics and limits its discussions of Islam strictly to political matters, it is conceivable that a Christian could have written it. The positive representation of Islam may simply reflect the need to appease the Islamic authorities.[70]

While it is difficult to exclude completely the possibility that the *Spanish Eastern Source* was composed in the Islamic West, its production in the eastern Mediterranean, and Syria in particular, seems far more likely for a variety of reasons. Theodor Nöldeke was the first to propose this, arguing in an "Epimetrum" to Theodor Mommsen's edition that this *Spanish Eastern Source* was most likely written in Greek by a Syrian Christian close to the center of Umayyad power.[71] More recently, this position has been argued by Hoyland, who explains that the *Spanish Eastern Source* "must have been composed in Syria, since the Umayyad caliphs are each described in a relatively positive vein, all reference to ʿAlī is omitted, Muʿāwiya II is presented as a legitimate and uncontested ruler, and the rebel Yazīd ibn al-Muhallab is labelled 'a font of wickedness.'"[72] Moreover, the *Spanish Eastern Source* shares a number of parallels with the Byzantine chronicle tradition, and if we suppose its composition in Spain, it is difficult to explain the circulation of so many Byzantine sources in Spain (or North Africa for that matter) at this time. By contrast, it is much easier to imagine that a single Eastern historical source had reached eighth-century Spain, most likely written in Greek, as this was the most common language of cultural exchange between East and West at the time.[73] Hoyland additionally identifies a number of common features shared by this *Spanish Eastern Source* and the *Syriac Common Source*, a now lost chronicle written around 750 by Theophilus of Edessa, whose contents are known from the extant chronicles of Theophanes, Agapius, Michael the Syrian, and the Syriac *Chronicle of 1234*, all of which depend on the *Syriac Common Source* (see the discussion below). Hoyland suggests the possibility that perhaps these Spanish chroniclers made use of the same Greek translation of the *Syriac Common Source* that Theophanes must have used when composing his Greek chronicle at the beginning of the ninth century.[74] While he makes this proposal somewhat tentatively, such apparent connections further indicate an eastern Mediterranean origin for the *Spanish Eastern Source*. Although much admittedly remains uncertain, Nöldeke's original suggestion of a Greek source written by a Syrian Christian still remains the most likely solution.

Of the two Spanish chronicles, the *Byzantine-Arab Chronicle* is generally regarded as the earlier, believed to have been written in 741. More accurately, however, this is not the date of the *Byzantine-Arab Chronicle* itself but is instead the date of the final entry from its eastern source. This would indicate that the *Spanish Eastern Source*, rather than the *Byzantine-Arab Chronicle*, was most likely produced in 741, while the *Byzantine-Arab Chronicle* was likely composed sometime later on the basis of this earlier source. For a western European chronicle of its time, the *Byzantine-Arab Chronicle* is rather peculiar in its overwhelming focus on events in the eastern Mediterranean, while devoting very little attention to either Spanish affairs or western Europe. According to Hoyland, only 9 percent of its contents concern Spanish affairs: there are six brief entries on the later Visigothic kings near the beginning (all taken from Isidore of Seville's *History of the Goths*), a brief mention of the conquest of Spain later on, and, near the chronicle's end, a description of the battle of Toulouse in 721.[75] Roughly one-third (29 percent) of the chronicle is devoted to Byzantine affairs, consisting of slightly more substantial notices regarding the Byzantine emperors from Phocas (610) to Leo III (717), although the reign of Heraclius alone commands approximately two-thirds of the total Byzantine material.[76] The majority of the chronicle, almost two-thirds of its total content (62 percent), focuses on Islamic history, with extended, favorable accounts of each ruler from Muhammad to Yazīd II (720–24).

Regarding Muhammad and the rise of Islam, the *Byzantine-Arab Chronicle* is remarkably favorable and free from polemic. As is the case in both chronicles, the account focuses largely on political matters, leaving religious affairs entirely to the side. Muhammad, however, is very clearly identified as the political leader of the Muslims at the time of the Islamic conquests of the Roman Near East. "When a most numerous multitude of Saracens had gathered together, they invaded the provinces of Syria, Arabia, and Mesopotamia, while one named Muhammad held the position of leadership over them [*Syriae, Arabiae et Mesopotamiae prouincias inuaserunt supra ipsos principatum tenente Mahmet nomine*]. Born of a most noble tribe of that people, he was a very prudent man and a foreseer of very many future events."[77] After a brief description of the conquest of Syro-Palestine,[78] the chronicle notes Muhammad's death and succession by Abū Bakr, who continued the conquests. "When Muhammad, the previously mentioned leader of the Saracens, had finished 10 years of rule, he reached the end of his life. [He is] the one whom they hold in such high regard and reverence until this day that they declare him to be the apostle and prophet in all their rituals and writings. In his place Abū Bakr of the Saracens (from which his predecessor also arose) was chosen by them. He organized a massive campaign against the Persians, which devastated cities and towns, and he captured very many of their fortifications."[79] The entire passage is extraordinarily positive for a Christian chronicle written under Islamic occupation. It is rather peculiar, however, in its apparent division of the Islamic conquest of the Near East into two successive stages: the first stage was begun by Muhammad in the "provinces of Syria, Arabia, and Mesopotamia," which context makes clear are Roman provinces, while the second stage commenced after Muhammad's death, when Abū Bakr led a massive campaign of conquest against the Persian Empire.[80]

This two-fold structure can perhaps be explained as the author's attempt to harmonize two different accounts of the Islamic conquest of the Near East, one an older tradition ascribing leadership to Muhammad, witnessed in the Christian historical tradition, and the other an ostensibly emerging Islamic tradition that identified the beginning of the Near Eastern conquests with Abū Bakr's reign. Roughly contemporary with the composition of the *Spanish Eastern Source* is the earliest Islamic biography of Muhammad, Ibn Isḥāq's *Sīra* of the Prophet, compiled sometime not long before the author's death in 767. According to Ibn Isḥāq's seminal account, Muhammad died in 632 in Medina and was not involved in the conquest of Syro-Palestine, as discussed further in the following chapter. During the mid-eighth century then, an Islamic biography of Muhammad had begun to form in the eastern Islamic lands, where the *Spanish Eastern Source* was most likely composed, and, as Lawrence Conrad has demonstrated, some Christian historical writers appear to have had access to these nascent Islamic traditions and occasionally made use of them.[81] The events of the Near Eastern conquests, however, were "only beginning to receive systematic historical attention" in the mid-eighth century, according to Conrad, and the Islamic historical tradition at this time could at best be characterized as "an emerging discipline." Nevertheless, it would appear that the earliest Islamic traditions of Muhammad's life and the Near Eastern conquests had possibly begun to circulate at this time, even though they may not have been written down yet, and some of these reports seem to have affected Christian historical writing of the period.[82]

Thus it seems possible that the author of the *Spanish Eastern Source* may have been aware of emerging Islamic traditions reporting Abū Bakr's leadership at the beginning of the conquests, and his two-stage account of the Islamic conquests could accordingly be understood as an effort to synthesize two divergent traditions that were circulating in his milieu.[83] An early tradition of Muhammad's leadership during the Palestinian campaign has perhaps come into contact here with the traditional Islamic account of Abū Bakr's leadership during the conquest of the Near East after Muhammad's death. The author of the *Spanish Eastern Source* has possibly preserved both traditions and harmonized them by locating Muhammad's leadership of a campaign against the Roman Near East slightly earlier in time, before the traditional date of his death, and then having Abū Bakr organize and execute the campaign against the Persian Empire only after Muhammad's death. This solution results in a somewhat inaccurate chronology, in seeming to make the Islamic conquest of the Roman Near East commence somewhat earlier than it actually did, instead of extending the date of Muhammad's death beyond its traditional date.[84] In any case, the *Spanish Eastern Source* clearly preserves the tradition of Muhammad's leadership at the beginning of the Islamic conquest of Syro-Palestine.

The same division of the conquest into two stages is also preserved in the *Hispanic Chronicle of 754*, although this chronicle adopts a considerably different attitude toward Islam, and consequently, its preservation of the *Spanish Eastern Source* differs in some significant details. In comparison with the *Byzantine-Arab Chronicle*, the *Hispanic Chronicle* is rather polemical, occasionally adding derogatory comments and, more frequently, omitting material from the *Spanish Eastern Source* that portrays Islam too favorably, as can be seen especially by comparing the citations that follow with those above. This chronicle is also considerably longer than the *Byzantine-Arab Chronicle*, since it includes extensive material on the Visigoths and focuses much more squarely on the Iberian Peninsula, while drawing on the *Spanish Eastern Source* to set events in Spain within a more global context. Moreover, the *Hispanic Chronicle* continues its record of eastern events until approximately 750, prompting the suggestion that perhaps the *Spanish Eastern Source* originally continued to this point, and the *Byzantine-Arab Chronicle* has for some reason truncated its source in 741.[85] Yet it is not at all clear why the author of the *Byzantine-Arab Chronicle* would have done this, and so it is just as likely that the *Hispanic Chronicle* has somehow supplemented the *Spanish Eastern Source* with additional information from another source.

In its basic outline, the *Hispanic Chronicle*'s account of the rise of Islam and the Islamic conquests of the Near East largely repeats that of the *Byzantine-Arab Chronicle*, but it clearly has edited the *Spanish Eastern Source* to reflect much more negatively on Islam.

> The Saracens rebelled in 618, the seventh year of the emperor Heraclius, and appropriated for themselves Syria, Arabia, and Mesopotamia, more through trickery than through the power of their leader Muhammad [*Siriam, Arabiam et Mesopotamiam furtim magis quam uirtute Mammet eorum ducatore rebellia adortante sibi*], and they devastated the neighboring provinces, proceeding not so much by means of open attacks as by secret incursions. Thus by means of cunning and fraud rather than power, they incited all of the frontier cities of the empire and finally rebelled openly, shaking the yoke from their necks. In 618, the seventh year of Heraclius, the warriors invaded the kingdom, which they forcefully appropriated with many and various consequences.[86]

Like the *Byzantine-Arab Chronicle*, the *Hispanic Chronicle* follows with a brief description of the Islamic conquest of Palestine, after which it notes the death of Muhammad and his replacement by Abū Bakr: "When Muhammad had completed his tenth year, Abū Bakr, from his own tribe, succeeded to the throne, and he too launched major attacks against the power of the Romans and the Persians."[87] Excepting the marked difference in tone, this report is remarkably similar to the *Byzantine-Arab Chronicle*'s description of the same events. Muhammad is clearly identified as the leader of the Muslims at the time of the initial campaign in Palestine, and there seems to be a two-fold structure to the campaign, beginning in Syro-Palestine and then expanding into Persia during the reign of Abū Bakr.

The most significant difference between these two accounts of the Islamic conquests is the *Hispanic Chronicle*'s indication that Abū Bakr led attacks against both the Romans and the Persians, in contrast to the *Byzantine-Arab Chronicle*, which describes Abū Bakr's massive new campaign against the Persians only. Yet this is not a particularly serious discrepancy, and in actuality it does not contradict the two-stage presentation of the Arab conquests found in the *Byzantine-Arab Chronicle* and, almost certainly, in the *Spanish Eastern Source* as well. Presumably, the author of the *Hispanic Chronicle* reflects here the fact that Islamic military operations against the Roman Empire did not cease with the conquest of Syro-Palestine. After taking control of Syria and Palestine, the Arabs continued to make advances against the Byzantines, proceeding to conquer Egypt, North Africa, and eastern Anatolia, and laying siege to Constantinople itself in 674.[88] Nonetheless, the *Hispanic Chronicle* clearly presents the Persian campaign as something begun only in the reign of Abū Bakr, and thus as a second stage in the Islamic conquest of the Near East. More importantly, the *Hispanic Chronicle*'s adherence to a two-phase description of the conquest is indicated again in its summation of the earliest Islamic conquests, which follows immediately after the notice concerning Abū Bakr. "After the tenth year of Muhammad's rule had expired in 628, in the seventeenth year of the emperor Heraclius, they chose the aforementioned Abū Bakr, of Muhammad's own tribe, in his place, and the Arabs fought with sword against Persia, which had been abandoned by the Roman empire. Abū Bakr ruled for almost three years, powerfully waging war."[89] Here the *Hispanic Chronicle* mentions Persia specifically in connection with Abū Bakr, essentially identifying the beginning of the campaign against Persia with the commencement of his reign. Furthermore, this passage bears a striking similarity to the *Byzantine-Arab Chronicle*'s description of Abū Bakr's reign, making it rather probable that this two-stage account of the Islamic conquests was present in the *Spanish Eastern Source*. Most likely then, this lost Greek chronicle described the initial Islamic assault on Palestine and Syria as occurring under Muhammad's leadership, while presenting the assault of Persia as a second stage in the conquests that commenced under Abū Bakr. Thus, the *Hispanic Chronicle*'s attribution of attacks against the Romans to Abū Bakr is best understood as an addition by its author, who no doubt was aware that conflict between the Byzantines and Muslims continued into the first caliph's reign and beyond.

In conclusion then, the *Spanish Eastern Source* was most likely a Greek chronicle written in Syria, sometime very close to 741. It is clear that this chronicle described the Islamic conquest of Syro-Palestine under Muhammad's leadership and then represented the conquest of Persia as a second stage of the conquests that commenced under Abū Bakr. This two-fold conception of the Islamic conquests possibly reflects an effort to reconcile an earlier tradition of Muhammad's leadership during the assault on Palestine with an emerging Islamic tradition that separated Muhammad from the Near Eastern conquests and identified their beginning with the reign of Abū

Bakr. We do not know the source of the *Spanish Eastern Source*'s information regarding the Islamic conquests and Muhammad's role therein, but given its later date and its apparent connections with the Eastern chronicle tradition, its report may derive from earlier literary sources.

There is no indication that this account of the rise of Islam has been doctored to suit any grand narrative, and perhaps most remarkably there is no trace of any apology or polemic in the *Spanish Eastern Source*, at least insofar as it is represented by the *Byzantine-Arab Chronicle*. There is hardly any reason to suspect that the redactor of the latter document was responsible for this favorable depiction of Islam, particularly in view of the comparative data afforded by the *Hispanic Chronicle*. In fact, so positive is the *Spanish Eastern Source*'s view of Islam that it is tempting to suspect that somehow there are Islamic sources lying just behind it. Perhaps some now lost early Islamic (Umayyad?) historical traditions also preserved a primitive tradition of Muhammad's leadership during the Palestinian campaign, such as we find attested in the non-Islamic sources. The Letter of ʿUmar discussed below certainly suggests this possibility. Furthermore, as noted above, the remarkably positive representation of Islam and its early leaders in the *Spanish Eastern Source* probably reflects an expectation of scrutiny by Islamic readers. In light of this, it seems rather unlikely that its author would either deliberately misrepresent Muhammad as the leader of the Palestinian conquests or would include information widely regarded as false by the Islamic authorities. This source in fact seems to be very close to the center of Umayyad power, and its use by these two early medieval Spanish chroniclers demonstrates not only that the tradition of Muhammad's leadership during the campaign in Palestine remained current in Christian historical writing over a century after the events themselves but also that this tradition had spread even to the West in early Islamic Spain.

The *Syriac Common Source*: The *Chronicle* of Theophilus of Edessa (ca. 750 CE)

The *Syriac Common Source* is a now lost medieval chronicle that we have already mentioned briefly in discussions of the *Doctrina Iacobi* and the *Spanish Eastern Source*. The first traces of this vanished chronicle began to emerge in the later nineteenth century, when it was discovered that the Greek chronicle of Theophanes (written 814 CE) and the Syriac chronicle of Michael the

Syrian (written 1195 CE) had used a common source in compiling their notices for the seventh century and much of the eighth, the so-called Eastern Source, or *Syriac Common Source*, as we have determined to call it. In Michael's case, it was further known that he had used this lost source at second hand, as it had been mediated to him through yet another lost chronicle, the *Chronicle* of Dionysius of Tellmahre (d. 845), which Michael implies was the only substantial source available to him for the seventh and eighth centuries.[90] The subsequent publication of the Christian Arabic chronicle of Agapius (written ca. 940) and the anonymous Syriac *Chronicle of 1234* have added further clarity to the picture. Agapius depends almost entirely on the lost *Syriac Common Source* for his description of events during the years 630–754, providing now a third independent witness to this missing source.[91] The *Chronicle of 1234*, in contrast, presents a second source that has drawn its seventh- and eighth-century material almost exclusively from Dionysius of Tellmahre's lost chronicle, preserving its contents in what many think is a less heavily edited version than is found in Michael's chronicle. Since Dionysius's chronicle is believed to have best preserved the *Syriac Common Source*, this anonymous thirteenth-century chronicle is an invaluable resource for reconstructing the contents of this now lost text.[92]

All of this makes determining the contents of the *Syriac Common Source* a rather complex and at the same time fairly straightforward endeavor. Since it is generally assumed that the *Chronicle of 1234* has most faithfully preserved the *Syriac Common Source*, via Dionysius of Tellmahre's vanished chronicle, one begins by looking at this chronicle, but at each point, one must also compare the data from Theophanes, Agapius, and Michael. Only after evaluating the various testimonies from all of these sources both with one another and with the tendencies of each individual chronicle can one come to a judgment as to what the *Syriac Common Source* most likely reported. When several sources converge very closely, we can be quite certain that this material has been faithfully preserved from the *Syriac Common Source*. By this means, an outline of this lost chronicle can be restored, as evidenced in Hoyland's very helpful summary of its contents.[93] Moreover, we now know the author of this important history of the seventh and eighth centuries to have been Theophilus of Edessa, an eighth-century Maronite scholar who served as court astrologer to the ʿAbbāsid caliph al-Mahdi.[94] Theophilus is said to have written several works on astrology, and his knowledge of Greek was such that he translated the *Iliad* and perhaps the *Odyssey* into Syriac, but all of these works are now lost, except for a few surviving fragments and excerpts. Most importantly for the present purposes, however, Theophilus also composed a chronicle, which, as Conrad has convincingly demonstrated, is almost certainly to be identified with the lost *Syriac Common Source*.[95]

Unfortunately, Theophilus of Edessa's account of Muhammad's life and the rise of Islam is somewhat difficult to determine, since the various witnesses to his *Chronicle* themselves preserve different descriptions of these events. Hoyland nicely summarizes the situation as follows: "Theophanes almost totally ignores Theophilus for his notice on Muhammad, drawing instead, indirectly, on Jewish and Muslim sources. Agapius abridges Theophilus, as he himself acknowledges, and supplements him with material from the Muslim tradition. That leaves Dionysius, who seems to me to best preserve Theophilus' entry."[96] Luckily, Dionysius's account of the rise of Islam is well preserved in both Michael the Syrian's *Chronicle* and the *Chronicle of 1234*: the two are either identical or very close in wording at this point. Michael's text does contain a few passages not found in the *Chronicle of 1234*, many of which are polemical in nature, but these are more likely to have been added by Michael than deleted by the latter.[97] Thus we may with some confidence regard the following passage from the *Chronicle of 1234* as representing something very close what once stood in Dionysius's *Chronicle*, and in turn as reflecting more or less what Dionysius likely found in Theophilus's now lost mid-eighth-century *Chronicle*.

> Therefore this Muhammad, while in the measure and stature of youth, began to go up and come down from his city Yathrib to Palestine for the business of buying and selling. And while he was engaged in this region, he encountered the belief in one God, and it was pleasing to his eyes. And when he went back down to the people of his tribe, he set this belief before them, and when he persuaded a few, they followed him. And at the same time he would also extol for them the excellence of the land of Palestine, saying that "Because of belief in the one God, such a good and fertile land has been given to them." And he would add, "If you will listen to me, God will also give you a fine land flowing with milk and honey." And when he wanted to prove his word, he led a band of those who were obedient to him, and he began to go up and plunder the land of Palestine, taking captives and pillaging. And he returned, laden [with booty] and unharmed, and he did not fall short of his promise to them.

> Since the love of possessions drives such behavior to become a habit, they began continually going out and coming back for plunder. And when those who were not yet following him saw those who had submitted to him becoming wealthy with an abundance of riches, they were drawn to his service without compulsion. And when, after these [raids], the men following him became numerous and were a great force, he no longer [went forth but] allowed[98] them to raid while he sat in honor in Yathrib, his city. And once they had been sent out, it was not enough for them to remain only in Palestine, but they were going much further afield, killing openly, taking captives, laying waste, and pillaging. And even this was not enough for them, but they forced them to pay tribute and enslaved them. Thus they gradually grew strong and spread abroad, and they grew so powerful that they subjugated almost all the land of the Romans and the kingdom of the Persians under their authority.[99]

The indication that the initial Islamic attacks on Palestine began during Muhammad's lifetime and under his leadership is quite clear here, and comparison with Michael's *Chronicle* confirms that Dionysius must have written something very similar in his early ninth-century *Chronicle*. Since Dionysius is believed to best preserve Theophilus's lost chronicle, it is further likely that this account bears a strong resemblance to Theophilus's description of the rise of Islam. Nevertheless, Theophanes and Agapius are not able to confirm the presence of this report in Theophilus's *Chronicle*, since they have both utilized other sources in their descriptions of the rise of Islam.[100] Fortunately, another source is available to verify that Theophilus's *Chronicle* almost certainly contained a passage similar to the one above and, more importantly, that it described Muhammad's leadership during the initial phase of the conquest of Palestine. The East Syrian *Chronicle of Siirt*, written in Arabic during the tenth century, also depends on Theophilus's lost *Chronicle* for its knowledge of many early seventh-century events, including the rise of Islam in particular.[101] Although many details found in Dionysius's account do not appear in the *Chronicle of Siirt*, the latter similarly indicates Muhammad's leadership during the initial assault on the Roman Near East in a report that almost certainly depends on Theophilus's earlier *Chronicle*. The *Chronicle of Siirt* begins its account of the rise of Islam by introducing Muhammad's appearance among the Arabs and briefly describing his religious teachings. Then it continues to relate the events of the conquests: "And Muhammad ibn ʿAbdullah was a strong and powerful leader. In the eighteenth year of Heraclius [627/28], Emperor of the Greeks, the year in which Ardasir the son of Siroe the son of Khosro Parvez reigned [629/30], the Arabs began their conquests, and Islam became powerful. And after that Muhammad no longer went forth in battle, and he began to send out his companions."[102] This passage is obviously much more terse than the account in Dionysius's *Chronicle*, but it is sufficient to confirm that the *Chronicle* of Theophilus, which was their common source, described Muhammad as initiating Near Eastern conquests and then withdrawing, entrusting the command during further expansions to others among his followers.

It would seem that Theophilus has perhaps here also combined two separate traditions about Muhammad's relation to the Near Eastern conquest: one reporting his direct involvement, as indicated in the first section, and a second that remembered Muhammad as remaining behind, sending forth his followers instead to assault the Roman and Persian empires. Quite possibly, this structure reflects an effort to merge the divergent accounts of the Christian historical tradition with the early biographies of Muhammad that were just beginning to emerge at this time. As Conrad has demonstrated, Theophilus appears to have had access to the nascent Islamic historical tradition in some form, and one would imagine that this was the source of his second tradition separating a still-living Muhammad from later events of the conquests.[103] Thus, in a schema that offers an intriguing parallel to the *Spanish Eastern Source*, which also seems to have had knowledge of the early Islamic historical tradition, Theophilus has possibly harmonized these disparate memories according to a two-stage narrative of the Islamic conquests that begins with Muhammad's leadership of the initial attacks on Palestine and then is followed by his withdrawal to Medina and a more extensive conquest of the Near East after his death under the leadership of Abū Bakr. Like the *Spanish Eastern Source*, Theophilus achieves this structure by advancing the onset of the Islamic conquests several years in order to place the initial Islamic attacks on Palestine within the traditional lifespan of Muhammad, that is, before 632, a date that Theophilus may also have learned from his Islamic sources.[104]

Theophilus's *Chronicle* is certainly not free from polemic in its description of the rise of Islam, at least if the *Chronicle of 1234* at all represents his account accurately. The earliest followers of Muhammad are depicted as being interested only in plunder, and their successful conquest of the Near East is ultimately accredited to their excessive greed. Moreover, Muhammad's early travels to Palestine as a merchant are clearly linked with a greater narrative having an apologetic agenda. These trips introduced him to the monotheistic beliefs of the Jews and Christians living there, and the chronicle identifies these as the source of his religious inspiration. The clear implication seems to be that Islam represents nothing more than a rehashing of the Judeo-Christian monotheistic traditions that Muhammad picked up during his visits to Palestine. Nonetheless, Muhammad's leadership during the conquest of Palestine plays no discernable role in this polemical narrative of Islamic origins: only Muhammad's travels to Palestine as a merchant are enlisted to mark Islam as derivative of Judaism and Christianity. Moreover, in contrast to his followers, Muhammad does not act out of greed but instead because of his devotion to the monotheistic traditions that he encountered in Palestine. Thus, his leadership of the initial attacks on Palestine is not ascribed to the covetous motives of his followers but instead to a prophetic call to lead them to the land of divine promise. In any case, Theophilus's identification of Muhammad as alive and leading the initial assaults on Palestine is clear, and the fact that he preserves this tradition perhaps in the face of new information issuing from the nascent Islamic historical tradition is a testament to how deeply engrained the tradition of Muhammad's leadership during the Palestinian campaign remained in Christian historiography approximately one century after the events.

The *Short Syriac Chronicle of 775* (ca. 775 CE)

Among several short Syriac chronicles from the eighth century is an anonymous chronicle sometimes known by the title that it bears in the unique manuscript preserving it: "An Account of the Generations, Races, and Years from Adam until the Present Day." This chronicle runs very quickly through the main events and figures of the Bible, following these with a list of Roman emperors and the length of their reigns. When it reaches the seventh century, the chronicle interrupts the reign of Heraclius with a brief mention of the Islamic conquests; then it continues to give a list of the early Islamic rulers and the number of years that each reigned, up until the accession of the caliph al-Mahdi in 775, which is the likely date of the chronicle's completion. The chronicle's transition from Roman and Muslim authorities, which hinges on the Islamic conquests, is related as follows:

> Maurice, 27 years and 6 months; Phocas, 8 years; Heraclius, 24 years. In the year 930 of Alexander, Heraclius and the Romans en-

tered Constantinople. And Muhammad and the Arabs went forth from the south and entered the land and subdued it [ܘܢܦܩܘ ܡܚܡܛ ܘܛܝ̈ܝܐ ܡܢ ܬܝܡܢܐ ܘܥܠܘ ܠܐܪܥܐ ܘܟܒܫܘܗ̇]. The years of the Hagarenes and the time when they entered Syria and took control, from the year 933 of Alexander. Each one of them by name as follows. Muhammad, 10 years; Abū Bakr, 1 year; 'Umar, 12 years; 'Uthman, 12 years; no king, 5 years; Mu'āwiya, 20 years; Yazīd, his son, 3 years; no king, 9 months; Marwan, 9 months; 'Abd al-Malik, 21 years; Walīd, his son, 9 years; Sulaymān, 2 years and 7 months; 'Umar, 2 years and 7 months; Yazīd, 4 years, 10 months, and 10 days.[105]

Unfortunately, the chronicler's knowledge of early seventh-century chronology was rather poor. As Palmer writes, "This text is full of oddities. Of the Byzantine emperors only Phocas reigned for a period approximately equivalent to that shown here. Of the Arab caliphs Abū Bakr is curtailed and 'Umar I is prolonged."[106] Perhaps the most peculiar item of all, however, is the implication that the Islamic conquest of Palestine took place in the year 618/19. While some of the Christian historical sources place the Islamic conquests before 632, none of them locates it this early: the date precedes even the *hijra* by three years. Strangely enough, however, a Syriac inscription from a north Syrian church dated to 780 bears the same information: "In the year 930 the Arabs came to the land."[107] Although Palmer and Hoyland both speculate as to possible explanations for this date, it remains a mystery. Nonetheless, for the present purposes the text is clear: in spite of its rather idiosyncratic dating, this short chronicle identifies Muhammad as leading the Islamic invasion of the Roman Near East. While the source of this information is completely unknown, it is conveyed without polemic and in the absence of any sort of apologetic agenda or totalizing explanation.

The *Zuqnin Chronicle* (ca. 775 CE)

Roughly contemporary with the preceding text is an anonymous chronicle written at the monastery of Zuqnin near Amida (modern Diyarbakır) sometime around 775. Unfortunately, these two chronicles have more in common than just their date of composition: the *Zuqnin Chronicle*'s chronology is also very weak during the period of the Islamic conquests. In fact, its author warns his readers that he was unable to find reliable sources for most of the seventh and eighth centuries: "From that point (574 CE) up to the present year (775 CE) . . . I have not found [a history] concerning events which is composed on such solid foundations as the former ones [that is, Eusebius, Socrates, John of Ephesus]."[108] In view of the author's own awareness of the rather poor sources at his disposal, one can hardly fault him for his mistakes in chronology.[109] In describing the rise of Islam, the Zuqnin chronicler, in spite of his expectedly weak chronology, nevertheless maintains the tradition of Muhammad's leadership during the invasion of Palestine:

> In 621 the Arabs conquered the land of Palestine all the way to the Euphrates River, and the Romans fled and crossed over to the east of the Euphrates, and the Arabs ruled over them in it [that is, Palestine]. Their first king was a man from among them whose name was Muhammad. They also called this man a prophet, because he turned them away from cults of every sort and taught them that there is one God, the maker of creation. And he established laws for them, because they were especially devoted to the worship of demons, the veneration of idols, and especially the veneration of trees. And because he had shown them the one God, and they had defeated the Romans in battle under his leadership [ܘܐܦ ܕܗܘ ܡܙܟܝܢܐ ܠܪ̈ܗܘܡܝܐ ܒܝܕ ܡܕܒܪܢܘܬܗ], and he had established laws for them according to their desire, they called him a prophet and a messenger of God.[110]

The entry for this year concludes with some brief polemical remarks accusing the Arabs of being "an especially greedy and carnal people," who follow only such laws as suit their desires.[111]

Excepting these final remarks, the *Zuqnin Chronicle*'s account of the rise of Islam is relatively free from polemic: it does not serve any obvious apologetic agenda and is not linked with any sort of totalizing explanation. With regard to Abū Bakr, the chronicle notes only his death and the length of his rule (five years), without any indication of his involvement in the conquest of the Near East. The conquests are not mentioned again until the second year of ʿUmar's reign, when "the Roman Emperor Heraclius went down to Edessa, and the battle of Gabitha took place, and the Persians were defeated and they left Mesopotamia." Following this is a notice that four years later the Arabs crossed into northern Mesopotamia and defeated the Romans there.[112] The chronology is in fact rather chaotic here as elsewhere in the chronicle, but its identification of Muhammad as alive and leading the Muslims during the conquest of Palestine is unmistakable.

A Report from the *Continuatio* of Abū l-Fatḥ's *Samaritan Chronicle* (seventh century?)

Among the sources signaled by Crone and Cook as witnessing to Muhammad's leadership of the assault on Palestine is the *Samaritan Chronicle* compiled by Abū l-Fatḥ al-Sāmirī al-Danafī at only the rather late date of 1355.[113] Yet despite the comparative youth of this collection, it is widely acknowledged that Abū l-Fatḥ's chronicle assembles much earlier material from a variety of older sources, several of which Abū l-Fatḥ identifies at the beginning of his composition.[114] Commissioned by the Samaritan high priest, the chronicle of Abū l-Fatḥ spans the period from Adam through the appearance of Muhammad, and it is generally regarded as one of the most important sources for the history of the Samaritan people. Although it was compiled only relatively recently, this chronicle is broadly recognized as preserving a great deal of much older material.[115] Abū l-Fatḥ's original composition concluded with Muhammad's appearance, drawing to a close with a Samaritan version of the Baḥīrā story, an Islamic legend according to which a Christian monk named Baḥīrā met the young Muhammad and identified him as a prophet on the basis of a distinctive birthmark on his back. In Abū l-Fatḥ's version, three astrologers, a Jew, a Christian, and a Samaritan, discerned Muhammad's appearance from the stars, and traveling together to his hometown, they each spoke with the young man, but it was (of course) the Samaritan who identified the sign on his back.[116] Immediately thereafter, Abū l-Fatḥ's chronicle appends a list of Samaritan high priests up until the appearance of Muhammad, concluding with the date at which the chronicle was completed.[117] Nevertheless, several of the most important manuscripts continue beyond this point, extending the narrative either to the reign of Hārūn al-Rashīd (786–809) or, in one manuscript, until the time of the caliph al-Rāḍī (934–40). There is a clear consensus that Abū l-Fatḥ's chronicle came to a close with Muhammad's discovery by the three astrologers,[118] and thus the account of the Islamic conquests often preserved in this Samaritan chronicle was not originally part of Abū l-Fatḥ's late medieval compilation. Rather, these reports belong to another anonymous Samaritan chronicle, known as the *Continuatio*, that has been appended to Abū l-Fatḥ's composition to extend its scope into the early Islamic period.

This *Continuatio* has recently been translated and subject to careful historical analysis by Milka Levy-Rubin, who determines that despite its distinction from Abū l-Fatḥ's original compilation, the *Continuatio* is in fact a particularly important source for the history of Palestine in the early Muslim period.[119] Levy-Rubin translates the most complete version of the *Continuatio*, known from only a single manuscript, which ends with the rule of al-Rāḍī, and her arguments for the value of this unique witness are convincing. The manuscript is reproduced following the translation, in lieu of an edition. Nevertheless, in the section covering the period between the Islamic conquests and the reign of Hārūn al-Rashīd, for which additional witnesses exist, Levy-Rubin has made comparative use of the other relevant manuscripts, as reflected in her extensive critical annotations. Even though almost nothing is known regarding the provenance or date of this nameless chronicle, Levy-Rubin's careful analysis has demonstrated the exceptional value of its witness to the history of early medieval Palestine.

The *Continuatio* opens with the events of the Islamic conquest of Palestine, and it names Muhammad as a key participant in the assault. Immediately after the "Baḥīrā" legend from Abū l-Fatḥ's chronicle, the *Continuatio* describes the Arab invasion and its consequences for the Samaritans in some detail.

> After this the Ishmaelites, Muḥammad and all his army, went forth to wage war against the Byzantines; they conquered the land and defeated the Byzantines and killed them as they fled before them. The *imām*[120] in those days was ʿAqbūn ben Elʿazar, who lived in Bayt Ṣāma. When the Muslims attacked and the Byzantines fled, all of the Samaritans who lived along the coast fled with the Byzantines from the advancing Muslims, [thinking] that they would return. When the Samaritans began to leave with the Byzantines for Byzantium (Rūmīya), they came to the *raʾīs* ʿAqbūn ben Elʿazar, to Bayt Ṣāma, because he lived there, and said to him, "You are a trustworthy man, so we will deposit our possessions with you until we return," thinking that they would be returning soon. . . . The people who deposited [their wealth] were the people of Caesarea, Arsūf, Maioumas, Jaffa, Lydda, Ascalon, Gaza, and all of the interior villages and those along the coast. And after this they left for Byzantium and remained there and have not returned to this day. The Muslims rose and entered the land of Canaan, and took control of it; they seized all the cities and inhabited them, and ruled

> over all the places until there was no place left which they had not taken over but Caesarea, which rebelled and did not submit to them because it was called the mother of cities and took precedence over them. [The Muslims] set up camp against it and besieged it for six years before they conquered it. . . . After they captured it, every place else stood in awe of them.[121]

As Levy-Rubin observes, this account has much to recommend it, and even at considerable historical distance from the events in question its verisimilitude is impressive.[122] Excepting only the indication that Muhammad participated in the assault, which Levy-Rubin regards as an error adopted from the Syriac chronicle tradition,[123] the details of this narrative comport well with the current understanding of how the conquest of Palestine unfolded. The *Continuatio* reports that while the Samaritans living on the coast felt threatened by the invaders and fled with the Byzantines, the inland areas were not as disrupted by the incursion: in fact, the region was sufficiently tranquil that the coastal Samaritans decided to entrust their belongings to the high priest living there. This description agrees with the apparent concentration of the Arab forces on the Byzantine cities along the coast, and the decision by many inhabitants to abandon their cities rather than offer resistance is consistent with the increasing recognition that the conquest of Palestine was largely a nondestructive affair.[124] Both literary evidence and the archaeological record suggest a picture of the Arab takeover as a mostly peaceful transition: numerous recent excavations have revealed "no sign of any traumatic break or crisis in the seventh century" that would indicate a pitched struggle for control of the region.[125] Moreover, the *Continuatio*'s indication that Caesarea in particular offered fierce resistance to the invaders is also confirmed by other sources, which describe the city's capture only after a long and arduous siege, as reflected in the text.[126]

More importantly, as Levy-Rubin notes, the author of this account "seems to have been familiar with the layout of the Byzantine city [that is, Caesarea], and was well informed about the story of its conquest."[127] Such knowledge of the city's plan as it existed during the Byzantine period is an impressive indication that this account was likely written by someone very close to the events described, perhaps with firsthand knowledge of what he relates.[128] This determination comports with the broader character of the *Continuatio*, whose reports generally exhibit "close proximity, both in time and place, to the events described in the text," often seeming to relate accounts provided by firsthand witnesses.[129] Although it is not known when or by whom this chronicle was first stitched together, its individual reports, as Edward Vilmar was the first to observe, appear to be contemporary with the events that they describe.[130] Comparison with the Islamic historical tradition reveals the *Continuatio* to be a reliable source in general, but with regard to events and activities in early Islamic Palestine, this Samaritan chronicle offers a unique source of particularly "detailed and trustworthy information."[131]

In view of the *Continuatio*'s overall quality as a historical source, and the general credibility of its description of the conquest of Palestine more specifically, one should perhaps reconsider Levy-Rubin's somewhat hasty dismissal of its report concerning Muhammad's involvement in the initial invasion. Levy-Rubin rejects this notice simply out of hand, on the basis that it contradicts the Islamic historical tradition, which consistently reports Muhammad's death prior to the assault on Palestine. Inasmuch as the Samaritans used a dialect of Aramaic as their primary language during the early Middle Ages, she proposes that this "mistake" owes itself to Samaritan knowledge of the Syriac historical tradition. Yet she does not elsewhere show evidence of influence from the Syriac tradition, nor does the *Continuatio* manifest any significant dependence on Christian historiography. Quite to the contrary, Levy-Rubin frequently appeals to the *Continuatio*'s independence and the uniqueness of its witness as evidence of its exceptional importance. To be sure, the *Continuatio* knows the same tradition regarding Muhammad's participation in the invasion of Palestine that is reflected in the Christian sources and the Shimʿōn b. Yoḥai complex. Nevertheless, there is no evidence to suggest that the *Continuatio*'s knowledge of this tradition is contingent on any of these other texts. Instead, the *Continuatio* seems to be an independent witness to this early tradition, which appears to have circulated among the different religious communities of early Islamic Palestine and the Near East more generally. Such an assessment fits well with the detailed and local character of the *Continuatio*'s report, and the apparent credibility of this account of the Palestinian conquest on other points invites some confidence in its notice of Muhammad's involvement. If this remark were merely the isolated witness of an anonymous Samaritan chronicle, it would rightly be disregarded. But when placed in the context of these other sources, it seems that the *Continuatio* confirms their collective witness, and together with the apocalypse of Rabbi Shimʿōn b. Yoḥai, it offers important evidence that this tradition was not simply a collective delusion of Christian historiography.

The *Continuatio*'s account of the Arab conquest is surprisingly free from polemic, and it does not interpret either the Muslim invasion or Muhammad's participation in it according to some apologetic interest or a totalizing narrative. On the whole, the *Continuatio* is quite favorable to the Arabs, and as Levy-Rubin observes, it exhibits a "positive evaluation concerning both conditions in Palestine during the Umayyad period and the positive attitude of these rulers towards the local population."[132] The Arab expulsion of the Byzantines is described with approval, and the terms of Islamic governance are met with neutral acceptance. Of Muhammad, the *Continuatio* says, rather astonishingly, that "the prophet of Islam did not cause anyone distress throughout his life. He would present his belief before the people, accepting anyone who came to him, [yet] not compelling one who did not." His immediate successors, the chronicle continues, ruled "according to what he had enjoined upon them; they did no more or less, and did not harm anyone."[133] It is a portrait of Islam's emergence within Palestine that comports rather well, as Levy-Rubin notes, with what can otherwise be known about this period.[134] Indeed, it is difficult to imagine that such a favorable account would have been composed much beyond the first several decades of Islamic rule, after which social and economic pressure on the *dhimmis* (that is, non-Muslim peoples) was increased. Consequently, when all the relevant factors are taken into consideration, this view of the early Islamic conquests from Samaria has much to recommend it, and its notice of Muhammad's involvement during the invasion warrants its inclusion alongside these other early witnesses to this tradition.

An Early Islamic Witness: ʿUmar's Letter to Leo (Eighth Century)

Important confirmation of this tradition of Muhammad's leadership during the invasion of the Near East emerges from a recently rediscovered early Islamic text, the alleged letter from the caliph ʿUmar II (717–20) to the Byzantine emperor Leo III (717–41). This letter was already known, albeit somewhat indirectly, from a précis of ʿUmar's correspondence composed by the Armenian chronicler Łewond in his eighth-century *History*.[135] Other historical sources, including the chronicles of Theophanes and Agapius make reference to this epistle, which ʿUmar purportedly sent in hopes of converting the emperor, but the original text was long presumed lost.[136] Leo's "reply," however, has been known since the beginning of the sixteenth century, when a brief Latin translation made from "Chaldean" (presumably Arabic) was first published.[137] The full extent of Leo's letter subsequently came to light only in Łewond's *History*, where it follows his summary of ʿUmar's letter.

This Armenian translation of Leo's letter is rather lengthy, and alone it amounts to more than one-fourth of Łewond's chronicle.[138] Its size not only revealed the Latin translation to be a mere summary of Leo's letter but also invited suspicions that the original version of ʿUmar's letter was likely of similar extent.

Fortunately, the complete text of ʿUmar's letter has recently come to light, having been pieced together from two partial manuscripts in different languages by Jean-Marie Gaudeul.[139] The second half of ʿUmar's letter was the first to be discovered, but since this fragment lacks the opening epistolary framework, the nature of this early Islamic text was not immediately recognized. In the mid-1960s, Dominique Sourdel found among a collection of materials from Damascus at the Turkish and Islamic Arts Museum in Istanbul ten stray parchment folios containing an Arabic text that appeared to be quite old. Sourdel published the text as an "Anonymous Muslim Pamphlet" against the Christians, and on the basis of the manuscript itself and the contents of the text, he convincingly argued for its composition sometime before the end of the ninth century.[140] Not long thereafter, Denise Cardaillac published a manuscript of Muslim anti-Christian polemics from the National Library of Madrid that includes the beginnings of a letter ascribed to ʿUmar, written to "Lyon, king of the Christian infidels."[141] Like the other polemics of this collection, the letter survives in Aljamiado, that is, a Romance dialect written using the Arabic script. Cardaillac compared this letter with Arthur Jeffrey's translation of ʿUmar's letter in Łewond's *History*, and, believing that Łewond's version was in fact the original, she concluded that the Aljaimado text had been more recently composed by Moriscos, using ʿUmar's letter as a basis and expanding it considerably.[142] Clearly, however, Łewond gives merely a "summary" (համառօտ), as he himself says, of ʿUmar's letter, and thus his account cannot form a reliable basis for such judgments.[143]

Gaudeul first came to suspect that Sourdel's "Anonymous Pamphlet" should be identified with ʿUmar's letter after comparing Leo's letter in Łewond very broadly with early Islamic polemical writings against the Christians from the ninth and tenth centuries. Gaudeul noted that many of the same themes and even similar expressions were found in both Leo's letter and the Anonymous Pamphlet, leading him to conclude that these two texts were in dialogue with one another and, by consequence, that the Anonymous Pamphlet was indeed the second half of ʿUmar's lost letter.[144] This hunch was confirmed unmistakably when Gaudeul began to compare ʿUmar's Aljaimado letter with Leo's letter in Łewond. At first Gaudeul began to notice connections between the

Aljaimado text and Leo's letter that were similar in nature to the former's parallels with the Anonymous Pamphlet. Then, in the final pages of the Aljaimado letter, Gaudeul found that its contents suddenly began to overlap with the first few pages of the Anonymous Pamphlet and that their contents were nearly identical.[145] This discovery revealed that the Aljaimado text was in fact no Morisco forgery but instead a very faithful translation of this early Arabic text, validating Gaudeul's identification of the Anonymous Pamphlet with ʿUmar's lost letter. Thanks to Gaudeul's meticulous research, ʿUmar's letter has now been recovered from these two manuscripts, thus restoring the other side of this interreligious debate from the early medieval Near East.

On the basis of this newly recovered text, Hoyland has introduced some important refinements to the dating of this early Islam polemic. Although Gaudeul largely follows Sourdel's initial dating of the Anonymous Pamphlet in assigning ʿUmar's letter to the late ninth century,[146] Hoyland's more thorough analysis of the Leo-ʿUmar tradition complex convincingly identifies the eighth century as the likely milieu for this epistolary contest.[147] First, Hoyland answers Stephen Gerö's proposal that Łewond's letter of Leo is a medieval Armenian forgery added to the text by a later reviser. According to Gerö, Łewond's *History* as we now have it is the work of an eleventh- or twelfth-century redactor, who heavily revised a now lost chronicle that was actually written by Łewond in the late eighth century. Among his amendments was the introduction of this epistolary exchange, inspired by brief mention of such correspondence in Thomas Artsruni's early tenth-century Armenian chronicle.[148] Łewond's editor, however, wanted to incorporate a more detailed account of the Leo-ʿUmar correspondence than he found in his source.[149] Consequently, Gerö postulates that the redactor took an existing Armenian anti-Islamic polemical tract and reshaped it to create the illusion of an exchange of letters. The scheme involved forging a letter from ʿUmar that corresponded with the main points of the anti-Islamic treatise and then "lard[ing] the Christian tract with allusions to the ʿUmar letter."[150]

Gerö's theories regarding Łewond's *History* and the Leo-ʿUmar correspondence in particular have not found much acceptance. Experts on the Armenian historical tradition continue to regard Łewond's chronicle as an authentic work of the late eighth century, and its genuine witness to an early tradition of a polemical exchange between Christians and Muslims in the guise of letters authored by Leo and ʿUmar seems widely conceded.[151] Nevertheless, Hoyland responds to each of Gerö's arguments point by point and convincingly demonstrates both that Łewond's *History* as we now have it is a work of the late eighth century and that his version of Leo's letter is not an adaptation of an Armenian work, but in fact translates an older Greek text that was part of an early tradition of epistolary polemic between Muslims and Christians.[152] Gaudeul's study, published subsequent to Gerö's work, is particularly decisive in this regard. Gaudeul's recovery of 'Umar's letter leaves Gerö's scenario rather improbable, and the close rhetorical connections between this Muslim text and Łewond's account of the correspondence suggests that they reflect an actual polemical exchange between Christians and Muslims in the early medieval Near East.[153]

Although Gaudeul (and Sourdel) would locate this exchange as late as the end of the ninth century, the date of Łewond's chronicle, the late eighth century, would seem to indicate that it had reached a fairly mature state more than a century earlier. Many of the main themes from this confrontation are in fact, as Hoyland notes, paralleled in other sources of the late eighth century and the early ninth.[154] Moreover, both letters have the appearance of responding to an earlier tradition of correspondence, which leads Hoyland to propose that over the course of the eighth century a series of Leo-'Umar / 'Umar-Leo letters were composed, and "what has come down to us is a compilation from or rehashing of such works."[155] Perhaps most importantly, however, the Aljaimado text of 'Umar's letter begins with an *isnād*, that is, a chain of the text's early transmitters. Although such efforts to authenticate Islamic traditions by providing an intellectual pedigree were frequently forged and are thus generally viewed with a high measure of suspicion, Gaudeul and Hoyland are both correct to note that in this instance the letter's *isnād* seems worthy of some historical consideration.[156] The *isnād* identifies a series of three scholars who are known to have been active in Ḥimṣ (Homs in western Syria), and the fact that the *isnād* does not attempt to link the letter with 'Umar himself seems to speak for its authenticity. The earliest of these transmitters died in 798, a date that would be consistent with the origins of these epistolary polemics in the eighth century. On the whole then, as Hoyland rightly concludes, the evidence strongly favors the emergence of a literary tradition of polemical correspondence between Leo and 'Umar, and more specifically the composition of 'Umar's letter, sometime before the end of the eighth century. This would make 'Umar's letter one of the oldest Islamic documents to have survived, making it a precious witness to the beginnings of Islam.

The relevant passage of 'Umar's letter for the present question comes at the very end of the text, in the early Arabic fragment published by Sourdel.

As the letter draws to a close, it undertakes an extended defense of Muhammad's prophethood. Invoking passages from the Qur'ān as evidence, "'Umar" contends that Muhammad was not taught by the Christian monks of the Baḥīrā legend but instead received his teaching directly from God. The nature of Muhammad's message is also defended. Muhammad brought the truth of monotheism to a people that "had never before received any prophet or any scripture, a nation of ignorant people . . . worshipping idols."[157] Muhammad's success in the face of his countrymen's immorality and infidelity is adduced as proof of the divine origin of his message. The conversion of these barbarous and faithless men to prayer, fasting, piety, and faithfulness verifies the authenticity of Muhammad's prophetic call and his preaching: "Indeed, only prophets, God's messengers, and the best of His servants can lead men in this way towards good, prescribing it, exhorting to it, while forbidding sins and transgressions."[158]

The letter then shifts to the Islamic conquests, which comprise its final theme. At God's command Muhammad taught his followers to fight against those who "give partners to God, refuse to recognize Him and worship another god until they come to honour the only God, the only Lord, adopt the one religion"; those who fail to do so are to pay the *jizya*, by which God will teach them to realize their infidelity (citing Qur'ān 9.29). As a consequence of this instruction, the letter explains that Muhammad led his followers forth out of Arabia against the Byzantine and Persian empires. "In this way, with him in whom we trust, and in whom we believe, we went off [فخرجنا معه تصديقا به وإيقانا به], bare foot, naked, without equipment, strength, weapon, or provisions, to fight against the largest empires, the most evidently powerful nations whose rule over other peoples was the most ruthless, that is to say: Persia and Byzantium."[159] Thus, this early Islamic text seems to confirm the witness of the non-Islamic sources that Muhammad was still leading his followers as they went forth and invaded the Byzantine Empire. Since 'Umar's letter is a Muslim text, Hoyland's questions are largely irrelevant: although it is a polemical text, there is no reason to think that the literary confrontation with Christianity has somehow determined Muhammad's involvement in the invasions. While the key passage unfortunately does not identify Muhammad specifically by name, using instead the third-person singular suffix pronoun, the immediate context leaves little doubt that he is the one with whom they went forth to fight, and both Sourdel and Gaudeul agree in translating the passage thus.[160]

Consequently, we have in 'Umar's letter to Leo an early Islamic text roughly contemporary with (or at least within a few decades of) Ibn Isḥāq's biography that appears to preserve a memory of Muhammad's leadership at the beginning of the Near Eastern conquests. This strongly invites the possibility that 'Umar's letter bears witness to the same early tradition signaled by the non-Islamic sources. Quite possibly, the tradition of Muhammad's leadership during the invasion of Palestine was still remembered by the Muslims of western Syria at the end of the eighth century, even as the Medinan traditions of Muhammad's pre-conquest death at Medina received official sanction at the court in Baghdad, in the form of Ibn Isḥāq's imperially commissioned biography.[161] Perhaps the author of 'Umar's letter did not yet know the new contours of Muhammad's biography as they were being formed in Medina and authorized at the 'Abbāsid capital. Or it may be that 'Umar's letter adheres to this tradition because it is in dialogue with the Christians, who seem to have known this early tradition rather well. In confronting these religious rivals, it would not be helpful to introduce revisionist history: such dramatic changes to the narrative of Islamic origins would likely not persuade Christians of the truth of Islam. Moreover, western Syria is precisely the location where one might expect to find such a traditional holdout: as will be seen in subsequent chapters, the tradition of Muhammad's leadership during the assault on Palestine seems to reflect the sacred geography of the earliest Muslims and Umayyads in particular. On the whole, the letter of 'Umar to Leo offers important and early confirmation from the Islamic tradition that the combined witness of the non-Islamic sources is not simply the result of an unlikely collective mistake. Instead, this anti-Christian polemical treatise, seemingly one of the earliest Islamic texts to have survived, vouches for the antiquity and authenticity of the tradition witnessed by these Christian, Jewish, and Samaritan sources.

Conclusion

These eleven witnesses from the seventh and eighth centuries all indicate in various ways that Muhammad was alive and leading the Muslims when the Islamic conquest of Palestine began.[162] While occasionally the years assigned to various events are not correct, this is not at all uncommon in medieval chronicles: such errors occur frequently in the chronicle tradition, and similar mistakes in chronology characterize the Islamic historical tradition as well.[163] Nonetheless, even when their chronologies are confused and inaccurate, medieval historical sources such as these are often reliable for their relative sequencing of events, and the consistency displayed with regard to Muhammad's involvement in the Near Eastern conquests is impressive to say the least. Some of these documents merely indicate Muhammad's death sometime after the Near Eastern conquests had begun, while others are more descriptive in noting Muhammad's actual leadership during the invasions. But when all of the sources are considered together, as they are here, their collective witness to Muhammad's continued leadership of the early Islamic community during the assault on the Roman Near East is unmistakable. While many scholars have rejected or ignored the evidence of these sources, no one has disputed that they do in fact report this.

For the most part, these reports are free from polemic and apologetic interests, and even when these qualities are evident elsewhere in a given text, they do not affect the notice of Muhammad's vitality and leadership of the military campaign in Palestine. None of these texts connects its report of Muhammad's leadership during the Near Eastern conquests with any sort of "totalizing explanation" of Islam or an apologetic agenda. Although a few of the authors display marked ideological tendencies elsewhere in their writing, in no instance are these themes linked with their observations that the conquest of Palestine or the Roman Near East began during Muhammad's lifetime. In every case, the notice of Muhammad's survival and leadership during the Near Eastern campaigns is mentioned almost in passing, so unobtrusively that its dissonance with the received tradition could easily be overlooked, as indeed it generally has been. The neutral, matter-of-fact manner with which the various sources convey this information suggests that this was the chronology that the authors had collectively received (or perhaps in some cases experienced?) rather than something that they were trying to impose onto their narratives. There is then little cause to suspect that any or all of these writers have invented a report locating the Islamic conquest of the Near East within Muhammad's lifespan to suit some broader ideological agenda: no evidence would suggest this, nor is there any obvious reason for them to have fabricated such information. Likewise, the possibility of a collective error by all eleven sources seems highly improbable, particularly in the case of the Letter of ʿUmar. While such an interpretation of course cannot be entirely excluded, it does not offer a very compelling explanation for the persistent and seemingly independent manifestations of this tradition linking Muhammad with the invasion of the Roman Near East.[164]

Several of these documents are of particularly high quality, including the first two and the final two especially. The *Doctrina Iacobi*, written within months of the invasion of Palestine it would seem, bears near contemporary witness to Muhammad's presence among the invading "Saracens." Although the text itself was composed in North Africa, its report concerning recent events in Palestine is said to rely on a document sent by a Jewish resident of Palestine, Abraham, who allegedly obtained his information about the Arabs and their prophet from eyewitnesses. In light of Abraham's notice that Muhammad was preaching the imminent arrival of the messiah, one wonders if some of his informants were among those Jews who saw Muhammad's religious movement as the fulfillment of their eschatological hopes. Such contemporary Jewish faith in Muhammad as a divinely appointed deliverer and herald of the messiah is clearly witnessed in the apocalyptic traditions ascribed to Rabbi Shimʿōn b. Yoḥai. Although these early traditions survive only in slightly more recent texts, their identification of Muhammad as one who conquers the land at God's will is so anomalous with later Jewish attitudes toward Muhammad and Islam that, as numerous scholars have noted, this apocalyptic vision must have been composed very close to the events of the conquest itself. Similarly, the *Continuatio* of the *Samaritan Chronicle*, which very clearly relates Muhammad's leadership during the invasion of Palestine, seems to preserve a particularly early account of the Islamic conquests, despite its survival only in a relatively late collection. Like the apocalypse of Rabbi Shimʿōn, the *Continuatio*'s strikingly positive attitude toward Muhammad and the invading Muslims, as well as its seemingly detailed and accurate knowledge of the conquests, suggests that its source for events of the mid-seventh century must have been composed in close proximity to the events themselves, perhaps on the basis of eyewitness accounts.

Finally, ʿUmar's Letter to Leo provides important confirmation of this early tradition from the Islamic side. Although this epistolary polemic is one of the later texts that we have considered, it is for an Islamic source particularly early. By way of comparison, the oldest extant narrative of Islamic origins, Ibn Isḥāq's biography of Muhammad, was composed only in the middle of the eighth century, and it is known only in two later recensions by ninth- and tenth-century authors. Moreover, as Hoyland notes, ʿUmar's letter shows signs of having compiled earlier "exchanges," and thus perhaps its tradition of Muhammad's leadership during the invasion of the Near East is even older than this version of the letter itself, similarly predating Ibn Isḥāq's biography. The apparent composition of ʿUmar's letter in western Syria is especially important, inasmuch as the Medinan traditions of Muhammad's pre-conquest death at Medina may have first spread into the Near East only at a later date largely through influence of Ibn Isḥāq's biography, a work composed by this Medinan scholar in Baghdad at the caliph's request. As a whole the canonical accounts of Islamic origins were composed under ʿAbbāsid rule almost entirely on the basis of Medinan and Iraqi authorities, and accordingly Syrian and (pro-)Umayyad traditions are very scarce in these eighth- and ninth-century collections.[165] Yet by contrast, ʿUmar's letter originates in the same geographic region as most of the sources considered in this chapter, that is, Syro-Palestine, the center of Umayyad rule. Quite possibly, this early Islamic apology preserves a common early memory of Muhammad's role in the invasion of Syro-Palestine from this region and this era, shared by Muslim, Christian, Jew, and Samaritan alike. Of utmost importance is the independence of these four reports from one another, which makes their convergence regarding Muhammad's leadership at the beginning of the Near Eastern conquests quite impressive to say the least. While it is of course possible that someone might have misunderstood Muhammad's significance for the invading Muslims, it is extremely unlikely that these four documents and their sources would all have made the same mistake independently, particularly in the case of ʿUmar's letter. Thus, in view of their high quality, these sources alone are compelling enough to warrant serious reconsideration of the traditional Islamic memory of Muhammad's death.

The remaining seven reports all come from the Christian historical tradition, whose accounts no doubt depend on earlier oral and written traditions about the Islamic invasions. Nonetheless, several of these texts bear witness even more clearly to Muhammad's leadership at the onset of the Near Eastern conquests. This agreement suggests that we are not misreading the earlier sources, or, at the least, we are interpreting their reports in the same way as the next generation of Near Eastern Christians and their historians. Like the previous four documents, these sources also represent the diverse religious communities of the early medieval Near East. Although one document, the short Syriac chronicle written in 775, was produced in an unknown context, the others were composed by authors from the Coptic, Maronite, East Syrian, and West Syrian communities, while one set of traditions survives in the Christian chronicles of early Islamic Spain. And most importantly, each of these witnesses appears to transmit this information independently.

We would add here briefly a later indication from the Islamic biographical tradition identifying Syria as the land of Muhammad's rule. In a report assigned to Kaʿb al-Aḥbār, a legendary bearer of Jewish lore in the early Islamic tradition, Ibn Saʿd identifies Mecca as the place of Muhammad's birth, Medina as the place of his migration, and Syria as the land of his rule (ملكه بالشأم).[166] Although it certainly is possible that this tradition merely reflects the eventual dominion of Muhammad's followers in Syria shortly after his death, this notice that Muhammad ruled over Syria is rather intriguing in light of the information above. The statement, which Kaʿb claims to know from "the Torah," identifies Syria as the area in which Muhammad established his political authority, seemingly in the same fashion that Mecca should be recognized as the place where he was born and Medina as the place to which he fled. Such parallels would appear to suggest that rule over Syria was one of the hallmarks, indeed the climax, of Muhammad's career: while other tendencies may have inspired this formulation, one certainly should not exclude the possibility that this report bears witness at greater distance to an earlier tradition associating Muhammad with the conquest of Syro-Palestine.

Yet while each of these early sources indicates in various ways the same chronology of Muhammad's survival into the period of the Near Eastern conquests, it should be noted that none of them actually relates any specific information concerning the manner and circumstances of his death. There are, however, a few Christian reports from the eighth or ninth century that in fact purport to describe the events of Muhammad's death. As one might expect, these accounts are highly polemical, offering narratives of Muhammad's demise that have been deeply colored by the Christian imagination. One of these, the Latin *Istoria de Mahomet*, is a brief biography of Muhammad that seems to have come into circulation in Spain sometime prior to the middle of the ninth century, when Eulogius of Cordova incorporated it into his *Liber apologeticus martyrum*.[167] Interestingly enough, like the sources considered above, the *Istoria de Mahomet* also seems to present the Islamic conquest of the Roman Near East within Muhammad's lifetime. This concise Christian "Life of Muhammad" begins with Muhammad "as an avaricious usurer," whose frequent business travels brought him into contact with Christian communities.[168] After drinking deeply of what he learned from the Christians, Muhammad was approached by "the spirit of error . . . in the form of a vulture," who persuaded Muhammad that he was the angel Gabriel and directed Muhammad to present himself to his people as a prophet. Muhammad then began to preach, convincing many to abandon idolatry and ordering them "to take up arms on his behalf, and . . . to cut down their adversaries with the sword." Then we learn that "first they killed the brother of the emperor who held dominion over the land and in recognition of the triumph of victory, they established the Syrian city of Damascus as the capital of the kingdom." Immediately thereafter, the *Istoria* continues to describe how Muhammad fabricated the Qur'ān, followed by notice of his somewhat irregular marriage to the wife of Zayd, which took place after he had already "subjected her to his lust."[169] Then with the commission of such a heinous sin, "the death of his soul and body approached simultaneously," and the *Istoria* concludes with an account of Muhammad's death.

The flow of the narrative certainly seems to suggest that the conquest of Syria took place during Muhammad's lifetime. It appears in this biography of Muhammad amid other major themes from his life, such as his career as a merchant, his doctrine of religious conquest, his composition of the Qur'ān, and his "irregular" marital life. If one did not know any better (from reading the accounts of the traditional Islamic sources), one would presumably understand the assault on Syria as also falling within Muhammad's lifespan. Standing squarely at the center of this polemical *vita*, the conquest of Syria seems very much to belong among the accomplishments of Muhammad's prophetic career. It is thus tempting to suppose that we meet here yet another witness to the early tradition of Muhammad's survival during the invasion of Syro-Palestine, albeit at a slightly greater chronological distance. Although the source is admittedly a hostile one, there is no obvious polemical motive for placing the Near Eastern campaign within—as opposed to immediately after—Muhammad's lifetime. That Damascus is here in focus, rather than Jerusalem, merely reflects its status as the first capital of the Islamic empire, and its capture in 634–35 fits with the time frame envisioned by the sources considered above. Likewise, Heraclius's brother Theodore did in fact lead, unsuccessfully, the defense of Syria, even though there is no evidence that he died in battle against the Arabs, as suggested by the *Istoria*.[170] Nevertheless, it must be admitted that the text does not explicitly associate Muhammad directly with the assault on the Roman Near East, and Damascus did not become the Islamic capital until 661. While these events do rather strangely intrude at the center of Muhammad's life story here, one cannot exclude the possibility that the author has "cut to the chase" by introducing what his audience would otherwise have known to be the final outcome of Muhammad's militant message. Yet by the same token, the *Istoria* does not otherwise clearly separate Muhammad from the conquests, and in light of the early tradition placing them within his lifetime, it seems very possible that we have here another relatively early witness to this rival tradition.[171]

As the *Istoria* continues to relate Muhammad's death, it explains that when he sensed that death had come upon him (immediately after his "sin" with Zayd's wife), he predicted that he would be resurrected three days after his death by the angel Gabriel. Following his death, Muhammad's followers maintained a vigil, guarding his body and awaiting its resurrection. When three days later this did not transpire, Muhammad's body began to stink, and his followers convinced themselves that their presence was preventing the angel's appearance. So they left the body alone, "and immediately instead of angels, dogs followed the stench and devoured his flank"; his disappointed followers then buried what was left of the body.[172] The Syriac versions of the Baḥīrā legend, a medieval Christian counter-narrative of Islamic origins, share a similar story, according to which Muhammad declared himself the Paraclete. By consequence, it seems, his followers expected that three days after his death "he would go up to heaven, to Christ, who sent him."[173] When he died, they brought his body to a large house and sealed it inside. Three days later, they returned only to find that they could not even enter the house on account of the stench of Muhammad's rotting corpse. Barbara Roggema, the text's most recent editor, dates this particular tradition tentatively to the eighth or ninth century, largely on the basis of its similarities to the *Istoria de Mahomet*, while Krisztina Szilágyi suggests a similar dating on the basis of the Baḥīrā legend's literary history.[174] It certainly seems possible, as Roggema suggests, that a Christian polemical tradition ascribing failed predictions of a bodily resurrection to Muhammad arose quite early, and that this episode from the Baḥīrā legend thus bears witness to an early anecdote about the end of Muhammad's life. As much would certainly seem to be suggested by an early Islamic tradition, discussed in the following chapters, that when ʿUmar initially refused to allow Muhammad's burial after his death, seemingly in hopes of his resurrection, al-ʿAbbās intervened to insist on his burial, noting that Muhammad's corpse had begun to stink.

Unfortunately, however, the Syriac Baḥīrā legend affords no indication of the timing of Muhammad's death in relation to either the Near Eastern conquests or any other major events from the history of early Islam. Nevertheless, the most striking feature of this alternative account of Muhammad's demise is its indication, in the East Syrian recension at least, that Muhammad's followers do not know anything about his grave, including, one would presume its location.[175] This feature would seem to suggest a particularly early date for this tradition, sometime before the tradition of Muhammad's death and burial in Medina had become well established. More to the point, particularly for present purposes, is that this brief polemical account seems to recall a time when Muhammad's followers were perhaps uncertain as to the location of his grave. It is difficult to imagine a Christian polemicist fabricating such Islamic ignorance concerning the site of Muhammad's death, particularly if the tradition of his death in Medina had been well established from early on. It is certainly not obvious, for instance, how this would serve the tendencies of this polemic: there is no reason why the location of the house where Muhammad failed to resurrect would need to remain a mystery, and indeed, the absence of a known grave could seem to validate an Islamic claim to his resurrection. Admittedly, this source is problematic on a number of fronts, and its polemical character raises substantial questions regarding its reliability. Nonetheless, its suggestion that there was a time when Muhammad's followers did not know the location of his grave is more than a little intriguing, and it certainly adds lateral support to the notion that Muhammad's life may have ended in rather different circumstances than his traditional biographies remember it.

In summary then, from 634 onward, the various religious communities of the Near East repeatedly report a memory of Muhammad's continued leadership of the Islamic community at the beginning of the Islamic conquests of the Near East. The consistency of this tradition and its persistence across confessional boundaries and over considerable distances are themselves quite persuasive. Moreover, there is no obvious reason for these authors to have fabricated this information, and the nature of the sources that transmit this information suggests that on this particular matter they are as reliable as one could reasonably expect of any historical source. To my knowledge, the earliest non-Islamic text to indicate that Muhammad died before the onset of the Near Eastern conquests is in fact Łewond's Armenian chronicle from the end of the eighth century, although Łewond's chronology of the conquest is itself highly erratic. Łewond locates the conquest of Syria and Palestine after Muhammad's death, although a little too far thereafter: according to Łewond, the Muslims did not invade Palestine until after the death of Heraclius, that is, 641.[176] This would place the invasion of Palestine well into ʿUmar's reign, which cannot be right.

Perhaps a more successful effort to "correct" the Christian historical tradition so that it would agree with the emergent Islamic historical tradition can be seen in the Greek chronicle of Theophanes, written at the beginning of the ninth century.[177] Although Theophanes is clear in signaling Muhammad's decease before the onset of the Palestinian campaign, Theophanes, or perhaps more correctly one of his sources, has made use of Islamic traditions for knowledge of the chronology of Muhammad's life, as Conrad has shown.[178] Thus, this Christian witness to the traditional Islamic chronology does not in fact offer independent attestation of Muhammad's death prior to the conquest but almost certainly reflects the author's direct knowledge of the emergent Islamic historical tradition and its memory of Muhammad's death in Medina in 632. Nevertheless, despite these "corrections," Theophanes additionally relates that Muhammad's life ended with his "slaughter" or "wounding" (σφαγή): could this anomaly perhaps suggest some vestige of an earlier tradition that Muhammad died in battle, possibly leading his followers in the conquest of the Holy Land?[179] To be sure, such a proposal is highly speculative, but the further indication in this passage that Muhammad's "slaughter" took place against a backdrop of Jewish messianic expectations would seem to comport with many of the early reports from the sources discussed above, as well other related traditions to be considered in Chapter 4. In any case, despite the eventual establishment of the canonical Islamic narratives of origins, the tradition of Muhammad's leadership during the conquest of Palestine died a hard death, and it continued to figure prominently in the Syriac historical tradition, where it appears in both Michael's *Chronicle* of the later twelfth century and the anonymous *Chronicle of 1234*, as we have already seen. Likewise, Thomas Artsruni's Armenian *History* from the turn of the tenth century also places the conquest of Palestine within Muhammad's lifetime.[180] Perhaps the tradition continued even later.

On the whole then, when considered purely on its own merits, the tradition that Muhammad survived to lead the invasion of Palestine would appear to be both early and trustworthy. The only problem, however, is that the Islamic historical tradition invariably reports Muhammad's death at Medina in 632, almost two full years before the Islamic armies first invaded Palestine and the rest of the Near East. Since these Islamic sources were essentially the only accounts of Islam's earliest history consulted or even available prior to the last century, the traditional Islamic account of the end of Muhammad's life has dominated Western historiography for centuries.[181] Now, however, thanks to the considerable efforts of both Western and Near Eastern scholars over the past century and a half, the literary heritage of other religious communities from the medieval Near East is becoming better known, and their writings have disclosed new perspectives on the rise of Islam. While much that these sources report is of use only for understanding internal responses to Christian defeat and the transition to Muslim rule, some of the information preserved by these texts also has value for understanding the earliest history of Islam itself, and the tradition of Muhammad's leadership at the beginning of the conquest of Palestine quite possibly stands among the latter. The high quality of the evidence demands that we take this witness seriously. But what are we to make of these two conflicting reports? To pursue this question further we must first and foremost consider both the nature and reliability of the sources responsible for transmitting the Islamic tradition of Muhammad's death in Medina as we have just done for the non-Islamic sources, a task to which we now turn in the following chapter.

CHAPTER 2

The End of Muhammad's Life in Early Islamic Memory

The Witness of the *Sīra* Tradition

Any effort to reconstruct the life of Muhammad and the origins of the religious movement that he founded must confront the difficult problem that there are only a handful of Islamic sources from the early period that convey any information regarding his life—or death, for that matter. Particularly troubling is the complete absence of any accounts from the first Islamic century. While the traditions of the Qur'ān rather probably belong to the first Islamic century, they convey virtually no information concerning the life of Muhammad and the circumstances of his prophetic mission.[1] Admittedly, many of Muhammad's later biographers claim to relate traditions on the authority of earlier sources, identifying their alleged informants in the chains of transmission, or *isnāds*, that generally accompany individual traditions about the prophet. Nevertheless, in the Islamic tradition such claims of authenticity through appeal to ancient experts are notoriously unreliable. *Isnāds* and the *ḥadīth* (that is, prophetic traditions) that they claim to validate were subject to forgery on a massive scale in early and medieval Islam, as discussed in more detail below, and among the most highly suspect and artificial elements in this system of legitimation are the transmitters named at the earliest stages, that is, the first-century "Companions of the Prophet" and their "Successors."[2] Moreover, while some later sources ascribe written biographies of Islam's prophet to certain renowned authorities from the later first century AH, many other reports offer contradictory testimony, and the balance of the evidence would appear to favor the latter. The issue of writing itself was the subject of considerable controversy in earliest Islam, and even though some more optimistic scholars have accepted at face value such testimonies of early written biographies, there is general consensus against the written transmission of traditions prior to the second Islamic century.[3] Despite some hints that early traditionists may have kept written notes for their own personal use, the transmission of knowledge remained almost exclusively oral for more than one hundred years after Muhammad's death.[4] ʿUrwa ibn al-Zubayr (d. 712), a renowned early authority on Muhammad's biography, is among those most frequently alleged to have written a narrative of Muhammad's life, but most scholars remain deeply skeptical of such reports.[5]

Nevertheless, a small group of researchers has recently attempted to locate certain biographical traditions credibly within the first Islamic century, focusing especially on traditions ascribed to ʿUrwa.[6] Avoiding the question of whether ʿUrwa actually wrote a biography of Muhammad, these scholars seek to identify ʿUrwa as the author of a corpus of oral tradition that is often assigned to his authority by much later sources. Yet despite a well-developed methodology and some very thorough analyses, their arguments are not persuasive. Indeed, the general failure of this approach to identify a significant corpus of early material presents one of the most troubling problems for efforts to reconstruct the history of primitive Islam on the basis of traditional Islamic sources.[7] The late formation of the earliest accounts of Islamic origins thus raises significant questions concerning their reliability as historical sources, particularly when they are studied in isolation from other non-Islamic witnesses. Excepting only the decidedly "ahistorical" witness of the Qurʾān, there are essentially no Islamic accounts describing the formation of Islam that can be convincingly dated prior to the turn of the second Islamic century, a circumstance greatly limiting historical-critical investigation of the beginnings of Islam.[8]

The manifold shortcomings of the early Islamic historical tradition, particularly with respect to the period of origins, invite the strong possibility that the beginnings of Islam differed significantly from their representation in the earliest biographies of Muhammad. Not only were the narratives first composed at only an arresting distance from the events that they describe, but modern scholarship on the traditional biographies of Muhammad has repeatedly found them to be unreliable sources. These writings present a highly idealized image of Muhammad and the early community suited to the beliefs and practices of Islam at the beginning of its second century and conformed to a number of literary and theological tendencies. Most importantly, however, the chronology of these narratives has long been recognized as one of the most artificial and unreliable aspects of Muhammad's canonical biographies, allowing for the real possibility that the sources considered in the previous chapter may indeed preserve an earlier tradition regarding the final years of Muhammad's life. The traditions of Muhammad's death contained in the oldest biographies are rather minimal, and in their earliest state they seem to have lacked any specific geographic or chronological context: these elements would appear to have been added only with the composition of the first written biographies around the middle of the eighth century. Consequently, these relatively recent documents cannot exclude the possibility that Muslims of an earlier age may indeed have remembered their prophet as leading his followers as they left Arabia and first entered into the land that had been promised to Abraham and his descendants. To the contrary, their failings as historical sources almost require that we look elsewhere to supplement our knowledge about the beginnings of Islam.

The Earliest Islamic Sources for the Life of Muhammad

The single most important early biography of Muhammad remains the *Maghāzī*, or *Campaigns*, of the Prophet by Ibn Isḥāq (d. 767), an account of Islamic origins compiled around the middle of eighth century, approximately 120 years after Muhammad's death.[9] Unfortunately, however, Ibn Isḥāq's biography does not itself survive: it is known only through later recensions, the most important of which are the *Sīra*, or *Life*, of the Prophet by Ibn Hishām (d. 833), composed at the beginning of the ninth century, and al-Ṭabarī's *History* from the turn of the tenth century. The mediated nature of Ibn Isḥāq's traditions must constantly be born in mind, particularly inasmuch as Ibn Hishām does not always reproduce Ibn Isḥāq's biography faithfully but has "abridged and vigorously edited" his source.[10] Nevertheless, through comparison of Ibn Hishām's transmission with that of al-Ṭabarī and others, it is frequently possible to recover significant amounts of Ibn Isḥāq's lost biography of Muhammad: when the sources coincide, it is highly likely that the material in question derives from Ibn Isḥāq's vanished *Life*. Of the various other early Islamic scholars who were reportedly engaged in the production and transmission of the *sīra* and *maghāzī* traditions (the two terms being largely interchangeable in this period), we generally know little more than their names. It would appear that only a handful of these early authorities actually produced written accounts, and with the exception of Ibn Isḥāq's biography, as mediated primarily by Ibn Hishām's later redaction, these early documents are witnessed by only a couple of fragments. A papyrus, for instance, has been discovered that relates traditions ascribed to Wahb b. Munabbih (d. 728), and while it remains uncertain whether these traditions actually derive from Wahb, there is no question that this document witnesses to early traditions, inasmuch as the artifact itself is contemporary with Ibn Hishām.[11] Unfortunately for present purposes, however, this fragment relates no information concerning the end of Muhammad's life.[12]

Working backward from the later recensions of Ibn Isḥāq's biography, one finds Ibn Shihāb al-Zuhrī (d. 742) frequently identified as one of Ibn Isḥāq's primary sources. Al-Zuhrī was a renowned Medinan authority on the life of Muhammad from the generation immediately prior to Ibn Isḥāq, and on the whole it seems likely that many of the traditions related by Ibn Isḥāq ultimately derive from al-Zuhrī's teaching, at least in terms of their general content. While it certainly is not at all impossible that later transmissions of Ibn Isḥāq's *sīra* have occasionally inserted al-Zuhrī's name on the basis of his reputation as a great scholar,[13] the probability that much of Ibn Isḥāq's information depends on al-Zuhrī seems rather high. In some instances, traditions from al-Zuhrī are further ascribed to ʿUrwa ibn al-Zubayr, and while it is not inconceivable that certain reports about Muhammad took their origin from ʿUrwa's teaching, this possibility has not been successfully demonstrated and remains highly speculative. It is doubtful that al-Zuhrī himself wrote either a history of early Islam or a biography of its prophet,[14] but several of his students in addition to Ibn Isḥāq composed biographies of Muhammad on the basis of traditions related from al-Zuhrī, the most important of these disciples being Mūsā b. ʿUqba (d. 758) and Maʿmar b. Rāshid (d. 770). Often by correlating traditions independently ascribed to al-Zuhrī in these and other sources with similar reports from Ibn Isḥāq's *Maghāzī*, it is possible to establish a measure of probability that al-Zuhrī may in fact have taught some of these traditions to his students.

Unfortunately, however, like Ibn Isḥāq's lost biography, neither Mūsā's or Maʿmar's *Maghāzī* survives, and we must rely primarily on the evidence of later writers for indirect knowledge of their contents, including especially al-Wāqidī (d. 823) and his disciple Ibn Saʿd (d. 845), as well as al-Ṭabarī (d. 923) and al-Balādhurī (d. 892). The only exception is perhaps a brief fragment purporting to transmit extracts from Mūsā's *Maghāzī*, which relates nineteen short and disconnected traditions concerning the life of Muhammad. Nevertheless, the authenticity of this document has been disputed, and given the paucity of its contents, the bulk of Mūsā's early biography must otherwise be derived indirectly from much later sources.[15] Despite the lack of a similar artifact, the prospects of recovering traditions from Maʿmar's *Maghāzī* are in fact much better than for Mūsā's lost work. Al-Wāqidī's *Maghāzī* from the close of the second Islamic century forms a particularly important witness to Maʿmar's biography, which seems to have served as one of its primary sources. Although al-Wāqidī's collection is somewhat marred by his occasionally irregular use of *isnād*s, as well as by the very strong possibility that he has made extensive—and often unacknowledged—use of Ibn Isḥāq's *Maghāzī*, al-Wāqidī's *Maghāzī* transmits considerable material from Maʿmar, at a chronological distance roughly equivalent to Ibn Hishām's separation from Ibn Isḥāq.[16] Unlike many earlier *maghāzī*s, however, al-Wāqidī's work is true to its title, taking focus on the campaigns of Muhammad during the period from his flight to Medina until his death, an event mentioned only briefly in passing.[17]

Al-Wāqidī is reported to have written several other works on Muhammad's life, including a collection on the *Death of the Prophet* (*Kitāb wafāt al-nabī*), but none of these writings is extant.[18] Presumably, many of the traditions from these lost works survive in the biography of Muhammad prepared by al-Wāqidī's student Ibn Saʿd. In the modern edition of the latter's *Ṭabaqāt*, the first two volumes comprise an extensive collection of traditions regarding the life of Muhammad, which seems to have been prepared by Ibn Saʿd himself (as opposed to his students). Although Ibn Saʿd has drawn from a number of authorities in compiling this biography, a large number of its traditions are given on al-Wāqidī's (and Maʿmar's) authority, many of which were likely taken from al-Wāqidī's now lost *sīra* works. Ibn Saʿd's collection is thus of particular importance since, as Horovitz notes, he is "the earliest author, after Ibn Isḥāq, from which a complete biography of the Prophet has come down to us."[19] In contrast to Ibn Isḥāq, however, Ibn Saʿd devoted considerable attention to the end of Muhammad's life, allotting roughly the last quarter of his biography to traditions concerning his death and burial. Here al-Wāqidī again figures prominently, and while his work on the *Death of the Prophet* was almost certainly a major source, Ibn Saʿd "has very greatly amplified" al-Wāqidī's earlier collection.[20] Thus, beyond its significance as a likely witness to al-Wāqidī's lost work on Muhammad's death, this final section of Ibn Saʿd's biography of Islam's prophet preserves the most extensive early Islamic collection of traditions about the end of Muhammad's life, first assembled nearly two centuries after the events themselves.

Despite the enormous value of both al-Wāqidī's and Ibn Saʿd's biographical works, the more recently published *Muṣannaf* of ʿAbd al-Razzāq al-Sanʿānī (d. 827), a collection of *ḥadīth* addressing a number of topics, presents a much more promising source for recovering some semblance of Maʿmar's lost *Maghāzī*. While this text includes a wealth of biographical traditions ascribed to Maʿmar, its attribution to ʿAbd al-Razzāq remains somewhat controversial, and there are significant unresolved issues regarding its authenticity. Most of this *Muṣannaf* is known only as transmitted by a somewhat later writer, Isḥāq al-Dabarī (d. 898), who in many respects can be seen as its potential author and furthermore seems to have been much too young to receive its contents directly from ʿAbd al-Razzāq, as alleged.[21] Nevertheless, Harald Motzki has recently argued that the published edition of ʿAbd al-Razzāq's *Muṣannaf* is in some sense "authentic" and can be relied upon as a source of traditions deriving from ʿAbd al-Razzāq in one form or another. Motzki willingly concedes that both Wansbrough and Calder are correct in noting considerable problems concerning the authorship of much early Islamic literature, acknowledging that "if the work [the *Muṣannaf*] is considered as a book with a definitely fixed text composed by ʿAbd al-Razzāq, the question must be answered in the negative." But Motzki argues that it was ʿAbd al-Razzāq who "spread the traditions" now compiled in the *Muṣannaf*, and in this more limited sense his authorship can be largely accepted.[22] Thus with some care it may be possible to recover early traditions from this collection, including perhaps many that were originally derived from Maʿmar's lost biography of Muhammad.

In its modern edition, the fifth volume of this *Muṣannaf* includes a sizable collection of traditions about Muhammad's *maghāzī*, here used in its broader sense to encompass the full span of Muhammad's life.[23] The overwhelming majority of these biographical traditions are ascribed to Maʿmar, suggesting that this section of the *Muṣannaf* may very well preserve a selection of traditions drawn from Maʿmar's *Maghāzī*. Although ʿAbd al-Razzāq is said to have studied with Maʿmar himself, in light of their considerable difference in age, one wonders if perhaps ʿAbd al-Razzāq has instead relied on a written version of Maʿmar's biography or some other intermediate source. ʿAbd al-Razzāq is reported to have died roughly fifty-seven years after Maʿmar, and if he studied with Maʿmar for seven or eight years as alleged by the later tradition, Maʿmar must have lived to at least eighty years old, instructing ʿAbd al-Razzāq just prior to his death while in his late seventies: although clearly not impossible, this detail certainly invites some question regarding the nature of ʿAbd al-Razzāq's relationship with Maʿmar.[24] Nevertheless, the prospect that the *maghāzī* section of the *Muṣannaf* transmits at least some material from Maʿmar's now lost work seems likely, particularly in those instances where other early sources can confirm this attribution.[25] Moreover, in contrast to al-Wāqidī's *Maghāzī*, ʿAbd al-Razzāq's *Muṣannaf* includes a short section of traditions related to Muhammad's death, a collection that adds an important and roughly contemporary supplement to Ibn Isḥāq's early assemblage of death and funeral traditions.[26] In making use of this source, however, it will be essential to bear in mind Motzki's caution that Ibn Hishām's *Sīra* must not be used "as if it were Ibn Isḥāq's original text," a warning that applies all the more so to ʿAbd al-Razzāq's unequaled witness to traditions from Maʿmar's early biography.[27]

Two additional early *muṣannaf* collections, the *Muṣannaf* of Ibn Abī Shayba (d. 849) and the *Ṣaḥīḥ* of al-Bukhārī (d. 870), include sections on the *maghāzī*, and while al-Bukhārī adheres to the more narrow meaning of this term, focusing largely on Muhammad's campaigns, both authors relate traditions about the end of his life. Like many other sources, these *ḥadīth* collections often convey traditions not otherwise attested in early Islamic literature, yet given the relatively late origins of all the surviving biographical compilations, it is difficult to assess the historical significance of such isolated traditions. The primary worth of these writings for recovering the earliest Islamic traditions about Muhammad's life and death tends to be found mainly in their convergences, when they collectively attest to a tradition that may be traced to an early authority, such as Ibn Isḥāq, Maʿmar, or perhaps even al-Zuhrī. Occasionally, however, some less well-attested reports may also be judged as early on the basis of their content, their "*matn*," particularly when they run counter to the prevailing doctrinal and literary tendencies of the earliest sources: such dissimilarities suggest an early tradition that has been preserved against these ideological interests on account of its relative antiquity. By carefully sifting these earliest sources according to such principles, it is possible to identify a rather basic account of the end of Muhammad's life as it was remembered by Medinan scholars of the mid-eighth century.

As will be seen, the resulting sketch of Muhammad's death and burial is disappointingly meager, and despite the frequent illusion of detailed specificity, the earliest accounts disclose remarkably little about the historical circumstances of Muhammad's departure from this life. Although repeated attention to concrete details can give these reports a feel of authenticity, their focus on minutia often comes at the expense of broader historical context. As much is in fact typical of the early Islamic historical tradition, whose fragmented, atomistic nature is one of its most characteristic features. By consequence, individual traditions, despite their occasionally remarkable attention to detail, are commonly transmitted without any connection to a broader historical narrative.[28] This quality often leaves the sequence of events uncertain, and accordingly, as will be discussed further below, the chronology of the early Islamic historical tradition is widely recognized as one of its most artificial features. Likewise, the narrative detail that occasionally seems to bring these biographical vignettes to life is a common literary device, named by Roland Barthes "the reality effect."[29] With specific regard to the early traditions of Muhammad's death, Leor Halevi observes that their attention to seemingly trivial details serves "to give the religious narrative a sense of verisimilitude, a certain tangibility that only such casual details could provide."[30] As interesting as such details are for what they reveal about the conceptual world of Muslim believers at the beginning of Islam's second century, one must take care not to be seduced by these nuances into accepting the veracity of these reports. Rather than validating the accounts in which they occur, they are instead very likely a sign of their literary construction.

Later Biographical Sources: *Isnāds*, Forgery, and *Isnād* Criticism

There are, of course, in addition to these early collections, innumerable traditions about the life of Muhammad that survive in only later sources, a great many of which concern his death. One need only consider, for example, the sizable collection of death and burial traditions gathered by Ibn Saʿd in his *Ṭabaqāt*, the vast majority of which find no parallels in other early Islamic sources.[31] More recent works, such as Ibn Kathīr's *Sīra*, are even more extensive in their knowledge of Muhammad's life and death: somewhat paradoxically, it would seem that as the distance from Muhammad's lifetime increased, so too did the Islamic tradition's knowledge of what he had said and done.[32] Each of the biographical traditions in these collections of course bears an *isnād* vouching for its authenticity, and these chains of transmitters generally conclude with an early authority, such as al-Zuhrī or ʿUrwa, or even ʿĀʾisha or some other Companion of the Prophet, who is identified as the ultimate source of the report in question. In light of the attribution of these reports to such early authorities, one may perhaps wonder why they are not equally valued as witnesses to the life of Muhammad and the history of Islamic origins. Should not these traditions be taken for what they purport to be, namely, reports from the earliest authorities on the beginnings of Islam, including many who were themselves participants in these very events? While there is certainly no reason to exclude the possibility that some early traditions may survive in these later collections, and unquestionably some do, the endemic forgery of *ḥadīth* and *isnāds* in medieval Islam means that neither these traditions nor their alleged transmissions can be taken at face value.

Consequently, the countless traditions ascribed to al-Zuhrī and ʿUrwa (among others) by later sources most likely do not reflect actual transmissions so much as the reputation of these two scholars as the earliest and most important authorities on Muhammad and the rise of Islam. Traditions conveying what the community believed to be true about earliest Islam would have been attracted magnetically to their names by sheer virtue of their fame. One need not imagine some sort of conspiracy or even a willful falsification, as some have wrongly maintained, to explain such developments: members of the Islamic community would rather "naturally" have assumed that traditions about the Prophet held to be true must have originated with one of these two sagacious men. As Harris Birkeland comparably observes with regard to Ibn ʿAbbās, whose reputation as a great authority on *tafsīr* inspired later transmitters to attribute a "great ocean" of exegetical traditions to his authorship, "so it is even today, for instance in traditionalistic, rural communities in Norway. Every accepted religious opinion is attributed to Christ, Paul, or Luther." He continues to note, perhaps even more tellingly, that "it would provoke great indignation if anybody should happen to express the opinion that Luther ever believed in predestination. Every believing peasant would deny that statement most decidedly."[33] Surely this is not the result of some widespread conspiracy to deceive. Accordingly, one would in fact expect to find that the chains of transmission in the *sīra* literature regularly ascribe much of their material to ʿUrwa and al-Zuhrī, and consistent attribution of traditions to these early authorities does not necessarily indicate the authenticity of these attributions. It is instead altogether likely that established patterns of authoritative transmission had become fixed according to traditional forms rather early on, and these patterns provided paradigms for the *isnāds* that were attached to later traditions. Insofar as the Islamic community believed such later traditions to be true, there was not so much a need to invent phony *isnāds* to justify their authenticity; rather, the "truth" of the traditions themselves would make their attribution to authoritative scholars such as ʿUrwa and al-Zuhrī mostly a foregone conclusion.[34]

In the face of such concerns, the methods of *isnād* criticism, especially as developed by Joseph Schacht, G. H. A. Juynboll, and, most recently,

Harald Motzki, can often be somewhat helpful for assessing the probability of attributions to such early authorities. Through an extensive correlation of the different *isnād*s assigned to a particular tradition in later sources, one can occasionally identify a plausible date for the tradition, as well as the individual who was most likely responsible for initially placing it into circulation. The Islamic tradition itself of course has long-established methods of *isnād* criticism designed to assess the authenticity of the numerous *ḥadīth* ascribed to Muhammad, the vast majority of which have been regarded as spurious even in the Islamic faith. Yet modern scholarship on Islamic origins generally approaches these chains of transmitters with a great deal more skepticism than the Islamic tradition, and consequently it has developed its own methods for evaluating both the *isnād*s themselves and the various traditions, or *matn*s, to which they are attached. There is certainly warrant for such suspicion, since forgery of *ḥadīth* and their *isnād*s was pandemic in early Islam: the ninth-century Islamic scholar of *ḥadīth* al-Bukhārī is said to have examined 600,000 traditions attributed to the Prophet by their *isnād*s, and of these he rejected over 593,000 as later forgeries.[35] Matters are even worse in regard to the *sīra* traditions, which medieval Islamic scholars regarded as having even less historical reliability than the rest of the *ḥadīth*.[36] With good cause, modern scholarship on Islamic origins has merely intensified the Islamic tradition's own internal skepticism of prophetic traditions in its efforts to reconstruct the beginnings of Islam.

Ignác Goldziher and Schacht after him were among the first Western scholars to draw attention to the artificial and historically problematic nature of very many *isnād*s that the Islamic tradition viewed as credible, casting considerable doubt on the authenticity of the traditions that these *isnād*s claimed to validate.[37] Schacht, however, developed a method of analysis that allowed for the extraction of historically valuable information from these partially fabricated lists of transmitters. This approach, generally known as common-source analysis, compares all the various *isnād*s assigned to a particular tradition in different sources in order to identify the earliest transmitter on whom all the highly varied chains of transmission converge, the so-called common link.[38] As Schacht rather reasonably concludes, this figure is most likely the person who first placed a particular tradition into circulation, since numerous *isnād*s all unanimously identify him as a source. Otherwise, it is difficult to explain how these highly variegated chains of transmission could converge on this single individual as their earliest common source. The alternative, that somehow all of these different *isnād*s have by chance invented the same early transmitter, is comparatively unlikely. Thus some degree of confidence may be placed in identifying the common link with the earliest history of a particular tradition, although as will be seen in a moment, even this seemingly fail-safe method is not without significant problems and uncertainties.

An inherent skepticism pertains to the list of transmitters preceding the common link, however. By definition these figures do not vary in any (or almost any) of the *isnāds* transmitting a particular tradition, which could on the surface seem to speak for their authenticity. Nevertheless, there are considerable reasons for doubting the historical accuracy of these earliest transmitters, and it seems rather likely that these oldest links in these chains were invented early in the process of transmission in order to give these traditions sanction by linking them with Muhammad and other revered figures from the earliest history of Islam. Particularly important is Schacht's famous observation that *isnāds* tend to grow backwards. Schacht has argued rather compellingly that the earliest links of many *isnāds*, particularly those identifying the Prophet, the Companions, and the Successors as sources, are in fact the most likely to be falsified. Moreover, he concludes that the closer the original source of the tradition is to the Prophet himself, the more likely that the *isnād* and the tradition itself are counterfeit and late, making traditions ascribed directly to Muhammad both the latest and most likely to be forged.[39] Recent studies by several scholars who are otherwise sympathetic to Schacht's methods have cast significant doubt on his second principle, and the notion that *isnāds* ascribed to earlier authorities are categorically more likely to be both recent and inauthentic has come into question.[40] Yet while many of these studies have shown that such traditions are not necessarily more recent than others, they nonetheless generally confirm that their ascriptions to early authorities are overwhelmingly false, verifying the most important aspect of Schacht's hypothesis. Suspicion of these earliest transmitters is further warranted by the fact that prior to the second Islamic century *isnāds* usually were not used in the transmission of early Islamic traditions, including the *sīra* traditions in particular.[41] At this late stage, chains of transmission suddenly had to be constructed, as is evident in Ibn Isḥāq's use of only a very basic and nascent form of *isnāds*.[42] When there was uncertainty regarding a tradition's origin, which surely was often the case after over a century of anonymous transmission, traditions were ascribed to great figures from the past, and from this chronological distance it seems rather likely that the nearer the *isnād* approaches to Muhammad, the less likely it is to reflect an actual pattern of historical transmission.

Despite the apparent promise of Schacht's approach, however, significant unresolved issues remain concerning its reliability, and several recent studies have raised important concerns about the accuracy of common-link analysis for dating early Islamic traditions. The most dramatic challenge to the method has come from an article by Michael Cook, which demonstrates that in certain instances where one can actually test the reliability of common-link analysis through alternate means of dating, the method fails to date material accurately.[43] Cook's study examines several early Islamic eschatological traditions, all of whose dates can be determined from their content, using a rather standard method for dating apocalyptic material. These traditions all purport to predict the future, and up to a certain point they exhibit astonishing accuracy, which is undoubtedly due to the fact that they were written after the events that they correctly predict. Then, suddenly, the author's prognostic powers fail, and his predictions of the future no longer correspond with the historical record. The point at which this transition occurs reliably indicates the time of the tradition's composition: here is where its author has truly begun to speculate regarding the future. This moment of the prophetic spirit's departure can thus be compared with the date of the tradition as determined by common-link analysis of the *isnād*s, and for each of the three traditions that Cook considers, the common link fails completely as a means of dating. How could such a seemingly well-reasoned method perform so poorly?[44]

The most common explanation for the common link's failure to provide consistently accurate and reliable dating of early Islamic traditions involves the so-called spread of *isnād*s during the process of transmission.[45] As Schacht first recognized, it is altogether likely that these authoritative chains of transmission were altered by the complications of transmission over an extended period of time as well as by the editorial interests of an evolving Islamic tradition. The result is that many *isnād*s are contaminated and do not preserve an accurate record of historical transmission, particularly in the earliest stages of this process. According to Schacht, the "spread of *isnād*s" involves "the creation of additional authorities or transmitters for the same doctrine or tradition." This phenomenon is particularly evident in material ascribed to Successors of the Prophet, and it can often create the illusion that the common link, and thus the tradition itself, circulated earlier than it actually did.[46]

Nevertheless, Motzki and others advocating the reliability of this method have largely rejected out of hand such concerns about any significant spread of *isnād*s, inasmuch as their approach demands accurate records of transmission. As these scholars seek to mine ever deeper within these transmission histories in hopes of securing traditions even closer to the beginnings of Islam, a much more optimistic view concerning the reliability of these textual genealogies is required, particularly in regard to the early transmitters. While occasionally this approach has convincingly dated certain traditions to the beginnings of the second Islamic century, Motzki often argues aggressively for an even earlier dating, to the first Islamic century. Yet in doing so he generally must engage in special pleading on behalf of early tradents,[47] and as several critics have noted, these efforts to push certain traditions into the seventh century are methodologically problematic and not very convincing.[48] Motzki seeks to further enhance these claims of authenticity by raising the stakes and forcing a decision between either accuracy and genuineness or outright forgery and vast conspiracy. If the reliability of these pedigrees is to be doubted, then one must suppose the existence of a widespread and deliberate conspiracy of forgery within the early Islamic community on a scale that is historically improbable.[49] The rhetorical effect of this position is effectively to shift the burden of proof, requiring any skeptics to account for what is reckoned to be the only alternative to "authenticity," a grand conspiracy of forgery.

These are not, however, the only two possibilities, as many less sanguine scholars have remarked, and generally one would not want to insist on such a severe bifurcation in analyzing the formative period of a religious tradition.[50] G. R. Hawting, for instance, has critiqued this falsely posed either/or well in his review of Motzki's book, the full extent of which is worth quoting:

> It seems unlikely that this stark contrast is an adequate view of what is a religious tradition, produced during a relatively long period of social and political disruption when the institutions for safeguarding the transmission were only beginning to be formed, subject to the vicissitudes of a still mainly oral culture, and committed to writing in the form in which we have it at the beginning of the third century of Islam at the earliest. Motzki seems to have little time for the effects of the continuous reworking of the tradition, the introduction of glosses and improvements, the abbreviation and expansion of material, the linking together of reports which originated independently, the adaptation of traditions which originate in one context with a particular purpose so that they may be used in another, let alone simple errors of scribes and narrators. One cannot rule out real forgery but what that might be in a society which revered authority and tradition above independence and

> innovation is not obvious. Students of the historical tradition (*ta'rīkh*) have been able to demonstrate the way in which the tradition could be manipulated to give significantly different messages even after it had been recorded in writing (cf., for example, the way in which al-Ṭabarī was used by the later compilers like Ibn al-Athīr). This sort of creative reinterpretation must have been much more possible in the stages before the appearance of written texts.[51]

One can in fact identify a variety of interests and tendencies within the early Islamic tradition, as well as certain features of the process of transmission itself, that may have effected the manipulation of *isnāds*. Michael Cook presents perhaps the most detailed explanation of this phenomenon, and he describes numerous mechanisms by which *isnāds* likely spread, none of which, it is important to note, involves a grand (or even modest) conspiracy of forgery. On the contrary, Cook identifies several very ordinary events from the process of transmission that likely have introduced the spread of *isnāds*, and all of these are "thoroughly in accordance with the character and values of the system [of transmission]."[52] Patricia Crone additionally explains how the rivalries between various centers of early Islamic scholarship (that is, Medina, Mecca, Kūfa, Baṣra, Syria) likely brought about the spread of *isnāds* in many instances.[53] Likewise, Norman Calder's study of the early Islamic legal tradition identifies still more factors that likely influenced the process of transmission and caused the spread of *isnāds*. Calder focuses particularly on doctrinal differences as a vector for such changes, and he presents a compelling example from the *ḥadīth* that clearly evidences the spread of *isnāds* occasioned by inter-Islamic dogmatic disputes.[54] Any one or a combination of these factors could easily have inspired adjustments to these records of transmission, introducing distortions that would lead to the identification of false common links and, by consequence, inaccurate datings.[55] Thus, while the use of common-link analysis to date material may be accepted somewhat provisionally, one must always bear in mind the failures of this method when it has been tested and the potentially deviating effect of the spread of *isnāds*.[56] In order to guard against such inaccuracies, this approach can be applied effectively only to traditions bearing an extremely dense pattern of transmission from multiple, intermediate common links, a threshold that few traditions prove capable of meeting. Moreover, while this approach has shown some success in locating a number of traditions at the beginnings of the second Islamic century, for many of the reasons noted above, it has not proven very effective for identifying traditions from the first century with much credibility.[57]

Despite these problems, a small group of scholars has recently applied this method to a selection of *sīra* traditions, not in an effort to recover early traditions from much later sources, where it may perhaps prove effective, but instead with the intent of securing elements of Muhammad's biography to figures from the first Islamic century. In particular, they have aimed at exhuming a core of tradition that can be assigned to 'Urwa ibn al-Zubayr's authorship, thus fixing the outline of Muhammad's career to this scholar from the end of the seventh century and the beginning of the eighth. In this way they would attempt to establish the historical accuracy and authenticity of at least some of the basic events from the traditional narrative of Islamic origins. At issue is the general reliability of the early *sīra* traditions for knowledge of Muhammad's life and the beginnings of Islam: the historical veracity of these accounts stands very much in question. As already noted, the narrative traditions of Muhammad's life were rather late in forming, and even the earliest sources, such as they are, can be known only indirectly through more recent transmissions. Accordingly, one must reckon with the fact that during the century that elapsed between the end of Muhammad's life and the first recoverable narratives of Islamic origins, the Islamic faith almost certainly underwent significant changes in its beliefs and practices. As the chapters to follow will argue, Islam's transformation during this first century seems in fact to have been considerable, involving the shift from an imminent eschatological belief focused on Jerusalem to become the religion of a global empire with a sacred geography centered on the Hijāz. Such developments were bound to have an effect on Islam's self-image, including particularly how it recalled its formative period and even perhaps how it remembered the ending of its founder's life. Indeed, as is widely conceded, the image of Muhammad presented in these early biographies reflects not so much a historical figure from the early seventh century as an idealized portrait of Islam's founding prophet designed to suit the needs and concerns of eighth- and ninth-century Islam.[58] Taking the second edition of the *Encyclopaedia of Islam* as a reflection of the *opinio communis*, the *sīra* traditions are here judged as being essentially worthless for reconstructing a historically credible biography of Muhammad or for the history of early Islam more generally.[59]

With this assessment, Muhammad runs the risk of vanishing from history, and taking with him any reliable knowledge concerning the origins of Islam. Against this general consensus, Gregor Schoeler and Andreas Görke, and to a lesser extent Motzki, have applied the methods of *isnād* criticism to several individual *sīra* traditions, in the hopes of preventing such an epistemological collapse.[60] If their analysis is correct, then the "basic framework" of Muhammad's biography, presumably including at least some of its chronology, may be ascribed to ʿUrwa and perhaps some other early figures. Since ʿUrwa was a nephew of Muhammad's favorite wife, ʿĀʾisha, as Görke and Schoeler frequently remind their readers, one can safely assume, they would argue, that his account is largely accurate. Although Görke and Schoeler do not include traditions concerning the end of Muhammad's life among their alleged corpus of ʿUrwan material, their proposal, if correct, would be of some significance for estimating the reliability of these biographical sources. In such a case it would certainly be more difficult, although by no means impossible, to raise significant doubts concerning the accuracy of the traditional Islamic memory of Muhammad's death. Nevertheless, the approach fails to deliver what its proponents have promised, largely because the biographical traditions generally lack the dense networks required to identify meaningful nodes of transmission, leaving them rather unsuited for this method of analysis. Consequently, Görke and Schoeler's claims that ʿUrwa may be identified as the author of a significant corpus of *sīra* traditions are not especially persuasive. Ultimately their investigations do little to advance our knowledge of the *sīra* traditions beyond what may already be determined from Ibn Isḥāq's *Maghāzī* and other early sources.

For example, Motzki applies this *isnād*-critical approach to a tradition in which Muhammad orders the assassination of a Jewish opponent, Ibn Abī l-Ḥuqayq, and while he convincingly assigns the tale to al-Zuhrī, his efforts to identify an earlier source are not persuasive.[61] To do so, he must conflate two traditions that in fact appear to be quite distinct and ignore the deeply problematic nature of one of his tradents, Abū Isḥāq.[62] Schoeler makes a similar analysis of the traditions of the beginnings of Muhammad's revelations (the *iqraʾ* episode) and the rumors that ʿĀʾisha had committed adultery (*ḥadīth al-ifk*),[63] while Görke has investigated the reports of Muhammad's treaty at al-Ḥudaybiya.[64] Görke and Schoeler have also published together a very brief article on an extensive tradition complex purportedly associated with the events of Muhammad's *hijra*.[65] In each instance they attempt to identify these traditions with ʿUrwa, whose biography of Muhammad they aim to reconstruct using the methods of common-link analysis.[66] While al-Zuhrī and occasionally other authorities of his generation can be persuasively linked with these traditions, the reach back to ʿUrwa is generally not convincing. Their arguments often require a great deal of optimism regarding the accuracy of certain *isnād*s and an occasional willingness to accept hypothetically reconstructed lines of transmission. In the case of the complex of traditions linked with the *hijra*, for instance, a large body of material transmitted by only a single source is identified as genuine, while *isnād*s belonging to only specific parts of the alleged tradition complex are occasionally represented as authenticating the entire block of material.[67]

Görke and Schoeler are most successful in arguing that the traditions of Muhammad's experience of visions and voices at the onset of his revelations and a basic narrative of his flight to Medina in the face of opposition had begun to circulate at the end of the seventh century. Likewise, the story of 'Ā'isha's suspected adultery and her subsequent acquittal is persuasively dated to this period through the study of its *isnād*s. Yet one should recognize just how meager these results are, particularly given the amount of effort involved. Even if all the methodological questions regarding such an *isnād*-critical approach to the *sīra* traditions are placed to the side, the resultant biography of Muhammad is disappointingly minimal. Motzki himself ultimately expresses some doubt whether "the outcome will justify the time and energy needed for such an enterprise," and he forecasts that "the historical biography which will be the outcome of all these source-critical efforts will be only a very small one."[68]

Perhaps even more important is the failure so far of this arduous method to reveal anything particularly new about the historical Muhammad that could not already be determined using simpler approaches. For instance, there can be little doubt that the early Muslims believed that Muhammad had been the recipient of divine revelation, and its representation as a vision of light and auditions merely reflects a well-established biblical pattern.[69] Moreover, dating according to the *hijra* is attested by early documentary sources, signaling the importance of a tradition of Muhammad's "flight" for the early Muslims.[70] The accusations against 'Ā'isha are also credibly early, inasmuch as they reflect negatively on a figure who later came to be revered as the "mother of the faithful," and one would thus imagine that the story had begun to circulate before 'Ā'isha had attained this status in Sunni piety.[71] Even if one were to accept the more problematic arguments presented on behalf of the traditions of al-Ḥudaybiya and Ibn Abī l-Ḥuqayq's murder, ultimately very little is added to our portrait of Muhammad. It is certainly believable that Muhammad may have concluded an unfavorable treaty regarding fugitives or ordered the assassination of an opponent, as reported in these accounts. But these traditions reveal almost nothing about the nature of Muhammad's religious movement and its early history. In these areas the *sīra* traditions remain not only unproven but suspect, leaving modern scholars with the difficult choice of either taking these biographies more or less at face value or looking elsewhere for more reliable evidence of primitive Islam. Such are the circumstances one must face in evaluating the early Islamic traditions of the end of Muhammad's life.[72]

Ibn Isḥāq's Account of Muhammad's Death and Burial

Taking Ibn Isḥāq's early biography as a basis, we gain a clear sense of how the Muslims of the mid-eighth century imagined the death and burial of their founding prophet and what they thought was important to "remember" about these events.[73] The story begins just as a band of soldiers under Usāma b. Zayd's leadership is dispatched to attack Syria, more specifically the region of Transjordan and the coastal plain of Palestine, in a report given without attribution according to Ibn Hishām's transmission.[74] Then, suddenly Muhammad became ill after returning home from Medina's graveyard, where he had offered prayers for the dead, an act that foreshadows the prayers offered over his own grave after his burial.[75] According to one account, Muhammad was posed with a choice at the cemetery, presumably by God, who offered him either "the keys of the treasuries of this world and long life here followed by Paradise,"[76] or the chance to meet the Lord in Paradise at once. As Ibn Isḥāq later explains, Muhammad often said that "God never takes a prophet to Himself without giving him the choice." Deciding for the latter option, Muhammad returned home to ʿĀʾisha, and then while making rounds among his wives, he suddenly fell ill in the house of Maymūna. Muhammad asked his wives for their permission to return to ʿĀʾisha's house and be cared for there by her, and when they agreed he was taken to ʿĀʾisha and spent his final days with her. At Muhammad's request, she placed him in a tub, and together with al-Faḍl b. al-ʿAbbās and ʿAlī, she poured "seven skins of water from different wells" over him until he cried "Enough, enough!" As ʿAlī left Muhammad's house, al-ʿAbbās warned him that Muhammad would soon die, and ʿAlī would find himself "a slave." Al-ʿAbbās suggested that they should go to Muhammad and ask him either to declare them as his successors or, if he had chosen someone else, "to enjoin the people to treat us well." Thereafter Muhammad went and "sat in the pulpit," revealing the choice that he was offered as well as his decision. Abū Bakr expressed alarm at the news, but Muhammad reassured him and underscored their unique bond of friendship, directing that all the doors to the mosque should be closed except for the one from Abū Bakr's house. According to Ibn Hishām (but not al-Ṭabarī), Muhammad also took the occasion to encourage the people to join in Usāma's expedition to Palestine, ordering that it be dispatched immediately.

When Muhammad returned home, his illness intensified, and he lost consciousness. His wives agreed to administer a medicine that had been brought from Ethiopia, and once Muhammad awoke, he was irritated and demanded to know who had forced the medicine upon him. They explained that they were afraid that he would develop pleurisy without the medicine. Muhammad protested that God would never afflict him with such a shameful disorder, and as punishment, he forced each of his wives to take the medicine themselves. Ibn Hishām then relates several stories in which Muhammad declares his preference that Abū Bakr should lead the community in prayers in his stead, some of which insist quite deliberately that Abū Bakr, rather than ʿUmar, was to fill this role. Although al-Ṭabarī also reports two similar traditions, he fails to do so on Ibn Isḥāq's authority, raising the question of whether these endorsements of Abū Bakr appeared in Ibn Isḥaq biography.[77] Nevertheless, the appearance of one of these traditions in al-Balādhurī's *Ansāb al-ashrāf* on Ibn Isḥāq's authority perhaps confirms its place in his *Maghāzī*.[78] A pair of related traditions further note that Muhammad peeked into the mosque while Abū Bakr was leading the prayers and was seen by the people one last time: according to one tradition Muhammad sat beside Abū Bakr as he led the prayers, concluding with an admonition to adhere strictly to the Qurʾān and to it alone, laying nothing to his charge. Abū Bakr and Muhammad returned to their houses, and Muhammad laid his head on ʿĀʾisha's bosom. When someone from Abū Bakr's family brought a toothpick (*siwāk*), ʿĀʾisha offered it to Muhammad and "chewed it for him to soften it and gave it to him. He rubbed his teeth with it more energetically than [she] had ever seen him rub before." Then, after this final act of oral hygiene, Muhammad cried out, "Nay, the most Exalted Companion is of Paradise," signaling his resolve to depart from this world, and he expired in ʿĀʾisha's arms. A rather peculiar story then follows, in which ʿUmar refuses to believe that Muhammad has died, insisting that, like Moses, he had ascended to God only temporarily and would soon return. Although more will be said about this intriguing episode especially in the following chapter, Abū Bakr arrives from his house and silences ʿUmar by citing a Qurʾānic verse predicting Muhammad's death. Astonishingly, however, Ibn Isḥāq reports that no one had ever heard that verse before Abū Bakr recited it at that very moment.

Muhammad's burial is then deferred by the ensuing struggle over who was to succeed him as the community's new leader. In a gathering at the hall (*saqīfa*) of the Banū Saʿīda, the prominent men of the community jockeyed with one another to determine Muhammad's successor, ultimately choosing Abū Bakr, who served as the first caliph. In the transition then to Muhammad's burial, ʿUmar twice offers apologies for his frenzied denials of Muhammad's death, one given immediately after the *saqīfa* meetings and a second ascribed to ʿUmar during the time of his own caliphate. In both accounts ʿUmar explains his behavior as a result of his firm belief that Muhammad would remain alive and leading his people until the arrival of the eschatological Hour. ʿAlī, it would appear, remained behind while Abū Bakr and the others contended over the caliphate, attending to Muhammad's body and preparing it for the grave. Assisted by al-ʿAbbās and his sons al-Faḍl and Qutham, as well as Usāma b. Zayd and Shuqrān, one of Muhammad's freedmen, ʿAlī washed Muhammad's body. When they could not decide whether or not to remove Muhammad's clothing before washing his corpse, divine intervention made clear that he should remain clothed. Following the washing, Muhammad's body was wrapped in three garments, and two gravediggers, a Meccan emigrant and a Medinan, prepared his grave in the characteristic Medinan style, with a distinctive niche. A dispute arose over Muhammad's place of burial that was resolved by Abū Bakr, who recalled Muhammad as having said, "No prophet dies but he is buried where he died." Thus the grave was dug immediately beneath his bed, in ʿĀʾisha's house, and the people came and began to pray over Muhammad. ʿAlī, the sons of al-ʿAbbās, al-Faḍl and Qutham, descended into the grave, as did Shuqrān and al-Mughīra b. Shuʿba, who purposefully dropped his ring in the grave as a ruse to allow him to descend and embrace Muhammad's body one final time. The scene draws to a close with recollections of Muhammad's censure against those "who choose the graves of their prophets as mosques" and his final injunction to eliminate all religions other than Islam from the Arabian Peninsula.

While the broader context of these events is somewhat obscured by the episodic and disconnected nature of the individual *ḥadīth*, it is clear that they collectively relate Muhammad's death in an urban setting, which is easily recognizable as the Medina of Muslim tradition. Moreover, Ibn Isḥāq's presentation of these events within the sequence of his collection locates them before the full-scale assault on Palestine had begun, although Usāma's expedition to Palestine just before Muhammad's illness and death presents an intriguing anomaly to be addressed later in this chapter. Muhammad's death seems to follow closely on his "farewell pilgrimage" to Mecca, which Ibn Isḥāq appears to locate in the year 10 AH.[79] Yet nothing in the death and burial traditions themselves specifies such timing, and the reports alone offer no clear indication of when Muhammad died, either in relative or absolute terms: this information must be derived from Ibn Isḥāq's arrangement.[80] His *Maghāzī* is the first witness to this chronology, and while there is no basis for concluding that the sequence is entirely Ibn Isḥāq's invention, the reports that he has gathered fail to present any evidence of its existence prior to his collection. The brief fragment purporting to relate selected traditions from Mūsā ibn 'Uqba's *Maghāzī* affords no confirmation of his ordering of events, inasmuch as these extracts contain nothing relevant to the end of Muhammad's life.[81] 'Abd al-Razzāq's *Muṣannaf* presents a relative chronology similar to Ibn Isḥāq's, but there is likewise no indication that his sequence reflects any earlier source. As is the case with so much of our information concerning the origins of Islam, it is not possible to date this chronology of Muhammad's death before the beginning of the second Islamic century. Perhaps Ibn Isḥāq inherited this schema from al-Zuhrī, but there is no evidence to indicate this. In any case, the received chronology of Muhammad's death in the Islamic historical tradition cannot be shown to have existed prior to the middle of the eighth century, over a century after the events in question took place.

Muhammad's Death According to al-Zuhrī

If this chronology is first witnessed only by Ibn Isḥāq, there are a number of death and burial traditions that can, with some measure of credibility, perhaps be linked with al-Zuhrī's teaching.[82] For instance, several other early sources link al-Zuhrī with the report of the sudden onset of Muhammad's illness while visiting his wives, in the house of Maymūna, after which his wives gave permission for him to be nursed in 'Ā'isha's house, where al-Faḍl b. 'Abbās and 'Alī assisted her as they poured water from seven wells over him. An account of these events almost identical to Ibn Isḥāq's is ascribed to al-Zuhrī through different channels in 'Abd al-Razzāq's *Muṣannaf*, Ibn Sa'd's *Ṭabaqāt*, and al-Bukhārī's *Ṣaḥīḥ*.[83] The convergence of these transmissions on al-Zuhrī suggests a likelihood that the tradition originated with his teaching. Likewise Muhammad's preaching in the mosque during his illness, in which he praises Abū Bakr as his closest friend and orders all the doors of the mosque closed except for Abū Bakr's, is also ascribed to al-Zuhrī by 'Abd al-Razzāq and Ibn Sa'd.[84] Muhammad's statement that "God never takes a prophet without offering him a choice" is imputed to al-Zuhrī by al-Bukhārī and Ibn Sa'd, as well as by a collection of traditions from al-Zuhrī surviving on a papyrus of the early ninth century.[85] The basic elements of the Ethiopian medicine story are placed under al-Zuhrī's authority by ʿAbd al-Razzāq and Ibn Saʿd,[86] and both identify al-Zuhrī as having circulated Muhammad's command to establish Islam as the only faith in the Arabian Peninsula.[87] Al-Bukhārī, ʿAbd al-Razzāq, and Ibn Saʿd all attribute Muhammad's denunciation of those who make the graves of their prophets into places of worship to al-Zuhrī,[88] and all three impute to him the traditions concerning Muhammad's appointment of Abū Bakr (rather than ʿUmar) as the community's new prayer leader.[89] The tradition of Muhammad peering into the mosque while Abū Bakr led the prayers on the day of his death was also known to ʿAbd al-Razzāq, al-Bukhārī, Ibn Saʿd, and al-Balādhurī from al-Zuhrī.[90] The conversation between ʿAlī and al-ʿAbbās concerning their status after Muhammad's death is also widely attested on al-Zuhrī's authority, appearing in ʿAbd al-Razzāq, Ibn Saʿd, and al-Bukhārī, as well as in al-Ṭabarī's *History*, where he cites the *ḥadīth* both from Ibn Isḥāq and according to a second, independent line of transmission from al-Zuhrī.[91] Finally, al-Zuhrī is credited with teaching the story of Muhammad and the toothpick by Ibn Saʿd, although ʿAbd al-Razzāq records only Muhammad's final words from this scene, "with the most Exalted Companion!," an exclamation that Ibn Saʿd and the ninth-century al-Zuhrī papyrus instead link with the tradition of Muhammad's choice.[92]

The same sources also agree in assigning to al-Zuhrī the story of ʿUmar's refusal to accept Muhammad's death and his correction by Abū Bakr, who persuaded ʿUmar and the others that Muhammad had indeed died through the recitation of a Qurʾānic verse that no one had ever heard before. Versions almost identical to Ibn Isḥāq's account appear in ʿAbd al-Razzāq, Ibn Saʿd, and al-Bukhārī.[93] A shorter version, which relates only ʿUmar's protests, absent any rebuttal from either Abū Bakr or the Qurʾān, is transmitted from al-Zuhrī through different channels by Ibn Abī Shayba and Ibn Saʿd, as well as by ʿAbd al-Razzāq.[94] Likewise, ʿUmar's initial apology for his actions in the wake of the *saqīfa* meetings is also ascribed to al-Zuhrī by ʿAbd al-Razzāq and Ibn Saʿd, while al-Balādhurī credits al-Zuhrī with ʿUmar's second explanation, allegedly given while he was caliph.[95] Presumably, some version of this story, at the very least in its shortened form, and ʿUmar's subsequent apologies belonged to al-Zuhrī's teaching. The nature of the story itself suggests a particularly early origin: it seems improbable that Muslims of the early second century or later would have invented such a strange tale, involving ʿUmar's violent denials of Muhammad's death. ʿUmar's mistaken rant casts this "rightly guided" caliph in a rather unfavorable light, and it does not fit with the tendencies of the early Islamic historical tradition. Accordingly, this tradition's preservation is a likely token of its early formation: its transmission by al-Zuhrī despite its awkwardness is most likely a consequence of the story's well-established status in the community's historical memory already by his time. As much is equally if not more true of Abū Bakr's Qurʾānic correction, particularly in light of the crowd's alleged ignorance concerning the recited passage. It is hard to imagine the invention of a tradition that so pointedly raises the question of the Qurʾān's integrity during the mid-eighth century.

There is, however, another account of ʿUmar's denial ascribed to Ibn ʿAbbās that appears to be even older than the al-Zuhrī version, a report that, although absent from Ibn Isḥāq's *Maghāzī*, is witnessed by ʿAbd al-Razzāq, Ibn Saʿd, and al-Balādhurī.[96] According to this tradition, it was al-ʿAbbās, rather than Abū Bakr, who opposed ʿUmar's ravings, countering them not with a Qurʾānic proof-text but instead with the observation that Muhammad's body had begun to stink. As Wilferd Madelung has argued, the chronology of Muhammad's burial in relation to the *saqīfa* meeting in this account favors the antiquity of the al-ʿAbbās version.[97] Moreover, failure to make recourse to the Qurʾān also strongly suggests its priority: it is difficult to account for the subsequent invention of a tradition that so inelegantly argues for Muhammad's mortality on the basis of his pungent corpse if Abū Bakr's Qurʾānic riposte was already in circulation. Al-ʿAbbās's complaints of Muhammad's stench are in fact seemingly belied by a widely circulated tradition from Ibn Isḥāq's collection that underscores the exceptional nature of Muhammad's body in death as well as life: such a body presumably would not stink so offensively immediately after dying.[98] Indeed, the sweet fragrance of Muhammad's incorruptible body after death is a frequent theme of the *ḥadīth* that seems to have developed over the course of the eighth century through influence from the Christian hagiographical tradition.[99] Moreover, the earliest Christian accounts of Muhammad's death and burial also note that his corpse began to stink when his followers did not bury him soon after his death: accordingly it would appear that these narratives show an awareness of the early Islamic tradition regarding ʿUmar and al-ʿAbbās, as well as the reported delay in burying Muhammad's festering body.[100] Consequently, a tradition indicating the initial denial of Muhammad's death by at least some within the earliest Islamic community not only can be traced back to al-Zuhrī's teaching, but there is evidence of an even older version of the story that ultimately seems to have required the invention of a Qurʾānic rebuttal to silence the protests of ʿUmar—and presumably others as well. These reports of a controversy surrounding the reality of Muhammad's death reflect perhaps the earliest extant Islamic traditions about the end of Muhammad's life, and as we will see in the following chapter, they appear to be intimately linked with the imminent eschatological expectations of Muhammad and his earliest followers.

ʿAbd al-Razzāq and Ibn Saʿd also ascribe to al-Zuhrī a tradition that Muhammad sought to write something down just before his death, a report that Ibn Isḥāq has possibly suppressed.[101] As Muhammad's illness grew worse, he asked for something to write on, in order to leave behind a document that would prevent his followers from going astray. ʿUmar opposed the request, suggesting that Muhammad's illness was clouding his judgment and that the existence of the Qurʾān obviated the need for any additional document to guide the community. Others, however, began to argue that Muhammad should be given something to write with. When the ensuing noise and confusion eventually began to disturb Muhammad, he dismissed the throng and ultimately failed to produce a document. While it is certainly possible that al-Zuhrī taught something of this nature, the absence of any ascription to al-Zuhrī independent of Maʿmar suggests that possibly the latter is its author. Nevertheless, in light of the controversies surrounding the issue of writing in earliest Islam, as noted above, as well as the politically volatile nature of the tradition with regard to issues of succession to Muhammad, it is certainly conceivable that Ibn Isḥāq may have chosen to omit the story from his collection.

As for the washing of Muhammad's corpse and his burial, Ibn Isḥāq's account of these events largely departs from al-Zuhrī's authority, ascribing its dozen or so reports mainly to other traditionists. Other early collections, such as al-Wāqidī's *Maghāzī*, Mālik's *Muwaṭṭaʾ*, al-Bukhārī's *Ṣaḥīḥ*, Muslim's *Ṣaḥīḥ*, and Abū Dāʾūd's *Sunan*, show little interest in the details of Muhammad's burial, and al-Ṭabarī's *History* merely reproduces Ibn Isḥāq's rather meager assemblage of funeral traditions, which appears to be the earliest such compilation. The reticence of these early sources on this topic suggests that perhaps Muhammad's burial did not arouse the interests of his earliest biographers until a relatively later date, and Ibn Isḥāq's shift away from al-Zuhrī at this point seems to signal that the latter did not concern himself particularly with this subject. One wonders if perhaps this early silence is somehow related to the tradition from the East Syrian Baḥīrā legend that Muhammad's followers knew nothing about his grave.[102] Nevertheless, the eventual proliferation of traditions about Muhammad's funeral can be witnessed especially in Ibn Sa'd's *Ṭabaqāt*, as well as to a lesser extent by 'Abd al-Razzāq, Ibn Abī Shayba, and al-Balādhurī.[103] Although Ibn Sa'd ascribes a significant number of funeral traditions to al-Zuhrī, the absence of any parallel transmissions from either earlier or contemporary collections makes it extremely difficult to judge the accuracy of these attributions. It may well be that as traditions about Muhammad's burial began to develop, they were attracted to al-Zuhrī's name and assigned to him largely on the basis of his reputation as an authority on Muhammad's biography.

Of the burial traditions gathered by Ibn Isḥāq, only a single report is given on al-Zuhrī's authority, a notice that after Muhammad's corpse had been washed, it was wrapped in three garments, "two of Ṣuḥār make, and a striped mantle wrapped one over the other."[104] Ibn Sa'd, 'Abd al-Razzāq, and al-Balādhurī report a similar tradition on al-Zuhrī's authority, indicating that Muhammad was buried in three pieces of cloth, two white and one striped.[105] The early ninth-century papyrus also ascribes to al-Zuhrī a tradition that Muhammad was buried in a striped woolen garment, adding further credence to the possibility that Ibn Isḥāq inherited such information from him.[106] Nevertheless, the early Islamic traditions about Muhammad's burial clothes vary widely, and as Halevi observes, these reports reveal a great deal more about the culture of burial in early Islam than they do about actual events from the early seventh century.[107] Ibn Sa'd, 'Abd al-Razzāq, and al-Balādhurī also ascribe 'Alī's exclamation while washing Muhammad's corpse ("you were excellent in life and in death") to al-Zuhrī,[108] while Ibn Abī Shayba joins these three collectors in ascribing to al-Zuhrī the traditions that 'Alī, al-'Abbās, al-Faḍl, and Ṣāliḥ (that is, Shuqrān) participated in Muhammad's burial.[109] 'Abd al-Razzāq and Ibn Abī Shayba further relate here the installation of a brick monument to mark the location of Muhammad's grave. Nevertheless, in both instances the report is given on Ma'mar's authority, and thus the attribution to al-Zuhrī is somewhat questionable.[110] Muhammad's statement that "no prophet dies but he is buried where he died," reported by Abū Bakr, and the ensuing decision to bury him beneath his bed are ascribed by 'Abd al-Razzāq, Ibn Abī Shayba, and al-Balādhurī not to al-Zuhrī but to one of Ibn Isḥāq's contemporaries, Ibn Jurayj (d. 767).[111] 'Abd al-Razzāq likewise joins Ibn Isḥāq in assigning the tradition of Muhammad's burial in the middle of the night between Tuesday and Wednesday to another contemporary traditionist, 'Abdallāh b. Abī Bakr (d. 753).[112]

One has the sense then that with perhaps the exception of Muhammad's burial in three garments, Ibn Isḥāq (and possibly Ma'mar as well) is collecting these funeral traditions for the first time, and on the whole, his account of Muhammad's burial consists of what appear to be "idealized memories of Muḥammad" aimed at normalizing Islamic funeral practices and distinguishing them from the practices of their non-Islamic neighbors.[113] Moreover, both these burial traditions and the traditions of Muhammad's illness and death are heavily overlaid by the political and sectarian struggles of early Islam that ensued immediately after Muhammad's death. As both Madelung and Halevi observe, the cast of characters and their various roles in Muhammad's death and burial are designed to bolster the claims of one party or the other in the contest for authority within the earliest community.[114] Muhammad's sickbed provided, as Juynboll remarks, a frequent topos for the expression of these and other interests.[115] Thus, many of the details from these accounts should be viewed as governed by such ideological concerns, rather than reflecting actual historical events.

Yet these observations aside, Ibn Isḥāq transmits a mosaic of traditions from al-Zuhrī that seem to envision Muhammad's death within an urban context, where his wives live in separate dwellings and the faithful gather regularly in a central mosque for prayers. In contrast to the implied witness of the non-Islamic sources, Muhammad does not appear to have been out on campaign when he suddenly became ill and died; rather his death is situated within a thoroughly domestic setting, where Muhammad is surrounded by the constant care and attention of his friends and family. While this backdrop certainly bears a credible resemblance to the Medina of Islamic tradition, the city itself is never named in the death and burial traditions ascribed to al-Zuhrī. Is it then possible that the later tradition has supplied this location and its urban ambiance as the setting for Muhammad's departure from this world, transferring these events from an original context somewhere outside the Ḥijāz? Could it be that the early Muslims had re-remembered the circumstances of Muhammad's passing so dramatically just under a century after the event itself? There are in fact reasons to suspect a possible relocation of Muhammad's death to Medina, but their consideration must be deferred until a later chapter. The remainder of this chapter will instead examine the historical reliability of the *sīra* tradition more broadly, focusing especially in the issue of its chronology. As it turns out, the chronology of Muhammad's life is one of the most artificial and unreliable features of these early biographies, a point that is widely conceded by modern scholarship and even, to a certain extent, by the Islamic tradition itself. Moreover, modern scholarship has identified a variety of literary tendencies that have markedly shaped Muhammad's traditional biography, and some of these may have influenced the early Islamic memory of his death, determining certain aspects of both its timing and location. Finally, we will consider certain passages from Ibn Isḥāq's *Maghāzī* that seem to link Muhammad with a military campaign in Palestine during the final years of his life. These textual anomalies may possibly reveal traces of an older Islamic tradition concerning the end of Muhammad's life that would comport with the witness of the non-Islamic sources.

Sīra Chronology and Its Reliability

On the whole, the Islamic reports concerning Muhammad's death and burial appear to have been rather late in forming, as seems to be typical of the Islamic historical tradition more generally. The earliest evidence suggesting that Muhammad died before the invasion of Palestine appears only in Ibn Isḥāq's biography, composed over a century after the events themselves, and while this sequence may perhaps depend on information that Ibn Isḥāq inherited from his teacher al-Zuhrī, even this possibility leaves a considerable interval of time. Despite this gap, certain earlier scholars of formative Islam, perhaps most notably Montgomery Watt, have occasionally invoked the existence of a historically reliable kernel of truth buried in the *sīra* traditions that can guarantee the "general framework" of their chronology, but such appeals are unwarranted.[116] Moreover, the success of Ibn Isḥāq's biography ensured that its relative chronology of Muhammad's life would come to prevail over the later tradition.[117] As a result, very little can be known about how the Muslims of the first century may have remembered the life and death of their prophet differently from Ibn Isḥāq's canonical account. Rather than securing a bedrock of chronology, as Watt would have it, Ibn Isḥāq's hagiography of Muhammad presents a mythical portrait of Muhammad that is quite removed from the actual events of the early seventh century, whatever they may have been.

As early as the work of Henri Lammens at the beginning of the twentieth century, the *sīra* traditions were recognized as being basically a "midrash" on the text of the Qur'ān: that is, the *sīra* developed largely from an effort to embellish and flesh out the rather terse contents of the Qur'ān by providing them with a context.[118] Lammens demonstrated that the *sīra*'s production took place at a considerable historical distance from the actual life of Muhammad, and that as a result its contents were formed to correspond with

Islamic belief and practice as they had developed almost a century after Muhammad's death.[119] Although it cannot be overlooked that Lammens has rightly been characterized as "filled with a holy contempt for Islam," his formative insights into the nature of the *sīra* have remained fundamental to its study: as F. E. Peters observes of Lammens's work on the *sīra*, "whatever his motives and his style . . . Lammens' critical attack has never been refuted."[120] More recent works by Wansbrough and Uri Rubin have similarly demonstrated in rather different ways that the representation of Muhammad in the *sīra* traditions is essentially a reflection of Islam and its concerns during the eighth and ninth centuries, having little to do with the historical figure of Muhammad.[121] Patricia Crone reaches the same conclusion in the opening pages of her *Slaves on Horses*, where she offers the following pithy, if devastating, assessment of the *sīra* traditions as historical sources:

> Thanks to its success, the *Sīra* of Ibn Isḥāq is practically our only source for the life of Muhammad preserved within the Islamic tradition. The work is late: written not by a grandchild, but a great-grandchild of the Prophet's generation, it gives us the view for which classical Islam had settled. And written by a member of the "*ulama*" the scholars who had by then emerged as the classical bearers of the Islamic tradition, the picture which it offers is also one sided: how the Umayyad caliphs remembered their Prophet we shall never know. That it is unhistorical is only what one would expect, but it has an extraordinary capacity to resist internal criticism, a feature unparalleled in either the *Skandhaka* [the life of the Buddha] or the Gospels, but characteristic of the entire Islamic tradition, and most pronounced in the Koran: one can take the picture presented or one can leave it, but one cannot *work* with it.[122]

Such rough dismissal of the historical reliability of the *sīra* traditions is not limited only to "skeptical" scholars but is shared by more sanguine scholars of early Islam as well. It is indeed widely conceded that the *sīra* traditions tell us almost nothing of actual events from Muhammad's life and times; they reflect instead the convictions and concerns of the communities and individuals that produced them during the second Islamic century.[123]

In spite of these not inconsiderable problems, one might be tempted to suppose, with Watt, that at the very least the basic chronology of the *sīra* tradition could hold some historical value. Even if the details of the *sīra* are more or less legendary, perhaps the chronological framework on which they are strung together might still be historically accurate. Unfortunately, this is simply not the case: on the contrary, of all the various features of the *sīra*, the chronology of Muhammad's life is regarded as one of its most artificial elements. Conrad identifies *sīra* chronology as among the most "vexed" issues of early Islamic historiography,[124] and even Schoeler, who has argued for greater confidence in the historicity of Muhammad's biographies, freely concedes the lateness and artificiality of the *sīra*'s chronology. According to Schoeler, all of the earliest transmitters display considerable carelessness and inconsistency with regard to chronology, and the relative chronology of Muhammad's life as we now have it is largely the work of a single individual, Ibn Isḥāq.[125] Donner similarly observes that the earliest Muslims appear to have been profoundly disinterested in history, perhaps as a consequence of imminent eschatological expectations. As a result, the primitive Islamic tradition took little care to preserve dates and other chronological information from Muhammad's prophetic career, and when historical writers were faced with the task of recounting Muhammad's life nearly a century later, they met with rather poor sources.[126] The first biographers essentially had to invent the chronology of Muhammad's life, resolving numerous matters themselves "in definitive fashion and in detail, regardless of whether or not sufficient evidence existed to do so," since thorough knowledge of Muhammad's life was required for both Qur'ānic exegesis and legal interpretation.[127] Such conditions would seem particularly ripe for the possible transformation—perhaps even without any deliberate reinvention—of an earlier memory concerning the end of Muhammad's life.

When taken on their own, the traditions of Muhammad's death ascribed to al-Zuhrī by Ibn Isḥāq and other early sources offer no sense of chronology. If one were to extract them from the collections in which they presently survive, one would not have the slightest idea when Muhammad was believed to have died, either in absolute or even relative terms. And while it certainly is possible that al-Zuhrī may have relayed some sequence of events to his students, such an arrangement is not evident from the traditions themselves. Only with Ibn Isḥāq's *Maghāzī*, as witnessed by later sources, do we gain any sense of a chronological order linking these isolated traditions. This circumstance is actually quite typical of the early Islamic historical tradition, whose individual units characteristically display an atomistic quality, possessing little to no historical context in themselves. The early Islamic historians have arranged these isolated fragments of tradition according to a sequential overlay of their own fashioning. The disjointed nature of early

Islamic historiography very often leaves the sequence of events uncertain, and as a result both relative and absolute chronology are among the weakest and most artificial elements of the early Islamic historical tradition. These uncomposed elements of the primitive Islamic historical tradition seem to reflect the general absence of historical consciousness within earliest Islam. As Fred Donner repeatedly observes, the early Islamic community appears to have been guided by a "markedly ahistorical" outlook, and only at the end of the first Islamic century do we find any evidence of a "historicizing impulse."[128] At this time, when the biography of Muhammad as we have it first began to take shape, the emergent scholars of early Islam "found themselves faced with a large body of material the exact chronological relationships of which had been forgotten or obscured by an overlay of fictitious material. It was in the matter of chronology, perhaps, that the early Muslims' essentially ahistorical outlook created the gravest obstacles for the development of Islamic historiography, and, for the early period at least, chronology constitutes one of the weakest points of the Islamic historiographical tradition."[129]

While there is sporadic evidence of dating according to the *hijra* already by the twenties and thirties AH from a few documentary sources, this system of dating appears to have been limited to official and court documents, and it had no impact on the "personal recollections of individuals" and "tribal oral traditions" that formed the basis of the Islamic historical tradition.[130] Moreover, there is evidence for the parallel use of other chronological systems during the first Islamic century, such as the dating according to the "Yazdegerd era" witnessed on early Arab-Sassanian coinage, or the reference to "year forty-two of the rule of Believers" in an early Islamic papyrus.[131] Indeed, the Arab-Sassanian coins very often appear to give a date for the *hijra* equivalent to 624–25, and the fact that an equivalent date is confirmed by the aberrant chronology of Sayf b. ʿUmar's history of the conquest of Arabia indicates that not all of the early Muslims agreed even on the dating of the *hijra*.[132] Moreover, the dating of traditions in relation to the *hijra* "became feasible for historians only after the lengthy process of establishing relative chronologies," a process that began only at the end of the first Islamic century.[133] According to Donner, it was al-Zuhrī more than anyone else who was "responsible for establishing the generally accepted version of the sequential order in which the main episodes of the Islamic origins story took place," that is, the *relative* chronology of events. Although it is perhaps a bit presumptive to credit al-Zuhrī with the invention of this full sequence (as noted above), there can be no question that Ibn Isḥāq had a fairly developed relative chronology as he composed his *Maghāzī*, some of which he possibly inherited from al-Zuhrī. Nevertheless, Donner rightly emphasizes the significant contributions made by both Ibn Isḥāq and al-Wāqidī to the traditional chronology of Muhammad's life: much of the basic chronology of Muhammad's life, including perhaps even the timing of his death, was determined only at this rather late date.[134] This long delayed interest in the order of events certainly raises significant questions about the reliability of the traditional chronology of Muhammad's life, particularly since, as Donner observes, the earliest history of the community, including Muhammad's career at Medina specifically, was "the most difficult to recover remembered information about."[135] Thus, given the radically ahistorical character of early Islamic memories concerning the time of origins, and the relatively late imposition of a sequential order onto this material, one would do well to cast a wary eye toward the chronology evident in the earliest biographical sources.[136]

Lammens was the first to tackle systematically the complex problems of the *sīra*'s chronology, and after sorting through its jumble of dates, he reached the conclusion that not only was its chronology completely unreliable, but it was also inconsistent.[137] Most importantly, Lammens recognized that the *sīra* tradition was driven above all else by a concern to preserve a strict numerical symmetry, not only in its division of Muhammad's career into proportioned phases, but with respect to all numbers.[138] Thus while the chronology of Muhammad's life varies considerably according to different witnesses, the division of time is consistently symmetrical and artificial in all the sources. The most frequently encountered chronology identifies Muhammad as 40 years old at the time of his prophetic vocation, attributing to him thereafter a prophetic career of 20 years, evenly divided between Mecca and Medina, with 10 years spent in each city for a total of 60 years at his death.[139] Recent studies by Conrad and Rubin illuminate certain aspects of the symbolism lying behind the construction of this numerical typology for Muhammad's life. Conrad, for instance, identifies the frequent use of the number 40 in antiquity as a topos to indicate plenitude and divine activity, as well as a widely held belief that 40 was the age at which a man was at the peak of his physical and intellectual powers.[140] Rubin pursues these same issues further in a major study devoted to examining the ways in which the early Islamic community shaped the *sīra* traditions to portray Muhammad in the image of a biblical prophet. In a chapter devoted to the chronology of Muhammad's life, Rubin uncovers a variety of highly symbolic numerical patterns that shape and control the chronological division of Muhammad's life. The most intriguing of these is the identification of a dramatic parallel between Muhammad's 40–10–10 chronology and the life of Moses. Since Moses traditionally began his prophetic career at the age of 80 and then died at 120, Muhammad's lifespan reflects the same division as Moses' life, only decreased by half. As Rubin explains, this scheme presumably fits with an Islamic tradition according to which successive prophets are called at an age half that of their predecessors.[141]

Yet not all of the various Islamic sources attribute 60 years to Muhammad according to such a 40–10–10 chronology. There is considerable variation within the early Islamic tradition regarding Muhammad's ultimate age: many sources report his death at 65, while others make him considerably older than this, and still others describe him as being much younger. As Conrad observes, "Well into the second century A.H. scholarly opinion on the birth date of the Prophet displayed a range of variance of 85 years."[142] Alternate schemas were also utilized to divide Muhammad's career between Mecca and Medina, some favoring a longer period of prophetic leadership, and others trying to break the symmetry of years in favor of one city or the other, presumably in order to indicate that city's spiritual superiority.[143] Yet in spite of all this chronological confusion, there is no clear evidence of any variation in the year of Muhammad's death in the Islamic tradition. Although one finds considerable diversity of opinion regarding the exact day of the week or month on which he died,[144] beginning with Ibn Isḥāq, the Islamic tradition quite consistently identifies 632 as the year of his death, so that even the skeptic Lammens believed that two key dates in the chronology of Muhammad's life, the *hijra* in 622 and his death in 632, "deserve to inspire confidence of a relative kind."[145]

Unfortunately, Lammens was not aware of the important counter-evidence from outside of the Islamic tradition suggesting that Muhammad was still alive as the conquest of Palestine began. Yet Lammens did discover certain peculiar *sīra* traditions that could suggest Muhammad's survival into the period of the Palestinian conquest, a memory that was perhaps subsequently effaced by the now traditional account of his death in 632 at Medina. Lammens found several long overlooked reports within the Islamic historical tradition that ascribe thirteen, rather than the traditional ten, years to the Medinan period of Muhammad's life.[146] In this case, if the date of the *hijra* remains 622, the end of Muhammad's life would come in 635, three years later than the traditional date and well after the beginning of the Islamic conquest of the Near East. Likewise, the uncertainties concerning the date of the *hijra* in this early period could also suggest Muhammad's death possibly as late as 635. As noted above, both the early historian Sayf b. ʿUmar and the Arab-Sassanian coins indicate a date for the *hijra* of 624–25, which would place Muhammad's death in 634–35 according to the traditional Islamic count of ten years after the *hijra*. Perhaps the notice in some of the non-Islamic sources considered in the previous chapter that Muhammad ruled for only seven years is related to this alternative chronology of the *hijra*. These reports, along with similar indications by a handful of Islamic sources, may possibly reflect an alternative strategy for revising the timing of Muhammad's death so that it would occur before the invasion of Palestine: if the *hijra* were in 624–25, then a seven-year reign would place his death in 632.[147]

Admittedly, there is an early Arabic papyrus with both a Greek date equivalent to 643 and an Arabic date "in the year twenty-two," revealing the early use of a calendar beginning in 621–22. Yet as Crone and Cook observe, there is no evidence that this particular chronology was widely adopted or that it signals a universal recognition of this year as the date of the *hijra* at this time. To the contrary, the variant tradition signaled by Sayf and the early coins indicates that some early Muslims dated this pivotal event three years later than the traditional date. Donner's remarks concerning the rather late implementation of *hijra* dating certainly invite the possibility that it was some time before the official date of the *hijra* became widely established. Moreover, as Crone and Cook further note, without this important early papyrus, "early Islamic chronology would be very much out to sea": its exceptional status certainly raises the question of whether early Islamic chronology was in fact during the first several decades a bit "lost at sea."[148] Thus, these deviant chronologies of the *hijra* further invite the possibility of an early memory that Muhammad survived into the period of the conquest of Palestine.

It is conceivable, however, that some of these chronological variants may simply reflect the contest between Mecca and Medina, as the two cities were vying with one another to lay claim to the status of Islam's holiest city.[149] One of the ways that this rivalry often manifested itself was in various adjustments to the chronology of Muhammad's life, aimed at shifting the symmetry of ten years in both cities in favor of one or the other. Certain Meccan traditions, for instance, sought to represent Mecca's spiritual primacy by extending the length of Muhammad's prophetic career there by three years, giving him a total of thirteen years in Mecca but only ten in Medina. While a similar adjustment in Medina's favor could potentially be the source of these traditions assigning thirteen years to Muhammad's Medinan period, this does not reflect the general pattern of the comparable pro-Medinan traditions. Adjustments favoring Medina generally subtract two years from Muhammad's time in Mecca, rather than adding time to his Medinan period, making for a total of eight years as a prophet in Mecca and ten in Medina.[150] This alternate strategy was almost certainly determined by the fact that the traditional dates of Muhammad's death and of the *hijra* were already well established by the time of this rivalry: Medina's time could not be similarly extended, since doing so would necessitate a change in either the date of the *hijra* or Muhammad's death. Thus Medina's partisans looked to shorten the length of Muhammad's Meccan period rather than extend his time in Medina. Nevertheless, it is admittedly possible that traditions giving Muhammad thirteen years in Medina have simply duplicated the Meccan extension without regard for the disruptions in chronology: Lammens, after all, has shown that the *sīra* traditions were not very concerned about such consistency.[151]

It is equally possible, however, that the tradition assigning Muhammad with thirteen years in Medina is primitive, since its creation after the dates of Muhammad's death and the *hijra* had become firmly established would be highly problematic.[152] Its survival in so few sources is to be expected in view of these circumstances: the tradition's blatant contradiction of the traditional chronology of Muhammad's death would assure its limited preservation. This evidence is admittedly somewhat complicated, and in isolation it could seem to be little more than scatter within the tradition. Nevertheless, the witness of the non-Islamic sources certainly invites the possibility that these reports preserve an early tradition that has somehow survived the process of revision. Such an interpretation finds support in certain traditions of the *sīra* that describe military engagements in Palestine during Muhammad's lifetime: these reports may in fact also witness to an older tradition that remembered Muhammad's vitality into the period of the Near Eastern conquests.

Vestiges of a Palestinian Campaign?

In addition to these stray reports assigning thirteen years to Muhammad's stay in Medina or the *hijra* to 624–25, there are some peculiar episodes from early Islamic historical tradition that may possibly preserve vestiges of older traditions associating Muhammad with the conquest of Palestine. On several occasions, for instance, the *sīra* tradition reports military engagements by Muhammad's followers in Palestine during his lifetime. Admittedly, none of these accounts matches exactly the report of the non-Islamic sources (and the Letter of ʿUmar) that Muhammad was leading the Muslims at the beginning of the Palestinian campaign, that is, at least not as they are presently embedded within the traditional narratives of Islamic origins. One wonders if perhaps these reports may reflect earlier traditions of an assault on Palestine under Muhammad's leadership that have been subsequently recast so as to dissociate Islam's founding prophet from the invasion of the Promised Land.[153] Certain features of these stories suggest that this may in fact be the case.

According to the *sīra* tradition, the first Islamic military activities in Palestine took place at the battle of Mu'ta, a location approximately fifteen kilometers south of Karak in modern Jordan and fifteen kilometers east of the Dead Sea. There Muhammad's followers fought and were defeated by "Byzantine" forces in September 629, roughly two and a half years before Muhammad's death.[154] While there is no indication that Muhammad himself was involved in this engagement, at his command an expedition of three thousand men set off into Byzantine territory, with an unspecified purpose. According to Ibn Isḥāq's account, once Muhammad's followers reached Roman Palestine, they learned that the Roman emperor Heraclius was operating in the area with one hundred thousand "Greek" troops, together with another one hundred thousand Arab auxiliaries.[155] Understandably intimidated by such odds, the Muslim army camped for two nights at Maʿān, roughly thirty kilometers east of Petra, deliberating over what they should do. The soldiers suggested that they send a message to Muhammad requesting either reinforcements or permission to withdraw, but their leaders persuaded them to attack instead, resulting in a crushing defeat for the Muslims.

While the numbers of the Byzantine army are certainly inflated, and it seems highly unlikely that Heraclius himself would have been involved, this tradition describes what was seemingly the initial confrontation between Muhammad's followers and some Byzantine confederates, over two years before Muhammad's death. Donner interprets the battle of Mu'ta as reflecting a larger pattern of raids into southern Palestine under Muhammad's direction, aimed at bringing the Arab tribes of this region under his authority.[156] Donner has recently reiterated his observation of Muhammad's clear and continued interest in the north, proposing further that this northward push may have been driven by imminent eschatological expectations and Jerusalem's prominent role in the drama of the end times. Inasmuch as the Final Judgment was soon to arrive, as Donner notes there would have likely been a strong impulse to secure control of Jerusalem.[157] Hoyland also concludes that the evidence of the *sīra* traditions seems to indicate at the very least that Muhammad himself initiated a military campaign aimed at controlling southern

Palestine, while Watt identifies Mu'ta and other related skirmishes as the beginning of Muhammad's "northern policy," a strategy aiming at expansion into Roman Syria.[158] Yet the testimony of the non-Islamic sources that Muhammad led the invasion of Palestine certainly invites the possibility that there may be more to these indications of a northern policy during the final years of Muhammad's life than either Watt or Donner could have determined on the basis of the Islamic sources alone. What appears in the traditional biographies as Muhammad's greater plans for invading Roman Palestine may originally have involved more than mere intent: these signs of a northern policy perhaps instead reflect altered remnants of older traditions that recalled Muhammad's involvement in the assault on Roman Palestine. While Muhammad is not identified as the leader of the expeditionary force at Mu'ta, the soldiers' proposal to send a message to Muhammad would seem to suggest that he is "in theater" somewhere nearby, since communication to and from Medina, some 750 kilometers away, would presumably have taken a considerable amount of time.[159] While this is quite possibly just a literary device designed to heighten the narrative's drama, the notion that the original audience would have found such a proposal plausible could indicate a rather different historical circumstance for the engagement at Mu'ta.

There are, moreover, problems with the dating of this episode that could suggest some adjustments have been made to its chronology. As Walter Kaegi notes, the *sīra* tradition's account of Mu'ta is complicated by certain details of the contemporary conflict between the Byzantines and the Persians. Although Hercalius had defeated the Persian army in Mesopotamia already by early 628, Persian troops remained in Palestine until July 629, when Heraclius reached an agreement with the Persian leaders to remove their soldiers from Palestine and other occupied Byzantine territories.[160] This leaves a pretty narrow window for the restoration of Byzantine military authority over Palestine, raising questions as to whether such an engagement between Muhammad's followers and a "Byzantine" force would even have been possible by September. Mu'ta was after all a fairly remote location on the southeastern desert frontier, and there is no evidence of any Roman military presence there in the later sixth century or early seventh, or even as far back as the later fourth century.[161] Yet Kaegi rather blithely assumes that the Byzantine army must have rushed back into Palestine, quickly reestablishing its presence even in remote areas, like Mu'ta, where it had not previously been active for some time. Despite the problems of logistics and timing, Kaegi concludes solely on the basis of these reports from the *sīra* tradition that in just two months' time "somehow the Byzantines had already resumed control of this relatively distant region that was east of the Jordan."[162] Yet such rapid restoration of Byzantine military control to a region that had not been actively defended for centuries seems highly unlikely. Instead, given the general weakness of *sīra* chronology, as well as the tradition of Muhammad's involvement in the invasion of Palestine, one might alternatively suspect that a tradition originally linking Muhammad to the larger assault on Palestine has possibly been moved up earlier in his biography to coincide with his death in Medina in 632. In such a case the chronological difficulties may reflect nothing so much as ignorance of the details of Byzantine military history on the part of Muhammad's early biographers as they sought to rewrite the history of this early engagement.

Equally peculiar is the account of Mu'ta from Theophanes' *Chronicle*, the first non-Islamic source to refer to this event.[163] According to Theophanes' report, Mu'ta does indeed mark the beginnings of the Islamic invasion of Palestine, and despite this initial defeat, the Muslims thereafter began to wrest control of Palestine from the Byzantines. Theophanes, however, locates the battle of Mu'ta in the year *after* Muhammad's death: although Muhammad is credited with planning the attack, it was realized only in the first year of Abū Bakr's rule. While it is conceivable that Theophanes has simply made a mistake, it seems more likely, as Conrad has persuasively argued, that Theophanes relies on early Islamic sources for his account of this battle.[164] Could it be then that Theophanes—or more probably, his Islamic source—has preserved an older tradition of Mu'ta's chronology and its relation to the conquest of Palestine? In such a case Theophanes' divergence from the *sīra* traditions may simply reflect a different interpretive strategy for revising an older tradition that originally associated Muhammad with the invasion of Palestine. While the *sīra* traditions may have adjusted the original accounts of this first assault on Palestine so that it would appear to have been a minor engagement occurring sometime well before Muhammad's death at Medina in 632, Theophanes' Islamic sources have perhaps harmonized the same early tradition with Muhammad's Medinan demise by removing Muhammad from the action and linking the battle instead with Abū Bakr.[165] On the whole, both the timing of Mu'ta and its relation to the Islamic conquest of Palestine seem to be much less certain than the confidence that Kaegi and others have placed in Ibn Isḥāq's account might suggest. Particularly in light of the tradition of Muhammad's leadership during the invasion of Palestine, it would appear that some of the rough spots in the various early accounts of Mu'ta may need to be rethought.[166]

Accounts of a military engagement at Tabūk approximately one and a half years before Muhammad's death similarly warrant reconsideration of

Muhammad's possible association with the Palestinian campaign.[167] According to the early Islamic biographies, Muhammad personally led an expedition to "Tabūk in Syria," about two hundred kilometers southwest from ʿAqaba, with the explicit purpose of assaulting the Byzantine Empire. Not only did Muhammad personally take charge of this intended invasion of Roman territory, but its scale was unprecedented. This was no raiding party: the army that marched against "the Greeks" at Tabūk was the largest, most well-equipped military force that Muhammad had ever assembled, numbering thirty thousand men according to al-Wāqidī and al-Balādhurī (compared, for instance, with the three thousand reportedly sent to Mu'ta).[168] The size of the undertaking, as well as Muhammad's personal leadership, certainly suggests that this expedition was more than an effort to subdue the local Arabs of the Byzantine borderlands. Rather, the goal would appear to have been a decisive and extensive attack on the Roman Empire. Although al-Wāqidī explains that Muhammad was responding to rumors that the Byzantines had begun to amass a powerful army on the empire's southern frontier to march against him and his followers, Tor Andrae is correct to note that plans for conquest and expansion into the Roman Empire instead were likely behind such a massive military campaign.[169] Both Muhammad's religious message and his prior pattern of conquest suggest that the expedition to Tabūk represents the beginnings of a northern strategy of much grander scale than most historians, both Islamic and modern, have been willing to envision.

Whatever Muhammad's motives and expectations may have been in attacking Rome, the Islamic historical tradition reports that events at Tabūk did not go as planned. According to Ibn Isḥāq, when Muhammad reached Tabūk he not only found no army, but he met with no resistance whatsoever. In fact, the Byzantine governor of ʿAqaba is said to have traveled to Tabūk in order to arrange terms for surrender with Muhammad. Other local tribes were similarly quick to submit, placing themselves under Muhammad's authority and agreeing to pay the poll tax.[170] The expedition would appear to have been a complete success: with no violence or loss of life, Muhammad had successfully extended his authority to the marches of Byzantium, securing the capitulation of the local imperial authorities. After such an auspicious beginning to his attack on the Roman Empire, it is difficult to imagine that Muhammad would have turned right around and headed back to Medina. Yet according to the Islamic historical tradition, that is exactly what he did. Having traveled over great distance with a battle-ready army, the largest he had yet assembled, Muhammad essentially met with no resistance as he approached the prosperous and sacred lands of the Bible. Then astonishingly and without much explanation, Muhammad rejected the incredible opportunity that lay seemingly before him, turning away from the biblical Holy Land in favor of returning to Medina.[171] The conclusion is so anomalous with Muhammad's initial intention for a massive invasion and military expedition against the Byzantines that one wonders if we really have the complete story here. Indeed, perhaps the engagement at Tabūk originally marked instead the beginning of a campaign in Palestine under Muhammad's leadership that occupied the final years of his life. This is admittedly a somewhat speculative proposal; nevertheless, it seems warranted inasmuch as the traditional accounts of Tabūk do not appear to reflect the full extent of Muhammad's political interests in a concerted northern strategy of military engagement with the Byzantines in Palestine.

Finally, even the very end of Muhammad's life itself, as related in the earliest biographies, is intersected by a major campaign aimed deep within Roman Palestine. Both Ibn Isḥāq and al-Wāqidī report that just before he suddenly became ill and died, Muhammad was planning an incursion into Palestine, an event to which Ibn Isḥāq rather strangely refers twice. Some sources indicate that Muhammad had initially planned to lead this campaign himself, which would certainly seem consistent with the reports of his actions at Tabūk.[172] Nevertheless, Muhammad instead placed Usāma b. Zayd in command of a force of cavalry, ordering them to attack, according to Ibn Isḥāq, "the territory of Balqā' and al-Dārūm in the land of Palestine": these regions lay deep within Byzantine territory, in central Transjordan and along the coastal plain of Palestine respectively.[173] Al-Wāqidī devotes considerable attention to this assault on "the Greeks" in Palestine at the end of his biography, inserting Muhammad's death into the account almost as an afterthought.[174] Al-Wāqidī, however, identifies the goal of Usāma's expedition as Mu'ta, making it into a second battle at Mu'ta, which took place after Muhammad's death. Presumably, this reflects an effort to harmonize Ibn Isḥāq's chronology of the battle of Mu'ta with the alternate tradition witnessed by Theophanes' *Chronicle*.

Nevertheless, many other collectors have preserved this tradition, and the majority name Ubnā as the target of this assault. Ibn Habīb describes Dārām, the fort nearby Gaza, as the army's objective, but Abū Dā'ūd, Ibn Ḥanbal, and Ibn Sa'd (among others) identify Ubnā as their goal.[175] While Ubnā's precise location has vexed Islamic historians, both medieval and modern, de Prémare convincingly argues that it is to be identified with the city Yubnā in Palestine, which lay to the north of Gaza along the coast.[176] These reports would appear to confirm Ibn Isḥāq's report that Muhammad's followers, at his command, were engaged in military activities on the coastal plain of Palestine, even before his death. The confusion regarding Ubnā's location in both the Islamic tradition and modern scholarship was likely generated by the apparent contradiction between these reports and the established narrative of Palestine's invasion only well after Muhammad's death. Al-Wāqidī, however, resolved the tension by using the alternative chronology for Mu'ta to relocate the battle to an area on the fringes of Roman Palestine.

Moreover, Ibn Isḥāq's rather peculiar positioning of Usāma's campaign within the narrative of his *Maghāzī* seems to suggest that the episode's chronology was perhaps still somewhat volatile in the middle of the eighth century. Ibn Isḥāq relates this tradition twice, once just before Muhammad's death, but also earlier in his narrative, immediately after Muhammad's "farewell pilgrimage."[177] In between the two accounts is a list of Muhammad's raids, which could certainly give the impression that Usāma's attacks should be understood within the context of Muhammad's broader military campaign. The tradition's reduplication could itself suggest that the mission's chronology had in fact been revised not very long before Ibn Isḥāq's biography: its repeated appearance may be symptomatic of an effort to find a new home for a tradition that originally had linked the invasion of Palestine with Muhammad's lifetime. The episode's instability within the structure of Muhammad's biography may indicate efforts to re-date these events from a campaign in Palestine so as to have them occur sometime before the story of Muhammad's death at Medina in 632. This point is underscored by having Muhammad ascend to the pulpit of Medina's mosque while in the throes of his illness in order to defend Usāma's incursion and to foster support for the mission.[178] It is as if, with this final prophetic plea, Ibn Isḥāq has sought to secure a chronologically troublesome incident to a more amenable position prior to the account of Muhammad's Medinan decease.

Thus, despite the absence of any direct evidence from the early *sīra* traditions that would indicate an invasion of Palestine under Muhammad's leadership, each of these military expeditions seems to hint at the beginnings of a concerted military campaign against Palestine within Muhammad's lifetime. The attack on Mu'ta describes the initial sally of Muhammad's followers into Byzantine Palestine already more than two years before his death, and a variant chronology reported by Theophanes suggests a possible older tradition locating this battle sometime after 632. The expedition to "Tabūk in Syria," approximately one and a half years before Muhammad's death, reportedly involved the largest military force that Muhammad had ever assembled. Muhammad himself led this army to the borderlands of Roman Palestine, with the express purpose of engaging the Byzantines militarily on a massive scale, according to the *sīra* tradition. Despite the peaceful resolution achieved with the ruler of ʿAqaba and other local tribes, this certainly sounds like the beginnings of a campaign directed against the Byzantines in Palestine. Likewise, Muhammad's dispatch of an army under Usāma's command to attack the Byzantines deep within their territory, along the coastal plain north of Gaza and in the center of Transjordan, certainly would appear to be a mission from a fairly advanced military campaign in Palestine, rather than a raid orchestrated from Medina. All of this suggests that perhaps there was once a great deal more to Muhammad's northern strategy than the earliest Islamic biographers have remembered. Indeed, the indication of certain authorities that Muhammad himself had initially intended to lead Usāma's assault may represent some vestige of such an earlier tradition: perhaps Muhammad was once described as leading this attack, and Ibn Isḥāq or one of his predecessors replaced him with Usāma. Muhammad's leadership of the assault on Roman Palestine is further suggested by Ibn Saʿd's report from Kaʿb al-Aḥbār that as Mecca was Muhammad's birthplace and Medina the place of his *hijra* so Syria was the land of his rule.[179] In any case, these reports from the *sīra* traditions that describe Muhammad as initiating significant military actions against the Byzantines in Palestine in the years before his death certainly present a striking parallel with what Christian and other non-Muslim writers report: accordingly, one must consider that these traditions may preserve traces of an older tradition that is witnessed more directly by the non-Islamic sources.[180]

Conclusion

Although the traditional Islamic biographies of Muhammad are unanimous in their agreement that Muhammad died at Medina in 632, the very nature of these sources invites serious questions about their reliability. The oldest recoverable Islamic traditions about the end of Muhammad's life cannot be dated much earlier than around a century after the events that they report, and while these reports often come with a pedigree assigning their content to earlier authorities, given the widespread fabrication of *isnād*s in the Islamic tradition, these alleged chains of transmission cannot guarantee their earlier circulation. Moreover, the rather atomistic form in which these earliest reports have survived yields almost no internal indication of chronology, and only with Ibn Isḥāq's *Maghāzī* from the middle of the eighth century is there a clear sequence of events that provides a basic chronology for the end of Muhammad's life. While one might perhaps be initially inclined to give the *sīra* tradition's chronology the benefit of the doubt, particularly when it speaks with such unanimity, *sīra* chronology has frequently been shown to be both weak and highly artificial, and even the medieval Islamic tradition looked upon the *sīra* traditions with considerable suspicion.

The chronology of the early conquests is certainly no better, as Noth, Conrad, and Donner, among others, have demonstrated.[181] For example, the date of Jerusalem's conquest is itself highly uncertain: despite the frequent acceptance of 638 as the year when the Arabs conquered the Holy City, Heribert Busse makes an excellent case, using Christian and Islamic materials together, for dating these events early in 635.[182] Indeed, the events of the invasion of Syria and Palestine more generally are so confused in the Islamic sources that, as Donner writes, their course is "impossible to reconstruct with confidence because the traditional Muslim sources provide conflicting reports that cannot be reconciled satisfactorily."[183] The discord and confusion of the early Islamic accounts of the Syrian campaign are undoubtedly tokens that the original sequence of events either had been largely forgotten or was subject to widespread revision by individual historians. In either case it would appear that the chronology of the early conquests, much like that of Muhammad's life, is the work of Islamic traditionists from the eighth and ninth centuries. In such circumstances, it is easy to imagine how a tradition of Muhammad's leadership during the invasion of Palestine could have either become lost or been re-remembered by his early biographers.

Certain literary tendencies of the early *sīra* tradition may have encouraged such revision of Muhammad's association with the conquest of Palestine, including most notably the influence of prophetic models from the biblical tradition. Modern scholarship has long recognized that the *sīra*'s depiction of Muhammad is frequently modeled directly after the life of Moses, in an effort to shape Muhammad's biography according to the pattern of a biblical prophet.[184] As noted already, this tendency is especially apparent in the *sīra*'s chronology of Muhammad's life, and the timing of his birth and death in particular has been harmonized to reflect the traditional boundaries of Moses' lifespan.[185] Understood in this context, a shift of Muhammad's death from after the invasion of Palestine in 634 to a pre-conquest death at Medina in 632 would also serve to conform the end of his life to the prophetic archetype established by the story of Moses. According to biblical tradition, Moses died before reaching the Holy Land and thus was not involved in the Israelite conquest of Canaan.[186] Yet while Moses neither entered the Holy Land nor led its invasion, he nevertheless did lead the Israelites during their earlier subjugation of the peoples east of the Jordan (in what was to become the Roman province of "Arabia"). Thus by locating Muhammad's death in 632, both before the invasion of Palestine and outside of the Holy Land, Muhammad, like Moses, leads the children of Abraham to reclaim the land of their inheritance, but does not himself enter it nor have a hand in its conquest. While Muhammad leads his followers in battle along their way to the Promised Land, the task of conquering the land, as in the biblical account, falls to a close friend: Joshua, in the case of Moses, and Abū Bakr (or Usāma b. Zayd?), in the case of Muhammad.

Such influence from biblical typology is especially evident in the traditions of Muhammad's leadership of the expedition to Tabūk. This intended assault on the Byzantines in Palestine links Muhammad more forcefully with the conquest of Palestine than perhaps any other moment in the *sīra* tradition; consequently it is no surprise that here the tradition also takes deliberate steps to separate Muhammad from the full-scale invasion of Palestine, particularly through associating him in certain ways with Moses. Ibn Isḥāq does not explain why Muhammad apparently called off the mission to launch a massive attack on the Byzantines in Palestine, only noting that he remained in Tabūk less than ten nights and then returned to Medina.[187] While traveling back, however, Muhammad makes a significant reprise of one of Moses' most famous and momentous miracles, his causing water to gush forth from a rock while the Israelites were wandering in the desert (Exod. 17:1–7; Num. 20:1–12). On the way back to Medina, Muhammad's followers discovered water issuing from a rock, but only enough for two or three people. Muhammad ordered that it be left alone until he arrived, but some of "the hypocrites" got there first and drew the water for themselves. Angered by their disobedience, Muhammad cursed these men and then placed his hand under the rock. At first only a small trickle issued forth into his hand, but when Muhammad sprinkled the rock with this water and prayed over it, water began to gush forth so that there was enough for everyone to drink. While this may appear to be nothing more than an innocent typological imitation of Moses, it should be noted that as Muhammad here turns his back to Palestine and seemingly abandons his intention to invade, he repeats the very act that, according to Numbers 20:12, ensured that Moses would not be allowed to enter the Promised Land. While no explicit connection is made between the miracle and Muhammad's failure, like Moses, to enter the Holy Land, surely the connection was readily apparent to an audience as steeped in prophetic traditions as were the *sīra* writers and their patrons. The placement of this particular miracle in the context of Muhammad's turning away from an invasion of Palestine certainly suggests that the tradition of Moses' failure to enter the Promised Land along with the Israelites had shaped the early Islamic memory of Muhammad's relation to the invasion of Palestine. His reprise of such a notorious miracle while inexplicably turning back from Palestine is surely no mere coincidence.

Biblical typologies alone, however, do not seem sufficient to explain the disconnect between the Islamic and non-Islamic sources with respect to Muhammad's association with the conquest of Palestine. If we are to entertain the possibility that the non-Islamic sources have preserved an earlier tradition that was subsequently revised by the Islamic tradition, certainly a much more powerful impulse, or set of impulses, seems required to explain this transformation. Donner is indeed right to raise such a demand in his criticism of the so-called "skeptical school."[188] Although Donner's critique will be addressed in some detail in the following chapter, he is correct that some sort of a profound ideological rupture within earliest Islam seems necessary to explain the scope of the changes that the skeptical approach envisions. The remainder of this study thus will focus on several important areas where the Muslims of the early second century AH appear to have come to rather different beliefs from those of Muhammad and his earliest followers, namely, with respect to eschatology, confessional identity, and sacred geography. Donner himself has made several important contributions to reevaluating the nature of earliest Islamic belief in some of these areas, and despite his protest, it does in fact appear that the evidence of considerable change is sufficient to warrant the skeptic's position that there is potentially significant discontinuity between the faith and practice of primitive Islam and the later memory of Islamic origins as reflected in the narratives of the mid-eighth and ninth centuries.

The remaining chapters will then argue that some fairly rapid changes to certain fundamental aspects of the early Islamic faith can possibly explain the differences in the source materials regarding the end of Muhammad's life and his connection with the conquest of Palestine. One of the most significant areas where the religious orientation of Muhammad's earliest followers quickly transformed seems to have been eschatology. As will be seen in the following chapter, Muhammad and the earliest Islamic community appear to have believed that they were living in the final moments of history, expecting to witness the final judgment of the Hour within their own lifetimes. The radical cognitive reorientation that must have ensued when the eschatological Hour failed to arrive on schedule would have required Muhammad's original followers to undertake a profound remaking of their faith. In the course of this transformation, it would appear that more than just their eschatological timetable was revised.

CHAPTER 3

The Beginnings of Islam and the End of Days

Muhammad as Eschatological Prophet

Insofar as the early *sīra* traditions preserve a memory of Islamic origins that has been deeply colored, if not completely determined, by the faith and practice of Islam during the eighth and ninth centuries, one must look elsewhere for evidence of what the "historical" Muhammad and his earliest followers may have believed. Only by somehow bypassing Muhammad's traditional biographies can we hope to discover any possible traces of the primitive Islam of the mid-seventh century. Unfortunately, however, the sources for such an undertaking are rather limited. One potential alternative to the *sīra* traditions is of course the Qur'ān, which provides a unique window into the first century of Islam. Although the Qur'ān reveals frustratingly little about the events of Muhammad's life and the early history of the religious community that he founded, it nevertheless is alleged to preserve a record of Muhammad's teaching. As the oldest surviving piece of Islamic literature, and the only literary document from Islam's first century, the Qur'ān presents a precious witness to Muhammad's religious beliefs as interpreted by his earliest followers. Thus, the Qur'ān offers the most promising chance of peering behind the veil of the Islamic myth of origins.[1] In particular, by attempting to read the Qur'ān against, rather than with, the traditional narratives of Islamic origins, it may be possible to excavate an older stratum in the development of the Islamic faith. This endeavor, of course, is not simply a matter of interpreting the Qur'ān at every instance in a manner opposite to the received tradition simply for the sake of doing so. Rather, the aim is to locate instances where the text of the Qur'ān appears to stand in tension with the traditional accounts of Islamic origins, while searching for parallel anomalies in the early Islamic tradition that similarly resist interpretive closure. By finding such hermeneutic gaps between the sacred text and tradition, we disclose a space that invites the potential discovery of a different sort of Islam at these earliest stages, a religious movement perhaps not completely discontiguous from what would follow but which has a distinctive character nonetheless.

What we might expect to learn from the Qur'ān, however, is necessarily limited. The Qur'ān is, as Fred Donner observes, a "profoundly ahistorical" text,[2] and in contrast to the gospels of the Christian New Testament, it does not relate the story of Muhammad's prophetic ministry or the early history of his followers.[3] Rather, the Qur'ān serves primarily to gather together much earlier biblical and Arabian traditions and funnel them through the person of Muhammad, excluding from its purview the "incidentals of time and space."[4] As Michael Cook effectively summarizes, based on the Qur'ān alone, "we could probably infer that the protagonist of the Koran was Muhammad, that the scene of his life was in western Arabia, and that he bitterly resented the frequent dismissal of his claims to prophecy by his contemporaries. But we could not tell that the sanctuary was in Mecca, nor that Muhammad himself came from there, and we could only guess that he established himself in Yathrib."[5] At the most general level, the Qur'ān reveals a monotheist religious movement grounded in the biblical and extra-biblical traditions of Judaism and Christianity, to which certain uniquely "Arab" traditions have been added. These traditions, however, are often related in an allusive style, which seems to presuppose knowledge of the larger narrative on the part of its audience. There is clear emphasis on articulating the boundaries of this new religious community, particularly in relation to other Arab "polytheists," but also with regard to Jews and Christians. The Qur'ān also regulates social practices and boundaries within the community, proclaiming God's divine law in a fashion reminiscent of the Jewish scriptures. Likewise, there is pressing concern with the impending arrival of the Hour, or "God's command (*amr*)," terms that designate the Final Judgment: Muhammad and his earliest followers seem to have believed that this eschatological event was about to take place or indeed had already begun. Muhammad thus appears as a monotheist prophet within the Abrahamic tradition who called his followers to renounce polytheism, to submit to the divine laws, and to prepare themselves for the impending doom: altogether, it is a portrait rather familiar from the Jewish and Christian scriptures.

Nevertheless, much recent scholarship on Islamic origins, particularly in English, has often failed to give the eschatological aspect of Muhammad's message the proper emphasis that it deserves. From the beginnings of Western study of Islam, scholars have generally recognized the importance of the Hour in Muhammad's preaching: the coming judgment is in fact the second most common theme of the Qur'ān, preceded only by the call to monotheism.[6] Yet despite the Qur'ān's frequent focus on the impending *eschaton*, many modern experts have sought to minimize the significance of this belief within the early community. In presenting Muhammad and his message to a modern audience, these scholars have often aimed to portray him as a great social reformer and preacher of ethical monotheism. Admittedly, neither of these qualities is inherently contradictory with belief in the world's imminent destruction: Jesus, for example, seems to have combined a message of eschatological urgency with a call to social justice and a critique of wealth. There is little question that the Qur'ān evidences much concern with social justice, yet as Donner observes, these elements, while not insignificant, "are incidental to the central notions of the Qur'an, which are religious."[7] Nonetheless, time and again for most of the last century, Muhammad's biographers have repeatedly cast him primarily in the mold of a great social reformer whose pragmatic mission was to challenge the social and economic inequities of this world rather than to issue an urgent warning before the world's impending judgment and destruction in the Hour. These modern scholars would not have Muhammad appear, as Richard Bell explains, as "a crack-brained enthusiast" ranting about impending doom, but instead as a great leader whose religious message was "from the very start quite a rational and practical one."[8] Yet in diminishing Muhammad's eschatological fervor, these studies efface what is perhaps one of the most clearly identifiable features of both the historical figure of Muhammad and the religious community that he founded. Moreover, the rapid transformation of Islam from an eschatological faith to the religion of an expanding empire provides an important context of change within which to situate the differences between the Islamic and non-Islamic sources concerning the end of Muhammad's life.

The idea that primitive Islam was an eschatological movement anticipating an imminent end to the world is thus not a new proposal, although one might perhaps be forgiven for perceiving it as such. The rather peculiar absence of this perspective from much contemporary literature on early Islam calls for renewed consideration of the importance of imminent eschatology in formative Islam. While the themes of divine judgment and the promised rewards and punishments of the afterlife are invariably identified as key elements of Muhammad's preaching, what often slips through in many accounts is the urgency with which Muhammad seems to have expected the impending arrival of the Hour or "God's command," even within his own lifetime it would appear. Several recent studies have called attention to individual elements of the early Islamic tradition that strongly suggest such eschatological belief to have been a core element of Muhammad's religious movement. Nevertheless, these traditions have so far been studied largely in isolation from one another, hindering a full appreciation of the various traces that this primitive eschatological impulse appears to have left within the later tradition. When collectively considered, this corpus of eschatological traditions from both the Qur'ān and the *ḥadīth* bears impressive witness to an early belief in the looming judgment and destruction of the world, presenting a body of evidence in many ways comparable to the early Christian traditions that have led scholars of the New Testament to identify Jesus of Nazareth as an eschatological prophet. Accordingly, methods and perspectives from biblical studies hold great potential to illuminate this aspect of the Qur'ān and earliest Islam, a quality whose significance has often been muted by the Qur'ān's prolonged sequestration from historical-critical study.[9]

From Portent of the Hour to Prophet of Social Justice: Muhammad in Modern Scholarship

The Eschatological Prophet of Early Western Scholarship

The first Western scholar to propose that an impending doom lay at the heart of Muhammad's preaching seems to have been Snouck Hurgronje. In an early publication on Mahdism (written in the context of the contemporary Mahdi revolt in the Sudan), Hurgronje observes that Muhammad "apparently always believed that the end of the world was quite close," to the effect that in the earliest Islamic tradition Muhammad's appearance itself was reckoned as one of "the signs of the imminent end of the world." So long as Muhammad remained alive, Hurgronje writes, it was unthinkable to his followers that he would die, and when he in fact died before the Hour's arrival, the community at first refused to believe it and was eventually persuaded only with great difficulty by Abū Bakr.[10] Several years later, in his response to Hubert Grimme's presentation of Muhammad as a socialist reformer, Hurgronje singled out Muhammad's belief in the impending divine destruction of the world as the primary inspiration for his prophetic activities.[11] According to Hurgronje, the coming Day of Judgment permeated all of Muhammad's thoughts and actions. Despite his pressing defense of the divine unity against those whom he believed to have strayed from this principle, such radical monotheism was not the impetus behind Muhammad's prophetic mission. Rather, he was "haunted" by the idea of an imminent universal judgment that would be preceded by dreadful catastrophes and the destruction of all living beings.[12] Other dogmas of Muhammad's preaching were "more or less accessories" to the doctrine of impending divine judgment, which always remained "the essential element of Muhammad's preaching." The various institutions and practices of the early Islamic community arose only gradually once a community of followers had begun to heed Muhammad's eschatological warnings, and while these topics were often subjects of his later teachings, the doctrine of judgment always remained central.[13] Thus Hurgronje argues for an understanding of both Muhammad's preaching and the religious movement that he engendered as profoundly eschatological in nature, expecting an imminent end of the world.

Not long thereafter, the great Danish Old Testament scholar Frants Buhl offered a similar interpretation of Muhammad as having been motivated above all else by belief in an impending judgment. It was, Buhl writes, "the thought of the imminent Judgment Day that made such a forceful impression on his mind and filled his imagination with the magnificent and baroque images that he tirelessly evokes in the oldest parts of the Qurʾān." Although Buhl admits that Muhammad's "profound religious sensibility was of course also receptive to gentler and more intimate voices," his overpowering concern with the looming *eschaton* and dread of the horrifying punishments that soon awaited the damned were the forces that set his mind in motion and gave rise to his religious movement.[14] According to Buhl, Muhammad first acquired this perspective through Christian influence and initially had no intention of founding a new religion, aiming only to warn his people of the coming judgment that had been announced before him by the Christian (and Jewish) scriptures. Only later did he develop an awareness of having himself been sent as a new prophet to warn the Arabs before the impending doom, and from this point on the swiftly approaching Day of Judgment "ruled all of his thoughts" and stood at the core of his message.[15] Even after Muhammad's immigration to Medina, at which point the Qurʾān seems to reflect a new concern with the more worldly affairs of the early Islamic community, Muhammad continued to preach the coming judgment, which remained a consistent theme of his religious movement from its beginning until his own death.[16]

A few years later, Paul Casanova developed this hypothesis further still, presenting an even more forceful and systematic argument that Muhammad was an eschatological prophet who expected an imminent end to the world in his important if largely overlooked monograph from the beginning of the twentieth century, *Mohammed et la fin du monde*.[17] It is unfortunate that Casanova's ideas received such rough dismissal from his contemporaries, inasmuch as they occasionally manifest great insights regarding the eschatological themes of the Qur'ān and early Islamic tradition that would not be rivaled until the later twentieth century.[18] No less important was his early suggestion that the collection of the Qur'ān was largely the work of the caliph ʿAbd al-Malik (685–705) and his notorious governor al-Hajjāj, a long discounted view that recently has come more into favor.[19] To be sure, *Mohammed et la fin du monde* is a rather uneven work, and in his effort to rethink the origins of Islam, Casanova occasionally wanders down a blind alley. In particular, Casanova's study is frequently marred by its engagement with Aloys Sprenger's earlier work, which leads Casanova to frame the broader questions between two rather extreme positions: either Muhammad was a charlatan who initially used threats of an impending doom to frighten the Meccans into following him, only to reverse course when this failed (Sprenger), or when Muhammad died before the Hour's arrival, his original teachings on the subject were "if not falsified, at least concealed with the greatest care" by Abū Bakr, ʿUthmān, and others (Casanova).[20] Yet, of course, these are not the only two possible explanations for the evidence. Moreover, one need not subscribe to Casanova's somewhat peculiar (and unpersuasive) views on the origins of the Mahdi or Muhammad's formation within an Arabian Christian group prior to his prophetic career in order to appreciate the broader outlines of the monograph's argument, which can be quite compelling when isolated from many of its more idiosyncratic positions.

In this regard, Casanova's argument is reminiscent of Hermann Reimarus's seminal eighteenth-century studies of the gospels, which identified Jesus as a prophet of the Kingdom of God's imminent arrival and imputed the subsequent alteration of Jesus' message to his immediate followers who thereby aimed to perpetuate the movement for their own political and economic gain.[21] Despite his somewhat crudely placed accusations against Jesus' disciples, Reimarus's fundamental observations concerning Jesus' eschatological message eventually emerged as a cornerstone of historical Jesus research, albeit after lying dormant for over a century.[22] Like Casanova's study, certain of Reimarus's insights seem to have been far ahead of their time, and his distracting and rather inflammatory charges against Jesus' earliest followers no doubt only made it easier for his contemporaries to disregard his important discoveries. In similar fashion, Casanova's charges of a deliberate conspiracy to falsify Muhammad's teaching mar his otherwise compelling reconstruction of Muhammad as a prophet of the end times. Yet notwithstanding these missteps, Casanova's study identifies a number of important traditions from both the Qur'ān and *ḥadīth* that are extremely difficult to explain in the absence of a pressing belief in the imminent end of the world on the part of Muhammad and his early followers. In retrospect, it is somewhat regrettable that, as with Reimarus, these idiosyncrasies prevented Casanova's peers from recognizing the otherwise profound insights of his study, which only recently have come to be fully appreciated by scholars of Islamic origins.

In view of contemporary developments within the study of Christian origins, especially Albert Schweitzer's pivotal rediscovery of an eschatological Jesus, it is somewhat surprising that Casanova's parallel findings did not at the time find a warmer reception among scholars of early Islam. By this time, various theories of the New Testament's formation advanced by higher biblical criticism, beginning especially with F. C. Baur (1792–1860) and the Tübingen school, had opened up a new understanding of the Christian scriptures as having been strongly shaped by the shifting religious beliefs and practices of the early communities that produced and collected them.[23] By the later nineteenth century, New Testament scholars had come to recognize that among the changes effected by the early community was a gradual transformation of Jesus' imminent eschatology to mitigate the failed arrival of "the Kingdom of God," an event that Jesus seems to have predicted within the lifetime of his initial followers.[24] As this first generation began to pass away and the world itself did not, the early Christians were forced to reinterpret what Jesus had meant when he foretold the coming of God's Kingdom: since they believed what he taught to have been true, it was necessary to adjust their understanding—and even their memory—of his preaching to coincide with this reality. When considered within such a context, Casanova's observations suggest not so much a deliberate conspiracy to conceal Muhammad's original teachings, as he himself proposes, but instead what was more likely an almost unconscious tweaking of the Qur'ānic text and its interpretation by the early community to meet the needs of its changing beliefs about the coming Hour (among other subjects). As much, at least, is strongly suggested by comparative evidence from the study of early Christianity. Nevertheless, it would appear that such perspectives never had much of a chance to influence the study of Islamic origins: by the time Casanova's monograph appeared, the Qur'ān's status as an absolutely authentic repository of Muhammad's teachings had emerged as a fundamental dogma of Islamic studies, and Casanova's transgression of this central tenet in particular appears to have occasioned the greatest ire from his more conventional colleagues.

The failure of comparative approaches from early Christian studies to make a significant impact on the study of formative Islam is perhaps largely consequent to the early wedding of the study of Islamic origins with philology, that is, "Semitics" or "Near Eastern languages and civilizations," and Old Testament studies, rather than religious studies and New Testament and early Christian studies, during the nineteenth century.[25] In this regard it would appear that Heinrich Ewald, who trained many of the field's "founding fathers," including such heavies as Julius Wellhausen and Theodor Nöldeke (his favorite student), left an especially lasting imprint on the discipline.[26] Ewald was an exceptionally doctrinaire *Doktorvater* whose traditionalism and Christian piety made him an ardent opponent of the new methodological perspectives that were emerging within the study of early Christianity and revolutionizing its investigation, including above all those of F. C. Baur and the Tübingen school.[27] Although Ewald was generally possessed of an agonistic temperament, his hatred for Baur and his radically critical approach to the study of Christianity was unparalleled: as one historian of the Tübingen school and its influence observes, "scarcely ever was a theologian attacked with such venomous invective or so spitefully maligned as Baur" was by Ewald.[28] Ewald was himself only very minimally accepting of higher criticism of the Bible, allowing for pseudonymous documents and discrepancies within the biblical canon, for instance, but he insisted, against Baur and his ilk, that the New Testament preserved a reliable historical record of the life and teachings of Jesus and the history of the early church. Baur's proposal that our knowledge of earliest Christianity is very limited, having been largely determined by the various "tendencies" within the communities of formative Christianity, was for Ewald a pernicious "overturning and destruction of all intellectual and moral life."[29]

Ewald's rejection of these approaches seems to have left an imprint on his students and, by consequence, on the field of early Islamic studies, perhaps accounting in some part for the initial dismissal and rather long incubation of Casanova's ideas. For example, Nöldeke, whose views on the Qur'ān (rather astonishingly) continue to dominate the field after nearly a century and a half of study,[30] followed closely in his master's footsteps by bringing only a very moderate amount of higher criticism to the Qur'ān and the traditional narratives of its origins. More or less mirroring his mentor's rather conservative view of the New Testament and its value as a historical source, Nöldeke firmly maintained the Qur'ān's attribution to Muhammad as it stands as well as its value as a reliable historical record of earliest Islam.[31] The approach could hardly be more different from the radical critique posed by Baur and the Tübingen school, whose ideas Ewald would surely have trained him to disregard if not despise: it was, after all, Ewald who supervised Nöldeke's prize-winning dissertation, and Nöldeke dedicated its published version to his mentor.[32] Nöldeke's work generally reflects instead the historical positivism characteristic of nineteenth-century philology, which aimed at reconstructing the past largely "from the visible surface of history" and stood in sharp "opposition to the *Geschichtskonstruktionen* of the enlightenment," reflected at the time primarily in Hegel's philosophy, and in the study of religion, in Baur and the Tübingen school. For Nöldeke, history was made by "great men," whose genius could be seen in the works that they had authored, making it important that Muhammad, and in no sense the Islamic community, had to be identified as the sole source of the Qur'ān.[33]

The imprint of such historiographical principles on Nöldeke's foundational work left the basic template for investigation of Islamic origins somewhat restricted, and the relative absence of approaches inspired by the hermeneutics of suspicion, which were bearing great fruit in other areas of historical study, meant that Casanova's work was not able to receive an entirely fair hearing at the time. Nevertheless, as David Cook has recently observed of Casanova's work, "It is interesting to note that ideas not accepted at the time, like Casanova's idea that Muhammad and the early Muslims were driven by a belief in the imminent end of the world, are clear and obvious now."[34] Clear and obvious as such ideas may indeed appear, they unfortunately have not yet found widespread acceptance among scholars of early Islam: as will be seen below, the study of formative Islam over the past several decades has expressed a strong preference for non-eschatological views of Muhammad and the Qur'ān. Yet the recent espousal of Casanova's primary thesis, that Muhammad and his followers seemingly did not expect that he would die before the end of the world, by other scholars of Islamic origins such as Fred Donner and Mahmoud Ayoub certainly invites renewed consideration of Casanova's arguments along lines similar to those taken in the study of earliest Christianity and its eschatological traditions.[35]

There were, however, other continental scholars who shared many of the broad outlines of Casanova's thesis, even if they could not accept it in all of its particulars. Régis Blachère gave Casanova's study perhaps the fairest hearing of any of his contemporaries, and while he found much therein to agree with, he ultimately could not accept Casanova's proposal that the early community had adjusted Muhammad's teachings on the impending doom. It was easier for him to believe that Muhammad himself had changed his mind when he arrived in new circumstances in Medina. Nevertheless, Blachère is quite clear in his assessment that "without any doubt, at the beginning of his mission, Muhammad appears in the Qur'ān solely as the herald of the utmost Hour: the essential theme of his preaching, then, consists of the description of the end of the world, of the Last Judgment, of Hell, and of Paradise."[36] Tor Andrae, although he appears to ignore Casanova's important study, also brings important emphasis to Muhammad's belief in an imminent eschatology, focusing on the "eschatological piety" that lay at the core of Muhammad's teaching.[37] As Andrae explains, "the basic conviction of Mohammed's preaching, and the heart of his prophetic message . . . is the *last day*—the day of judgment and retribution. For him the Day of Judgment is not an occurrence far off in the hazy uncertain future, belonging to a different sphere from that of mundane events. It is a reality that is threateningly near."[38] Andrae is somewhat more cautious in this regard than Casanova, however, and he maintains that "Mohammed never stated directly that the judgment would fall upon his own generation," referring to passages in the Qur'ān indicating that God alone knows when the Hour will arrive. Nevertheless, as Andrae notes, "[Muhammad] often shows that he regarded it as possible that he himself might yet experience it."[39] Andrae's Muhammad is thoroughly eschatological and driven above all else by a conviction that the end is very near, and even if he hesitates to ascribe to Muhammad a belief that the *eschaton* would come within his lifetime, it quite clear that Muhammad viewed the Final Judgment as menacingly close for those to whom he preached. If by some chance he did not live to see the Hour's sudden arrival, he seems to have expected that the human race would not walk upon the earth very much longer.

Bell, Watt, and the Non-Eschatological Prophet of Social Reform

Thanks to the translation of Andrae's biography into English (among other languages) and its wide dissemination throughout much of the twentieth century, his vision of Muhammad as an eschatological prophet enjoyed a fairly broad readership. Nevertheless, despite this study's popularity, it would appear that a rather different view of Muhammad's preaching has come to prevail in more recent scholarship on early Islam, where the idea of Muhammad as a prophet of ethical monotheism, interested in reforming the world rather than heralding its impending dissolution, has largely taken root. This view owes itself largely to the work of Richard Bell, who in his 1925 Gunning Lectures, published as *The Origin of Islam in Its Christian Environment*, made a forceful argument that the heart of Muhammad's preaching was not in fact eschatological but instead had its basis in a call "to recognize and worship the one true God and show thankfulness for His bounties." According to Bell, it was only when this initial message failed that Muhammad subsequently began to proclaim "the threat of judgment and punishment to come," a message that he later would drop after gathering enough followers.[40] It would appear that this hypothesis was driven at least partly by Bell's admiration for Muhammad as someone possessing above all else "a very practical character." Although Muhammad was a "visionary," as Bell writes, "he was not a crack-brained enthusiast. . . . Even in Mecca the practical direction of this thought is very marked." Since Bell believed that Muhammad's enterprise was "from the very start quite a rational and practical one," it would not do to have him ranting about an impending doom that never came, as Hurgronje and Casanova in essence portray him.[41] Although Bell addresses each of these scholars only once by name, and without specific reference to their views concerning Muhammad's eschatology, it would appear that his reconstruction of Islamic origins aims at recovering an alternative portrait of Muhammad more agreeable to modern tastes, making of him a religious genius of sorts instead of a prophet who mistakenly foretold the world's imminent destruction.[42]

According to Bell, Muhammad began his preaching with "an appeal to the gratitude of men and their recognition of the bounties in creation."[43] When this appeal to the Meccans' better instincts fell flat, Muhammad quickly turned to different tactics, emphasizing God's wrath and the promise of divine punishment for disobedience. Circumstances then pressed Muhammad to intensify his rhetoric, and he began to adduce prior examples of God's castigation, noting God's destruction of the Arabian peoples of ʿĀd and Thamūd, as well as God's vengeance against Pharaoh and the Egyptians. Only somewhat later did Muhammad stumble upon the Judeo-Christian apocalyptic tradition, which he found ideally suited to his task of calling the Meccans to divine obedience. All of Muhammad's apocalyptic material is directly borrowed from Judaism and Christianity according to Bell, from some unknown source that Muhammad apparently held in the highest regard. His encounter with these traditions made a deep impression on him, so much so that he temporarily came to identify these apocalyptic traditions with the content of the divine revelation that he had been charged to deliver. For a time the idea of divine judgment appears to have been central to Muhammad's preaching, but eventually, once he achieved authority over a community of believers in Medina, the idea of the Last Judgment "passe[d] into the realm of assured dogma in Muhammad's mind," says Bell. Thus, while Muhammad did not drop the notion entirely, new concerns occasioned by a community of followers pushed what had for a time been the central theme of Muhammad's preaching, impending judgment, to the side, as it became one among many articles of faith.[44]

This reconstruction of Muhammad's unfolding message, in which its eschatological elements are downgraded considerably, depends profoundly on Bell's idiosyncratic efforts to date various traditions within the Qur'ān, an endeavor that even his most sympathetic disciple, Montgomery Watt, found questionable on certain points.[45] Bell's hypothesis rests on his identification of a very specific order to Muhammad's revelations, according to which he privileges certain non-eschatological traditions focused on the revelation of "signs" as the most primitive layer within the Qur'ānic collection.[46] Despite some important advances achieved by Bell's often insightful research on the Qur'ān, his peculiar views regarding the exact order of its revelations have not found much acceptance among scholars of early Islam, and there seems to be fairly broad consensus that a precise chronology of the earliest Qur'ānic *sūras* cannot be achieved. Although Nöldeke proposed a widely accepted division of the Qur'ānic *sūras* into four successive chronological periods (based largely on earlier work by Gustav Weil), even those adopting his reconstruction generally acknowledge that the absolute sequence of Nöldeke's earliest *sūras* cannot be known, and they must be "understood as a group rather than as standing in the exact chronological order of their revelation."[47] Nöldeke's four-period schema is itself merely hypothetical, owing a sizeable debt to traditional Islamic views about the formation of the Qur'ān, and Alford Welch is right to observe that scholars embracing this approach to the Qur'ān "have not demonstrated the validity of the historical framework or the development of ideas and key terms assumed by their system."[48] Nevertheless, despite such broader methodological issues that remain concerning the Qur'ān's internal chronology, Bell's marginalization of the eschatological themes within Muhammad's preaching continues to guide many modern studies of Islamic origins, particularly in English, where Bell's demotion of Muhammad's "apocalyptic" preaching to secondary status remains prevalent.

Montgomery Watt, in his highly influential monograph *Muhammad at Mecca*, reproduces his mentor's relegation of Muhammad's eschatology almost slavishly. Watt's isolation (following Bell) of "the small group of passages which appear to be earliest of all" allows him to conclude that Muhammad's core message relates the benevolence and power of the God who created the universe, absent any concern with an impending judgment.[49] Such limited references to the Final Judgment as do occur within these earliest passages look not to its imminent arrival, according to Watt, but instead witness "to the reality and certainty of it at some unspecified future time."[50] Only when the Meccans resisted this initial message did Muhammad begin to threaten them with temporal calamities, following the pattern established by other prophets before him. Yet the Final Judgment remains ever a distant future event according to Watt's reconstruction, which, even more so than Bell, minimizes the eschatological element of Muhammad's preaching as witnessed by the Qur'ān. Such occlusion of Muhammad's eschatological urgency allows Watt to transform Muhammad from an apocalyptic preacher into the social and moral reformer for which his work is so famous.[51] If indeed Grimme's Muhammad can be said to resemble "a sort of nineteenth-century German Social Democrat," this Anglican clergyman's prophet perhaps looks suspiciously like a twentieth-century liberal Protestant, striving after social justice and an increase of personal piety.[52]

Seemingly in ignorance of the previous work by Bell and Watt on this topic, Harris Birkeland advanced what amounts to an almost identical hypothesis, namely, that Muhammad's "fundamental religious experience" consisted not of concern for an impending judgment, but was instead rooted in "the recognition of God's merciful guidance in the life of himself [that is, Muhammad] and his people."[53] In order to reach this conclusion, however, Birkeland undertakes a much more detailed analysis than either Bell or Watt, focusing on five Qur'ānic *sūra*s that he believes have preserved Muhammad's earliest preaching (93, 94, 108, 105, 106). If one accepts Birkeland's premise, that these five *sūra*s are in fact somehow primary, then his argument largely succeeds. But therein lies the problem: the rather narrow privilege of primacy that Birkeland (as well as Bell and Watt) extends to a handful of *sūra*s seems inescapably arbitrary. When taken on its own terms, Birkeland's reconstruction of Muhammad's early religious experiences is entirely plausible, but ultimately his hypothesis founders on the seemingly capricious nature of its underpinnings. Simply by selecting five alternate *sūra*s to represent the very oldest layer within the Qur'ān, one could discover a rather different basis for Muhammad's earliest religious experience and preaching. Yet even in the event that the handful of *sūras* privileged by Birkeland (or Bell or Watt) could persuasively be identified as the earliest, it is not entirely clear why this finding should diminish the fervent eschatological warnings dispersed elsewhere throughout the Qur'ān.

Such objections are raised by Rudi Paret in his brief popular biography of Muhammad, published just shortly after the monographs by Birkeland and Watt.[54] Paret notes especially the uncertainties underlying these efforts to isolate certain *sūras* as uniquely preserving the most primitive stage of Muhammad's religious teaching. Of the forty-eight *sūras* that Nöldeke assigns to the earliest Meccan period, for instance, a clear majority address eschatological themes, seeming to indicate the relative importance of eschatology within Muhammad's earliest preaching. Perhaps more important, however, is Paret's observation that even in the *sūras* that Bell identifies as being the very earliest, one finds eschatological content alongside the themes of God's creative power and benevolence. This recognition leads Paret to propose the simple yet obvious—and no doubt largely correct—solution that both ideas must have occurred together at the core of Muhammad's initial preaching. The textual evidence of the Qur'ān itself seems to suggest this conclusion. Moreover, the two ideas are highly complementary to one another, and their frequent concurrence in both Jewish and Christian circles supports the conclusion that Muhammad began to preach by simultaneously invoking God's benevolence and creation as well as warning against divine judgment.[55] There is in fact no compelling reason why these ideas should be segregated so that only one can be primitive, as Bell, Watt, and Birkeland propose, forcing a choice between either a benevolent creator or divine judgment. Given the current state of the evidence, Paret's proposal that Muhammad initially offered a message of divine judgment that was grounded in an ethical monotheism seems to be the most reasoned deduction. Nevertheless, and most importantly, Paret resists any notion that Muhammad believed the Final Judgment to be imminent. Rather, Paret views the Qur'ān's warnings of impending judgment as Muhammad's threats against his opponents that they would soon suffer temporal chastisement, while the Final Judgment was an event belonging to the distant future. In this regard, Paret ultimately does not depart very far from Bell's and Watt's uneschatological prophet: Muhammad may have preached eschatological ideas from the very start, but according to Paret these were lacking any sense of urgency.[56]

One can only imagine that some sort of apologetic interest (perhaps unconscious) lurks behind these efforts to cleanse eschatology, and particularly imminent eschatology, from Muhammad's teaching. It would seem that their ultimate goal is a more "practical" and "rational" prophet, instead of a "crack-brained" eschatological enthusiast, whose core message of ethical monotheism is simply overlaid, rather than defined, by belief in an impending doom, as Bell suggests.[57] In this manner, one can understand Muhammad, with Birkeland, as a true religious "genius," worthy of founding one of the world's "great religions." Rather than being a misguided eschatological prophet, Muhammad instead achieved the great "new insight" of recognizing "the Lord's wonderful and merciful guidance of the life of men," which enabled him to "drive out pagan semi-religiosity" among his countrymen.[58] As Bart Ehrman notes of the quest for the historical Jesus, the recent impulse to discover a non-eschatological Jesus seems to have been driven primarily by interest in finding a Jesus who is relevant to the social and political concerns of the modern world; similar concerns no doubt underlie these sketches of Muhammad as a non-eschatological prophet of divine benevolence and social reform.[59] Moreover, such portraits have the further advantage of allowing for smooth continuity between Muhammad's initial religious movement and the Islamic tradition as it came to be established in its classic form under the ʿAbbāsids: if in fact Muhammad was the harbinger of an impending judgment that never arrived then one must acknowledge a considerable disconnect between his teaching and the religion that ensued. By alternatively securing the essence of Muhammad's preaching in an ethical monotheism, carved out against the "pagan semi-religiosity" of his cultural heritage, one can perhaps more readily imagine his prophecy as providing the germ for a great civilization.

Muhammad's warnings of impending judgment thus amount to little more than an extraneous, if somewhat distracting, digression from this fundamental theme. Indeed, it is rather difficult to imagine Muhammad as primarily a social reformer, as Watt suggests, if in fact he expected the social order itself to disintegrate soon along with the rest of the world. Yet while the theme of divine judgment is too central to the Qur'ān simply to be ignored, its apparent proximity for Muhammad can be rather effortlessly displaced into an unknown, distant future, a hermeneutic strategy frequently employed by the early Islamic tradition. In similar fashion, most modern studies have preserved Muhammad's role as a preacher of divine judgment, but all too often the Final Judgment is postponed until the distant end of time, allowing for a portrait of Muhammad as a champion of social justice to fill out the canvas of his life. Although this image of Muhammad may be appealing to modern historians and Muslims alike, it fails to do justice to the eschatological urgency signaled by the Qur'ān. In this regard, such portrayals of Muhammad cannot help but recall the various nineteenth-century "liberal" biographies of Jesus, which buried his eschatological warnings of the Kingdom of God's imminent arrival in favor of a more rational and relevant Jesus, who echoed the ideals of many among the nineteenth-century intelligentsia in preaching a message of social justice and ethical living.[60]

Watt is clearly the individual most responsible for this prevailing view of Muhammad, particularly inasmuch as it bears the strong imprint of his *Muhammad at Mecca* and *Muhammad at Medina*.[61] In subsequent works Watt remained faithful to the position of these early studies,[62] and his revision of Bell's *Introduction to the Qur'ān* continues his teacher's abatement of Muhammad's eschatological fervor in order to underscore themes of "God's bounties in creation" and their occasion for human gratitude.[63] In combination then with important lateral support from Birkeland's study, Watt's extension of Bell's vision of Muhammad has determined a marked shift away from eschatology that pervades most modern scholarship on primitive Islam. Perhaps there is no better evidence of this reorientation than Welch's revision of Buhl's article on Muhammad for the second edition of the *Encyclopedia of Islam*: although Buhl retains primary authorship according to the article's signature, Welch has introduced significant revisions to this entry, perhaps most notably in displacing the eschatological prophet of Buhl's original article with the social reformer imagined by Watt, his own *Doktorvater*.[64]

Likewise, F. E. Peters's biography of Muhammad seems to follow the Bell-Watt model more or less tacitly in presenting the concepts of divine guidance and benevolence at the beginning of Muhammad's preaching, before moving on to discuss the themes of divine judgment in the following section.[65] Much more explicit, however, is Peters's endorsement of Birkeland's hypothesis, according to which Muhammad initially preached God's providential guidance, without any mention of divine judgment: this topic and other eschatological themes, Peters explains, would emerge only subsequently as "characteristic teachings of the somewhat later Muhammad the 'warner.'"[66] Muhammad's warnings before the divine judgment, however, are not presented here as having any particular chronological urgency about them, and it is very telling that the Hour is never mentioned in Peters's study. By contrast, Peters's recent comparative study, *Jesus and Muhammad*, is quite direct in this regard. Here Muhammad is identified as primarily a social and economic reformer in the mold of Watt, and although he taught that God will one day bring judgment and punishments against the unbelievers, he did not proclaim these events as being especially imminent but saw them as belonging to the more distant future.[67] Moreover, while Peters at least mentions the Hour once in this study, he does so oddly enough only to deny its importance, maintaining that in comparison with Jesus, "there is no similar sense of anticipation in the Quran, neither of the breaking in of a new age nor of a cataclysmic final hour. The Quran speaks often of the judgment, of the reward of the virtuous and the punishment of the wicked; but though the language is eschatological, it is not apocalyptic. The judgment is no closer and no farther than it has been for any human being."[68]

Maxime Rodinson's popular biography of Muhammad, although written in French, has been widely available and influential in English, and Rodinson also hews to the line of Bell and Watt in presenting Muhammad as a non-eschatological prophet of social change.[69] Likewise, Tilman Nagel's recent biography of Muhammad, the sprawling *Mohammed: Leben und Legende*, also essentially follows the model established by Bell and Watt. Muhammad was not the "chiliastisch" prophet envisioned by the *Doctrina Iacobi* and Casanova; in fact, Nagel maintains, his political ambitions were already present during the Meccan phase of his career. Again like Watt (and Paret), Nagel understands the Qur'ān's references to eschatological events as indicating things that will take place in the distant future, while its threats of impending punishment refer to God's temporal chastisements that will come against Muhammad's opponents.[70] More specialized studies by Miklos Muranyi and Ahmed Afzaal have similarly adopted Watt's perspective in arguing that primitive Islam was at its root a social movement, in which concern for the approaching Hour was not of particular importance.[71] Although there have been pockets of dissent, some of which will be noted below, scholarship on Muhammad and the origins of Islam during the second half of the twentieth century has for the most part remained firmly in the grip of Bell's and Watt's marginalization of eschatology.

Other more popularly oriented works have taken a similar tack, including Karen Armstrong's widely read and influential biography of Muhammad, which immediately sweeps eschatology aside, proposing that "the Last Judgment was only mentioned briefly in the earliest suras, or chapters, of the Qur'an but the early message was essentially joyful."[72] In the chapter that follows, Armstrong's study describes Muhammad instead as a preacher of God's goodness, manifest in the created order, identifying him further as a champion of the poor and oppressed who campaigned for social justice against the rich and powerful merchants of Quraysh. The End, however, is practically nowhere in sight, and Armstrong maintains that the Qur'ān's references to "the approaching Last Judgment are essentially symbolic representations of divine truths and should not be understood as literal facts"—a rather sweeping and subjective assessment to say the least.[73] Similarly, Fazlur Rahman's *Major Themes of the Qur'ān* also presents primitive Islam as concerned above all else with the establishment of social justice: although Rahman's decidedly theological study includes a chapter dedicated to Qur'ānic eschatology, the Final Judgment here is cast as a distant future event, interpreted primarily within the context of a call to moral responsibility and justice.[74]

In even the most recent popular works, the liberal reformer of the Bell-Watt hypothesis continues to prevail. Irving Zeitlin's somewhat superficial effort to uncover the "historical Muhammad" essentially amounts to a survey of selected previous scholarship on Muhammad, and, unsurprisingly, summaries of Bell's and Watt's theories stand as the centerpiece of the volume.[75] Eschatology was simply not a theme of particular importance to Zeitlin's "historical Muhammad," who seems to have had no sense of an impending judgment. The same is also true of Tariq Ramadan's *In the Footsteps of Muhammad*, where the Hour is mentioned only a single time, in the quotation of a *ḥadīth* that is cited as evidence of Muhammad's concern for the environment and his advocacy of an "upstream ecology."[76] The Final Judgment, which Ramadan discusses only very briefly, was apparently for Muhammad a distant future event whose primary function was to ground his ethical teaching in a belief in the afterlife.[77] By contrast, Muhammad's program of social justice and reform permeates Ramadan's biography: the book's index, for instance, includes nineteen different subheadings under the entry for "social justice and equity." Omid Safi's recent book *Memories of Muhammad* similarly presents the historical Muhammad as a thoroughly non-eschatological founder of what he names "the Muhammadi Revolution," a revolution of spiritual awakening and social reform that aimed first to transform the heart and then the social order. Muhammad was not, it seems, especially concerned with the impending Hour but rather with "the suffering of the poor and downtrodden in his society."[78] Likewise Asma Afsaruddin's new popular history of early Islam directly dismisses the recent suggestions by Donner and Ayoub that Muhammad and his followers expected the end of the world in their lifetimes, lightly shrugging off their arguments as "hardly convincing."[79] Instead, "the Qur'an's clear and powerful message" addressed not the impending judgment of the Hour but "egalitarianism and social justice," a message that was aimed especially "to those who were on the periphery of society."[80]

The overwhelming impact of these studies is to normalize a portrait of Muhammad as a non-eschatological social reformer whose gaze was not fixed on the hastening Hour and impending divine destruction and judgment, but whose mission instead immersed him in the concerns of the world, where he labored to establish a brighter future for generations to come. The pervasive influence of the Bell-Watt hypothesis has had the effect, it would appear, of squeezing to the margins any serious consideration of the powerful eschatological belief that saturates the Qur'ān, particularly in the so-called "Meccan" *sūras*.[81] Yet while the traditional Islamic biographies of Muhammad certainly foster such reconstructions of Muhammad's activities, the Qur'ān itself, which remains the single best source for knowledge of Muhammad's preaching and the nature of earliest Islam, clearly and consistently conveys the image of Muhammad and his religious movement as oriented around strong belief in the imminent end of the world and impending divine judgment. Moreover, when the traditions of the *ḥadīth* are mined for eschatological proclamations ascribed to Muhammad, one finds a significant body of complementary evidence witnessing to a primitive belief in a swiftly approaching doom, and the preservation of these reports against the interest of the later tradition strongly suggests their authenticity, according to a well-established cornerstone of historical criticism, the criterion of discontinuity, or criterion of embarrassment, as it is sometimes named.[82] Indeed, when the eschatological traditions of the Qur'ān and early Islam are evaluated according to the same standards used in reconstructing the historical Jesus, the results suggest a need to move beyond modern scholarship's prophet of social justice in order to recover, as once was similarly necessary in the study of the historical Jesus, the eschatological warner who stands at the origin of this global religious tradition.

Codifying a Prophet's Speech: The Qur'ān as Text

In order to peer through the Qur'ān into Islam's primeval history, it is necessary to better understand the nature of the text itself, as well as its relation to the historical figure of Muhammad. Despite the sureties that many modern scholars of Islam hold regarding the Qur'ān as a transparent record of Muhammad's preaching, the history of the Qur'ānic text remains very much uncertain, becoming all the more so when evaluated according to the standards applied to early Christian literature. The Islamic tradition professes that the Qur'ān was collected into its present form just twenty or so years after the death of Muhammad, during the second half of the caliph ʿUthmān's reign (644–56), a tenet that has been adopted almost wholesale by most modern scholarship on the Qurʾān and Islamic origins. Nevertheless, the early Islamic tradition itself exhibits considerable diversity of opinion on this matter, and on the whole the historical evidence would seem to favor the Qurʾān's collection and standardization only at a later date, most likely during the reign of ʿAbd al-Malik, as Casanova first proposed. While there is then little doubt that the traditions of the Qurʾān reflect the preaching of Muhammad as remembered by the Muslims of the seventh century, such a lengthy period of transmission invites the possibility that the early community played a significant role in shaping the contents of the Qurʾān according to its own interests and concerns.

Likewise, the general consensus of modern scholarship regarding the Qurʾān's internal chronology similarly mimics the traditional Islamic view of the sequence of revelation, and although this prevailing schema is frequently deployed to reconstruct the development of Muhammad's religious views, its validity is largely assumed rather than demonstrated. As an alternative to this confessionally derived framework for interpreting the Qurʾān, the methodological toolkit of biblical studies, and New Testament studies in particular, could be brought more fully to bear on the analysis of the Qurʾān.[83] Unfortunately, Wansbrough's observation that the Qurʾān "as a document susceptible of analysis by the instruments and techniques of Biblical criticism . . . is virtually unknown" is still as true today as it was over thirty years ago.[84] Yet insofar as the methods and perspectives of New Testament scholarship have proven highly effective in analyzing the eschatological traditions of Christianity's sacred texts, which formed over the course of twenty to fifty years after its founder's death, their utility for developing a critique of Qurʾānic eschatology based on criteria external to the Islamic tradition seems quite promising. Such an approach would certainly allow for the potential discovery of new perspectives on the Qurʾān and formative Islam that the traditional narratives of Islamic origins have largely obscured, particularly with regard to the tenor of eschatological urgency present in Muhammad's prophetic message.

As even the most superficial reading of the Qurʾān will disclose, the Islamic sacred text is suffused with eschatology. Although not every *sūra* manifests the same level of concern with the coming climax of history, themes of divine judgment, the rewards of the just, and the punishments awaiting the wicked, occasioned by the end of the world, comprise one of the two most prominent topics of Qurʾānic discourse, rivaled only by its doctrine of God.[85] Modern scholars have frequently observed that this eschatological element is particularly prominent in those *sūra*s assigned by Nöldeke to Muhammad's

Meccan period, while in the *sūras* traditionally associated with Medina, concern with the last things becomes more attenuated, although it nonetheless persists.[86] These eschatological differences among the *sūras* are thus often made to conform, more or less, to a chronological progression in Muhammad's thought, whereby he preached a message of the coming eschatological judgment in Mecca that in Medina was superseded by the more pressing concerns of a new polity, as reflected in the "Medinan" *sūras*. Of course, this narrative of theological development depends quite heavily on the four-period scheme devised primarily by Nöldeke, which affords a less than ideal basis for historical analysis. Nöldeke's system of classification and its various other derivative models were developed not on the basis of an exogenous critique of the Qur'ān, but instead they largely reproduce the traditional Islamic datings of individual *sūras*.[87] While this four-fold classification is occasionally somewhat useful for its grouping of different *sūras* with similar themes and styles, there is certainly "no guarantee that all *sūras* with the same style belong to the same period."[88] Moreover, given the later Islamic tradition's general (and quite understandable) resistance to locating a message of imminent eschatology at the core of Muhammad's revelation, it may be helpful to identify an alternative framework for analyzing the eschatological traditions of the Qur'ān.

Biblical Criticism and the Qur'ān

Perhaps a more generally useful approach would involve an extensive form critical and tradition critical investigation of the Qur'ānic text, initially aimed at classifying the different types of material present in the Qur'ān, followed by an effort to determine the *Sitz im Leben* of individual traditions as well as their possible development during the process of oral transmission.[89] The seeds of such an analysis can be seen in part in Wansbrough's studies and also Alfred-Louis de Prémare's recent work on the Qur'ān, but more systematic study is clearly needed.[90] The particular advantage of such an approach is that it would not rest on traditional Islamic materials, as does Nöldeke's schema, but would instead be grounded in the methods of modern biblical studies. Unfortunately, it would seem that any possibility of applying form criticism or tradition criticism to the Qur'ān has long been forestalled by Nöldeke and Schwally's sweeping conclusion that the "development of the Islamic canon is utterly unique—one could say that it took place in the opposite fashion [from the biblical texts]": this effective divorce between the Bible and Qur'ān was unlikely to foster such an undertaking.[91]

The separation of Qur'ānic studies from biblical studies remains strongly in place, as evidenced, for example, by F. E. Peters's outright rejection of methods from biblical studies, including form criticism in particular, as having no pertinence to study of the Qur'ān in his article "The Quest of the Historical Muhammad." According to Peters, "Our copy of the Qur'ān is, in fact, what Muhammad taught, and is expressed in his own words." Following the traditional Islamic account of the Qur'ān's collection almost to the letter, Peters explains that these teachings were committed to writing very shortly after Muhammad's death, under the caliph 'Uthmān, and they were transmitted during this brief interval by men who "were convinced from the outset . . . that what they were hearing and noting 'on scraps of leather, bone and in their hearts' were not the teachings of a man but the *ipsissima verba Dei* and so they would have been scrupulously careful in preserving the actual wording." Furthermore, Peters argues that early Islam had no "Easter miracle" to inspire reflective revision of the past, and so one may simply assume that "the Qur'ān is convincingly the words of Muhammad," obviating any need for form or tradition critical study.[92] Thus he concludes,

> if Form criticism proved valuable as a clue to the transmission and the secondary *Sitz im Leben* of the New Testament, that is, "the situation in the life of the Church in which those traditions were found relevant and so preserved (as it turned out) for posterity," it can have no such useful purpose in Islam since there is no conviction that the Qur'anic material was in any way being shaped by or for transmission. On our original assumption that Muhammad is the source of the work, what is found in the Qur'an is not being reported but simply recorded; consequently, modern Form criticism amounts to little more than the classification of the various ways in which the Prophet chose to express himself.[93]

Yet this premise is built on a series of presumptions that, despite their widespread acceptance and frequent repetition, do not seem particularly warranted. The precise circumstances of the Qur'ān's origins are in fact quite uncertain, and as will be seen below, its collection and standardization likely took place over an interval of time comparable in length to the gospel traditions. Moreover it is not at all certain that the Qur'ān may be taken simply as a transparent record of Muhammad's *ipsissima verba* or that its traditions have somehow remained entirely untouched by the process of oral transmission. Indeed, as Peters himself acknowledges here with remarkable candor, such principles are purely matters of "conviction" and "assumption." Nor can it be assumed that the later Islamic view of the Qur'ān as *ipsissima verba Dei* prevailed within the earliest community, and the failed arrival of the promised final Hour, while no "Easter miracle," certainly invites reflection on how attitudes toward the Qur'ānic traditions might have shifted over time, inviting revisions and additions in light of the *eschaton*'s unexpected delay. Indeed, once the overlay of traditional Islamic views about the Qur'ān is removed, the possibilities of form and tradition critical analysis of the Qur'ān emerge as somewhat promising.

More recently François de Blois has sustained the argument that the Qur'ān should remain shielded from the approaches of biblical historical criticism: the Qur'ān's exemption from such analysis is warranted, de Blois maintains, by the radically different nature of the Muslim and Christian scriptures.[94] Yet by the same logic, methods developed in the study of the Hebrew Bible, such as form criticism and tradition criticism, should not be applicable to the study of the New Testament. As the Qur'ān differs from the traditions of the New Testament, so the writings of the New Testament differ significantly (perhaps even more so) both in their nature and in the process of their formation from the writings of the Hebrew Bible. And yet methods developed for studying the traditions of the Pentateuch have proven extremely fruitful when applied, for instance, to the sayings traditions of the synoptic gospels, in spite of the radical differences between these two corpora. Likewise, form critical analysis of the rabbinic traditions has yielded provocative, if controversial, results that have decisively affected the study of early Judaism.[95] Might this also prove true with the Qur'ān? Moreover, despite the significant literary differences between certain elements of the New Testament (such as Paul's letters) and the Qur'ān, the material of the synoptic sayings traditions is in fact remarkably similar, a point largely overlooked by de Blois. In both instances we have to do with a collection of religious teachings that, after a brief period of oral transmission, were committed to writing only somewhat later by the teacher's followers, all against a backdrop of imminent eschatological expectation.

De Blois is certainly right to note the stark difference between the variety of gospel traditions that circulated in the earliest Christian centuries and the striking uniformity of the Qur'ān as it has come down to us. Nevertheless, this difference seems to hinge not so much on the intrinsic nature of the texts themselves, but rather on the matter of when a centralized polity became involved in promulgating a standard text. From early on, the Qur'ān had the forceful backing of a powerful state, which seems to have ensured its textual homogeneity. Yet by comparison, once the Roman authorities embraced Christianity, and it became the religion of an empire, the "Byzantine text" of the New Testament came to prevail widely, pushing out other variants impressively.[96] And while it is true that many non-canonical gospels were aggressively censured by imperial and ecclesiastical authorities, this textual stability of the canonical Gospels (and other New Testament writings) emerged despite the remarkable diversity of the earliest witnesses and in the absence of imperial coercion, let alone a centralized campaign to round up and destroy all evidence of any variant readings, as the early Islamic authorities are reported to have done. In any case, it is not at all clear why the absence of textual variants should preclude a critical investigation of the Qur'ānic traditions and the process of their formation using methods and approaches from the study of the New Testament.

Yet for Peters and many others as well, the most decisive issue appears to be an abiding conviction in the Qur'ān's authenticity as a record of Muhammad's teaching, a principle first laid down forcefully by Nöldeke and widely echoed ever since.[97] In this regard de Blois would contrast with the Qur'ān the teachings of Jesus in the gospels, which are "at least in part, theologically dependent on Pauline doctrine. They cannot therefore be seen as records of the actual teachings of Jesus, but reflect certain defined positions in the history of Christian doctrine."[98] While there can be no doubt that the synoptic sayings traditions have been heavily shaped by the theological interests of the early Christian community, and they certainly are not a transparent record of Jesus' teaching, it seems something of an overstatement to maintain that they are simply a product of the early community, having no relation to what Jesus taught. Indeed, the dependence of the sayings tradition on Pauline doctrine is a rather dubious assertion and is in fact an old saw from the tradition of Islamic anti-Christian polemic with little basis in modern biblical scholarship.[99] Likewise, the notion that the Qur'ān is, to the contrary, an accurate record of Muhammad's teachings untouched by the later interests and concerns of his followers remains largely unsubstantiated, despite its frequent assertion.

A similar understanding of the Qur'ān governs the work of Angelika Neuwirth, whose literary approach to the Qur'ān, in her own words, "presupposes the reliability of the basic data of the traditional accounts about the emergence of the Qur'ān, assuming the transmitted qur'ānic text to be the genuine collection of the communications of the Prophet as pronounced during his activities at Mecca and again at Medina."[100] On this basis Neuwirth admittedly offers an intriguing reading of the Qur'ān as a text formed largely in a liturgical setting, where Muhammad and his followers regularly performed the "early" *sūra*s of the "Meccan" period. Yet her fidelity to the traditional Islamic account of the Qur'ān's initial formation during Muhammad's ministry in Mecca, including also the sequence of the *sūra*s (as adopted by Nöldeke largely from the Islamic tradition) presents a critical weakness in her overall approach. Likewise, despite the painstaking micro-philological analysis of various individual *sūra*s, Neuwirth's often subjective approach to the text does not persuasively establish its literary integrity.

According to Neuwirth, Muhammad from the start delivered his prophetic teachings in the form of carefully crafted rhyming discourses that were composed with a great deal of literary sophistication, a view embraced recently also by Peters.[101] These artful compositions now survive as the "Meccan" *sūra*s of the Qur'ān, whose authorship Neuwirth assigns to Muhammad not just in terms of general content but even at the level of the individual *sūra*s. Such poetic expressions of Muhammad's religious vision, as Neuwirth interprets them, reveal a prophet of some literary skill, who already in Mecca sought to refine his message into elaborate theological hymns.[102] Yet it is somehow difficult to imagine Muhammad as the deliberate poet-theologian that Neuwirth's study seems to envision. While one certainly need not accede to the Islamic tradition's characterization of Muhammad as illiterate, which is probably an apologetic invention in any case, Neuwirth's image of Muhammad nonetheless seems somewhat improbable. Muhammad's career appears to have been filled with frequent struggle and conflict, certainly if the early Islamic sources have any merit at all, and although such circumstances could perhaps inspire poetry, a more ad hoc style of leadership is instead suggested. Indeed, it is not entirely clear how Neuwirth and others adopting her hypothesis would reconcile this image of Muhammad with the somewhat different portrait of the traditional biographies. More importantly, if Muhammad was primarily an eschatological prophet warning before the impending doom of the Hour, as argued here, it is somewhat difficult to imagine him meticulously honing his urgent message into complex poetic hymns.

Neuwirth's understanding of the Qur'ān's literary integrity would thus seem to preclude its thoroughgoing analysis using the methods of biblical studies in the manner Wansbrough and others have proposed. As the work largely of a single author, Muhammad, even in the formation of its *sūras*, many of the methods of biblical criticism, particularly those focusing on the oral transmission and compilation of independent traditions, simply do not apply.[103] Indeed, according to Neuwirth, scholars who would adopt such an approach in studying the Qur'ān are accordingly guilty of a "flagrant breach" of their own methodological principles: they have never subjected the Qur'ān to "what biblical scholars refer to as 'literary criticism' [that is, *Literarkritik* or "source criticism"] in order to examine in a methodologically principled way whether it really does constitute a secondary compilation" of earlier written sources.[104] Admittedly, we do not have the literary sources to examine the formation of the Qur'ān with the same depth as the synoptic gospels: the comprehensive elimination of any variant codices seems to have ensured that.[105] Yet *Literarkritik* or "source criticism" is concerned primarily with the identification of earlier written transmissions, and while this approach does not exclude the possibility of earlier oral stages in the history of the text, "they are reconstructed in a different way, particularly on the basis of their genres and their *Sitz im Leben*," that is, using the methods of form and tradition criticism.[106] In fact, some biblical critics of the last century argued that these newer methods for studying the history of the text should now displace the "antiquated" approach of source criticism.[107]

Accordingly, the mere absence of earlier written sources does not at all warrant the conclusion that the Qur'ān could not have been composed over a period of decades out of much shorter "sayings" ascribed to Muhammad: there is in fact much to suggest that this was the process by which the Qur'ān came into being. And while the relative absence of parallel versions of the same tradition excludes the application of certain perspectives from form critical (and source critical and redaction critical) analysis, this deficiency should in no way proscribe wholesale the use of methods from biblical studies. Certainly, individual traditions from the synoptic gospels have been analyzed using form and tradition criticism in the absence of any doublet, for instance, and the Gospel according to John, whose traditions are quite independent from the Synoptics, has similarly not been spared historical-critical study. As with these traditions from the New Testament, it is possible to analyze the literary form of various traditions imbedded in the Qur'ān, to ask questions about their *Sitze im Leben* and the impact of the early community on their formation, and to compare different perspectives emerging from within the Qur'ān, even lacking recourse to parallel transmissions or knowledge of earlier written sources.[108]

While Neuwirth's reading of the Qur'ān has found a number of ardent followers, others have noted the relatively subjective nature of her interpretations, in light of which her approach fails to demonstrate the literary integrity of the "Meccan" *sūra*s convincingly.[109] Indeed, as Motzki notes, the prevailing view among scholars of the Qur'ān remains, contra Neuwirth, that its traditions initially circulated as short, individual sayings that only later on were woven together into *sūra*s during the process of their collection.[110] In contrast then to Neuwirth's alternative hypothesis, the Qur'ān's status as a composite text fashioned from earlier, much shorter units of tradition is widely acknowledged. For instance, Bell and Watt's influential *Bell's Introduction to the Qur'ān* includes a section identifying the various literary forms appearing in the Qur'ān. According to Bell and Watt, these are primarily of a "didactic" rather than "poetic or artistic" nature, and frequently these smaller formal units of tradition are found in a state of disjointed juxtaposition.[111] The elements of literary unity within the Qur'ān, such as they are, including various rhyme schemes, are held to have been introduced by those who sought to stitch these smaller fragments together.[112] De Prémare has more recently articulated a rather similar model of the Qur'ān's formation. Beginning with a literary approach to the text, de Prémare persuasively identifies various heterogeneous styles within the Qur'ān, cataloguing these discursive forms with somewhat greater precision than Bell and Watt. Likewise, de Prémare notes the different literary strategies by which these individual traditions were later woven together into larger textual units, thus creating a sense of cohesion among the Qur'ān's still noticeably disparate elements.[113] When understood in this manner, the Qur'ān holds great potential for analysis using the methods of biblical studies, including form and tradition criticism in particular. As Andrew Rippin observes of the Qur'ān, "Muslims speak of the Qur'ān as being written prior to its collection on 'stones, palm leaves and the hearts of men'; a literary hypothesis for the origins of the text, one which would account for the text's apparent disjointedness, virtually jumps out at the scholar familiar with form criticism. . . . On the evidence of the Muslim tradition itself, the same could be envisioned for the Qur'an: a weaving together of a text, involving duplications and abrupt breaks, just as in the Bible."[114]

It is certainly true that some basic elements of form and tradition criticism can be witnessed in earlier studies of the Qur'ān, particularly in Hartwig Hirschfeld's work as well as in Bell's translation and his only rather recently published commentary. Both scholars brought great insight to the study of the Qur'ān by treating individual units of tradition independently, rather than attempting to read each *sūra* as a cohesive whole, and also by considering the impact that the process of oral transmission may have had on the development of individual traditions.[115] Yet to the rather limited extent that form criticism has had any significant impact on the study of the Qurʾān, such influence has come primarily from form critical analysis of the Hebrew Bible. Nevertheless the model of New Testament form criticism seems much better suited to analysis of the Qurʾān than its Old Testament precursor.[116] In contrast to the Hebrew Bible, whose contents reflect a process of sedimentation that took place over several centuries with discrete periods of redaction, the Qurʾān, like the canonical gospels, was more hastily compiled from various independent fragments of tradition after a relatively brief period of oral transmission, within the context, it would seem, of imminent eschatological belief. Indeed, comparison with the New Testament suggests that the formation of the Qurʾān was not nearly so *völlig abweichend* as Nöldeke was once able to imagine.[117]

While a form critical analysis after the model of New Testament studies would unquestionably fail to produce a chronology of the Qurʾānic text in the manner that Nöldeke, Blachère, and Bell have sought, parsing the building blocks of Qurʾānic tradition according to different forms of discourse and considering their possible *Sitze im Leben* and the impact of the process of oral transmission would afford an avenue for investigating the history of this material prior to its compilation in the *textus receptus*. Nevertheless, this approach would require Qurʾānic studies to abandon its more or less tacit acceptance of the traditional Islamic accounts of the Qurʾān's serial revelation and its wholesale ascription to Muhammad in largely the same format that it has come down to the present day. The hermeneutics of suspicion, it would appear, have yet to transform Qurʾānic study in the way they have biblical studies: as Rippin recently observes, "when modern scholars approach the Qurʾān, the core assumptions of the Muslim tradition about the text are not challenged."[118] Yet as form critical study of the Bible provided scholars with a means of analyzing the history of Israel and early Christianity in a manner that was free from "the church's traditional view of biblical history,"[119] so too might its more thoroughgoing application to the Qurʾān afford the possibility of an analysis freed from the traditional Islamic view of Qurʾānic history. This endeavor would necessitate, however, that, *pace* Peters (et al.), the traditional Islamic framework be shelved. Form critical and tradition critical analysis of the Qurʾān would require consideration of at least the possibility that certain Qurʾānic pericopes had their origin (that is, their *Sitz im Leben*) not in Muhammad's ministry but in the life of the early community, or that perhaps they were shaped during the period of oral transmission to meet the changing conditions of the community: to date only John Wansbrough's *Quranic Studies* has adopted such an approach, albeit with much debated success.[120] Nevertheless, despite certain shortcomings of Wansbrough's study, such as, for instance, his somewhat unlikely late date for the final establishment of the *ne varietur* text of the Qur'ān, the overarching brilliance of his effort to rethink the origins of the Qur'ān in the terms of modern historical criticism should not be cast aside so lightly (as has often been the case). Indeed, even if it seems unlikely that the Qur'ānic text was still in flux as late as the third century AH, as Wansbrough has proposed, his general arguments for dating the Qur'ānic compilation significantly later than currently envisioned both by the Islamic tradition and most Western scholars of Islam remain valid.[121]

ʿUthmān, ʿAbd al-Malik, and the Collection and Standardization of the Qur'ān

According to the prevailing Islamic and Western view of the Qur'ān's collection, the caliph ʿUthmān oversaw its compilation during the second half of his reign, establishing the final, *ne varietur* consonantal text roughly twenty years after Muhammad's death. ʿUthmān then disseminated this new standard text together with instructions that all other copies of the Qur'ān should be destroyed, an order that was allegedly obeyed everywhere except for at Kūfa.[122] This scenario of course affords only a small window for any possible redaction by the early Islamic community, leaving relatively secure the firm association between the Qur'ānic *textus receptus* and Muhammad's religious teaching. Nevertheless, the almost wholesale acceptance that this scenario has found in modern scholarship is not so much warranted even by the witness of the early Islamic tradition itself, which conveys a wide range of opinions concerning the collection of the Qur'ān. If it is somewhat understandable that the later Islamic tradition eventually resolved the matter more or less unanimously in favor of the ʿUthmānic collection, the sheer diversity of information regarding the formation of the Qur'ān in the early tradition should perhaps occasion less certainty from modern Qur'ānic scholarship.[123]

For instance, as is well known, a widely attested tradition attributes the collection of the Qur'ān to the first caliph, Abū Bakr, who had the entire corpus collected on "sheets" (*ṣuḥuf*) of paper. Looking to Welch's article on the Qur'ān in *The Encyclopaedia of Islam* as something reflecting the *status quaestionis*, the consensus of modern scholarship rejects this tradition, since, as Welch notes, "there are serious problems with this account," not the least of which is that "most of the key points in this story are contradicted by alternative accounts in the canonical *ḥadīth* collections and other early Muslim sources." Nevertheless, when he comes to assess the traditions of an ʿUthmānic collection, Welch concludes almost identically that "this second collection story stands up to critical analysis no better than the first [that is, Abū Bakr's collection]. . . . We thus have before us another story whose particulars cannot be accepted." Despite this fully negative assessment, Welch explains that "the unanimity with which an official text is attributed to ʿUthmān, in the face of a lack of convincing evidence to the contrary" leads Western scholars to conclude that both the number and arrangement of the *sūra*s as well as the "basic structure of the consonantal text" may be assigned to the reign of ʿUthmān.[124] Nonetheless, it was only over the course of about three centuries, according to Welch, that this text gradually supplanted various other rival codices and was fine-tuned into the canonical *textus receptus*.[125]

Notwithstanding Welch's seemingly prosaic observation that the ʿUthmānic collection is essentially uncontested, there is in fact significant evidence challenging this widely accepted tenet of Qurʾānic studies. Wansbrough, for instance, presents a rather persuasive case against the ʿUthmānic collection on the basis of the Qurʾānic text itself, as well as the early Islamic literature about the Qurʾān: the data assembled by Wansbrough are not so easily overlooked as their absence from many discussions of the Qurʾān might seem to suggest.[126] Likewise, Patricia Crone and G. R. Hawting, working from a different angle, have both argued that certain elements of the legal tradition suggest a later redaction for the Qurʾān,[127] and Claude Gilliot has in numerous articles suggested that the Qurʾān was a collective work, drawing particular attention to the role of Muhammad's "informants" in shaping the text.[128] Perhaps the most compelling recent challenge to the tradition of ʿUthmānic codification, however, has come from Alfred-Louis de Prémare, whose works have been inexplicably ignored by so many recent studies of the Qurʾān.[129]

In essence, de Prémare has revived Casanova's thesis that the text of the Qurʾān was codified and disseminated primarily by ʿAbd al-Malik, during whose reign the Qurʾānic text was still very much in flux.[130] A substantial body of evidence suggests that ʿAbd al-Malik, working together with the governor of Iraq, al-Ḥajjāj, undertook the standardization of the Qurʾānic text in hopes of displacing the variant codices that were being used in different cities, aiming to establish religious unity as a means of unifying the Islamic polity under his authority.[131] The relative instability of the Qur'ānic text even at this late date is substantiated by the thousands of variant readings preserved by early Islamic authors or recorded on coinage. Yet perhaps the most prominent and inescapable such evidence appears in the inscriptions of the Dome of the Rock: these citations from the Qur'ān diverge from the *ne varietur textus receptus*, which had allegedly been codified almost forty years prior under 'Uthmān, at least according to the traditionally accepted account.[132] If the Qur'ānic text had been already established for nearly four decades by this time, it is difficult to explain how or why this variant text came to be inscribed on one of Islam's most sacred and prominent monuments. To the contrary, it would seem that even in the centers of power, the codification of the *textus receptus* had not yet been achieved.[133]

The legend of an 'Uthmānic collection, as de Prémare explains, was most likely invented to bolster the prestige and authority of the Umayyad dynasty by assigning this uniquely significant task to the first member of the family to attain the caliphal throne, 'Uthmān, who was also the only Umayyad counted among the first four "rightly guided" caliphs. The legend's pervasive sanction in later tradition is merely a result of its canonization by al-Bukhārī in his *Saḥīḥ* rather than any reflection of its historical merits.[134] Although Harald Motzki has recently presented a case for ascribing the tradition of an 'Uthmānic collection to al-Zuhrī, who appears as a common link in its *isnād*s, it should be clear that this determination in no way decides the issue of the Qur'ān's origins.[135] Motzki's article merely identifies a probability that the narrative of 'Uthmān's collection was in circulation by the middle of the eighth century; he does not, however, establish the accuracy of the story, which remains just one among several different versions of the Qur'ān's collection.[136] By way of comparison, one might consider the earliest Christian account of the formation of the canonical gospels, written by Papias at the beginning of the second century, approximately fifty years after the gospels' composition and one hundred years after the death of Jesus, a roughly comparable interval of time.[137] Yet despite Papias's relative proximity to the events in question and his appeal to eyewitnesses, his report is contradicted by other sources of information about the gospels' formation as well as by the nature of gospel texts themselves. Consequently, in stark contrast to the prevailing assumptions of Qur'ānic studies, no modern scholar of the New Testament would accept Papias's account, excepting only certain Evangelical Christian scholars for whom the authenticity of the gospels is theologically necessary.[138] As de Prémare himself rightly concludes, Motzki's discovery in no way impinges on his own arguments, which rather persuasively identify the reign of ʿAbd al-Malik, rather than ʿUthmān, as the era that "marked a decisive step" in the constitution of the standard Qurʾānic text. As much is also indicated, it would appear, by various contemporary Christian sources.[139]

Chase Robinson has recently added additional support for this view in his brief monograph on ʿAbd al-Malik, whom he also identifies as the most likely source of the *textus receptus* of the Qurʾān. Robinson points especially to the inherent improbabilities of the ʿUthmānic account, noting that ʿUthmān was simply in no position to achieve what the tradition has ascribed to him. "ʿUthman was deeply unpopular in many quarters; his reign was short and contentious. His successor's was longer, and one can imagine that the task of enforcing an ʿUthmanic version would have fallen in practice to Muʿawiya. But in a polity that lacked many rudimentary instruments of coercion and made no systematic attempt to project images of its own transcendent authority—no coins, little public building or inscriptions—the very idea of 'official' is problematic."[140] Likewise, the instabilities of the Qurʾānic text still in the age of ʿAbd al-Malik suggest that a standard text had not yet been achieved. When such circumstances are considered according to the same standards used in evaluating non-Islamic traditions, Robinson concludes that "*taken as a whole*, the reliable evidence suggests that Qurʾānic texts must have remained at least partially fluid through the late seventh and early eighth century." In contrast to ʿUthmān, ʿAbd al-Malik had both the means and motive to undertake standardization of the Qurʾānic text. "Here," writes Robinson, "the events make some real sense. For ʿAbd al-Malik had a clear interest: . . . his imperial program was in very large measure executed by broadcasting ideas of order and obedience in a distinctly Islamic idiom. What is more, unlike previous caliphs, ʿAbd al-Malik had the resources to attempt such a redaction and to impose the resulting text, which, amongst all its competitors, we inherit."[141] Consequently, Robinson concludes that "instead of speaking of an ʿUthmanic text, we should probably speak of a Marwanid one."[142] David Powers's recent monograph has brought further support to this view, presenting convincing evidence that "the consonantal skeleton of the Qurʾān remained open and fluid for three-quarters of a century between the death of the Prophet and the caliphate of ʿAbd al-Malik."[143] Indeed, the case for the Qurʾān's redaction under ʿAbd al-Malik increasingly seems more plausible than the traditionally received account of its ʿUthmānic origins.

Evidence for the standardization and promulgation of the Qurʾānic *textus receptus* under ʿAbd al-Malik and al-Ḥajjāj is in fact sufficiently strong that

Omar Hamdan has recently sought to harmonize their activities with the tradition of an ʿUthmānic collection by interpreting al-Ḥajjāj's efforts as a second major phase in the process of canonization ("the second *maṣāḥif* project"). While Hamdan seems to have little doubt that the Qurʾānic text as we have it was produced under ʿUthmān during the middle of the seventh century, he nevertheless surveys some compelling evidence that during al-Ḥajjāj's rule as governor of Iraq (694–713), this official text was not in use not only "in Basra and Kufa, but also in the other major cultural centers of early Islam."[144] Still at this late date, the "ʿUthmānic" text was not widely utilized, and its standardization across the early Islamic empire was achieved primarily through al-Ḥajjāj's enforcement and destruction of any rival versions. One thing then is clear from Hamdan's analysis: the Qurʾānic *textus receptus* was not widely in use before the beginning of the eighth century. Although Hamdan does not question the origin of the *textus receptus* under ʿUthmān, there seems to be no escaping the conclusion that the text of the Qurʾān remained relatively varied throughout the seventh century, and that the text that we now have today only displaced its rivals through the direct and concerted efforts of government authorities at a later date. Whether or not the text that ʿAbd al-Malik and al-Ḥajjāj promulgated actually originated with ʿUthmān is not at all certain, and it seems rather plausible instead that this recension was in fact produced under imperial patronage only at the end of the seventh century.

Even Angelika Neuwirth appears increasingly willing to allow for the possibility that the Qurʾānic text remained in flux and was not standardized until the reign of ʿAbd al-Malik. In the survey of recent Qurʾānic research that opens the republication of her *Studien zur Komposition der mekkanischen Suren*, Neuwirth acknowledges, albeit somewhat begrudgingly, the prospect that perhaps it was only under ʿAbd al-Malik's direction that the Qurʾān achieved its current shape. Although she clearly remains partial to the traditional view of an ʿUthmānic recension, in a bow to de Prémare's recent studies Neuwirth concedes the possibility of a final redaction during ʿAbd al-Malik's caliphate.[145] Nevertheless, she is quick to insist that this would afford at the maximum only sixty years between what she rather presumptively declares to be "the completion of the text" (seemingly at the end of Muhammad's life) and its publication in an authoritative edition. This leaves, Neuwirth avers, "a period which, contrary to de Prémare's conclusions, is too short to allow sufficient room for significant, that is, deliberate, theologically relevant modifications of the text."[146] Such a pronouncement is quite unwarranted, however, and one can only imagine that here we witness once again the persistent influence of Hebrew Bible studies—as opposed to methods and concepts from New Testament studies—on the analysis of the Qur'ān. As much is quite clear, for instance, in Fred Donner's critique of the "skeptical approach" (discussed below), when he rejects its use of methods from biblical criticism by explicitly stating that they are not "applicable to the study of the Islamic materials, which crystallized much more rapidly than the Old Testament tradition."[147] To be sure, if one's model is the formation of the Hebrew Bible, the period in question is indeed comparatively much shorter.

When viewed from the perspective of New Testament studies, however, Neuwirth's statement is rather astonishing. A fundamental principle of modern studies of the canonical gospels is the hypothesis that the early Christian community shaped and reshaped—even "invented"—traditions about the life and preaching of Jesus during the so-called "tunnel period" of their oral transmission, a process that still did not cease even after these traditions began to be collected in writing.[148] During this relatively brief interval—only about twenty years before the "Q" collection of Jesus' sayings and just forty to fifty years before the first of the canonical gospels were compiled—the early Christian traditions were subjected to significant, often deliberate, and theologically relevant modifications on a wide scale: according to a recent estimate by a particular group of New Testament scholars, 82 percent of the words attributed to Jesus in the canonical gospels were *not* actually spoken by him.[149] Consequently, if as Robinson advocates, scholarship on early Islam should be "committed to the idea that the history made by Muslims is comparable to that made by non-Muslims," the possibility that similar evolution is reflected within the Qur'ān should not be ruled out as a matter of principle, as Neuwirth has resolved.[150] Indeed, even if one were to allow for a period of only twenty years prior to a collection of the Qur'ān under 'Uthmān, the comparanda of the Q sayings collection offer a rather sobering analogue: very many of the sayings in this early collection of Jesus' teachings, compiled just twenty years after his death, are widely regarded by New Testament scholarship as either inauthentic or having been subjected to heavy redaction.[151]

Despite Neuwirth's rather forceful proscription, there appears to be no good reason to exclude the possibility of similar redaction of the Qur'ānic traditions over an equivalent period of time, particularly if, as is argued here, earliest Islam was, like earliest Christianity, suffused with imminent eschatological belief. As with primitive Christianity, early Islam's expectation of the world's impending judgment and destruction would likely have forestalled any effort to produce an authoritative, written collection of Muhammad's teachings: with so little time remaining, preparation for the Hour would surely have taken precedence over the standardization of a sacred text in order to ensure its transmission to future generations. Only as the Hour was continuously deferred, and the community's collective memory grew ever distant from the time of Muhammad and began to dim, did it become necessary to codify these sacred traditions.[152] This process need not have happened all at once, however, and as both Wansbrough's analysis of the Qur'ān's many textual repetitions and the existence of rival codices suggest, compilation of the Qur'ānic text likely occurred initially in several, independent stages, culminating in an official standardization of the text only under ʿAbd al-Malik.[153]

One should note, however, that Donner has lately advanced several arguments against such skeptical views of the Qur'ān that have persuaded many scholars to continue to look past the kinds of difficulties identified by Wansbrough, de Prémare, and Robinson, and to accept instead the traditional account of the Qur'ān's ʿUthmānic origin.[154] Despite his willingness to engage at least certain aspects of what he names the "skeptical approach," Donner has steadfastly maintained the traditional account of the Qur'ān's formation and the attribution of its contents to Muhammad, even though by his own admission certain of his findings regarding the changing nature of the early community seem to require a rather different model.[155] In this regard, Donner has certainly posed some legitimate questions deserving of answers, and although his primary target appears to be Wansbrough, whose deferral of the *textus receptus* to the early ninth century seems rather doubtful, Donner's critique nevertheless has some bearing for the more moderate proposal of a collection at the end of the seventh century as well.

The bulk of Donner's arguments aim to establish that the traditions of the Qur'ān appear to be somewhat older than those of the *ḥadīth*, a strategy seemingly determined by his understanding of Wansbrough's basic thesis as involving the identification of the Qur'ān as a small subset of the *ḥadīth* that eventually came to be canonized. Although I am not persuaded at all that this formulation represents an accurate summation of Wansbrough's hypothesis,[156] Donner's points with regard to comparison of the Qur'ān and the *ḥadīth* are well made, and I think it may be conceded that the material collected in the Qur'ān does in fact appear to be generally older than the traditions of the *ḥadīth*. The Qur'ān does indeed represent the earliest layer of the Islamic tradition, developed over the course of the seventh century, while the bulk of the *ḥadīth* (although by no means *all* of them) appear to have come into circulation only after the first Islamic century.[157] As Robinson and others have rightly observed, the literary form in which the earliest *ḥadīth* survive is without question the work of authors from the mid-eighth century and later, and it is thus no surprise to find abundant evidence that these prophetic traditions are more recent than the Qurʾān.[158]

Donner also notes the absence of any anachronisms in the Qurʾān that would betray its later formation. The *ḥadīth*, for instance, are full of references to people and events long after Muhammad's lifetime, in which Muhammad predicts events that will come to pass in later generations. Inasmuch as the Qurʾān makes no references to events beyond the lifetime of Muhammad, Donner suggests it is likely that the Qurʾān must have been collected shortly after Muhammad's lifetime and was already a "closed" text by the time of the First Civil War (656–61) "at the latest."[159] Yet following an identical logic, one could similarly make the argument that the Christian Gospel according to John, which does not assign any predictions to Jesus beyond his own lifespan (or a few days thereafter), must accurately reflect his life and teaching and date to sometime before 60 CE. To my knowledge, however, no serious New Testament scholar has proposed such an argument, and in general John is thought to be perhaps the latest canonical gospel.[160] Accordingly, the mere absence of predictive material in a text cannot be used to date it close to the events that it purports to describe or to verify its authenticity.

It is nonetheless true that such future elements are lacking from the Qurʾān, but their absence may simply reflect the fact that the Qurʾān is generally not a predictive text. The revelations that the early Muslims believed Muhammad to have received from God seem not to have been understood as foretelling the future; to the contrary, they reflect the restoration of an ancient faith that had been practiced by Abraham and Moses, and had been revealed to humanity before several times in the past. If this was in fact the early community's understanding of the Qurʾān, as seems to be the case, then it is hardly surprising that they did not fill it with *ex eventu* predictions about the future, and the absence of such forecasts does not guarantee either Muhammad's authorship of the Qurʾān or its collection under ʿUthmān. Moreover, as will be seen below, it does not appear that the Qurʾānic traditions actually envisioned much at all in the way of a future: the end of the world was near at hand, and in the Qurʾān God had unveiled one final time a revelation of truth that had previously been delivered to Abraham and others, warning humanity of its imminent judgment and destruction. Consequently, the Qurʾān's temporal orientation is generally focused more on events of the past than the future (excepting, of course, the immediate eschatological events of the impending judgment).

The only potentially predictive statement in the Qur'ān occurs at the opening of *sūra* 30, which remarks that "the Greeks have been vanquished in the nearer part of the land [that is, the Holy Land]," following then with a forecast that "after their vanquishing, they shall be the victors in a few years" (2–4). The last verse continues to explain that "on that day the believers shall rejoice in God's help," seeming to convey deep sympathy, if not even a sort of spiritual common cause, with the Byzantines. Traditionally, this passage has been interpreted as referring to the brief Persian conquest and occupation of the Byzantine Near East, which coincided with the lifetime of Muhammad, lasting from 614 until the Byzantine reconquest in 628. The joy at the Byzantines' victory in this interpretation is explained as the triumph of a monotheist people of the book over the heathen Persians. Nevertheless, an alternative vocalization of these verses, first attested by al-Tirmidhī (d. 892), renders the passage instead, "the Romans have vanquished in the near part of the Land. They, after their victory, will be vanquished in a few years."[161] According to this reading, the passage begins by noting the Byzantine victory over the Persians in 628 (or perhaps over Muhammad's followers at Mu'ta), followed by a prediction of their defeat several years later at the hands of Muhammad's followers.[162] Nöldeke predictably rejected this reading, since "Muhammad could not have foreseen this," but Bell and others have noted that "it is also difficult to explain Muhammed's favourable interest in the political fortunes of the Byzantine Empire in this early period," as seemingly indicated in the final verse.[163] Alternatively, however, if the verse refers to the victory of the Muslims over the Byzantines, the rejoicing of the Believers makes perfect sense. Quite possibly then, these verses were added to the Qur'ān only sometime after Muhammad's death, as the Muslims found themselves increasingly in competition with Christianity. In this context, such a tradition may have been invented in order to have Muhammad successfully predict future world events, as Jesus, for instance, had predicted the destruction of the temple and Jerusalem (Luke 19:41–44, 21:5–24). The later commentary tradition certainly remembers the fulfillment of this prophecy as having convinced many of the truth of Muhammad's message.[164]

Yet not only are future predictions largely missing from the Qur'ānic text, but Muhammad himself is strangely absent, excepting only a few passages. As Donner himself observes, "Muḥammad and his prophethood are very much in the background in the Qur'ān, overshadowed by other figures and themes."[165] Muhammad is in fact named only four times in the Qur'ān, always in the third person, and while other parts of the Qur'ān are readily interpreted with the broader context afforded by the *sīra* tradition, there is no guarantee that these later biographies are able to fill in the blanks of the Qur'ān with any accuracy.[166] Hartwig Hirschfeld has even proposed, not entirely without good reason, that these four mentions of Muhammad are likely insertions by the later community, based on a hypothesis that the name Muhammad, meaning, "he who is praised," was not Muhammad's birth name, but rather an honorific title subsequently bestowed on him by his followers.[167] While Hirschfeld's proposal has not gained a significant following, Muhammad's infrequent appearances in the Qur'ān could, if one follows Donner's reflections on the absence of anachronisms a bit further, suggest that much of the Qur'ān seems not only pre-Fitna but perhaps even pre-Muhammad. In recent years, as much has been proposed, first by Günter Lüling and more recently by the pseudonymous "Christoph Luxenberg,"[168] and while neither effort has met with much success, the proposal that the Qur'ān has in places incorporated significant pre-Islamic textual materials certainly merits further study.[169] Nevertheless, just as Muhammad's faint presence within the Qur'ān does not require chronological distance between him and a largely preexistent text, so too the absence of historical anachronisms in the form of predictions does not anchor a fixed text of the Qur'ān to the period before the First Civil War.[170]

Donner's observations regarding the Qur'ān's lack of anachronisms can be largely explained by the Qur'ān's focus primarily on the timeless message of a prophetic past and a present defined especially by inter-religious conflicts, the need for community order, and an impending doom that will soon bring history to a close. As Rippin observes of the Qur'ān, its contents largely serve to "bring strands of earlier biblical and Arabian traditions together through the person of Muhammad," and thus it is no surprise to find predictions of the future lacking.[171] In contrast to the *ḥadīth*, "the Qur'ān was highly selective in its choice of subject matter," Leor Halevi observes. "Searching for transcendence and *gravitas*, it excluded from its purview incidentals of time and space."[172] Moreover, the Qur'ān's apparent forecast of an imminent end to the world seems to have left the whole issue of "future history" a rather moot point.[173] Even Donner himself elsewhere notes that the Qur'ān is "profoundly ahistorical," having only two definite points of chronological reference, "the Creation and the Last Judgment." As Donner remarks, the Qur'ān seems to regard this final judgment as imminent, forcing its readers to choose between good and evil before it comes crashing down upon them.[174] The category of *ḥadīth*, however, afforded a younger genre that was considerably more flexible in terms of content, and, as evidenced by the prolific forgery of *ḥadīth*s, there was little hesitance to invent new traditions on a wide range of topics and attribute them to Muhammad using this vehicle. Consequently, it is no surprise to find a difference in regard to forged predictions between the Qur'ān and the *ḥadīth*. Nevertheless, this observation by no means warrants the conclusion that the Qur'ān itself was not subject to significant redaction and addition during the process of oral transmission; rather, it merely signals that predictive prophecies were neither a significant element of Qur'ānic text nor a major tendency of its redaction. By way of contrast, however, material relating various aspects of "earlier biblical and Arabian traditions" may well have been added to the Qur'ān after Muhammad's lifetime, such as seems to be the case with the Qur'ānic traditions of Jesus' Nativity, for instance.[175] Furthermore, if one supposes, as Donner himself has suggested, that Muhammad and his followers expected an imminent end to the world, to the extent that the issue of Muhammad's successor was largely irrelevant,[176] then presumably the Qur'ān's reference to Muhammad's mortality in 3:144 should be viewed as an interpolation, a possibility for which there is significant evidence in later tradition, as will be seen below.

Finally, in a more general critique of the skeptical approach as a whole, Donner raises an objection not dissimilar to the "Vincentian Canon" avowed by the triumphant orthodoxy of late ancient Christianity: in defending the truth of the orthodox Christian faith, Vincent of Lérins (d. 445) famously upheld its accuracy on the basis that it had been believed "everywhere, always and by all."[177] Hurgronje invokes Vincent's principle explicitly in his rejection of Casanova's new hypotheses,[178] and here Donner essentially returns to it, arguing against the skeptics that inasmuch as the earliest Islamic traditions have been held in common by all Muslims across the ages and the globe, in spite of considerable religious, political, and social tensions within the community, these memories must indeed reflect the beginnings of Islam with accuracy. Donner further proposes that there were in early Islam no "authorities" with "the power to impose a uniform dogmatic view," and he chides the skeptics for their failure to identify the agents behind the alleged changes in the early Islamic tradition prior to its crystallization in the received form. It is extremely unlikely, Donner continues, that these "unnamed 'authorities,' whoever they were, could have tracked down every book and tradition contained in every manuscript in the whole Islamic community, from India to Spain."[179]

The problem here, however, is very much with the sort of model of development that Donner seems to envision, at least in this study. While these observations may complicate certain aspects of Wansbrough's hypotheses regarding the nature and formation of the Qur'ān, such concerns do not preclude considerable revision of Muhammad's religious vision and the beliefs of his earliest followers over the course of the first sixty years, along the lines of what occurred in earliest Christianity. Indeed, Donner himself, when considering the shifting sectarian boundaries of the early community in subsequent studies, is willing to propose that once Islamic self-identity had evolved "to form a separate confessional group distinct from Christians, Jews, and others," "*the Muslim community* . . . would have taken great pains to project back into the story of its origins those features that had come to be decisive in establishing that separate identity and to obliterate or disguise any obvious traces of the 'pre-confessional' character of the community of believers."[180] At times Donner seemingly overstates the level of the early community's intentionality in this revision of origins by characterizing its efforts as having "taken great pains," or as he also writes, "carefully attempt[ing] to bury, or 'forget'" this past; more plausible is his suggestion elsewhere that such early changes were "not done intentionally to deceive later readers about the true state of affairs in the early community of the Believers, but merely because later Muslim copyists simply took for granted" that the truth as they believed it was the same truth held by the earliest Muslims.[181] If such significant changes could occur relevant to the confessional nature of the early community, then there is certainly no reason to exclude similarly dramatic changes regarding other important issues.[182]

As for the agents of such early changes, it simply is not possible or even important to identify the specific individuals, but that certainly does not mean that therefore there were no changes: even Donner himself seems to allow as much in other contexts. At present, not enough is known about the earliest Islamic community to expect discovery of such information,[183] and, following the analogue of earliest Christianity, the process of oral transmission (even alongside of some rudimentary written transmission) is rife with possibilities for both the revision and introduction of traditions. This is particularly the case in a context as rapidly changing as was primitive Islam, where the success of conquest and the continued delay of the anticipated Hour, among other developments, undoubtedly effected adjustments in the collective memory of the past and the community's vision of both its present and the future. In this regard, Robinson's assessment of the conditions in which the earliest Muslims first relayed the history of their origins is especially instructive. "It is true that oral history can extend back three or four generations with some accuracy, but this seems to be the exception rather than the rule, and even in those exceptional cases, what is remembered is generally what is socially significant. What is more, a relatively accurate oral history is predicated on a more or less stable social system, one that holds to old truths and conventions; in societies undergoing rapid social and political change (such as early Islam), oral history tends to be much less accurate."[184]

The final authorities behind the eventual standardization of Islam following this initial period of oral transmission would of course be the Umayyads (and especially ʿAbd al-Malik) and the ʿAbbāsids following after them. The fact that the early caliphs appear to have commanded considerably more authority in the religious sphere than the later (Sunni) tradition would care to remember, as Crone and Hinds have convincingly argued,[185] certainly suggests their potential influence on the development of the early Islamic tradition. Moreover, after only sixty years of what had been a largely oral tradition, there would be fairly little in the way of books or manuscripts to hunt down, although, as the Islamic tradition frequently makes note, variant codices of the Qurʾān remained for some time a vexing problem for the authorities who struggled to eliminate them, ultimately with great success.[186] As Michael Cook correctly observes, "The fact that for all practical purposes we have only a single recension of the Koran is thus a remarkable testimony to the authority of the early Islamic state."[187] Nevertheless, despite the Qurʾān's eventual standardization as a *ne varietur* codex, the possibilities for significant transformations of both the Qurʾān and the broader tradition during the early "tunnel period" of Islam's first several decades are in fact significant and ought not to be disregarded. Even if the application of such a hermeneutics of suspicion may ultimately determine that much of the Qurʾān can be in some sense ascribed to Muhammad, it must be allowed that additions and modifications may have been made by the community during the process of the text's transmission and formation, as was the case with the sacred scriptures of other religious traditions.

"The Imminent Is Imminent": Eschatology in the Qurʾān

While the present analysis of the Qurʾān will by no means attempt a thoroughgoing form and tradition critical study of the Qurʾānic text, its investigation of the Qurʾān's eschatology will operate primarily according to the basic principles of these methods, insofar as possible. It will focus particularly on eschatological pronouncements within the Qurʾān, which will be considered alongside various other formal elements, a parable for instance, that share a focus on eschatology. The study will raise questions about the *Sitz im Leben* of individual traditions, as well as about their possible transformation within the early community during the process of transmission. Moreover, it will apply many of the basic form and tradition critical criteria of dating traditions, including especially the important criterion of dissimilarity or criterion of embarrassment, not only to the Qurʾān but also in the following section to certain eschatological *ḥadīth*. This approach will make it possible to isolate elements of the early Islamic tradition that probably belong to the earliest layer of the tradition, presumably originating with even Muhammad himself as core elements of his religious movement. While perhaps not entirely unproblematic, such an approach certainly provides a less arbitrary framework for the analysis of Qurʾānic eschatology than the four-period scheme of Weil and Nöldeke, particularly since, as David Cook observes, the Islamic exegetical tradition on which their model is based "was basically hostile" to the eschatological matrix of the Qurʾān, a point recently demonstrated by Uri Rubin.[188] The traditional parsing of the *sūra*s according to different periods of Muhammad's activity in Mecca or Medina can thus be disregarded.[189]

Nevertheless, as David Cook rightly notes, there is some degree of tension between the Qurʾān's frequent eschatological exclamations, with their vision of impending doom, and other material focused on defining the nature and structure of the early community, particularly in those *sūra*s traditionally associated with Medina. It is not entirely clear how to relate the differences of tone and content reflected in the communal and political orientation of many so-called "Medinan" *sūra*s and the more ecstatic, apocalyptic mood of much "Meccan" material. Yet any perceived tension between this imminent eschatological belief and a concern for maintaining order and stability in the community is certainly more imagined than real. As Donner explains, the Qurʾān seems to envision the collective judgment of the community of the Believers at the Hour, and accordingly, "one who believes that the End is nigh and that one's salvation in the afterlife depends on the righteous conduct of his community in the world would, for this very reason, pay meticulous attention to the details of social conduct in the community."[190] Likewise, comparison with Paul's writings in the New Testament, and most especially his correspondence with the church at Corinth, demonstrates that details of community order could remain a high priority even during the fleeting moments before the end of time.[191] Other writings from the New Testament similarly reflect the concurrence of imminent eschatological belief and concern for community structure and maintenance,[192] and thus there is no reason to assume that early Islamic belief in the world's imminent destruction would exclude attention to matters of community order and practice.

In any case, the traditional analysis of the Qur'ān's history, both Islamic and Western, seems largely correct in identifying the eschatological traditions of the "Meccan" *sūras* as in some sense primary: their unfulfilled forecast of imminent judgment and destruction makes their invention by Muhammad's later followers highly improbable. The "Medinan" *sūras*, by contrast, frequently presuppose an evolution of the religious movement to encompass a sizeable community, and it is not inconceivable that many of the traditions gathered in these *sūras* could postdate the life of Muhammad and reflect the development of the community beyond the period of his apocalyptic apostolate: likely candidates for later redaction would include the change of *qibla* and polemics against Jews and Christians, for instance. Such possibilities obviously require a more detailed analysis, however,[193] and for now it will suffice to focus on the eschatological substrate spread across the Qur'ān, whose warnings of the Hour's impending arrival appear even in many of the *sūras* traditionally connected with Medina.

The Qur'ān repeatedly proclaims the threatening immediacy of the eschatological Hour, and the directness with which it warns urgently against an impending doom demands that one take this imminent eschatology seriously on its own terms, rather than seeking to harmonize it with the later tradition, as many modern biographers have done. Belief in the swiftly approaching end of the world pervades the Qur'ān with a clarity that is unmistakable: indeed, according to the Qur'ān itself, the very subject of its revelation "is knowledge of the Hour; doubt not concerning it" (43:61).[194] "Nigh unto men has drawn [اقْتَرَبَ] their reckoning," warns the opening verse of *sūra* 21. Likewise, *sūra* 16 begins with the pronouncement that "God's Judgment is coming," or even more literally, "God's rule [أَمْر] has arrived": the Arabic verb أَتَى (*atā*) appears here in the past tense, according to M. A. S. Abdel Haleem, to emphasize the immediacy of its coming arrival.[195] Indeed, it is somewhat difficult not to hear in these verses echoes of the eschatological warning with which Jesus supposedly began his ministry, "the Kingdom of God is at hand."[196] Such similarities likewise appear in the Qur'ānic "parable of the two men" (18:31–44), whose resemblance to Jesus' parable of the rich fool is striking (Luke 12:13–21), not in the least for its dramatic representation of the Hour's imminence.[197] "The matter of the Hour is as a twinkling of the eye, or nearer" (16:79), warns the Qur'ān. The Day of Judgment is "imminent" (40:18: الْآزِفَة), or, as stated elsewhere with even greater force, "the

Imminent is imminent" (53:57: أَزِفَتِ الْآزِفَةُ).[198] The "Lord's chastisement"—or "judgment" or "the terror"—"is about to fall" (لَوَاقِعٌ) upon the world; "none denies its descending," and "there is none to avert it" (52:7–8; 51:6; 56:1–2). The chastisement is in fact near (78:40; see also 27:72, 36:49), and the Qur'ān promises that the punishments of hell and the bliss of paradise will be known soon "with the knowledge of certainty," that is, at first hand (102:3–5). The Qur'ān rebukes those who disregard its warning, threatening that they will soon behold the Hour and its punishments with their own eyes (19:75).

The Qur'ān also refers frequently to certain signs, particularly astronomical events, that will herald the Hour's arrival (for example, 45:17), and some of these, it would appear, had already occurred within recent memory.[199] *Sūra* 77 warns, "Surely that which you are promised is about to fall! When the stars shall be extinguished, when heaven shall be split, when the mountains shall be scattered and when the Messenger's time is set, to what day shall they be delayed? To the Day of Decision" (7–13). On this last day, "the sun shall be darkened" and "the stars shall be thrown down"; the Hour will come "when the heaven is split open" and "when the stars are scattered" (81:1–2; 82:1–2). It will arrive "upon the day when heaven spins dizzily" (52:9), "when the sight is dazed and the moon is eclipsed, and the sun and moon are brought together" (75:7–9). The Hour is likened to an earthquake (22:1), presumably the meaning of "the mountains shall be scattered": "when the Terror descends (and none denies its descending) . . . the earth shall be rocked and the mountains crumbled and become a dust scattered" (56:1–6). Many of these signs had already occurred "in the heavens and on the earth" and yet had gone unheeded (12:105). In response to those who disbelieve in the Hour and its immediacy, the Qur'ān often appeals to such signs. "The Hour has drawn nigh: the moon is split. Yet if they see a sign they turn away" (54:1–2; cf. 69:16). Presumably, as David Cook notes, this proclamation refers to some dramatic astronomical event(s) that had recently appeared, which the Qur'ān interprets as a portent of the impending Hour. According to Cook, this was perhaps the appearance of Haley's comet in 607, just before the beginnings of Muhammad's preaching in the traditional chronology, while Rubin suggests that the passage refers to the observance of a partial lunar eclipse that was "taken as a warning of the oncoming eschatological cataclysm."[200] Confronted with such skepticism, the Qur'ān asks, "Are they looking for aught but the Hour, that it shall come upon them suddenly? Already its tokens have come; so, when it has come to them, how shall they have their Reminder?" (47:20).

A number of other Qur'ānic passages respond similarly to disbelief concerning the Hour and its imminent appearance: when some in its audience doubt the Hour's impending arrival, the Qur'ān warns, "Soon they shall know! Already Our Word has preceded to Our servants. . . . So turn thou from them for a while, and see them; soon they shall see! What do they seek to hasten Our chastisement?" (37:170–79). Those desiring to continue in their sinful ways ask "When shall be the day of Resurrection?" (75:5–6), to which the Qur'ān responds, the Calamity is "nearer to thee and nearer, then nearer to thee and nearer!" (75:34–35), warning elsewhere, "No indeed; they soon shall know! Again, no indeed; they soon shall know!" (78:4–5). When the Hour comes, "it shall be as if, on the day they see it, they have tarried for an evening, or its forenoon" (79:46): "leave them to eat, and to take their joy, and to be bemused by hope; certainly they will soon know!" (15:3). In the face of such doubts the Qur'ān counsels the faithful "be thou patient with a sweet patience; behold they see it as far off; but We see it is nigh" (70:5–7). The Hour will come suddenly upon the unbelievers and "seize them while they are yet disputing" (36:49).

Although the Qur'ān so insistently proclaims the Hour's looming immediacy, it nonetheless refuses to specify exactly when it will arrive. When the unbelievers seek to know the precise moment of the End's arrival, the Qur'ān occasionally responds that knowledge of the Hour lies with God alone (7:187; cf. 31:34, 41:47, 43:85). Such sentiments need not, however, signal waning confidence in the Hour's imminence: even if God alone knows the precise moment, the Final Judgment still lies threateningly near. Although "the knowledge is with God," says the Qur'ān, "assuredly you will soon know who is in manifest error" (67:26–29; cf. 33:63, 79:44–46). Jesus, for example, appears to have similarly preached that the Kingdom of God was at hand but that the precise moment of its arrival was known to the Father alone (for example, Matt. 24:32–25:12).[201] Nevertheless, these statements could possibly reflect an effort by the early community, or even Muhammad himself, to soften the impact of the Hour's continued delay. Several other passages in the Qur'ān may also indicate such a redactional tendency. For instance, even though the Hour is imminent, the Qur'ān reminds its audience that a day for God is one thousand years (22:47; cf. 32:5), or fifty thousand years according to an alternative reckoning (70:4). This formula would appear to borrow a strategy from the Christian tradition, explaining the end's unforeseen deferral through an appeal to the unfathomable differences between celestial and terrestrial time (cf. 2 Pet. 3:8, referring to Ps. 90:4).

Nevertheless, in both instances, despite such horological differences, the Hour's impending arrival is once again underscored as something threateningly close: "they see it as if far off, but We see it is nigh" (70:6–7; cf. 22:55).

A handful of other passages, however, express some slight hesitance regarding the Hour's proximity, softening its immediacy by introducing a note of uncertainty while still maintaining a strong sense of urgency. "It is possible [عسى أن] that it may be nigh," although when it comes "you will think you have tarried but a little" (17:51–52). Indeed, "it may be [عسى أن] that riding behind you already is some part of that which you seek to hasten on" (27:72). Elsewhere the Qur'ān warns somewhat more cautiously that while God alone knows when the Hour will descend, "Haply [لَعَلّ] the Hour is nigh" (33:63; cf. 42:17). Yet while various other passages appear to encourage continued patience in the face of unanticipated delay (for example, 11:8, 40:77), only in one instance does the Qur'ān suggest the possibility that the Hour's arrival may in fact not be so immediate. Despite the heated warnings of the Hour's imminence scattered across the Qur'ān, a single passage equivocates, confessing, "I do not know whether that which you are promised is nigh, or whether my Lord will appoint it for a space" (72:25).

As already noted, Western scholars have often invited readers to find in these differing shades of urgency evidence of a progression in Muhammad's teaching, as his thoughts concerning the *eschaton* evolved to meet changing circumstances.[202] This interpretation, which certainly is a possibility, is bolstered by the faith that many scholars place in the reconstructed chronology of the Qur'ān's *sūras*, as well as in the traditional biographies of Muhammad (or at least their historical core). Yet even if one analyzes the traditions above according to Nöldeke's influential division of the Qur'ānic *sūras*, it is in fact difficult to discern such a pattern: imminent eschatology maintains a presence (albeit somewhat diminished) in the "Medinan" material, while many of those passages expressing some hesitancy about the Hour's immediacy actually belong to the so-called "Meccan" periods. If, however, one were to abandon Nöldeke's framework, the validity of which is rather dubious in any case, it becomes even more difficult to impute any such ordered theological development to Muhammad's teachings on eschatology. No less of a problem is the dogmatic belief in Muhammad's authorship of the Qur'ānic *textus receptus* that has (with few exceptions) gripped the Western study of early Islam for the past century and a half.[203] The interpretive consequences of this tenet offer a particularly illustrative example of Michel Foucault's "author function": assignment of the complete text to Muhammad affords a locus for the construction of unity and coherence out of the Qur'ān's rather diverse assemblage of a wide range of textual material and traditions.[204] Muhammad's life and personality become a site allowing for a kind of hermeneutic closure of the text: his biography presents a metanarrative within which to fix its contents and provide them a rational ordering. In the case of eschatology, we are invited to conceive of a "rational and practical" man, whose pragmatism leads him to experiment for a time with eschatological preaching, in hopes that it would bring the Meccans' conversion, but when he finally achieves success in Medina, any concern for divine judgment "passes into the realm of assured dogma in Muhammad's mind," enabling him to focus more completely on his real mission of social reform.

Yet as much as Bell (and Watt) in responding to Casanova asks for consideration of the possibility that changes "must have occurred in Muḥammad's attitudes through twenty years of ever-changing circumstances,"[205] one certainly would be justified (as was Casanova) in turning the question around to ask what changes must have been effected within the early Islamic community in the face of its ever-changing circumstances. Over the course of sixty years (or even just twenty) of rapidly changing social and political conditions, it hardly stretches the imagination to envision significant shifts in the early Islamic community's worldview, particularly in light of the eschatologically charged milieu signaled by the Qur'ān. Nevertheless, as many scholars have noted, it is exceptionally difficult to gauge any conceptual or theological developments within the earliest community or their potential impact on the transmission of sacred tradition, particularly when faced with the extreme paucity of evidence for primitive Islam.[206] Any such reconstructions must of necessity be somewhat hypothetical. But this qualification does not concede any ground to more traditional approaches that would accept more or less at face value the salvation history fashioned by the later Islamic tradition. Studies assuming the validity of this framework are no less conjectural; they simply draw their conjecture from the mythology of origins constructed by the Islamic tradition itself instead of attempting an exogenous critique. As suggested already above, methods from the study of the New Testament, which has faced its own similar, albeit somewhat less bleak, crisis of evidence, can provide possible models for investigating the impact of the early community on the formation of Islamic scripture. Given the centrality of eschatology to Jesus' message as witnessed by the gospels, this topic and its reception within the early Christian communities have been particularly well studied. Thus, in this instance, as well as in others presumably, comparison with the evidence from and approaches to earliest Christianity can both guide and ground efforts to find a path through the relatively uncharted territory of early Islamic religious history.

Although numerous studies have dealt with the subject of eschatology in earliest Christianity, E. P. Sanders's treatment of the issue stands out as one of the best and most authoritative.[207] The evidence that Sanders must confront is both more complex and ample than is the case with early Islam, but his analysis presents an excellent model for assessing similar traditions within the Qur'ān. For instance, Sanders has the advantage of consulting multiple contemporary sources from the early Christian movement, an opportunity denied to the student of early Islam in the current state of our evidence. Likewise, he must examine the nuances of the concept of "the Kingdom of God" as witnessed both in early Christian literature and within the context of Judaism of the Second Temple period: different traditions describe the Kingdom as belonging to either the future or the present, and as having its location either on earth or in heaven. Consequently, Sanders parses the early Christian traditions about the Kingdom according to both time and location, with the aim of discerning which conception(s) most probably belonged to Jesus and his earliest followers and which most likely arose within the early Christian community. Through a careful analysis, Sanders persuasively argues that Jesus taught the Kingdom of God's imminent arrival, seemingly within the lifetime of his initial followers, and a similar approach to the Qur'ān and the early Islamic tradition reveals Muhammad also as an eschatological prophet who appears to have expected the Hour's immediate advent, perhaps even within his own lifetime.

Despite the somewhat more meager evidence for the origins of Islam, the Qur'ān itself is, as we have seen, rich in eschatological traditions. Innumerable passages from the Qur'ān relate eschatological content of a general nature, describing the events of the last day or the punishments and rewards awaiting the wicked and the just, for example. And while these traditions are not directly relevant to the question of the Hour's imminence, the Qur'ān's saturation with eschatological traditions is itself an important sign of eschatology's axial position within earliest Islam. As for those passages giving some time frame for the Hour's arrival, the overwhelming majority warn urgently that it should be expected any moment in the immediate future. A single passage indicates that this eschatological event has in fact already come (أَتَى), while numerous others repeatedly describe it as near (قَرِيبًا) or imminent (الْآزِفَةُ) or about to fall (لَوَاقِعٌ). Some of these traditions respond to doubts from the Qur'ān's audience, in the face of which the Qur'ān responds with renewed insistence on the Hour's imminence. Another group of passages identifies signs that will herald the Hour's arrival, and several among these traditions report that some of the signs had recently occurred. Two passages respond to questions about the Hour's arrival by explaining that a day to God is either as a thousand years or fifty thousand years to humankind, although both persist in maintaining the Hour's immediate proximity. Several passages reserve precise knowledge of the Hour's arrival to God alone, occasionally either in response to doubts or with reassurance of its propinquity. Only in four instances does the Qur'ān introduce any measure of uncertainty by suggesting that the Hour is "perhaps" near (عَسَى أَنْ or لَعَلَّ), while a single passage allows that the Hour may in fact not be near but postponed to some indefinite time.

As with the Kingdom sayings attributed to Jesus, there is some measure of diversity here; nevertheless, it is possible to sort through the different perspectives and identify what in all likelihood is the primitive element. First, as Sanders observes of the Jesus traditions, one outlook clearly predominates.[208] The preponderance of this evidence overwhelmingly speaks to belief in a cataclysmic eschatological event looming just on the horizon, presumably expected within the lifetime of Muhammad and his audience. The response of the unbelievers as portrayed in the Qur'ān particularly suggests that the context in which the Hour had been preached led them to conclude that they would soon witness the Hour's arrival themselves; indeed, the Qur'ān itself warns its opponents that they in fact will soon behold the Hour and its punishments with their own eyes (for example, 19:75; 37:170–79; 102:3–5). It is quite unlikely that later redaction of the Qur'ān would be responsible for this imminent eschatology, inasmuch as the promise of the Hour's prompt arrival within such a narrow time frame would have been contradicted by the subsequent community's experience of its delay. Thus, the criterion of dissimilarity (that is, dissimilarity with the lived experience of the early community) speaks very highly for the antiquity if not authenticity of this perspective: although strong eschatological elements persisted in early Islam beyond Muhammad's death, it seems rather improbable that the later tradition would insert traditions into the Qur'ān wrongly predicting the Hour's appearance in the immediate future, as scholars have similarly concluded with respect to Jesus.[209]

Also like the Jesus traditions, however, the Qur'ān preserves a minority view that the *eschaton* has in some sense already arrived. *Sūra* 16 opens rather oddly with the announcement that God's "rule" or "command" has in fact come, joined with a warning not to seek to hasten it. Similarly, other passages report that the portents of its arrival have already begun to appear (12:105;

47:20; 54:1). Perhaps these proclamations are best understood in a manner analogous to Sanders's explanation of comparable sayings from the Jesus traditions. It may well be that Muhammad saw the beginnings of "God's rule" as being made manifest in his own ministry, as Sanders suggests of Jesus.[210] Several of the *ḥadīth* discussed below that identify Muhammad's own appearance as concomitant with the Hour's arrival would appear to confirm this interpretation. Or, alternatively, it could be that *sūra* 16 merely wishes to emphasize the *eschaton*'s proximity—that it had come near. In any case, such passages are not at all inconsistent with the majority tradition locating the Hour in the immediate future.

On several occasions, however, the Qur'ān remarks that "knowledge of the Hour" belongs to God alone, generally in response to its critics who seem to have expected it much sooner. Western scholars have occasionally appealed to such traditions as providing evidence that Muhammad and the Qur'ān did not in fact expect or announce the Hour's arrival within the lifetime of the immediate audience.[211] One has the sense, however, that some scholars, by emphasizing these few passages, are looking for a way to avoid the uncomfortable conclusion that the Qur'ān and, by consequence, Muhammad inaccurately forecast the imminent judgment and destruction of the world, a tendency that Sanders (as well as Ehrman) has also observed in the work of many New Testament scholars.[212] Nevertheless, as noted above, there is no reason why such statements should be seen as contradictory to imminent eschatological belief. To the contrary, they complement rather well the Qur'ān's emphasis on the sudden and unexpected arrival of the Hour. These verses, if authentic, indicate nothing more than that Muhammad did not specify a precise moment in the immediate future when the Hour would arrive: just because the exact timing of the Hour was known to God alone does not mean that Muhammad saw it as anything other than threateningly imminent.[213]

Such sentiments could also, however, serve apologetic interests when the Hour in fact did not arrive as foretold: one finds similar circumstances in the earliest surviving Christian document, Paul's first letter to the Thessalonians, written just some twenty years after the death of Jesus. Already by this time, delay in the fulfillment of Jesus' promises about the Kingdom had begun to arouse serious concerns within the Christian communities, and Paul attempts to put such doubts to rest with confident assurances that "the day of the Lord will come like a thief in the night," even though its exact timing is unknown.[214] One can well imagine similar appeals to uncertain knowledge of the Hour's timing by the earliest Muslims, and it is not impossible that this motive could also underlie the appearance of Qur'ānic verses expressing similar sentiments. Yet more importantly, Paul's letters and the New Testament as a whole call attention to how in the face of eschatological disappointment a religious community could begin to reconfigure its sacred history and its vision of the future to meet these new circumstances. As Sanders notes, already from this very early stage in their history, the Christians had begun to adjust their traditions to comport with the problem that Jesus (and ultimately Paul as well) was wrong in predicting that the *eschaton* was imminent: often even the most minor adjustments could put a new eschatological spin on a tradition.[215] It would be altogether surprising if something similar did not occur within formative Islam.

Those verses invoking the vast difference between divine and human time are quite possibly the result of a similar apologetic impulse. While such verses do not directly contradict the Qur'ān's imminent eschatology, the prefigurative Christian use of this tradition to explain the delay of the *parousia* suggests a potential precedent for imitation.[216] Although each passage occurs in the immediate context of proclamations announcing the Hour's proximity, it could be that these statements are insertions designed, as even Bell suggests, "to obviate the difficulty of the delay in the coming event."[217] Likewise, the four verses sounding a faint note of uncertainty about the Hour's imminence are probably the result of minor interpolations. Their hedging stands in marked contrast to the rest of the Qur'ān, which vigorously proclaims the Hour's immediacy, inviting the possibility that in their current form these verses have drifted somewhat from the original message. One could readily imagine how in the course of transmission (particularly oral transmission) a word or two could easily slip into the text, shifting its meaning slightly to soften the Qur'ān's otherwise rigorous forecast of impending doom, which was increasingly confuted by experience of the Hour's unexpected delay. Excising just a word or two (either عَسَىٰ أَن or لَعَلَّ) from these passages in no way disturbs the sense of the broader context in which they appear, but, to the contrary, in each case their removal potentially improves the text by bringing it more into conformity with statements about the Hour found elsewhere in the Qur'ān.[218] Thus, there is the very real possibility that such minor insertions may have been made during the course of transmission, transforming what were perhaps originally proclamations warning of the Hour's imminence into more guarded statements that convey a relative uncertainty. Other passages forecasting the divine judgment's immediate proximity may have been similarly softened by joining them with traditions that relate temporal punishments (*Straflegende*) directed against specific individuals and nations: such intertextual positioning effectively recasts these warnings before the end of time so that they might instead suggest God's intra-historical punishments of the unrighteous. Nevertheless, Rubin convincingly argues that these warnings of earthly calamities and punishments should instead be understood as "complementary to the eschatological warnings," serving as portents of the oncoming judgment.[219]

Finally, the single verse expressing ignorance of whether "that which you are promised is nigh, or whether my Lord will appoint it for a space" almost certainly reflects a later addition. The notion is so out of step with the Qur'ān's otherwise confident declaration that judgment and the Hour are at hand that this formulation must have originated within the early Islamic community as it struggled to make sense of the Hour's continued deferral. Such alterations are not so much a matter of "forgery," however, as some more traditional scholars would have it. As the early Islamic believers remembered the words of the Qur'ān and transmitted them, they were confident both in the absolute truth of the words that had been revealed and in the prophet who revealed them. Thus, if the Hour was increasingly delayed beyond the lifetime of Muhammad and his original audience, then his followers would have to discover a more conditional sense within the eschatological traditions of the Qur'ān. The result was then not some sort of deliberate falsification, but rather a gradual, perhaps even subconscious, transformation to effect the harmonization of revealed truth with the dissonant experience of the Hour's postponement.

In sum, the Qur'ān affords considerable evidence that imminent eschatology stood as one of the primary tenets of earliest Islam. Most likely this belief in impending divine judgment and destruction goes back to Muhammad himself, whom we may rightly characterize as an eschatological prophet. Like many other religious visionaries before him, including Jesus in particular, Muhammad seems to have preached that the end of time had arrived, and he and his followers expected the *eschaton* to break in at any moment bringing history to a close, seemingly within their own lifetime. The earliest Muslims, as viewed through the Qur'ān, believed themselves to be living in the last days, and it seems likely that neither they nor Muhammad expected to die before the Hour's arrival. The final point, admittedly, is not explicit in the Qur'ān, although it frequently seems implicit, and circumstantial evidence, such as Muhammad's apparent failure to plan for his succession, certainly suggests this conclusion (so Donner and Ayoub observe), as do certain traditions from the *ḥadīth*, to be discussed momentarily. Nevertheless, it is quite clear that the earliest recoverable layer of the Islamic tradition is suffused with imminent eschatological belief similar in nature to that expressed by Jesus and the early Christian movement.

It would of course be helpful to have a broader understanding of the *religionsgeschichtliche* context in which Islam first arose in order to better understand the nature of early Islamic eschatology, but unfortunately we have no clear Islamic counterpart to Qumran, Josephus, or John the Baptist to provide such a backdrop. Despite the confidence that many modern scholars have placed in the traditional Islamic accounts of the *jāhiliyya*, that is, the historical backdrop of Muhammad's prophetic activities, these are far too late and tendentious to be of any historical use, leaving the nature of the religious milieu that produced the Qur'ān and Muhammad very much open to question.[220] One can merely point to the proliferation of apocalyptic literature and eschatological expectation in the seventh-century Near East as a general background that can at least partly explain the emergence of Muhammad's eschatological movement in this time and place.[221] Equally lacking for a more complete understanding of early Islamic eschatology and its development is something comparable to the broad spectrum of independent sources that survive from first-century Christianity. The polyphony of early Christian literature, limited as it is, affords the possibility of examining how individual traditions were appropriated by different sources; such evidence not only can verify the antiquity of certain traditions (that is, the criterion of multiple independent attestation) but also can disclose the redactional tendencies of the sources preserving them (that is, redaction criticism). Perhaps the Qur'ān's frequent repetitiveness will someday be mined for evidence of independent reception and redaction of certain traditions, particularly in light of Wansbrough's promising suggestion that these redundancies likely signal the existence of earlier collections of traditions that have been merged according to very conservative editorial principles, a conservatism determined by the authority that these proto-collections had already acquired in various communities.[222] Nevertheless, given the peculiar nature of the Qur'ān's allusive style and the general lack of context for its prophetic *logia*, such an approach is unlikely to yield a framework for the study of earliest Islam comparable to what has been achieved in early Christian studies.

Lacking such navigational beacons to guide an analysis of the earliest Islamic traditions, one must turn instead to the most promising alternatives, the prophetic traditions of the *ḥadīth* and the witness of seventh-century

Near Eastern literature to the nature of emerging Islam. While the latter will come more into focus again in the following chapter, the *ḥadīth* are quite rich in eschatological traditions, some of which relate directly to the current question of the Hour's imminence. The traditions of the *ḥadīth* are admittedly rather problematic historical sources in their own right, since, as already noted, they were late in forming and subject to forgery on a massive scale. Nevertheless, it is often possible to identify very early traditions among the *ḥadīth* not so much through analysis of an extensive network of transmission, an approach discussed in the previous chapter, but instead using the somewhat less arcane methods of *matn* analysis advanced particularly by Ignác Goldziher and Joseph Schacht.[223] In contrast to *isnād* criticism, *matn* analysis looks to the content of the tradition itself for signs of the historical context in which it was produced. Among the chief principles of *matn* criticism is that material contradicting key principles of the later tradition or that casts Muhammad or the early community in an unfavorable light is likely to be very early or even authentic.[224]

The logic here is identical to the so-called criterion of dissimilarity or embarrassment from the study of the historical Jesus. Traditions that are embarrassing or contradictory to established beliefs and practices are unlikely to have been invented in a setting where their content would have created dissonance. Instead, it is much more likely that such reports transmit older material that has been preserved against the later tradition's interest, perhaps only in a handful of minor sources, on account of their antiquity. *Ḥadīth* conveying Muhammad's predictions of an imminent end to the world certainly belong in this category, and there are in fact numerous reports, some more widely attested than others, indicating that Muhammad had promised his followers that the Hour would indeed arrive very soon. Such material is highly unlikely to be the invention of the later tradition, as many others have noted, and it offers important confirmation of the Qur'ān's imminent eschatology. Moreover, such reports of continued eschatological expectation within the early Islamic community belie the efforts of some modern interpreters to confine imminent eschatology to a specific interval of Muhammad's Meccan period. These *ḥadīth* suggest instead a sustained eschatological trajectory extending beyond Muhammad's lifetime and into the early Islamic community. Consequently, it is to these *ḥadīth* that we now turn for further evidence revealing earliest Islam as an eschatological movement driven by an apparent belief in the Hour's imminent arrival.

"He Has Been Sent with the Hour": Imminent Eschatology in the Early Islamic Tradition

Casanova was the first, it seems, to draw attention to the importance of various eschatological traditions among the *ḥadīth* that appear to confirm Muhammad's proclamation of imminent judgment and destruction as reflected in the Qur'ān. Despite David Cook's somewhat surprising criticism of Casanova's hypothesis on the basis that he "relies on the conjunction of the Qur'ān and *ḥadīth* to prove his point," to the contrary, their correlation is one of the main strengths of Casanova's proposal.[225] It is extremely difficult to account for the existence of these eschatological traditions unless Muhammad and his earliest followers actually anticipated the Hour's appearance in the near future, an expectation that the later tradition had to explain and adjust in light of its failed arrival. In recent years, several scholars have revived Casanova's investigation of such eschatological *ḥadīth*, generally with impressive results that are supportive of his initial observations. There is in fact strong evidence in the *ḥadīth* for primitive belief in the Hour's imminent advent, and this evidence forms an important compliment to Qur'ānic proclamations about the Hour that almost certainly derives from Muhammad himself and his earliest followers.

Even with the limited number of texts available to him at the turn of the twentieth century, Casanova was able to discover a number of *ḥadīth* that depict Muhammad as promising his followers that his ministry among them was intrinsically linked to the Hour's imminent arrival. A passage from Ibn Sa'd's *Ṭabaqāt*, which serves as one of two epigrams opening Casanova's study, says of Muhammad that "he has been sent with the Hour, in order to avert you from a severe punishment."[226] Casanova additionally notes another similar tradition, from a rather late source, Maqrīzī's *History of Egypt* (which he had translated), reporting that Muhammad had pronounced, "My coming and that of the Hour are concomitant; indeed, the latter almost arrived before me."[227] More recently, however, Meir Kister and Suliman Bashear have located this tradition in a number of other sources, where it often is coupled with Muhammad's statement that he had been "sent on the breath of the Hour."[228] The idea that Muhammad's mission was itself virtually simultaneous with the Hour's arrival also found expression in the widely circulated *ḥadīth* of the "two fingers." According to this tradition, as cited by Ibn Ḥanbal for instance, Muhammad said to the faithful, "'The hour has come upon you; I have been sent with the Hour like this,' and he showed them his two fingers, the index finger and the middle finger," joining them together to illustrate their coincidence.[229] Casanova cites this tradition from a number of important sources, to which Bashear adds quite a few more, the most authoritative and widely disseminated perhaps being Muslim's *Ṣaḥīḥ*. As Bashear further notes, the two fingers *ḥadīth* was often combined with Muhammad's statements that he had been "sent on the breath of the Hour" and that the Hour was so close that it had nearly outstripped his own arrival.[230]

The two fingers tradition is so widely attested that one could probably construct an impressive *isnād* bundle diagramming its transmission in the manner that Juynboll, Motzki, and others have sought to authenticate early prophetic traditions. Yet in the case of this particular tradition, such a laborious undertaking seems rather unnecessary, inasmuch as the *matn* itself speaks rather strongly for the tradition's antiquity if not authenticity. It is extremely difficult to imagine someone from a later generation inventing this statement and placing it in Muhammad's mouth: only shortly after his death such melding of the Hour with Muhammad's mission would have already become quite dissonant with the reality of the Hour's delay. Casanova and Bashear both note the struggles encountered by the early interpretive tradition as it sought to make sense of these *ḥadīth* and their failed promise of the Hour's imminent arrival. Perhaps the most famous effort to reconcile the two fingers tradition with the Hour's delay occurs at the beginning of al-Ṭabarī's *History*, where he rather cleverly deploys this tradition in order to place his work within an extended version of Islam's eschatological calendar.[231] This he achieves by transforming these eschatological warnings of imminent doom into an orderly model of historical periodization that frames his historical narrative. Al-Ṭabarī here concludes that since the index finger is one-fourteenth shorter than the middle finger, and the total length of the world's existence is known to be seven thousand years, Muhammad clearly meant to signal that the Hour would arrive five hundred years after him, thus leaving another two hundred years or so beyond al-Ṭabarī before the world would come to an end.

In the same context, al-Ṭabarī also identifies a second eschatological tradition that he employs to similar effect. According to this report, Muhammad once addressed his followers at a time "when the sun had almost set and only a small sliver of it remained visible," and he explained to them that "as compared to what remains of our world, that which has passed is like what remains of this day as compared to what has passed of it, and you will see only a little (more) of the sun."[232] The eschatological immediacy of this *ḥadīth* is rather clear, and once again it seems quite unlikely that such a prediction would have been ascribed to Muhammad very long after his death. Yet here al-Ṭabarī deploys a similar hermeneutic strategy that enables him again to push the Hour into the future. When Muhammad spoke these words, according to al-Ṭabarī, the day was half past, and since a day with God is as a thousand years, the Hour's advent could be expected five hundred years after the time when Muhammad spoke. In this way, what was presumably a very early expression of Islamic belief in the Hour's immediacy could be reconciled with the centuries that had elapsed between Muhammad's warnings and al-Ṭabarī himself. By reinterpreting the tradition's "small sliver" of the sun as somehow the equivalent of midday, al-Ṭabarī postpones the Hour into a distant future.

Casanova additionally notes two eschatological *ḥadīth* that had already been signaled in Sprenger's earlier study, both of which Bashear has since shown to have circulated widely in a number of important early collections.[233] In the first of these traditions, Muhammad is questioned as to when the Hour will arrive, and he responds by identifying the youngest man present and saying, "If this young man lives, the Hour will arrive before he reaches old age."[234] Clearly this *ḥadīth* also signals a primitive belief in the impending *eschaton*, whose arrival Muhammad seems to have promised within the generation of his initial followers, if not even sooner: indeed, the forecast is strikingly reminiscent of Jesus' similar promise to his followers that "this generation will not pass away" before the eschatological appearance of the Son of Man and the Kingdom of God (Matt. 16:28, 24:34 et par.). If, however, Muhammad preached the Hour's arrival before his own death, as some have thought, one could see this *ḥadīth* perhaps as an early effort to mitigate the Hour's unexpected delay, by extending the period of its anticipated arrival to encompass the lifespan of those who had first followed Muhammad. In either case, this *ḥadīth* clearly indicates a primitive belief in the Hour's imminent arrival sometime within the lifetime of Muhammad's initial followers. For the same reason that similar remarks can be confidently assigned to Jesus (in particular, their unmitigated inaccuracy), we must also assume the great antiquity, if not even authenticity, of Muhammad's prophetic promise.[235] Sprenger's second tradition attributes to Muhammad the statement that "at the end of one-hundred years there will be no one alive on the earth."[236] Although Casanova presents this tradition as further evidence of imminent eschatology in early Islam, and it certainly reflects as much, Bashear perhaps more accurately interprets this tradition as an early corrective aimed at extending the Hour's window even further, beyond Muhammad and the initial generation. Even so, the *ḥadīth* almost certainly belongs to the first Islamic century, where it attests to a persistent presence of imminent eschatological belief among the second generation of believers. In both cases, Bashear draws attention to the problems that later interpreters faced in confronting these traditions, with their seemingly clear predictions of the Hour's imminent arrival, noting also the different strategies employed to harmonize these failed predictions with the Hour's continued delay.

Casanova equally identifies a number of early biographical traditions that seem to indicate belief in the impending end of the world. Ibn Hishām, for instance, reports an anecdote concerning a Himyarite king that refers to Muhammad as the prophet who will appear "at the end of time."[237] Likewise, according to the Baḥīrā legend Muhammad is foretold as the prophet who will come "at the end of time."[238] Numerous other traditions, Casanova notes, signify Muhammad as the "prophet of the end of time," a title that certainly would appear to have originated within a context of imminent eschatological expectation.[239] Altogether, Casanova presents a fairly compelling assemblage of traditions (particularly given the somewhat limited sources at his disposal) that appear to have originated out of the eschatological hopes of the earliest community, and these generally confirm the Qur'ān's warnings against the Hour's impending doom. Nevertheless, Casanova's important insights from the tradition unfortunately have long been overlooked by scholars favoring the more rational and practical prophet of Bell and Watt over the eschatological enthusiast suggested by these *ḥadīth*.

Not until the early 1960s did the idea of Muhammad as an eschatological prophet resurface, in an important and compelling article by Meir Kister on early traditions about the construction of Medina's first mosque. Kister's brief study unearths an unusual *ḥadīth*, which despite its absence from the canonical collections survives in a number of minor collections as part of "a large body of early traditions omitted by later collectors."[240] By its very nature this particular *ḥadīth* seems to belong to the earliest traditions of Islam: as Kister notes, its pronounced eschatological urgency reflects a *Sitz im Leben* where belief in the Hour's imminence was paramount. The basic tradition describes efforts to build the first mosque in Medina, and as construction was underway, Muhammad ordered the workers, "Nay, a booth like the booth of Moses: *thumān* and wood, because the affair [*al-amr*] will happen sooner than that."[241] The apparent meaning of this directive, which survives in a number of sources, perhaps most notably Ibn Sa'd's *Ṭabaqāt*,[242] is that the builders were instructed not to bother with constructing a proper roof for the mosque, since the end was close at hand. Instead they were enjoined "to build the mosque in a provisional way, like the booth of Moses," apparently with a roof of thatch, because "God's command" would soon arrive, putting an end to life in general and, consequently, worship as well.[243] The tradition's omission from many standard collections is readily understandable, as Kister observes: "the Day of Judgment did not come in the days of the Prophet and there was no reason to quote a tradition which stated clearly that the Prophet believed that the *sāʿa* [the Hour] would happen in his own lifetime."[244] Moreover, it is extremely unlikely that believers in later generations would invent such a tradition and ascribe it to Muhammad, since it was so patently contradicted by the passing of time: the most probable explanation is that the tradition originated from Muhammad's own eschatological teaching. Thus, Kister concludes that this *ḥadīth* accurately reflects Muhammad's eschatological perspective even during the Medinan period, when he continued to expect the Hour's imminent arrival, seemingly before his own death.[245]

Following another lapse of several decades, Bashear brought renewed focus to the eschatological traditions of early Islam, followed more recently by David Cook, and both have exhumed a number of additional *ḥadīth* that witness to a primitive belief in the Hour's immediate arrival. While Bashear's article picks up very much where Casanova's study left off, in expanding considerably on Casanova's earlier references, Bashear also signals several new *ḥadīth* that reveal the eschatological context in which Islam was born. For instance, one tradition reports that Muhammad described himself in regard to the Hour as "somebody sent to his people as a watchman. Seeing a sudden swift raid already on the move and worrying that he would be surpassed by it, he started to wave his shirt/sword to his people."[246] Muhammad then continues to explain, as above, that the Hour had nearly outstripped his own arrival. Other traditions have Muhammad announcing that he "was sent in the presence of the Hour,"[247] or asking, "How would I rest happily while [knowing that] the man with the horn has taken it to his mouth waiting for the order to blow?"[248] Likewise, David Cook uncovers a tradition in which Muhammad promises his followers that some of them will live to see the Dajjāl (the Antichrist), again recalling Jesus' similar assurance to his followers (Matt. 16:28, 24:34): "there has been no prophet after Noah who has not warned his audience of the Dajjāl, and I (Muhammad) warn you of him as well. The Messenger of God described him to us and said: 'Some of those who see me or hear my words will live to see him.'"[249] Although other traditions explicitly state that people of Muhammad's generation would not live to see the Antichrist, these are almost certainly correctives to the earlier tradition, and as Cook notes, this promise that the Dajjāl and thus the Hour would appear within the lifetime of those who had followed Muhammad must belong to the very earliest traditions of Islam.[250] While many of these eschatological *ḥadīth* appear in only a handful of sources, their exclusion from the canonical collections is again quite understandable, and their survival at the margins of the tradition affords further evidence of primitive Islam's eschatological matrix. It is rather improbable that later generations would have dreamed up such pronouncements and placed them in Muhammad's mouth, when they were so plainly contradicted by the flow of history; to the contrary, the persistence of traditions ascribing to Muhammad a belief in the Hour's imminent arrival, despite their manifest inaccuracy, attests to the prominence of this idea within earliest Islam, confirming the evidence of the Qur'ān.

Bashear and Cook equally note that the early Islamic tradition was quick in adjusting expectations of the Hour's arrival to meet the circumstances of its prolonged delay, all the while keeping its appearance just on the horizon and continuing to anticipate its imminent advent. The narrow time frame initially envisioned by the Qur'ān and certain ancient *ḥadīth* could be readily expanded to encompass another generation or two as needed, and the fact that the early Islamic tradition appears to have continually made such minor adjustments, rather than abandoning belief in the Hour's proximity altogether, is yet another sign that imminent eschatology was central to primitive Islam. For example, numerous eschatological predictions survive in Islamic religious literature promising the Hour's arrival before the end of the first Islamic century. Casanova knew the tradition that no one would remain alive on the face of the earth at the end of one hundred years, as already noted, and both Bashear and Cook have drawn attention to a number of other traditions promising the Hour's arrival before the completion of a century.[251] Ultimately, these traditions too would require adjusting, and Bashear has charted the various hermeneutic strategies devised to accommodate both these early *ḥadīth* and the Qur'ān itself to the *eschaton*'s continued deferral. The interpretive work required to reconcile the Qur'ān with the Hour's delay is itself compelling testimony to the eschatological promise rooted in Islamic scripture.[252] Yet as various deadlines passed, new predictions of the Hour's approaching arrival arose, continuing to foretell its imminent appearance.[253] Undoubtedly much more research remains to be done on early Islamic eschatology, and although these studies have perhaps only scratched the surface, their findings are highly significant, revealing a fairly consistent pattern.

The persistence of imminent eschatology across the first Islamic century and beyond reveals this notion as embedded in the very fabric of formative Islam, thus confirming the Qur'ān's witness to a religious movement of eschatological expectation that began under Muhammad's prophetic leadership.

Muhammad's Death and the Hour's Delay: A Qur'ānic Intervention

According to Casanova's eschatological reconstruction of Islamic origins, Muhammad and his earliest followers not only expected that the world would come to an end very soon but that the Hour would arrive even before Muhammad's own death, a hypothesis more recently favored by both Donner and Ayoub, as noted above. Certainly the Qur'ān expresses an immediacy concerning the Hour that anticipates its arrival at any moment, quite possibly overtaking Muhammad and his followers before their natural deaths. Moreover, as both Donner and Ayoub observe, Muhammad's apparent failure to designate a clear successor and the Qur'ān's silence regarding such matters as political succession are "most cogently explained" by a primitive Islamic belief that the world would come to an end before such issues could arise: in light of the world's imminent judgment and destruction, "worrying about long-term leadership . . . was simply irrelevant."[254] It is somewhat hard to dispute such logic. If indeed Muhammad was the rational and pragmatic social reformer imagined by Bell and Watt and so many others following in their wake, it is extremely difficult to comprehend the confusion and disorder that ensued after Muhammad's death. Surely such a great social organizer who aimed at building a better society for future generations would have given more thought to how this community was to be led in his absence, if in fact he expected it to survive beyond his own lifespan. Yet the image of early Islam that emerges from the Qur'ān and these early *ḥadīth* suggests to the contrary that Muhammad and his followers believed themselves to be living on the remote edge of history, which was about to come to a close at any moment. While the Qur'ān fails to specify precisely when the Hour is to arrive, its extreme proximity is readily apparent, and judging from the Qur'ān's excited eschatological pronouncements, it seems very likely that Muhammad did not in fact expect his community of followers to outlast him but rather that the end would come before the issue of succession could arise.

The main problem with this hypothesis, however, is that in a single instance the Qur'ān indicates explicitly that Muhammad would someday die, in *sūra* 3:144: "Muhammad is naught but a Messenger; Messengers have passed away before him. Why, if he should die or is slain, will you turn about on your heels? If any man should turn about on his heels, he will not harm God in any way; and God will recompense the thankful." The gist of this is clear: as a Messenger himself, Muhammad will, like other Messengers before him, eventually die. Such a direct Qur'ānic forecast of Muhammad's death would seem to preclude any possibility that Muhammad and his followers might have believed that he would not die before the Hour's arrival. Is this passage then evidence that Muhammad himself foretold his own demise (in the third person?), meaning that he was fully aware not only of the fact that he would ultimately die but also that his community would require a successor to take his place as its leader (an event for which he seemingly failed to plan)?

While this Qur'ānic verse could appear to settle the question of whether Muhammad expected to die before the Hour's arrival rather decisively, the matter is actually not so easily resolved. The textual status of this passage is in fact very much open to question, and it is not at all clear that it was a part of "Muhammad's" Qur'ān. From almost the beginnings of Western research on the Qur'ān, scholars have raised the possibility that this verse is a later interpolation of the Qur'ānic text, and only the normative status of Nöldeke's opinions seems to have arrested this idea. The first investigator to identify signs of a textual problem with this passage was Antoine-Isaac Silvestre de Sacy, the founding father of Arabic philology in Europe. In reviewing the first volume of J. G. L. Kosegarten's *editio princeps* of al-Ṭabarī's *History*, Silvestre de Sacy reflects briefly on its report of 'Umar's agitated response to the news of Muhammad's death, an episode that provides rather interesting information regarding the status of this Qur'ānic verse. According to this tradition from Ibn Isḥāq's *Sīra*, transmitted by both al-Ṭabarī and Ibn Hishām, when 'Umar heard the news of Muhammad's passing, he forcefully denied that Muhammad had died, swearing, "By God he is not dead: he has gone to his Lord as Moses b. 'Imrān went and was hidden from his people for forty days, returning to them after it was said that he had died. By God, the apostle will return as Moses returned and will cut off the hands and feet of men who allege that the apostle is dead."[255] As Ibn Isḥāq relates, when Abū Bakr learned of this commotion, he came to the mosque, and after venerating Muhammad's remains he sought to restrain 'Umar, who nonetheless persisted in his ranting. Abū Bakr then addressed the crowd directly, hoping to defuse the disturbance that ʿUmar was creating, first by insisting on the reality of Muhammad's death, followed then by recitation of Qur'ān 3:144, which relates Muhammad's death. The throng apparently was quieted, although Ibn Isḥāq additionally and tellingly notes that "it was as though the people did not know that this verse had come down until Abū Bakr recited it that day. The people took it from him and it was (constantly) in their mouths."[256] This tradition is more than a little peculiar, as Silvestre de Sacy observes, and Ibn Isḥāq's report that no one had ever heard the verse before certainly suggests rather strongly that the verse was a late addition to the Qur'ānic text, whose inclusion required this elaborate literary device to justify its introduction.[257] In light of Abū Bakr's personal closeness to Muhammad, his sterling reputation, and his status within the early community, he would of course present a logical vehicle for such a textual addition, and placing the verse in his mouth would certainly be an effective means of quickly establishing its authenticity.

Not long after Silvestre de Sacy's initial remarks, Gustav Weil also proposed that Abū Bakr's Qur'ānic verse was most likely a later interpolation, first in his biography of Muhammad, and then in his groundbreaking *Historisch-kritische Einleitung in den Koran*.[258] In the latter work, as well as his *Geschichte der Chalifen*, Weil further suggests the possibility that Muhammad had allowed doubts about his mortality to arise among the faithful, prompting Weil to further question the authenticity of verses 3:185, 21:35, 29:57, and 39:30, all of which almost identically assert the notion that "every soul shall taste of death."[259] Yet before scholarly reflection on this unusual tradition and the questions that it raises about the integrity of the Qur'ān was allowed to mature, Nöldeke cut the discussion short, imposing his rather dogmatic and sweeping judgment that "der Koran enthält nur echte Stücke," a pronouncement that has continued to forestall historical critical analysis of the Qur'ānic traditions.[260] With respect to Qur'ān 3:144, Nöldeke rejects out of hand the suspicions previously raised by Silvestre de Sacy and Weil, basing his argument largely on a second version of the confrontation between ʿUmar and Abū Bakr preserved by al-Ṭabarī, but not by Ibn Hishām or Ibn Isḥāq. According to this alternate account, Abū Bakr initially cited Qur'ān 39:30–31,[261] followed then immediately by 3:144, prompting "some people from among the companions of Muḥammad" to affirm that they had never heard those verses before Abū Bakr spoke them on that day.[262] In commenting on this version, Nöldeke remarks that it is in fact perfectly reasonable to expect that these two passages, both authentic pronouncements of Muhammad in his view, would have been completely unfamiliar to ʿUmar and the others: taking the entire episode at face value, Nöldeke leans on his own dating of the Qurʾānic *sūras* to argue that not only were both verses over seven years old at the time but also that traditions dealing with such a grim subject as Muhammad's death were unlikely to have been recited very often.[263] Consequently, only very few people, such as Abū Bakr, would have had any knowledge of these verses, a rather odd conclusion that, if extended to many other passages of the Qurʾān, would invite some rather interesting questions about the nature of the Qurʾān and its earliest transmission. Such logic would suggest that Abū Bakr and this handful of individuals were possibly continuing to reveal passages of the Qurʾān in Muhammad's name to the rest of the community after his passing.

As for Weil's suggestion that Muhammad had allowed his followers to think that he was immortal, Nöldeke rejects this hypothesis on the basis that if it were true, his death would have brought an end to the Islamic religious movement on the spot. In addition, Nöldeke notes the unambiguous assertions of universal mortality in 3:185, 21:35, 29:57, and 39:30–31. Although Weil regards each of these passages as an interpolation, their authenticity is admittedly somewhat less in question. Nöldeke, however, considers it utterly preposterous that all five of these verses (including 3:144) could have somehow been "smuggled into" the Qurʾānic text.[264] If then the other four verses, or even any one of them, were already present in the Qurʾān, Nöldeke asks why there would have been any need to invent *sūra* 3:144 to provide clear Qurʾānic testimony regarding Muhammad's mortality: it would have been much simpler, he suggests, to invoke instead Qurʾān 39:30–31, as witnessed in al-Ṭabarī's alternate version of the story, or for that matter, any one of the other three verses (3:185, 21:35, 29:57). On the surface, this could seem to be a rather reasonable argument, but it does not, unfortunately, resolve either the issue of 3:144's authenticity or even the Qurʾān's position on Muhammad's death. First, the appearance of Qurʾān 39:30–31 in al-Ṭabarī's second account of Abū Bakr's confrontation with ʿUmar is almost certainly an accretion, added here as a supplement to 3:144, which Abū Bakr also cites: one would imagine that the verse was added to assuage any doubts that might arise from the crowd's astonishing unfamiliarity with 3:144. The fact that this alternate account does not appear in Ibn Hishām's biography or—more importantly—in Ibn Isḥāq's itself seems to indicate that this is a more recent tradition, a point seemingly overlooked by Nöldeke. Likewise, this version of the *ḥadīth* also mutes the crowd's reaction, reporting that only some of those present had never heard the verse before, a clear sign that this narrative has improved on the earlier account, presumably Ibn Isḥāq's, by smoothing out some rough edges.

Nevertheless, the question remains: if the other four verses were already present in the Qur'ānic text, do they not in fact afford clear evidence of a Qur'ānic belief in Muhammad's mortality, thereby obviating any need to fabricate a verse such as 3:144? In this case Abū Bakr could have spoken any one of these four verses in rebutting 'Umar, as Nöldeke suggests—and yet, in Ibn Isḥāq's version, he did not. Was there perhaps some reason why none of these verses seemed altogether appropriate in addressing Muhammad's sudden death prior to the Hour's arrival, thus inviting the creation of a new verse that would address the event more directly? Looking at 39:30–31, for instance, while the notion of universal mortality is unmistakably clear, so too is the eschatological context of this pronouncement. Although the passage begins with an address in the second person singular, there is no guarantee that the addressee was Muhammad, as the Islamic tradition has routinely understood this and other such passages. More to the point, however, is the articulation of the concept of human mortality within the context of the Day of Resurrection and the punishments of Gehenna: the message is that all human beings must die before they enter into either eternal reward or eternal punishment. Likewise, Qur'ān 3:185, 21:35, and 29:57, which on closer inspection appear to be three separate iterations of a more or less identical tradition,[265] bespeak the mortality of all humanity in the face of the universal judgment awaiting at the end of time. Thus these passages signal not Muhammad's personal death, but the eschatological necessity of mortality.[266] They contain no warning that Muhammad would die as other prophets before him had died, but rather a general notice that all human beings share in the quality of mortality, including Muhammad presumably. Yet this information comes not as notice that one day Muhammad would in fact die, leaving the community without his leadership, but instead it affords a description of the eschatological process, which will require the deaths of all humankind in passing from this life to the next one.[267]

Weil unfortunately muddled this question somewhat from the start by proposing a primitive belief in Muhammad's immortality, that he could not die, as opposed instead to the faith that the Hour's arrival would simply outpace his own personal death, and Weil's formulation of this particular hypothesis determined in large part the direction of Nöldeke's reflections on 3:144's authenticity. If indeed the issue at hand were a belief in Muhammad's immortality, then surely any of these verses would have sufficed to establish him as a mere mortal who like others would die before his passing into the heavenly realm. Yet Muhammad's mortality as such does not seem to have been the primary issue underlying the portrayed confrontation between ʿUmar and Abū Bakr. As Casanova rightly observes in correcting both Weil and Nöldeke, it was not Muhammad's mortality itself that was in question, but rather it was the *timing* of his death that seems to have caused an uproar within the early community.[268] It would appear, as ʿUmar himself later clarifies (see below), that the early community expected Muhammad to live until the Hour's arrival. Presumably, when the Final Judgment came, he too was expected to perish in the destruction of the Hour, in order to be resurrected into new life, in accordance with the views expressed in Qurʾān 3:185, 21:35, 29:57, and 39:30–31. Yet in view of the Hour's immediate proximity, as expressed by the Qurʾān and the eschatological *ḥadīth* considered above, there is a strong impression that the earliest Muslims did not believe it possible that Muhammad would die an ordinary death before the Hour's arrival, leaving them behind to await the end without him. Consequently, as insistent as these four verses are on the universality of human mortality, their eschatological context in no way places them at odds with what appears to have been a primitive belief that Muhammad would not die *before* the end's arrival. Muhammad's demise in the final conflagration was seemingly anticipated, but his sudden, quiet departure from the world before its arrival came as a shock that required explanation. In all likelihood, the alarmingly unfamiliar Qurʾānic verse placed in Abū Bakr's mouth at Muhammad's death was in fact a later interpolation designed to adjust the early community's eschatological calendar around their leader's unanticipated passing.

Despite Nöldeke's effective monopoly on this particular issue as well as many other fundamental questions regarding the Qurʾān, the matter of *sūra* 3:144's authenticity remained unsettled at least through the beginning of the previous century. Hirschfeld, for instance, regarded Nöldeke's blanket rejection of any Qurʾānic insertions whatsoever as too severe. In response, Hirschfeld outlined how the conditions of earliest Islam were actually ripe for possible additions to the Qurʾānic text, and he examined a series of verses that he believed were later accretions, including 3:144 in particular.[269] Hirschfeld adds to the arguments advanced by Silvestre de Sacy and Weil before him the idea that the name Muhammad is perhaps not a proper name, but a religious title, meaning "he who is praised," bestowed only later on the Arabian prophet by his followers. Consequently, as noted above, those verses in the Qurʾān mentioning the name Muhammad, or Aḥmad, including 3:144, are insertions in Hirschfeld's estimation. Although the value of this particular criterion is debatable, it certainly remains worthy of further consideration.[270] More to the point, however, are Hirschfeld's remarks concerning the potential mutability of the Qur'ānic text, which offer a welcome tonic to Nöldeke's rather stultifying proscription of any possible developments within the Qur'ān. Nöldeke's confidence that the Qur'ān contains only authentic material does not seem to have sufficient warrant, and looking to the Christian gospels for comparison, as suggested above, there is every reason to think that a certain level of dynamism remained present during the early transmission of the Qur'ānic text, particularly if the final recension was established only under 'Abd al-Malik's authority.

Casanova, as already noted above, similarly regards Qur'ān 3:144 as an interpolation, offering perhaps the most compelling argument for this status by folding the matter of the verse's authenticity, as well as the episode that so acutely raises the issue, into his broader hypothesis: Casanova's eschatological perspective illuminates rather well many nuances of the question. For Casanova, Ibn Isḥāq's report of the reaction to Muhammad's death serves primarily as a remarkable witness to an impassioned response of disbelief and cognitive disorientation within the early Islamic community at his passing. In this regard 'Umar's reaction would appear to confirm the sway that imminent eschatological belief held over the earliest Islamic believers: with the end so threateningly near, the thought that Muhammad might pass away before the Hour's arrival seems to have been far removed from their minds.[271] It is difficult to imagine any other tendency that would have effected the production and preservation of such an unusual narrative; absent widespread incredulity at Muhammad's death, it is hard to determine a purpose behind the creation and circulation of such an awkward story.[272]

Of course, there is no need to imagine that Ibn Isḥāq's account accurately reports real historical events that transpired between 'Umar and Abū Bakr in the moments immediately following Muhammad's death, as Nöldeke seems to presume, and for a variety of reasons this seems to be unlikely in any case. Presumably, the story instead reflects an ideological conflict within the earliest community as it sought to reconcile itself to Muhammad's unanticipated passing, here voiced by its two earliest leaders after Muhammad. One finds similar narratives throughout ancient Christian literature, where Peter and Paul, for example, are made to stand for different ideological positions with early Christianity, and such literary portrayals of theological disagreement and conflict played an important role as the early Christian communities worked through their differences and struggled to define themselves, as first recognized by F. C.

Baur and the Tübingen school.[273] Here the early Islamic tradition is most likely using ʿUmar and Abū Bakr in similar fashion "to think with," to borrow a phrase from Claude Lévi-Strauss,[274] allowing the portrayed drama between them to resolve the cognitive dissonance resulting from Muhammad's death and reorient the community's eschatological horizon. ʿUmar's voice represents the tattered faith of the early believers, who expected the Hour to arrive before Muhammad's death, while Abū Bakr brings a necessary doctrinal adjustment, accounting for Muhammad's death with the authority of a new and unfamiliar Qur'ānic verse.[275]

Qur'ān 3:144 forms the climax of Ibn Isḥāq's account of this incident, affording a scriptural proof-text capable of bringing the controversy over Muhammad's death to a speedy and decisive resolution. It is in fact the only verse in the Qur'ān where Muhammad's death is considered as "a real likelihood to be reckoned with," and not just "an abstract possibility" implicit in generic statements of human mortality.[276] Ibn Isḥāq's report, however, that "the people did not know that this verse had come down until Abū Bakr recited it that day," is rather alarming to the historian. Here the early tradition itself seems to be alerting readers that this passage is in fact a later accretion, which was added to the Qur'ānic text only after Muhammad's death. Taken at face value, it is difficult to avoid this conclusion: even if Muhammad once voiced this third-person pronouncement regarding his own death, it would appear that until he died it remained in the knowledge of Abū Bakr alone, at which point "the people took it from him," having it "(constantly) in their mouths." The verse only became a part of the public Qur'ān, according to this story, after Muhammad's death, when Abū Bakr unveiled the verse to silence ʿUmar. And while Muhammad may indeed have actually spoken these words, it seems rather misguided to insist that this *must* have been the case. On the whole, the nature of this story and the controversy surrounding Muhammad's death that it reveals suggest that the verse is most likely an interpolation designed specifically to address the issue of Muhammad's death, which is not otherwise directly considered in the Qur'ān. It is hard to imagine, for instance, that if there were a similar case regarding words ascribed to Jesus in the canonical gospels, New Testament scholars would similarly resist the seemingly obvious evidence that the verse is a later invention whose introduction required such direct acknowledgment and apology.

Moreover, other traditions concerning ʿUmar's protest at Muhammad's death, which are almost certainly older than Ibn Isḥāq's report, offer important evidence that this Qur'ānic verse is indeed an interpolation. As noted in the previous chapter, certain early collections preserve an account reporting that it was al-ʿAbbās, not Abū Bakr, who confronted ʿUmar and rebutted his rantings that Muhammad had not died,[277] and as Wilferd Madelung has argued, manipulation of the events of Muhammad's burial in Ibn Isḥāq's narrative to position its timing after the Saqīfa meeting reveals the al-ʿAbbās tradition to be more primitive.[278] In this older account, no reference is made to any Qurʾānic testimony in order to silence ʿUmar; rather, al-ʿAbbās simply remarks that Muhammad's corpse had begun to smell and thus required prompt burial, and if in fact Muhammad was not dead, it would be no trouble for God to bring him forth from the tomb. This tradition's failure to invoke a Qurʾānic resolution to the problem suggests that originally there was no scriptural passage perceived as relevant to Muhammad's personal demise. One would imagine that if Qurʾān 3:144 had been in circulation among the faithful prior to Muhammad's death, al-ʿAbbās would have referenced this verse as offering a clear resolution to the conflict, but he does not. This certainly would seem preferable to his somewhat inelegant contention that Muhammad had begun to stink, a point that, while seemingly confirmed by the earliest Christian accounts of Muhammad's death and burial, is directly contradicted by other Islamic traditions from the eighth century insisting on the sweet fragrance of his immaculate corpse.[279] Of course, this earlier tradition cannot prove that this Qurʾānic passage is in fact an interpolation, but its absence from the al-ʿAbbās account certainly offers persuasive lateral support for this hypothesis. Indeed, the Qurʾānic silence of this early version suggests a textual void wherein the early tradition might have invented such a verse. In the end, however, Ibn Isḥāq's narrative itself remains the most crucial evidence for this possibility. If the Qurʾānic verse is not a more recent interpolation, it is extremely difficult to imagine why the tradition would acknowledge with such candor the verse's unfamiliarity to the faithful. Such a forthright and awkward apology seems unimaginable for something that was already an established part of the Islamic scripture.

In a very revealing coda to this episode, which Ibn Isḥāq sandwiches between the struggle for succession to Muhammad at the Saqīfa meeting and Muhammad's burial, ʿUmar continues to serve as a mouthpiece for the primitive community's belief that Muhammad would live until the Hour: here, however, ʿUmar himself directly corrects such false expectations, offering a pair of apologies for his own mistaken views.[280] One of these accounts offers a flash-forward to ʿUmar's reign as caliph, when ʿUmar is afforded the opportunity to clarify his behavior at Muhammad's death. As he was walking one day with

Ibn ʿAbbās, ʿUmar explained that he reacted thus because he truly believed that Muhammad would remain with the people until the Hour to serve as a witness for them regarding their final deeds, citing Qurʾān 2:143 in support of this position. Yet in the second of his apologies, delivered before the assembly at the Saqīfa, ʿUmar offers a slightly different justification for his actions. In adding his endorsement to Abū Bakr's selection as the community's new leader, ʿUmar also apologizes for his behavior at Muhammad's death with a confession that what he said had no basis "in God's book," nor was it something that Muhammad had promised to him, seeming to contradict his statement as caliph that Qurʾān 2:143 had inspired his response. More importantly, however, in the version of this episode transmitted by Ibn Saʿd from al-Zuhrī through Maʿmar and Yūnus, ʿUmar explains that he could not believe that Muhammad had died, "because he [Muhammad] said that he thought that he would be the last of us [alive]."[281] Once again, this report almost certainly reflects a very early tradition, inasmuch as it is quite unlikely that some later traditionist would ascribe such a patently false prediction to Muhammad, even indirectly through ʿUmar. By contrast, Ibn Isḥāq's version has ʿUmar confess, "I thought that the Messenger of God would conduct our affairs until he was the last of us [alive]," making ʿUmar himself, rather than Muhammad, responsible for this false prophecy.[282] Presumably, Ibn Isḥāq's version is the more recent of the two, having made adjustments to shield Muhammad from error, while Ibn Saʿd's account preserves yet further evidence of a primitive belief that the Hour would arrive prior to Muhammad's death, a position here ascribed to Muhammad himself.

Judging from these reports, one would hardly imagine that ʿUmar was the only person to have held such a view prior to Muhammad's death, and it is unimaginable that the later Islamic tradition would address such beliefs so directly if in fact they were not widespread within the early community. Here again ʿUmar represents the expectation that Muhammad would survive to see the Hour's imminent arrival, a view that ʿUmar ultimately repudiates, disarming any potential arguments for this belief by explicitly denying them any basis in either the Qurʾān or a "promise" (عهد) by Muhammad. Clearly such a decisive intervention was necessary: as already seen, numerous early *ḥadīth* appear to suggest that Muhammad's mission and the Hour would overlap, and the eschatological pronouncements of the Qurʾān generally seem to envision a very short time frame for the Hour's arrival. One would imagine that such traditions were readily adduced by partisans of this primitive view as Islam struggled to adjust to the reality of Muhammad's unexpected demise. Moreover, ʿUmar himself mouths an interpretation of Qurʾān

2:143 as a promise that Muhammad would survive until the Hour; presumably this verse appears not just as some idle exegetical exercise but in order to counter an older hermeneutic tradition built around expectation that the world would end before Muhammad died. Indeed, Casanova additionally signals a number of Qur'ānic passages that could appear to hold forth the possibility that Muhammad would live to see the coming judgment (for example, 10:46, 13:40, 40:77).[283]

This complex of Qur'ānic and prophetic traditions likely served to ground the belief that Muhammad would not die prior to the Hour's arrival, requiring the kind of strong, direct response evident in the early *sīra* traditions. In order to dislodge this early eschatological hope, it was necessary to enlist both of Muhammad's first two successors, Abū Bakr and 'Umar, whose combined authority is invoked to abrogate these older traditions. 'Umar stands as the model for the individual believer's eschatological reorientation: so strong was 'Umar's conviction that Muhammad would live to see the Hour that even when confronted with Muhammad's death he threatened with violence anyone who dared to allege that Muhammad had died. Yet if even 'Umar could eventually admit that he had believed wrongly and Muhammad was indeed dead, then his eschatological conversion paved the way for other believers to follow his example. The centerpiece of this campaign, however, was the mysterious verse cited by Abū Bakr on the occasion of Muhammad's death. Although no one else could recall having heard the verse before, this clear affirmation that Muhammad would die like other prophets before him seems to have played a pivotal role in resolving the controversies occasioned by Muhammad's untimely death. The reported ignorance of the crowd, however, is too much to overlook, and despite its presence in the *textus receptus* of Qur'ān, *sūra* 3:144 is most likely a later interpolation, arising from the Hour's failure to arrive, as expected, before Muhammad's death.

Conclusion

Despite a prevailing mood in English-language scholarship that favors the more sedate portrait of Muhammad as a pragmatically minded social reformer, evidence that earliest Islam was a movement driven if not even defined by imminent eschatological belief is simply too strong to ignore. Since the ascendency of Bell and Watt's reconstruction of Islamic origins, the powerful eschatological impetus behind primitive Islam has frequently been marginalized, reduced at best to a passing phase of Muhammad's early career that is of no particular importance for understanding the beginnings of Islam. This disregard for the eschatological urgency of the early Islamic tradition is perhaps most clearly evident in Bell and Watt's collective dismissal of Casanova's study as so insignificant that "it is unnecessary to refute it in detail."[284] One hopes that the recent attention directed to early eschatological traditions by David Cook, Donner, Rubin, and Bashear, as well as the passing remarks from Ayoub, signal a new willingness to engage this aspect of formative Islam. This is not a matter of mere emphasis, however. The influential narrative of social and economic reform advanced particularly since Watt depends very much on pushing early expectations of an imminent *eschaton* to the periphery. If Muhammad and his followers believed the world was about to end in final judgment and destruction, it is rather difficult to imagine Muhammad as the practical social reformer building a brighter tomorrow for future generations that emerges from many modern studies. However attractive this reasoned social reformer may be to both modern Muslims and scholars alike, serious engagement with the eschatological traditions of the Qur'ān and early *ḥadīth* seems to require an understanding of Muhammad as someone who saw the social order and the world itself as swiftly passing away. With such a narrow eschatological horizon, it is somewhat difficult to envision Muhammad as engaging in protracted struggle to bring equality and social justice to those on the margins of society. As the discovery of eschatology forced scholars of Christian origins to abandon the much more palatable vision of Jesus as primarily a prophet of social justice to find instead a man who believed himself to be living in the last days, so too will the recovery of early Islamic eschatology necessitate significant revision of traditional narratives of Islamic origins.

In this respect, the "quest of the historical Muhammad" presently seems to stand in much the same circumstances as Albert Schweitzer found the "quest of the historical Jesus" at the turn of the twentieth century. While the portrait of Muhammad as a social reformer remains ascendant, many scholars have introduced serious questions about the nature of the early Islamic sources on which it is based. Watt's prophet of social justice and its many derivatives depend heavily on the traditional accounts of Muhammad's life, whose supposed "solid core of fact" guarantees the "general framework" that makes these reconstructions of Muhammad's career possible.[285] Yet as noted in the previous chapter, scholarship on the *sīra* traditions has repeatedly shown these traditional Islamic biographies to be extremely poor historical sources. They are late productions that present a highly idealized image of Muhammad suited to the needs and interests of eighth- and ninth-century Islam. Accordingly, many more critically minded scholars of Islamic history have judged these early narratives of Islamic origins to be more or less worthless for reconstructing the actual events of the early seventh century. Even Donner's cautiously optimistic approach to the sources in his *Narratives of Islamic Origins* yields little more than the conclusion that earliest Islam was characterized by an emphasis on personal and corporate piety. Despite the many merits of Donner's excellent study, one must admit that this is something of a rather banal result: presumably even the most ardent skeptic would willingly concede that piety was of great importance in primitive Islam.[286] More troubling, however, is Donner's parallel conclusion that other topics, such as "tribal ties, politics, confessionalism, or systematic theology" and even the history of the community itself, seem to have held very little concern for the earliest Muslims.[287] Only their piety is clearly witnessed by the sources.

Like the Christian gospels—indeed, perhaps even more so—the earliest narratives of Islamic origins were heavily determined by the theological interests of the later community (that is, salvation history), inviting the conclusion, with Wansbrough, that all historical knowledge of Muhammad and the origins of Islam has essentially been lost, obscured by the imagination of medieval Islam. For those willing to accept this critique of the traditional sources, the results are particularly devastating. While disputes remain as to just how much of a basic "historical kernel" can possibly be exhumed from the heavy theological overlay, for many scholars engaged in the historical-critical study of early Islam a veil of uncertainty has descended over the lifetime of Muhammad as well as much of the seventh century. The result is a frequent resignation in the face of traditional Islamic accounts of the beginnings of Islam as hopelessly tendentious and colored by a highly theologized narrative of history: some recent studies of early Islam simply skip past the seventh century in light of this crisis of the early sources.[288] Consequently, many scholars are resigned to a certain quiet ignorance regarding the nature of earliest Islam, a "thoroughgoing skepticism" or the "literary" approach as Schweitzer characterized the equivalent position in the work of William Wrede and other contemporary biblical scholars.[289]

Nevertheless, the eschatological traditions of early Islam offer a potential alternative to the traditional narratives of Islamic origins, capable of shedding some light into the murkiness of Islam's earliest history. The Qur'ān, which is widely acknowledged as preserving the earliest layer of the Islamic tradition, likely having some connection with Muhammad himself, is rife with eschatological material, including numerous pronouncements regarding the imminence of the Hour's arrival. Given the Hour's extended delay, it is extremely unlikely that such predictions would have been invented by later believers and ascribed to Muhammad when they had been so manifestly falsified. Moreover, related evidence from the early *ḥadīth* further attests to the prominence of imminent eschatological belief in earliest Islam, and the dissonance of such expectations with the lived experience of the Hour's delay again makes their invention by the early community similarly improbable. Altogether, these data from the primitive Islamic tradition yield a credible portrait of Muhammad as an eschatological prophet, who appears similar in many respects to the historical Jesus.

Accordingly, this alternative understanding of primitive Islam confronts the historian with a dilemma not unlike that identified by Schweitzer at the end of his seminal study of the historical Jesus: the choice lies between either a "thoroughgoing skepticism" (articulated in its most radical form by Wansbrough's "literary solution") or a "thoroughgoing eschatology."[290] In view of the highly ideological nature of early Christian literature, Schweitzer observed that one can either abandon all hope of knowing who the historical Jesus was ("thoroughgoing skepticism") or, through embracing the position of "thoroughgoing eschatology," find an historically probable Jesus who, nevertheless, has little relevance for modern Christianity. "There is," he explains, "on the one hand the eschatological solution, which at one stroke raises the Marcan account as it stands, with all its disconnectedness and inconsistencies, into genuine history; and there is, on the other hand, the literary solution, which regards the incongruous dogmatic element as interpolated by the earliest Evangelist into the tradition and therefore strikes out the Messianic claim altogether from the historical Life of Jesus. *Tertium non datur.*"[291] The same options exist, it would appear, with respect to Muhammad: the highly theological nature of the early sources invites either skeptical resignation or the recovery of an eschatological prophet of the end times, whose message was preserved against the interest of later tradition to yield at least a credible approximation of the "*ipsissima vox Machometi.*" While this historical Muhammad may prove of little use to modern Muslims, it nevertheless represents a plausible reconstruction worthy of standing alongside of the historical Jesus, having been discovered using comparable methods.

With regard to the broader questions of this study, namely, the divergent traditions concerning the chronology of Muhammad's death, this finding holds a deep significance that is perhaps not immediately apparent. The imminent eschatological expectations of earliest Islam present a circumstance that was likely to result in the rapid transformation of the primitive tradition on a considerable scale. The Hour's failed arrival and its continued deferral present a likely catalyst that would have invited and to a certain extent even required sweeping revisions of early Islamic faith and practice. If Muhammad and the earliest Muslims saw themselves as living within a relatively short span of remaining time, expecting the end of the world at any moment, then one would imagine that their focus was overwhelmingly directed toward the Hour's imminence, and all other aspects of community life and religious doctrine were viewed within this ever narrowing horizon. Yet as the climax of history failed to appear within the first generation(s), the end of the world slowly receded further and further into the future. Consequently, Muhammad's followers were soon compelled to rethink the nature of their religious movement. The rapid acquisition of an enormous empire would only have intensified this need. The eschatological movement of Islam's initial decades could no longer simply wait for the world to pass away, but it would have to metamorphose into a civilization, and while the precise details of this transformation of the Islamic religion from its primitive form to its classical one are unknown, there is every reason to think that the differences would have been considerable.

In the conclusion to his study of traditional narratives of Islamic origins, Donner again remarks on the apparent consensus with which the different Islamic groups remembered their beginnings, identifying three possible explanations for this apparent unanimity. One possibility, which Donner identifies with the "radical revisionist historians," is that this common narrative is "the product of a process of myth-making in the Islamic community at a much later date," that is, "during the second and subsequent centuries AH." As a result, "the real events lying at the origins of Islam . . . were either completely forgotten, or have been completely suppressed and obscured by the later myth, and can never be satisfactorily recovered from the evidence available today."[292] No doubt Donner is largely correct in his critique of this view, and it seems rather improbable (although by no means impossible) that "the outlines of the consensus view" regarding origins were not yet in place by the end of the first Islamic century, at which time al-Zuhrī in particular appears to have been actively engaged in the construction of such a narrative of origins on the basis of earlier traditions. Indeed, even Crone and Cook in *Hagarism* conclude "that the outlines of Islam as we know it had already appeared by the beginning of the eighth century."[293] Alternatively, in the view favored by Donner, it may be "that the consensus exists because the events actually did happen in the way described by our sources, and were so well known in the early community that all groups were required to accept the basic 'script' of events."[294] One certainly should not discount this possibility altogether, but Donner also describes an intermediate hypothesis, which he is perhaps a bit too hasty in dismissing. It is conceivable, he suggests, "that the consensus represents a fiction that arose *before* the coalescence of the Islamic historiographical tradition and the diverse political and theological points of view that it embraces," the somewhat more modest proposal advanced by Crone and Cook in *Hagarism*.[295]

Donner rejects this possibility on the grounds that the outlines of this consensus would need to have formed no later than about 75 AH, when there would potentially have been individuals still alive who might have remembered some of Muhammad's activities in Medina. Surely such people would have opposed any accounts that were at variance with their own memories, he supposes. Moreover, Donner once again raises questions about agency, asking "who could have had the authority and power to impose a spurious narrative of this kind on the community."[296] Nevertheless, both objections fail when subjected to closer analysis, leaving room for some significant doubts regarding this "consensus narrative." There certainly is no reason to assume that any changes regarding early Islam's memory of its origins could only be the consequence of a "spurious narrative" or "fiction" that was "imposed" on an unwilling community of the Believers. To the contrary, one would expect that this consensus evolved over time within the early community itself as its beliefs and circumstances changed, in a manner paralleled by many other religious traditions, as Donner himself seems to allow elsewhere.[297] Moreover, as noted already above, the strong linkage between early Islam and political authority points to the early Islamic polity as a likely mechanism by which a standard account of Islamic origins could be promulgated and authorized: it is surely no coincidence that both al-Zuhrī and Ibn Isḥāq were both working under direct imperial patronage.[298] As for the supposed objections from older witnesses who could be relied upon to correct any attempted divergence from "what really happened," this argument is not as reassuring as it might seem. If, for instance, one looks to earliest Christianity for a point of comparison, such memories of the past as it "actually happened" did not in fact prevent the significant transformation of its founder's biography only forty years after his ministry and death. Memories, it would seem, have a tendency to change considerably over time.

Indeed, primitive Christianity presents a remarkably helpful, if often overlooked, analogue for understanding earliest Islam, inasmuch as it similarly had to adapt rather quickly to the failed eschatological expectations of its first generation(s). Thanks to the more abundant and diverse (and datable) literary record of ancient Christianity, it is possible to observe the radical transformation of Christianity as it changed quickly from a Jewish apocalyptic movement awaiting the world's imminent demise into a deeply Hellenized religious community seeking to establish its place within the Roman world and beyond. If one compares, for instance, the Christian literature of the later first century, such as the Deutero-Pauline letters, the Acts of the Apostles, and the letters of Ignatius of Antioch, with Jesus' eschatological movement as it can be reconstructed from the canonical gospels, the differences are astonishing. Over this interval, roughly equivalent to the period between Muhammad and ʿAbd al-Malik's reign, the changes in Christian faith and practice with regard to Jewish law, ethics, eschatology, community structure and leadership, and theology are profound. Perhaps nowhere is this more evident than in the changing ideas about the nature of Jesus himself, as this eschatological warner soon became the divine object of Christian worship.[299] By the time a century had elapsed (roughly the interval between Muhammad and al-Zuhrī), the differences had become even greater, as reflected in the sophisticated philosophical-theological systems of Basilides, Justin Martyr, and Valentinus: one may rightly wonder if any of these early Christians and the historical Jesus would even have recognized the other as coreligionists! Similarly, as Wansbrough notes, the radically different visions of the Christian faith that Marcion and Ignatius of Antioch (not to mention Valentinus) could both profess on the basis of Paul's teaching (who also believed that the world was about to end) further attest to the rapid pace of transformation within a nascent religious tradition.[300] And while many of these Christians disagreed sharply with one another regarding the origins of Christianity, such diversity in comparison with early Islam undoubtedly reflects not only the comparatively abundant literary sources surviving from formative Christianity, but also the lack of a central authority within earliest Christianity that could establish such a consensual narrative.

When Christianity eventually became the official ideology of an empire, it was again further transformed, and the fact that Islam underwent this double transformation from an eschatological faith to the religion of an empire over such a short span of time suggests that changes in Islam during the first fifty to one hundred years were likely even more radical than what can be witnessed more clearly in the development of early Christianity. Although some scholars have protested that such drastic transformation of the early Islamic tradition would have required a widespread and deliberate conspiracy of forgery of a massive scale within the early Islamic community,[301] the comparative evidence of ancient Christianity suggests that this simply is not the case. Indeed, as Robinson articulates well, these objections—themselves overly skeptical in their own right—assume a far too simplistic view of the nature of religious traditions and their transmission.[302] In addition, while such changes in early Christianity occurred more or less spontaneously within its various, often loosely linked communities, the centralized authority of the early Islamic state presents a likely agent through which such transformations could be widely disseminated and authorized. Judging then from the perspectives of comparative religion, such dynamic transformation of the early Islamic tradition during its first century is not some sort of improbable deception requiring a conspiracy or special pleading, but instead it reflects a fairly ordinary phenomenon that is more or less to be expected of an eschatological religious movement that was able to adapt—and survive.

The radical reorientation of the Islamic faith from an eschatological movement awaiting the end of the world to the forward-looking faith of an expanding empire provides a very likely context for dramatic revision to its narratives of origins, including especially the life of its founder, Muhammad. In contrast to Donner's concerns regarding the "skeptical" approach, such a hypothesis does not appeal to an argument from silence but instead rests on direct evidence from the Qur'ān and the *ḥadīth*.[303] There is no phantom conspiracy demanding the widespread fabrication and dissemination of an alternative myth of origins; rather, early Islam seems to have undergone a fairly typical, yet extensive, reconfiguration as its imminent eschatological hopes passed into an ever distant future, a dramatic reorientation paralleled by similar fundamental changes within earliest Christianity. Comparison with the early Christian gospels further suggests the possibility that the chronology and circumstances of Muhammad's death were revised in this process of re-remembering: the gospel writers often similarly adapted the chronology of Jesus' life to suit ideological and literary purposes.[304]

The prominence of imminent eschatological belief within the earliest tradition and its failure to be fulfilled thus present circumstances in which the meaning of Muhammad's death would potentially need to be rethought and given new meaning. Particularly if the end was expected to come before Muhammad died, as seems to be the case, his passing before the Hour's arrival, as well as the Hour's prolonged delay, would require that new significances be sought for this traumatic event that was never supposed to have happened. With Islam's transformation from an eschatological movement into an ecumenical civilization, Muhammad's death would need to be recast to embody the values of the imperial faith of classical Islam. This is all the more so given that Muhammad's eschatological preaching was likely a primary impetus to the Near Eastern conquests themselves, as Donner and David Cook have proposed (and Casanova before them).[305] As will be seen in the following chapter, certain tendencies of the early Islamic tradition suggest the possibility that a memory of Muhammad's continued vitality at the beginning of the Palestinian campaign was effaced by a re-imagination of his death at Medina in 632 in order to suit ideological patterns and convictions that had come to prevail in the Islam of the early eighth century. Dramatic changes in early Islamic confessional identity and a related reorientation of its sacred geography provide the likely catalyst for the emergence of new memories describing Muhammad's pre-conquest death in the Ḥijāz.

CHAPTER 4

From Believers to Muslims, from Jerusalem to the Ḥijāz

Confessional Identity and Sacred Geography in Early Islam

The Hour's failure to arrive in a timely fashion certainly must have required Muhammad's early followers to undertake a profound reinterpretation and revision of his original message, much as one similarly finds in the wake of early Christianity's failed eschatological expectations. Inasmuch as Muhammad seems to have forecast the Hour's proximate advent with great urgency, one would expect that the transformation of primitive Islam began rather quickly: as this core conviction, which seems to have partly fueled the Near Eastern conquests, became increasingly untenable with each year that passed, the early Muslims would have been forced to rethink the focus of their faith, presumably within a couple of decades after Muhammad's departure. Moreover, in light of Muhammad's strong personal associations with the advent of the Hour, as seen in the previous chapter, one can imagine that the events of his death were accordingly recast to better comport with the emerging new vision of Islam. There is, as we have seen, good evidence to suggest that Muhammad's earliest followers expected the Hour to arrive before his death: indeed, it appears that Muhammad himself may have preached this message. Consequently, the shock of Muhammad's unexpected death before the Hour's arrival would have impelled his followers to begin a process of profoundly rethinking the nature of their faith almost immediately. Muhammad's eschatological promise had been fractured by his own death, and as a result, his followers would need to re-imagine his quietus as an event that exemplified, rather than undermined,

Islam's core beliefs. The evidence that Muhammad's death posed a stumbling block for early Muslims certainly invites the possibility that alternative memories of the incident had to be invented. What had originally been an unimaginable, devastating blow to the eschatological faith of the early believers would need to be recast according to the more eschatologically patient form of Islam that had begun to take shape in the wake of its founder's departure and the Hour's steady retreat into the future.

Nevertheless, as upsetting as Muhammad's death before the Hour seems to have been for the early community, this experience alone does not seem likely to have occasioned the kind of shifts in memory regarding the end of his life that are suggested by comparison of the Islamic and non-Islamic sources. Moreover, while the chronology, both relative and absolute, of the traditional Islamic narrative of origins is so artificial and unreliable that it often may be generally disregarded, this fact alone does not automatically invite credence in the alternative reports of Muhammad's association with the Near Eastern conquests. Likewise, although the peculiar accounts of Usāma's expedition to Palestine just before Muhammad's death and other anomalies from the early *sīra* traditions may suggest potential vestiges of an older configuration placing the assault on Palestine within Muhammad's lifespan, it seems necessary to identify some sort of strong tendency within the early Islamic tradition that could have inspired such significant revisions to the circumstances of Muhammad's death. Only a profound ideological shift affecting the very nature of the Islamic faith would seem capable of having transformed the memory of the end of Muhammad's life so dramatically. Unfortunately, the orthodox and orthoprax interests that control most of the earliest sources generally work to obscure any potential evidence of primitive deviancies from the established faith of classical Islam. Nevertheless, traces of an earlier formation occasionally slip past the filter of censorship to reveal the existence of beliefs and practices within the earliest Islamic community that are at variance with the traditional Islam of the eighth and ninth centuries. Collectively, these anomalies offer persuasive evidence that the primitive Islamic tradition underwent some profound ideological changes during its first several decades in areas that impinged significantly on self-identity, and this process of transformation suggests a context that was capable of generating the kinds of revisions to the conclusion of Muhammad's life indicated by the non-Islamic sources.

More specifically, certain apparent changes in both the confessional identify of the early community and its sacred geography, particularly with regard to Jerusalem, suggest clear tendencies that may have inspired a re-remembering of the circumstances of Muhammad's death. Insofar as primitive Islamic beliefs in both of these areas appear to have been closely linked with the eschatological faith of Muhammad and his earliest followers, the rapid revision of the early community's eschatological vision would likely have occasioned a parallel reorientation of confessional identity and sacred geography. Islam's sudden control of a vast, sophisticated empire and its frustrated eschatological hopes undoubtedly provided important accelerants in this process of resynthesis. As has become increasingly clear, considerable evidence both within the Islamic tradition itself and from contemporary non-Islamic sources suggests earliest Islam to have been an eschatological movement focused on Jerusalem and the Holy Land, whose membership was open to a wide range of "Believers" united by their common commitment to a generic form of Abrahamic monotheism. The subsequent erasure of these primitive elements and their replacement by an imperial faith whose confessional identity was grounded in Arab ethnicity and a distinctively Islamic holy land in the Ḥijāz were likely to have required significant adjustments to the narrative of origins, including, very possibly, a revised memory of Muhammad's pre-conquest death in Medina that was better suited to this new configuration of Islamic belief.

The Community of the Believers: Confessional Boundaries in Early Islam

One of the earliest and most important witnesses to the inter-confessional or nonsectarian nature of the earliest Islamic community and its Palestinian sacred geography is the anonymous Armenian chronicle misidentified for many years with the lost *History of Heraclius* ascribed to a certain bishop Sebeos.[1] Although the attribution to Sebeos has long been disproven, it has nevertheless become accepted practice to refer to this mid-seventh-century chronicle as the history of "Sebeos."[2] Whoever its author may have been, Sebeos's history is one of the most valued historical sources for events in the Near East during the early seventh century, not only because historical sources for this period are somewhat scarce, but particularly in light of the high quality of Sebeos's historical writing. As James Howard-Johnston remarks, "Sebeos' contribution to our knowledge of the ending of classical antiquity is greater than that of any other single extant source."[3] Covering the period from the 480s to 661, the chronicle is generally dated to the early 660s, as suggested by its description of certain events from 652 as if they had just taken place, and its conclusion with Muʿāwīya's victory in the First Civil War (656–61) in a fashion that Hoyland describes as "stop-press news."[4]

Sebeos's account of the rise of Islam is extremely valuable not only for its antiquity and detail, but also for its generally high quality as a source. Sebeos is, as Hoyland notes, "the first non-Muslim author to present us with a theory for the rise of Islam that pays attention to what the Muslims themselves thought they were doing."[5] In an account somewhat at odds with the Islamic historical tradition, but not completely irreconcilable with it, Sebeos reports that just prior to the rise of Islam, a group of Jewish refugees from Edessa settled among the Arabs. These Jews explained to the "sons of Ishmael" their common descent from Abraham, seemingly in an effort to convert them. Although the Arabs were persuaded of their kinship with the Jews, they were for the most part reluctant to adopt the religious practices of Judaism.[6] This all changed rather suddenly, however, with the appearance of Muhammad, as Sebeos explains in the following passage.

> At that time a man appeared from among these same sons of Ishmael, whose name was Muhammad, a merchant, who appeared to them as if by God's command as a preacher, as the way of truth. He taught them to recognize the God of Abraham, because he was especially learned and well informed in the history of Moses. Now because the command was from on high, through a single command they all came together in unity of religion, and abandoning vain cults, they returned to the living God who had appeared to their father Abraham. Then Muhammad established laws for them: not to eat carrion, and not to drink wine, and not to speak falsely, and not to engage in fornication. And he said, "With an oath God promised this land to Abraham and his descendants after him forever. And he brought it about as he said in the time when he loved Israel. Truly, you are now the sons of Abraham, and God is fulfilling the promise to Abraham and his descendants on your behalf. Now love the God of Abraham with a single mind, and go and seize your land, which God gave to your father Abraham, and no one will be able to stand against you in battle, because God is with you."[7]

Immediately after Muhammad's preaching, these "sons of Israel" dispatch a letter to the Byzantine emperor, informing him that "God gave that land to our father Abraham and to his descendants after him as a hereditary possession. We are the sons of Abraham. You have occupied our land long enough. Leave it in peace, and we will not come into your land. Otherwise, we will demand that possession from you with interest."[8] The emperor of course refuses, and the conquest of Palestine ensues, without, however, any notice of Muhammad's involvement in the campaign. Yet Sebeos equally fails to record Muhammad's death, and he makes no mention of Abū Bakr, identifying 'Umar (634–44) as the community's next leader.[9]

Despite Sebeos's significant disagreements with the received narratives of Islamic origins on certain points, his report is not to be lightly dismissed. As a historian, Sebeos earns the highest marks. For instance, Howard-Johnston observes, with explicit comparison to the early Islamic sources, that "no other extant source which touches on the Arab conquests can match his account in its range, coherence, precision, and apparent sobriety," adding further that Sebeos in fact "offers the best hope of reaching back to seventh-century historical reality."[10] Critical study has revealed that Sebeos made extensive use of earlier documentary sources, that he chose these sources very wisely, and that his editing of these sources appears to have been minimal.[11] Moreover, Sebeos presents a historical narrative that, in comparison with other contemporary historians, is remarkably free from bias. Excepting only two specific incidents, Sebeos describes the events of this period with an impartiality that few if any among his peers were able to equal.[12] Sebeos does, however, like most historians, have a clearly identifiable *Tendenz* in his history: viewing the turbulent events of his day through the eyes of the Christian apocalyptic tradition, he believed that the world was nearing its end, an opinion in which he was by no means alone.[13] Yet even this theme colors his narrative in only a few instances, most of which amount to only "a small number of editorial interjections" that are easy to separate from the rest of his record.[14]

Particularly important is the notice that Sebeos's account of the rise of Islam derives from eyewitness reports: its sources are identified as "men who had been taken as captives from Arabia to Khuzistan. And having been eyewitnesses of these things themselves, they told us this account."[15] Equally important, however, is the fact that Sebeos himself does not appear to have been the author of this account, but rather it derives from an earlier written source that he incorporates, the so-called Palestinian Source, an account of Islamic origins composed somewhere in Palestine, most likely in Jerusalem. Thus, Sebeos's description of the rise of Islam reproduces an even earlier written account that was produced in early Islamic Palestine, seemingly within a decade or at most two of both Muhammad's life and the conquest of Palestine, a primitive account that identifies its basis in the eyewitness testimony of multiple informants.[16] The fact that these alleged eyewitnesses were taken captive in "Arabia" (presumably the Roman province of Arabia), where the Near Eastern conquests began, and then remained in the company of these "sons of Israel" as prisoners until they reached Khuzistan indicates that their observations of formative Islam were made over a rather extended period of time. Given that these reports are said to derive from prisoners of war, however, one should certainly be on the alert for any signs of polemical slander aimed at their captors. Yet there are no hints of any anti-Islamic polemic in this description of Islamic origins, and if, reprising Hoyland's criteria for evaluating non-Islamic sources, this account passes beyond the mere conveyance of "facts" to offer an explanation for the rise of Islam, then it should be noted that it is a non-apologetic explanation. Likewise, none of the broader tendencies guiding Sebeos's historical vision seems to have left an impact on this account,[17] and the basic legal teachings that it ascribes to Muhammad are confirmed by similar injunctions in the Qur'ān.[18]

Nevertheless, a handful of scholars has more or less dismissed Sebeos's description of the rise of Islam as an invention largely inspired by Christian anti-Judaism. Sebeos's report of a Jewish-Arab "cabal" is to be discharged, they suggest, as a malicious fabrication governed by Christian polemics against the Jews.[19] Such quick dismissals, however, fail to do justice to the quality of Sebeos's report, as well as to the breadth of lateral evidence supporting his account, both from the Islamic tradition and from other sources. In contrast to judgments that Sebeos has invented an insidious cabal or that his account "fairly seethes with anti-Jewishness," his even-handedness in describing the alliance of some Jews and Arabs around the idea of a common monotheism and a shared claim to the Holy Land hardly seems vitriolic or polemical. Even if the role that he ascribes to certain Jews as a sort of catalyst for Islam is perhaps somewhat exaggerated, his report certainly is not a slander implicating the Jews as a whole. Moreover, his remarks that some Jews formed a significant part of the early Islamic community are neither malicious nor, it would appear, misinformed: as will be seen, the Islamic tradition itself offers much support for something like what Sebeos describes in this regard.

Hoyland in particular has persuasively defended Sebeos's account against charges that it is simply an anti-Jewish fabrication, noting that many of its details are paralleled in other contemporary Christian sources.[20] Even before the rise of Islam, in the fifth century, there are reports that some Arabs living in the borderlands of the Roman Empire had rediscovered their common descent with the Jews and returned to the observance of Abrahamic monotheism by adopting the laws and customs of Judaism.[21] Likewise, Hoyland points to certain Jewish sources that relate a Jewish presence among the Arabs at the time of the invasion of Palestine.[22]

Harald Suermann follows Hoyland in rejecting the notion that Sebeos's account may be dismissed as a product of anti-Judaism, arguing instead that Sebeos (or more precisely his source) seems surprisingly well informed and that the prospect of such a Jewish-Arab alliance is indeed highly credible.[23] As Steven Wasserstrom similarly concludes, "To be sure, large numbers of Jews surely did recognize the Qur'an and did believe in the new prophet [that is, Muhammad]. . . . Various Jewish compromises with the new dispensation were attempted. . . . The Prophet Muhammad recognized the value of such compromises and declared to the community: 'Believe in the Torah, in the Psalms, and in the Gospel, but the Qur'an should suffice you.'"[24]

Perhaps the single most important Jewish witness to the inter-confessional nature of the early Islamic community is the much cited *The Secrets of Rabbi Shim'ōn b. Yoḥai*, which describes the rise of the "Kingdom of Ishmael" and its rule over the Holy Land as the workings of Divine Providence, seeming to draw on an earlier source that originally interpreted the Arab conquest within a messianic context.[25] As noted already in the first chapter, when the text's seer "began to sit and expound (the passage) 'and he beheld the Kenite' (Num. 24:21)," he perceived the coming reign of the kingdom of Ishmael over Israel and was alarmed. The angel Metatron then came to him and explained, "Do not be afraid, mortal, for the Holy One, blessed be He, is bringing about the kingdom of Ishmael only for the purpose of delivering you from that wicked one (that is, Edom [Rome]). In accordance with His will He shall raise up over them a prophet. And he will conquer the land for them, and they shall come and restore it with grandeur. Great enmity will exist between them and the children of Esau."[26] When Rabbi Shim'ōn is perplexed and asks for further clarification, Metatron answers his concerns with an ingenious reconfiguration of the traditional messianic interpretations of Isaiah 21:6–7 and Zechariah 9:9 concerning "the rider of an ass" and "the rider of a camel," combining these traditions to cast the Ishmaelite prophet as a messianic deliverer.[27] Shortly thereafter the vision prophesies that a "second king who will arise from Ishmael will be a friend of Israel," apparently indicating 'Umar. "He will repair their breaches and (fix) the breaches of the Temple and shape Mt. Moriah and make the whole of it a level plain. He will build for himself there a place for prayer [שתחויה] upon the site of the 'foundation stone' [אבן שתיה]."[28] The vision then continues to relate the rule of the Umayyads, ending with reference to the 'Abbāsid revolution and the fallen dominion of "the children of Ishmael in Damascus." Thereafter will follow a period of rule by the "wicked kingdom" (that is, Rome) for nine months, after which several messiahs will arise to defeat "Armilos" (Rome) in a final confrontation, ending in a two-thousand year messianic rule that will be followed by the Final Judgment.[29]

This early Jewish text is of course highly significant for understanding both Sebeos's report specifically and the rise of Islam more generally. Although in its present form *The Secrets of Rabbi Shimʿōn b. Yoḥai* dates to sometime around the 'Abbāsid revolution, scholars are widely agreed that its description of the Arab conquests reveals a much earlier source that is seemingly contemporary with the invasion itself, and thus also roughly contemporary with Sebeos's Palestinian Source. The rather positive assessment of Muhammad and his followers in this initial section suggests its early formation, as does the contrast with more negative complaints against the oppressive rule of the Muslims later in the document. This original source appears to give, as John Reeves observes, "a qualified endorsement of nascent Islam as a type of Jewish messianic movement."[30] Hoyland suggests that these "messianic interpretations of the Arab conquerors" seem to have been occasioned "by 'Umar's building activity on the temple mount," while another Jewish apocalypse from the seventh century identifies Muʿāwiya as the one who, under divine guidance, "will restore the walls of the Temple," and 'Abd al-Malik is forecast as the leader who "will rebuild the Temple of the eternal God of Israel."[31] The Temple's restoration was a common theme in the Jewish apocalyptic literature that had begun to proliferate on the eve of Islam,[32] and there are even some indications in the early *piyyutim* (Jewish liturgical poetry) that Jewish worship on the Temple Mount was indeed briefly restored during the period of Sassanian rule over Palestine.[33]

As will be seen below, early Islamic apocalyptic traditions describing expectations of the Temple's restoration appear to confirm the indications of *The Secrets of Rabbi Shimʿōn b. Yoḥai* and these other sources, bearing a parallel witness to the presence of both Jews and Jewish eschatological hopes within the earliest Islamic community. And as Bashear and Donner have both noted (with differing force), 'Umar's traditional title, al-Fārūq, meaning "the savior," was likely bestowed on him by Jewish members of the early "Islamic" community. As both scholars observe, the Jews in this early community of the Believers likely interpreted the eschatological fervor of primitive Islam in accordance with their own messianic expectations.[34] Accordingly it seems likely that ʿUmar's title reflects "an Islamic fossilization of a certain Jewish idea of messianism," undoubtedly contributed by Jewish members of the early community.[35] Presumably, the same phenomenon is also evident in the *Doctrina Iacobi*'s report that Muhammad was "preaching the arrival of the anointed one who is to come, the Messiah."[36] While Crone and Cook take such statements as evidence that earliest Islam had strong messianic expectations, Donner correctly notes that while primitive Islam seems to have been thoroughly eschatological, there is no evidence of any faith in a coming messiah who will accompany the *eschaton*.[37] Rather, the *Doctrina Iacobi* seems to reflect here the imminent eschatology of primitive Islam as seen by Jewish members of the early community, who understood it according to their own apocalyptic traditions.

Yet Jewish participation during the early stages of Muhammad's religious movement is even more strongly apparent in the early Islamic sources. As Donner in particular has recently argued, these early sources seem to reveal a primitive community that was inter-confessional, comprised not just of "Muslims," but inclusive of Jews and even Christians in a sort of "ecumenical" monotheism that identified itself as "the community of the Believers."[38] Muhammad's followers, Donner maintains, did not initially seek to distinguish themselves as "a separate religious confession distinct from others."[39] Rather, Muhammad appears to have organized a confederation of Abrahamic monotheists "who shared Muhammad's intense belief in one God and in the impending arrival of the Last Day, and who joined together to carry out what they saw as the urgent task of establishing righteousness on earth—at least within their own community of Believers, and, when possible, outside it—in preparation for the End."[40] These two points, belief in the one God and the imminence of the last day, seem to have been the defining tenets of the community of the Believers, and in the face of the Hour's immediacy, other differences faded into insignificance, at least for a time. Other hallmarks of the Believers' faith, namely, emphasis on regular prayer, fasting, charity, and purity, were also part of the common piety of late ancient Judaism and Christianity, and thus would have formed a bridge rather than a boundary between the Believers and these other monotheist communities.[41] Accordingly Muhammad's religious movement, as Donner explains, was not so much "a new and distinct religious confession" but rather was a "monotheistic reform movement" advocating increased piety in the face of a rapidly approaching divine judgment.[42]

Prior to the third quarter of the first Islamic century, "Muslims" were merely one subset of the early Believers, Donner maintains. As much is indicated, for instance, by several Qur'ānic passages that seem to distinguish two such overlapping groups within the early community.[43] Likewise, some early *ḥadīth* indicate that the only requirements for membership in the community were the profession of monotheism and paying one's dues,[44] while others reference the Torah and other "scriptures" belonging to the people of the book favorably, further suggesting such an inter-confessional quality to the early community.[45] Indeed, the category of "scripture" seems have been rather fluid for the early Believers. Christians and Jews in the community were expected to follow their own scriptures, whose authority was seen as parallel to, rather than supplanted by, Muhammad's revelations. As Wansbrough astutely observes, the emphasis on Muhammad's unique status among the prophets is in fact a later development, not present in the Qur'ān, which seems to regard all prophets as equals.[46] Muhammad's prophetic activity was thus merely the last in a long line of monotheist prophets, including Moses and Jesus, whose revelations from the one true God were in their essentials identical with Muhammad's message, as certain passages from the Qur'ān itself seem to indicate.[47] Such a conception of Muhammad's revelation in relation to other "scriptures" would certainly comport with the Qur'ān's later collection under ʿAbd al-Malik, as argued in the preceding chapter: only with the emergence of a distinctively Islamic sectarian identity at this time did it become necessary to codify the Qur'ān into a uniquely Islamic scripture that would distinguish Islam from its monotheist siblings and their "inferior" scriptural collections.

Perhaps the most famous and dramatic witness to the full participation of Jews within this early community of Believers is the so-called Constitution of Medina, or as Donner prefers to call it, "the *umma* document."[48] This early Islamic document survives in three different versions in much later sources, but its authenticity as a witness to primitive Islam is almost universally recognized, particularly on the basis of its discontinuity with other early sources regarding the ethnic and religious boundaries of the early community.[49] This agreement between Muhammad and the people of Yathrib made provisions for the inclusion of at least some Jews within Muhammad's eschatological community. According to the Constitution, the Jews comprise a distinct group within the larger community of the Believers, who nevertheless are allowed to maintain their own religion.[50] In defining the relations between the Believers (*Muʾminūn*) and the Muslims (*Muslimūn*), the Constitution declares the Jews to be "a people (*umma*) with the *Muʾminūn*, the Jews having their law (*dīn*) and the *Muslimūn* having their law. [This applies to] their clients (*mawālī*) and to themselves, excepting anyone who acts wrongfully (*ẓalama*) and commits crimes/acts treacherously/breaks an agreement, for he but slays himself and the people of his house."[51] The Jews are also expected to "pay [their] share," while the Constitution's only doctrinal stipulation requires belief "in God and the Last Day."[52] These and many other passages seem to describe precisely the sort of inter-confessional community that Donner envisions, to the effect that even the Islamic tradition itself does not deny that the Jews were initially welcomed into the "Islamic" community on such terms, as least for a short time.[53]

Nevertheless, according to the traditional accounts, inclusion of the Jews was only a short-lived experiment, which Muhammad allowed as a concession in hopes that the Jews of Yathrib would soon convert to "Islam." Not long thereafter, Muhammad and his followers are said to have turned against the Jews and rejected their participation within the community of the Believers, redrawing its confessional boundaries more narrowly.[54] Yet there is no reason to assume that Muhammad in fact abandoned the Jews and expelled them from the community so quickly just because the later Islamic tradition imagines it thus. The anti-Judaism of the early Islamic historical tradition, and especially the *sīra* tradition, has deeply colored Islamic memories of this earlier inclusiveness, and the sectarian contentions of these later writers should not control the interpretation of this primitive document.[55] Indeed, as Donner remarks, the later "Muslim tradition would carefully attempt to bury, or 'forget,' the absence of strict confessional barriers that marked the early days of the community of Believers," taking "great pains to project back into the story of its origins those features that had come to be decisive in establishing [its] separate identity and to obliterate or disguise any obvious traces of the 'preconfessional' character of the community of Believers."[56] With this in mind, it is in fact somewhat remarkable that such significant memories of the early community's inter-confessional nature have somehow escaped this censorship. Presumably, their survival attests to just how profound and pronounced this nonsectarian quality was, and when the later tradition could not simply erase this feature of its past, the only strategy of containment available was to diminish this early program of inclusion by reinventing it as a brief attempt to accommodate the obstinate Jews of Medina.

Donner uncovers similar evidence of the early community's inter-confessional nature in the Qur'ān as well. A surprising number of passages refer to the *ahl al-kitāb*, the "people(s) of the Book" in a very positive manner, often seeming to imply their inclusion among the Believers. Qur'ān 2:62 and

5:69, for instance, associate those Jews, Christians, and Sabians "who Believe in God and the Last Day" with the community of the Believers: like the Believers, they will have nothing to fear or regret. Faith in God and the last day here again are the defining qualities of the community, and this belief both "secures salvation" and "transcends the communal distinctions between Jew, Sabian, Christian, etc."[57] Similar sentiment emerges elsewhere in the Qur'ān, as Donner demonstrates, implying that there were at least some Jews and Christians who were counted among the Believers, all the while retaining their identities as Jews and Christians. Basic belief in God and faith in the approaching *eschaton*, together with moral behavior, were the only requirements for salvation, a simple creed that transcended membership in a particular monotheist community. Muhammad appears to have served largely as an arbiter within this inter-confessional community, and the Qur'ān expects that its Jewish and Christian members will continue to adhere to their own covenants, which will lead them to salvation.[58] "If the *ahl al-kitāb* believe and are pious (*ittaqaw*), We shall efface their evil deeds from them (*la-kaffarnā ʿanhum sayyi'ātihim*) and shall admit them to the garden of delight. If they obey the Torah and the Gospel and that which was sent down to them from their Lord, they shall eat from above, and from beneath their feet. Among them is a provident/moderate community (*ummatun muqtaṣidatun*), but many of them do evil" (Qur'ān 5:65–66).[59]

As is clear from the final remarks of this passage, however, not all Jews and Christians were welcomed by the community of Believers, and there were some among the *ahl al-kitāb* that the Qur'ān considered evil and to be shunned. Although many Jews and Christians appear to have joined Muhammad's religious movement while retaining their confessional identities, others refused and seem to have opposed it. The nature of this confrontation is not entirely clear, but the Qur'ān appears to suggest that some Jews and Christians were insistent on the exclusive truth of their unique covenants (for example, 2:111, 2:135). Others perhaps would not accept the Believers' faith in the imminence of the last day; the Qur'ān repeatedly responds to such doubts among its audience. Still others presumably found themselves excluded by their failure to meet the Believers' standard of piety. Whatever its basis, the Qur'ān's division of the *ahl al-kitāb* according those who "believed" and those who spurned Muhammad's message can largely explain the often ambivalent attitude of the Qur'ān and the early Islamic tradition to Jews and Christians. Following on an observation by Albrecht Noth, Donner notes that "when the Qur'an refers to the *ahl al-kitāb* in general, the tone of the passage is usually positive, whereas verses with negative overtones usually refer to *a part* of the *ahl al-kitāb*."[60] Such positive references would seem to reflect the nonsectarian nature of Muhammad's religious movement, while Qur'ānic attacks against Jews and Christians appear to be aimed at only a part, the disbelieving part, of those communities.

Donner largely adopts this hermeneutic strategy in addressing the handful of Qur'ānic passages that could seem to contradict his hypothesis regarding the early community's inter-confessional nature. When read within their broader context, many seemingly negative statements are seen as being directed only against opponents of the Believers within these religious communities.[61] More problematic, however, are certain passages ostensibly directed against the Christian doctrine of the Trinity, a belief that is condemned as a transgression of monotheism. Such pronouncements would seem to preclude any Christian participation in Muhammad's early religious movement, inasmuch as the doctrines of the triune God and Christ's full divinity had come to prevail within Christianity by the early seventh century. Any non-Trinitarian Christians who may have found a temporary home within the early community of Believers would have been an extremely small minority. Despite occasional theories that some sort of non-Trinitarian Jewish-Christian group played a significant role in the formation of Islam,[62] there is essentially no evidence for the existence of such groups in the Near East at this time.[63] Indeed, any Christians that Muhammad and his early followers encountered would have been overwhelmingly, if not exclusively, Trinitarian. How then are the Qur'ān's occasional polemics against the Trinity to be reconciled with this view of the early community?

Donner suggests that perhaps such theological tensions could be overlooked during the early history of the community, as these differences were pushed to the side in favor of emphasis on the core themes of the impending last day, faith in the God of Abraham, and a call to piety. As the movement evolved, however, "it was precisely the theological implications of such passages as these in the Qur'an text that made inevitable the eventual crystallization of Muslims as a religious confession distinct from other monotheisms." Moreover, prior to the establishment and dissemination of a standardized Qur'ānic text, Donner suggests that "Muslims actually knew very little of the Qur'an," which could perhaps explain apparent tension between these Qur'ānic passages and the more open boundaries of the early community.[64] Nevertheless, Donner insists on retaining the traditional account of the Qur'ān's codification under ʿUthmān, which allows for a somewhat shorter interval than he would like in order to explain these developments. If, however, the Qur'ānic text was not fixed until somewhat later, perhaps as late as the reign of ʿAbd al-Malik, as seems more likely, then it is possible to view these anti-Christian polemics instead as symptomatic of the early community's evolving identity.

Such a model of Islamic origins would allow for the existence of an interconfessional community of the Believers through the reign of the early caliphs, roughly corresponding with the period of around seventy years envisioned by Donner. During this time one would imagine that this new religious movement transformed significantly as it began to engage the diverse religious landscape of the late ancient Near East. In such a context one can readily imagine swift and sweeping changes to the emergent Islamic faith and its self-identity, fueled by the failed arrival of the *eschaton* and determined largely by competition within the "sectarian milieu" of Near Eastern monotheism.[65] Even if Wansbrough's timeline for the Qur'ān's formation is improbably long, the kinds of development within the Islamic tradition that he suggests need to be considered within this relatively shorter interval. During the period between the death of Muhammad and the rise of the Marwānids, it seems that Muhammad's followers increasingly saw themselves as a community separate from the other monotheisms of the Near East, ultimately emphasizing the rejection of Christianity's Trinitarian monotheism as a principle point of distinction. Consequently, Qur'ānic traditions opposing the Trinity most likely arose or at the very least found new emphasis in concert with the early community's evolving identity from Believers to Muslims. Together with a new emphasis on Muhammad's status as a prophet of unique stature, opposition to the Trinity formed one of the two basic principles that carved out a distinctly Islamic identity from the Abrahamic monotheist traditions of the Near East.[66]

The emergence of these themes around the beginning of ʿAbd al-Malik's reign is consistent with the apparent consolidation of Islam and the promotion of "a distinctly Islamic idiom" under his rule.[67] Around this same time Muhammad's name appears for the first time in documentary evidence, as does the earliest evidence for the traditional Islamic confession of faith, the *shahāda*, "There is no God but God; Muhammad is the apostle of God."[68] There is ample evidence, however, as Donner in particular has noted, that the *shahāda* originally consisted only of a simple profession of monotheism: "There is no God but God." Such a general affirmation of monotheism, absent any specific pronouncement regarding Muhammad's prophetic status, would have been widely acceptable to the various members of the inter-confessional community of the Believers. Donner further suggests that occasional references to the two *shahāda*s in the Islamic legal tradition likely preserve a vestigial witness to such confessional development, reflecting the addition of a second *shahāda* concerning Muhammad in order to demarcate Islam from these other monotheisms.[69] Likewise, Bashear's identification of an early Islamic *shahāda* naming Jesus also seems to reveal the nonsectarianism of the earliest community; indeed, Bashear's article on this phenomenon identifies the resilience of this older interconfessional orientation even into the second Islamic century, particularly in Syria.[70] Yet it is surely no accident that the earliest documentary evidence of Islam's sectarian self-definition on the basis of Muhammad's unequaled prophetic status appears almost simultaneously with ʿAbd al-Malik's great building project, the Dome of the Rock. This monument dramatically laid claim to the sacred space of the Temple Mount for Muhammad's followers, complete with inscriptions proclaiming the full *shahāda* and bearing anti-Trinitarian propaganda.[71] Moreover, as noted previously, the Dome's inscriptions do not correspond exactly with the received text of the Qurʾān, a difference that not only suggests a later standardization of the Qurʾānic text but also possibly indicates the relatively recent, and thus textually unstable, nature of these anti-Christian pronouncements themselves at this time.[72] On the whole, the religious developments of ʿAbd al-Malik's reign seem highly consistent with the transformation of an originally nonsectarian movement of Abrahamic believers into a distinctly Islamic form of monotheism, lending further support to Donner's hypothesis concerning Islamic origins.

Testimonies from several contemporary Christian writers would also appear to confirm Donner's reconstruction of the earliest Islamic community. The Syriac writers of the seventh century, for instance, rarely identify Muhammad as a prophet, describing him instead as the "king of the Arabs."[73] Likewise, there is little evidence of any polemic in these Christian sources directed against this new religious group, which they name the "Hagarenes." This could suggest, Donner notes, that the "Believers" or "Hagarenes" did not yet constitute a clearly defined religious community in the seventh century.[74] Donner points specifically to the chronicle of John bar Penkaye, written in northern Mesopotamia toward the end of the seventh century, which conveys rather clearly the non-confessional nature of the "Islamic" community even at this late date. For example, John's chronicle describes Muhammad as the community's "guide" (ܡܗܕܝܢܐ) rather than as a prophet or apostle, and he reports that Muhammad held the Christians and their monastics in high regard. More importantly, however, John says of this new religious movement that "they required only tribute (*madattā*) of each person, allowing him to remain in whatever faith he wished. Among them were also Christians in no small numbers: some belonged to the heretics [that is, the miaphysites], while others to us."[75] Not only does John report the presence of significant numbers of Christians within this new religious movement, but he notes even more specifically that those who joined were allowed to remain in whatever faith tradition they wished. Although John himself stood outside of the community of Believers, this Christian inhabitant of the Umayyad Empire perceived the new faith as having a profoundly nonsectarian nature, as well as considerable overlap with his own religious community, even still at this later date.

In a letter written several years earlier, the East Syrian patriarch Isho'yahb III remarked that not only did these new rulers not oppose Christianity, but quite to the contrary, they praised it and honored Christian priests and saints, as well as their churches and monasteries.[76] The Samaritan *Continuatio* similarly reports remarkable tolerance by Muhammad and the early caliphs toward other monotheist communities: perhaps this also is a reflection of the early community's nonsectarian quality.[77] Likewise, John of Damascus's assessment of early Islam as a Christian heresy should perhaps be reconsidered in this light.[78] Although one can easily understand how such characterization could have arisen purely from polemical motives, Donner's findings suggest the possibility that John's perspective may reflect, at least in part, the inter-confessional nature of the community under the Umayyads, as well as some considerable overlap with his own Christian community. John of all people would certainly have been in a position to have a particularly well-informed view of emergent Islam. Not only had his father served as secretary and chief financial administrator to each of the early Umayyad caliphs in their capital at Damascus, including Mu'āwiya, Yazīd, Mu'āwiya ibn Yazīd, Marwān ibn al-Ḥakam, and 'Abd al-Malik, but John himself had served as a high-ranking financial official in the Umayyad administration before becoming a priest and monk. Despite its highly polemical tone then, perhaps John's classification of early Islam as a deviant form of Christianity preserves some trace of its inter-confessional origins: as Hoyland notes of John's description, "though unsympathetic, the author is well informed."[79]

The involvement of John and other members of his family in the Umayyad government at high levels would itself also appear to provide evidence of the primitive community's lingering nonsectarianism. It is indeed difficult to imagine members of a prominent Christian family being placed in such authoritative positions if the beginnings of Islam were truly as sectarian as the later tradition has remembered it. John's own service in Hishām's administration and that of his father to earlier caliphs are best understood as reflecting the early inclusion of Christians within an inter-confessional community of the Believers. The same is also true of Muʿāwiya's intermarriage with the powerful Christian Kalb tribe, from which his successor, the caliph Yazīd, was produced. Such relations to the Christian community certainly suggest a rather permeable boundary still at this date. Yet perhaps even more remarkable is the presence of Christian troops in the "Islamic" military as late as the Second Civil War: members of the Kalb and Taghlib tribes are said to have marched with Yazīd's army into the Ḥijāz bearing as standards the cross and the banner of their patron, St. Sergius. Such participation in the military campaigns of the Umayyads, particularly while bearing these openly Christian symbols, would seem to presume the full membership of these Christians—as Christians—within the community of the Believers.[80]

Although Donner himself freely concedes that there is much evidence that either complicates or contradicts his reconstruction of Islamic origins, it is difficult not to agree with him that the hypothesis of a primitive, inter-confessional Abrahamic monotheism comports much better with the majority of the evidence concerning the early Islamic period than does the traditional Islamic account of origins.[81] For instance, the improbable success of the early "Islamic" conquests is more readily explained if they were propelled by an ideology similar to what Donner has reconstructed. "If we assume that the conquerors were from the start representatives of an alien and hostile new creed, Islam, it seems highly improbable that they would have succeeded; the local populations would have resisted the Muslims from the outset, and it would have been difficult for the latter to secure a foothold. If we see the conquerors not as confessionally exclusive Muslims, however, but rather as monotheist Believers who might have been sympathetic to other monotheists among the conquered peoples, the long-term success in the aftermath of the conquests appears more plausible."[82] In his recent monograph, Donner develops this hypothesis further, arguing that the nonsectarianism of the community and its inclusion of pious Jews and Christians can effectively explain the relatively peaceful transition of power in the seventh-century Near East. Although the Islamic (and some non-Islamic) literary sources are replete with accounts of widespread destruction, the archaeological record tells a strikingly different story, offering almost no evidence of violent conquest. The non-confessional quality of the early community of the Believers suggests a context in which the Jews and Christians of the Near East would likely have offered little resistance, eliminating any need for violence and destruction of property. While the Byzantine army assuredly met the Believers on multiple occasions with great force, most locales seem to have negotiated their surrender to these new rulers peacefully. The Believers' tolerance and even inclusion of Jews and Christians within their community would likely have made their rule an acceptable alternative to Byzantines and Sassanians, particularly for the Jewish and non-Chalcedonian Christian communities that had suffered state persecution by the Roman authorities in recent memory. This inter-confessional monotheistic reform movement striving for an increase in piety offered little to which these religious communities would have objected, and indeed, at the local level it would appear that there was very little change in the administrative structures of civic life.[83]

A number of other more circumstantial elements would also seem to favor Donner's hypothesis, including the use of "Believers" rather than "Muslims" as the earliest self-designation of this community. The lack of any formal ritual for conversion to Islam may reflect the tradition's beginnings as a sort of monotheist confederacy. The similarities of certain aspects of Islamic cultic practice (including the Friday prayer service in particular) to Jewish and Christian practices also seem to indicate the presence of Jews and Christians within the early community of the Believers.[84] Likewise the "allusive style" of the Qur'ān, which suggestively and indirectly evokes traditions and narratives from the Bible, also implies very close relations with Jews and Christians at the beginnings of Islam.[85] Similarly, G. R. Hawting's work on the idea of idolatry in early Islam suggests a primitive community that was struggling to draw its boundaries not according to prophetic allegiance but at the acceptable limits of monotheism, and only somewhat later did this religious movement emerge from the context of a broader monotheism as a separate and distinct monotheist faith.[86] More recently, Patricia Crone has extended Hawting's insights by exploring further the nature of the Qur'ānic "pagans," who in fact seem to have been worshiping the "biblical" God. Moreover, as both Hawting and Crone observe, their "association" of other beings with this God does not amount to polytheism but instead looks very similar to the practice of angel veneration within early Judaism. Such characteristics then would suggest the emergence of Muhammad's movement within a broader context that was already permeated by Abrahamic monotheism, in which Muhammad's opponents were not "pagans" but other monotheists who worshipped the same God in a different manner.[87]

The early Believers' appropriation of Christian sacred space for their worship, either cooperatively or through cooption, further suggests close relations between this new religious movement and certain elements of the Christian communities of the late ancient Near East. Perhaps the most famous example is the Believers' use of the Church of St. John the Baptist in Damascus, which they ultimately appropriated in the construction of the Umayyad Mosque.[88] Examples of such inter-confessional condominium of sacred space are especially common in reports from early Islamic Jerusalem. Although the sources are understandably complex, particularly in light of their tension with later Islamic confessional identity, it would appear that the early Believers in Jerusalem initially joined the Christians in the Holy Sepulcher for their worship. After taking the Holy City on Palm Sunday, as Heribert Busse argues, the Believers joined in the Christian celebrations of Holy Week; it was not very long, however, before they abandoned this practice and turned their attention to the Temple Mount, where they would ultimately build the al-Aqṣā Mosque and the Dome of the Rock.[89] Suliman Bashear has collected numerous other reports of early Muslims praying in Jerusalem's churches, including Golgotha and the Tomb of the Virgin in particular; the latter, in which both ʿUmar and Muʿāwiya are alleged to have prayed, to this day has a *miḥrāb* signaling the direction of Islamic prayer for visitors to the shrine.[90] This phenomenon was not unique to Jerusalem, and Bashear notes additional examples of this practice from other early Islamic centers such as Edessa, Kūfa, and Damascus.[91] The practice apparently continued into the second Islamic century in some locations, proving one of the most lasting vestiges of Islam's inter-confessional origins, and as Bashear notes, early Islamic prayer in churches seems to be linked with the issue of sacred direction in primitive Islam, an issue to which we will turn very shortly.[92]

Finally, apparent confirmation of the early community's inter-confessional nature also emerges at a somewhat greater distance in some intriguing reports of Aḥmad ibn Ḥanbal's (d. 855) teachings, where the issue of Jewish and Christian members of the early *umma* remained a matter of great concern and consternation, even two or three centuries later. The topic arises in Ibn Ḥanbal's *responsa*, that is, his answers to various questions posed by the faithful, which were collected two generations later by Abū Bakr al-Khallāl (d. 923), the great consolidator of the Ḥanbali school of jurisprudence.[93] Although much of al-Khallāl's collection of *responsa* has unfortunately been lost, certain sections have nonetheless survived, including the recently published *Kitāb ahl al-milal*, which frequently addresses relations between Muslims and their non-Muslim neighbors. The exchanges on this subject cover a wide variety of topics, and while the content of some inquiries occasionally disturbed or surprised Ibn

Ḥanbal, his response to the question of whether Muhammad allowed Jews and Christians membership in his religious community is especially remarkable both for its absolutism and its vehemence. Indeed, the unyielding and unwavering force with which Ibn Ḥanbal is said to have rejected this very question suggests that the subject remained a particularly vexing issue, a matter extremely sensitive to address even at this distance from the apostolic age. When asked "whether there were Jews and Christians among the *umma* of Muhammad," Ibn Ḥanbal "became enraged" at the question and responded, "This is a filthy question, and one must not discuss it!"[94] The inquirer then asks if he should similarly rebuke anyone else who might introduce such a question, and Ibn Ḥanbal repeats the same response, making clear that it is forbidden even to discuss the subject. When another of Ibn Ḥanbal's students poses the same question, Ibn Ḥanbal is surprised to learn that anyone would possibly claim such a thing. When the student assures him that there are indeed those who claim that Jews and Christians had been included in Muhammad's primitive religious community, Ibn Ḥanbal commands his followers to respond with a sharp rebuke and refutation, putting such nonsense quickly and completely to rest without further discussion.[95]

Thomas Sizgorich has recently explored the significance of these Ḥanbali legal traditions within the context of ʿAbbāsid society, arguing that they reflect the heightened social and cultural status of Jews and especially Christians in this age.[96] The prominence of many Christians and Jews presented circumstances threatening to Islamic cultural identity insofar as certain members of these groups were enabled to transgress the boundaries that defined the Islamic religious community against its nearest rivals. Likewise, Sizgorich explains that increasingly sophisticated Jewish and Christian knowledge of the Qurʾān and Islamic tradition further exacerbated the problem, as members of these communities began to offer rival articulations of Islamic identity and otherness. Ibn Ḥanbal's sharp rejection of even raising the question of whether Jews and Christians had belonged to Muhammad's religious community is thus explained as a response to these developments within ʿAbbāsid society.[97]

Sizgorich is undoubtedly correct that the high status of many elite non-Muslims would have posed a disturbing challenge to certain traditional ideas about Islamic identity in Ibn Ḥanbal's age. Nevertheless, these circumstances alone do not seem sufficient to have engendered significant debate regarding the presence of Jews and Christians within Muhammad's primitive religious community. Moreover, it is not entirely clear how the prominent status of certain non-Muslims would have provoked the forceful and repressive response that Ibn Ḥanbal is said to have given. Rather, it seems far more likely that this question and its juristic proscription reflect a persistent memory of the primitive community's inter-confessional nature, as signaled by the various sources considered above. Indeed, Ibn Ḥanbal's fervent rejection of even allowing the issue to be discussed suggests that this was a question that had some traction. If this notion were only the mere fancy of certain Christians and Jews hoping to further advance their social status, then it would be difficult to comprehend why Ibn Ḥanbal and others would not simply have dismissed the question outright as a risible fiction. But the absolute prohibition against even discussing the matter suggests a fear that such conversations might unearth older memories about the primitive Islamic community that had to stay buried and forgotten in order to sustain the faith and practice of Islam in its ninth- and tenth-century configuration. Consequently, this treatment of the issue of whether Jews and Christians had belonged to Muhammad's early religious community by early Ḥanbali scholars seemingly provides further confirmation that the primitive *umma* did indeed welcome Jewish and Christian members. Apparently, the Jews, Christians, and Muslims of the ʿAbbāsid era had not completely forgotten the religious hybridity of Muhammad's community of the Believers, a point causing no small annoyance to the Islamic jurists of the age.

In itself, however, the discovery that earliest Islam appears to have been an inter-confessional movement inclusive of Jews, Christians, and other monotheists is of somewhat indirect consequence for understanding the divergent traditions about the end of Muhammad's life. Yet the shared Abrahamic monotheism of the Believers seems to have included a conviction that as Abraham's descendants they were destined to inherit the land of divine promise, the Holy Land, and its sacred center, Jerusalem, as Sebeos and other related early sources indicate.[98] Given the enormous significance of both Jerusalem and the Holy Land in Jewish and Christian sacred geography, it is certainly no surprise to find that the Believers initially focused their eschatological hopes on the restoration of their ancestral inheritance. Numerous early sources reveal Jerusalem and the Holy Land as the goal of early Islamic aspirations: there, according to Jewish and Christian—as well as Islamic—eschatology, the Final Judgment will transpire, and accordingly Muhammad and the Believers, it would seem, aimed to secure control of Jerusalem, "the apocalyptic city *par excellence*,"[99] in advance of the Hour's rapidly approaching arrival. Likewise the complicated question of sacred direction in earliest Islam and the early Islamic interest in the Temple

Mount further indicate an initial orientation toward this sacred city. These elements of the early tradition, which are rooted in Islam's primitive interconnectedness with Judaism and Christianity, certainly have bearing for understanding the early reports of Muhammad's survival into the period of the invasion of Palestine and Syria.

Nevertheless, according to the traditional accounts of Islamic origins from the eighth and ninth centuries, the cities of Mecca and Medina in the Ḥijāz were of paramount importance in the formation of Islam, and any evidence of Jerusalem's primitive significance has been reduced to the odd vestigial trace. As numerous scholars have suggested, it would appear that by the end of its first century Islam had largely abandoned its original fixation on Jerusalem and the Holy Land in order to define a distinctively Arabian holy land of its own. This transition to a sacred geography anchored in the Arabian Ḥijāz formed, it seems, a crucial element in Islam's effort to define itself confessionally from the other monotheisms that it once had welcomed as its spiritual partners. One must therefore consider the very real possibility that, in the process of revising this aspect of its memory of origins, the Islamic tradition also re-remembered the end of Muhammad's life so that it no longer overlapped with the Believers' eschatological campaign to reclaim their Abrahamic inheritance in the Holy Land. Instead, the tradition came to remember Muhammad as being soundly laid to rest in the Islamic holy city of Medina, amid the newly consecrated landscape of an Arabian—and Abrahamic—Ḥijāz.

The Holy Land of Divine Promise: The Sanctity of Jerusalem in Formative Islam

One of the most remarkable aspects of Sebeos's near contemporary account of Islam's emergence within the late ancient Near East is its indication that the liberation of the biblical Holy Land lay at the heart of Muhammad's preaching. According to Sebeos, Muhammad exhorted his followers, a group comprised of Jews and Arabs, to rise up and conquer the sacred land that God had promised to them. "Truly, you are now the sons of Abraham, and God is fulfilling the promise to Abraham and his descendants on your behalf. Now love the God of Abraham with a single mind, and go and seize your land, which God gave to your father Abraham, and no one will be able to stand against you in battle, because God is with you."[100] Similar sentiments are expressed much later in the *Chronicle* of Dionysius of Tellmahre (d. 845), which reports that Muhammad would "extol for them the excellence of the land of Palestine, saying that 'Because of belief in the one God, such a good and fertile land has been given to them.' And he would add, 'If you will listen to me, God will also give you a fine land flowing with milk and honey.'"[101]

Much more importantly, however, the Qur'ān itself seems to advance the same idea, suggesting that this theme may indeed have formed an important element of Muhammad's preaching. *Sūra* 33:27 proclaims that "He made you heirs to their land [أَرْضَهُمْ] (of the 'people of the Book') and their dwellings and to a land which you have not yet trodden," a land that the Qur'ān elsewhere names "the Holy Land" (الْأَرْضَ الْمُقَدَّسَةَ).[102] *Sūra* 10:13–14 similarly relates: "We destroyed generations before you when they acted oppressively while their apostles brought them proofs, yet they did not Believe. Thus do we repay a guilty people. Then we made you successors in the land [الْأَرْضِ] after them, so we may see how you behave."[103] Likewise, *sūra* 21:105–6, citing Psalm 37:29, promises, "We wrote in the Psalms, as We did in [earlier] Scripture, 'My righteous servants will inherit the land [الْأَرْضَ].' There truly is a message in this for the servants of God!"[104] According to these Qur'ānic passages, God has chosen the Believers to inherit the Promised Land, and they were called to liberate it from the rule of the wicked and once again establish righteousness in the sacred lands: indeed, *sūra* 10:14 rather oddly seems to speak of these events as if they had already occurred. The similarities to Sebeos's account of Muhammad's preaching are certainly quite striking, and accordingly one must imagine that the liberation of the Holy Land likely formed a core element of the early Believers' religious ideology. Al-Ṭabarī's report that the leaders of the Arab armies justified their invasion of the Near East to their opponents by insisting that the land had been promised to them by God would seem to confirm the presence of this mindset among the early Believers.[105]

On the basis of these and many other traditions, including the Jewish apocalypses considered above, Uri Rubin determines that the earliest Islamic self-identity was grounded primarily in the traditions of the ancient Israelites, including especially their exodus from a land of exile and their entry into the land of divine promise. Rubin's careful and convincing analysis reveals a primitive stratum in the Islamic sources, according to which the "Jews and Arabs share the sacred mission of carrying out the divine scheme, which is to renew the ancient Exodus and to drive the Byzantines out of the Promised Land. The messianic goal is shared with the Arabs not only by contemporary 'Judeo-Muslims,' but also by the Biblical Children of Israel," who are expected "to assist the Muslims in the eschatological anti-Byzantine holy war."[106] Although many of the traditions considered by Rubin survive only in somewhat later sources, their anomalous focus on the Holy Land as the primary object of early Islamic aspirations seems to indicate their early formation. Indeed, these ideas appear to have been sufficiently forceful within formative Islam to leave a strong impression in the early Islamic historical tradition, despite their manifest tension with the canonical narratives of Islamic origins. Most importantly, however, these reports concerning the theological significance of the "Islamic" conquest of the Holy Land are largely confirmed by other evidence from the early Islamic tradition indicating the preeminence of Jerusalem and the Holy Land for the early community of the Believers.

As Rubin's comments indicate, the Believers' promised inheritance of the land seems to have been strongly linked with their belief in the impending *eschaton*, and Donner similarly identifies the imminent eschatology of the early community as a primary motivation for the invasion of the Holy Land and also as the source of Jerusalem's exalted status in primitive Islam. According to Donner, the Believers' firm conviction that the Hour had drawn nigh seemingly impelled them to strive northward toward Jerusalem, a view also shared by David Cook.[107] That such an impulse was evident already during Muhammad's lifetime would appear to be confirmed by the *sīra* tradition's reports of his particular interest in a northern campaign.[108] And considering the broader religious context of formative Islam, Jerusalem's draw must have been compelling. In the various eschatological scenarios outlined by late ancient Judaism and Christianity, Jerusalem stood at the center of the map: there the Final Judgment would take place, culminating in the restoration of God's rule over the righteous. In traditional Jewish expectation the Messiah would restore the Davidic kingship and rebuild the Temple at Jerusalem, establishing divine law and eliminating the wicked from the earth. Likewise, according to a popular early Byzantine eschatological scheme, the "Last Emperor" would vanquish the enemies of Christianity, establish righteousness on the earth, and then hand over imperial authority to Jesus at Jerusalem in the Second Coming.[109]

Undoubtedly these apocalyptic scripts must have influenced the expectations that Muhammad and the Believers held regarding the impending Hour, and in fact, as we will see, Islam's eschatological vision has focused squarely on Jerusalem until the present, a correspondence that surely is no mere coincidence. Consequently, Donner suggests that "the Believers may have felt that, because they were in the process of constructing the righteous 'community of the saved,' they should establish their presence in Jerusalem as soon as possible." There they perhaps expected "that the *amir al-mu'minin* [the commander of the Believers], as leader of this new community dedicated to the realization of God's word, would fulfill the role of that expected 'last emperor' who would, on the Last Day, hand earthly power over to God."[110] In such a way the forcefulness of eschatological belief within primitive Islam must have drawn the Believers to focus their hopes on a restoration to the Holy Land where the final events of history were soon to unfold. As much is indicated, for instance, in an early eschatological tradition from the *Faḍā'il al-Quds* literature (a corpus discussed in more detail below) that identifies the beginnings of the final conflict in the battle between the descendants of Abraham and the Romans for control of the Promised Land. Here God promises Abraham, "In the end of days I will bring there the best of my servants to fight the sons of Esau [the Romans]. Ibrāhīm asked: O Lord in which place there? He answered, On the shore which is at the southern side of Jerusalem."[111] As Ofer Livne-Kafri observes, this tradition would appear to refer to the persistent fighting between the army of the Believers and the Romans in the coastal towns of Palestine during the 640s, events appearing here "in eschatological colours" that suggest their association with an impending end of the world.[112]

Of course, this understanding of earliest Islam suggests a rather different impetus for the Near Eastern "conquests" from what has generally been assumed both in the traditional sources and in traditional scholarship, as Donner additionally notes. The underlying purpose for the "expansion of the Believers' rule" (as Donner renames the "Islamic conquests") was not to spread the distinctive religious confession of "Islam," especially since such a monotheist sect did not yet exist in the era of the Believers. Indeed, "if the Believers already embraced a clearly defined and distinct new creed," he remarks, "and had tried to demand that local communities observe it, those populations of the Fertile Crescent would have resisted their arrival stubbornly." And yet it would appear that they did not: otherwise, it is difficult to comprehend how such a small number of conquerors could have succeeded in subduing and maintaining authority over a very large population, if there had in fact been fierce resistance. Consequently, it would seem that the Believers, rather than seeking to expand the membership of a newly formed monotheist confession through conquest, instead sought to extend their political hegemony over new populations, "requiring them to pay taxes, and asking them, at least initially, to affirm their belief in one God and the Last day, and to affirm their commitment to living righteously and to avoid sin."[113]

Nevertheless, even the Believers' efforts to expand their political authority were not so much with the aim of creating a powerful empire that would rule over the peoples of the earth. After all, the world itself was fleeting away and such earthly power would soon vanish with the Hour's arrival. Instead, as Donner explains, "The early Believers were concerned with social and political issues but only insofar as they related to concepts of piety and proper behavior needed to insure salvation."[114] Fear before the impending judgment, not a lust for political power, seems to have inspired Muhammad and his followers to form "a community of the saved, dedicated to the rigorous observance of God's laws as revealed to His prophets." Following the guidance of Muhammad, God's most recent prophet, they hoped to attain both individual and collective salvation when the last day soon would appear. The early Believers appear to have understood that the events of the *eschaton* were in fact beginning to unfold even in the very formation of their righteous community. Accordingly, they were to struggle against the unbelievers and the wicked to eliminate them from the earth and to spread the influence and dominion of their faithful polity, rooting out sinfulness and establishing obedience to God's law in advance of the impending judgment. It was thus imperative to expand the community as quickly as possible and to as many people as possible in order to meet the swiftly approaching divine justice of the Hour.[115]

Donner further observes that all this "sounds like a program aimed at establishing 'God's kingdom on Earth,' that is, a political order (or at least a society) informed by the pious precepts enjoined by the Qur'an and one that should supplant the sinful political order of the Byzantines and Sasanians."[116] Although Donner remarks that the Qur'ān never uses the phrase "kingdom of God," both it and the Islamic tradition frequently refer to the *eschaton* as the "*amr* of God," that is, "God's command" or even "God's rule/reign/dominion."[117] Indeed, as scholars of the New Testament have often remarked, the phrase "Kingdom of God" in the gospels seems to refer more to the idea of God's sovereignty or kingship rather than an actual kingdom.[118] Particularly in light of the fact that the early Believers were led after Muhammad's death by an individual with the title "*amir al-muʾminin*," or "commander of the Believers," whose authority appears to have been at least partly religious, it seems quite likely that the approaching "*amr allāh*" does indeed indicate something on the order of God's eschatological reign or kingdom.[119] Consequently, the Believers likely saw the military success and the rapid expansion of their devout polity not only as divine validation of their movement but also as events themselves marking the "beginning of the End," drawing them ever closer to the eschatological climax of history just over the horizon. Central to this final arc of history was the Believers' inheritance of the Holy Land, as evidenced by both the Qur'ān and other early sources. There, and in Jerusalem more specifically, God was expected to fulfill God's divine rule, God's *amr*, thus making the expansion to Jerusalem of utmost importance to the Believers as they raced to meet the Hour together as a community righteous before God. The "Islamic conquests" then were not an effort to spread the sectarian faith of "Islam" by force or to establish an enduring empire that would rival Rome in its glory and might. Rather, the militant piety of Muhammad's early followers was directed above all else toward the elimination of the sinful polities around them, and against Byzantine rule in the Holy Land in particular, as well as toward the expansion of their community of the saved in advance of the Hour's arrival, almost certainly with Jerusalem, the eschatological nexus of Abrahamic monotheism, as their ultimate goal.

It is presumably for such reasons that Muhammad and the Believers originally prayed not facing Mecca but toward Jerusalem, itself a particularly telling sign of the Holy City's exceptional importance in earliest Islam. Numerous sources indicate Jerusalem as the original direction of Islamic prayer or "*qibla*," a tradition so anomalous with later Islamic practice that it undoubtedly must be primitive. The Qur'ān itself notes that at some point there was a change of *qibla*, but its notice is frustratingly vague: neither the occasion nor the original direction is named, and the new direction is identified only as "toward the sacred place of worship" (الْمَسْجِدِ الْحَرَامِ).[120] The early Islamic tradition, however, is predictably less taciturn, and Ibn Isḥāq's biography, for example, notes that while Muhammad had originally prayed toward Jerusalem, he began to face Mecca during the seventeenth or eighteenth month after his arrival in Medina.[121] Later interpreters often disagreed as to whether Jerusalem was actually the original direction of prayer, and some commentators instead describe the Jerusalem *qibla* as merely another temporary experiment aimed at recruiting the Jews of Medina.[122] One of Ibn Isḥāq's reports resolved the issue by explaining that although Muhammad had originally prayed toward Jerusalem while he was in Mecca, he did so by placing the Kaʿba between himself and the Holy Land.[123] Yet such traditions were presumably designed to minimize the "embarrassment" that Mecca was not originally the focus of the Believers' prayers.[124]

Other traditions make quite clear that before the change of *qibla* in Medina, Muhammad had prayed toward Jerusalem: for instance, when one of his early followers decides to pray toward the Kaʿba, Muhammad corrects him, and he returns to the "apostle's *qibla*," that is, Jerusalem.[125] According to another tradition, attributed to al-Zuhrī, the Jerusalemite *qibla* was the norm for all of the prophets who preceded Muhammad, since "from the time Adam descended into this world, Allāh has never sent a prophet without making the Rock [in Jerusalem] his *qibla*." The tradition continues to explain that the Islamic *qibla* was changed to Mecca only by divine concession, after Muhammad had repeatedly requested this from God, presumably reflecting Qur'ān 2:144 ("We will surely turn thee to a direction that shall satisfy thee").[126] Certain other reports indicate that even before Muhammad's arrival, the Medinans had built a mosque in Qubā with the *qibla* facing Jerusalem, and that once he came to Medina Muhammad prayed in the mosque without changing its orientation. There is even a tradition from al-Wāqidī that Muhammad's mosque in Medina was originally built to face in the direction of Jerusalem.[127] Such reports of the Jerusalem *qibla*'s priority seem unlikely to have arisen once the Meccan *qibla* had become established, while traditions suggesting a brief Jerusalemite interlude would appear to serve an apologetic interest. As Frants Buhl observes of the diverse opinions in the Islamic sources regarding Muhammad's *qibla* in Mecca, "surely no one would have invented such a thing if the direction of prayer at that time had actually been the same as the later canonical direction."[128]

In any case, these traditions make clear Jerusalem's status as an important sacred center in primitive Islam whose prestige rivaled and indeed seemingly surpassed that of Mecca in the earliest stages. Moreover, they equally underscore the point that Mecca did not emerge as the center of Islam's sacred geography until somewhat later in the movement's history. Although the *sīra* tradition would have us believe that this reorientation was effectively and efficiently achieved by Muhammad's instruction at Medina, there is certainly no reason to take these much later memorializations of Islamic origins at face value. By Ibn Isḥāq's time, in the middle of the eighth century, it would have been essential to validate the established practice of praying toward Mecca by placing it under prophetic authority, as well as to disarm any memories of Jerusalem's importance by diminishing this earlier *qibla* as only a very brief, experimental phase in the tradition's formation.[129] Yet as will be seen, there is significant evidence to suggest that prayer toward Jerusalem was not just some short-lived fad of the Meccan and early Medinan periods: it is clear that Jerusalem remained an important sacred center of Islam, and the aim of Islamic prayer, for several decades after the death of Muhammad.

Of course, it should be noted that Jerusalem and Mecca were not the only two options for sacred direction in nascent Islam. There is scattered evidence of other early trajectories, leading Bashear to conclude, "As far as the first century is concerned, one cannot speak of 'one original *qibla* of Islam,' but rather of several currents in the search for one."[130] Perhaps such early diversity is signaled by the Qur'ānic pronouncement, "To God belongs the East and West; whithersoever you turn, there is the face of God" (2:115; cf. 2:177). There are numerous hints in the early tradition, for instance, of an eastern *qibla*. Bashear presents a philological argument for the existence of an early eastern *qibla*, noting the Islamic usage of various terms derived from the root associated with the east (or more precisely, the sunrise: ŠRQ) as synonyms for certain activities and locations involved in prayer.[131] Many years earlier, Tor Andrae had proposed that Muhammad's original *qibla* in Mecca had been toward the east, believing that he had adopted this custom from Christian practice, a position also endorsed by Buhl and, following a slightly different argumentation, Vasily (or Wilhelm) Barthold.[132] Nevertheless, such reasoning in part passes over the difficult question of whether Christianity actually had a significant presence in the seventh-century Ḥijāz, when in fact this seems rather doubtful. Although Christianity had literally encircled the Ḥijāz by Muhammad's lifetime, there is no evidence of a significant Christian community in either Mecca or Medina.[133] While scholars of Near Eastern Christianity routinely assert that Christianity had penetrated the Ḥijāz by the seventh century, this is largely assumed on the basis of the much later Islamic source materials, whose accounts are quite suspect in this matter.[134] Yet even taking these reports more or less at face value, they afford no evidence of Christian communities in Mecca and Medina, but only anecdotes concerning a few individual converts.[135] Indeed, it is rather telling that, as Wansbrough observes, any Christian characters appearing in the narratives of Islamic origins are "always from outside the Ḥijāz" and their introduction "is always gratuitous, and their alleged place of origin suspect."[136] Consequently, any Christian influence on the *qibla* would likely have come not in Mecca or Medina, but only after the Believers had entered the confessional diversity of the Roman and Sassanian Empires, as Moshe Sharon has more plausibly speculated.[137]

Whatever may have been the inspiration for an eastern *qibla*, Sharon has drawn attention to possible archaeological evidence for such practice in what appears to be the remains of an early mosque at Be'er Orah in the southern Negev. Sharon describes this rectangular building as "an open mosque with two miḥrābs, one facing east and one facing south. The one facing south was clearly a later addition made after 'Abd al-Malik's reforms came into effect."[138] Although some have suggested the possibility that this structure may be a converted church, whose eastern niche was simply the church's apse, the archaeology of the site confirms its original construction as a mosque with an eastward *miḥrāb*.[139] Two early Iraqi mosques have also been found with aberrant *miḥrāb*s, the mosques of al-Ḥajjāj in Wāsiṭ and of Uskaf bani Junayd near Baghdad, both of which are oriented approximately thirty degrees too far to the north, pointing almost due southwest to somewhere in northwestern Arabia. While it is difficult to assess the significance of these deviant *miḥrāb*s, they certainly add support to Bashear's proposal of different currents searching for an Islamic *qibla*.

According to various reports in the Islamic tradition, the mosque of ʿAmr b. al-ʿĀs at Fusṭaṭ in Egypt originally had an eastward *qibla*: the sources relate that it was "very much turned toward the east."[140] Important confirmation of these reports comes from Jacob of Edessa (d. 708), who as a young man had studied in Egypt for several years. In a letter written while he was serving as bishop of Edessa (684–88), Jacob reveals some interesting information concerning the Islamic *qibla* in answering the question of why the Jews (in Edessa) prayed toward the south.

> Your question is vain . . . for it is not to the south that the Jews pray, nor either do the Muslims (*mhaggrāyē*). The Jews who live in Egypt, and also the Muslims there, as I saw with my own eyes and will now set out for you, prayed to the east, and still do, both peoples—the Jews towards Jerusalem and the Muslims towards the Kaʿba (*kʿbtʾ*). And those Jews who are to the south of Jerusalem pray to the north; and those in the land of Babel, in Ḥira and in Baṣra, pray to the west. And also the Muslims who are there pray to the west, towards the Kaʿba; and those who are to the south of the Kaʿba pray to the north, towards that place. So from all this that has been said, it is clear that it is not to the south that the Jews and Muslims here in the regions of Syria pray, but towards Jerusalem or the Kaʿba, the patriarchal places of their races.[141]

As Hoyland notes, Jacob's observations appear to have been based on his own firsthand experiences and are thus likely to report accurately the practice of Egyptian and Mesopotamian Muslims in the later seventh century. And although Jacob identifies something named the "Kaʿba" as the focus of their prayers, this certainly does not seem to be the Meccan shrine of later Islamic tradition. Indeed, it would appear from Jacob's observations of practice within these early Islamic communities that the Muslims of the Near East turned to face a sanctuary in a rather different location.

Judging from Jacob's account, it would seem that the Kaʿba, the focus of Muslim prayer, was located either in Jerusalem or somewhere nearby: in each instance, the Muslims are said to pray in the same direction of the Jews, whose focus is Jerusalem.[142] Particularly interesting is the notice that Muslims in Ḥira and Baṣra pray toward the Kaʿba facing the west. Accounts describing the construction of Kūfa's mosque in 638 clearly indicate that the direction of the *qibla* was to the west, seemingly due west, exactly the direction of Jerusalem, leading Hoyland to conclude that the original direction of prayer in Kūfa was indeed westward.[143] When paired with Jacob's report of western prayer in Ḥira and Baṣra, it seems highly likely that the early Muslims of Mesopotamia were praying toward the west, in the direction of Palestine rather than the Ḥijāz. A report that Islamic prayers in Khurasan and Transoxania were similarly directed toward the west at the time of their initial conquest could seem to confirm an orientation toward the Holy Land, if not toward Jerusalem itself.[144] Although this practice perhaps did not aim these Central Asian prayers precisely toward Jerusalem, the custom of the earliest Muslims seems to have been to pray "in the general direction of the Kaʿba rather than trying to be accurate," as both Jacob and the Islamic tradition appear to indicate.[145]

Certain rare but important variants in early Islamic burial practice additionally seem to indicate the existence of a Jerusalem *qibla* well beyond Muhammad's early months in Medina. One of the most distinctive features of Islamic burial is the orientation of the deceased within the grave to face the Meccan *qibla*. According to Leor Halevi, this practice "represented for Muslims a ritual form expressive of their own particular confessional identity" with respect to Judaism and Christianity.[146] Yet the excavation of an early Islamic cemetery at Qasṭal al-Balqāʾ in Jordan has revealed burials very clearly oriented toward Jerusalem.[147] As Halevi notes, "This evidence suggests that the abrogation of the *qibla* of Jerusalem in favor of the *qibla* of Mecca did not have an immediate effect on burial practices everywhere in the world of Islam."[148] Indeed, such burials would seem to indicate the existence of a Jerusalem *qibla* well into the Umayyad period. Perhaps the accusation against ʿAbd al-Malik that he sought to "transfer" the *qibla* to Jerusalem reflects not so much an effort on his part to innovate but is instead indicative of the continued practice of a Jerusalem *qibla* by many Muslims still at the end of the seventh century.[149] Likewise, in a widely circulated tradition, ʿUmar, after his arrival in Jerusalem, asked Kaʿb, the legendary early Islamic authority on Jewish traditions, for advice regarding prayers offered on the Temple Mount. When Kaʿb suggested that prayers should be offered from the north side of the Rock, thereby uniting the two *qiblas* of Jerusalem and Mecca, ʿUmar refused and directed that prayers instead should be made to the south of the Rock, on the site where the al- Aqṣā Mosque eventually was built.[150] This tradition too could suggest the late survival of a Jerusalem *qibla*, as well as the search for a compromise and the need to authorize the switch to an exclusively Meccan *qibla*.

Nevertheless, the *qiblas* of the early mosques at Wāsiṭ and Uskaf bani Junayd are truly aberrant, pointing neither toward the Holy Land nor the Ḥijāz but somewhere in between. Largely on this basis, Crone, Cook, Hawting, and others have argued for the existence of an early Islamic sanctuary somewhere in northwest Arabia, whose traditions (including possibly the title "Kaʿba") were only later conferred on the Meccan shrine.[151] Cook and Crone further attempt to align the Egyptian evidence with the two Iraqi mosques by interpreting the Islamic sources as describing Egyptian prayer "facing slightly south of east."[152] But the pertinent reports, while not certainly excluding this possibility, do not specify such direction, only noting prayer toward the "Kaʿba" in the east, according to Jacob, or "very much turned toward the east" (قبلة مشرقة جدا), according to the Islamic sources.[153] Thus, it seems equally if not perhaps even more likely that these early Muslims were turning in prayer toward a sacred location in the Holy Land, quite possibly in Jerusalem itself, as the preponderance of the evidence, both Islamic and non-Islamic, would appear to suggest. Still, the two early Iraqi mosques and the potential evidence of the Beʾer Orah mosque are important reminders that, as Bashear and others have noted, sacred direction in early Islam does not appear to have been entirely uniform. Nevertheless, the sacred status of Jerusalem and the Holy Land in earliest Islam and the observance of a Jerusalem *qibla* by a significant number of early Muslims, including Muhammad himself, are well attested by these sources, and it seems clear that these practices cannot simply be relegated to a passing moment in Muhammad's career, as many of the traditional Islamic sources would suggest.

Other vestiges of Jerusalem's early significance manifest themselves in a variety of forms and forums, ranging from eschatological expectations to funerary customs to early liturgical traditions. J. W. Hirschberg was perhaps the first scholar to recognize Jerusalem's early primacy in formative Islam, concluding largely on the basis of traditions concerning the Temple Mount's sacred rock and its Islamic shrine that "the sanctity of Jerusalem is older than that of Mecca" in the Islamic tradition.[154] Meir Kister has similarly identified early legal traditions indicating both Jerusalem's prominence in primitive Islam and a related effort to conceal or diminish its early importance. In an article examining an early *ḥadīth* restricting Islamic pilgrimage to only three holy mosques, Kister notes the shifting attitudes toward Jerusalem's sanctity within the later Islamic tradition. According to the most widely attested version of this *ḥadīth*, Muhammad limits pilgrims to only "the Sacred Mosque (in Mecca), [his] mosque (in Medina) and al-Aqṣā mosque."[155] Although initially deployed to prohibit pilgrimage to various lesser shrines, such as the Miḥrāb Da'ūd in Jerusalem, the mosque of Qubā near Medina, and al-Ṭūr (that is, Mount Sinai), this tradition eventually developed into a controversy largely over the status of Jerusalem.[156] A number of counter-traditions survive that seek to minimize the sanctity of Jerusalem while exalting Mecca and Medina at its expense. Traditions naming only the mosques of Mecca and Medina as legitimate objects of Islamic pilgrimage, along with others discouraging pilgrimage to Jerusalem, "bear evidence to the fact that among scholars of Islam in the first half of the second century there was some reluctance to give full recognition to the third mosque and to grant Jerusalem an equal position with the two holy cities of Islam, Mecca and Medina." Many traditions insist that prayers offered in the holy mosques of Mecca and Medina are better than a thousand prayers in any other mosque, Jerusalem seemingly left deliberately off the list.[157] Other traditions elevate the mosque of Qubā above Jerusalem, while still others name the mosque of al-Khayf near Mecca in its place as the third legitimate goal of a pilgrimage: such traditions also seem designed to advance the sanctity of Mecca and Medina at Jerusalem's expense.[158] Yet unless Jerusalem was especially revered by the earliest Muslims, as equal to or even above Mecca and Medina, it is difficult to understand why traditions such as these would have arisen in the first place.

At the same time, certain related traditions seek to emphasize Jerusalem's equality with Medina and its mosque, with some occasionally even asserting its superiority over "the city of the Prophet" and its mosque. One tradition explains, for instance, "that a prayer in the mosque of Mecca is worth a hundred thousand prayers, a prayer in the mosque of Medina a thousand prayers and a prayer in Jerusalem twenty thousand prayers."[159] Moreover, Jerusalem is often paired with Mecca in a manner that suggests its superiority to Medina and its equality with the latter, at least in the minds of some early Muslims. A verse ascribed to the early Islamic poet al-Farazdaq (d. 728), for instance, places the two sanctuaries of Mecca and Jerusalem seemingly on equal footing as the two "Houses of God." Other reports reflect a concern that some early Muslims viewed pilgrimage to Jerusalem as an acceptable alternative to Mecca, which conferred equal merits on its devout visitors.[160] Similar anxieties appear to be reflected in the strict regulations imposed on pilgrims to Jerusalem, seemingly designed to underscore the difference—and inferiority—of pious visits to the shrines of Jerusalem's Noble Sanctuary (*al-Ḥaram al-Sharīf*).[161] On the whole, these traditions reveal the heightened sanctity of Jerusalem in formative Islam, together with the high level of apprehension that this status occasioned among many scholars of the second Islamic century. Such concerns about the veneration of Jerusalem would seem to presuppose a strong early tradition of its holiness that was in need of being diminished. Yet while such traces of Jerusalem's exalted position in the primitive tradition occasionally seem to slip through in the course of this early debate, ultimately Jerusalem came to be ranked beneath the two sacred centers of the Ḥijāz, Mecca and Medina. Nevertheless, the apparent effort from some quarters to remove Jerusalem entirely from its elite status within the hierarchy of Islam's most sacred shrines was not successful, and despite its demotion, the early Islamic reverence for the Holy Land and its Holy City could not be completely overcome.

An early exegetical tradition identified by Suliman Bashear similarly seems to indicate the importance of Jerusalem and its sanctuary for the early community of the Believers. Qur'ān 2:114 condemns "those who prohibit the mention of God's name in His places of worship and strive to have them deserted."[162] According to Bashear's analysis, the prevailing opinion of the *tafsīr* tradition associates the revelation of this verse with Jerusalem, where it was the Byzantines who were preventing the "Muslims" from entering the Jerusalem sanctuary, that is, the area of the Temple Mount. It is certainly no surprise to find that some authorities linked the revelation of this verse instead with a Meccan context, suggesting that it referred to Muhammad's persecution by Quraysh, which prevented him from observing the *ḥajj*.[163] Yet Bashear is surely right in judging the tradition of a Byzantine context as the more primitive interpretation: while it is easy to understand the Meccan tradition as an effort to correct the sharply dissonant report of a Byzantine setting, it is very difficult to imagine that a verse already bound to the Meccan sanctuary would become so widely associated with Jerusalem by later commentators. The Qur'ān's reference to the "destruction" (فِي خَرَابِهَا) of these holy places certainly suggests the Jerusalem Temple, which lay in ruins at the beginnings of Islam. Less clear, however, are the precise circumstances to which this interpretation refers, inasmuch as Byzantine control over the Temple Mount would seem to presume a time before the Muslims had captured Jerusalem. Exactly who then were the "Muslims" that the Byzantines were believed to have barred from entering Jerusalem's "mosque"? Although one can only speculate, a likely source would be those Jews who joined themselves to the early community of the Believers. Under Byzantine rule, the Jews were not only banned from the Temple Mount, but were prohibited from even entering the city of Jerusalem. Perhaps this interpretation of the verse—and possibly even the verse itself—arose during the early interconfessional stage of Islam's formation, having been introduced by those Jews who had attached themselves to this new religious movement. Yet whatever its origin may have been, this interpretive tradition forms an important witness to the high esteem in which the early Islamic tradition initially held both Jerusalem and its sanctuary.

In recent decades, a number of scholars have profitably mined the Islamic literary traditions on *The Merits of Jerusalem*, the *Faḍā'il al-Quds*, in order to recover a clearer sense of Jerusalem's sacred status in earliest Islam. Inasmuch as the earliest work preserving such material dates only to the early eleventh century, this genre was long disregarded by students of early Islam as merely local collections of medieval traditions praising Jerusalem.[164] Recent studies, however, have shown that many of these traditions can be persuasively dated to the later seventh century. Indeed, one of the most striking signs of their antiquity is the very high regard in which they hold Jerusalem and the Holy Land, an anomalous tendency that contradicts more recent traditions seeking to diminish Jerusalem's status in favor of a sacred topography concentrated in the Ḥijāz.[165] Not only is Jerusalem described in these traditions as "the land that God has chosen from among all other lands," but the foundation stone of its Temple, "the Rock of Jerusalem (*ṣakhrat Bayt al-Maqdis*) is from Paradise, and it is the navel of the earth."[166] Such notions, which strain against Islam's sacred geography in the Ḥijāz, must be early, from the period when Jerusalem was still the focus of the Believers' spiritual aspirations. "No less ancient," writes Kister, "is the *ḥadīth*, 'The establishment of the site of the Temple will be the destruction of Yathrib.'"[167] Here we find Jerusalem's exalted sanctity forcefully invoked at the expense of Yathrib, the city (*medina*) of the Prophet; as much is imaginable only prior to the ascendency of the Ḥijāz in the mythology of Islamic origins. Other related traditions indicating "that Muhammad's nation will build the Temple" and describing its anticipated reconstruction must similarly date, according to Kister, to around the middle of the first Islamic century.[168] Likewise, frequent reference in these traditions to "the Torah" and the "Books of the Prophets" suggests a circumstance in which the Jewish scriptures were viewed as authoritative.[169] Such traditions could only have formed within the inter-confessional context of the early community of the Believers, with their common focus on a shared Abrahamic inheritance.

Among the most prominent themes of the *Faḍāʾil al-Quds* literature is eschatology: following a pattern already well established in Judaism and Christianity, numerous events connected with the Hour's arrival are joined to Jerusalem and its holy sites.[170] Jerusalem is the location where the gathering for the Final Judgment and the resurrection will take place.[171] On the last day its Rock will be center stage: the Rock will serve as "the place for the foot of Allāh," and God Godself declares that it will serve as God's Throne of Glory.[172] From the Rock the angel Isrāfīl will sound the final trumpet, and hearing his call, all living creatures will assemble in Jerusalem.[173] Hell will be opened up from the Valley of Joshaphat, or Gehenna, while Paradise will open up beneath the al-Aqṣā mosque.[174] Jerusalem will serve as a refuge against the Dajjāl, the antichrist, and there Jesus the son of Mary will appear and defeat him.[175] Moreover, as noted above, a number of these early eschatological traditions emphasize Jerusalem's superior sanctity at the expense of its main urban rivals, Mecca and Medina. On the day of resurrection, according to several traditions, the Kaʿba "will be conducted to Jerusalem like a bride conducted to her husband," at which point both will ascend together to heaven with their inhabitants.[176] The nuptial metaphor certainly would seem to suggest Jerusalem's superiority to the Kaʿba, its bride.

Particularly remarkable in this regard is the tradition concerning the "destruction of Yathrib," noted above. This forecast, which survives in a number of sources, proclaims that "the building of *Bayt al-Maqdis* (*bunyān bayt al-maqdis*) is the destruction of Yaṯrib [Medina], and the destruction of Yaṯrib is the coming of the *malḥama* [that is, the apocalyptic battle], and the coming of the *malḥama* is the conquest of Constantinople, and the conquest of Constantinople is the coming out of the *daǧǧāl*."[177] Although *Bayt al-Maqdis* is a common designation for Jerusalem in the Islamic sources, one should note that the title itself derives from the Hebrew name for the Jewish temple, *Beit HaMikdash* (בית המקדש), "the Holy House." As such this tradition probably originated within Jewish eschatological hopes for the Temple's restoration that, as we have noted, formed a prominent impulse within the early community of Believers. According to one tradition, for instance, the Jewish convert Kaʿb al-Aḥbār is said "to have found in one of the books," presumably referring here to some "Jewish" writing, the following prediction:

> Rejoice, Jerusalem (ʾĪrūšalāyim), that is to say *bayt al-maqdis* and the Rock (*al-ṣakhra*) and it is called the Temple [*al-haykal: hekhal* in Hebrew]. I will send you my servant ʿAbd al-Malik and he will

> build you and embellish you, and I shall restore *bayt al-maqdis* to its former sovereignty (*mulk*) and I shall crown it with gold and silver and pearls, and I shall send you to my people, and I shall place my throne on the Rock, and I am God, the Lord, and David is the king of the sons of Israel.[178]

Likewise, another early tradition ascribed to Kaʿb proclaims that "God revealed himself to Jacob and said: I shall send from your descendants kings and prophets, till I send the Prophet of the *ḥaram* whose nation will build the Temple (*haykal*) of Jerusalem, and he is the seal of the prophets and his name is Aḥmad," that is, Muhammad.[179]

With the coming restoration of the "Temple," Yathrib would thus be destroyed or abandoned, or at the very least would have its religious significance usurped by this renewed sanctuary. This prophecy quickly became more than just some apocalyptic fantasy once the Believers came into possession of the Holy City and constructed a series of ever grander edifices on the Temple Mount. Palestine was not merely the land of their promised inheritance, but its sacred center, Jerusalem and the Temple Mount in particular, seems to have held an important cultic significance for the earliest Believers. Not very long after Jerusalem came under their control, Muhammad's followers set to work building a place of worship on the Temple Mount. As much is indicated, for instance, by an early tradition that survives in an appendix to the Georgian version of John Moschus's *Spiritual Meadow*, a collection of anecdotes concerning the monks and holy men of sixth- and seventh-century Palestine.[180] According to this report, the invading "Saracens" quickly proceeded to the Temple Mount after taking the city. "They took some men, some by force and some willingly, to clean the place and to build that cursed thing, which is for prayer and which they call a mosque."[181] As the account continues, it locates these events within the lifetime of Patriarch Sophronius of Jerusalem, who died in 639, and the tradition itself dates to sometime before 668, making for a particularly early witness to Muslim religious activities on the Temple Mount.[182]

Other sources appear to confirm the construction of a Muslim sanctuary on the Temple Mount shortly after the conquest of Jerusalem. For instance, the roughly contemporary *History* of Sebeos describes the Jews as building a structure on the site of the Holy of Holies initially with Arab support, only to have the Arabs later expel them and seize the building for themselves.[183] Likewise, around the middle of the seventh century (ca. 660), Anastasius of Sinai reports having witnessed further construction work on the Temple Mount, noting that he had observed demons assisting the "Saracens."[184] When the English pilgrim Arculf visited Jerusalem sometime during the 670s, he saw a large rectangular building on the Temple Mount, capable of holding at least three thousand people, which the "Saracens" regularly used for worship, describing the structure as an *orationis domus*.[185] At a somewhat greater distance, the *Chronicle* of Theophilus of Edessa (ca. 750) similarly relates that shortly after the Arabs' capture of Jerusalem, they sought to rebuild the Temple, adding further credence to these earlier reports.[186] When joined to the evidence from the Jewish apocalyptic literature of the seventh century that contemporary Jews understood the building activities on the Temple Mount under the early caliphs as a restoration of the Temple, the site's primary religious significance for the early Believers seems unmistakable.[187]

The culmination, however, of the early Islamic building program on the Temple Mount was ʿAbd al-Malik's new shrine over the Temple's sacred Rock, completed in 691–92. Many among the Believers appear to have viewed its erection as an actual restoration of the Temple, and it may in fact be that this was ʿAbd al-Malik's intent.[188] Yet however the Dome's precise relation to the Temple may have been conceived by ʿAbd al-Malik and other early Muslims, it seems clear that the shrine's initial purpose and significance were quite different from how this sacred space came to be interpreted and used in later Islam. Far from serving as merely a memorial to the spot from which Muhammad began his heavenly journey, the sanctuary was apparently in the late seventh century and the early eighth the site of an actual cult. Some accounts relate that worshippers in Jerusalem originally circumambulated the Dome's holy Rock in a fashion similar to the circumambulation of the Kaʿba during the traditional Islamic *ḥajj*.[189] Although these reports may be nothing more than polemical fabrications, designed to denigrate ʿAbd al-Malik's shrine as an illegitimate attempt to redirect the *ḥajj* to Jerusalem (an accusation discussed further below), the Dome is, like the Kaʿba, seemingly designed "for circumambulation around a sacred rock," and the existence of legal traditions forbidding this and other related rituals in the Dome could suggest a response to such practices.[190]

There is compelling evidence, however, for the observance of elaborate ritual ceremonies in the Dome of the Rock during the Umayyad period. These rites are described almost identically in the *Faḍāʾil al-Quds* literature as well as in an account from the *Mirʾāt al-Zamān* of Sibṭ b. al-Jawzī published by Amikam Elad.[191] According to these reports, the shrine and its Rock were served by a corps of three hundred ritual "attendants" (الخدم), as well as two hundred gatekeepers, ten for each of its gates, and a staff of Jews and Christians who cleaned the Ḥaram and provided glass and wicks for its lamps and goblets.[192] The Dome was open for public worship only on Mondays and Thursdays; on other days the attendants alone were allowed inside. The public services began in private the evening before, when the attendants prepared a complex perfume that was allowed to sit overnight. The following morning they purified themselves with ritual washing and donned ceremonial garments. After these preparations, they rubbed the Rock with perfume and burned incense all around it, thereafter lowering the curtains that surrounded the Rock "so that the incense encircles the *Ṣakhra* [the Rock] entirely and the odour [of the incense] clings to it."[193] When the curtains were subsequently raised, the public was invited in to pray in the presence of the sacred Rock and its intense fragrance, but only for a brief time, allowing for just two *Rakʿah*s (prayers) or perhaps at most four according to Wāsiṭī's account. Wāsiṭī continues to describe the Dome's cleansing following the public's departure, which seems to mark the conclusion of these biweekly ceremonies.[194]

Unfortunately, we are not given to know the full significance of these rituals, and to my knowledge only Moshe Sharon has offered an interpretation of their broader meaning.[195] Nevertheless, these liturgical practices make clear that the Dome was originally much more than just another place of prayer and was instead considered a sacred space of the highest sanctity in earliest Islam. The rites are clearly centered on the Rock itself, which had been a central feature of the Jewish Temple(s). According to the Mishnah, the Rock was considered the "foundation rock" (אבן שתיה) of divine creation, and upon it the Ark of the Covenant had originally rested within the Temple's Holy of Holies; after the Ark's removal, the high priest would enter the Holy of Holies on the Day of Atonement, Yom Kippur, and place incense upon the Rock.[196] The practice apparently continued into the Byzantine period, inasmuch as the fourth-century "Bordeaux Pilgrim" notes in his *Itinerary* that once a year the Jews anointed this stone on the Temple Mount, mourning and rending their garments.[197] The intensive perfuming and incensing of the Rock in ʿAbd al-Malik's shrine are highly redolent of this Jewish practice, and the regular attention to the Rock by a professional band of liturgical specialists certainly recalls the cult of the Jewish Temple much more than anything associated with the Meccan Kaʿba. Likewise, the days of the week on which the ceremonies were observed, Monday and Thursday, held special meaning in the Jewish tradition: on these days the Torah was read publicly before the morning prayer, an activity that was joined with fasting and special prayers.[198] Indeed, the distinctive rites belonging to the Dome of the Rock in the Umayyad period strongly suggest that it was not erected as a substitute for the Kaʿba, in order to provide an alternate site for the rituals that came to be associated with the Meccan shrine. Rather, the Dome had its own significance that was commemorated by distinctive ritual practices that were reminiscent of the Jewish Temple and corresponded to the patterns of Jewish observance.

Of course, there was no sacrifice involved, and this had been the primary function of both Jewish Temples. Yet since the destruction of the Second Temple, Judaism and Christianity had both reoriented themselves—in different ways—away from the Temple's sacrificial cult. Perhaps after so many centuries, Jewish ideas of a restoration of this sacred space did not expect a resumption of the sacrifices. As Sharon observes, in Jewish eyes "the true Temple could only be built by the Messiah"; the Jews likely saw the Dome as merely a "symbol of the Temple" and viewed this rescue of the Temple's site from the "humiliating devastation" under Christian rule as "the beginning of redemption." Although the sacrifices could not be restored, "the holy ointment and lighting of oil lamps were rituals that could symbolize the Temple" as they awaited the Messiah's coming.[199] Indeed, these connections between the Dome and the Temple in the *Faḍāʾil al-Quds* literature strongly affirm the indications of the Jewish apocalypses considered above, leaving little question that the two structures were genetically linked not only in the eyes of certain Jewish "Believers" but in the early Islamic understanding as well.[200]

This early Islamic veneration of the Rock, however, suggests something much more than just an ersatz Temple erected in anticipation of an impending messianic restoration. The Rock, as already noted, originally lay within the Holy of Holies, and as the last remaining vestige of the dwelling place of the divine presence within the Temple, the Rock itself possessed an inherent holiness that would have resonated immediately with many of the early Believers. The Islamic traditions describing the Rock as God's terrestrial throne and as the intersection of the earthly and heavenly realms undoubtedly take their origin from the Rock's association with the Holy of Holies in the Jewish Temple. According to the early traditions of the *Faḍāʾil al-Quds*, God had sat on the Rock after completing the creation and ascended to Heaven from the Rock after dwelling there for forty years.[201] There are even faint traces, as Josef van Ess notes, of an early Islamic tradition that the "footprint" on the Rock is not Muhammad's but God's, which the latter left just before ascending. The tradition's blatant anthropomorphism would appear to be a sign of its relative antiquity.[202] Consequently, even though the Dome of the Rock was certainly not erected as a formal restoration of the Jewish Temple and its sacrificial cult, the building's location and its ritual practices certainly suggest a sort of renewal or reformation of the Temple tradition in an "Islamic" guise. One can readily imagine how such developments would have inspired many among the early Believers to envisage the Dome as realizing in some way the Temple's reconstruction.

Presumably, many among Muhammad's earliest followers would have seen this progressive restoration of cult to the Temple Mount as setting in motion the events of the end times, as indicated by the apocalyptic traditions of the *Faḍā'il al-Quds* collections (as well as the apocalypse of Rabbi Shim'ōn and other sources). According to their eschatological vision, this final sequence was expected to unfold over a rather short span of time after the "Temple's" restoration, again suggesting a rather primitive tradition. Myriam Rosen-Ayalon's compelling interpretation of the Dome of the Rock's architecture and decoration as reflecting traditions about the end of times certainly suggests its construction within an eschatologically charged atmosphere.[203] According to somewhat later reports, the Dome was originally decorated with images pertaining to the last days, including "the picture of *al-Ṣirāṭ* [that is, the bridge to Heaven], the Gate of Paradise and the footprint of the Messenger of God (Ṣ) and the Valley of Gehenna," which would seem to affirm the building's association with the coming "end of days."[204]

The early traditions of the *Faḍā'il al-Quds* literature thus would appear largely to confirm the reconstruction of primitive Islam that we have proposed in this as well as the preceding chapter: these traditions reveal an inter-confessional movement, with a strong Jewish (and perhaps Christian) presence, guided by belief in an impending and unfolding *eschaton*, whose primary events are centered on Jerusalem and the Holy Land. Indeed, these reports seem remarkably consistent with Sebeos's description of this religious movement. Moreover, if earliest Islam was an eschatological movement expecting an imminent end to the world, as the Qur'ān and other early traditions strongly seem to suggest, the fact that the events of Islam's eschatological drama have remained so firmly anchored to Jerusalem, rather than being foretold against a Ḥijāzī backdrop, is yet another forceful sign of Jerusalem's paramount importance in the formative tradition.[205] As David Cook notes, there were in fact efforts to supplant Jerusalem's eschatological primacy, replacing it with some other center, such as Medina, Damascus, or Kūfa, but these were all unsuccessful, thwarted by Jerusalem's exceptional holiness and the apparent force of its connection in early Islamic culture to traditions about the end of times.[206]

Closely related to Jerusalem's unique eschatological status are presumably the various traditions recommending burial in Jerusalem and the Holy Land. Dying in Jerusalem is "like dying in the first sphere of heaven, and dying in the vicinity is like dying in [Jerusalem itself]"; consequently, burial in Jerusalem is equivalent to being "buried as if in the first sphere of heaven." Those buried in Jerusalem will be "saved from the test of the grave and its agony" and "are held to have crossed the 'bridge of Hell' [*al-Ṣirāṭ*]."[207] More importantly, however, Jerusalem was believed to be the resting place of the prophets. Abraham, Isaac, and Jacob were buried there, as was Adam, whose legs lie beside the Rock and whose head was near the mosque of Abraham (in Hebron).[208] Only Muhammad, with his traditional burial in Medina, seems to have been left out. There is, however, evidence in the *Faḍā'il al-Quds* literature of a "dispute over Muḥammad's place of burial, in which a group of his friends demanded that he be brought to Jerusalem, the resting place of the prophets."[209] Wāṣiṭī preserves a similar tradition in his collection, involving a confrontation between al-Zuhrī and a *qāṣṣ* (storyteller) while the former was a pilgrim in Jerusalem:

> When al-Zuhrī came to Jerusalem I took him to pray at the holy sites. I said to him: There is a sheikh here called 'Uqba b. Abī Zaynab who relates traditions from the Books [that is, Jewish and Christian sources]. Would you like to meet him? We sat beside him and he began to extol the virtues of Jerusalem. At length al-Zuhrī said to him: O sheikh! You will never be able to outdo Allāh's words in praise of Jerusalem "Glory be to Him, who carried His servant by night from the Holy Mosque to the Further Mosque" [Qur'ān 17:1]. This angered the sheikh, who said: The hour of the resurrection will never arrive until the bones of Muhammad (Ṣ) are transferred to Jerusalem.[210]

Could such a story reflect vestiges of a tradition linking the end of Muhammad's life and possibly even his burial originally with the Holy Land? Admittedly, these reports say nothing concerning the location of Muhammad's death, and their invention could be easily explained by the broader tradition of prophetic burial in Jerusalem. Nevertheless, they may possibly represent some trace of a connection between the end of Muhammad's life and the

Holy Land, offering at least faint evidence for a tradition of his death somewhere outside of the Ḥijāz, perhaps following the invasion of Palestine, as seems to be suggested by the sources analyzed at the outset of this study.

In light of Jerusalem's exceptional sanctity within formative Islam, one would almost anticipate the existence of a tradition joining the culmination of Muhammad's life with the Holy Land and its liberation by the faithful children of Abraham. As we have seen, the earliest evidence, from both non-Islamic and Islamic sources, strongly indicates that the Holy Land and its sacred center in Jerusalem were the primary focus of the early Believers' aspirations. As much is indicated by the early selection of Jerusalem, instead of Mecca, as the *qibla* for Islamic prayer, a point that even the early Islamic tradition itself must acknowledge. There is no reason to believe, as the *sīra* tradition relates, that this choice of sacred direction was only a brief, early experiment: a variety of sources bear witness that the Jerusalem *qibla* was practiced even after Muhammad's death, while prayer toward Mecca became the universal standard only somewhat later. Moreover, the early traditions of the *Faḍāʾil al-Quds* literature, which almost certainly date to the later seventh century, reveal a religious movement that is imbued with the traditions of early Judaism, presumably having a large "Jewish" element within its community of the Believers. The early Islamic emphasis on restoring worship and a sanctuary to the site of the Temple shows a remarkable connection with both Judaism and Jerusalem. Such elements would have powerfully drawn Muhammad to Jerusalem and the Holy Land in early Islamic memory, whether he actually ever made it there or not. For example, Hirschberg suggests that the story of Muhammad's Night Journey to Jerusalem is a primitive tradition, perhaps circulated by Muhammad himself, designed to place Muhammad somehow in the Holy Land, since, according to Jewish tradition, "there could be no prophecy outside of Palestine."[211] While it seems more likely, as discussed below, that this tradition emerged to displace Islam's early connection with the Holy Land and secure its origins more firmly in the Ḥijāz, Hirschberg's hypothesis rightly recognizes the pull that the early Islamic—and Jewish—traditions concerning Jerusalem and Palestine must have had on the earliest memories of Muhammad's life. The conceptual world of Abrahamic monotheism essentially demanded his presence, in some capacity, in the Promised Land. Thus it is understandable that we find Kaʾb declaring Syria (*al-Shām*), and not the Ḥijāz, as the land of Muhammad's prophetic rule. Indeed, it makes perfect sense to find such words voiced by Kaʾb, who not only was, according to tradition, close to the early Umayyad leaders but also serves as the mouthpiece of early "Judeo-Islam" in the traditional materials.[212]

Jerusalem's fusion with Islam's eschatological hopes is also particularly significant in this regard. If Muhammad was in fact an eschatological prophet, whose earliest followers expected an imminent end to the world, then one would almost expect to find the completion of his life merged with the sacred landscape that would be the setting for history's conclusion. Even if Muhammad had died in rather different circumstances, it is easy to imagine the emergence of an early Islamic tradition remembering him as the one who led his followers into the eschatological land of promise. A tradition of his death and perhaps even burial after the beginnings of the campaign to reclaim the Holy Land would fit the eschatological narrative of early Islam quite well: presumably his death would present a harbinger of the *eschaton*'s arrival, as his life came to an end in the land where the prophets lie buried. Even if such a tradition of Muhammad's leadership during the invasion of Palestine is not verifiable as a historical "fact," it is certainly quite likely that this detail may have formed part of the earliest community's narrative of its beginnings, whether or not it actually happened.

The context of an eschatological movement focused on reclaiming the Holy Land of promised inheritance would strongly invite the memory of Muhammad's involvement in its liberation, and perhaps the reports considered in the first chapter of this study indeed report such a tradition stemming from the primitive community of the Believers. While there is no guarantee that this information accurately describes the historical reality of the mid-630s, there is good reason to believe that Islam's earliest traditions about its prophet may very well have remembered his involvement in the conquest of the Holy Land. The eschatological confidence of earliest Islam and its apparent focus on Jerusalem and the Holy Land as the site of the final conflagration would have almost required Muhammad's presence as his followers attained their ultimate goal. Even if it had not actually happened thus, it must have seemed entirely logical for his followers to remember the beginnings of Islam in this way. Nevertheless, once Islam developed a sacred geography anchored in the Ḥijāz as a central element of its confessional self-definition that was distinct from the other Abrahamic monotheisms that it had once welcomed, the end of Muhammad's life would have to be radically re-remembered. The rival tradition of Muhammad's pre-conquest death in Medina can thus be understood as a memorialization of his death within this new, distinctively Islamic—and Arab—sacred landscape.

Muhammad at Mecca: Remembering the Origins of Islam in an Arabian Holy Land

Jerusalem's importance as a sacred center in formative Islam is thus widely reflected in early Islamic, as well as non-Islamic, sources, and there can be little question that for much of Islam's first century, the Holy Land figured rather prominently on its sacred map. Yet despite Jerusalem's unmistakable sanctity during the period of Umayyad rule, the question of its status, particularly in relation to the Islamic holy cities of the Ḥijāz, was the subject of considerable dispute in sources of the second, third, and subsequent centuries, as noted already from Kister's analysis of the "Three Mosques" *ḥadīth*. Although the sacredness of Jerusalem and its surroundings for the early Believers and the Umayyads could not simply be overlooked or forgotten, the predominant voice within the Islamic historical tradition has remembered the sanctity of Jerusalem rather differently. According to the prevailing view, the Islamic sources evaluate this focus on Jerusalem and the Holy Land during the formative period essentially as a deviant innovation introduced by the Umayyads in an effort to develop and promote the sanctity of the lands from which they ruled, Syria and Palestine, at the expense of the traditional cradle of the Islamic faith, the cities of Mecca and Medina in the Ḥijāz. Inasmuch as the later historical tradition was often rather unkind to the Umayyads, routinely reproaching them for impiety and un-Islamic behavior, such an assessment comports well with this broader tendency of Islamic historiography.[213] These later traditionists accuse the Umayyads of engaging in a propaganda campaign to elevate the religious significance of Jerusalem and the Holy Land to equal status with the Ḥijāz. The effort allegedly reached its peak during the Second Civil War, when ʿAbd Allāh ibn al-Zubayr proclaimed himself caliph in 683, with effective sovereignty over the Ḥijāz and its sanctuaries. It was at this time, according to a number of reports, that ʿAbd al-Malik had the Dome of the Rock constructed in an effort to divert the Islamic pilgrimage from Mecca, which was under his rival's control, to Jerusalem.[214] The sanctity of Jerusalem thus was viewed by many later Muslims as a secondary development, largely manufactured to serve the political needs of the notorious Umayyad caliphs, and its sacred precincts certainly were not equal in holiness to the shrines of the Ḥijāz.

The perspective of these later Islamic historians, with its criticism of the Umayyads and their motives, was highly influential on early Western accounts of the origins of Islam. Drawing on these sources, scholars of the late nineteenth and early twentieth centuries estimated the sanctity of Jerusalem and the Holy Land in early Islam to be primarily a product of Umayyad political interests. Moreover, they accepted more or less at face value the tradition that ʿAbd al-Malik constructed the Dome of the Rock as a rival to the Meccan Kaʿba, in hopes of diverting the pilgrimage to Jerusalem. Although others had proposed this explanation before him, Ignác Goldziher is perhaps most closely associated with this hypothesis, and it was primarily through his influence that it came to prevail.[215] Nevertheless, around the middle of the twentieth century, S. D. Goitein upended Goldziher's theory with a pair of articles calling attention to the likely anti-Umayyad bias underlying such reports.[216] Against Goldziher, Goitein argues that the sanctity of Jerusalem and Palestine in formative Islam was not the product of Umayyad political machinations but instead had its basis in the genuine religious beliefs of the early Muslims. As Goitein rightly observes, it is highly unlikely that ʿAbd al-Malik would have attempted something as outrageous and potentially inflammatory as diverting the *ḥajj* when he was in such a politically tenuous situation: if in fact the *ḥajj* to Mecca were already established as a standard practice, such actions would have marked him as a *kāfir*, a heretic, and only strengthened the cause of his Meccan rival.[217] Moreover, Goitein adduces considerable positive evidence from the early Islamic tradition revealing a high regard for the sanctity of Jerusalem and the Holy Land in general, irrespective of the *ḥajj* or the Ḥijāz. It is highly improbable, Goitein concludes, that such extensive belief in the holiness of Jerusalem could have been manufactured in the brief interval when ʿAbd al-Malik and Ibn al-Zubayr were contending for the caliphate.[218]

On the whole it would appear that Goitein's arguments have carried the day, and since the publication of his articles, only very few Western scholars have continued to adhere to Goldziher's hypothesis.[219] As a result, scholars of formative Islam during the past half century have by and large come to recognize the sanctity of Jerusalem as a principle feature of the primitive tradition.[220] Even the English translation of Goldziher's *Muhammedanische Studien* (1966) includes an editorial remark correcting his views, explaining that there is "no doubt" that the tradition accusing ʿAbd al-Malik of attempting to divert the *ḥajj* "is an anti-Umayyad invention."[221] The only major dissent to this consensus would appear to come from Amikam Elad, who has recently attempted a revival of Goldziher's theory concerning the status of Jerusalem and the Dome of the Rock.[222] Nevertheless, Elad's arguments are not fully persuasive, inasmuch as they fail to answer many of the key problems that Goitein identifies, and he does not provide sufficient evidence for accepting the accusation that ʿAbd al-Malik sought to divert the *ḥajj*.

While Elad is correct to stress the political context of ʿAbd al-Malik's shrine, the Dome's political impact certainly does not exclude the basis of its veneration in actual Islamic piety. Indeed, one would imagine that ʿAbd al-Malik sought to promote the existing sanctity of Jerusalem and the Holy Land in order to gain support against his Ḥijāzī rival. The fundamentally religious origin of early Islamic veneration of Jerusalem and Palestine in no way precludes the politicization of these elements under the Umayyads; yet such political exploitation of the Holy Land would seem to presume a forceful religious belief in its sanctity.[223] In the end, Elad himself concedes that genuine religious convictions underlay ʿAbd al-Malik's building program and his promotion of Jerusalem's sanctity, including its status as the site of the former Temple and its eschatological significance, although he maintains that the "immediate cause" for ʿAbd al-Malik's actions was political.[224] Such conclusions, however, are not really at odds with Goitein's basic hypothesis, and while the catalyst for the Dome's construction may have been partly political, the sanctity of Jerusalem (and the Dome) remains grounded in pre-existing religious beliefs, which were not ʿAbd al-Malik's invention.

Much more problematic is Elad's contention that ʿAbd al-Malik's motives for building the Dome of the Rock were in fact to divert the *ḥajj* to Jerusalem. Although Elad repeatedly asserts that this was ʿAbd al-Malik's intention, he does not offer convincing evidence for this conclusion, particularly in light of the issues raised by Goitein and others sharing his views. The earliest sources making this accusation are only from the late ninth century (al-Yaʿqūbi) and the early tenth (Eutychius), and Elad adds a number of other authorities largely from the twelfth and later centuries to this list.[225] Nevertheless, the sources in question frequently show signs of a Shīʿī (and sometimes ʿAbbāsid) bias, both of which would involve a measure of prejudice against both the Umayyads and Jerusalem.[226] Despite such tendencies in the sources, Elad suggests, against Goitein, that sectarian allegiances rarely affected the narratives of the early Islamic historians, and their accounts generally reflect a balance and moderation that eschews factional bias. Moreover, since later "Sunni" authors did not hesitate to include this tradition, Elad concludes that its report of ʿAbd al-Malik's intention to divert the *ḥajj* must in fact be reliable.[227] Unfortunately, however, these arguments are not sufficient to allay concerns that the tradition is in fact a polemical fabrication, a product of either pro-Shīʿī, pro-ʿAbbāsid, or anti-Umayyad bias. Any one—or perhaps more likely, some combination—of these three tendencies could have generated this calumnious report, and such later interests in defaming the Umayyads seem a much more likely source of this report than an actual attempt by ʿAbd al-Malik to divert the *ḥajj*.[228]

Perhaps more important, however, is the question of whether there even was by this time a well-established and exclusive practice of annual pilgrimage to Mecca or the Ḥijāz for ʿAbd al-Malik to have attempted to divert. It is not at all clear that primitive Islam had a single sacred center, and it is doubtful that Mecca had been identified as a unique focus of Islamic piety by the middle of the first Islamic century. One cannot assume that the *ḥajj* to Mecca had become established as a canonical practice of the Islamic faith prior to ʿAbd al-Malik's reign, nor is it certain that by this time Mecca had eclipsed Jerusalem's sanctity to emerge as the preeminent sacred center of the Islamic tradition. Yet earliest Islam's special veneration for Jerusalem and the Holy Land clearly emerges from the sources considered above. Accordingly, ʿAbd al-Malik's shrine on the Temple Mount was almost certainly not a deviant innovation designed to radically reorient the sacred geography of Islam; rather, the Dome's construction seems instead to have been grounded in the traditional piety of primitive Islam, whose reverence for Jerusalem and the Jewish Temple it was erected to commemorate. Far from introducing an aberrant practice, the Dome of the Rock is more likely the final flowering of the Jerusalem-centered piety of the Believers during Islam's first several decades. If anything, it is the *ḥajj* that seems to be something of a novelty in this period, and Mecca's sanctity appears to be emergent.

"As far as Mecca is concerned," Chase Robinson explains, "it must be emphasized that there is no clear evidence that pilgrimage to the Kaʿba and/or the environs of Mecca had become a fixed feature of Muslim belief and practice at the end of the seventh century."[229] The Qurʾān speaks only vaguely of a pilgrimage, generally identifying its object rather plainly as "the House," *al-Bayt* (for example, 2:158, 3:96–97). Although the later Islamic tradition confidently assumes that these references indicate the Meccan Kaʿba, absent such hindsight, this meaning often is not clear from the texts themselves, and perhaps in earliest Islam this *Bayt* was understood to be the *Bayt al-Maqdis*, Jerusalem and its Holy House, the Temple. Admittedly, *sūra* 5:95–97 twice invokes the name "Kaʿba," in one instance identifying it with the "Holy House" (*al-bayt al-ḥarām*), yet its absence from related passages in other *sūra*s certainly invites the possibility that this is an interpolation. Alternatively, one should recall the witness of Jacob of Edessa, whose description of early Islamic prayer seems to locate the "Kaʿba" either in Jerusalem or somewhere nearby in the later seventh century. Moreover, as Robinson concludes, "we should not assume that early

Muslims acted in accordance to a text that itself had not become fixed or authoritative," a status that the Qur'ān achieved only during ʿAbd al-Malik's reign, according to Robinson.[230] While Mecca may also have held special significance for the early Believers, in order to understand the evolving nature of sacred geography in formative Islam, one must, as Robinson suggests, "set aside presumptions that prescribed fixed pilgrimage rites to a centre (Mecca), which enjoyed pride of place over all others": it took some time, it would appear, for Mecca "to eclipse Jerusalem as the focus of pilgrimage."[231] And although it was a contest that Mecca would ultimately win, the practice of sacred pilgrimage to Jerusalem would persist, and, as already noted, traditions asserting that Jerusalem's holiness equaled or even surpassed that of Medina or Mecca continued to circulate in later centuries.[232] Thus, despite Mecca's eventual ascendency, Jerusalem's foremost importance for the early Believers proved indelible, and its sanctity could not be completely eclipsed by the holy sites of the Ḥijāz. Indeed, Jerusalem's apparently primitive veneration in the Islamic faith serves partly to highlight the secondary status of the Ḥijāz's eventual emergence as a distinctively Islamic holy land.

Increasingly over the past several decades, scholars have called attention to the fact that traditions relating the unique sanctity of the Ḥijāz generally have an air of novelty about them. Perhaps more significant, however, is the related observation that the traditional representation of Islamic origins as unfolding against an exclusively Ḥijāzī backdrop seems to be a more recent invention rather than a simple reflection of historical realities. The first to suggest such a radical rethinking of the beginnings of Islam seems to have been John Wansbrough, who proposed that Islam's memories of an Arabian origin are not so much a record of historical fact as part of a broader strategy of self-legitimation aimed at distinguishing Islam from its monotheist rivals in the early medieval Near East. Through analysis of the Qur'ān and other early sources, Wansbrough arrives at the conclusion that these writings reveal a faith formed within the crucible of Middle Eastern monotheism that was shaped by extensive dialogue with the traditions of Judaism and, to a lesser extent, Christianity.[233] As Wansbrough observes, the traditional narrative of Islam's rise in Mecca and Medina is attested only rather late, in sources composed over a century after the events in question, which themselves are known only as transmitted by authors of the ninth century and later. This interval allowed ample time for significant changes in Islamic self-understanding to arise so that by the time these traditions were gathered the community's memory of its own genesis had altered considerably. As a result, according to Wansbrough, Islam's initial emergence within the "sectarian milieu" of the Near East has been displaced by the myth of Ḥijāzī origins. No less controversial is Wansbrough's contention that the Qur'ān did not emerge in its *ne varietur* form as the inviolable sacred text of Islam until sometime around the turn of the ninth century. Yet even if the Qur'ānic *textus receptus* likely became fixed about a century earlier, as argued in the previous chapter, this circumstance does not significantly affect Wansbrough's theories regarding the historical circumstances of the Islamic tradition's origins. When taken on its own terms, the Qur'ān shows almost no trace of any connection with the Ḥijāz, and one of the primary achievements of Wansbrough's *Quranic Studies* lies in its demonstration of just how much the Ḥijāzī background of the Qur'ān text is a product not of the text itself, but instead of the Islamic exegetical tradition.[234]

Regardless of how one may estimate some of Wansbrough's broader conclusions regarding the origins of Islam, his work persuasively identifies a pattern evident in the earliest legal, historical, and exegetical traditions of Islam, all of which "reflect a single impulse: to demonstrate the Hijazi origins of Islam."[235] Even if one is unwilling to accept Wansbrough's implication that the beginnings of Islam had nothing to do with the Ḥijāz, this forceful tendency of the tradition to situate formative Islam entirely within the Ḥijāz is discernable and requires explanation. Many of the sources seemingly "protest too much" in the effort to link every aspect of the rise of Islam unambiguously with the Ḥijāz, as if there could be some doubt. One possible solution, initially proposed by Crone and Cook in *Hagarism*, would locate the beginnings of Islam in northwest Arabia, along the fringes of the Roman Empire.[236] Certain elements could seem to favor such an hypothesis, including the *qibla* of the early Mesopotamian mosques, the spread of monotheism among the Arabs of Rome's borderlands, the inclusion of significant numbers of Jews within the early community, and the primitive focus on the Holy Land, as noted above. Likewise, Crone offers additional support for this theory in her study of *Meccan Trade and the Rise of Islam*; there she presents further evidence of the Islamic tradition's effort to concretize the Qur'ān within a Ḥijāzī setting, concluding once again that the evidence concerning trade and the sanctuary is a better fit with northwest Arabia than with Mecca and the Ḥijāz.[237] Moreover, Yehuda Nevo, together with various colleagues, has similarly argued that archaeological and inscriptional evidence from the central Negev seems to comport better with the data of early Islam than does the Ḥijāz, offering somewhat debatable support for Crone and Cook's proposal.[238]

Yet as intriguing as such hypotheses undeniably are, they have not proved compelling, nor have they decisively resolved the question of where Islam was born. Although Roman Arabia and its environs certainly present a favorable setting for the genesis of Islam, it is difficult to bind Islam's origins exclusively to this region. For the moment at least, it seems somewhat unlikely that we will succeed in finding the actual location where Muhammad's religious movement first took shape with such precision, and it certainly is not possible to rule out Muhammad's origin in the Ḥijāz. Nevertheless, whatever connection the Ḥijāz and its two sacred cities, Mecca and Medina, may have had with the beginnings of Islam, it is increasingly clear that this region was not as uniquely important in formative Islam as the later tradition remembers it. To the contrary, it would appear that the community of the Believers first emerged within a very different setting, as persuasively argued in Crone's recent article on the livelihood of the Qur'ān's "pagan" opponents (the *mushrikūn*), for instance. Although Crone is here more cautiously agnostic regarding the exact location of Islam's genesis, she convincingly demonstrates that the Qur'ān's representation of its opponents as agriculturalists (as opposed to traders) is incompatible with barren landscape of Mecca and its environs.[239] As Watt himself notes at the very beginning of *Muhammad in Mecca*, "at Mecca . . . no agriculture at all was possible—an important fact that should be kept in mind."[240] Thus this aspect of the Qur'ān's message clearly indicates its formation within a context rather different from what the later tradition imagines: it is evidence strongly suggestive that the Qur'ān, and hence Islam, may have first taken shape somewhere outside of the Ḥijāz (or at least not in Mecca).

Likewise, Hawting's numerous studies of early traditions related to the Meccan shrine have reached similar conclusions. While Hawting has remained largely noncommittal regarding the precise birthplace of Muhammad's religious movement, his research frequently identifies the origins of certain traditions associated with the "Meccan" shrine within a Jewish milieu. It would thus appear that Islamic ideas about the holiness of this sanctuary did not just borrow from, but were initially formed within, a Jewish context and were only later transferred to the Meccan shrine at a secondary stage. Otherwise, it is difficult to understand how certain distinctively Jewish notions came to be associated with the Meccan sanctuary, if this shrine had been the focus of a distinctively Islamic veneration from the very beginning.[241] Other scholars likewise have observed that numerous Jewish traditions regarding the sanctity of Jerusalem have similarly been transferred to Mecca and its shrine by the early Muslims.[242] Such findings are not only highly compatible with the inter-confessional nature of the early community of the Believers, as well as the apparent early focus on Jerusalem and the Holy Land, but they also strongly seem to suggest the emergence of Mecca and the Ḥijāz at the center of Islam's sacred geography only at a later stage.

Hawting takes a similar position in his monograph on the question of idolatry in earliest Islam, proposing that Islam first emerged within the context of a larger monotheist religious group (or groups), developing into a distinctly Islamic form of monotheism only "over an extended period of time and, thus, a quite wide geographical area."[243] According to Hawting, "The area in which these key developments took place was not Arabia but the wider Middle East, and in particular Syria and Iraq. Whatever religious ideas the Arabs brought with them into the lands they conquered, it is likely that it was from the social, political and religious interaction of the Arabs and the peoples over whom they ruled that Islam as we know it was formed."[244] On the whole, the primary thesis of Hawting's book has been rather well received. As he persuasively argues, the Qur'ān's religious opponents appear in fact to have been monotheists whose belief in the intercessory efficacy of certain intermediary beings separated them from the more austere monotheism outlined in the Qur'ān. Only somewhat later was their "association" (*shirk*) of other intermediate beings with God transformed into the Meccan paganism imagined by the Islamic traditional sources. The broader framework, however, within which Hawting situates these findings, has drawn a fair amount of criticism: while some scholars have embraced his reassessment of the Qur'ān's opponents, many have balked at his related contention that these developments occurred outside of the Ḥijaz, in Syria and Mesopotamia.[245]

Although Hawting does not exclude the possibility of a Ḥijāzī context, the lack of evidence for any significant concentration of monotheists in this area of the Arabian Peninsula leads him to conclude that Syria (including Palestine) and Mesopotamia present a more plausible setting. As we have already noted, while Christianity had in fact surrounded the Ḥijāz, there is no evidence of its spread into this region. Likewise, although the Islamic tradition describes a sizable Jewish community in Yathrib (Medina), its existence is not confirmed by any non-Islamic sources. The legend of the Jews' expulsion from Medina under ʿUmar and their relocation to Iraq is quite possibly a convenient apologetic device designed to reconcile their absence from the Ḥijāz with traditional accounts of Islamic origins. More importantly, however, there is no evidence at all of any significant Jewish (or Christian) presence in Mecca, where the Qur'ān's "pagan" opponents are reputed to have lived.[246] Of course, it is not impossible that monotheist belief was in fact quite diffuse in the early seventh-century Ḥijāz but has simply failed to register in our source materials. Yet given the present state of our evidence, the kind of intense inter-monotheist polemic that Hawting recovers from the Qur'ān is more conceivable in seventh-century Syria and Mesopotamia than in the seventh-century Ḥijāz. Accordingly, Hawting interprets the Islamic tradition's invention of a vibrant Meccan paganism out of the Qur'ān's attacks against these monotheist "associators" as an effort to re-imagine the origins of Islam within a uniquely Ḥijāzī and thoroughly polytheist setting, where the birth of Islam was isolated from any possible influence coming from Judaism or Christianity. Such a narrative, Hawting observes, not only established Islam as confessionally distinct from its monotheist rivals but also underscored the purity of its unique revelation, which came directly from God and not from the religious traditions of Islam's predecessors.[247]

Nevertheless, the locational aspect of Hawting's reconstruction, as well as those of Wansbrough, Crone, and Cook, is not so much important for what it may indicate about where Islam really did or did not originate; rather, its primary significance lies in what it reveals about the development of sacred geography within earliest Islam. If the beginnings of Muhammad's religious movement perhaps took place somewhere in the Ḥijāz, which certainly is a distinct possibility, it nonetheless appears that neither this region nor the cities of Mecca and Medina were the focus of its earliest religious aspirations. Formative Islam does not seem to have been grounded in a sacred geography that viewed the Ḥijāz as a uniquely Islamic holy land with its cultic center at the Meccan sanctuary. To the contrary, as we have seen above, a wide range of evidence indicates that the earliest Muslims regarded Palestine, Jerusalem, and the Temple Mount as particularly holy. Even if Muhammad's followers originally rode forth from the Ḥijāz, their faith appears to have been looking forward, to Jerusalem, where presumably the Hour awaited, rather than gazing backward, in a memorialization of the Ḥijāz as the sacred landscape of the Qur'ān and its prophet.

One should of course not discount the possibility that in this formative period many of the early Believers also considered the Ḥijāz to be a land of some religious significance. Perhaps Mecca and Medina shared some measure of sanctity within a sacred landscape that appears to have given pride of place, at least initially, to Palestine, the land of promise and prophets, and to Jerusalem, the site of the Temple and the impending judgment of the Hour. Yet as Crone and Cook have famously noted, no source outside of the Islamic tradition makes any mention at all of Mecca prior to the *Byzantine-Arab Chronicle of 741*, and this text refers to it only in passing in the context of the Second Civil War between ʿAbd al-Malik and Ibn al-Zubayr. If Mecca had been of central importance for the early Believers, such lengthy silence is rather puzzling. Moreover, the Qurʾān itself identifies the specific location of "the House" (*al-Bayt*) just once, in which case it mysteriously names not Mecca but instead "Bakka" as its site (3:96). Although "the Islamic tradition is naturally at pains to identify this place with Mecca," this certainly is not clear from the text itself.[248] In any case, whatever the early status of Mecca and Medina may have been, a primitive orientation toward the holiness of Jerusalem as the Believers' principal sacred center seems unmistakable.

If in fact earliest Islam was, as we have argued, an inter-confessional movement that included a sizable Jewish contingent and perhaps at least some Christians, one certainly would expect to find Jerusalem and Palestine at the center of its sacred geography. Evidence suggesting that the early Believers were impelled by a religious conviction in their shared Abrahamic right to inheritance of this land would essentially require such convictions. Moreover, the apparent eschatological fervor that inspired Muhammad and his earliest followers to expect the Hour's imminent arrival would have drawn their hopes to focus on Jerusalem. Jerusalem's eschatological status as the location of history's final events in the Jewish, Christian, and—ultimately—Islamic traditions would have brought this city's unique sanctity immediately to the fore. Yet as the Hour continued to be delayed and the force of its immediate expectation accordingly began to diminish, this important pillar of Jerusalem's sanctity was weakened. Nevertheless, as an apparent vestige of the early Believers' reverence for this city, Jerusalem remains the focus of Islam's now postponed eschatological expectations. Moreover, once formative Islam began to separate itself confessionally from the other monotheisms of the Near East, it became unacceptable to have a sacred center whose significance was defined primarily by Jewish and Christian traditions. Islam would have to discover its own distinctive sacred geography, one that would distinguish it from—and herald its superiority to—the monotheistic traditions it had previously embraced as fellow Believers.

Presumably, the Ḥijāz offered a welcome blank slate, onto which a new sacred geography and a new salvation history could be inscribed. Yet there must have been some sort of an early connection between formative Islam and the Ḥijāz. It is hard to imagine, as some theories may seem to suggest, that there was no prior association between Muhammad's religious movement and this area. Clearly, Muhammad or a significant portion of his followers must have hailed from this region; otherwise, it is difficult to understand why the Islamic tradition would ultimately have settled on the particular sacred geography that came to define it. Perhaps the religious movement had some early connection with Yathrib (Medina) or even Mecca.[249] At the outset, however, this territory of origins seems to have been less esteemed than the land of eschatological promise, Jerusalem and the Holy Land. Only when the expected imminent destruction failed to arrive did the early Muslims find a need to re-remember the landscape of the Ḥijāz as the sacred cradle of Islam. Here Islam's peerless prophet, Muhammad, had revealed its unique scripture, the Qur'ān. No longer was Islam a nonconfessional movement of eschatological anticipation centered on the Final Judgment in Jerusalem. The Hour's prolonged deferral transformed the apocalyptic faith of the early Believers into a monotheist sect that transposed the sacred history of its Jewish and Christian antecedents onto the new landscape of the Ḥijāz. Thus was a distinctively Islamic faith born out of the sectarian milieu of the late ancient Near East, defined by its singular prophet and its own holy scriptures, which had been revealed in a distinctive sacred language, Arabic, against the consecrated landscape of the Arabian Ḥijāz. These were the markers of a new Islamic identity that would distinguish this nascent religious tradition from the fellow monotheists with whom it had once had freely associated.

Inasmuch as the Ḥijāz lay largely outside the orbit of the Jewish and Christian traditions, mapping the origins of Islam onto this region would underscore Islam's originality and independence from these earlier monotheist traditions. Yet the cultural isolation of the Ḥijāz presented Islam with another problem. Its sacred text, the Qur'ān, is so thoroughly suffused with traditions drawn from the Jewish and Christian traditions that by adopting a sacred geography anchored in the Ḥijāz, Islam effectively severed its scriptural traditions from the land of their origins. If Islam wished to present itself as the renewed faith of Abraham, it would somehow have to reconcile its sacred geography with the traditional associations of Abraham with Mesopotamia and Palestine. This it would largely achieve through an effort at the wholesale transfer of many biblical traditions to the Ḥijāz. There was, as Rubin notes, a general attempt "to elevate the status of the Ḥijāz to the rank of the Promised Land and to show that sacred history started to unfold not in Syria, but rather in Arabia."[250] Mecca is equated with Zion, and its sanctuary is made into an important pilgrimage destination for the prophets, including both Moses and Elijah in particular.[251] The Lost Tribes were also "found" in the Ḥijāz, linking its past securely with the Israelites.[252] The traditions from the Jerusalem Temple and its sacred rock were likewise assigned to Kaʿba.[253]

Particularly important, however, were traditions concerning Abraham and the near sacrifice of his son. Although a number of early Islamic accounts reproduce a version of the traditional Jewish legend of Abraham's near sacrifice of his son Isaac in or nearby Jerusalem, other accounts move these events into the Ḥijāz, where Abraham almost sacrifices his son Ishmael, the legendary ancestor of the Arabs. These Ḥijāzī-Ishmaelite traditions were, as Bashear notes, "part of the process of the rise of Mecca as the Abrahamic cultic center of Islam, where the symbolic act of sacrifice should annually be repeated as part of the *ḥajj* rituals."[254] These revised traditions were essential to justify the transfer of Islam's primary sacred center from Jerusalem to Mecca. Likewise, the traditions of the pre-Islamic *ḥanīfs*, the legendary rogue monotheists of the Arabian Ḥijāz, played a key role in the establishment of the Meccan sanctuary that ultimately would succeed in undermining Jerusalem's status. The *ḥanīfs* allowed for belief in a certain undercurrent of continuity between the religion established long ago by Abraham himself in the Ḥijāz and its alleged revival in the revelations of Muhammad: their persistent witness offered important validation of Islam as a restoration of God's original revelation in the consecrated land, the Ḥijāz.[255]

It is somewhat difficult to determine when the Ḥijāz first emerged as the primary focus of Islamic piety and identity. Quite possibly, it had been reverenced to some degree from the outset, perhaps alongside of Jerusalem. There are, as noted already, signs that earliest Islam perhaps did not have only a single sacred center, evidenced especially by the confusion about the *qibla*, as well as certain traditions that seem to assume the existence of two sacred centers, one in the north (Jerusalem?) and a second to the south (Mecca?).[256] Nevertheless, it would appear that for the first several decades, many among the Believers held Jerusalem and the Holy Land in much higher regard, as the site of the impending judgment and the promised patrimony of Abraham. In Bashear's estimation, the shift from Jerusalem to the Ḥijāz began in the early second/eighth century, as part of a broader program of Arabizing this new faith.[257] Likewise, Bashear dates the interpretive work of merging the rites of the Meccan *ḥajj* with the story of Abraham and Ishmael to this period.[258] Goldziher too observed that the intensive effort to consecrate the Hijāzī landscape appears to have coincided with the rise of the ʿAbbāsids around this same time.[259]

Nevertheless, there are reasons to suspect that the transition to a primarily Ḥijāzī sacred geography began somewhat earlier, ironically perhaps, under ʿAbd al-Malik and his Marwānid successors. Despite their condemnation in the later traditions as innovators who sought to promote Jerusalem and Syria at the expense of the Ḥijāz, it would appear that these Umayyad leaders were instrumental in the shift to an Arabian holy land. As noted above, it was near the beginning of ʿAbd al-Malik's reign when the early inter-confessional community of the Believers seems to have dissolved, and a distinctly Islamic version of Abrahamic monotheism first began to emerge from this "ecumenical" eschatological movement. At this time Islam came to be distinguished from its monotheist rivals by a rejection of the Trinity and the proclamation of Muhammad as a prophet of unequalled significance. This new religious configuration was seemingly embraced by ʿAbd al-Malik, who sought to merge Islamic identity with the Arab polity, both Islamicizing the Arab state and, by consequence, Arabizing Islam.[260] Moreover, it seems that this period also saw the collection and promulgation of a uniquely Islamic sacred scripture, written in a distinctive sacred language, Arabic. As emergent Islam began to distance itself confessionally from Judaism and Christianity, adopting an increasingly Arabic identity in the process, one would suspect that the notion of a uniquely Islamic and Arabian holy land became increasingly attractive.

The events of the Second Civil War present a likely catalyst for this shift. While this hypothesis could seem somewhat improbable on the surface, given ʿAbd al-Malik's victory over his rivals in the Ḥijāz, Ibn al-Zubayr's southern caliphate instead reveals the significance that many Muslims attached to this region and its shrines at the close of the seventh century. As Hawting observes of this confrontation, "One has the impression that it is not just that the conflict took place in the area where the holy places lay, but rather that ideas about the pilgrimage and the sanctuary were involved in the conflict."[261] Although the first caliphs seem to have paid little attention to Mecca and its shrine, it would appear that by the latter half of the first Islamic century, Mecca and its sanctuary had become the focus of intense devotion, even if at this time neither the Kaʿba nor the city itself was yet included in the rites of *ḥajj*.[262] This Meccan piety seems to have played more than a small role in Ibn al-Zubayr's revolt against the Umayyads. As Rubin observes, reports concerning this Ḥijāzī rebellion indicate that the uprising was in large part a response to the Israelite and Jerusalemite piety of the Umayyads.[263] Hoyland likewise concludes that the sources appear to indicate that "the revolt of ʿAbd Allāh ibn al-Zubayr had religious implications."[264] For instance, an apocalyptic *ḥadīth* dating to the height of this conflict identifies Ibn al-Zubayr as "the Restorer who, after the corruption of Islam at the hands of ʿAlī, Muʿāwiya, and Yazīd, would return it to its pristine purity of the time of the Medinese caliphate; who would, as the *ḥadīth* puts it, 'act among the Muslims according to the Sunna of their Prophet' so that Islam would 'settle down firmly on the ground.'"[265] Even a contemporary Christian chronicler notes that Ibn al-Zubayr rose up against the Umayyads "out of zeal for the house of God, and he was full of threats against the Westerners [that is, the Umayyads], claiming that they were transgressors of the law. He came to a certain locality in the South where their sanctuary was, and lived there."[266]

It is thus perhaps no mere coincidence that Ibn al-Zubayr was also the first Islamic leader to issue coins bearing the full "double *shahāda*," that is, the confession that "there is no God but God" *and* "Muhammad is the messenger of God."[267] As noted above, the second phrase does not appear to have been an element of the original confession of faith advanced by the early Believers. For them, a simple profession of monotheism seems to have sufficed for membership in the community. Affirmation of Muhammad's unique status as a prophet was added only toward the end of the seventh century, seemingly as part of a broader effort to differentiate "Islam" from its monotheist siblings as a separate and distinctive faith community. The issue of such coinage marks a notable inclination by both Ibn Zubayr and his rebellion toward an Islamic sectarianism and away from the early inter-confessional faith of the Believers, represented in the late seventh century by the Umayyad rulers. Proclamation of the double *shahāda* formed a significant parallel to the construction of a distinctly Islamic holy land in the Ḥijāz, both of which served to establish the sectarian identity of this "new" Arabian form of monotheism.

More than just a political struggle then, this early conflict between Jerusalem and Mecca had deep roots in "differing religious attitudes" that were distinguished especially by competing sacred geographies, one Ḥijāzī/Meccan and the other Syrian/Jerusalemite.[268] Partisans of the southern shrine rallied around Ibn al-Zubayr, seemingly alarmed at the Umayyad neglect of the Ḥijāz in favor of Syria and Jerusalem.[269] The resulting confrontation was thus not merely a dynastic struggle between the Marwānid and Zubayrid clans; it was apparently also a contest over the very nature of Islam and the location of its holy land. Here Wansbrough's recommendation of Walter Bauer's approach to the study of earliest Christianity for analyzing formative Islam is particularly helpful. Bauer's model postulates "the *coexistence* of variant and competing confessional expressions, each potentially and, from a local point of view perhaps actually, 'orthodox,'"[270] and it seems that something of this nature likely underlies the Second Civil War and the related conflicts over sacred geography. Much as the earliest Christians struggled over the precise relationship of their new faith to its Jewish matrix and the Jerusalem cult, it would appear that formative Islam was divided between those favoring a more Israelite and Jerusalemite identity for the movement (that is, the Umayyads and their supporters) and others who increasingly conceived of their faith as distinctively Arab and Ḥijāzī (Ibn al-Zubayr and his followers). The fact that many sources and traditions reflecting the former point of view have an association with Syria and Palestine (and to a lesser extent, Mesopotamia) seems to support such a conclusion.

Of course, ʿAbd al-Malik emerged the victor in this confrontation, and yet the sacred geography and ritual norms of Islam came to focus not on Jerusalem but on Mecca and the Ḥijāz, the region championed by his opponents. Nevertheless this outcome is not as incongruous as it may at first appear. Hoyland concludes that the powerful influence of religious piety fueling Ibn al-Zubayr's insurrection inspired ʿAbd al-Malik and his successors to take more seriously the religious positions espoused by their opponents. This experience led the Marwānids to break with the more religiously neutral pattern of governing exemplified by the Sufyānid line of the Umayyads and to establish a distinctively "Islamic" version of monotheism as the ideological basis of the Arab polity. This strategy, Hoyland observes, offered ʿAbd al-Malik "a way to rally the competing parties of this divisive civil war and to steal the thunder from his opponents."[271] Yet the decision that ʿAbd al-Malik faced was not just whether to Islamicize the state or not, but more fundamentally, what kind of "Islam" he would embrace. Under his predecessors, the inter-confessional model of the community of the Believers appears to have held sway, with a related focus on the sanctity of Jerusalem and the Jewish traditions of the Temple in particular. In the wake of the Second Civil War, ʿAbd al-Malik appears to have begun the process of reorienting the faith of the early Believers away from an inter-confessional monotheism and toward the more sectarian and Arabian vision of Islam with a sacred geography fixed in the Ḥijāz, an ideology that seems to have given strength to Ibn al-Zubayr's rebellion.[272] Having recognized its potentially disruptive force, ʿAbd al-Malik sought to neutralize this threat by embracing it.

Nevertheless, the Jerusalem-oriented faith of the early community of the Believers was eclipsed neither immediately nor entirely by this new model. After all, ʿAbd al-Malik completed the Dome of the Rock just as the Second Civil War came to a close, and as we have seen, this shrine and its early rituals had strong connections with the Jewish Temple and the eschatological, inter-confessional faith of the early Believers. Yet ʿAbd al-Malik's reign appears to mark the beginnings of a profound shift in the direction that formative Islam would ultimately take, toward a more confessionally narrow movement with an Arabian sacred geography centered in the Ḥijāz. Immediately after his victory, ʿAbd al-Malik took steps to establish religious ties with the Ḥijāz. He is said to have repaired the Kaʿba, which had been damaged during the siege of Mecca, and removed changes made by Ibn al-Zubayr, restoring it to the form that it had before the war.[273] Perhaps it was directly as a consequence of these activities that the Kaʿba became integrated into the rituals of the *ḥajj*.[274] Only two or three years later, ʿAbd al-Malik personally led the *ḥajj* to Mecca, sealing the relationship between the caliphate and the Ḥijāz.[275] His son and successor, Walīd I (705–15), continued this building program in the Ḥijāz, sponsoring a reconstruction of Muhammad's mosque in Medina.[276] Perhaps many of the traditions associating the Umayyads more positively with the Ḥijāz reflect this new initiative after the conclusion of the Second Civil War.[277]

Such elevation of the Ḥijāz, however, ultimately had to come at the expense of Jerusalem and its sacred "temple" shrine, the Dome of the Rock. Once the true Islamic "temple," the site of Abraham's near sacrifice of Ishmael, had been identified in the Kaʿba, a new significance would have to be discovered for the Dome and its Rock, one that would complement Islam's new sacred geography. The solution was to associate Jerusalem's Temple Mount, its mosque, and the Dome of the Rock no longer with Jewish Temple, but instead with the story of Muhammad's Night Journey (*isrāʾ*) and his Ascension (*miʿrāj*). Originally, these traditions seem not to have been connected with Jerusalem, and there is fairly broad agreement that the earliest interpretation of Qurʾān 17:1 understood the *masjid al-aqṣā*, the "farthest place of prayer" to which Muhammad is said to have miraculously traveled, as a heavenly temple.[278] This view prevailed during the first Islamic century, and the absence of Qurʾān 17:1 from the Dome of the Rock's earliest inscriptions appears to confirm that this shrine was not build to commemorate the Night Journey and Ascension. As Busse argues persuasively, it was not until sometime after the reign of Walīd (d. 715) that the buildings of the Temple Mount came to be associated with the *masjid al-aqṣā* of this Qurʾānic verse.[279] This new understanding of the Islamic shrines on the Temple Mount fit perfectly with the move away from Judaism and Jerusalem and toward a uniquely Islamic sacred history grounded in a Ḥijāzī holy land.[280] By redefining the Temple Mount as the goal of Muhammad's Night Journey and the site of his heavenly Ascent, the exceptional holiness of these shrines could be maintained, but with a significance that was entirely Islamic, grounded in the Qur'ān and the life of its peerless prophet rather than the traditions of the Jewish Temple.[281] No less important was the implicit subordination of Jerusalem to Mecca and the Ḥijāz: Jerusalem's Ḥaram drew its significance from a miraculous diversion that brought Muhammad from the consecrated land of the Ḥijāz to Jerusalem for only a brief visit before his heavenly ascent and ultimate return to the Ḥijāz. It was an effective strategy by which Jerusalem's holiness could be accommodated to a new sacred geography fixed (almost) entirely in the Ḥijāz.

Muhammad at Medina: A Prophet *Is* Welcome in His Hometown

If this devotional turn toward the south began under the Marwānids, it would seem that it was the 'Abbāsids who completed the consecration of the Ḥijāz, filling it with monuments to Muhammad and his prophetic mission. In the Umayyad period, for instance, the house where Muhammad was born appears to have been used as an ordinary dwelling, and it was made into a mosque only in the later eighth century. Yet as the veneration of Muhammad increased, memorials proliferated across the Ḥijāz honoring even the most trivial moments of his life, such as "the place where his cooking pot stood, when in the first year of the flight he prepared food under a tree for himself and his companions, in Baṭḥā ibn Azhar."[282] Numerous graves of prophets, especially from the era of the Patriarchs, were "discovered" in the vicinity of the Ka'ba, and Medina soon abounded in memorials to Muhammad and the early caliphs. On the whole, the effect was to inscribe the life of Muhammad and the beginnings of Islam physically onto the Hijāzī landscape, marking it unmistakably as the land of Islamic (and Abrahamic) origins.[283] Of these various shrines, however, Muhammad's tomb eventually emerged as the most revered site in Medina, and veneration of his grave was often equated with veneration of Muhammad himself. There were even some Muslims who believed that Muhammad's grave was holier than the Ka'ba, and accordingly that pilgrimage to his tomb was more meritorious than pilgrimage to Mecca. It was further believed that Muhammad had been created from the very earth of the Medinan grave in which he rested. Not surprisingly, there were also rival traditions claiming that Muhammad had been formed from Meccan clay.[284] Yet in either case one can hardly imagine a tradition that would bind Muhammad more intimately or more dramatically to the sacred landscape of the Ḥijāz.

It is not entirely clear, however, when the Mosque of the Prophet in Medina came to be identified as Muhammad's burial place. The Christian Baḥīrā legend, it will be recalled from the first chapter, alleges that there was a time when Muhammad's followers did not know where his grave was.[285] Yet more importantly, the earliest traditions describing Walīd's reconstruction of this site identify its significance in relation to Muhammad's dwelling places and the early place of worship that he had established nearby, but they do not connect Walīd's new mosque with the tomb of Muhammad.[286] Al-Ṭabarī and Balādhurī, for instance, make no mention at all of Muhammad's burial in their descriptions of Walīd's shrine, while Ibn Saʿd's report includes only a single tradition (ascribed to al-Wāqidī) that refers to "the grave" as a point of reference for locating some of the original dwellings.[287] The omission is surely significant: if Muhammad's death and burial were already associated strongly with his Medinan home by the early eighth century, one would certainly expect to find some notice of this in the earliest accounts of Walīd's building efforts there. This silence suggests instead that the connection between Muhammad's tomb and the Medinan mosque did not become well established until the tradition about his death in ʿĀʾisha's apartment entered into circulation, together perhaps with the related tradition that "no prophet dies but he is buried where he died." Although the former report can plausibly be linked with al-Zuhrī's teaching (d. 742), the latter tradition cannot be dated earlier than Ibn Isḥāq's *Maghāzī* (d. 767). The link between Muhammad's tomb and the Medina mosque thus seems to be somewhat later than Walīd's reconstruction, and like most of the burial traditions, it cannot be securely dated before the middle of the eighth century, a century or so after the actual events.

The traditional location of Muhammad's death in Medina, instead of in Mecca, the Holy Land, or anywhere else, may be as much as anything else a consequence of the fact that the earliest biographical traditions of the Prophet developed in Medina and were put into circulation elsewhere by natives of that city. Virtually all the early authorities on the life of Muhammad hailed from Medina, and it seems likely that on more than one occasion their biographies of Muhammad may have been colored by local boosterism.[288] Al-Zuhrī and Ibn Isḥāq were both native sons of this "City of the Prophet," as was the legendary authority ʿUwra ibn al-Zubayr, who was brother to none other than ʿAbd Allāh ibn al-Zubayr, the Ḥijāzī caliph who rose up in revolt against the Marwānids and their Jerusalemite vision of Islam. By consequence one would expect their early biographies of Muhammad to reflect a sharp Ḥijāzī and Medinan bias, and in fact their work, as Rubin observes, "seems to have been designed to secure the status of Arabia in the collective historical memory as the birthplace of Islam."[289] The fact that Ibn Isḥāq and other early *sīra* authors composed their works under the direct sponsorship of the ʿAbbāsid caliphs, who had begun to aggressively develop the holy sites of the Ḥijāz, would only have fueled this tendency.[290] The canonical account of Muhammad's death should thus be understood against the backdrop of Yathrib's successful campaign to secure its unique status as the "City of the Prophet": there Muhammad made his home from the birth of the Islamic community until his death. By situating the end of Muhammad's life within its limits, the city of Yathrib would have intensified its identification with the formation of Islam under Muhammad's leadership. Related to Yathrib's emerging prestige is of course the nascent cult of the Prophet in Islam, and particularly the veneration of his relics and tomb in Medina. Although we know frustratingly little as yet about the initial emergence of Muhammad and his tomb as specific foci of Islamic piety, it is rather likely that such practices had begun to appear by the mid-eighth century, around the same time when the *sīra* traditions were being developed by the scholars of Medina.[291] Such at least is the indication of Ibn Isḥāq's *Maghāzī*.

In its narrative of Muhammad's burial, Ibn Isḥāq's *Maghāzī* describes behavior by the participants that appears to prefigure and establish precedent for the veneration of his grave and bodily relics: "So the bed on which he died was taken up and they made a grave beneath it. Then the people came to visit the apostle praying over him by companies: first came the men, then the women, then the children. No man acted as imām in the prayers over the apostle."[292] These events appear to present the mythic prototype that both authorizes and establishes the patterns for the veneration of the Prophet at his tomb by his followers.[293] Nevertheless, not long after this passage, Ibn Isḥāq records a rather different tradition according to which Muhammad is reported to have said, "'God slay a people who choose the graves of their prophets as mosques,' warning his community against such a practice."[294] One can reasonably deduce from this condemnation that such practices had already arisen within the Islamic community: this saying was undoubtedly placed in Muhammad's mouth because by Ibn Isḥāq's time some had begun to venerate the grave of the Prophet. It is admittedly peculiar to find in the same text both this archetypal representation of the veneration of Muhammad's relics and his tomb together with an explicit condemnation of such practices. Nonetheless, the dissonance between the two traditions may simply reflect a diversity of opinion within the early Islamic community regarding the appropriateness of the cult of the

Prophet and his relics, much as one still today finds great division over such issues in contemporary Islam. Perhaps Ibn Isḥāq has merely collected the different traditions concerning the Prophet's burial that were available to him without attempting to decide the issue.

In any case, there is good reason to suspect that the veneration of Muhammad's tomb and relics had already begun by Ibn Isḥāq's time, as his own *Maghāzī* indicates, and consequently this phenomenon presents yet another motive for the potential relocation of Muhammad's death to Medina. Quite possibly this tradition arose in tandem with the cult, in order to authenticate the veneration of the Prophet's tomb in Medina. Similar stories abound within the Christian tradition, for instance, which aim to link a holy person and her or his death with a particular location claiming to possess her or his relics or shrine. The various stories of the end of the Virgin Mary's life present a good analogue: alternative traditions locate the end of her life in Jerusalem and Ephesus, while a third set of legends links her passing through her grave clothes with Constantinople. All three locations have preserved different traditions of the end of Mary's life that support the authenticity of their relics and shrines, identifying both her departure and her favor uniquely with their locale.[295] By the same token, one would suspect that the narratives of Muhammad's death in Medina developed alongside the emergent veneration of Muhammad's grave and the related transformation of Yathrib into the "City of the Prophet."

Conclusion

The evidence that earliest Islam differed in significant ways from what eventually became its classical formation is, from a historical-critical perspective, quite compelling, and it would appear that Muhammad's religious movement underwent some profound changes as it evolved from the inter-confessional, eschatological faith of the early Believers into an imperial religion defined by Muhammad's unique prophecy and Arabian identity. These dramatic developments in the nature of early Islam provide an important context within which to evaluate the different traditions concerning the end of Muhammad's life that emerge from comparison of the Islamic and non-Islamic sources. As noted in the previous chapter, Muhammad's earliest followers seem to have shared a fervent belief in the imminent arrival of the Hour and the world's impending judgment and destruction. Their timetable was extremely short, and there are signs that the *eschaton* was expected even within Muhammad's own lifetime: several *ḥadīth* describe the Hour's arrival as concomitant with Muhammad's prophetic mission, and ʿUmar's reaction to Muhammad's sudden demise, as recorded in Ibn Isḥāq's *Maghāzī*, gives dramatic voice to the early community's struggle to come to terms with Muhammad's unexpected passing before the Hour. Nevertheless, despite Muhammad's personal association with the Hour's appearance in the early tradition and the shock of his death before the climax of history, it is not clear how these failed eschatological hopes alone could explain the differences between the Islamic and non-Islamic sources concerning Muhammad's leadership during the Near Eastern conquests. In order to better understand this discrepancy, one must also consider the broader religious circumstances in which this urgent eschatological belief found expression.

As seen above, there is substantial evidence that the early Islamic community was not sectarian but was confessionally diverse, welcoming both Jews and, it seems, even Christians to membership in the community of Believers. Certain elements of the Qurʾān as well as other early sources, both Islamic and non-Islamic, reveal the hybrid nature of the earliest "Islamic" community, as Donner in particular has persuasively demonstrated. Among the most important of these early witnesses is the Constitution of Medina, which clearly spells out the terms for full inclusion of certain Jewish groups within the earliest community while allowing them to maintain their own beliefs and practices. Nevertheless, the biographical collections that preserve the Constitution of Medina paint this arrangement as merely a temporary measure aimed at persuading more Jews to acknowledge Muhammad's leadership, explaining that it was quickly annulled once it proved unsuccessful. Yet numerous other sources indicate that the inter-confessional nature of the early community persisted until about the end of the seventh century. The Constitution of Medina's history, it would appear, has been edited to disguise the nonsectarian quality of the early community of the Believers in order to hew more closely to the canonical narrative of Islam's origins as a distinctive monotheist sect from the very outset. The same can be said of the Jerusalem *qibla*. Although traditional narratives of Islamic origins often remember this practice as a brief, temporary compromise designed to appease the Jews of Medina, other sources indicate that prayer in the direction of Jerusalem was both a primitive and enduring custom in earliest Islam. This early ritual focus on Jerusalem reveals much about the nascent "Islamic" community and its incongruity in certain key areas with what would ultimately become the classical formation of the Islamic faith.

The early Believers thus were united by a common faith in the God of Abraham and their shared belief that God was working through Muhammad during the final moments of history to warn Abraham's descendants of the Hour's impending judgment. Not surprisingly Jerusalem, the aim of their daily prayers, was identified as the site where this final conflagration would take place: as the traditional focus of both Jewish and Christian eschatological hopes, it was only natural that Muhammad and the early community of the Believers would have similarly expected to witness the end of history in the Holy City. Likewise it appears that Jewish expectations of the Temple's restoration prior to the *eschaton* were embraced by the early community of the Believers. Both Jewish and Islamic traditions describe the Temple's restoration as a portent of the Hour, and it would appear that such expectations were partially met through ʿAbd al-Malik's construction of the Dome of the Rock. The Rock's significance as the central focus of both Jewish Temples and the complex rituals apparently devised in the early Islamic period to venerate the Rock suggest the Dome's construction to serve as kind of provisional replacement of the Temple in Islamic guise while awaiting the coming divine restoration of the Temple at the *eschaton*. Yet once Islam had shed both this early hybridity and its eschatological fervor, a new significance would have to be discovered for Jerusalem, the Temple Mount, its sacred rock, and its shrine that would distinguish Islam from Judaism (and Christianity) and also correspond with the emergence of a distinctly Islamic holy land in the Ḥijāz. These ends were seemingly achieved through the story of Muhammad's Night Journey and Ascension, which maintained a sort of lesser sanctity for Jerusalem while anchoring Islamic identity to the Ḥijāz and subordinating Jerusalem to its sacred cities, Mecca and Medina. Jerusalem's religious significance was subsequently rooted in Muhammad's brief visit there, on a miraculous journey that both began and ended in the Islamic holy land of the Ḥijāz.

The eschatological traditions of Islam also signal rather tellingly the primacy of Jerusalem in earliest Islam. The Qur'ān's unyielding focus on the Hour's imminence reveals eschatology to have been at the center of Muhammad's preaching and the beliefs of his earliest followers. Yet even today Islam's eschatological hopes remain soldered to Jerusalem and its Temple Mount: despite the ensuing displacement of eschatology and the extension of the Hour into the distant future, Jerusalem still remains the focus of Islam's beliefs about the last days. It is difficult to comprehend how or why Jerusalem would have attained this status within the Islamic tradition unless Islam had from the very beginning fixed its eschatological expectations to Jerusalem and its environs. If, for instance, the Ḥijāz had from the very beginning been revered as Islam's unique holy land, as it is in the later tradition, it is hard to understand why Jerusalem, instead of one of the cities of the Ḥijāz, became the nexus of Islam's eschatological vision. Moreover, despite frequent attempts to relocate Islamic eschatology to the Ḥijāz, Jerusalem has maintained its firm hold on the Islamic imagination in this area. While so many other Abrahamic traditions from the Holy Land were quickly transferred into the Ḥijāz, eschatology alone proved intractable.[296] Presumably, this unbreakable bond between Jerusalem and the *eschaton* reflects the antiquity of these traditions: only an especially early and forceful connection between Jerusalem and the events of the Hour could have resisted the powerful draw of the Ḥijāz in the centuries to come.

Such circumstances make it difficult to escape the conclusion that Jerusalem and the Holy Land were almost certainly Islam's original sacred center. If primitive Islam was profoundly eschatological in its worldview, and Jerusalem has stood from the beginning as the focus of its eschatological aspirations, then the probability is extremely high that Jerusalem and Palestine, rather than the Ḥijāz, was the original Islamic holy land. It is hard to imagine that Muhammad and his followers, focused as they were on the impending Hour, would have remained fixed on Mecca and Medina as they rode forth from Arabia. To the contrary, Jerusalem, the city where their eschatological hopes would soon be realized, must have loomed before them as the center of an Abrahamic holy land where God's ancient promises were coming to fulfillment. The apparently inter-confessional nature of the community likewise must have inspired Muhammad's early followers to venerate Palestine and Jerusalem as the land of their common sacred inheritance, intensifying the sanctity of the Promised Land as Islam's original holy land. Only after the eschatological confidence of the early Believers began to fade and the Hour was deferred to sometime in the more distant future did Jerusalem's unique sanctity and significance diminish, paving the way for a new sacred landscape in the Ḥijāz. In its new, non-eschatological guise, Islam carved out a distinctively sectarian and Arabian holy land in which to ground the faith of an emerging empire.

It is within the context of these rapid changes in eschatological orientation and sacred geography that the different reports about the final years of Muhammad's life and his relation to the conquest of Palestine can perhaps be understood. In its earliest configuration, the eschatological faith of the Believers almost necessitated that Muhammad would lead them into the Promised Land. Muhammad, as the herald of the Hour's imminent arrival, should be the one who leads them to meet the climax of history in Jerusalem. As already suggested, even if Muhammad was not in fact leading his followers as they entered the Holy Land, the logic of their faith would very likely have inspired them to remember him as leading the eschatological restoration of Abraham's descendants to the land of their divine inheritance. In this religious framework, Muhammad's death in the Ḥijāz prior to the Hour's arrival not only would have held no religious significance in itself, but such a memory would have contradicted the faith of his earliest followers, who seem to have believed that the *eschaton* was linked specifically with his person and was to arrive within his lifetime. Only after Islam's transformation into a distinctive monotheist sect defined by Arabian identity and Muhammad's unique prophecy would it have made sense to locate Muhammad's death at Yathrib in the Ḥijāz. In the context of the wholesale transfer of Jewish and Abrahamic traditions into a newly fashioned Islamic holy land, it suddenly became essential to have Islam's unequaled prophet laid to rest within its distinctive sacred landscape. Thus, the traditional account of Muhammad's death in Medina would appear to be a more recent tradition, while the reports coming from the non-Islamic sources—and the letter of ʿUmar—suggesting that Muhammad survived to lead the Islamic conquest of Palestine likely witness to an older tradition. Even if this rival account may not in fact be historically accurate, it is witnessed by much earlier sources and comports well with the shape of the Islamic tradition in its earliest stages. Its displacement by the canonical narrative of Muhammad's death in Medina can be readily explained by the reorientation of Islamic sacred geography from Jerusalem to the Ḥijāz and the resultant "Ḥijāzification" of the traditional narratives of Islamic origins.

More sanguine scholars will perhaps object that the uniformity with which the traditional Islamic sources record the death of Muhammad in Medina before the invasion of Palestine should sufficiently guarantee the authenticity of this received account. If this memory is so consistently attested by the early Islamic witnesses to the beginnings of Islam, one might argue, surely this speaks to its accuracy. Yet the problem with such reasoning is that the pace of change within earliest Islam appears to have been especially rapid, while the earliest narratives of Islamic origins are both few and exceptionally late in their formation. In less than a century, Islam quickly transformed itself from an eschatological movement with roots in Judaism and the Holy Land into an imperial religion grounded in Arabian identity. By way of comparison, early Christianity took roughly three and a half centuries to make a comparable—and well-documented—transition. The swift pace of such sweeping changes within earliest Islam, as well as the relatively quick emergence of a strong central authority governing the Islamic polity, often makes it difficult to recover clear evidence concerning the nature of earliest Islam. Moreover, the relatively late production of the first surviving narratives of Islamic origins and their authorization and dissemination by a strong, centralized authority (that is, the ʿAbbāsids) only after this transformation had occurred seem to have ensured that older memories of Islam's earliest faith and practice were largely forgotten or even erased.

Consequently, the fact that there is such apparent uniformity in the Islamic community's memory of its period of origins is no guarantee of its authenticity. In fact, given such circumstances it is all the more remarkable that any traces whatsoever survive to reveal the primitive faith of Muhammad's earliest followers. These anomalies, such as the eschatological urgency of the Qurʾān and certain early *ḥadīth*, as well as the inter-confessional nature of the community of Believers and the focus on Jerusalem and the Abrahamic Promised Land, combine to reveal a very different religious formation at the beginnings of Islam. The traditions of Muhammad's leadership during the invasion of Palestine would appear to be a related anomaly, and when considered in this context, they appear to bear credible witness to an early memory of Muhammad as leading the children of Abraham into the land of divine promise to meet the destiny of the Hour.

CONCLUSION

Jesus and Muhammad, the Apostle and the Apostles

The Islamic tradition reports Muhammad's death at Medina in 632 before the Near Eastern conquests with remarkable consistency, a fact that might appear to inspire some sort of confidence in the historical accuracy of this account. Nevertheless, at present we do not have any evidence that this particular tradition is much earlier than Ibn Isḥāq's mid-eighth-century *Maghāzī*, the first written source to relate this information. It may very well be that Ibn Isḥāq's biography has largely determined this date for all subsequent sources, since, as numerous scholars have observed, the basic chronology of Muhammad's life as we now have it is largely the work of Ibn Isḥāq. We simply do not know what other traditions might have been in circulation during the first century AH, and it remains quite possible that the memory of Muhammad's leadership during the assault on Palestine indicated by the non-Islamic sources and the letter of ʿUmar in fact reflects an older tradition. The notorious artificiality and historical unreliability of the *sīra* tradition, particularly in regard to its chronology, give cause to doubt its witness almost prima facie with respect to most dates. Furthermore, the deviant reports from a handful of early Islamic sources that the length of Muhammad's Medinan period was either seven years or thirteen years or that the *hijra* was in 624/25 certainly invite the possibility of an earlier tradition that Muhammad lived somewhat longer than Ibn Isḥāq has remembered. But in light of the uniformity with which the Islamic tradition otherwise relates Muhammad's Medinan demise in 632, one would perhaps rightly expect more specific and compelling reasons for questioning the accuracy of this traditional account. Indeed, it seems that only a broader process of rapid and radical change within the early Islamic religious movement could explain the kind of revisions to the narrative of origins implied by these other sources.

The imminent eschatology revealed by the Qur'ān and a number of eschatological *ḥadīth* certainly presents a context that would have required some sweeping changes to the early Islamic tradition within a relatively short period of time. Muhammad and his followers appear to have expected the world to end in the immediate future, seemingly within their own lifetimes. When the Hour failed to arrive on schedule and continued to be deferred into an ever distant future, the meaning of Muhammad's message and the faith that he established had to be fundamentally rethought by his early followers. In the process of this reconfiguration, Islam seems to have shed an early inter-confessional identity that initially welcomed Jews and even Christians within the primitive "community of the Believers." Somewhat predictably, this early pan-Abrahamic religious movement appears to have focused its eschatological hopes on the Promised Land and Jerusalem, and thus the invasion of the Roman Near East seems to have been joined to the expectation of the Hour. Yet in the course of this eschatological movement's sudden transformation into the religion of an emerging empire, Islam's sacred geography appears to have shifted dramatically. Mecca and Yathrib in the Ḥijāz replaced Jerusalem and Palestine as the Islamic holy land as part of a swift and profound revision of the Islamic faith into a distinctively Arab confession defined by Muhammad's unique prophecy. While the earlier creed of the Believers certainly would have favored Muhammad's participation in the conquest of Palestine, Islam's new orientation required Muhammad to die instead in this Arabian holy land, within the sacred confines of the Prophet's own city.

Although certain more sanguine scholars of the origins of Islam have often expressed their own brand of skepticism in objecting that such dramatic changes could not possibly have occurred over such a short interval, the history of primitive Christianity strongly suggests otherwise. One need only compare the Jewish apocalyptic worldview of Jesus and his earliest followers with the Hellenized Christianity of Justin Martyr or Valentinus in order to understand the rapid pace with which an eschatological movement rooted in the Abrahamic traditions could transform itself. Christianity changed dramatically during its first one hundred years as it spread from its origins among the Jewish peasants of Palestine out into the culturally sophisticated and ethnically diverse Roman Empire: one would hardly expect anything less from Islam as it made essentially the same transition. Sticking with this comparison, perspectives gained from the investigation of early Christianity may also help to explain the considerable interval between the events of Muhammad's life and preaching and the first efforts to commit them to writing. Insofar as earliest Islam was, like formative Christianity, a religious movement whose adherents expected an imminent end to the present world, the eschatological fervor of the primitive community likely discouraged any process of beginning to codify and record the early history of Islam for nearly a century, much as was also the case with earliest Christianity. With the end of the world so near, it must have seemed that there was little point in documenting the events of the recent past for posterity. The collection and promulgation of the Qur'ānic text only at the end of the seventh century under ʿAbd al-Malik can be similarly explained.

Nevertheless, the relative silence of the Islamic tradition for much of its first century may not be entirely the fault of such imminent eschatological expectations. Indeed, it is quite possible that there was a significant body of traditions from the earliest community that have not survived simply because they did not match the needs and interests of eighth-century Islam. David Cook suggests, for instance, that in the process of editing the Qur'ān many of the earliest community's apocalyptic beliefs were possibly "cut out at an early stage, perhaps when the early caliphs (assuming that they were really responsible for the collection of the Qur'ān) realized that the End was not going to come immediately . . . , and a system or state had to be founded," a proposal, one should note, that is strikingly reminiscent of Casanova's hypothesis.[1] At this later stage in its history, the Islamic tradition would have required a decidedly different understanding of its origins, much as Christian writers of the second century (and even earlier) radically transformed the imminent eschatology of Jesus and the earliest Christians into an institutionalized and deeply Hellenized faith.[2] Given the very real possibility that the theology and concerns of the primitive community of the Believers differed significantly from the faith of the early ʿAbbāsid empire in other areas as well, it is likely that when the Islamic scholars of the eighth and ninth centuries composed their histories, they generally did not preserve early traditions that were at variance with what Islam had become. Rather, they have selectively shaped the material at their disposal into a narrative of origins that comports more directly with the Islamic faith and practice of the eighth and ninth centuries, re-mythologizing the movement's formative history to meet these new circumstances. Once again it is important to emphasize, however, that this process need not be understood as some sort of grand conspiracy to deceive, as some have wrongly insisted: quite to the contrary, these authors were assured of the truth of Islam as they believed and practiced it in the eighth and ninth centuries, and material contradicting this faith would rather naturally be excluded from their accounts.

Such an understanding of early Islamic history is certainly suggested by comparison with Walter Bauer's groundbreaking and seminal study of earliest Christianity, *Orthodoxy and Heresy in Earliest Christianity*, which has not inaccurately been characterized as "possibly the most significant book on early Christianity written in modern times."[3] By analyzing the evidence for earliest Christianity from different regions independently, Bauer proposed that the puzzling historical silence regarding the beginnings of Christianity in Egypt and eastern Syria, for instance, reflects the fact that the original Christian traditions of these areas were likely quite different from what eventually came to be "orthodox" Christianity. Consequently, later "orthodox" writers did not preserve the earliest Christian traditions of these and other areas, which not only contradicted their own interpretations of Christianity but, perhaps even more importantly, called into question the historical primacy of those beliefs eventually defined as orthodox. In place of these now lost primitive traditions, later orthodox writers offered new accounts of Christian origins, which they constructed around a core of carefully selected sources and traditions from the ancient church that supported their narrative of "orthodox" Christianity as the aboriginal form of the faith in every land: *quod semper, quod ubique, quod ab omnibus*.[4]

The numerous skeptical interpretations of early Islamic history have much in common with this approach to early Christianity: they share both its suspicion of traditional narratives of origins and its insistence on interpreting them in light of the editorial interests of later orthodoxies. In fact, Wansbrough explicitly identifies Bauer's work as an influential model for his own important reevaluation of the beginnings of Islam.[5] Bauer's conception of a primitive condition of heterodoxy that focuses on regional diversity has great potential for illuminating the earliest history of Islam. Unfortunately, however, some contemporary scholars of Islam (as well as many Muslim intellectuals) have reacted to any such skeptical inquiries into the origins of Islam with a measure of hostility or dismissal that seems unwarranted. Given the broad range of competing opinions that are welcomed within New Testament studies, some of which are highly speculative and fundamentally contrary to the received narratives of origins, the forceful resistance to such ideas by certain scholars of Islamic origins is not only surprising but somewhat disheartening. Nonetheless, in spite of its controversial status within Islamic studies, this so-called skeptical approach to the study of early Islam offers the most methodological continuity with the study of other religious traditions from late antiquity, and for this reason alone it should be more actively pursued.

The differing approaches to Christian and Islamic origins can perhaps be brought into greater relief by extending an earlier observation by Patricia Crone in the "Historiographical Introduction" to her *Slaves on Horses*. Here Crone completes her insightful analysis of the sources available for studying earliest Islam through a comparison of the *sīra* traditions with similar material from a variety of different cultures, including the earliest biography of the Buddha, the Icelandic sagas, and the Christian gospels. Regarding the latter in particular, she asks in a footnote that we "consider the prospect of reconstructing the origins of Christianity on the basis of the writings of Clement or Justin Martyr in a recension by Origen."[6] With this brief remark, Crone succinctly captures the stark difference in the quality of the sources available for the study of earliest Christianity and earliest Islam. In essence, Crone asks that we imagine that the earliest extant gospel was written not by "Mark" sometime around 70, roughly four decades after the crucifixion of Jesus, but rather by Clement of Alexandria (ca. 150–ca. 211), and moreover that this earliest biography survives only in an edition revised by Origen of Alexandria (ca. 185–ca. 254). For the sake of comparison, one should perhaps presume that in addition we actually have a copy of the lost "Q" gospel, a collection of sayings with no narrative context or passion narrative that was compiled approximately twenty to thirty years after the death of Jesus. The Q gospel reveals no information regarding the death of Jesus, nor really any knowledge of his activities or their setting, making it roughly analogous to the Qur'ān.[7] For this information, we would depend entirely on this hypothetical "Gospel according to Clement" as now revised in the "Gospel according to Origen."

One can only imagine what such a gospel might have looked like, but presumably Jesus would have appeared much more like a Hellenistic philosopher and somewhat less as a Jewish eschatological prophet. Perhaps the following reflections from Clement of Alexandria give some indication of how different such a gospel might have looked. "But in the case of the Savior, it would be ludicrous [to suppose] that the body, as a body, demanded the necessary aids in order for its duration. For he ate, not for the sake of the body, which was kept together by a holy energy, but in order that it might not enter into the minds of those who were with Him to entertain a different opinion of him; in a manner as certainly some afterwards supposed that He appeared in a phantasmal shape. But he was entirely impassible; inaccessible to any movement of feeling—either pleasure or pain."[8] Apparently, Clement's Christ did not need to eat, and he did so only in order to prevent people from falling into error concerning the reality of his body. Moreover, Clement believed Christ to have been "entirely impassible," experiencing neither pleasure nor pain. Although Clement writes here to oppose "docetism" (an early Christian belief that Christ only appeared to have physical body), his own understanding of the radical difference between Christ's body and the bodies of other human beings skirts very close to this early Christian heresy. If we take this passage as symptomatic of what a hypothetical gospel according to Clement might have looked like, one would expect that the agonies and doubts of Christ in Gethsemane and on the cross would have been remembered rather differently—if at all—and the centrality of suffering and embodiment in Christian piety and theology would be accordingly diminished. The fact that Clement could re-imagine Christ thus to better fit with Platonic ideas of God—despite the existence of several earlier written accounts—is itself a testimony to how radically religious traditions can change over a relatively short period of time. Origen's "gospel" seems to have similarly entertained some rather peculiar notions about Christ's body, which he claims to have received as established "tradition": according to Origen, Jesus could change his body's appearance at will, making it appear simultaneously in different forms according to the unique capacity of each individual to see it, an understanding echoed in other contemporary sources.[9] One wonders how such a notion might have affected later Christological reflection if this idea were at the heart of Christianity's canonical "gospel." One also wonders what the first-century Palestinian Jewish peasants who followed this eschatological prophet would have made of such a notion. Surely other topics similarly would have been remembered quite differently from the canonical gospels in this deeply Hellenized biography of Jesus.

Yet in order to fully comprehend the value of this comparative perspective, it may be useful to extend Crone's initial thought experiment to imagine a similar evidentiary discrepancy concerning the end of Jesus' life. Let us suppose, for the sake of argument, that this Origenist revision of Clement's gospel reports Jesus' death at Jerusalem in the year 31 (which is in fact the date indicated in Luke's gospel);[10] there are no earlier Christian reports, and all subsequent Christian writers repeat the same information with confidence. Nevertheless, continuing with this premise, let us additionally assume that there are ten independent non-Christian sources mentioning Jesus, all of which indicate the end of his life sometime later, say around 33 or 34, in Tiberias, as well as a stray early Christian document that appears to confirm the same information (the actual date is sometime between 28 and 33, as determined by correlating the gospel traditions with Roman historical sources).[11] Moreover, some of these non-Christian sources were written within twenty or thirty years of the events that they describe and may depend at some level on firsthand reports. Furthermore, many of these non-Christian authors are known to be generally reliable, and there is no obvious reason why any of them would have falsified the circumstances of the end of Jesus' life. Let us additionally assume that in contrast to the non-Christian sources, Origen's revision of Clement's gospel and later related Christian traditions are well known to portray Jesus' life through the lens of second- and third-century Christianity, and more importantly, that their chronology is notoriously unreliable, characterized almost universally by scholarship as "internally weak, schematized, [and] doctrinally inspired."[12] Furthermore, there are several significant ideological motives, as well as certain minor literary tendencies, that would likely have encouraged the Christian tradition to have altered the date and location as indicated by the non-Christian sources. Given such circumstances, one wonders whether historians of Christian origins would continue to maintain the unquestioned accuracy of Jesus' death in 31 at Jerusalem. It seems much more likely that instead, given the tendencies of New Testament criticism, scholars would have by now developed various elaborate and comprehensive theories to account for this divergence of the textual traditions.

In fact, New Testament scholars have often expressed deep skepticism concerning the canonical accounts of Jesus' death and burial, even though they were first written down approximately forty years after the events that they purport to describe. John Dominic Crossan, for instance, argues that the death and burial narratives of the canonical gospels are pious fictions, with essentially no basis in history. Following the crucifixion, Crossan provocatively suggests, the body of Jesus was most likely left at the foot of the cross where it was eventually consumed by crows and dogs: as much is indicated, Crossan maintains, by comparative evidence concerning Roman treatment of capital criminals.[13] The members of the Jesus Seminar reach similar conclusions following the same reasoning.[14] Although these views certainly do not reflect any kind of consensus of New Testament scholarship, many readers, both academic and otherwise, have found them persuasive. Yet more mainstream scholars, while perhaps rejecting any idea that Jesus' body was eaten by wild dogs, would nonetheless concede that many details from the death and burial accounts are not historical but have instead been generated to fit certain typological and theological expectations.[15] This skepticism, and particularly the more radical version expressed by Crossan and the Jesus Seminar, stands in marked contrast to the confidence that many scholars of early Islam have placed in the Islamic traditions of Muhammad's death and burial, which first seem to have been compiled more than a century after the events themselves. There is on the whole a remarkable difference in the amount of suspicion that scholars of early Christianity and early Islam are willing to bring to the earliest textual sources. Indeed, scholarship on the New Testament has even gone so far as to argue that the Q traditions were originally not teachings of Jesus but instead John the Baptist. The fact that such bold and intriguing arguments concerning the traditional source materials are welcomed in New Testament studies, even though they might meet with respectful disagreement, certainly presents a bracing contrast to the methodological conservatism and often outright hostility to skeptical approaches to the sources frequently evident in the study of formative Islam.[16]

Of course, such comparisons largely serve to underscore just how different the source materials are for studying the origins of Christianity and Islam. Despite frequent assertions to the contrary, our historical knowledge concerning Muhammad and first-century Islam is far more limited and uncertain than is the case with respect to Jesus and first-century Christianity. While no modern scholar believes any longer, as Ernest Renan naïvely proposed, that Islam was born "in the full light of history,"[17] one nevertheless meets in many writings on early Islam a presumption that the evidence for the beginnings of Islam is in fact superior to that for formative Christianity. For example, F. E. Peters, in his article "The Quest of the Historical Muhammad," argues that we are in a much better position to recover the historical figure of Muhammad than is the case with Jesus, on the basis that the Qur'ān is Muhammad's own composition, in contrast to the Christian gospels.[18] Matters are not so simple, however. Leaving aside for the moment the complex question of the Qur'ān's authenticity, it is certainly questionable to maintain that the sources for our knowledge of Muhammad and the formation of his religious movement are better than they are for Jesus and earliest Christianity. A major problem is that the Qur'ān, as Peters himself acknowledges, reveals almost nothing about Muhammad himself or the history of the early community.

For this information, we are entirely dependent on the early biographies of Muhammad, the *sīra* traditions, sources that are not at all equal in their historical quality to the canonical Christian gospels. Despite perhaps a superficial, generic similarity to the prophetic biographies of the New Testament, the early *sīra* traditions instead resemble much more the apocryphal acts of the apostles, and their historical value as witnesses to the beginnings of Islam should be measured accordingly. Much like the earliest *sīra* collections, the fantastic, novelistic narratives of the earliest apocryphal acts were composed on the basis of oral tradition and legend roughly a century or two after the events that they describe. Moreover, these apocrypha reflect the values and assumptions of the literate, upper-class Roman Christian audience for which they were composed: if these were our only sources for knowledge of the beginnings of Christianity, we would know precious little about the Jewish eschatological movement that Jesus and his followers began in first-century Galilee.[19] While these fanciful biographies of the Christian apostles may occasionally preserve authentic traditions from the origins of Christianity that have not otherwise survived, such instances tend to be the exception rather than the rule, and no serious scholar of early Christianity would accept these narratives as reliable representations of the actual lives and missionary activities of the early Christian apostles.[20] Yet many scholars of Islam, such as Montgomery Watt, have routinely turned to the comparable narratives of the *sīra* tradition for knowledge of the life of Muhammad and the early history of his religious movement, taking more or less for granted the accuracy of at least their "basic framework."

It is not then that the sources for knowledge of the historical Muhammad are considerably better than those for the historical Jesus, but to the contrary, on the whole they are seemingly worse. Yet the primary difference lies in the approach to the sources and more specifically in the measure of skepticism that scholars in each field bring to such late, tendentious sources whose purpose is to mythologize the time of origins. As Chase Robinson rightly asks with respect to this difference, "Would anyone seriously argue now that Peter founded the Papacy, that, as Stephen I (254–57 CE) describes it, its basis is the *cathedra Petri*?"[21] One might note that such claims are in fact advanced even earlier by Tertullian (ca. 160–ca. 220).[22] Even more to the point are the *Acts of Peter*, a biography of the apostle Peter written sometime around the middle of the second century that describes his preaching and martyrdom in Rome.[23] No respectable scholar would interpret this narrative as a more or less accurate record of Peter's activities in Rome, even in its "basic framework." In fact, it is strongly debated whether or not the "historical Peter" ever even was in Rome, let alone died there, despite the consistency with which the early Christian tradition maintains these "facts." As one scholar summarized, "Doubts concerning the precise details of Peter's life extend to the manner, date, and location of his death, for while there is a body of literary and liturgical evidence that he died as a martyr in Rome during the reign of Nero, a fact held to be supported by the results of archaeological excavations in Rome, there has always been a good deal of scholarly debate and polemic concerning such data."[24] It is at the very least peculiar that the biographies of Muhammad have not yet been the subject of similar scrutiny, particularly in regard to questions where non-Islamic sources offer a contradictory witness.

Perhaps the apostle Paul presents a better point of comparison: like the apostle of Islam, Paul left behind a corpus of writings (many of which he actually seems to have written) and was perhaps more than any other early figure responsible for determining the future shape of Christianity. There was for Paul himself, like Muhammad, no "Easter miracle," and yet the life of Paul remains largely a mystery. Outside of the few details that can be gleaned from his letters, very little is certain. The canonical Acts of the Apostles describes his conversion as well as some of his missionary activities in the period from roughly 47 to 60. Nevertheless, the narrative of the canonical Acts was composed much later, most likely sometime around the year 100 (if not perhaps even a little later). Moreover, the Acts of the Apostles has been exposed as being highly tendentious, and on virtually every point where its accuracy can be tested against the letters of Paul, this earliest history of Christianity fails.[25] Although scholars have often used Acts provisionally to fill in the gaps between Paul's letters and to supply them with some additional context, in critical scholarship the problematic nature of Acts is constantly present in the scholar's mind. More to the point, particularly for the present purposes, little is known concerning the end of Paul's life. Although the tradition of Paul's death in Rome is widely accepted, its timing is uncertain. Many scholars assume that Paul was martyred in Rome shortly after he was brought there in chains, in the early 60s, as seems to be implied by the canonical Acts. Yet Paul himself wrote of his intention to travel to Spain and spread the gospel there (Rom. 15:22–27), and certain early Christian sources, including one written in Rome around 95, suggest that this goal was in fact realized.[26] In this case, Paul must have been released from captivity in Rome (at least if one follows the account in Acts) and allowed to travel to Spain, only to return to Rome and suffer martyrdom there in the later 60s. Whether or not Paul actually made it to Spain is not particularly relevant to the present subject, nor is the question of whether he died at the beginning or the end of the 60s. What is important, however, is the ambiguity and uncertainty that scholars of early Christianity have uncovered through the careful analysis of their sources, by noting both their tendencies and the presence of conflicting voices. The study of Islamic origins would be greatly enriched, I believe, by the more frequent application of a similar approach.

Admittedly, the historical evidence for the origins of Christianity is vastly different from the material available for reconstructing the rise of Islam, and no doubt the comparative abundance of sources for understanding earliest Christianity has given rise to the forceful methodological skepticism with which early Christian studies approaches its subject. The rather limited nature of the source material for understanding the rise of Islam, by way of contrast, has somewhat understandably necessitated a much more trusting stance toward to the evidence that is available. Yet in spite of these differences, such comparisons are quite illuminating, and they suggest a real need to take seriously the perspectives on earliest Islam offered by non-Islamic literature, even when they disagree with the traditional Islamic accounts. In view of the complexities of all these data then, it does not seem that we can give a precise date for Muhammad's death any more. This is not all that surprising, however: such is the case for numerous historical figures from the late ancient world, including Jesus, Peter, Paul, Clement of Alexandria, Origen, and Tertullian, among many others. While it is entirely possible that the non-Islamic sources are somehow wrong, I think it is just as likely that the *sīra* tradition has adjusted an earlier tradition of Muhammad's death for one or more of the various reasons identified in this study. In view of the irresolvable uncertainty, it would seem that the earliest evidence concerning the date of Muhammad's death is most accurately represented as either 632–35 or at the very least circa 632.

Nevertheless, as stated at the outset, the significance of this conclusion lies well beyond just a minor adjustment in the date of Muhammad's death. To the contrary, such findings validate the importance of using non-Islamic sources in conjunction with the early Islamic witnesses to reconstruct the history of formative Islam. It is not just the year of Muhammad's death that stands here in question; rather we find in these two early traditions possible evidence of the primitive Islamic community's evolving memory of the end of its founder's life. The circumstances in which the early Muslims imagined Muhammad to have lived out the final years of his life potentially reveal much about the changing beliefs and ideals of this religious movement. While the tradition of Muhammad's death in Medina underscores various conventional Islamic beliefs, including especially its Ḥijāzī holy land and Arab identity, the tradition witnessed by the non-Islamic sources and the Letter of ʿUmar suggests a rather different configuration. Yet perhaps more importantly, the reliability of traditional Islamic sources for understanding Islam's earliest history is also at stake here. If something as basic and widely acknowledged in the Islamic sources as the date of the Prophet's death turns out to be uncertain, and can be shown to be so on the basis of non-Islamic sources, then it would seem that we need to reevaluate the methods and approaches used in studying formative Islam, which all too often have been trusting of Islamic sources.

In his brief book on Muhammad, Michael Cook identifies three major differences between the Islamic and non-Islamic sources: the chronology of Muhammad's death, a sustained inclusion of Jews within the early community, and the religious importance of Jerusalem and Palestine for Muhammad and his earliest followers. Cook then concludes that "if the external [that is, non-Islamic] sources are in any significant degree right on such points, it would follow that the tradition is seriously misleading on important aspects of the life of Muhammad, and that even the integrity of the Koran as his message is in some doubt. In view of what was said above about the nature of the Muslim sources, such a conclusion would seem to me legitimate; but it is only fair to add that it is not usually drawn."[27] As we have argued in this study, these three points appear to be intertwined, and the complimentary witness of the non-Islamic sources to certain anomalous elements that survive in the early Islamic tradition seems to confirm the hypothesis that earliest Islam was an inter-confessional eschatological movement focused on Jerusalem. Only after Muhammad's death and the prolonged delay of the Hour did his followers shed these early ideas, exchanging them for a more sectarian identity defined by Arab ethnicity, Muhammad's unique prophecy, and a sacred geography in the Ḥijāz. Although these findings diverge considerably from the traditional narratives of Islamic origins, the difference is certainly no more radical than what scholars of Christian or Jewish origins have postulated about the beginnings of those traditions. Moreover, it is particularly significant that this reconstruction of primitive Islam has been determined using an approach similar to that used in studying early Christianity and early Judaism. Accordingly, this study has hopefully demonstrated the value of critically questioning the traditional narratives of Islamic origins using perspectives developed in biblical and early Christian studies, as well as the usefulness of comparing these results with the evidence of external historical sources, long a standard practice in these fields. Such an approach to the beginnings of Islam, along lines similar to the study of formative Christianity and Judaism, has the potential, I would argue, to bring greater methodological (and ultimately pedagogical) unity to the academic study of religion.[28]

NOTES

INTRODUCTION

1. Crone and Cook, *Hagarism*.

2. Unless otherwise indicated, all dates in this study are CE. On the nature of the sources for this period, see, e.g., Haldon, *Byzantium in the Seventh Century*, 1–2; Herrin, *The Formation of Christendom*, 133. Regarding the particular value of the Syriac historical tradition for this period, see Conrad, "Varietas Syriaca"; and Robert Hoyland's contribution to Palmer, *The Seventh Century*, xxiv–xxvi.

3. Wansbrough, *Quranic Studies*; Wansbrough, *The Sectarian Milieu*. A brief and helpful introduction to Wansbrough's methods and conclusions can be found in Rippin, "Literary Analysis of Qurʾān." One should also see the special issue of *Method and Theory in the Study of Religion* that was devoted to Wansbrough's legacy in the study of early Islam: Berg, "Islamic Origins Reconsidered." On the significance of both Crone and Cook's *Hagarism* and Wansbrough's works for integrating Islam better into the study of religion in the early medieval Near East, see esp. Hawting, "John Wansbrough, Islam, and Monotheism."

4. See, e.g., Wansbrough, "Review of *Hagarism*," 155–56; Hoyland, *Seeing Islam*, 547.

5. Wansbrough, *The Sectarian Milieu*, 116–17.

6. In fact, some recent archaeological studies suggest something like Crone and Cook's hypothesis in *Hagarism*: see Pentz, *The Invisible Conquest*; and Magness, *The Archaeology of the Early Islamic Settlement*. Pentz's analysis of the archaeology of sixth- and seventh-century Syro-Palestine essentially argues that the transition to Arab rule came primarily as a result of economic changes and took place gradually as the nomadic cultures on the margins of civilization came to exercise increasing authority over the settled communities. Pentz additionally concludes that the archaeological evidence contradicts the Islamic historical tradition's account of a massive campaign of conquest, involving major battles and considerable destruction of property: "The 7th century 'conquest' of Syria is—in archaeological terms—totally invisible. That is to say, archaeological evidence is abundant, while the archaeologist looking for a break in the material is searching in vain" (74). This observation is largely confirmed by Magness in her study, which concludes that there is no archaeological evidence for the widespread violence and destruction described in the Islamic accounts of the conquest of Palestine. The implication

of both studies would seem to be that the Arabs who took political control of the Near East came not in a massive invasion from the Ḥijāz but were instead Arabs living on the fringes of the Roman and Persian empires who gradually assumed control without the dramatic and destructive battles recorded by the Islamic historical tradition. See also in this regard now Walmsley, *Early Islamic Syria.*

7. For a range of negative reactions, see, e.g., Rahman, *Major Themes of the Qurʾān*, xiii–xiv; Stover, "Orientalism and the Otherness of Islam"; Abdul-Rauf, "Outsiders' Interpretations of Islam"; Rahman, "Approaches to Islam"; Serjeant, "Review of John Wansbrough"; Wansbrough, *The Sectarian Milieu*, 116–17.

8. See Wansbrough, *The Sectarian Milieu*, 116–19.

9. Hoyland, *Seeing Islam*, 597–98.

10. The famous phrase is from Leopold von Ranke, the nineteenth-century founder of modern, critical history. For more on van Ranke and his significance for modern history, see White, *Metahistory*, 163–90, esp. 163–64.

11. See, e.g., Hoyland, *Seeing Islam*, and numerous works by Lawrence I. Conrad, esp., e.g., Conrad, "The Conquest of Arwad."

12. Crone and Cook, *Hagarism*, 3–4, 24, 152–53 n. 7. Nevertheless, Crone and Cook do elsewhere (p. 24) assess the significance of this tradition, which they assume to be correct, considering how and why the later Islamic tradition has revised its earliest history on this point.

13. See also the helpful survey of sources in Penn, "Syriac Sources."

14. Hoyland, *Seeing Islam*, 592–94.

15. Ibid., 594–95.

16. Ibid., 595–97.

17. For a discussion of the importance of this particular criterion in historical Jesus studies, see Porter, *The Criteria for Authenticity*, 82–89, 102; see also the following representative examples: Meier, *A Marginal Jew*, 1: 174–75; Theissen and Merz, *The Historical Jesus*, 116–17; Ehrman, *Jesus*, 90–91.

18. See, e.g., Ehrman, *Jesus*, 91–94; Meier, *A Marginal Jew*, 1: 168–71. In the study of early Islam, this principle was perhaps first and most influentially articulated by Goldziher: see Goldziher, *Muslim Studies*, 2: 39–40.

19. Hoyland, "Writing the Biography," 585.

20. Watt, *Muhammad at Mecca*, 103.

21. Hoyland, "Writing the Biography," 585; see Burton, "Those Are the High-Flying Cranes."

22. Rubin, for instance, evaluates Burton's hypothesis as "an oversimplified view that the traditions were invented merely to provide a Quranic basis for one of the formulas of the *naskh* theories": Rubin, *The Eye of the Beholder*, 162 n. 16. See also Hawting, *The Idea of Idolatry*, esp. 134–35.

23. Hawting, *The Idea of Idolatry*, esp. 130–49.

24. These arguments are directed primarily against Rubin, *The Eye of the Beholder*, 156–66. Although Rubin does not directly address the issue of historicity, the implication of his study seems to be that the whole episode is fabricated on the basis of the Qurʾān.

25. See, e.g., Clark, *History, Theory, Text.*

26. Hoyland, "The Earliest Christian Writings," esp. 277–81, 290. This section of the article is entitled "Muhammad the Instigator of the Conquests."

27. Spuler, "La 'Sira' du Prophète."

28. So Toby Lester reports in his *Atlantic Monthly* article, "What Is the Koran?," 46.

29. Bowersock, Brown, and Grabar, *Late Antiquity*, s.v. "Muhammad" by Michael Cook. See also M. Cook, *Muhammad*, 75–76.

30. Crone, "What Do We Actually Know about Mohammad?" In a personal communication of 16 June 2004, Crone informed me that she has not given up on the idea that Muhammad may have survived beyond the traditional date of his death, as seems to be indicated by these sources.

31. See esp. Conrad, "The Conquest of Arwad"; Hoyland, "Sebeos"; Hoyland, *Seeing Islam*, 545–90.

32. Perhaps Peter Brown was the first to move things in this direction by including early Islamic civilization in his classic study, P. Brown, *The World of Late Antiquity*. In particular, the various works published in the Darwin Press series "Studies in Late Antiquity and Early Islam" have contributed much to this reorientation, among numerous other studies. The need for such a perspective and the value of so-called skeptical scholarship for achieving it are well articulated in Hawting, "John Wansbrough, Islam, and Monotheism." See also Griffith, "Disputing with Islam," sec. 1; and Donner, *Narratives of Islamic Origins*, 293–96, both of which describe the problems of this divide between late antiquity and early Islam from the perspectives of Christian studies and Islamic studies respectively.

33. Exemplary in this regard is Sizgorich, *Violence and Belief*. Nevertheless, despite this study's careful elucidation of various connections between late ancient Christianity and early Islam, Sizgorich largely avoids the complicated issues of the first Islamic century and focuses instead on the more abundant materials of the second and third, leaving an unfortunate, if somewhat understandable, gap in the study. Although the study treats narratives describing the beginnings of Islam, it analyzes these traditions within the context of their production, rather than as sources for the events of the first century. The same is also true of the related articles, Sizgorich, "Do Prophets Come with a Sword?"; and Sizgorich, "Narrative and Community." Nevertheless, the relative absence of the Qurʾān as an object of analysis in these studies is rather peculiar.

34. Raven, "Sīra." Raven cites the Salman Rushdie affair as "a striking illustration of the attitude of modern Muslims towards the *sīra*."

35. See, e.g., Berlinerblau, *The Secular Bible*, 116–28, which notes the pivotal role of "believing critics" in the establishment of modern biblical criticism. In this chapter on "The Secular Qurʾān?" Berlinerblau forecasts that a similar cadre of "believing critics" emerging from within the Islamic community itself will be necessary to achieve a comparable transformation in the study of Islamic origins.

36. This approach to the historical-critical discussion of religious traditions and their internal truth claims rests heavily on the cultural-linguistic model for understanding religion proposed in Lindbeck, *The Nature of Doctrine*, esp. 30–46. Lindbeck's work in turn depends a great deal on certain ideas in Wittgenstein's philosophy of religion,

which also has influenced the above remarks: see Clack, *An Introduction to Wittgenstein's Philosophy of Religion*, esp. 78–89; Malcolm, *Wittgenstein*; Kerr, *Theology after Wittgenstein*, esp. 29–52.

37. For a compelling critique of secular knowledge and its truth claims, particularly in relation to religious belief, see, e.g., Milbank, *Theology and Social Theory*.

38. Peters, *Jesus and Muhammad*, 14–17, 24–37; although see 196.

39. See, e.g., R. Brown, *The Death of the Messiah*, 2: 1350–78; Meier, *A Marginal Jew*, 1: 372–409.

40. See, e.g., R. Brown, *The Birth of the Messiah*, 513–16, 547–56; Meier, *A Marginal Jew*, 1: 214–16; Ehrman, *Jesus*, 36–49.

41. Zwierlein, *Petrus in Rom*.

42. E.g., Kümmel, *Introduction to the New Testament*, 234–46.

43. See, e.g., R. Brown, *The Birth of the Messiah*, 32–38; R. Brown, *The Death of the Messiah*, 1: 13–25; Ehrman, *Jesus*, 30–40.

44. For this reason the sources surveyed in Kohlberg, "Western Accounts" are largely irrelevant to the present study. The medieval Western European accounts of Muhammad's death surveyed by Kohlberg are from the twelfth century or later, and, as Kohlberg himself notes, either they are the fanciful imaginings of Christian polemicists or they depend directly on the Islamic historical tradition, including Ibn Isḥāq's biography especially. The only earlier source signaled by Kohlberg is the *Istoria de Mahomet*, an anonymous Latin text written sometime before the mid-ninth century whose contents are largely polemical fiction. Nevertheless, as will be seen in the following chapter, this Christian "Life of Muhammad" also seems to suggest the conquest of the Roman Near East by Muhammad's followers during his lifetime.

45. The sources considered in Kohlberg's article were all composed several centuries after the traditional Islamic biography of Muhammad had become well established and widely dispersed: ibid., 165–77. Even if any one of these later authors may have been aware of the earlier reports associating Muhammad with the invasion of Palestine (in the case of Western sources, perhaps from the Spanish chronicle tradition, which Kohlberg oddly overlooks, and the *Istoria de Mahomet*, whose placement of the conquest of Syria within Muhammad's lifetime Kohlberg also fails to note), one certainly would not be surprised to find that they have adhered to the chronology of the Islamic historical tradition. Lacking the skepticism of modern historiography, they doubtless would have assumed that the Muslims remembered these events with great accuracy and then adjusted their own collective memories accordingly. The same sort of deference would appear to hold even in the case of modern historiography, such as, for instance, when Hoyland in his article on the life of Muhammad in Christian sources first notes that the relevant writings clearly describe Muhammad as still alive at the time of the conquests but then immediately concludes that the contradictory information from Islamic tradition is of course correct: Hoyland, "The Earliest Christian Writings," 277–81, 290.

46. Although it is not uncommon to find "apocalyptic" used in this sense, when considered historically (as in this study) "apocalyptic" instead refers most properly to a genre of early Jewish and Christian literature. Although this literature often contains

eschatological material, it should not be simply equated with eschatology, as scholars of biblical studies are largely agreed. See, e.g., J. Collins, *Apocalypse*, esp. p. 9; and J. Collins, *Apocalyptic Imagination*, 1–42.

47. Unfortunately, Donner, *Muhammad and the Believers* appeared well after this monograph had been composed and was near the end of a very lengthy review process. Nevertheless, the core hypothesis of this study had already been well articulated in Donner, "From Believers to Muslims." In light of the significance of Donner's new monograph for the present study, however, I have made an effort to incorporate its findings as much as possible.

48. Cf. Crone and Cook, *Hagarism*, 24.

49. An important critique originally raised by Said, *Orientalism.*

50. See, e.g., Stover, "Orientalism and the Otherness of Islam." See also Abdul-Rauf, "Outsiders' Interpretations of Islam," 179–88; Rahman, "Approaches to Islam," 189–202.

51. The need for such critical approaches in the discipline of religious studies is well expressed in McCutcheon, *Manufacturing Religion.*

52. C. Robinson, *ʿAbd al-Malik*, 103.

CHAPTER 1

1. Hoyland, *Seeing Islam*, 59. Here Hoyland argues persuasively against Dagron's suggestion that the text was composed sometime in the early 640s, which seems unlikely: Dagron and Déroche, "Juifs et Chrétiens," 246–47. In his article on the life of Muhammad as reflected in Christian sources, Hoyland relegates this text to a footnote because Muhammad is not specifically named: Hoyland, "The Earliest Christian Writings," 277 n. 6. Nevertheless, there can hardly be any question that he is indeed the prophet to whom the *Doctrina Iacobi* refers.

2. This is essentially the thesis of Olster, *Roman Defeat.* Nonetheless, while Olster maintains that there is no correlation between this literature and the real relations of Jews and Christians in late antiquity, I have argued elsewhere that both Jewish and Christian polemics from this period reveal some awareness of the other's polemics and what they believe, and moreover that they are at least indirectly related to the social situation of the Jews in the Roman Empire: see Shoemaker, "Let Us Go and Burn Her Body," esp. 778–88. See also the review of Olster's book in Cameron, "Byzantines and Jews."

3. Olster, *Roman Defeat*, 175.

4. Ibid., 158–75, esp. 159–61.

5. Ibid., 159–64; cf. also Hoyland, *Seeing Islam*, 56; Dagron and Déroche, "Juifs et Chrétiens," 240–46. The specific attention given to the cities of Ptolemais and Sykamine in Palestine leads Hoyland and Dagron and Déroche to conclude that the author is likely a native of their environs.

6. Hoyland, *Seeing Islam*, 56. Hoyland later notes of these details: "The *Doctrina Jacobi* distinguishes itself by its attention to narrative and topical detail, but it is a common trait of the anti-Jewish treatises of the sixth and seventh centuries that rather than simply rehearse traditional arguments and citations, they dress them up with a storyline and

discussion of contemporary issues" (60). To a somewhat limited extent, Hoyland is correct here, in that this literature often works to create an aura of plausibility around the events of a Jewish / Christian debate. But, as Olster has quite convincingly demonstrated, the anti-Jewish literature of this period generally does in fact "simply rehearse traditional arguments and citations," avoiding direct mention of contemporary issues, and most notably, the fact of the Christian empire's defeat. What Hoyland apparently misses here is that the *Doctrina Iacobi* truly does stand out within the genre of early Byzantine anti-Jewish literature in its remarkable preservation of details regarding contemporary social and political issues: see Olster, *Roman Defeat*, 158–75, esp. 158–59, 175.

7. In discussing the nineteenth-century French realist novel, Roland Barthes observed that there was a tendency to pile up details that were insignificant for either plot or character development; he concluded that "the significance of the insignificance" lay in deploying this sort of "thick description" to bolster the illusion of reality in the reader's mind. See Barthes, "The Reality Effect," 141–48. In relation to late ancient Christian literature, see also the discussion of this concept in Clark, "Holy Women, Holy Words," 419. Nevertheless, even on the outside chance that the details of this text are designed merely to increase the verisimilitude of what were ultimately fictional events, it stands to reason that the author would have made these surrounding details, including the reference to the rise of Islam, as accurate as possible in order to create the maximum "reality effect."

8. Olster, *Roman Defeat*, 158–59.

9. The name Sergius appears only in the Church Slavonic version of the *Doctrina Iacobi*, but comparison with other sources suggests that this probably was the name of the Roman official to which the text here refers. See the discussion below. On the different versions of the *Doctrina Iacobi*, which also survives in Arabic and Ethiopic in addition to Greek and Church Slavonic, see Dagron and Déroche, "Juifs et Chrétiens," 47–68.

10. The Greek word used here is Ἑρμόλαος, which is a Greek form of the name Armilus. Armilus is the name given to the Antichrist in Jewish apocalyptic literature of this period. In Christian apocalyptic, Armilus (from Romulus) is instead the name of the emperor who receives the promise of Rome's eternal rule. This is one of the many details that demonstrates the author's considerable knowledge of contemporary Judaism: a Christian would not name the anti-Christ Armilus. See Olster, *Roman Defeat*, 173–74. For a contemporary example of such Jewish usage, see the seventh-century *Sefer Zerubbabel*: Lévi, "L'Apocalypse de Zorobabel," 68 (1914): 136; Himmelfarb, "Sefer Zerubbabel," 75.

11. *Doctrina Iacobi* V.16 (Dagron and Déroche, "Juifs et Chrétiens," 209–11). This translation and all others are my own, unless otherwise indicated.

12. In addition to the extended discussion of the *Syriac Common Source* below, see also Hoyland, *Seeing Islam*, 400–409. The reference from the second chronicle can be found in Thomas the Presbyter, *Chronicle* (Brooks, *Chronica minora II*, 1: 147–48). Although Thomas's *Chronicle* does not actually give the name Sergius, it is widely agreed that the report refers to his death: see, e.g., Donner, *The Early Islamic Conquests*, 115–16; Gil, *A History of Palestine*, 38–39; Kaegi, *Byzantium and the Early Islamic Conquests*, 88–89; Dagron and Déroche, "Juifs et Chrétiens," 246 n. 105; Hoyland, *Seeing Islam*, 60 (esp. n. 19), 120; Palmer, *The Seventh Century*, 19 n. 119.

13. Many scholars have identified this Sergius with a Sergius mentioned in the *Brevarium* of the Patriarch Nicephorus (d. 828) who was killed by the "Saracens": Nicephorus, *Brevarium* 20 (Mango, *Nikephorus*, 68). Nevertheless, both Mango and Hoyland caution, rightly I think, that there is no clear indication that these two individuals are the same, despite their common names: see Nicephorus, *Brevarium* 20 (Mango, *Nikephorus*, 187); and Hoyland, *Seeing Islam*, 59–60.

14. Crone and Cook, *Hagarism*, 4, 152 nn. 5 and 6.

15. Ibid., 4.

16. Theophanes, *Chronicle* (de Boor, *Theophanis chronographia*, 1: 333); Sebeos, *History* 42 (Abgarian, Պատմութիւն Սեբէոսի, 135).

17. Donner, "La question du messianisme"; Bashear, "The Title '*Fārūq*.'"

18. Donner, "La question du messianisme," 24, suggests that the Christian author has ascribed false information to the Jews in order to discredit them. As attractive as this might seem on the surface, it is not a sufficient explanation, above all because Olster has shown convincingly that the author does not appear to have adopted this strategy but is instead remarkably accurate in his portrayal of Judaism. Furthermore, it is difficult to explain the corroboration of this information in other sources where anti-Judaism is not directly in evidence.

19. Hoyland, "The Earliest Christian Writings," 290.

20. Ibid.

21. Hoyland, *Seeing Islam*, 130.

22. Harald Suermann rather strangely asserts that the *Doctrina Iacobi* "certainly refers to Muhammad's military raids" in this instance, presumably indicating his campaigns in Arabia(?). Yet it is not at all clear on what basis he would sever this report from the invasion of Palestine and move it earlier into the Arabian career of Muhammad. While this would perhaps comport with the much later Islamic biographies of Muhammad, there is certainly nothing in the *Doctrina Iacobi*'s report that would suggest Suermann's interpretation of this passage: presumably he is aiming to harmonize the account with later Islamic tradition. See Suermann, "Early Islam," 139.

23. Crone and Cook, *Hagarism*, 4–5.

24. Lewis, "An Apocalyptic Vision," 321–22.

25. On the Kenite's identification with the Arabs, see Crone and Cook, *Hagarism*, 35–37.

26. *The Secrets of Rabbi Shimʿōn b. Yoḥai* (Jellinek, *Bet ha-midrash*, 3: 78; Reeves, *Trajectories*, 78–80, slightly modified).

27. See the discussions of this passage in Lewis, "An Apocalyptic Vision," 323–24; Crone and Cook, *Hagarism*, 4–5; Gil, *A History of Palestine*, 63; Hoyland, *Seeing Islam*, 310–11; Reeves, *Trajectories*, 80–81. See also the broader analysis of these traditions in Bashear, "Riding Beasts."

28. *The Secrets of Rabbi Shimʿōn b. Yoḥai* (Jellinek, *Bet ha-midrash*, 3: 79; Reeves, *Trajectories*, 81–82).

29. *The Secrets of Rabbi Shimʿōn b. Yoḥai* (Jellinek, *Bet ha-midrash*, 3: 79–80; Reeves, *Trajectories*, 84–85).

30. E.g., Even-Shmuel, *Midreshe ge'ulah*, 167–69, 175–77; Lewis, "An Apocalyptic Vision," 323; Baron, *A Social and Religious History*, 3: 93, 274 n. 27; Crone and Cook, *Hagarism*, 4–5; Dagron and Déroche, "Juifs et Chrétiens," 43; Gil, *A History of Palestine*, 61–62; Hoyland, "Sebeos," 92; Hoyland, *Seeing Islam*, 308.

31. Crone and Cook, *Hagarism*, 4.

32. Lewis, "An Apocalyptic Vision," 321.

33. *The Secrets of Rabbi Shimʿōn b. Yoḥai* (Cairo Geniza fragment, Wertheimer, *Bate midrashot*, 2: 25–26; Lewis, "An Apocalyptic Vision," 322 n. 1; reprinted in Wertheimer and Wertheimer, *Bate midrashot*, 2: 506–7).

34. *The Secrets of Rabbi Shimʿōn b. Yoḥai* (Munich MS Hebr. 222, ff. 107b–111a, 107b). See Lewis, "An Apocalyptic Vision," 322 n. 1; and Steinschneider, "Apocalypsen mit polemischer Tendenz," 635 n. 18.

35. Even-Shmuel, *Midreshe ge'ulah*, 162–74; Lewis, "An Apocalyptic Vision," 323.

36. Buttenwieser, *Outline of the Neo-Hebraic Apocalyptic Literature*, 42.

37. *Ten Kings Midrash* (Eisenstein, *Otsar midrashim*, 2: 465; Lewis, "An Apocalyptic Vision," 322, 324). Lewis suggests that the *Ten Kings Midrash* has here confused Muhammad with the early caliphs, an interpretation driven no doubt by a desire to maintain a consistency with the traditional Islamic narratives of the conquests (323).

38. ועומר איש שוטה ובעל הרוח ומדבר על הקב"ה כזבים והוא מכבש את הארץ. *The Prayer of Rabbi Shimʿōn b. Yoḥai* (Jellinek, *Bet ha-midrash*, 4: 119; Lewis, "An Apocalyptic Vision," 312).

39. The chronicle has also been called the "*Anonymous Guidi*"" after its first editor.

40. See the discussion in Hoyland, *Seeing Islam*, 182–85.

41. Ibid., 183.

42. Nautin, "L'auteur de la 'Chronique Anonyme.'"

43. Hoyland, *Seeing Islam*, 184–85.

44. Ibid., 185.

45. Most likely the "Mrwnaye" are the inhabitants of the region of Merv, in light of the fact that Yazdgerd III is known to have died there.

46. The *Khuzistan Chronicle* (Guidi, *Chronica minora I*, 1: 30–31). The Syriac word ܡܕܒܪܢܐ generally denotes a secular, rather than religious, leader: see Payne Smith, *Thesaurus Syriacus*, 1: 817.

47. Hoyland, *Seeing Islam*, 182.

48. Such is the assessment offered in Wright, *A Short History of Syriac Literature*, 143. This was repeated more recently in Albert et al., *Christianismes orientaux*, 357: "a tenu en Orient une place équivalente à celle de Jérome dans le monde latin."

49. His considerable oeuvre is discussed in Wright, *A Short History of Syriac Literature*, 141–54. Of all the authors covered in this work, only the discussion of Bar Hebraeus is as lengthy.

50. Jacob of Edessa, *Chronological Charts* (Brooks, Guidi, and Chabot, *Chronica minora III*, 1: 263); translated in Hoyland, *Seeing Islam*, 163–64.

51. Jacob of Edessa, *Chronological Charts* (Brooks, Guidi, and Chabot, *Chronica minora III*, 1: 326). In the left margin of the chart, Jacob further clarifies that the beginning of

the Arab kingdom happened when Heraclius was in his eleventh year and Khosro was in his thirty-first year. On the conversion of Jacob's years into CE dates, see Palmer, *The Seventh Century*, 41–42, 255–59. Hoyland's treatment of this text is rather brief: Hoyland, *Seeing Islam*, 163–65.

52. Jacob of Edessa, *Chronological Charts* (Brooks, Guidi, and Chabot, *Chronica minora III*, 1: 327).

53. Palmer, *The Seventh Century*, 43.

54. *Short Syriac Chronicle of 705* (Land, *Anecdota Syriaca*, 2: 11). See the discussion and translation in Palmer, *The Seventh Century*, 43–44; and Hoyland, *Seeing Islam*, 394–95. Regarding the *Hispanic Chronicle*, see below.

55. Jacob of Edessa, *Chronological Charts* (Brooks, Guidi, and Chabot, *Chronica minora III*, 1: 326).

56. See the discussions of this battle in Kaegi, *Byzantium and the Early Islamic Conquests*, 67–74; Donner, *The Early Islamic Conquests*, 101–11. Nevertheless, see also the reinterpretation of the Mu'ta traditions proposed in the following chapter.

57. Kaegi, *Byzantium and the Early Islamic Conquests*, 72. On relations between the *Chronicle* of Theophanes and the Islamic historical tradition, see Conrad, "Theophanes and the Arabic Historical Tradition."

58. Donner, *The Early Islamic Conquests*, 111–19.

59. Hoyland, *Seeing Islam*, 446.

60. Johnson, "Further Remarks."

61. Ibid., 114–15. Fragments of this history have been published in Orlandi, *Storia della Chiesa*.

62. Johnson, "Further Remarks," 113.

63. *History of the Patriarchs of Alexandria* (Evetts, *History of the Patriarchs*, 2: 492).

64. Or perhaps, "altered it (for the worse)": see Lane and Lane-Poole, *Arabic-English Lexicon*, 1334b, c. The sense here is somewhat unclear, as evidenced by the fact that the version preserved in the earliest manuscript has here instead وبين النلهرين سباداميه, the meaning of which is unknown: Seybold, *Severus ibn al Muqaffa'*, 99.

65. *History of the Patriarchs of Alexandria* (Evetts, *History of the Patriarchs*, 2: 492–93).

66. Hoyland, *Seeing Islam*, 446.

67. R. Collins, *The Arab Conquest of Spain*, 56, 60. Note that while Collins suggests the existence of two separate sources that were shared by the chronicles, one for Byzantine affairs, and another covering Islamic history, Hoyland posits the existence of only one source that contained information regarding both Byzantium and the Islamic empire: Hoyland, *Seeing Islam*, 424–25.

68. Hoyland, *Seeing Islam*, 425.

69. Dubler, "Sobre la crónica arábigo-bizantina," 331. See the criticisms of Dubler's proposal in R. Collins, *The Arab Conquest of Spain*, 56, 62; Hoyland, *Seeing Islam*, 425; Barkai, *Cristianos y musulmanes*, 55 n. 2.

70. R. Collins, *The Arab Conquest of Spain*, 57, 62–63; see also the discussion of the *Hispanic Chronicle of 754* in Wolf, *Conquerors and Chroniclers*, 31–45.

71. Nöldeke, "Epimetrum." See also Mommsen, *Chronica minora*, 2: 324, where Mommsen notes connections with Byzantine sources.

72. Hoyland, *Seeing Islam*, 424. Michael McCormick also favors an eastern original, probably in Greek: Kazhdan, *The Oxford Dictionary of Byzantium*, s.v. "Continuationes Isidorianae," by Michael McCormick.

73. Hoyland, *Seeing Islam*, 425: see additional reasons for a Greek original in n. 122. See also R. Collins, *The Arab Conquest of Spain*, 56. The connections with Byzantine sources are extensively displayed in a series of charts published by Dubler, "Sobre la crónica arábigo-bizantina," esp. 298–332; see esp. the elaborate stemma on 332, which should not be taken at face value. For instance, Collins himself remarks of this article that "great caution is needed in considering some of the specific claims Dubler makes as to Byzantine and other Eastern Mediterranean texts being currently available in Spain": R. Collins, *The Arab Conquest of Spain*, 55 n. 11. On the limited cultural exchange between East and West at this time, see especially Mango, "La culture grecque et l'Occident."

74. Hoyland, *Seeing Islam*, 425.

75. Ibid., 423. For the date, see R. Collins, *The Arab Conquest of Spain*, 55–56.

76. Heraclius's entry accounts for 62 percent of the Byzantine material and 18 percent of the entire chronicle: Hoyland, *Seeing Islam*, 423.

77. *Byzantine-Arab Chronicle of 741* 13 (Gil, *Corpus*, 1: 9); Theodor Mommsen's edition is still useful, since it presents the *Byzantine-Arab Chronicle* synoptically with the *Hispanic Chronicle* in places where they have used the *Spanish Eastern Source*: Mommsen, *Chronica minora*, 2: 337.

78. *Byzantine-Arab Chronicle of 741* 14–16 (Gil, *Corpus*, 1: 9; Mommsen, *Chronica minora*, 2: 337–38; trans. in Hoyland, *Seeing Islam*, 616).

79. *Byzantine-Arab Chronicle of 741* 17 (Gil, *Corpus*, 1: 9; Mommsen, *Chronica minora*, 2: 338).

80. See also Hoyland, *Seeing Islam*, 555 n. 46, which similarly understands the passage as indicating Muhammad's leadership of this initial invasion of Roman territory. Note that Mesopotamia was a Roman province in the late sixth century and the early seventh.

81. Conrad, "Theophanes and the Arabic Historical Tradition," 7, 16–20.

82. Ibid., 7–8, 21–42.

83. Note also that a list of the early caliphs in Syriac also places the end of Muhammad's life ten years after he began to rule in Medina: *Short Syriac Chronicle of 724* (Land, *Anecdota Syriaca*, 1: 40–41; and Brooks, *Chronica minora II*, 1: 155). Although it is frequently dated to 724, this is in fact a terminus post quem, and it could be as late as 743. Likewise, scholars have maintained that this list is in fact the Syriac translation of an Islamic document, inasmuch as it uses the word *rasul* in reference to Muhammad. It is not impossible, however, that this usage could reflect a Christian provenance close to the Umayyad authorities. This list, like the *Spanish Eastern Source*, makes no mention of ʿAlī. Nevertheless, it also makes no reference to the Islamic conquest of the Near East, thus making it more or less irrelevant for present purposes. As the *Spanish Eastern Source* and the *Chronicle* of Theophilus of Edessa (both roughly contemporary sources) demonstrate, in this era there

were sources that ascribed ten years to Muhammad's rule while also identifying him as the leader of the initial invasion of the Roman Near East. See the discussions of this text in Palmer, *The Seventh Century*, 49–50; and Hoyland, *Seeing Islam*, 395–96.

84. The chronology of the *Byzantine-Arab Chronicle*, and apparently the *Spanish Eastern Source* as well, is far from perfect in any case. In the *Byzantine-Arab Chronicle*, the initial conquests are indicated just before an event dated to 621; in the *Hispanic Chronicle of 754*, the first stage of the Islamic conquest began in 618, and Muhammad died ten years later in 628: *Byzantine-Arab Chronicle of 741* 13–14 (Gil, *Corpus*, 1: 9; Mommsen, *Chronica minora*, 2: 337); *Hispanic Chronicle of 754* 8 (López Pereira, *Crónica mozárabe*, 28). The latter date agrees with Jacob of Edessa's date for Muhammad's death, but the first date is not the same, since Jacob gives Muhammad only seven years.

85. Hoyland, *Seeing Islam*, 426.

86. *Hispanic Chronicle of 754* 8 (López Pereira, *Crónica mozárabe*, 28; Wolf, *Conquerors and Chroniclers*, 113–14).

87. *Hispanic Chronicle of 754* 10 (López Pereira, *Crónica mozárabe*, 30; Wolf, *Conquerors and Chroniclers*, 114).

88. Haldon, *Byzantium in the Seventh Century*, 54–56, 63–64.

89. *Hispanic Chronicle of 754* 11 (López Pereira, *Crónica mozárabe*, 30; Wolf, *Conquerors and Chroniclers*, 115).

90. These points were demonstrated definitively in Brooks, "The Sources of Theophanes." There is also evidence for a mediating source between Theophanes and the *Syriac Common Source*, which extended the latter up to 780, but this matter is of interest only for studying Theophanes' chronicle. The history of the investigation of Theophanes' "eastern sources" is briefly surveyed in Conrad, "Theophanes and the Arabic Historical Tradition," 5–6.

91. See Hoyland, *Seeing Islam*, 440–43.

92. This is the common wisdom regarding the *Chronicle of 1234*: Palmer, *The Seventh Century*, 90, 101–3; Conrad, "The Conquest of Arwad," 328–34, 347–48. Palmer presents in English translation his reconstruction of Dionysius of Tellmahre's lost chronicle based on this principle in Palmer, *The Seventh Century*, 85–221, where he translates the relevant portions of the *Chronicle of 1234*, giving supplementary quotations from Michael in the footnotes, together with references to Agapius and Theophanes. But see now some important issues regarding the reliability of the *Chronicle of 1234* raised by Hoyland, *Seeing Islam*, 419, which suggest that careful comparison with the other related sources is still very important.

93. Hoyland, *Seeing Islam*, 631–71.

94. Theophilus was first proposed by Brooks as one of two possibilities: Brooks, "The Sources of Theophanes," 583–86. Subsequent study has been able to eliminate the competition, making Theophilus's identification as the author almost certain. See Conrad, "Theophanes and the Arabic Historical Tradition," 43; Conrad, "The Conquest of Arwad," 322–48; Hoyland, *Seeing Islam*, 401–2; Palmer, *The Seventh Century*, 96–98.

95. Conrad, "Varietas Syriaca," 91–94; Conrad, "The Conquest of Arwad," 331; Hoyland, *Seeing Islam*, 400–401.

96. Hoyland, *Seeing Islam*, 404–5. Hopefully, Conrad's long anticipated work on eastern Christian historiography concerning the rise of Islam during the ʿAbbāsid period will further clarify this topic: Conrad, *Muhammadanea Edessensis*.

97. Hoyland, "The Earliest Christian Writings," 280 n. 16.

98. The *Chronicle of 1234* actually reads here "he no longer allowed," which does not make very much sense in light of the following descriptions of increasing raids by Muhammad's followers. Furthermore, comparison with other related chronicles makes it rather unlikely that the *Chronicle of 1234*'s phrase "he no longer allowed" actually reflects the text of Theophilus's *Chronicle*. For instance, Michael's *Chronicle* has instead: "When many had sworn allegiance to him, he no longer went up in person as leader of those who went up to plunder, but he sent others at the head of his armies while remaining himself in his city on the seat of honor." Michael the Syrian, *Chronicle* 11.2 (Chabot, *Chronique de Michel le Syrien*, 4: 405–6; translated in Palmer, *The Seventh Century*, 130 n. 294). Likewise, the *Chronicle of Siirt* (see below), which also depends on Theophilus's *Chronicle*, has here: "In the eighteenth year of Heraclius, Emperor of the Greeks, the year in which Ardasir the son of Siroe the son of Khosro Parvez reigned, the Arabs began their conquests, and Islam became powerful. And then Muhammad no longer went forth in battle, and he began to send out his companions." *Chronicle of Siirt* 101 (Scher, *Histoire nestorienne*, 4: 600–601). Thus the translation above reflects what was most likely in Theophilus's now lost *Chronicle* at this point, as determined through comparison with all of the dependent sources, rather than simply reproducing the *Chronicle of 1234*.

99. *Chronicle of 1234* (Chabot, *Chronicon ad annum Christi 1234*, 1: 227–28).

100. The report in Theophanes' *Chronicle* does bear a slight structural resemblance to Dionysius's account, which may be of some limited significance. Theophanes begins his account of the rise of Islam by first summarizing the earliest events of the Islamic campaign in Palestine, after which he notes Muhammad's death under the entry for the following year: Theophanes, *Chronicle* (de Boor, *Theophanis chronographia*, 1: 332–33). Theophanes is quite clear, however, that the conquests in fact began only after Muhammad's death, and the initial description of the conquests before the notice of Muhammad's death seemingly figures as foreshadowing of the events to follow. Nonetheless, this peculiar structure may reflect the fact that one of Theophanes' sources attributed the beginning of the Palestinian campaign to the final years of Muhammad's life, which is indeed likely since he utilized a version of Theophilus's *Chronicle*.

101. Hoyland, *Seeing Islam*, 401 n. 52, 405 n. 62.

102. *Chronicle of Siirt* 101 (Scher, *Histoire nestorienne*, 4: 600–601).

103. Conrad, "Theophanes and the Arabic Historical Tradition," esp. 7–8, 31–32, 39–42.

104. The exact date that Theophilus assigned to Muhammad's death is somewhat uncertain, although there is good reason to suspect that it was 631–32. Palmer notes that Dionysius of Tellmahre attributes a ten-year reign to Muhammad: Palmer, *The Seventh Century*, 36, 144. The same information appears in the *Chronicle of 1234*, which assigns ten years to Muhammad and gives 631/32 as the year of his death: Chabot, *Chronicon ad annum Christi 1234*, 1: 238–39 (CE dates determined using the chart in Palmer, *The*

Seventh Century, xxxviii). Agapius agrees: his *Chronicle* is damaged at the key point that recorded Muhammad's death and the transfer of power to Abū Bakr, but elsewhere it is clear that Abū Bakr died in 634/35 after reigning for three years, placing Muhammad's death in 631/32: Agapius, *Chronicle* (Vasiliev, *Kitab al-ʿUnvan / Histoire universelle*, 3: 468–69). Nonetheless, Michael's *Chronicle* says that Muhammad ruled for seven years, implying his death in 628/29. He further states that Abū Bakr reigned for two years and seven months, identifying 630 as the second year of his reign, all of which agrees with Jacob of Edessa, whom Michael identifies as a source: Michael the Syrian, *Chronicle* 11.3 (Chabot, *Chronique de Michel le Syrien*, 4: 410; see also 4: 378, scholion for the reference to Jacob). Nonetheless, later on Michael (correctly) notes the death of Abū Bakr in 635!: *Chronicle* 11.5 (ibid., 4: 414). Theophanes, in contrast, attributes nine years of rule to Muhammad (see the explanation of this in Conrad, "Theophanes and the Arabic Historical Tradition," 16–20), identifying the date of Muhammad's death as 622 AD, but 630 CE according to the *annus mundi* and the regnal year of Heraclius: Theophanes, *Chronicle* (de Boor, *Theophanis chronographia*, 1: 332–33). The agreement of Agapius and the *Chronicle of 1234* is impressive, and we can attribute Michael's error to his use of Jacob, and Theophanes' to his Islamic sources (as Conrad explains). But it is equally possible that Agapius and the *Chronicle of 1234* have independently corrected earlier mistakes, particularly since Agapius had access to a Muslim chronology, and the latter shows evidence of having used Islamic sources: Hoyland, *Seeing Islam*, 419, 441.

105. *Short Syriac Chronicle of 775* (Brooks, Guidi, and Chabot, *Chronica minora III*, 1: 348).

106. Palmer, *The Seventh Century*, 52; see also Hoyland, *Seeing Islam*, 396–99, who reaches similar conclusions.

107. Palmer, "The Messiah and the Mahdi," 45–84; see also Hoyland, *Seeing Islam*, 398–99, 415–16.

108. The *Zuqnin Chronicle* (Chabot, *Incerti auctoris Chronicon*, 2: 146), following the textual emendations and translation in Palmer, *The Seventh Century*, 69; see also the translation in Harrak, *The Chronicle of Zuqnīn*, 138. For more on the *Zuqnin Chronicle*'s somewhat problematic chronology during this period, see Palmer, *The Seventh Century*, 65–70; and Hoyland, *Seeing Islam*, 409–14. This chronicle is sometimes referred to as the chronicle of Ps.-Dionysius, but this is confusing and should be avoided (particularly since there is already another Ps.-Dionysius). The source of this is F. Nau's mistaken identification of this chronicle with the lost chronicle of Dionysius of Tellmahre. Others have identified the author as Joshua the Stylite, but this is disputed. Therefore it seems best for now to identify the chronicle by the monastery where it was composed. See the discussion in Palmer, *The Seventh Century*, 53.

109. As he apologizes: "If [someone] has consulted a history which does not match this one, he should realize that not even the authors of former times agree with one another. One gives a low figure, another gives a high figure. It causes no injury to the discerning and the god-fearing if a date is one or two years out either way. It should be enough for the god-fearing to see the castigation of former generations and themselves turn away from wickedness, lest they too should have to endure such castigation." The

Zuqnin Chronicle (Chabot, *Incerti auctoris Chronicon*, 2: 147; translated in Palmer, *The Seventh Century*, 54; see also Harrak, *The Chronicle of Zuqnīn*, 139).

110. The *Zuqnin Chronicle* (Chabot, *Incerti auctoris Chronicon*, 2: 149). See also the translations in Palmer, *The Seventh Century*, 56; Harrak, *The Chronicle of Zuqnīn*, 141–42.

111. The *Zuqnin Chronicle* (Chabot, *Incerti auctoris Chronicon*, 2: 149–50).

112. The *Zuqnin Chronicle* (ibid., 2: 150). These events are identified as taking place in 633 and 637 respectively. Note that the notice indicating that the Arabs captured Caesarea in Palestine in 642 (identified as the tenth year of 'Umar's reign) probably originally referred instead to the capture of Caesarea in Cappadocia: see Palmer, *The Seventh Century*, 69.

113. Crone and Cook, *Hagarism*, 152–53 n. 7.

114. Abū l-Fatḥ, *Samaritan Chronicle* (Vilmar, *Abulfathi Annales Samaritani*, 5); cf. Levy-Rubin, *Continuatio*, 24–26.

115. Levy-Rubin, *Continuatio*, 3.

116. Abū l-Fatḥ, *Samaritan Chronicle* (Vilmar, *Abulfathi Annales Samaritani*, 172–75). The same episode is also in Levy-Rubin, *Continuatio*, 121–23; trans. 46–50.

117. Abū l-Fatḥ, *Samaritan Chronicle* (Vilmar, *Abulfathi Annales Samaritani*, 178; Stenhouse, *The Kitāb al-Tarīkh*, 248).

118. The grounds for this determination are well explained in Levy-Rubin, *Continuatio*, 5–7.

119. Ibid., xi, 3, 7, 10–19.

120. I.e., the Samaritan high priest.

121. *Continuatio* of the *Samaritan Chronicle* (Levy-Rubin, *Continuatio*, 123–24; trans. 50–53); cf. Vilmar, *Abulfathi Annales Samaritani*, 179–80.

122. Levy-Rubin, *Continuatio*, 27–29.

123. Ibid., 51 n. 32.

124. Elad, "The Coastal Cities of Palestine," esp. 146–51.

125. Levy-Rubin, *Continuatio*, 28. In addition to the numerous archaeological studies cited by Levy-Rubin, see also Pentz, *The Invisible Conquest*; Magness, *The Archaeology of the Early Islamic Settlement*; and Walmsley, *Early Islamic Syria*. As Pentz concludes, "The 7th century 'conquest' of Syria is—in archaeological terms—totally invisible. That is to say, archaeological evidence is abundant, while the archaeologist looking for a break in the material is searching in vain" (74).

126. Gil, *A History of Palestine*, 59–60.

127. Levy-Rubin, *Continuatio*, 29.

128. The detailed description of Caesarea, omitted from the quotation above, is correlated with what is known of the Byzantine city's layout in ibid., 52–53 n. 45.

129. Ibid., 10–12, 15, 23, 26.

130. Vilmar, *Abulfathi Annales Samaritani*, lxxvii: "Sed libri, e quibus depromtae sunt, a scriptoribus rerum narratarum aequalibus compositi esse videntur. . . . Horum igitur addiamentorum antiquissimi sunt fontes."

131. Levy-Rubin, *Continuatio*, 15–16, 19.

132. Ibid., 29.

133. *Continuatio* of the *Samaritan Chronicle* (Levy-Rubin, *Continuatio*, 53, 125).

134. See, e.g., the references in Levy-Rubin, *Continuatio*, 29 n. 131.

135. Łewond, *History* 13 (Ezeantsʿ, Պատմութիւն Ղեւոնդեայ, 42–45; Jeffery, "Ghevond's Text," 277–78; Arzoumanian, *History of Lewond*, 70–71).

136. Theophanes, *Chronicle* (de Boor, *Theophanis chronographia*, 1: 399); Agapius, *Chronicle* (Vasiliev, *Kitab al-ʿUnvan / Histoire universelle*, 3: 503).

137. Ps.-Leo III, *Letter to ʿUmar II* (PG 107: 315–24). This edition does not publish the complete introduction to the text, for which one must still consult the early sixteenth-century (and unpaginated) edition: Champier, *De triplici disciplina*.

138. Łewond, *History* 14 (Ezeantsʿ, Պատմութիւն Ղեւոնդեայ, 45–98; Jeffery, "Ghevond's Text," 281–330; Arzoumanian, *History of Lewond*, 72–105).

139. Gaudeul, "The Correspondence between Leo and ʿUmar."

140. Sourdel, "Un pamphlet musulman anonyme." I thank Patricia Crone for initially drawing my attention to this text.

141. Cardaillac, "La polemique anti-chrétienne," 1: 92–103, 145–52, 2: 194–267.

142. Ibid., 1: 145.

143. Łewond, *History* 13 (Ezeantsʿ, Պատմութիւն Ղեւոնդեայ, 42; Arzoumanian, *History of Lewond*, 70).

144. Gaudeul, "The Correspondence between Leo and ʿUmar," 119–23.

145. Ibid., 123–27, 144–48.

146. Ibid., 127.

147. Hoyland, *Seeing Islam*, 490–501. See also Hoyland, "The Correspondence," which is largely identical to the discussion in *Seeing Islam*.

148. Gero, *Byzantine Iconoclasm during the Reign of Leo*, 132–41.

149. Ibid., 150–71.

150. Ibid., 171.

151. E.g., Arzoumanian, *History of Lewond*, 25–47; Thomson and Howard-Johnston, *The Armenian History*, 1: xxxv–xlvii; Gaudeul, "The Correspondence between Leo and ʿUmar," 111–19. Robert Thomson, however, while he accepts Łewond's *History* as a chronicle of the late eighth century, elsewhere follows Gerö's hypothesis that the letters themselves are a later interpolation: Thomson, "Muhammad and the Origin of Islam," 831, 839.

152. Hoyland, *Seeing Islam*, 491–93, 498.

153. Gaudeul, "The Correspondence between Leo and ʿUmar," 116–23, 130–31.

154. Hoyland, *Seeing Islam*, 499–501.

155. Ibid., 496.

156. Gaudeul, "The Correspondence between Leo and ʿUmar," 126, esp. n. 27; Hoyland, *Seeing Islam*, 493–94.

157. Ps.-ʿUmar II, *Letter to Leo III* (Sourdel, "Un pamphlet musulman anonyme," 32; trans. 24–25; Eng. trans. Gaudeul, "The Correspondence between Leo and ʿUmar," 154).

158. Ps.-ʿUmar II, *Letter to Leo III* (Sourdel, "Un pamphlet musulman anonyme," 33; trans. 25; Eng. trans. Gaudeul, "The Correspondence between Leo and ʿUmar," 155).

159. Ps.-ʿUmar II, *Letter to Leo III* (Sourdel, "Un pamphlet musulman anonyme," 33; trans. 25; Eng. trans. Gaudeul, "The Correspondence between Leo and ʿUmar," 155).

160. See also Gaudeul, *La correspondance*, 29. Sizgorich also gives a translation of this passage at the beginning of his recent book. Nevertheless, it is peculiar that his translation simply omits the important initial phrasing, "In this way, with him in whom we trust, and in whom we believe," without any explanation: Sizgorich, *Violence and Belief*, 1.

161. Sellheim, "Prophet, Chalif und Geschichte," 39–46; C. Robinson, *Islamic Historiography*, 26–27, 122.

162. Hoyland also identifies the *Chronicle* of Thomas the Presbyter (ca. 640 CE) as witnessing to Muhammad's leadership during the conquest of Palestine: Hoyland, "The Earliest Christian Writings," 277–78. The text, however, only refers to the "Arabs of Muhammad" in the context of describing the initial assault on Palestine. While Hoyland writes of this phrase that "the implication here is that Muhammad was a military leader of some kind," this interpretation is not in fact clear from the text. It may be simply that these Arabs were identified as those "of Muhammad" in order to distinguish them from other Arab groups. See Thomas the Presbyter, *Chronicle* (Brooks, *Chronica minora II*, 1: 147–48).

163. Noth and Conrad, *The Early Arabic Historical Tradition*, 40–42.

164. Neal Robinson in particular has suggested precisely this explanation in his textbook on the Qur'ān: "The mistaken notion that he was alive at the conquest of Palestine, which seems to have gained currency in some circles, may have arisen because his name was so often on the lips of the conquerors, whose basic creed was that there is no deity but Allah and that Muhammad is the Messenger of Allah." N. Robinson, *Discovering the Qur'an*, 54. One must admit that this is a possibility, but the persistence of this tradition and its failure to be contradicted for over a century—as well as its apparent confirmation in an Islamic source—strongly suggest otherwise. Robinson claims that there are Christian sources from the same period that indicate that Muhammad's death occurred before the conquest of Palestine and accuses Cook and Crone of withholding them. Nevertheless, Robinson is in fact mistaken on this point. It is true that Jacob of Edessa's charts "imply that his reign began in 622 but lasted for only seven years not ten." Yet Robinson fails to note that Jacob nonetheless signals the beginning of the conquest of Palestine within Muhammad's lifetime, as noted above. Indeed, it is highly significant that no source from the first Islamic century "correctly" relates Muhammad's death before the conquest of Palestine. If this chronology were a well-established tradition by this time, it seems likely that at least one or two sources would report his death before the invasion of Palestine. But to my knowledge, there is in fact no such witness prior to Ibn Isḥāq's mid-eighth-century biography of Muhammad.

165. See, e.g., Humphreys, *Muʿawiya*, esp. 15–18; Donner, Narratives of Islamic Origins, 10–11; Crone, *Slaves on Horses* 4.

166. Ibn Saʿd, *Ṭabaqāt* (Sachau, *Biographien Muhammeds*, 1.2: 87).

167. See Thomas and Roggema, *Christian Muslim Relations*, 721–22; Hoyland, *Seeing Islam*, 512–15.

168. *Istoria de Mahomet* (Wolf, "The Earliest Latin Lives," 96–99); cf. Eulogius of Cordova, *Liber apologeticus martyrum* 16 (Gil, *Corpus*, 2: 483–86).

169. See the recent discussion of this episode in Powers, *Muḥammad Is Not the Father*, 35–71.

170. Kaegi, *Byzantium and the Early Islamic Conquests*, 133.

171. It is also possible that the *Istoria* has borrowed this chronology from the two Spanish chronicles discussed above, the *Byzantine-Arab Chronicle of 741* and the *Hispanic Chronicle of 754*.

172. *Istoria de Mahomet* (Wolf, "The Earliest Latin Lives," 97–99).

173. *Legend of Sergius Baḥīrā (East-Syrian)* 21 (Roggema, *The Legend of Sergius Baḥīrā*, 302–3); see also the same story in the *Legend of Sergius Baḥīrā (West-Syrian)* 9 (ibid., 332–35).

174. Thomas and Roggema, *Christian Muslim Relations*, 401–2; cf. ibid., 600–603; Roggema, *The Legend of Sergius Baḥīrā*, 302–3, n. 106; Szilágyi, "Muḥammad and the Monk," esp. 178, 191, 207.

175. *Legend of Sergius Baḥīrā (East-Syrian)* 21 (Roggema, *The Legend of Sergius Baḥīrā*, 302–3).

176. Łewond, *History* 1 (Ezeantsʿ, Պատմութիւն Ղեւոնդեայ, 3–4; Arzoumanian, *History of Lewond*, 48).

177. Theophanes, *Chronicle* (de Boor, *Theophanis chronographia*, 1: 332–36). Nonetheless, Theophanes does mention the earliest events of the Arab campaign in Palestine before signaling Muhammad's death, as noted above.

178. Conrad, "Theophanes and the Arabic Historical Tradition," 16–20.

179. Theophanes, *Chronicle* (de Boor, *Theophanis chronographia*, 1: 333).

180. Thomas Artsruni, *History* 2.4 (Patkanean, Պատմութիւն տանն Արծրունեաց, 98–103; Thomson, *History of the House of the Artsrunikʿ*, 164–69).

181. The clear dependence of the Western tradition on the accounts of the early Islamic sources for this information, from the beginnings in writers of the twelfth century through the scholars of the nineteenth, is well demonstrated in Kohlberg, "Western Accounts," 168–84.

CHAPTER 2

1. E.g., Rippin, "Muḥammad in the Qurʾān," esp. 299–302, 307–8; M. Cook, *Muhammad*, 69–73; Peters, "The Quest of the Historical Muhammad," 301–5; Peters, *Muhammad and the Origins of Islam*, 261; Wansbrough, *Quranic Studies*, 56; Paret, "Der Koran als Geschichtsquelle" (although note Wansbrough's important critique of Paret's attempt to recover Muhammad's psychological development from the Qurʾān); Hodgson, *The Venture of Islam*, 160–61.

2. On the status of the *sīra* traditions as a subset of *ḥadīth*, see Rubin, *The Life of Muhammad*, xxv–xxvii.

3. In favor of an early written transmission are Horovitz, *The Earliest Biographies of the Prophet*, 23–27; Sezgin, *Geschichte des arabischen Schriftums*, 1: 53–84, 275–87; and Duri, *The Rise of Historical Writing*, 72–75. Most scholars, however, including many more "sanguine" scholars, favor the development of a written historical tradition sometime

after the first century: e.g., Sellheim, "Prophet, Chalif und Geschichte"; Schoeler, *Charakter und Authentie*, 28–32; Donner, *Narratives of Islamic Origins*, 16–18, 280–81; C. Robinson, *Islamic Historiography*, 20–30.

4. See M. Cook, "The Opponents of the Writing"; Schoeler, "Die Frage"; Schoeler, "Wieteres zur Frage"; Schoeler, "Mündliche Thora"; Schoeler, "Schreiben und Veröffentlichen"; Schoeler's articles have recently been translated into English in Schoeler, *The Oral and the Written.*

5. See, e.g., C. Robinson, *Islamic Historiography*, 23–24; Schoeler, *Charakter und Authentie*, 28–32.

6. Görke, "The Historical Tradition about al-Ḥudaybiya"; Görke and Schoeler, "Reconstructing the Earliest *Sīra* Texts"; Motzki, "The Murder of Ibn Abī l-Ḥuqayq"; Schoeler, *Charakter und Authentie*; Schoeler, "Mūsā b. ʿUqbas *Maghāzī*"; Schoeler, "Character and Authenticity"; Schoeler, "Foundations for a New Biography."

7. See the extended critique of this approach in Shoemaker, "In Search of ʿUrwa's *Sīra*."

8. Donner, for instance, describes the Qurʾān as having "a profoundly ahistorical view of the world and of mankind": Donner, *Narratives of Islamic Origins*, 80–85, quotation at 80. Likewise, Watt remarks that "the Qurʾān in isolation from the *Sīra* yields hardly any historical information": Watt, "The Reliability of Ibn Ishaq's Sources," 31–32.

9. On the date of Ibn Isḥāq's biography, see, e.g., Sellheim, "Prophet, Chalif und Geschichte," 33. For general discussions of the early *sīra* traditions, see Rubin, *The Life of Muhammad*, xiii–xxxvi; Rubin, *The Eye of the Beholder*, 5–17; J. Jones, "The *Maghāzī* Literature," 343–36; Humphreys, *Islamic History*, 77–80; and esp. Hinds, "'Maghāzī' and 'Sīra.'"

10. C. Robinson, *Islamic Historiography*, 25. Likewise, Harald Motzki recently cautioned against using Ibn Hishām's version "as if it were Ibn Isḥāq's original text," as many scholars have tended to do: Motzki, "The Author and His Work," 174. Sadun Mahmud al-Samuk argues, on the basis of comparison between Ibn Hishām's "epitome" and al-Ṭabarī, that Ibn Isḥāq never gave his *sīra* collection a definitive written form and transmitted his traditions only orally (although some portions may have been fixed in writing by himself or others). Synoptic comparison of traditions reveals that by the time Ibn Isḥāq's traditions reached written form, innumerable variants in style, length, and content are to be found. On this basis al-Samuk concludes that a precise historical reconstruction of Ibn Isḥāq's assemblage of traditions is not possible. Al-Samuk, "Die historischen Überlieferungen nach Ibn Ishaq," 160–61. See also Conrad, "Recovering Lost Texts," 260–61, where similar issues are briefly addressed.

11. Khoury, *Wahb b. Munabbih.*

12. The same is also true of the fragment of Ibn Isḥāq's *sīra* as transmitted from al-ʿUṭāridī < Yūnus b. Bukair, which equally fails to relate the end of Muhammad's life: "Ibn Isḥāq," *Kitāb al-siyar*. See also the English summary by Guillaume, *New Light on the Life of Muhammad.*

13. See Juynboll, *Muslim Tradition*, 146–60.

14. E.g., Goldziher, *Muslim Studies*, 2: 195–96. Schoeler, however, is more confident that al-Zuhrī was one of the first scholars to commit traditions to writing, suggesting

that his notes may have been available to later scholars: Schoeler, "Mündliche Thora," 227–31; Schoeler, *Charakter und Authentie*, 32–37. Nevertheless, Michael Cook is more careful in noting the very contradictory nature of the evidence regarding al-Zuhrī's role in producing written materials: M. Cook, "The Opponents of the Writing," 459–66. See also C. Robinson, *Islamic Historiography*, 25, who is similarly skeptical.

15. Sachau, "Das Berliner Fragment," trans. in Guillaume, *The Life of Muhammad*, xliii–xlvii. The manuscript refers to these traditions collectively as a "selection." Against the fragment's authenticity, see Schacht, "On Mūsā." Schoeler has recently defended its authenticity in Schoeler, "Mūsā b. ʿUqbas *Maghāzī*."

16. On al-Wāqidī's knowledge and use of Ibn Isḥāq, see Horovitz, *The Earliest Biographies of the Prophet*, 114–15, esp. n. 111, where Conrad notes various opinions as to the precise nature of al-Wāqidī's use of Ibn Isḥāq. See also, for conflicting opinions, J. Jones, "Ibn Isḥāq and al-Wāqidī"; and Schoeler, *Charakter und Authentie*, 134–42.

17. Hence the title of Wellhausen's abridged translation: Wellhausen, *Muhammed in Medina*.

18. Horovitz, *The Earliest Biographies of the Prophet*, 108–11.

19. Ibid., 120.

20. Ibid., 121.

21. See Hawting, "Review of Harald Motzki," 142–43; Conrad, "Recovering Lost Texts," 261; and Calder, *Studies in Early Muslim Jurisprudence*, 194–95. Even Motzki acknowledges the problems with chronology, and he must assume that Isḥāq al-Dabarī "probably received it in written form from his father, a pupil of ʿAbd al-Razzāq, but skipped his father in the *riwāya*": Motzki, "The *Muṣannaf* of ʿAbd al-Razzāq," 2; Motzki, "The Author and His Work," 182.

22. Motzki, "The Author and His Work," 171, 193–94. Motzki claims this conclusion as vindication against Calder, who, according to Motzki, maintained "that these books have nothing at all to do with ʿAbd al-Razzāq," a position that Motzki attributes to Calder's complete rejection of the value of *isnād*s (ibid., 194–95; see also 177, where Calder's concerns about the accuracy of attribution are represented as an "argument" that "denies" the authenticity). Such caricature is not, however, an accurate representation of Calder's position or his concerns. Calder does not reject but rather poses important unanswered questions about the authenticity of ʿAbd al-Razzāq's *Muṣannaf*, concerns that he raises based not so much with respect to the value of *isnād*s, but instead in light of frequency of "organic texts, pseudepigraphy, and long-term redactional activity as features of *some* third-century material" (Calder, *Studies in Early Muslim Jurisprudence*, 194). Although Motzki does in fact answer some of Calder's doubts in his article, in actuality he also concedes to a certain extent the "organic" nature of the texts as well as the effects of long-term redactional activity that Calder's remarks seek to highlight. In reaching his conclusions, however, Motzki represents Calder's position as rather more extreme than it actually is, creating the false effect of a stark "either/or" choice between his own view that there is some authenticity to the *Muṣannaf* and the position (incorrectly) imputed to Calder that "these books have nothing at all to do with ʿAbd al-Razzāq." Calder neither states nor implies the latter position in his critique of Motzki;

rather, he advocates further critical reflection before taking these attributions at face value. Such reflection is in fact what Motzki provides in this more recent article, presenting a more nuanced understanding of the relation between these texts and the jurisprudence of this late second-century scholar than appears in some of his earlier works. It should perhaps be noted, however, that Motzki often presents such extreme "either/or" dichotomies in the attempt to persuade readers of his position: either we must accept his arguments for the reliability of Islamic tradition or we must assume a grand conspiracy of forgery and deception on the part of the early Islamic community. See, e.g., Hawting, "Review of Harald Motzki," 142; C. Robinson, *Islamic Historiography*, 53–54.

23. Rubin, *The Eye of the Beholder*, 11–12.

24. See Motzki, "The *Muṣannaf* of ʿAbd al-Razzāq," 5. ʿAbd al-Razzāq's approximate age is determined by assuming, with Fred Donner, that transmitters "needed to be at least fifteen years old to fully comprehend" what they were learning and that "few people lived beyond the age of sixty": Donner, *Narratives of Islamic Origins*, 204 n. 3. According to the Islamic tradition, ʿAbd al-Razzāq began to study *ḥadīth* at the age of twenty: Ṣiddīqī, *Ḥadīth Literature*, 52. See also Juynboll, "On the Origins of Arabic Prose," 170, which is similarly skeptical about some of the advanced ages required by the alleged lines of early transmission for many *ḥadīth*.

25. Hinds, "'Maghāzī' and 'Sīra'" 62, 65; Schoeler, *Charakter und Authentie*, e.g., 15, 20, 37; Zaman, "*Maghāzī* and the *Muḥaddithūn*," 2.

26. The account of Muhammad's death and burial is found in ʿAbd al-Razzāq, *Muṣannaf*, 5: 428–39.

27. Motzki, "The Author and His Work," 174.

28. Donner, *Narratives of Islamic Origins*, 253–63.

29. See Barthes, "The Reality Effect," 141–48.

30. Halevi, *Muhammad's Grave*, 49. Halevi cites here Kermode, *The Genesis of Secrecy*, chap. 5, which deals specifically with the use of this device in the context of religious "scripture."

31. Ibn Saʿd, *Ṭabaqāt* (Sachau, *Biographien Muhammeds*, 2.2: 1–98).

32. See Ibn Kathīr, *The Life of the Prophet Muḥammad*.

33. Birkeland, *The Lord Guideth*, 7.

34. See Donner's similar remarks with regard to the Constitution of Medina: Donner, "From Believers to Muslims," 39–40.

35. Crone, *Roman, Provincial, and Islamic Law*, 33.

36. Rubin, *The Life of Muhammad*, xxvi–xxvii.

37. Goldziher, *Muslim Studies*, vol. 2; Schacht, *The Origins of Muhammadan Jurisprudence*; Schacht, "A Revaluation of Islamic Traditions"; Donner, *Narratives of Islamic Origins*, 257.

38. Schacht, *The Origins of Muhammadan Jurisprudence*, esp. 163–75.

39. Ibid., esp. 5, 30, 33, and 166.

40. See Rubin, *The Eye of the Beholder*, 234–60; M. Cook, "Eschatology and the Dating of Traditions," esp. 35; Crone, *Roman, Provincial, and Islamic Law*, 122–23 n. 53, although Crone attempts to defend Schacht's "rule of thumb" particularly against evidence

coming from eschatological traditions, arguing quite reasonably that, in contrast to other types of tradition, eschatology was not subject to the same kind of evolution evident in other areas. Nonetheless, Rubin argues that this "rule of thumb" does not hold up in respect to the biographical traditions, which were subject to such evolution.

41. Burton, *An Introduction to the Hadith*, 116–18; Juynboll, *Muslim Tradition*, 5, 72–73. See also Donner, *Narratives of Islamic Origins*, 121, where a slightly earlier date is suggested, ca. 80 AH.

42. J. Jones, "The *Maghāzī* Literature," 347. Al-Zuhrī, who is Ibn Isḥāq's primary source, is often credited with being the first to use *isnāds*: see Donner, *Narratives of Islamic Origins*, 121.

43. M. Cook, "Eschatology and the Dating of Traditions." See also Crone, *Roman, Provincial, and Islamic Law*, 122–23 n. 53.

44. Görke has recently attempted to answer this question, but many of his observations were already recognized as problems and addressed in Cook's article. A number of the problems identified by Görke, however, impinge on arguments that he himself has made in other articles attempting to assign authorship of certain *sīra* traditions to ʿUrwa. Görke, "Eschatology, History, and the Common Link"; see also Shoemaker, "In Search of ʿUrwa's *Sīra*," 279, 290.

45. M. Cook, *Early Muslim Dogma*, 107–16; see also M. Cook, "Eschatology and the Dating of Traditions," 24 and 40 n. 19, where he answers some objections by Juynboll to his explanation of this phenomenon; Schacht, *The Origins of Muhammadan Jurisprudence*, esp. 163–75; Crone, *Roman, Provincial, and Islamic Law*, 27–34.

46. Schacht, *The Origins of Muhammadan Jurisprudence*, 166–75; M. Cook, "Eschatology and the Dating of Traditions," 24.

47. E.g., Motzki, "The *Muṣannaf* of ʿAbd al-Razzāq," 3–4, 6–7, 9, etc; Motzki, "*Quo vadis, Ḥadiṯ*-Forschung?"; Motzki, "*Quo vadis, Ḥadiṯ*-Forschung?, Teil 2."

48. Calder, *Studies in Early Muslim Jurisprudence*, 194–95; Hawting, "Review of Harald Motzki"; Berg, *The Development of Exegesis*, 36–38, 112–14; Melchert, "The Early History of Islamic Law," 301–4; Hoyland, "Writing the Biography," 587. A particularly detailed and convincing critique can be found in Schneider, "Narrativität und Authentizität." Nevertheless, Motzki has recently published a collection of several extensive responses to scholars who have disagreed with his methods, including two directed at Schneider, in a volume also containing two essays by other scholars: Motzki, Boekhoff-van der Voort, and Anthony, *Analysing Muslim Traditions*. Here Motzki notes (229) that Schneider has responded to his most recent critique with the suggestion that continuation of the debate would not be fruitful, and given the fundamentally different methodological presuppositions of both scholars, it is hard not to agree.

49. See, e.g., Motzki, "The *Muṣannaf* of ʿAbd al-Razzāq," 3–4, 6–7, 9, etc. Such pleading is particularly evident in Motzki, "The Prophet and the Cat," esp. 32 n. 44, 63. To a more limited extent Donner also employs this sort of argument in his recent study of early Islamic historical writing: Donner, *Narratives of Islamic Origins*, esp. 25–29, 283, 287.

50. E.g., "The frequent references to concepts such as authenticity and forgery indicate a very undynamic view of the tradition. In Motzki's approach there seem to be only

two sorts of material to be found in Muslim traditional literature: authentic and forged. And if forged, then the work must be the work of an individual forger." Hawting, "Review of Harald Motzki," 142. See also C. Robinson, *Islamic Historiography*, 53–54.

51. Hawting, "Review of Harald Motzki," 142.

52. M. Cook, *Early Muslim Dogma*, 111.

53. Crone, *Roman, Provincial, and Islamic Law*, 27–30.

54. Calder, *Studies in Early Muslim Jurisprudence*, 236–41.

55. Juynboll has defended the accuracy of common-link analysis against such concerns by arguing that the spread of *isnād*s was not widespread. Cook, however, explains why Juynboll's arguments fail to exclude this considerable possibility. Juynboll, "Some *Isnad*-Analytical Methods," 354–57; M. Cook, "Eschatology and the Dating of Traditions," 40 n. 19.

56. Motzki has attempted a defense of the reliability of *isnād*s, aimed primarily at Calder, although it is not especially persuasive. Here especially Motzki grounds his arguments in protests that such skepticism would require "a high measure of 'criminal energy,'" insisting that the high ethical standards of the medieval transmitters would preclude such a possibility. Also, rather astonishingly, Motzki maintains that such conclusions regarding the spread of *isnād*s, "would only make sense if it were evident that the majority of the *isnād*s were forged." Al-Bukhārī's rejection of 593,000 traditions out of the 600,000 that he allegedly examined as forgeries would seem to lay this objection to rest. In Motzki's terms this does indeed suggest a great deal of "criminal energy." Motzki, "The Prophet and the Cat," esp. 32 n. 44, 63. Motzki's arguments with regard to the *Muwaṭṭa*''s attribution to Mālik in this article are somewhat more persuasive, however.

57. See, e.g., Juynboll, "Some *Isnād*-Analytical Methods," esp. 382..

58. See, e.g., Buhl, *Das Leben Muhammeds*, 372–77; Rodinson, *Mohammed*, xi; Wansbrough, *The Sectarian Milieu*; Crone, *Slaves on Horses*, 4–15; Crone, *Meccan Trade*, 214–30; Peters, "The Quest of the Historical Muhammad," 301–6; Rubin, *The Life of Muhammad*, xv–xxi; C. Robinson, *Islamic Historiography*, 10, 23–25.

59. Raven, "Sīra," esp. 662.

60. Görke and Schoeler, "Reconstructing the Earliest *Sīra* Texts." A more general description of the project can be found in Schoeler, "Foundations for a New Biography." See now also Görke and Schoeler, *Die ältesten Berichte*.

61. Motzki, "The Murder of Ibn Abī l-Ḥuqayq."

62. On the separateness of the two accounts, see Mattock, "History and Fiction"; Newby, "The *Sirah* as a Source"; regarding the problems surrounding the tradent "Abū Isḥāq," see Juynboll, "On the Origins of Arabic Prose," 170–71; Juynboll, *Muslim Tradition*, 141–42. For further discussion of these and other points, see Shoemaker, "In Search of 'Urwa's *Sīra*," 331–9.

63. Schoeler, *Charakter und Authentie*.

64. Görke, "The Historical Tradition about al-Ḥudaybiya."

65. Görke and Schoeler, "Reconstructing the Earliest *Sīra* Texts."

66. Schoeler, "Foundations for a New Biography"; Görke and Schoeler, "Reconstructing the Earliest *Sīra* Texts."

67. A more extended discussion and critique of both this method and its application to the biographical traditions can be found in Shoemaker, "In Search of ʿUrwa's *Sīra*." Unfortunately, Görke and Schoeler's recent book on traditions ascribed to ʿUrwa appeared too late to take into account in this article. Nevertheless, with respect to the traditions covered in my article, nothing is added to the discussion in this book that would impinge on the arguments that I have made. Moreover, with regard to the four traditions additionally ascribed to the ʿUrwan "corpus" in their monograph (the battles of Badr, Uḥud, and the Trench, and the conquest of Mecca), each of these, as predicted in the article, is even less persuasively assigned to ʿUrwa. Indeed, Görke and Schoeler both concede this point in the conclusion to their own study, judging the attribution to ʿUrwa more questionable in each case: Görke and Schoeler, *Die ältesten Berichte*, 256–57, 286. Thus, these traditions pose no challenge to the broader critique of this approach to the early *sīra* traditions presented in the article, which could easily be extended to include these traditions.

68. Motzki, "The Murder of Ibn Abī l-Ḥuqayq," 234–35.

69. Rubin, *The Eye of the Beholder*, 103–12.

70. Crone and Cook, *Hagarism*, 7, 157 n. 39; Humphreys, *Islamic History*, 19.

71. Schoeler, "Character and Authenticity," 362; Schoeler, *Charakter und Authentie*, 164.

72. In this respect Peters's rather prosaic assertion that the traditions of Muhammad's death are reliable and "derived from his wife Aisha" is rather astonishing: Peters, *Jesus and Muhammad*, 152.

73. Ibn Isḥāq's account of Muhammad's death and burial is preserved by Ibn Hishām, whose report is largely confirmed by traditions in al-Ṭabarī's *History*. See Ibn Hishām, *Kitāb sīrat Rasūl Allāh* (Wüstenfeld, *Das Leben Muhammed's*, 1: 999–1026). Al-Ṭabarī's account includes many more traditions, among which are found most of the reports attributed by Ibn Hishām to Ibn Isḥāq: al-Ṭabarī, *Ta'rīkh* (de Goeje et al., *Annales* I: 1794–1837).

74. Al-Ṭabarī identifies one of Ibn Isḥāq's contemporaries, but not Ibn Isḥāq himself, as his source for this tradition.

75. Regarding the suddenness with which Muhammad's death is portrayed by Ibn Isḥāq and in other early sources, see, e.g., Buhl [and Welch], "Muḥammad," 374b. Note, however, that Ibn Isḥāq seems to have related a tradition outside of this death and burial account that suggests a connection between Muhammad's final illness and his attempted (but unsuccessful) poisoning four years prior by a Jewish woman in Khaybar named Zaynab bt. al-Ḥārith: Ibn Hishām, *Kitāb sīrat Rasūl Allāh* (Wüstenfeld, *Das Leben Muhammed's*, 1: 764–65); and al-Ṭabarī, *Ta'rīkh* (de Goeje et al., *Annales*, I: 1583–84). In this context, immediately after Muhammad's attempted poisoning, Ibn Isḥāq adds a tradition that at the time of his illness, some four years later, Muhammad remarked that he had begun to "feel a deadly pain" from the attempted poisoning. Western scholarship, however, has persistently dismissed this tradition as unhistorical; in particular, the four year interval between the attempted poisoning and Muhammad's sudden, fatal illness renders the story highly unlikely. The failure of this tradition to recur later in Ibn Isḥāq's

narrative, and particularly in his account of Muhammad's illness and death, perhaps reflects the apparent tension between this report and the suddenness with which Muhammad's death is described in this final section, not to mention his "choice" to die. For more concerning the negative assessment of this tradition in modern scholarship, see esp. the overview in Kohlberg, "Western Accounts," 184–88.

76. The quotations from Ibn Hishām's account of Muhammad's illness, death, and burial in this section are taken from the translation by Guillaume, *The Life of Muhammad*, 678–90. A translation of al-Ṭabarī's account can be found in al-Ṭabarī, *The History of al-Ṭabarī: Volume IX*, 163–209.

77. Al-Ṭabarī, *Ta'rīkh* (de Goeje et al., *Annales*, I: 1810–12).

78. Al-Balādhurī, *Ansāb*, 1: 559.

79. Ibn Hishām, *Kitāb sīrat Rasūl Allāh* (Wüstenfeld, *Das Leben Muhammed's*, 1: 965–70).

80. Although Ibn Hishām's *Sīra* ends with Muhammad's death, Ibn Isḥāq's *Maghāzī* seems to have continued in relating events under the early caliphs, as witnessed particularly by al-Ṭabarī's *History*.

81. Tradition seventeen in this collection is a brief notice that "the apostle made the pilgrimage of completion in A.H. 10. He showed the men the rites and addressed them in ʿArafa sitting on his camel al-Jadʿā" (Sachau, "Das Berliner Fragment," 466, translated in Guillaume, *The Life of Muhammad*, xlvi). Yet this report in no way signals his death, and taken on its own terms, the designation of this pilgrimage as one "of completion" (التمام) likely refers to the pilgrimage itself, rather than the "completion" of Muhammad's life, which is in no way indicated. The phrase "pilgrimage of completion" is probably intended to signal the importance and perfection of the pilgrimage itself. Even traditions recorded by Ibn Isḥāq that identify this pilgrimage as a "pilgrimage of farewell" explain that the pilgrimage was named thus not because Muhammad died soon thereafter, but because "he did not go on pilgrimage after that" (perhaps because he had gone to campaign in Palestine?): Ibn Hishām, *Kitāb sīrat Rasūl Allāh* (Wüstenfeld, *Das Leben Muhammed's*, 1: 970; Guillaume, *The Life of Muhammad*, 652). The tradition that Muhammad fell ill and died suddenly while preparing for another military expedition (according to Ibn Isḥāq) would appear to indicate that this pilgrimage was in no way intended by Muhammad as a "farewell" in preparation for his impending death, serving instead primarily to authorize the traditional rites of the *ḥajj*.

82. Only one of Ibn Isḥāq's al-Zuhrī traditions is ascribed to ʿUrwa—the scene of the toothpick and Muhammad's final exclamation. Although a handful of other sources attribute one or the other of these traditions to ʿUrwa through different channels, often independently of one another, the alleged transmissions do not display a consistent pattern that would identify the tradition with ʿUrwa.

83. < al-Zuhrī, without any intermediary: ʿAbd al-Razzāq, *Muṣannaf*, 5: 429–30; < Aḥmad b. al-Ḥajjāj < ʿAbdallāh b. al-Mubārak < Maʿmar and Yūnus < al-Zuhrī: Ibn Saʿd, *Ṭabaqāt* (Sachau, *Biographien Muhammeds*, 2.2: 29); < Saʿīd b. ʿUfayr < al-Layth < ʿUqayl < al-Zuhrī: al-Bukhārī, *al-Jāmiʿ*, Kitāb al-Maghāzī, bāb 83, ḥadīth 14 (Krehl and Juynboll, *Le Recueil*, 3: 187; Khan, *Ṣaḥīḥ al-Bukhārī*, 5: 517–18).

84. < al-Zuhrī, without intermediary: ʿAbd al-Razzāq, *Muṣannaf*, 5: 430–31; < Aḥmad b. al-Ḥajjāj < ʿAbdallāh b. al-Mubārak < Yūnus and Maʿmar < al-Zuhrī: Ibn Saʿd, *Ṭabaqāt* (Sachau, *Biographien Muhammeds*, 2.2: 26).

85. < Abū al-Yamān < Shuʿayn < al-Zuhrī: al-Bukhārī, *Jāmiʿ*, Kitāb al-Maghāzī, bāb 83, ḥadīth 9 (Krehl and Juynboll, *Le Recueil*, 3: 186; Khan, *Ṣaḥīḥ al-Bukhārī*, 5: 514); < Maʿmar < Muḥammad b. ʿAbdallāh < al-Zuhrī: Ibn Saʿd, *Ṭabaqāt* (Sachau, *Biographien Muhammeds*, 2.2: 27); < ʿUqayl < al-Zuhrī: Abbott, *Studies in Arabic Literary Papyri*, 2: 167 (doc. 6, verso, no. 16).

86. < Maʿmar < al-Zuhrī: ʿAbd al-Razzāq, *Muṣannaf*, 10: 359–60; < al-Wāqidī < Muḥammad b. ʿAbdallāh < al-Zuhrī: Ibn Saʿd, *Ṭabaqāt* (Sachau, ed., *Biographien Muhammeds*, 2.2: 32).

87. < Maʿmar < al-Zuhrī: ʿAbd al-Razzāq, *Muṣannaf*, 5: 428–29; < al-Wāqidī < Maʿmar < al-Zuhrī: Ibn Saʿd, *Ṭabaqāt* (Sachau, *Biographien Muhammeds*, 2.2: 44).

88. < Saʿīd b. ʿUfayr < al-Layth < ʿUqayl < al-Zuhrī: al-Bukhārī, *al-Jāmiʿ*, Kitāb al-Maghāzī, bāb 83, ḥadīth 14 (Krehl and Juynboll, *Le Recueil*, 3: 187; Khan, *Ṣaḥīḥ al-Bukhārī*, 5: 518); < al-Zuhrī, without intermediary: ʿAbd al-Razzāq, *Muṣannaf*, 5: 431–32; < Yaʿqūb b. Ibrāhīm b. Saʿd al-Zuhrī < Ibrāhīm b. Saʿd b. Ibrāhīm al-Zuhrī < Ṣāliḥ b. Kaysan < al-Zuhrī: Ibn Saʿd, *Ṭabaqāt* (Sachau, *Biographien Muhammeds*, 2.2: 34).

89. < al-Zuhrī, without intermediary: ʿAbd al-Razzāq, *Muṣannaf*, 5: 432–33; < Aḥmad b. al-Ḥajjāj < ʿAbdallāh b. al-Mubārak < Yūnus and Maʿmar < al-Zuhrī; and < Muḥammad b. ʿUmar al-Aslami < Muḥammad b. ʿAbdallāh < al-Zuhrī; and < al-Wāqidī < Muḥammad b. ʿAbdallāh < al-Zuhrī: Ibn Saʿd, *Ṭabaqāt* (Sachau, *Biographien Muhammeds*, 2.2: 18, 20–21); < Saʿīd b. ʿUfayr < al-Layth < ʿUqayl < al-Zuhrī: al-Bukhārī, *al-Jāmiʿ*, Kitāb al-Maghāzī, bāb 83, ḥadīth 14 (Krehl and Juynboll, *Le Recueil*, 3: 187–88; Khan, *Ṣaḥīḥ al-Bukhārī*, 5: 518). Al-Bukhārī, however, notes only Muhammad's selection of Abū Bakr and ʿĀʾisha's resistance, without any mention of ʿUmar or a number of other elements common to the other accounts.

90. < al-Zuhrī, without intermediary: ʿAbd al-Razzāq, *Muṣannaf*, 5: 433; < Saʿīd b. ʿUfayr < al-Layth < ʿUqayl < al-Zuhrī: al-Bukhārī, *al-Jāmiʿ*, Kitāb al-Maghāzī, bāb 83, ḥadīth 16 (Krehl and Juynboll, *Le Recueil*, 3: 188; Khan, *Ṣaḥīḥ al-Bukhārī*, 5: 520); < Aḥmad b. al-Ḥajjāj < ʿAbdallāh b. al-Mubārak < Yūnus and Maʿmar < al-Zuhrī; also < Yaʿqūb b. Ibrāhīm b. Saʿd al-Zuhrī < Ibrāhīm b. Saʿd b. Ibrāhīm al-Zuhrī < Ṣāliḥ b. Kaysan < al-Zuhrī; and < Saʿīd b. Manṣūr < Sufyān b. ʿUyayna < al-Zuhrī: Ibn Saʿd, *Ṭabaqāt* (Sachau, *Biographien Muhammeds*, 2.2: 17–19); al-Balādhurī, *Ansāb*, 1: 561.

91. < al-Zuhrī, without intermediary: ʿAbd al-Razzāq, *Muṣannaf*, 5: 435–36; < Yaʿqūb b. Ibrāhīm b. Saʿd al-Zuhrī < Ibrāhīm b. Saʿd b. Ibrāhīm al-Zuhrī < Ṣāliḥ b. Kaysan < al-Zuhrī: Ibn Saʿd, *Ṭabaqāt* (Sachau, *Biographien Muhammeds*, 2.2: 36); < Isḥāq < Shuʿayb b. Abī Ḥamza < al-Zuhrī: al-Bukhārī, *al-Jāmiʿ*, Kitāb al-Maghāzī, bāb 83, ḥadīth 15 (Krehl and Juynboll, *Le Recueil*, 3: 188; Khan, *Ṣaḥīḥ al-Bukhārī*, 5: 518–19); < Aḥmad b. ʿAbd al-Raḥmān b. Wahb < ʿAbdallāh b. Wahb < Yūnus < al-Zuhrī: al-Ṭabarī, *Taʾrīkh* (de Goeje et al., *Annales*, I: 1807–8).

92. < al-Wāqidī < Jaʿfar b. Muḥammad b. Khālid b. al-Zubayr < Muḥammad b. ʿAbd al-Raḥman b. Nawfal < al-Zuhrī: Ibn Saʿd, *Ṭabaqāt* (Sachau, *Biographien Muhammeds*, 2.2:

30); < al-Zuhrī, without intermediary: ʿAbd al-Razzāq, *Muṣannaf,* 5: 436; < Maʿmar < Muḥammad b. ʿAbd Allāh < al-Zuhrī: Ibn Saʿd, *Ṭabaqāt* (Sachau, *Biographien Muhammeds,* 2.2: 27); < ʿUqayl < al-Zuhrī: Abbott, *Studies in Arabic Literary Papyri,* 2: 167 (doc. 6, verso, no. 16).

93. < Maʿmar < al-Zuhrī: ʿAbd al-Razzāq, *Muṣannaf,* 5: 436–37; cf. ibid., 3: 596; < Aḥmad b. al-Ḥajjāj < ʿAbdallāh b. al-Mubārak < Yūnus and Maʿmar < al-Zuhrī; and < Abū Bakr b. ʿAbdallāh b. Abī Uways < Sulayman b. Bilāl < Muḥammad b. ʿAbdallāh b. Abī ʿUtayq al-Taymi < al-Zuhrī: Ibn Saʿd, *Ṭabaqāt* (Sachau, *Biographien Muhammeds,* 2.2: 54–56); < Yaḥyā b. Bukayr < al-Layth < ʿUqayl < al-Zuhrī: al-Bukhārī, *al-Jāmiʿ*, Kitāb al-Maghāzī, bāb 83, ḥadīth 20 (Krehl and Juynboll, *Le Recueil,* 3: 190; Khan, *Ṣaḥīḥ al-Bukhārī,* 5: 523); also < Bishru b. Muḥammad < ʿAbdallāh < Yūnus and Maʿmar < al-Zuhrī: al-Bukhārī, *al-Jāmiʿ*, Kitāb al-Janāʾiz, bāb 3, ḥadīth 1 (Krehl and Juynboll, *Le Recueil,* 1: 314; Khan, *Ṣaḥīḥ al-Bukhārī,* 2: 188–89).

94. < ʿAbd al-ʿAzīz b. Abān b. ʿUthmān < Maʿmar < al-Zuhrī: Ibn Abī Shayba, *Muṣannaf,* 14: 558–59; < Yaʿqūb b. Ibrāhīm b. Saʿd al-Zuhrī < Ibrāhīm b. Saʿd b. Ibrāhīm al-Zuhrī < Ṣāliḥ b. Kaysan < al-Zuhrī: Ibn Saʿd, *Ṭabaqāt* (Sachau, *Biographien Muhammeds,* 2.2: 53); < al-Zuhrī, without intermediary: ʿAbd al-Razzāq, *Muṣannaf,* 5: 433.

95. < Maʿmar < al-Zuhrī: ʿAbd al-Razzāq, *Muṣannaf,* 5: 437–38; < Aḥmad b. al-Ḥajjāj < ʿAbdallāh b. al-Mubārak < Yūnus and Maʿmar < al-Zuhrī: Ibn Saʿd, *Ṭabaqāt* (Sachau, *Biographien Muhammeds,* 2.2: 56); < Ibn Saʿd < Wāqidī < Muḥammad b. ʿAbdallāh < al-Zuhrī: al-Balādhurī, *Ansāb,* 1: 568..

96. All three ascribe the tradition to ʿIkrimah: ʿAbd al-Razzāq, *Muṣannaf,* 5: 433–35; Ibn Saʿd, *Ṭabaqāt* (Sachau, *Biographien Muhammeds,* 2.2: 53–54); al-Balādhurī, *Ansāb,* 1: 567.

97. Madelung, *The Succession to Muḥammad,* 256–60.

98. Ibn Hishām, *Kitāb sīrat Rasūl Allāh* (Wüstenfeld, *Das Leben Muhammed's,* 1: 1019). See also Ibn Saʿd, *Ṭabaqāt* (Sachau, *Biographien Muhammeds,* 2.2: 63); Ibn Abī Shayba, *Muṣannaf,* 14: 558; al-Balādhurī, *Ansāb,* 1: 571.

99. This was recently argued by Szilágyi, "The Incorruptible and Fragrant Corpse."

100. *Istoria de Mahomet* (Wolf, "The Earliest Latin Lives," 97–99); *Legend of Sergius Baḥīrā (East-Syrian)* 21 (Roggema, *The Legend of Sergius Baḥīrā,* 302–3); see also the same story in the *Legend of Sergius Baḥīrā (West-Syrian)* 9 (ibid., 332–35).

101. < Maʿmar < al-Zuhrī: ʿAbd al-Razzāq, *Muṣannaf,* 5: 438–39. Al-Bukhārī cites this tradition from ʿAbd al-Razzāq, but with some slight differences: al-Bukhārī, *al-Jāmiʿ*, Kitāb al-Maghāzī, bāb 83, ḥadīth 5 (Krehl and Juynboll, *Le Recueil,* 3: 185; Khan, *Ṣaḥīḥ al-Bukhārī,* 5: 512–13); < al-Wāqidī < Usāma b. Zayd al-Laythi and Maʿmar < al-Zuhrī: Ibn Saʿd, *Ṭabaqāt* (Sachau, *Biographien Muhammeds,* 2.2: 37).

102. *Legend of Sergius Baḥīrā (East-Syrian)* 21 (Roggema, *The Legend of Sergius Baḥīrā,* 302–3).

103. Ibn Saʿd, *Ṭabaqāt* (Sachau, *Biographien Muhammeds,* 2.2: 61–81); Ibn Abī Shayba, *Muṣannaf,* 14: 553–62; al-Balādhurī, *Ansāb,* 1: 569–79. The relevant traditions in ʿAbd al-Razzāq's *Muṣannaf* are scattered throughout his *Kitāb al-janāʾiz*: ʿAbd al-Razzāq, *Muṣannaf,* 3: 385–600.

104. Ibn Hishām, *Kitāb sīrat Rasūl Allāh* (Wüstenfeld, *Das Leben Muhammed's*, 1: 1019; Guillaume, *The Life of Muhammad*, 688).

105. Ibn Sa'd, *Ṭabaqāt* (Sachau, *Biographien Muhammeds*, 2.2: 65); 'Abd al-Razzāq, *Muṣannaf*, 3: 420–22; al-Balādhurī, *Ansāb*, 1: 572.

106. Abbott, *Studies in Arabic Literary Papyri*, 2: 167–68, 171–72 (doc. 6, verso, no. 16). Abbott notes, however, that this particular tradition "has no identical parallel."

107. See Halevi, *Muhammad's Grave*, 84–92. The topic of Muhammad's grave clothes features rather prominently in a number of early collections: see the various references in ibid., 281 n. 5.

108. 'Abd al-Razzāq, *Muṣannaf*, 3: 403; al-Balādhurī, *Ansāb*, 1: 571; Ibn Sa'd, *Ṭabaqāt* (Sachau, *Biographien Muhammeds*, 2.2: 63). Ibn Isḥāq attributes this information to other authorities.

109. 'Abd al-Razzāq, *Muṣannaf*, 3: 475–76; al-Balādhurī, *Ansāb*, 1: 570; Ibn Sa'd, *Ṭabaqāt* (Sachau, *Biographien Muhammeds*, 2.2: 61); Ibn Abī Shayba, *Muṣannaf*, 14: 556. Ibn Isḥāq again attributes this information to other authorities.

110. Ibn Sa'd, however, ascribes a rather different tradition concerning a brick monument to al-Zuhrī through Ibn Jurayj: Ibn Sa'd, *Ṭabaqāt* (Sachau, *Biographien Muhammeds*, 2.2: 74).

111. 'Abd al-Razzāq, *Muṣannaf*, 3: 516–17; al-Balādhurī, *Ansāb*, 1: 573; Ibn Abī Shayba, *Muṣannaf*, 14: 553–54.

112. 'Abd al-Razzāq, *Muṣannaf*, 3: 520; Ibn Hishām, *Kitāb sīrat Rasūl Allāh* (Wüstenfeld, *Das Leben Muhammed's*, 1: 1020).

113. Halevi, *Muhammad's Grave*, 3, 10; see also 45–55, 183.

114. Madelung, *The Succession to Muḥammad*, 23–37, 356–60; Halevi, *Muhammad's Grave*, 45–50.

115. Juynboll, "Early Islamic Society," 187–88.

116. E.g., J. Jones, "The Chronology of the Maghazi"; and Watt, *Muhammad at Mecca*; Watt, *Muhammad at Medina*; Watt, "The Reliability of Ibn Ishaq's Sources." See also Donner, *Narratives of Islamic Origins*, 16–20. In his most recent work, however, Donner advocates a somewhat similar position, advancing the general reliability of the *sīra* and conquest narratives. According to Donner, "we can indeed draw from them a basic skeleton of the course of historical events": Donner, *Muhammad and the Believers*, 51–52, 91. Despite the many considerable merits of this groundbreaking new study, its account of the beginnings of Islam occasionally relates material from the *sīra* traditions uncritically (e.g., 92–96).

117. The Islamic historical tradition, which developed shortly after the *sīra* traditions and depends on them, also uniformly reports the death of Muhammad prior to the narration of the Near Eastern conquests. Nevertheless, not only are these accounts of Muhammad's death derivative of the *sīra* traditions, but their descriptions of the Near Eastern conquests are themselves also notoriously problematic and inaccurate: see, e.g., Conrad, "The Conquest of Arwad"; see also Pentz, *The Invisible Conquest* and Magness, *The Archaeology of the Early Islamic Settlement*, both of which find in the archaeological record a very different set of circumstances than those described by the Islamic historians.

118. Rubin has recently argued to the contrary that the *sīra* is not merely an exegetical expansion of the Qurʾān, but is in fact earlier than the Qurʾān. See Rubin, *The Eye of the Beholder*, 226–33; also Rubin, "The Life of Muhammad." Nevertheless, rather than suggesting the *sīra*'s priority to the Qurʾān, Rubin's findings would seem to indicate instead the parallel and independent development of the Qurʾānic traditions alongside of historical traditions about the life of Muhammad and the beginnings of Islam. Rubin's research points toward the revision of certain early biographical traditions to reflect the contents of the Qurʾān once it had become established as the Islamic sacred scripture.

119. Most fundamental is his article Lammens, "Qoran et tradition," now translated into English as Lammens, "The Koran and Tradition." See also Lammens, *Fatima*, and the English translation, Lammens, "Fatima."

120. Peters, "The Quest of the Historical Muhammad," 302–3.

121. Wansbrough, *The Sectarian Milieu*; Rubin, *The Eye of the Beholder.*

122. Crone, *Slaves on Horses*, 4.

123. According to Patricia Crone, "That the bulk of the *Sīra* and lives of the Rashidun consists of second-century ḥadīths has not been disputed by any historian, and this point may be taken as conceded": ibid., 14–15. As evidence of this consensus, see Raven, "Sīra." Nevertheless, note also the studies by Motzki, Görke, and Schoeler mentioned above, which I do not find persuasive.

124. Conrad, "Theophanes and the Arabic Historical Tradition," 16. See also J. Jones, "The *Maghāzī* Literature," 349–50.

125. Schoeler, *Charakter und Authentie*, 15, 23, 32, 40, 131–34. See also Donner, *Narratives of Islamic Origins*, 242–43.

126. Donner, *Narratives of Islamic Origins*, 231; also 75–85, 94–97, 114–15, 276, 282. See also Donner, *Muhammad and the Believers*, 51–52, where he also notes the general artificiality and confusion of chronology in the Islamic narratives of origins.

127. Conrad, "Theophanes and the Arabic Historical Tradition," 17.

128. Donner, *Narratives of Islamic Origins*, 231; also 75–85, 94–97, 114–15, 276, 282.

129. Ibid., 231.

130. Ibid., 237. See also Noth and Conrad, *The Early Arabic Historical Tradition*, 40–42.

131. Album and Goodwin, *Sylloge of Islamic Coins*, 56–60; Donner, "From Believers to Muslims," 48. See also Popp, "Die frühe Islamgeschichte," 38–45; and now also Popp, "The Early History of Islam," 36–43.

132. Mordtmann, "Zur Pehlevi-Münzkunde," esp. 97; Wellhausen, "Prolegomena zur ältesten Geschichte des Islams," 6; cf. Crone and Cook, *Hagarism*, 157 n. 39; Donner, *Narratives of Islamic Origins*, 244–45; Crone, "What Do We Actually Know about Mohammad?" For more concerning Sayf b. ʿUmar, see al-Ṭabarī, *The History of al-Ṭabarī: Volume X*, xiv–xix. Although modern Western scholarship has frequently followed the medieval Islamic tradition in dismissing Sayf as untrustworthy, recently more considered examination has shown that this prejudice is no longer warranted, and Sayf's traditions are on the whole no more problematic than those transmitted by Ibn Isḥāq or al-Wāqidī. See esp. Landau-Tasseron, "Sayf ibn ʿUmar."

133. Donner, *Narratives of Islamic Origins*, 231.

134. Ibid., 168, 232, 242–43. See also Schoeler, *Charakter und Authentie*, 15, 23, 32, 40, 131–34.

135. Donner, *Narratives of Islamic Origins*, 279.

136. See also Conrad, "Theophanes and the Arabic Historical Tradition," 16–17; and J. Jones, "The *Maghāzī* Literature," 349–50.

137. Lammens, "L'Âge de Mahomet," and the English translation: Lammens, "The Age of Muhammad"; see also Wansbrough, *Quranic Studies*, 38–43; Wansbrough, *The Sectarian Milieu*, 32–36; M. Cook, *Muhammad*, 64–65.

138. Lammens, "L'Âge de Mahomet," 212–15, and the English translation: Lammens, "The Age of Muhammad," 189–91. See also Sellheim, "Prophet, Chalif und Geschichte," 70–71, 75–78. Conrad discusses the topic of numerical topoi and symbolism generally in Conrad, "Seven and the *Tasbīʿ*," focusing on their impact on biographical literature in pp. 62–73.

139. Lammens, "L'Âge de Mahomet," 215; Lammens, "The Age of Muhammad," 190–91; Rubin, *The Eye of the Beholder*, 196–99.

140. Conrad, "Abraha and Muḥammad," esp. 230–37.

141. Rubin, *The Eye of the Beholder*, 189–214, esp. 196–99. Of course, this overlooks Jesus as an obviously intervening prophet, but this would by no means impede such an interpretation by the authors and readers of Muhammad's biographies.

142. Conrad, "Abraha and Muḥammad," 239.

143. Rubin, *The Eye of the Beholder*, 203–9.

144. See the discussion in ibid., 190–94.

145. Lammens, "L'Âge de Mahomet," 217; Lammens, "The Age of Muhammad," 192.

146. Lammens, "L'Âge de Mahomet," 215; Lammens, "The Age of Muhammad," 191. The sources cited by Lammens are al-Balādhurī, al-Tirmidhī, and Ibn ʿAbd al-Barr. Hoyland in Palmer, *The Seventh Century*, 51, n. 164 invokes these reports of thirteen years in Medina in an effort to reconcile the chronology of the Christian chronicles with the Islamic historical tradition.

147. Concerning the Islamic reports, see Lammens, "L'Âge de Mahomet," 217; Lammens, "The Age of Muhammad," 192; Crone and Cook, *Hagarism*, 157 n. 39.

148. See Crone and Cook, *Hagarism*, 7 and esp. 157 n. 39; Donner, *Narratives of Islamic Origins*, 168, 232, 242–43.

149. For a thoroughgoing analysis of the rivalry between these two cities, see Arazi, "Matériaux pour l'étude du conflit."

150. Rubin, *The Eye of the Beholder*, 203–9.

151. Lammens, "L'Âge de Mahomet," 215; Lammens, "The Age of Muhammad," 190.

152. In his discussion of the variant chronologies regarding Mecca and Medina (Rubin, *The Eye of the Beholder*, 203–9), Rubin does not discuss the traditions assigning thirteen years to Medina, nor, for that matter, does his study appear to make any reference at all to Lammens's work.

153. Although modern historians have long viewed the accounts of these battles as describing concrete historical realities of military engagements from the lifetime of Muhammad, David Powers is right to note that although such episodes have been "widely

treated as history," as represented in the *sīra* collections they are "better understood as salvation history." See Powers, *Muḥammad Is Not the Father*, 10.

154. Regarding the date and location, see Kaegi, *Byzantium and the Early Islamic Conquests*, 71–72. See also the helpful maps at pp. 48–49, as well as Knauf, "Aspects of Historical Topography."

155. The account can be found in Ibn Hishām, *Kitāb sīrat Rasūl Allāh* (Wüstenfeld, *Das Leben Muhammed's*, 1: 791–802); and al-Ṭabarī, *Ta'rīkh* (de Goeje et al., *Annales*, I: 1610–18). Cf. al-Wāqidī, *Kitāb al-maghāzī*, 2: 755–69.

156. Donner, *The Early Islamic Conquests*, 101–11.

157. Donner, *Muhammad and the Believers*, 50, 96–97, 143–44.

158. Hoyland, *Seeing Islam*, 555; Watt, *Muhammad at Medina*, 105–17.

159. For example, the well-organized and efficient Roman postal service would have required approximately three weeks for such a return journey; one would imagine that it might take even longer in these circumstances. See Ramsay, "The Speed of the Roman Imperial Post"; Eliot, "New Evidence for the Speed of the Roman Imperial Post."

160. Kaegi, *Byzantium and the Early Islamic Conquests*, 72–73.

161. Ibid., 72.

162. Ibid., 73.

163. Theophanes, *Chronicle* (de Boor, *Theophanis chronographia*, 1: 335–36).

164. Conrad, "Theophanes and the Arabic Historical Tradition," 23–26.

165. Powers has alternatively proposed that Mu'ta was merely an early skirmish during the Islamic assault on Palestine that took place after Muhammad's death, as reported by Theophanes. Its chronology and significance were later revised so that it fell within Muhammad's lifetime in order to provide an occasion for Zayd, Muhammad's adopted son, to die before Muhammad's own death. This was necessary, Powers explains, to validate Muhammad's status as the final prophet. If Zayd were still alive when Muhammad expired, he would have been expected to inherit the "prophetic mantle." While I propose a rather different reconstruction of the battle of Mu'ta on the basis of these divergent accounts, I strongly concur with Powers's observation that the chronology of Muhammad's biography was first being established by the scholars of Medina only around the beginning of the second century and was being manipulated to serve ideological purposes. See Powers, *Muḥammad Is Not the Father*, 72–93. I thank Professor Powers for sharing his work with me in advance of its publication in 2009.

166. Alfred-Louis de Prémare comes to largely similar conclusions regarding Mu'ta in de Prémare, *Les fondations de l'islam*, 138–40. Beck, "Die Sura *ar-Rūm*," 339 and Gallez, *Le messie et son prophète*, 2: 459–61 suggest that *sūra* 30 of the Qur'ān ("The Byzantines") refers to the battle of Mu'ta: their alternative vocalization of verses 2–5 reflects an established Islamic reading of these verses.

167. Regarding the date, see Kaegi, *Byzantium and the Early Islamic Conquests*, 82.

168. Watt, *Muhammad at Medina*, 105. For Ibn Isḥāq's account of these events, see Ibn Hishām, *Kitāb sīrat Rasūl Allāh* (Wüstenfeld, *Das Leben Muhammed's*, 1: 893–913); and al-Ṭabarī, *Ta'rīkh* (de Goeje et al., *Annales*, I: 1692–1705). On the number of troops, see al-Wāqidī, *Kitāb al-maghāzī*, 3: 1002, 1041; and al-Balādhurī, *Ansāb*, 1: 368.

169. Al-Wāqidī, *Kitāb al-maghāzī*, 3: 989–92; Andræ, *Mohammed*, 168–69.

170. Ibn Hishām, *Kitāb sīrat Rasūl Allāh* (Wüstenfeld, *Das Leben Muhammed's*, 1: 902); and al-Ṭabarī, *Ta'rīkh* (de Goeje et al., *Annales*, I: 1702).

171. Al-Wāqidī, however, explains that once Muhammad realized that there was in fact no gathering military threat from the Byzantine army in southern Palestine, he no longer had any interest in the area and returned home to Medina: al-Wāqidī, *Kitāb al-maghāzī*, 3: 1019. While Donner, *The Early Islamic Conquests*, 107 and Kaegi, *Byzantium and the Early Islamic Conquests*, 80 both take this report more or less at face value, Watt, *Muhammad at Medina*, 105 and Andræ, *Mohammed*, 168 are right to be considerably more skeptical of this rather late report from al-Wāqidī that seems designed to fill in the explanation that is missing from Ibn Isḥāq's report and other early accounts.

172. Buhl [and Welch], "Muḥammad," 374.

173. Ibn Hishām, *Kitāb sīrat Rasūl Allāh* (Wüstenfeld, *Das Leben Muhammed's*, 1: 970, 999); al-Ṭabarī, *Ta'rīkh* (de Goeje et al., *Annales*, I: 1794; al-Ṭabarī, *The History of al-Ṭabarī: Volume IX*, 163, where the locations are clarified in notes 1131 and 1132). See also Schick, *The Christian Communities of Palestine*, 257–58, 280–81.

174. Al-Wāqidī, *Kitāb al-maghāzī*, 3: 1117–27; cf. Wellhausen, *Muhammed in Medina*, 433–37.

175. Ibn Ḥabīb, *Kitāb al-muḥabbar*, 125; Abū Dā'ūd, *Sunan Abī Dāwūd*, 3: 38 (no. 2616); Ibn Ḥanbal, *Musnad*, 5: 205, 209; Ibn Sa'd, *Ṭabaqāt* (Sachau, *Biographien Muhammeds*, 4: 66).

176. De Prémare, *Les fondations de l'islam*, 140–45.

177. Ibn Hishām, *Kitāb sīrat Rasūl Allāh* (Wüstenfeld, *Das Leben Muhammed's*, 1: 970, 999); cf. al-Ṭabarī, *Ta'rīkh* (de Goeje et al., *Annales*, I: 1794–95). Although al-Ṭabarī only reports this event in the immediate context of Muhammad's death, and he gives his second report on the basis of other authorities, it is more likely that he has "corrected" Ibn Isḥāq than it is that Ibn Hishām has introduced such a problematic doublet to his source.

178. Ibn Hishām, *Kitāb sīrat Rasūl Allāh* (Wüstenfeld, *Das Leben Muhammed's*, 1: 1006–7); cf. al-Ṭabarī, *Ta'rīkh* (de Goeje et al., *Annales*, I: 1796–97).

179. Ibn Sa'd, *Ṭabaqāt* (Sachau, *Biographien Muhammeds*, 1.2: 87).

180. It does not seem possible, however, to understand the non-Islamic reports of Muhammad's leadership during the Palestinian campaign as some sort of collective misinterpretation of these traditions. The *sīra* traditions reporting Muhammad's involvement are much too late to exert such an influence on most of the reports examined above.

181. E.g., Noth and Conrad, *The Early Arabic Historical Tradition*, 40–45; Conrad, "Theophanes and the Arabic Historical Tradition"; Conrad, "The Conquest of Arwad"; Donner, *Early Islamic Conquests*, 116, 124–28, 142–46; Donner, *Narratives of Islamic Origins*, 94–97, 230–48; Bashear, "Apocalyptic," 199.

182. Busse, "'Omar b. al-Ḥaṭṭāb," esp. 111–16; Busse, "'Omar's Image as the Conqueror," esp. 160–64.

183. Donner, *Muhammad and the Believers*, 123.

184. See, e.g., Rubin, *The Eye of the Beholder*. The same tendency is also quite apparent in the Gospel according to Matthew's portrayal of Jesus: see, e.g., Allison, *The New*

Moses. Recently Ze'ev Maghen has explored parallels between the lives of David and Muhammad, particularly with regard to the traditions about Bathsheba and Zaynab: see Maghen, "Intertwined Triangles." I thank David Powers for this reference. See now also Maghen, "Davidic Motifs."

185. See, e.g., Mittwoch, "Muhammeds Geburts- und Todestag"; Rubin, *The Eye of the Beholder*, 107–10, 191–96.

186. See esp. Deut. 31–34.

187. Ibn Hishām, *Kitāb sīrat Rasūl Allāh* (Wüstenfeld, *Das Leben Muhammed's*, 1: 904); al-Ṭabarī, *Ta'rīkh* (de Goeje et al., *Annales*, I: 1703–4).

188. Donner, *Narratives of Islamic Origins*, 283–88.

CHAPTER 3

1. Perhaps the best effort to reconstruct the beginnings of "Islam" primarily on the basis of the Qur'ān alone is Donner, *Muhammad and the Believers*, esp. 56–89, a work that, unfortunately, appeared only after the present study had been completed.

2. Donner, *Narratives of Islamic Origins*, 75–85, esp. 80.

3. Peters, "The Quest of the Historical Muhammad."

4. Wansbrough and Rippin, *Quranic Studies*, xvii; Halevi, *Muhammad's Grave*, 207.

5. M. Cook, *Muhammad*, 70.

6. Nöldeke observes the frequency of this theme, especially in the early "Meccan" *sūras*, but does not focus on it as a particularly central element of Muhammad's preaching, nor does he draw attention to the judgment's apparent immediacy: Nöldeke and Schwally, *Geschichte des Qorāns*, e.g., 1: 98–99. See also Nöldeke, *Das Leben Muhammed's*, 36. Sprenger saw impending doom as a core element of Muhammad's early preaching, which he believed Muhammad had employed to frighten the Meccans into following him, only to abandon this strategy later for a different approach: Sprenger, *Das Leben und die Lehre*, 1: 504, 529–36. On the prominence of the judgment of the Hour within the Qur'ān, see Bell and Watt, *Bell's Introduction to the Qur'ān*, 158; more recently, see Donner, *Muhammad and the Believers*, esp. 58–59.

7. Donner, *Muhammad and the Believers*, 88–89; see also xii.

8. Bell, *The Origin of Islam*, 71–72, 80, 83.

9. Many of the same themes of this chapter are addressed much more briefly in Shoemaker, "Muḥammad and the Qur'ān."

10. Hurgronje, "Der Mahdi," 26. Reprinted in Hurgronje, *Verspreide geschriften*, 1: 145–81.

11. Hurgronje, "Une nouvelle biographie de Mohammed." Reprinted in Hurgronje, *Verspreide geschriften*, 1: 319–62. Hurgronje responds here to Grimme, *Mohammed*.

12. Hurgronje, "Une nouvelle biographie de Mohammed," 149–51.

13. Ibid., 161–62.

14. Buhl, *Das Leben Muhammeds*, 126–27. Originally published in 1903 as Buhl, *Muhammeds liv*, and recently republished in 1998, in which see 96–97. See also the English summary of Buhl's study in Buhl, "Muḥammad."

15. Buhl, *Das Leben Muhammeds*, esp. 132–33, 144–45, 157; Buhl, *Muhammeds liv* (1998), 98, 104–5, 113. Here Buhl is especially influenced by Hurgronje, "De Islam," 263; reprinted in Hurgronje, *Verspreide geschriften*, 1: 206.

16. Buhl, *Das Leben Muhammeds*, 196–97; Buhl, *Muhammeds liv* (1998), 138–39.

17. Casanova, *Mohammed*. The study was published in three parts, the last two of which consist of extensive notes to the first thirty pages of the initial volume.

18. Particularly surprising, especially in light of his previous remarks on the topic, are the undeservedly dismissive comments in Hurgronje, *Mohammedanism*, 15–18. See also, e.g., Gottheil, "The Beginnings of Islam"; Z. [*sic*], "Review of Paul Casanova, *Mohammed*"; M. B. [*sic*], "Review of Paul Casanova, *Mohammed*"; McNeile, "Review of Paul Casanova, *Mohammed*"; Bergsträsser and Pretzl, *Geschichte des Qorāns III*, 6–8; Bell, *Introduction to the Qurʾān*, 46–47; Bell and Watt, *Bell's Introduction to the Qurʾān*, 53–54.

19. Casanova, *Mohammed*, 103–42. See further discussion below regarding this hypothesis of the Qurʾānic text's origin.

20. Sprenger, *Das Leben und die Lehre*, 504, 532–36; Casanova, *Mohammed*, 4.

21. These writings were published anonymously only after Reimarus's death by G. E. Lessing as *Fragmente eines Ungenannten* between 1774–78. The most important of these, the seventh fragment, was published in 1778 as *Von dem Zwecke Jesu und seiner Jünger*.

22. Baird, *History of New Testament Research*, 1: 170–77. Albert Schweitzer writes of the final and most important of these fragments that "to say that the fragment on 'The Aims of Jesus and His Disciples' is a magnificent piece of work is barely to do it justice. This essay is not only one of the greatest events in the history of criticism, it is also a masterpiece of general literature." Schweitzer, *The Quest of the Historical Jesus*, 15.

23. Regarding the importance of the Tübingen school, which has been called "*the most important theological event in the whole history of theology from the Reformation to the present day*" (Harris, *The Tübingen School*, v, emphasis in the original), see, in addition to Harris's monograph, Baird, *History of New Testament Research*, 1: 244–330; and Kümmel, *The New Testament*, 120–205.

24. This position is of course most famously represented in Schweitzer, *Von Reimarus zu Wrede*; English trans., Schweitzer, *The Quest of the Historical Jesus*. Schweitzer's paradigm-shifting book was itself largely inspired by the earlier work of Weiss, *Die Predigt Jesu vom Reiche Gottes*. Yet the basic notion that eschatology was the central component of Jesus' teaching was, as noted above, proposed much earlier by Reimarus (1694–1768): it was some time before New Testament scholarship was ready to accept Reimarus's radical insight. See the discussion in Schweitzer, *The Quest of the Historical Jesus*, 13–26. On the decisive impact of Schweitzer's book, see, e.g., Sanders, *Jesus and Judaism*, 23–27; and Ehrman, *Jesus*, 125–28.

25. See Fähndrich, "Invariable Factors"; and Irwin, "Oriental Discourses," esp. 91–101, 104–7. See also Lüling, "Preconditions," 73–79. Although this latter article is quite polemical and often engages in *ad hominem* attacks (which may or may not be justified in some instances), Lüling's remarks on the early marriage of Qurʾānic studies with Semitic philology (or "Near Eastern studies") rather than religious studies are helpful. Stefan Heidemann traces back even further the formation of Islamic studies in Germany within study of the

Hebrew Bible and its eventual emergence as a primarily philological endeavor: Heidemann, "Zwischen Theologie und Philologie."

26. Fück, *Die arabischen Studien in Europa*, 167; Irwin, "Oriental Discourses," 93, 104. Heidemann focuses especially on Ewald's mentor, Johann Gottfried Eichhorn, in tracing the lineage from Hebrew Bible to philology; regarding Ewald in particular, see esp. Heidemann, "Zwischen Theologie und Philologie," 166–67. Regarding Ewald's determining influence on the emergence of "Oriental studies" in nineteenth-century Germany, see Preissler, "Die Anfänge," passim.

27. On Ewald's fierce opposition to the new approaches that had emerged within early Christian studies, as well as his nature as a mentor, see Davies, *Heinrich Ewald*, 23, 36–40, 63–64, 68–71; Fück, *Die arabischen Studien in Europa*, 167, 217; Harris, *The Tübingen School*, 43–48; Baird, *History of New Testament Research*, 1: 287–93; Hurgronje, "Theodor Nöldeke," 245; Preissler, "Die Anfänge," 258. For remarks concerning Ewald's methodological conservatism and resistance to the emergent historical-critical approaches within early Christian studies from perhaps the two greatest innovators of the field, see Baur, *Die tübinger Schule*, 122–71; and Schweitzer, *The Quest of the Historical Jesus*, 116 (esp. n. 4), 135.

28. Harris, *The Tübingen School*, 43.

29. Ibid., 45.

30. Angelika Neuwirth recently has described Nöldeke's work rather tellingly as "the rock of our church": Higgins, "The Lost Archive." See also, e.g., Rippin, "Western Scholarship and the Qurʾān," 240: Nöldeke's *Geschichte des Qorāns* "is the work that set the tone, approach, and agenda for most of the European and American scholarship that has been produced since." See also Neuwirth, *Studien zur Komposition*, esp. 7*, 27*.

31. Nöldeke and Schwally, *Geschichte des Qorāns*, 2: 1–5.

32. According to Nöldeke's own assessment of his *Doktorvater*, "Ewald war, als Lehrer unmethodisch, dictatorisch, verlangte gleich vom Anfänger sehr viel; aber er regte gewaltig an, imponirte [*sic*] durch seine ganze Persönlichkeit: und, wer sich Mühe gab, lernte viel bei ihm. Freilich wenn man selbstständig geworden war, dann ward es kaum möglich, auf gutem Fuss mit ihm zu bleiben, denn er sah die kleinste Abweichung von seinen Ansichten als einen Abfall von der Wahrheit an, und zörnte darüber mächtig." Davies, *Heinrich Ewald*, 37.

33. Fähndrich, "Invariable Factors," 148, 152–53. See also Johansen, "Politics and Scholarship," 75–83; Fück, *Die arabischen Studien in Europa*, 217–20.

34. D. Cook, *Studies in Muslim Apocalyptic*, 30. See also D. Cook, "Muslim Apocalyptic and *Jihād*," 66.

35. Donner, "From Believers to Muslims," esp. 10–13; Donner, *Narratives of Islamic Origins*, 30 n. 78, 46; Donner, *Muhammad and the Believers*, esp. 79–82, 97; Ayoub, *The Crisis of Muslim History*, 145–46. See Casanova, *Mohammed*, 12. Ayoub makes no mention of Casanova's study in connection with this hypothesis, while Donner's article signals Casanova's work only briefly in a footnote without engaging it. Donner's earlier monograph also does not refer to Casanova in this context, although he elsewhere notes Casanova's hypothesis that Muhammad believed the Last Judgment was imminent (Donner, *Narratives of Islamic Origins*, 75 n. 50). Here Donner explains that while Casanova finds an "apocalyptic

eschatology" in the Qur'ān, others have reached a "non-apocalyptic understanding of Qur'ānic eschatology." The precise meaning of "apocalyptic" in this context is unclear to me. Donner's more recent monograph (*Muhammad and the Believers*) does not address Casanova at all. Note also that while Donner has elsewhere argued against the idea that early Islam was a messianic movement, this conclusion by no means entails any rejection of the strong presence of an imminent eschatology, as he himself allows: Donner, "La question du messianisme"; also Donner, "The Sources of Islamic Conceptions of War," 43–50.

36. Blachère, *Introduction au Coran*, 22–25. See also Blachère, *Le problème de Mahomet*, 43–51.

37. Andræ, "Der Ursprung des Islams," esp. 213–47. See also the French translation of this study: Andræ, *Les origines de l'Islam*, 67–100.

38. Andræ, *Mohammed*, 53–63; quotation at 53 (originally published in 1932 as Andræ, *Mohammed, sein Leben und sein Glaube*).

39. Andræ, *Mohammed*, 53.

40. Bell, *The Origin of Islam*, 72.

41. Ibid., 71–72.

42. Ibid., 80, 83. While Bell does in fact refer to Hurgronje's article responding to Grimme, he does not address its view of Muhammad as primarily a herald of impending judgment; Casanova's work is not specifically cited.

43. Ibid., 102.

44. Ibid., 102–7.

45. Watt's most direct critique of his mentor's theories appears in Watt, "The Dating of the Qur'ān."

46. Bell's views are articulated in Bell, *Introduction to the Qur'ān*, 72–138, and again by Watt in Bell and Watt, *Bell's Introduction to the Qur'ān*, 101–47.

47. See, e.g., Böwering, "Chronology and the Qur'ān," 322–26. The system was outlined initially in Weil, *Historisch-kritische Einleitung in den Koran*, 54–81, and then more fully developed in Nöldeke and Schwally, *Geschichte des Qorāns*, 1:74–164.

48. Welch, "Al-Ḳur'ān," 416–18, esp. 417. Recently Nicolai Sinai has attempted a defense of Nöldeke's system of dating, but I do not find the argument persuasive. The article successfully argues that there are literary and conceptual similarities among the different groups of *sūra*s that Nöldeke has grouped according to four chronological strata, which is in fact often the case. Yet Sinai argues that certain "hybrid" *sūra*s exhibit the transition from one grouping to another and then proceeds to argue that the sequence proposed by Nöldeke (and, in essence, the Islamic tradition) presents "the most plausible evolutionary narrative," finally proposing to validate this conclusion with reference to the "outline" of Muhammad's life as presented in the *sīra*. This particular "evolutionary narrative" of the traditions is indeed plausible, but it is not especially more plausible than other alternative explanations (some of which are noted by Sinai), and the ultimate appeal to the chronology of the *sīra* to secure this understanding of the Qur'ān is particularly unpersuasive. There still is not sufficient evidence for the precise ordering that Nöldeke would assign to the individual *sūra*s, nor even for the alleged sequence of the four groups of *sūra*s. See Sinai, "The Qur'ān as Process," esp. 408–16.

49. Watt, *Muhammad at Mecca*, 62–65.

50. Ibid., 66.

51. See esp. ibid., 72–85; see also 1–25. Nevertheless, the historical framework of a "Meccan spice trade" underlying Watt's larger hypothesis is profoundly flawed, and the fallacies of the economic context that he imagines for Muhammad's mission of reform are well described in Crone, *Meccan Trade*. See also Crone's response to R. B. Serjeant's rather *ad hominem* attacks against her in Crone, "Serjeant and Meccan Trade." Note also that Crone has modified her position on Meccan trade slightly in a recent article, although without any need to soften her broader critique, which still stands: Crone, "Quraysh and the Roman Army."

52. Regarding Grimme, see, e.g., Wheatley, *The Places Where Men Pray*, 364 n. 187; see also Rodinson, *Mohammed*, 76. Early critics saw in Watt's monograph a "Marxist" version of Muhammad, and he himself suggests the influence of "an elementary knowledge of Marxism" on his reconstruction: Watt, *Islam and the Integration of Society*, 2.

53. Birkeland, *The Lord Guideth*, 5.

54. Paret, *Mohammed und der Koran*, 69–79 (originally published in 1957).

55. Ibid., 76–79.

56. Ibid., 96–98.

57. Bell, *The Origin of Islam*, esp. 71–72.

58. Birkeland, *The Lord Guideth*, 132.

59. Ehrman, *Jesus*, 127; see also Sanders, *Jesus and Judaism*, 154. Both of course echo Schweitzer, *The Quest of the Historical Jesus*, esp. 402–3. As Ehrman notes, a small minority of New Testament scholars have recently labored to recover a non-eschatological Jesus, yet Ehrman dispenses with such hypotheses swiftly and judiciously: Ehrman, *Jesus*, 132–34.

60. On the portrayal of Jesus in nineteenth-century Protestant liberalism, see, e.g., Baird, *History of New Testament Research*, 2: 85–136; Kümmel, *The New Testament*, 162–84. Regarding liberalism's strong resistance to the idea of Jesus as an eschatological prophet, see esp. the chapter "The Struggle against Eschatology" in Schweitzer, *The Quest of the Historical Jesus*, 242–69.

61. Peter van Sivers rightly identifies Watt's work as a "secular" version of the "sacred vulgate" of the Islamic tradition concerning the period of origins, noting as well its prevailing influence on modern Western scholarship on early Islam: van Sivers, "The Islamic Origins Debate Goes Public," 3.

62. Watt, *Muhammad: Prophet and Statesman*, 19–28; Watt, *Islam and the Integration of Society*, 5–14.

63. E.g., Bell and Watt, *Bell's Introduction to the Qur'ān*, 115–18.

64. Buhl, "Muḥammad," esp. 645–46; Buhl [and Welch], "Muḥammad," 363–64. In this respect especially Tilman Nagel's assessment of the second edition's article as "eine nur unwesentlich überarbeitete Version" of Buhl's earlier article is most peculiar: Nagel, *Mohammed*, 835.

65. Peters, *Muhammad and the Origins of Islam*, 152–56.

66. Ibid., 152–53. In an endnote addressing a later subject, Peters eventually notes that in fact there is not complete agreement among scholars regarding "the nuances of

the *sequence* of revelation, and hence of Muhammad's own spiritual evolution," and he identifies Hurgronje and Paret as important dissenters: p. 292, n. 39. It is unfortunate that this information is buried in a remote endnote while the views of Birkeland are positioned as authoritative.

67. Peters, *Jesus and Muhammad*, 111, 115.

68. Ibid., 123.

69. Rodinson, *Mohammed*, 81–98; but see also 120–23, where judgment is in fact identified as a theme of the early stages that was abandoned later on.

70. Nagel, *Mohammed*, e.g., 462–63, 844, 909–10.

71. Muranyi, "Die ersten Muslime"; Afzaal, "The Origin of Islam."

72. Armstrong, *Muhammad*, 91–107, esp. 91.

73. Ibid., 99. Armstrong suggests, however, that a belief in divine judgment (sometime in the distant future) gradually assumed a place in some of Muhammad's "revelations" and may in fact have been the topic that aroused resistance to his teaching at Mecca (pp. 106–7). Armstrong is quick to note, however, that Muhammad borrowed this idea from the Jews and Christians, and so presumably it is not to be estimated a part of his marvelous "spiritual genius" (p. 98).

74. Rahman, *Major Themes of the Qurʾān*, 37–64, 106–20.

75. Zeitlin, *The Historical Muhammad*. The views of Bell and Watt are summarized in chapters 7 and 8 respectively, where together they cover the period of Muhammad's activity in Mecca. To his credit, however, Zeitlin accepts the critique of Crone, *Meccan Trade*, although he attempts to salvage something of Watt's thesis in its wake. Clinton Bennett's *In Search of Muhammad* is likewise a summary of previous scholarship that is similarly accepting of Watt's conclusions: Bennett, *In Search of Muhammad*, 19, 128–32.

76. Ramadan, *In the Footsteps*, 202–3. The *ḥadīth* in question teaches that "if the hour of Judgment Day comes while one of you holds a sapling in his hand, let him hurry and plant it."

77. Ibid., 43–44.

78. Safi, *Memories of Muhammad*, e.g., 33, 97–101, 115, 123.

79. Afsaruddin, *The First Muslims*, 26.

80. Ibid., 3. See also Chase Robinson's extended and excellent critique of Afsaruddin's book in Robinson, "The Ideological Uses."

81. It is somewhat telling that a recent "companion" volume to the Qurʾān addresses under the heading "Content" seven different themes, none of which concerns eschatology: Rippin, *The Blackwell Companion to the Qurʾān*.

82. For a brief presentation of the criterion of embarrassment and the related criterion of discontinuity (i.e., discontinuity with the later tradition in this case), see Meier, *A Marginal Jew*, 1: 168–74. For a more popular presentation, see Ehrman, *Jesus*, 91–94. For a more thorough discussion of these criteria and their history within biblical studies, see Theissen and Winter, *The Quest for the Plausible Jesus*, esp. 1–171.

83. A recent article by Herbert Berg and Sarah Rollens draws some interesting comparisons between the study of the historical Muhammad and the historical Jesus: Berg and Rollens, "The Historical Muḥammad." Nevertheless, the article and its conclusions

are rather problematic, particularly as a result of the limited range of scholarship engaged on both ends. Although the more mainstream position of scholars such as Ehrman, Sanders, and others who follow in the tradition of Schweitzer's eschatological Jesus is briefly mentioned, the article primarily engages those scholars, such as Kloppenborg, Crossan, Borg, and the Jesus Seminar, who have sought to find a more theologically relevant, non-eschatological Jesus. While I would agree with much of the critique that they level against this minority position within historical Jesus studies, it certainly is not correct to present this position as characteristic of the field of study as a whole and to evaluate it primarily on this basis. Likewise, with respect to Muhammad, the article significantly engages only the approach of Görke and Schoeler, without addressing many other studies of the sort considered above. Thus, the basis for their rather sweeping conclusions is not sufficient.

84. Wansbrough, *Quranic Studies*, ix. Devin Stewart is at least partly justified in correcting some perhaps overly enthusiastic remarks by Robert Phenix and Cornelia Horn hailing Christoph Luxenberg's book as the "critical turn" that will finally usher in a "Higher Criticism" of the Qur'ān comparable to developments in biblical studies over the past two centuries. Nevertheless, Stewart's retort that such a "critical turn" was made during the middle of the nineteenth century by Nöldeke's study certainly will not persuade many trained in biblical studies that Qur'ānic studies has indeed achieved this critical turn. As noted above, Nöldeke's study emerged from a conservative methodological context largely resistant to the perspectives of higher criticism that were emerging within biblical studies at the time. Moreover, the fact that Qur'ānic studies has remained essentially stalled at this point for a century and a half certainly does not help Stewart's argument, and if Phenix and Horn perhaps overestimate Luxenberg's study, their assessment of the state of Qur'ānic studies in comparison with biblical studies seems rather fair. See Stewart, "Notes on Medieval and Modern Emendations," 225–26, critiquing Phenix and Horn, "Review of Christoph Luxenberg." See also the remarks by Donner and Gilliot in the same volume as Stewart that essentially affirm the deficiencies of Qur'ānic Studies in this regard: Donner, "The Qur'ān in Recent Scholarship," 29–30; Gilliot, "Reconsidering the Authorship of the Qur'ān," 88.

85. As acknowledged, e.g., by both Bell and Watt: Bell, *Introduction to the Qur'ān*, 155; Bell and Watt, *Bell's Introduction to the Qur'ān*, 158. For surveys of Qur'ānic eschatology, see Rüling, *Beiträge zur Eschatologie*, 6–40; Attema, *De mohammedaansche opvattingen*, 6–43; J. Smith, "Eschatology"; D. Cook, *Studies in Muslim Apocalyptic*, 169–75.

86. This division was most clearly articulated by Bell, who wrote that while "the idea of the Last Judgment maintains itself to the end," by "the close of the Meccan period it passes into the realm of assured dogma." Bell, *The Origin of Islam*, 107. Casanova envisioned three periods: one in which the Qur'ān declares the imminence of the Hour, followed by a period in which there is some question whether it was near or distant, and finally, a third period when the Qur'ān is preoccupied with issues from the early community: Casanova, *Mohammed*, 71. See also Buhl, *Das Leben Muhammeds*, 196–97; Buhl, *Muhammeds liv* (1998), 138–39; and Bell and Watt, *Bell's Introduction to the Qur'ān*, 54, 158. Rodinson and Armstrong go too far, however, in seeking to contain Muhammad's

eschatological concerns entirely within the early part of the Meccan period: Rodinson, *Mohammed*, 123; Armstrong, *Muhammad*, 91.

87. Welch describes this schema as "little more than a European variation of the traditional dating": Welch, "Al-Ḳurʾān," 417a. See also Reynolds, "Introduction," 9; Donner, "The Qurʾān in Recent Scholarship," 29.

88. Welch, "Al-Ḳurʾān," 417a. See also the sharp critique raised by Wansbrough, *Quranic Studies*, 126. For a particular example of this system's failings, see Firestone, "Disparity and Resolution." Again, for reasons identified in the notes above, the recent attempt to defend Nöldeke's dating of the various *sūras* in Sinai, "The Qurʾān as Process" is not persuasive.

89. John J. Collins suggested in a communication at the annual meeting of the American Academy of Religion in 2007 that such an undertaking would likely be worthwhile, a proposal that seemed to be well received by those in the audience: J. Collins, "Response to Session on 'Islamicate Apocalypsis.'" For more on the methods of form and tradition criticism, particularly as developed in the study of the Hebrew Bible, see, e.g., Sweeney, "Form Criticism"; and Knight, "Traditio-Historical Criticism."

90. De Prémare, *Aux origines du Coran*, esp. 35–45. See also earlier sketches in Bell and Watt, *Bell's Introduction to the Qurʾān*, 75–82; and Welch, "Al-Ḳurʾān," 421–25. Equally important for such an endeavor will be consideration of the different addressees of Qurʾānic material, as Andrew Rippin has recently suggested: Rippin, "Muḥammad in the Qurʾān."

91. Nöldeke and Schwally, *Geschichte des Qorāns*, 2: 120. See, however, Wansbrough's thoughtful critique of Nöldeke's largely unwarranted assumptions: Wansbrough, *Quranic Studies*, 43–44.

92. Peters, "The Quest of the Historical Muhammad," esp. 293–95.

93. Ibid., 297.

94. De Blois, "Islam in Its Arabian Context," 616–19.

95. See, e.g., Saldarini, "Form Criticism."

96. See, e.g., Metzger and Ehrman, *The Text of the New Testament*, 218–22, 279–80, 306–7.

97. "Der Koran enthält nur echte Stücke": Nöldeke, *Orientalische Skizzen*, 56.

98. De Blois, "Islam in Its Arabian Context," 617. See, however, the somewhat different views in Peters, "The Quest of the Historical Muhammad."

99. See, e.g., ʿAbd al-Jabbār, *Tathbīt* (Reynolds and Samir, *Critique*, 90–91, 98–105). See also Anthony, "Sayf ibn ʿUmar's Account." As an example of the sharp *differences* between Paul and the synoptic tradition, see, e.g., the remarks in Ehrman, *Lost Christianities*, 98–99 concerning Paul's "gospel" and the Gospel according to Matthew, where he concludes, "It is hard to imagine Paul and Matthew ever seeing eye to eye." Likewise, Peters, despite some missteps in reading the gospels and New Testament scholarship, gets right the important differences between Paul and the Synoptics: Peters, *Jesus and Muhammad*, 147–48.

100. Neuwirth, "Structural, Linguistic and Literary Features," 100.

101. Neuwirth, *Studien zur Komposition*, esp. 175–321. Cf. Peters, *Jesus and Muhammad*, 74–79.

102. Neuwirth characterizes the Meccan *sūras* as "technically sophisticated" compositions with "highly sophisticated phonetic structures." Neuwirth, "Structural, Linguistic and Literary Features," 98–99. Although Neuwirth allows for the possibility of occasional minor revisions by the later community, "Neuwirth concludes that it must have been the Prophet himself who composed the bulk of the Meccan sūras in the form which they have now": Motzki, "Alternative Accounts," 63–65.

103. Neuwirth has shown some interest in variant versions of the same story in the Qurʾān, but not so much as independent variants arising through an extended process of oral transmission, as Wansbrough and form and tradition criticism would approach such variants. Instead, she sees these variant traditions as "chronologically consecutive renditions that might adapt and modify one and the same story in the light of changing historical circumstances and on the basis of an ever-growing textual nucleus of past prophetic promulgation." Thus she seems to understand these variants as deliberate retellings by Muhammad in the context of the earliest community that respond to new circumstances or an encounter with new traditions. See, e.g., Sinai and Neuwirth, "Introduction," 9 n. 24, and also the articles cited there.

104. Ibid., 9. See also Neuwirth, *Studien zur Komposition*, 13*, where she uses the term *Literarkritik* in this same context, a word that is more accurately translated into English as "source criticism," i.e., the analysis of a text in order to detect its use of earlier written sources, rather than "literary criticism," which suggests a rather different approach to the text. See, e.g., Barton, "Reflections," esp. 523–25, which identifies the German *Literarkritik* with the English "source criticism," although note also that Barton here concludes by drawing some interesting parallels between *Literarkritik* and the various methods of interpretation known more generally in English as "literary criticism" of the Bible. Furthermore, Neuwirth's (and Sinai's) remark that "Wansbrough simply assumes that the Qurʾān is a textual corpus whose genesis *postdates*, rather than *parallels*, the formation of a nuclear Islamic community" does not seem entirely accurate. I certainly understand Wansbrough's interpretation of the Qurʾān to involve its development in parallel with the early community's development and its "crystallization." The difference here would seem to be rather the length of the time frame within which the beliefs and practices of the early community "crystallized." For Neuwirth, it would seem that this took place during the last two decades of Muhammad's life; according to Wansbrough this took several decades if not centuries.

105. As Omar Hamdan concludes of this campaign, "the results were so extensive that one could only wonder in disbelief if after the second *maṣāḥif* project any remnant of a differing recension were to come to light": Hamdan, "The Second Maṣāḥif Project," 829.

106. See, e.g., Levin, "Source Criticism," 39.

107. Knight, "Traditio-Historical Criticism," 103–4.

108. Neuwirth remarks that her study has used *Formkritik* to analyze the Qurʾān, but it would seem that such a claim can only be maintained to a rather limited extent. While she does indeed identify a *Sitz im Leben* for the traditions that she analyzes in the liturgical recitation of the early community (at the Kaʿba in the case of the earliest *sūras*), and she notes their "funktionale und ornamentale Form," many of the most important

elements of traditional form criticism are lacking from her approach: for instance, her understanding of the Qurʾān would seem to proscribe any analysis of *Formgeschichte*. On the whole, Neuwirth's *Formkritik* of the Qurʾān thus amounts, as Peters writes in the quotation above, "to little more than the classification of the various ways in which the Prophet chose to express himself." See Neuwirth, "Structural, Linguistic and Literary Features," 110–11; Neuwirth, *Studien zur Komposition*, 26*, 37*; Sweeney, "Form Criticism," 18.

109. See, e.g., Welch, "Review of *Studien zur Komposition*"; and Rippin, "Review of *Studien zur Komposition.*"

110. Motzki, "Alternative Accounts," 63.

111. Bell and Watt, *Bell's Introduction to the Qurʾān*, 75–82.

112. Ibid., 38–39, 89–98.

113. De Prémare, *Aux origines du Coran*, 29–45.

114. Rippin, "Reading the Qurʾān," 642.

115. Hirschfeld, *New Researches*; Bell, *The Qurʾān*; Bell, *A Commentary on the Qurʾān*. Bell's proposed division of the Qurʾānic *sūra*s into smaller units has not met with much acceptance, yet even if his reconstruction is rather imperfect and highly idiosyncratic, the approach is undoubtedly correct: see, e.g., Welch, "Al-Ḳurʾān," 417–18; Rippin, "Reading the Qurʾān." An interesting approach to the *ḥadīth* using elements of form criticism was published by Speight, "The Will of Saʿd b. a. Waqqāṣ."

116. Rippin, who has briefly commented on the limited influence of form criticism on Qurʾānic studies, particularly as evident in Bell's work, notes the impact of ideas only from Old Testament form criticism and from Wellhausen's work in particular (although strictly speaking, Wellhausen's work is an example of source criticism [*Literarkritik*] rather than form criticism): see Rippin, "Literary Analysis of Qurʾān," 158; Rippin, "Reading the Qurʾān," esp. 641–43. For more on the importance of form criticism within modern New Testament study, see Baird, *History of New Testament Research*, 2: 269–86; Kümmel, *The New Testament*, 325–41. A somewhat more guarded summary can be found in Neill and Wright, *The Interpretation of the New Testament, 1861–1986*, 253–69. Nevertheless, as the authors note (themselves both bishops in the Anglican Church), form criticism was never as well received in Britain as it was by scholars in Germany and the United States: ibid., 269–76; see also Baird, *History of New Testament Research*, 2: 269. The classic example of the method's application to the gospels is Bultmann, *The History of the Synoptic Tradition*. A more basic overview of the method can be found in Fossum and Munoa, *Jesus and the Gospels*, 66–77.

117. Frank van der Velden's recent warning against any approach to formative Islam that might "look into the kind of hermeneutical abyss that misled some Christian biblical exegetes of the 'new form critical school' in the 1970s" seems a bit presumptive and misguided. Not only has the Qurʾān so far been relatively shielded from the critical perspectives of form criticism, but it seems somewhat inappropriate to proscribe a valuable and well-established method of historical analysis simply because one does not particularly like the results ("hermeneutical abyss") that it yields. See van der Velden, "Relations between Jews," 31.

118. Rippin, "Western Scholarship and the Qur'ān," 240–47, esp. 242. See also, e.g., Rippin, "Literary Analysis of Qur'ān," 153, 158–59; Rippin, "Reading the Qur'ān," 641–42; Arkoun, "Bilan et perspectives"; Wansbrough, *Quranic Studies*, ix.

119. Koch, *The Growth of the Biblical Tradition*, 70.

120. For a brief and helpful introduction to Wansbrough's methods and conclusions, see Rippin, "Literary Analysis of Qur'ān." See also the special issue of *Method and Theory in the Study of Religion* that was devoted to Wansbrough's legacy in the study of early Islam: Berg, "Islamic Origins Reconsidered." Regarding the controversial reception of Wansbrough's ideas, see esp. Berg, "The Implications." On Wansbrough's use of methods from New Testament form criticism, see Adams, "Reflections on the Work of John Wansbrough," esp. 80–81. Note, however, that despite Wansbrough's embrace of such approaches, he expressed skepticism that earliest Islam was an eschatological community, although he did not discuss the issue in any depth: Wansbrough, *Quranic Studies*, x.

121. Rippin's remarks in his foreword to the recent republication of *Quranic Studies* summarize well the distraction that this rather aggressive claim has posed for many readers, who seem unable to see past it to grasp the much broader significance of the work: "It is those points that have led to many exchanges and debates among scholars and others, most of them unprofitable in my view, regarding the most 'outrageous' claim that the Qur'ān was written (down) at the beginning of the third-century *hijrī*. Indeed, some people seem to have reacted to *Quranic Studies* solely on the basis of this matter, as though Wansbrough wrote the book in order to prove that point but that he buried it within the text in an obscure manner in order to lessen the impact. To me, this is a misreading of the book." Wansbrough and Rippin, *Quranic Studies*, xiv. See also Reynolds, "Introduction," 12.

122. See, e.g., the summary in Welch, "Al-Ḳur'ān," 405.

123. De Prémare, *Les fondations de l'islam*, 281–88; Modarressi, "Early Debates."

124. Welch, "Al-Ḳur'ān," 405. I find Gregor Schoeler's recent article defending the traditional accounts of the Qur'ān's codification unpersuasive. In essence, the article merely rehashes various elements from the traditionally received account while professing a belief in their "general core" and "consistent general picture of the Qur'ān's compilation." This argument reflects a somewhat weaker version of the sort of *petitio principii* that is evident in Watt's approach to the *sīra* literature. After summarizing individual points from the traditional account, Schoeler pronounces the reports credible and consistent with the "overall picture," without ever raising questions about the credibility of this "overall picture" itself or considering whether the credibility of these accounts as seen from the viewpoint of the Islamic tradition affords any assurance of their historical accuracy. See Schoeler, "The Codification of the Qur'an," e.g., 780, 782, 784–85.

125. Welch, "Al-Ḳur'ān," 406–8.

126. Wansbrough, *Quranic Studies*, esp. 43–51. See also Rippin, "Literary Analysis of Qur'ān"; Rippin, "*Qur'anic Studies*, Part IV"; Wansbrough and Rippin, *Quranic Studies*, xiv–xviii; Berg, "The Implications"; Hawting, "John Wansbrough, Islam, and Monotheism"; Mojaddedi, "Taking Islam Seriously"; Reynolds, "Introduction," 12.

127. Crone, "Two Legal Problems"; Hawting, "The Role of the Qur'ān."

128. See the recent summary in Gilliot, "Reconsidering the Authorship of the Qur'ān," esp. 88–94, 100–101. See also Gilliot, "Les 'informateurs' juifs et chrétiens"; Gilliot, "Le Coran, fruit d'un travail collectif?"; Gilliot, "Les traditions sur la composition."

129. De Prémare, *Les fondations de l'islam*, 278–306; de Prémare, *Aux origines du Coran*, esp. 57–136; de Prémare, "Coran et Hadîth"; de Prémare, "La constitution des écritures"; de Prémare, "'Abd al-Malik b. Marwān et le Processus"; and now also de Prémare, "'Abd al-Malik b. Marwān and the Process." See also de Prémare, "Les textes musulmans."

130. See Casanova, *Mohammed*, 103–42. Nevertheless, de Prémare nowhere explicitly acknowledges Casanova's influence or cites his work. De Prémare's presentation of this argument is strengthened considerably by his inclusion of a number of relevant texts in translation, to which he often refers in the course of his study: de Prémare, *Les fondations de l'islam*, 442–68.

131. De Prémare, *Les fondations de l'islam*, 294–302; de Prémare, *Aux origines du Coran*, 72–99; C. Robinson, *'Abd al-Malik*, 100–104. See also in this regard Mingana, "Transmission of the Kur'ān" (1916); reprinted as Mingana, "Transmission of the Kur'ān" (1917); Crone and Cook, *Hagarism*, 17–18; Hoyland, *Seeing Islam*, 500–501.

132. See M. Cook, *The Koran*, 118–22; Welch, "Al-Ḳur'ān," 404b (which refers to "thousands of textual variants" in classical literature). The inscriptions of the Dome of the Rock were most recently published with translation in Grabar, *The Shape of the Holy*, 92–99. Rather astonishingly, Estelle Whelan has attempted to establish an early date for the Qur'ān on the basis of the Dome of the Rock's inscriptions: Whelan, "Forgotten Witness." Nevertheless, her special pleading that canonical verses have been adapted to a missionary purpose in this setting is not persuasive.

133. Recently François Déroche has published a very early version of the Qur'ān reconstructed from several related manuscript fragments, the culmination of his extensive work in this area: Déroche, *La transmission écrite*. The results are impressive, and they indeed bear witness to an early and important recension of the Qur'ān. Nevertheless, the author's dating of this text to the first Islamic century is not fully persuasive. As Fred Leemhuis recently notes, "A few qur'ānic manuscripts have been attributed by some specialists to the seventh century, but as yet no extant manuscript has been unequivocally dated to a period before the ninth century on the basis of firm external evidence. Such external evidence would provide a powerful argument in the controversy that exists in Western scholarship about when the codification of the Qur'ān took place, whether this was at the beginning of Islamic history, as related by the traditional view, or about two centuries later, according to John Wansbrough's hypothesis." Leemhuis, "From Palm Leaves to the Internet," 146. Likewise, Chase Robinson correctly observes that "there is not a single Qur'ānic manuscript, Yemeni or otherwise, that has been dated to the seventh century on anything other than palaeographical grounds, which, given the paltry evidence that survives, remain controversial in the extreme. One scholar's seventh-century leaf, another may assign to the eighth or ninth." Although Robinson concedes that it is likely that scholarship will succeed in identifying a handful of Qur'ānic folios from the seventh century, this will be "a far cry from establishing the traditional account of Qur'ānic origins or, for that matter, its collection and editing." C. Robinson, "The Ideological Uses," esp. 212–14. See also de Prémare, *Aux origines*

du Coran, 58–60; M. Cook, *The Koran*, 120. Moreover, the very earliest possible date for this text would appear to be toward the end of ʿAbd al-Malik's reign, in which case this manuscript may possibly be understood as having been produced within the broader context of his efforts to create a standardized text. Indeed, as David Powers concludes, this manuscript itself affords important evidence "that the consonantal skeleton and performed reading of the Qurʾān remained open and fluid until the end of the first/seventh century": Powers, *Muḥammad Is Not the Father*, 166–96, esp. 193.

134. De Prémare, *Aux origines du Coran*, 70–73; de Prémare, *Les fondations de l'islam*, 289.

135. Motzki, "The Collection of the Qurʾān."

136. See de Prémare, *Aux origines du Coran*, 72–73; de Prémare, *Les fondations de l'islam*, 281–88; Modarressi, "Early Debates."

137. The fragments of Papias are most readily accessible in Ehrman, *The Apostolic Fathers*, 2: 85–120. The most important fragments, regarding the gospels of Mark and Matthew, are preserved in Eusebius, *Ecclesiastical History* III.39. Regarding Papias's dates, see Ehrman, *The Apostolic Fathers*, 2: 86–87.

138. See, e.g., Kümmel, *Introduction to the New Testament*, 53–56, 94–97, 241–44; Schoedel, "Papias"; Ehrman, *Jesus*, 42–45. For a recent example of an evangelical scholar who appeals to Papias to authenticate the gospels, see Bauckham, *Jesus and the Eyewitnesses*; for a more popular example—and one more directly apologetic in tone—see T. Jones, *Misquoting Truth*, esp. 83–94, 102–5, 147–48.

139. De Prémare also draws the comparison to Papias: de Prémare, "La constitution des écritures," 176, 183. Regarding the evidence from Christian sources, see also de Prémare, *Aux origines du Coran*, 72–73, 93–97; de Prémare, *Les fondations de l'islam*, 299; de Prémare, "ʿAbd al-Malik b. Marwān et le Processus," 184–89; de Prémare, "ʿAbd al-Malik b. Marwān and the Process," 194–97. See also Mingana, "The Transmission of the Kurʾān."

140. C. Robinson, *ʿAbd al-Malik*, 102. As Hoyland recently notes, "It has become almost a dogma now that the pre-ʿAbd al-Malik Muslim state was very decentralized," that is, "a weak state": Hoyland, "New Documentary Texts," 398. Hoyland seeks to add some nuance to this view, pointing to accomplishments and innovations under previous rulers; nevertheless, the various exceptions that he identifies, while interesting, do not fully undermine the striking differences in the Islamic polity before and after ʿAbd al-Malik. In any case, Hoyland identifies nothing that would suggest the reign of ʿUthmān was in fact capable of producing and enforcing the standard text of the Qurʾān, and moreover, his conclusions reinforce the idea that the thorough Islamicization of the state was indeed ʿAbd al-Malik's innovation (410).

141. C. Robinson, *ʿAbd al-Malik*, 103. On ʿAbd al-Malik's role in the consolidation of Islam and its fusion with the state, see also Hoyland, *Seeing Islam*, 551–56.

142. C. Robinson, *ʿAbd al-Malik*, 104.

143. Powers, *Muḥammad Is Not the Father*, 155–96, 227–33, esp. 227.

144. Hamdan, "The Second Maṣāḥif Project," 828.

145. Neuwirth, *Studien zur Komposition*, 18*–22*.

146. "Auch wenn man nicht von einer Redaktion ʿUthmāns ca. 650 ausgehen will, so liegen doch auf keinen Fall mehr als 60 Jahre zwischen dem Abschluss des Textes und seiner verbindlichen Veröffentlichung—eine Frist, die, entgegen den Schlussfolgerungen von de Prémare, zu kurz ist, um hinreichend Raum für maßgebliche, d. h. gezielte, theologisch relevante Modifikationen des Textes . . . zu bieten." Ibid., 19*. The supposition here that any such changes must have been "deliberate" (*gezielte*) seems largely to miss the point of how such religious traditions often evolve in accordance with the changing beliefs and practices of a given community, particularly in a formative period such as this.

147. Donner, *Narratives of Islamic Origins*, 29.

148. See, e.g., Sanders, *The Historical Figure of Jesus*, 57–63; Ehrman, *Jesus*, 21–53; Dunn and McKnight, *The Historical Jesus*; Koester, *Introduction to the New Testament*, 2: 59–64.

149. Funk and Hoover, *The Five Gospels*, 5. Although the perspectives of the Jesus Seminar that are presented in this volume lie somewhat outside the mainstream in their belief in a non-eschatological Jesus and a rather early dating of the Gospel of Thomas, this work has the advantage of reflecting the collective views of a number of New Testament scholars on the authenticity of specific sayings when studied using, among other methods, form and tradition criticism. In general terms, the findings of this group are reflective of the field as a whole regarding the transmission of the sayings of Jesus in the first decades of Christianity. Concerning the dates of these early Christian writings, see, e.g., Koester, *Ancient Christian Gospels*, 87; Ehrman, *Jesus*, 48, 82. The "Q" gospel is a lost collection of Jesus' sayings that was most likely compiled sometime around the year 50. Its contents are largely known from the comparison of the gospels of Matthew and Luke, both of which have independently utilized this early written collection. Certain traditions known to both Matthew and Luke, but apparently not to Mark, are understood to derive from this lost collection. As it is currently understood, Q was essentially a list of sayings ascribed to Jesus, without any narrative context or a Passion narrative. For more information, see, e.g., Kümmel, *Introduction to the New Testament*, 38–80.

150. C. Robinson, *ʿAbd al-Malik*, 103.

151. This result of gospel criticism is perhaps most easily appreciated by non-specialists again through consulting the discussion of various Q traditions in Funk and Hoover, *The Five Gospels*. A good starting place would perhaps be the large collection of sayings in the Sermon on the Mount: Matt. 5–7 (pp. 138–59). It should again be noted, however, that the findings of the Jesus Seminar, which produced this volume, are not always representative of scholarship more broadly. For example, a not inconsiderable amount of material is rejected on the basis of the Jesus Seminar's idiosyncratic view of Jesus' eschatology. Nevertheless, the process by which such early materials are tested for "authenticity" is largely representative of the broader field of study. Peters draws a similar comparison between Q and the Qurʾān, and to be fair, he seems almost as confident that Q relates actual teachings of Jesus as he is that the Qurʾān is a repository of Muhammad's teaching: see Peters, *Jesus and Muhammad*, 62–73. Nevertheless, such a sanguine approach to the Q traditions is largely out of step with most New Testament scholarship from the past century.

152. Cf. Sanders, *The Historical Figure of Jesus*, 58–60.

153. See Wansbrough, *Quranic Studies*, 20–52, esp. 50–51. See also de Prémare, *Les fondations de l'islam*, 302–13, 463–66; de Prémare, *Aux origines du Coran*, 83–93; Welch, "Al-Ḳurʾān," 406–8.

154. Donner, *Narratives of Islamic Origins*, 20–63.

155. Donner, "From Believers to Muslims," 17–18.

156. Donner's formulation arises, it would appear, from his assumption that Wansbrough's use of the term "prophetical *logia*" to describe the Qurʾānic material should simply be taken as a shorthand for "what we usually call *ḥadīth*" (Donner, *Narratives of Islamic Origins*, 36, esp. n. 2; cf. Wansbrough, *Quranic Studies*, 1). Yet it is not at all clear that Wansbourgh makes such an equation. Wansbrough has borrowed the term *logia* from New Testament form criticism, whose methods he has in large part employed, and its usage here is part of the move to begin reconceptualizing this material within a new context. In the recent reissue of *Quranic Studies*, with additional material from Rippin, the latter appends a glossary, particularly of the technical terms that Wansbrough applies from biblical criticism, and he defines *logia* as "oracles, divine utterances, specifically sayings of Jesus that lie behind the Gospels" (Wansbrough and Rippin, *Quranic Studies*, 312). Halevi adds further clarity to Wansbrough's usage of the term with his description of Wansbrough's Qurʾānic *logia* as "discrete statements, disjoint from narrative," that were ascribed to Muhammad, reflecting a seemingly different category from the *ḥadīth*: Halevi, *Muhammad's Grave*, 23. See also in regard to Wansbrough's use of the term *logia*, Adams, "Reflections on the Work of John Wansbrough," 82; Motzki, "Alternative Accounts," 60–61. Note that Mohammad Benkheira has recently raised a similar critique of de Prémare's reconstruction of early Islamic history by similarly accusing him of following Wansbrough in considering the collection of the Qurʾān as contemporary with the collection of the *ḥadīth* and identifying the Qurʾānic corpus as essentially a subset of the *ḥadīth*: Benkheira, "L'analyse du *ḥadīṯ*." Fortunately, de Prémare was able to respond and correct what are inaccurate representations of his thesis: de Prémare, "Mise au point."

157. Uri Rubin has developed the hypothesis that the Qurʾān appears to be later than the earliest *ḥadīth*, seemingly favoring a date for the Qurʾān along the lines that Wansbrough has proposed. His argument rests largely on the observation that many early *ḥadīth* lack Qurʾānic elements while more recent traditions appear to have adapted earlier reports to conform to the traditions of the Qurʾān. Nevertheless, what Rubin's research more probably discloses is the formation of these early *ḥadīth* within a context where the authority of the Qurʾān was not yet fully established, and as the Qurʾān's authority became more and more absolute, its contents were gradually written into these earlier traditions. See Rubin, *The Eye of the Beholder*; Rubin, *Between Bible and Qurʾān*.

158. C. Robinson, *Islamic Historiography*, 20–30. Even if some basic elements of the earliest *ḥadīth* may perhaps derive from various oral traditions and legends circulating in the later seventh century, the oldest *ḥadīth* seem to have been given their "literary" form only at the beginning of the eighth century, at the earliest. Beginning at this time it is occasionally possible to identify very early "common-links" (e.g., al-Zuhrī, d. 742) who may be associated with the "authorship" of a particular tradition as it is preserved in later sources. Thus, the literary and other stylistic features of the *ḥadīth* that Donner compares with the

Qur'ān do in fact reflect a different *Sitz im Leben* after the beginning of the eighth century. See also the earlier studies of Schacht, *The Origins of Muhammadan Jurisprudence*; and Wensinck, *The Muslim Creed*, e.g., 59.

159. Donner, *Narratives of Islamic Origins*, 49.

160. For more on the Gospel according to John and its date, see, e.g., Kümmel, *Introduction to the New Testament*, 188–247.

161. Al-Tirmidhī, *Al-Jāmiʿ al-ṣaḥīḥ*, 5: no. 3192.

162. See the discussion of the vocalization and interpretation of this verse in El Cheikh, "Sūrat al-Rūm." Edmund Beck suggests that the "Byzantine" victory refers to Mu'ta: Beck, "Die Sura *ar-Rūm*," 339.

163. Nöldeke and Schwally, *Geschichte des Qorāns*, 1: 149 n. 7; Bell, *The Qur'ān*, 2: 392.

164. El Cheikh, "Sūrat al-Rūm," 357.

165. Donner, *Narratives of Islamic Origins*, 51.

166. E.g., Rippin, "Muḥammad in the Qur'ān," esp. 299–302, 307–8; M. Cook, *Muhammad*, 69–73; Peters, "The Quest of the Historical Muhammad," 301–5; Peters, *Muhammad and the Origins of Islam*, 261; Wansbrough, *Quranic Studies*, 56; Hodgson, *The Venture of Islam*, 160–61.

167. Hirschfeld, *New Researches*, 138–40.

168. Lüling, *Über den Ur-Qur'an*; in English as Lüling, *A Challenge to Islam*; Luxenberg, *Die syro-aramäische Lesart*; in English as Luxenberg, *The Syro-Aramaic Reading of the Koran*.

169. Donner, in a recent article, offers a somewhat sympathetic description of Luxenberg's approach (as well as Lüling's), and although he evaluates the hypothesis as "unproven," he also notes that it "deserves to be fully tested to see if it may apply for at least some Quranic passages." Donner's article offers evidence that at least the Qur'ānic usage of the word *furqān* suggests that "the Qur'ān text, as we have it today, at some point underwent a process of purely *written* transmission, without the advantage of any controlling oral recitation, at least in part": Donner, "Quranic *Furqān*," 297–300. See also Donner, *Muhammad and the Believers*, 56. In a recent article, Uri Rubin has argued for a genuinely Arabic meaning for the word *furqān* as it is used in the Qur'ān, but his recourse to significantly later sources for evidence renders the argument less than fully persuasive: Rubin, "On the Arabian Origins." For recent critiques of both Lüling's and Luxenberg's theories from a traditional perspective, see Motzki, "Alternative Accounts," 65–71; and Neuwirth, *Studien zur Komposition*, 13*–16*. For more positive assessments of Luxenberg's work, see Phenix and Horn, "Review of Christoph Luxenberg"; Gilliot, "Review of Christoph Luxenberg"; van Reeth, "Le vignoble du paradis." See also several of the essays in Reynolds, *The Qur'ān in Its Historical Context*.

170. See also the interesting recent article by Patricia Crone, which observes that the "polytheists" of the Qur'ān appear to have been involved in agricultural practices that do not seem viable in the Mecca area. Although she refrains from drawing conclusions from this aspect of the text, the point is clearly made. Crone, "How Did the Quranic Pagans Make a Living?"

171. Wansbrough and Rippin, *Quranic Studies*, xvii.

172. Halevi, *Muhammad's Grave*, 207.

173. As David Cook writes, "The Qur'an is an eschatological book and not an apocalyptic book. This would seem apparent on the basis of our research, and would indicate that Muḥammad believed in the immediacy of the end to such an extent that the whole issue of apocalyptic 'future history' was a moot one for him. His eyes were upon the Day; the specific portents preceding that Day were so blindingly clear to him that there was no need to mention them, and, indeed, he virtually does not do so. This fact could explain the silence of the Qur'an as far as apocalyptic goes." D. Cook, *Studies in Muslim Apocalyptic*, 301.

174. Donner, *Narratives of Islamic Origins*, 75–85, esp. 80.

175. See Shoemaker, "Christmas in the Qur'ān." Note, however, that more recent excavations have determined that even though a *mihrab* was added to the sanctuary of the Kathisma church, it nevertheless remained in use primarily by Christians. Furthermore, the uppermost mosaic floors now appear to have been added in the ninth century, altering their relation to the mosaics of the Dome of the Rock. See esp. Di Segni, "Christian Epigraphy." Nevertheless, the apparent connections between the traditions of this particular shrine and the unique formation of the account of Jesus' Nativity in the Qur'ān remain highly significant.

176. Donner, *Narratives of Islamic Origins*, 46.

177. "Quod ubique, quod semper, quod ab omnibus": Vincent of Lérins, *Commonitorium* 2.3 (Migne, *Patrologiae cursus completus, Series Latina*, 50: 640).

178. Hurgronje, *Mohammedanism*, 17.

179. Donner, *Narratives of Islamic Origins*, 26–28. See also pp. 37–38 where the issue of agency surfaces again, and the reprise of the ubiquity argument at pp. 286–90.

180. Donner, "From Believers to Muslims," 12, 52, emphasis added. Cf. now Donner, *Muhammad and the Believers*.

181. Donner, "From Believers to Muslims," 39.

182. Indeed, Donner himself adopts a much more dynamic view of earliest Islam in his recent monograph: see Donner, *Muhammad and the Believers*, esp. 220–24.

183. Wansbrough and Rippin, *Quranic Studies*, xvii–xviii.

184. C. Robinson, *Islamic Historiography*, 10.

185. Crone and Hinds, *God's Caliph*.

186. See, e.g., de Prémare, *Les fondations de l'islam*, 302–13, 463–66; de Prémare, *Aux origines du Coran*, 83–93; Welch, "Al-Ḳur'ān," 406–8; Hamdan, "The Second Maṣāḥif Project," 829.

187. M. Cook, *The Koran*, 124. For comparison, one should again consider the remarkable convergence of the New Testament text once Christianity became the faith of an empire, despite both the lack of imperial coercion and the remarkable diversity of the earliest witnesses: Metzger and Ehrman, *The Text of the New Testament*, 218–22, 279–80, 306–7.

188. D. Cook, *Studies in Muslim Apocalyptic*, 274; Rubin, "Muḥammad's Message."

189. Donner has similarly chosen to cast aside this traditional interpretive framework: Donner, "From Believers to Muslims," 18; Donner, *Muhammad and the Believers*, 53–54.

190. Donner, *Muhammad and the Believers*, 79–80.

191. Regarding the various issues concerning community order and stability within the early church at Corinth, see, e.g., Martin, *The Corinthian Body*; Theissen, *Studien zur Soziologie des Urchristentums*; English trans., Theissen, *The Social Setting of Pauline Christianity*.

192. As much is reflected in the very title of Gager, *Kingdom and Community*. See also, e.g., Overman, *Matthew's Gospel and Formative Judaism*; Saldarini, *Matthew's Christian-Jewish Community*; Balch, *Social History of the Matthean Community*; Neyrey, *The Social World of Luke-Acts*.

193. These issues will be considered to some extent in the following chapter, but see also Bashear, "Qur'ān 2:114 and Jerusalem"; Bashear, "Qibla Musharriqa"; Hoyland, *Seeing Islam*, 560–73; Donner, "From Believers to Muslims"; Donner, *Muhammad and the Believers*; Wansbrough, *The Sectarian Milieu*; D. Cook, "The Beginnings of Islam as an Apocalyptic Movement."

194. Unless otherwise indicated, translations of the Qur'ān are from Arberry, *The Koran Interpreted*. Nevertheless, I have followed the Egyptian system of numbering the verses to facilitate easier reference to the Arabic text.

195. Abdel Haleem, *The Qur'ān*, 166. On the difficulties in translating the term أَمْر, which clearly has an eschatological significance in the Qur'ān, see D. Cook, *Studies in Muslim Apocalyptic*, 271–72.

196. ἤγγικεν ἡ βασιλεία τοῦ θεοῦ: Mark 1:15 and par.

197. Bell also noted the similarities of these two parables: Bell, *The Origin of Islam*, 114–15.

198. Alternatively one might translate the passage as "the hastening [Hour] is at hand."

199. See also D. Cook, "Messianism and Astronomical Events," esp. 45–47.

200. Ibid., 46–47; D. Cook, *Studies in Muslim Apocalyptic*, 273, esp. n. 7; D. Cook, "Muslim Materials on Comets and Meteorites," 134–35; Rubin, "Muḥammad's Message." See also Aḥmad, "Did Muḥammad Observe the Canterbury Meteor Swarm?"; Aḥmad, "The Dawn Sky on Laylat al-Qadr"; Rada and Stephenson, "A Catalogue of Meteor Showers in Medieval Arab Chronicles," 9–10. Nevertheless, as Cook rightly observes, these studies place a little too much confidence in the traditional Islamic accounts of the beginnings of Muhammad's revelations.

201. See, e.g., Schweitzer, *The Quest of the Historical Jesus*, 239.

202. E.g., Bell, *The Origin of Islam*, 86–90, 102–7; Bell and Watt, *Bell's Introduction to the Qur'ān*, 54; Rodinson, *Mohammed*, 120–23; Blachère, *Introduction au Coran*, 24–25.

203. See, e.g., Hurgronje, *Mohammedanism*, 15–17; Bell, *The Qur'ān*, 1: vi; Bell and Watt, *Bell's Introduction to the Qur'ān*, 50–54; Watt, *Muhammad at Mecca*, 52–58; Paret, "Der Koran als Geschichtsquelle"; Welch, "Al-Ḳur'ān," 402–4; Welch, "Qur'ānic Studies"; Welch, "Muḥammad's Understanding of Himself"; Peters, "The Quest of the Historical Muhammad," 293–94; Rippin, "Muḥammad in the Qur'ān"; Motzki, "The Collection of the Qur'ān," 1–5; Neuwirth, "Structural, Linguistic and Literary Features," 100; Berg, "Context: Muḥammad."

204. Foucault, "What Is an Author?," esp. 111–12, 118–20.

205. Bell and Watt, *Bell's Introduction to the Qur'ān*, 54.

206. Perhaps the definitive statement regarding both the lack of evidence for the nature of earliest Islam and the nature of the Islamic sources as reporting a kind of "salvation history" (*Heilsgeschichte*) is Wansbrough, *The Sectarian Milieu*; now republished with extensive annotations: Wansbrough and Hawting, *The Sectarian Milieu*.

207. Sanders, *Jesus and Judaism*, 123–56, although one could still explore Weiss, *Die Predigt Jesu vom Reiche Gottes* or Schweitzer, *The Quest of the Historical Jesus*, 330–97 on this topic with profit, even at such chronological distance. For a more popular presentation of the same ideas, see Sanders, *The Historical Figure of Jesus*, 169–88 and Ehrman, *Jesus*, 125–39.

208. Sanders, *Jesus and Judaism*, 152–53; Sanders, *The Historical Figure of Jesus*, 176–77.

209. Schweitzer, *The Quest of the Historical Jesus*, 360–63; Sanders, *The Historical Figure of Jesus*, 180.

210. Sanders, *Jesus and Judaism*, 140–41, 153–54; Sanders, *The Historical Figure of Jesus*, 177–78.

211. E.g., Rüling, *Beiträge zur Eschatologie*, 11; J. Smith, "Eschatology," 46. Cf. Bell and Watt, *Bell's Introduction to the Qur'ān*, 53–54; Watt, *Muhammad at Mecca*, 65–66.

212. Sanders, *Jesus and Judaism*, 154; Sanders, *The Historical Figure of Jesus*, 178–79; see also Ehrman, *Jesus*, 127.

213. See also Rubin, "Muḥammad's Message," 42–43, which reaches a similar conclusion.

214. Sanders, *The Historical Figure of Jesus*, 179. See 1 Thess. 4:12–5:11.

215. Sanders, *The Historical Figure of Jesus*, 179–82.

216. See ibid., 180.

217. Bell, *The Qur'ān*, 2: 604. *Sūra* 22 appears to have mixed together here traditions about the eschatological Hour and the temporal punishments that God has brought against peoples in the past and threatens to bring against the Meccans. See, e.g., ibid., 1: 316–23.

218. E.g., using Arberry's translation as modified appropriately: 17:51–52: "Then they will shake their heads at thee, and they will say, 'When will it be?' Say: 'It is nigh. It will be on the day when He will call you, and you will answer praising Him, and you will think you have but tarried a little.'" 27:71–72: "They say, 'When shall this promise come to pass, if you speak the truth?' Say: 'Riding behind you already is some part of that you seek to hasten on." 33:63–64: "The people will question thee concerning the Hour. Say: 'The knowledge of it is only with God; what shall make thee know? The Hour is nigh.' God has cursed the unbelievers, and prepared for them a Blaze." 42:17–18: "God it is who has sent down the Book with the truth, and also the Balance. And what shall make thee know? The Hour is nigh. Those that believe not therein seek to hasten it; but those who believe in it go in fear of it, knowing that it is the truth. Why, surely those who are in doubt concerning the Hour are indeed in far error."

219. Rubin, "Muḥammad's Message," 41–42.

220. The problems with the traditional Islamic accounts of the *jāhiliyya* are well discussed in Hawting, *The Idea of Idolatry*, whose views seem to have met largely with acceptance on this particular issue.

221. See, e.g., Reeves, *Trajectories*, 1–110; Morony, *Iraq after the Muslim Conquest*, 325–31; van Bekkum, "Jewish Messianic Expectations"; Rubin, *Between Bible and Qurʾān*, 20–35; Donner, "La question du messianisme," 24; Donner, "The Sources of Islamic Conceptions of War," 43–46; Donner, *Muhammad and the Believers*, 14–16; D. Cook, "The Beginnings of Islam as an Apocalyptic Movement"; D. Cook, *Studies in Muslim Apocalyptic*, 4–9; Hoyland, "Sebeos," 91–92; Reinink, *Syriac Christianity*; Stemberger, "Jerusalem in the Early Seventh Century."

222. Wansbrough, *Quranic Studies*, 20–52, esp. 21–29, 50–51.

223. See esp. Goldziher, *Muslim Studies*, 2: 33–40; Schacht, *The Origins of Muhammadan Jurisprudence*, 176–89.

224. Goldziher, *Muslim Studies*, 2: 39–40.

225. D. Cook, *Studies in Muslim Apocalyptic*, 273–74 n. 8.

226. Ibn Saʿd, *Ṭabaqāt* (Sachau, *Biographien Muhammeds*, 1.1: 65).

227. Casanova, *Mohammed*, 18; Maqrīzī, *Description historique*, 3: 18.

228. Kister, "A Booth Like the Booth of Moses," 152; Bashear, "Muslim Apocalypses," 78.

229. Ibn Ḥanbal, *Musnad*, 3: 310–11.

230. Muslim, *Ṣaḥīḥ*, 4: 1794–95. See also the various other examples of this tradition cited in Casanova, *Mohammed*, 15–17, 196–99; and Bashear, "Muslim Apocalypses," 76–80.

231. Al-Ṭabarī, *Ta'rīkh* (de Goeje et al., *Annales*, I: 8–18).

232. Al-Ṭabarī, *Ta'rīkh* (ibid., I: 9–10; al-Ṭabarī, *The History of al-Ṭabarī: Volume I*, 175–76).

233. Casanova, *Mohammed*, 17, citing Sprenger, *Das Leben und die Lehre*, 1: 535–36. See also Bashear, "Muslim Apocalypses," 89.

234. E.g., Ibn Abī Shayba, *Muṣannaf*, 15: 168; Ibn Ḥanbal, *Musnad*, 3: 192, 213, 228, 269–70, 283; Muslim, *Ṣaḥīḥ*, 4: 1795–96.

235. For a comparative perspective concerning the eschatological teachings of Jesus, see, e.g., Meier, *A Marginal Jew*, 2: 289–397, esp. 336–48.

236. Casanova, *Mohammed*, 17, citing Sprenger, *Das Leben und die Lehre*, 1: 535–36. See also Bashear, "Muslim Apocalypses," 90–91.

237. Ibn Hishām, *Kitāb sīrat Rasūl Allāh* (Wüstenfeld, *Das Leben Muhammed's*, 1: 13–14). Although Guillaume translates this passage (في اخر الزمان) as "in the time to come" (Guillaume, *The Life of Muhammad*, 7), "at the end of time" seems to be a preferable translation.

238. Casanova, *Mohammed*, 208.

239. See the various examples collected in ibid., 207–13.

240. Kister, "A Booth like the Booth of Moses," 150.

241. Al-Ṭurṭūshī, *Al-Ḥawādith wa-al-bidaʿ*, 94; trans. Kister, "A Booth like the Booth of Moses," 150.

242. Ibn Saʿd, *Ṭabaqāt* (Sachau, *Biographien Muhammeds*, 1.2: 2); see also Kister, "A Booth like the Booth of Moses," 151–54.

243. Kister, "A Booth like the Booth of Moses," 151.

244. Ibid., 152.

245. Ibid., 155.

246. E.g., Ibn al-Mubārak, *Kitāb al-zuhd*, 554; trans. Bashear, "Muslim Apocalypses," 79, where other sources are indicated.

247. E.g., Ibn Ḥanbal, *Musnad*, 2: 50, 92; trans. Bashear, "Muslim Apocalypses," 80, where other sources are indicated.

248. E.g., Ibn al-Mubārak, *Kitāb al-zuhd*, 557; trans. Bashear, "Muslim Apocalypses," 80, where other sources are indicated.

249. E.g., Ibn Abī Shayba, *Muṣannaf*, 15: 135, 168; Ibn Ḥanbal, *Musnad*, 1: 195; trans. D. Cook, *Studies in Muslim Apocalyptic*, 4 n. 7, where other sources are indicated.

250. D. Cook, *Studies in Muslim Apocalyptic*, 4. See also Livne-Kafri, "Some Notes on the Muslim Apocalyptic Tradition," 76 n. 22.

251. Bashear, "Muslim Apocalypses," 87–92; D. Cook, "The Beginnings of Islam as an Apocalyptic Movement."

252. Bashear, "Muslim Apocalypses," 80–87.

253. Ibid., 92–98.

254. Donner, *Narratives of Islamic Origins*, 46; Ayoub, *The Crisis of Muslim History*, 145–46.

255. Ibn Hishām, *Kitāb sīrat Rasūl Allāh* (Wüstenfeld, *Das Leben Muhammed's*, 1: 1012; Guillaume, *The Life of Muhammad*, 682–63); cf. al-Ṭabarī, *Taʾrīkh* (de Goeje et al., *Annales*, I: 1815–17).

256. Ibn Hishām, *Kitāb sīrat Rasūl Allāh* (Wüstenfeld, *Das Leben Muhammed's*, 1: 1012–13; Guillaume, *Life of Muhammad*, 683).

257. Silvestre de Sacy, "Taberistanensis," 536–37.

258. Weil, *Mohammed der Prophet*, 350–51; Weil, *Historisch-kritische Einleitung in den Koran*, 43–44.

259. Weil, *Geschichte der Chalifen*, 1: 15 n. 1. Cf. Goldziher, *Muslim Studies*, 2: 261.

260. Nöldeke, *Orientalische Skizzen*, 56. See also Gilliot's critique of this position, in which he notes that even Nöldeke himself eventually came to concede the possibility of interpolations in the Qurʾān: Gilliot, "Reconsidering the Authorship of the Qurʾān," 100.

261. "Thou art mortal, and they are mortal; then on the Day of Resurrection before your Lord you shall dispute."

262. Al-Ṭabarī, *Taʾrīkh* (de Goeje et al., *Annales*, I: 1818–19; trans. al-Ṭabarī, *History of al-Ṭabarī: Volume IX*, 187–88).

263. Nöldeke, *Geschichte des Qorâns*, 198.

264. Ibid., 199–200.

265. Bell, *A Commentary on the Qurʾān*, 2: 66.

266. See O'Shaughnessy, *Muhammad's Thoughts on Death*, 14–15, 21–23.

267. Bell, *A Commentary on the Qurʾān*, 1: 102. See also O'Shaughnessy, *Muhammad's Thoughts on Death*, 56–57, 80–81.

268. Casanova, *Mohammed*, 19–20. It is unfortunate that Schwally completely ignores Casanova's important arguments regarding this passage in his revision of Nöldeke's study: Nöldeke and Schwally, *Geschichte des Qorāns*, 2: 81–84. Insofar as Schwally's discussion has continued to carry the day regarding the issue of the verse's authenticity, it is particularly regrettable that he fails to engage the most convincing arguments for the verse's secondary status, presented in Casanova's unfairly neglected study. In light of this omission, Nöldeke and Schwally should not be regarded as definitive on this particular issue.

269. Hirschfeld, *New Researches*, 136–42, esp. 137–39.

270. Two recent essays have pursued this theme, although both rather unpersuasively: Popp, "Die frühe Islamgeschichte"; see also Popp, "The Early History of Islam"; and Luxenberg, "Neudeutung"; see also Luxenberg, "A New Interpretation."

271. So also even Wansbrough acknowledges in *The Sectarian Milieu*, 145.

272. Donner, *Muhammad and the Believers*, 97, also suggests this interpretation.

273. See, e.g., Harris, *The Tübingen School*, 181–237. For more recent studies in this vein, see, e.g., Luedemann, *Opposition to Paul*; Luedemann, *Early Christianity*. For other examples involving the literary representation of apostles as a part of theological conflict and definition, see e.g., MacDonald, *The Legend and the Apostle*; Parrott, "Gnostic and Orthodox Disciples"; A. Brock, *Mary Magdalene*.

274. Lévi-Strauss, *Structural Anthropology*, 61–62; via P. Brown, *The Body and Society*, 153–54.

275. Perhaps the lament of an early Islamic tombstone (from 691) signals a late vestige of this tradition: "The greatest of misfortunes for the people of Islam is their loss of the prophet Muḥammad." Rached, Hawary, and Wiet, *Catalogue général*, 9: no. 3201. Such phrasing seems to suppose that the loss was perhaps unexpected. The translation is from Halevi, *Muhammad's Grave*, 20–21, which notes that such laments over Muhammad's death commonly appear on later tombstones as well.

276. O'Shaughnessy, *Muhammad's Thoughts on Death*, 54, 80.

277. ʿAbd al-Razzāq, *Muṣannaf*, 5: 433–35; Ibn Saʿd, *Ṭabaqāt* (Sachau, *Biographien Muhammeds*, 2.2: 53–54); al-Balādhurī, *Ansāb*, 1: 567.

278. Madelung, *The Succession to Muḥammad*, 356–60.

279. *Istoria de Mahomet* (Wolf, "The Earliest Latin Lives," 97–99); *Legend of Sergius Baḥīrā (East-Syrian)* 21 (Roggema, *The Legend of Sergius Baḥīrā*, 302–3); see also the same story in the *Legend of Sergius Baḥīrā (West-Syrian)* 9 (ibid., 332–35). Szilágyi, "The Incorruptible and Fragrant Corpse."

280. Ibn Hishām, *Kitāb sīrat Rasūl Allāh* (Wüstenfeld, *Das Leben Muhammed's*, 1: 1017–18); al-Ṭabarī, *Taʾrīkh* (de Goeje et al., *Annales*, I: 1828–30; trans. al-Ṭabarī, *History of al-Ṭabarī: Volume IX*, 200–201).

281. Ibn Saʿd, *Ṭabaqāt* (Sachau, *Biographien Muhammeds*, 2.2: 56). See also the translation in al-Ṭabarī, *History of al-Ṭabarī: Volume IX*, 200 n. 1378. ʿAbd al-Razzāq preserves a rather similar version attributed to al-Zuhrī through Maʿmar, although it differs slightly at this point, having ʿUmar (and not Muhammad himself) express the idea that Muhammad would be the last one remaining alive: ʿAbd al-Razzāq, *Muṣannaf*, 5: 437–38.

282. Ibn Hishām, *Kitāb sīrat Rasūl Allāh* (Wüstenfeld, *Das Leben Muhammed's*, 1: 1017–18); al-Ṭabarī, *Ta'rīkh* (de Goeje et al., *Annales*, I: 1828–29; trans. al-Ṭabarī, *History of al-Ṭabarī: Volume IX*, 200–201).

283. See verses signaled in Casanova, *Mohammed*, 35–41, some of which are more persuasive than others.

284. Bell, *Introduction to the Qurʾān*, 47; Bell and Watt, *Bell's Introduction to the Qurʾān*, 53.

285. E.g., Watt, "The Reliability of Ibn Ishaq's Sources," 32. See also the discussion of other similar efforts to recover the "kernel of historical fact" from these sources in Donner, *Narratives of Islamic Origins*, 16–20. For an example of how the *sīra* traditions have reinterpreted Qurʾānic eschatological traditions in order project this image of Muhammad, see now Rubin, "Muḥammad's Message."

286. Donner, *Narratives of Islamic Origins*, 64–97, esp. 85–89. In a more recent study, however, Donner draws attention also to the apparent eschatological immediacy of the primitive Islamic faith: Donner, *Muhammad and the Believers*, e.g., 78–82.

287. Donner, *Narratives of Islamic Origins*, 88, 94–97..

288. E.g., Sizgorich, *Violence and Belief*; and Halevi, *Muhammad's Grave* (which does make note of a couple of seventh-century tombstones).

289. See, e.g., C. Robinson, *Islamic Historiography*, 8–12, 19–24; M. Cook, *Muhammad*, 61–76; cf. Schweitzer, *The Quest of the Historical Jesus*, 330–403.

290. Schweitzer, *The Quest of the Historical Jesus*, 330–403.

291. Ibid., 337.

292. Donner, *Narratives of Islamic Origins*, 287.

293. Crone and Cook, *Hagarism*, 29.

294. Donner, *Narratives of Islamic Origins*, 289.

295. Ibid., 288.

296. Ibid.

297. Donner, "From Believers to Muslims," 12, 52.

298. Sellheim, "Prophet, Chalif und Geschichte," 39–46; C. Robinson, *Islamic Historiography*, 26–27, 122; Lecker, "Biographical Notes."

299. This difference is sharply articulated already by Schweitzer in the famous conclusion to his pivotal study: Schweitzer, *The Quest of the Historical Jesus*, 398–403. See also Sanders, *The Historical Figure of Jesus*, 1–9; Fredriksen, *From Jesus to Christ*; Grant, *Jesus after the Gospels*.

300. Wansbrough, *The Sectarian Milieu*, 125.

301. See, e.g., Motzki, "The *Muṣannaf* of ʿAbd al-Razzāq," 3–4, 6–7, 9, etc.; Donner, *Narratives of Islamic Origins*, esp. 25–29, 283, 287; Versteegh, *Arabic Grammar*, 48. See also, however, the thoughtful critique of Versteegh's methodological assumptions in Rippin, "Studying Early *Tafsir* Texts"; Rippin, "*Qurʾanic Studies*, Part IV," 43–45.

302. C. Robinson, *Islamic Historiography*, 53–54. See also Berg, "The Implications," 14–15; Hawting, "Review of Harald Motzki," 142.

303. Donner, *Narratives of Islamic Origins*, 283.

304. See, e.g., Meier, *A Marginal Jew*, 1: 372–433.

305. Donner, "The Sources of Islamic Conceptions of War," 43–50; Donner, *Muhammad and the Believers*, 82, 85, 88, 96–97, 143–44; D. Cook, "Muslim Apocalyptic and *Jihād*," 66; cf. Casanova, *Mohammed*.

CHAPTER 4

1. On this attribution, its history, and its inaccuracy, see now Thomson and Howard-Johnston, *The Armenian History*, 1: xxxiii–xxxviii. This publication presents a complete translation and extensive historical commentary on Sebeos's chronicle. See also Greenwood, "Sasanian Echoes," esp. 325–26.

2. See, e.g., Hoyland, *Seeing Islam*, 124–25; Thomson and Howard-Johnston, *The Armenian History*, 1: xxxv, n. 20; Greenwood, "Sasanian Echoes," 326. For reasons made clear by Thomson, "Pseudo-Sebeos" is not a possible alternative.

3. Thomson and Howard-Johnston, *Armenian History*, 1: lxxvii.

4. See the discussions in Hoyland, *Seeing Islam*, 125; Thomson and Howard-Johnston, *The Armenian History*, 1: xxxviii–xxxix; Greenwood, "Sasanian Echoes," 389.

5. Hoyland, *Seeing Islam*, 128.

6. Sebeos, *History* 42 (Abgarian, Պատմութիւն Սեբէոսի, 134).

7. Sebeos, *History* 42 (ibid., 135). Similar accounts, which depend either on Sebeos or his "Palestinian Source," can be found in Łewond, *History* 1 (Ezeantsʿ, Պատմութիւն Ղեւոնդեայ, 3–6); and Thomas Artsruni, *History* 2.4 (Patkanean, Պատմութիւն տանն Արծրունեաց, 98–103; Thomson, *History of the House of the Artsrunikʿ*, 164–69). See Thomson and Howard-Johnston, *The Armenian History*, 1: 94 n. 585; 2: 237.

8. Sebeos, *History* 42 (Abgarian, Պատմութիւն Սեբէոսի, 135–36). In Artsruni's account, Muhammad himself sends the letter to Theodore, the brother of Heraclius: Artsruni, *History* 2.4 (Patkanean, Պատմութիւն տանն Արծրունեաց, 101; Thomson, *History of the House of the Artsrunikʿ*, 167). There is a parallel Islamic tradition that Muhammad sent a letter to Heraclius, demanding that he convert to Islam or lose his lands. Although Conrad dates this letter to "the mid-Umayyad period, perhaps to early in the career of al-Zuhrī," it is clear that a basic form of this tradition was known to Sebeos in the middle of the seventh century. See Conrad, "Heraclius," 125–30.

9. Sebeos, *History* 42 (Abgarian, Պատմութիւն Սեբէոսի, 139).

10. Thomson and Howard-Johnston, *The Armenian History*, 2: 237.

11. Ibid., 1: lxv–lxxiv; Greenwood, "Sasanian Echoes," 326–74.

12. Thomson and Howard-Johnston, *The Armenian History*, 1: lxiv. See also Hoyland, *Seeing Islam*, 125–28 on Sebeos's trustworthiness.

13. Greenwood, "Sasanian Echoes," 382–88. See also the various apocalyptic texts discussed in Hoyland, *Seeing Islam*, 257–335.

14. Thomson and Howard-Johnston, *The Armenian History*, 1: lxxvi; Greenwood, "Sasanian Echoes," 383–85.

15. Sebeos, *History* 42 (Abgarian, Պատմութիւն Սեբէոսի, 139).

16. Thomson and Howard-Johnston, *The Armenian History*, 1: lxviii–lxx; 1: 102 n. 634; and 2: 238–40. See also Greenwood, "Sasanian Echoes," 365–66.

17. Thomson and Howard-Johnston, *The Armenian History*, 1: lxxvi.

18. Ibid., 2: 238; Hoyland, *Seeing Islam*, 131, 593.

19. Moshe Gil characterizes the report as describing a "cabal" in Gil, *A History of Palestine*, 61 n. 64. See also Wansbrough, *The Sectarian Milieu*, 117; Griffith, "Jews and Muslims," 87; Cameron, "Blaming the Jews," 65–66.

20. Hoyland, "Sebeos," esp. 89–90. See also, e.g., V. Déroche, "Polémique anti-judaïque," 158–59.

21. Sozomen, *Ecclesiastical History* (Hussey, *Sozomeni Ecclesiastica historia*, 2: 671–72).

22. Hoyland, "Sebeos," 91–92. See also Rubin, *Between Bible and Qurʾān*, 32–34.

23. Suermann, "Early Islam," 141–44.

24. Wasserstrom, *Between Muslim and Jew*, 51. See also Kister, "Ḥaddithū ʿan banī isrāʾīla."

25. Lewis, "An Apocalyptic Vision"; Crone and Cook, *Hagarism*, 4–5; Hoyland, *Seeing Islam*, 308–12.

26. *The Secrets of Rabbi Shimʿōn b. Yoḥai* (Jellinek, *Bet ha-midrash*, 3: 78; Reeves, *Trajectories*, 78–80, slightly modified).

27. *The Secrets of Rabbi Shimʿōn b. Yoḥai* (Jellinek, *Bet ha-midrash*, 3: 78; Reeves, *Trajectories*, 80). See also in this regard Bashear, "Riding Beasts."

28. *The Secrets of Rabbi Shimʿōn b. Yoḥai* (Jellinek, *Bet ha-midrash*, 3: 79; Reeves, *Trajectories*, 81–82).

29. *The Secrets of Rabbi Shimʿōn b. Yoḥai* (Jellinek, *Bet ha-midrash*, 3: 79–80; Reeves, *Trajectories*, 84–85).

30. Reeves, *Trajectories*, 77.

31. Hoyland, *Seeing Islam*, 311–12, 317; *Jewish Apocalypse on the Umayyads* (Lévi, "Une apocalypse judéo-arabe," 178–79).

32. As witnessed most dramatically perhaps in the early seventh-century *Sefer Zerubbabel* (Lévi, "L'Apocalypse de Zorobabel"), which is translated in Reeves, *Trajectories*, 40–66. See also Grossman, "Jerusalem in Jewish Apocalyptic Literature," 295–305; van Bekkum, "Jewish Messianic Expectations," 103–6.

33. Fleischer, "New Light on Qiliri"; Fleischer, "Solving the Qiliri Riddle." See also Dagron and Déroche, "Juifs et Chrétiens," 26–27; Yahalom, "The Temple and the City," 278–80; Grossman, "Jerusalem in Jewish Apocalyptic Literature," 300.

34. Donner, "La question du messianisme"; Bashear, "The Title '*Fārūq*'."

35. Bashear, "The Title '*Fārūq*'," 48. See also Hoyland, "Sebeos," 97.

36. *Doctrina Iacobi* V.16 (Dagron and Déroche, "Juifs et Chrétiens," 209).

37. Donner, "La question du messianisme"; cf. Crone and Cook, *Hagarism*, 5–6.

38. Donner, "From Believers to Muslims." See now also Donner, *Muhammad and the Believers*, esp. 68–77, 108–19.

39. Donner, "From Believers to Muslims," 9. See also D. Cook, "The Beginnings of Islam as an Apocalyptic Movement."

40. Donner, "From Believers to Muslims," 10–11. Hints in certain early Islamic apocalyptic traditions of a primitive self-identity as a sort of "new Israel" also could suggest such a community: Livne-Kafri, "Some Notes on the Muslim Apocalyptic Tradition," 85–86.

41. Donner, *Muhammad and the Believers*, 61–69.

42. Ibid., 87.

43. Donner, "From Believers to Muslims," 12, 14–16; Donner, *Muhammad and the Believers*, 57–58, 71–72, 203–4. Initially, the term "muslim," meaning "one who has submitted," was used in reference to Jewish and Christian members of the community as well as those who had newly converted to "monotheism" as a result of Muhammad's teaching. Over time, however, the name "muslim" came to apply primarily to these new monotheist converts. While Jewish and Christian Believers could continue to be identified as such, converts from "paganism" could no longer be known by their former confession. Consequently, "muslim," a term that originally applied to all of the Believers, slowly gravitated to these new monotheists who had renounced their former faith. When Muhammad's followers later began to distance themselves from Judaism and Christianity and establish a confessionally distinct monotheist sect, "Islam" and "Muslim" were thus the terms adopted to distinguish this new monotheism from those of the Jews and Christians it had once welcomed. See also Hoyland, "New Documentary Texts," 409–10, where something similar is proposed.

44. Kister, ". . . *Illā Bi-ḥaqqihi*. . . ."

45. Kister, "Ḥaddithū ʿan banī isrāʾīla."

46. Wansbrough, *Quranic Studies*, 55.

47. Donner, "From Believers to Muslims," 13–16; Donner, *Muhammad and the Believers*, 69–70, 75–77, 87, 134, 204, 206.

48. For text, translation, and analysis of the most important version, see Lecker, *The "Constitution of Medina."* See also Wensinck, *Muhammad and the Jews of Medina*; Watt, *Muhammad at Medina*, 221–60; Serjeant, "The *Sunnah, Jāmiʿah*"; and Donner, *Muhammad and the Believers*, 227–32.

49. Regarding the Constitution of Medina's early date, see, e.g., Watt, *Muhammad at Medina*, 225; Crone, *Slaves on Horses*, 7; Crone and Cook, *Hagarism*, 7–8; Wellhausen, "Muhammads Gemeindeordnung," 80; Caetani, *Annali dell'Islām*, 1: 402–3; and Humphreys, *Islamic History*, 92–98.

50. See also Hoyland, "Sebeos," 95; Rubin, "The 'Constitution of Medina.'" Rubin has recently expressed some doubts about the "authenticity" of the Constitution; nevertheless, he concludes that it reflects a very early conceptualization of Islamic identity in the context of the Near Eastern conquests, which identifies its inter-confessional program as especially early: Rubin, *Between Bible and Qurʾān*, 48–49.

51. Citing Donner's slight modification of Serjeant's translation: Donner, "From Believers to Muslims," 30–31; cf. Serjeant, "The *Sunnah, Jāmiʿah*," 27.

52. Donner, "From Believers to Muslims," 38. See also Donner, *Muhammad and the Believers*, 230–31.

53. See the discussion of other relevant passages in Donner, "From Believers to Muslims," 30–33.

54. See, e.g., the summaries in Watt, *Muhammad at Medina*, 192–228; and Paret, *Mohammed und der Koran*, 113–24. According to most estimations based on the traditional sources this experiment lasted roughly for Muhammad's first year in Medina.

55. Hoyland, "Sebeos," 94.

56. Donner, "From Believers to Muslims," 52, 12.

57. Ibid., 19.

58. See the complete discussion in ibid., 17–24. See also Donner, *Muhammad and the Believers*, esp. 69–71, 74–77, 111–12; and Hoyland, "Sebeos," 95.

59. Adopting Donner's translation: Donner, "From Believers to Muslims," 20. See also Comerro, "La nouvelle alliance." For a translation that renders the passage in a manner that comports with Islam's eventual confessional distinction from Judaism and Christianity, see Abdel Haleem, *The Qurʾān*, 74.

60. Donner, "From Believers to Muslims," 18; cf. Donner, *Muhammad and the Believers*, 74.

61. Donner, "From Believers to Muslims," 23–25.

62. See, e.g., Sprenger, *Das Leben und die Lehre*, 1: 21–45; Bell, *The Origin of Islam*, 12–14; Schoeps, *Theologie und Geschichte des Judenchristentums*, 334–42; Roncaglia, "Élements Ebionites et Elkésaïtes"; Lüling, *Über den Ur-Qurʾan*. Cf. Harnack, *Dogmengeschichte*, 2: 537. For more recent efforts to establish such a connection, see de Blois, "*Naṣrānī*"; Gallez, *Le messie et son prophète*; Gnilka, *Die Nazarener und der Koran*; and Peters, *Jesus and Muhammad*, 117–18, 199–200. De Blois' work in particular is a linguistic tour de force, but his efforts to connect the Qurʾānic *naṣrānī* with a specific Jewish-Christian sect described by certain early Christian heresiologists are problematic. For instance, the attempt to link the Qurʾān's apparent indication that some Christians had deified Mary with Elchasaite mythology as described by Epiphanius of Salamis is a bit of a stretch. More importantly, however, much of the information concerning these Jewish-Christian groups is taken from Epiphanius and other heresiologists, whose reports are generally regarded with deep suspicion: see, e.g., Jacobs, *Remains of the Jews*, 44–51; Cameron, "How to Read Heresiology."

63. See, e.g., Wansbrough and Hawting, *The Sectarian Milieu*, vii; Pritz, *Nazarene Jewish Christianity: From the End of the New Testament Period until Its Disappearance in the Fourth Century* (the subtitle says it all). Even Bellarmino Bagatti, whose optimism about the possibility of recovering information concerning the Jewish Christians is perhaps unrivaled, concludes that by the early fifth century Jewish Christianity had disappeared: Bagatti, *The Church from the Circumcision*, 143–47. See also the important critique of Bagatti's work raised by Taylor, *Christians and the Holy Places*, 5–47.

64. Donner, "From Believers to Muslims," 26–27. See now also Donner, *Muhammad and the Believers*, 77.

65. See Donner, "From Believers to Muslims," 42.

66. Ibid., 12 n. 2; Donner, *Muhammad and the Believers*, 212–14. To these two points should also be added a parallel geographic reorientation to focus on Arabia and the Ḥijāz as discussed in the following section. Regarding Muhammad's changing status, see Donner, "From Believers to Muslims," 34–48. Other examples of the Islamic effort to differentiate culturally from Judaism and Christianity are discussed in Kister, "'Do Not Assimilate Yourselves.'"

67. E.g., C. Robinson, *ʿAbd al-Malik*, 103. See also Hoyland, *Seeing Islam*, 551–56; Hoyland, "New Documentary Texts," 397, 409–10; Donner, *Muhammad and the Believers*, 194–224.

68. Crone and Hinds, *God's Caliph*, esp. 27–32, also locates the emergence of Muhammad's unique prophetic status at the same time, following a slightly different thread.

69. Donner, "From Believers to Muslims," 47–48; Donner, *Muhammad and the Believers*, 111–12, 249. See also Wensinck, *Concordance et indices*, s.v. "shahāda," which indicates many instances of the *shahāda* that mention only profession of God's oneness; also Kister, ". . . *Illā Bi-ḥaqqihi* . . ."; and D. Cook, "The Beginnings of Islam as an Apocalyptic Movement."

70. Bashear, "Jesus in an Early Muslim Shahāda."

71. C. Robinson, *ʿAbd al-Malik*, 77–79; Donner, *Muhammad and the Believers*, 199–202, 205, 208, 213. The inscriptions of the Dome of the Rock were most recently published with translation in Grabar, *The Shape of the Holy*, 92–99. A translation can also be found in Donner, *Muhammad and the Believers*, 233–35. See also Busse, "Monotheismus und islamische Christologie."

72. M. Cook, *The Koran*, 118–22; C. Robinson, *ʿAbd al-Malik*, 102–3.

73. S. Brock, "Syriac Views," 14; Donner, *Muhammad and the Believers*, 111.

74. Donner, "From Believers to Muslims," 43; Donner, *Muhammad and the Believers*, 222–23. See also Griffith, "The Prophet Muhammad," esp. 122–24; Reinink, "The Beginnings of Syriac Apologetic Literature," esp. 167–70.

75. John bar Penkaye, *Riš Mellē* (Mingana, *Sources syriaques*, 146*–147*; S. Brock, "North Mesopotamia," 61 [slightly modified]).

76. Ishoʿyahb III, *Letter* 14 (Duval, *Išoʿyahb Patriarchae III Liber epistularum*, 251).

77. *Continuatio* of the *Samaritan Chronicle* (Levy-Rubin, *The Continuatio*, 53, 125).

78. John of Damascus, *On Heresies* 100/101, 60–67 (PG 94: 764–73); see also Sahas, *John of Damascus on Islam*; concerning John, his family, and his account of Islam, see Hoyland, *Seeing Islam*, 480–89.

79. Hoyland, *Seeing Islam*, 488.

80. Donner, *Muhammad and the Believers*, 176–77, 180–81, 192–93, 222.

81. Donner, "From Believers to Muslims," 48–52.

82. Ibid., 50–51.

83. Donner, *Muhammad and the Believers*, 106–18, 130. On the relative absence of destruction in the archaeological record, see esp. Pentz, *The Invisible Conquest*; Magness, *The Archaeology of the Early Islamic Settlement*; and Walmsley, *Early Islamic Syria*.

84. Donner, "From Believers to Muslims," 49; Donner, *Muhammad and the Believers*, 214–15. See also Becker, "Zur Geschichte"; and Mittwoch, *Zur Entstehungsgeschichte*.

85. Adams, "Reflections on the Work of John Wansbrough," 87.

86. Hawting, *The Idea of Idolatry*, e.g., 11.

87. Crone, "The Religion of the Qurʾānic Pagans," esp. 191–200.

88. Donner, "From Believers to Muslims," 51–52; Donner, *Muhammad and the Believers*, 115. See also Creswell and Allen, *A Short Account*, 65–67. In Jerusalem, the Church of the Ascension on the Mount of Olives was similarly appropriated and transformed into a mosque: Murphy-O'Connor, *The Holy Land*, 124–25. Likewise, during the early Islamic period, a *miḥrāb* was added to the Church of the Kathisma, an early Nativity shrine dedicated to the Virgin Mary midway between Jerusalem and Bethlehem. Nevertheless, the most

recent excavations indicate that this feature was added in the eighth or ninth century, at which time the building still remained in use by Christians. Whether or not the early Believers may have used this space in common with the Christians of Jerusalem during the seventh century remains uncertain, however. See Di Segni, "Christian Epigraphy," 248–50; and also Avner, "ירושלים, מר אליאס – כנסיית הקתיסמה"; Avner, "The Recovery of the Kathisma Church."

89. Busse, "'Omar b. al-Ḥaṭṭāb"; Busse, "'Omar's Image"; Busse, "Die 'Umar-Moschee."

90. Bashear, "Qibla Musharriqa," 267–68, 274–77. For more on the Virgin's tomb and its *miḥrāb*, which appears to have been added in the seventeenth century, see Murphy-O'Connor, *The Holy Land*, 129–31; Bagatti, Piccirillo, and Prodomo, *New Discoveries*, 43–44.

91. Bashear, "Qibla Musharriqa," 267–68, 277–78.

92. Ibid., 268, 280–81.

93. On al-Khallāl's importance and concerning the *responsa*, see Melchert, *The Formation*, 137–56; and M. Cook, *Commanding Right*, 87–113.

94. Al-Khallāl, *Ahl al-milal*, 1: 54–55. Ibn Ḥanbal's *responsa* on this topic occupy 1: 53–62 of this collection. The translation is from Sizgorich, *Violence and Belief*, 242, where three such *responsa* are translated.

95. Al-Khallāl, *Ahl al-milal*, 1: 56.

96. Sizgorich, *Violence and Belief*, 241–71.

97. E.g., ibid., 267.

98. Conrad, "The Arabs," 697–98.

99. McGinn, *The Meanings*, 10; cited in Donner, *Muhammad and the Believers*, 97, 248.

100. Sebeos, *History* 42 (Abgarian, Պատմութիւն Սեբէոսի, 135).

101. *Chronicle of 1234* (Chabot, *Chronicon ad annum Christi 1234*, 1: 227–28).

102. Hoyland, "Sebeos," 97, citing Hoyland's translation. Cf. *sūra* 5:21.

103. Translation from Donner, *Muhammad and the Believers*, 81.

104. Abdel Haleem, *The Qur'ān*, 208, slightly modified: Abdel Haleem writes instead, "'My righteous servants will inherit the earth,'" which disguises the connection to the biblical land of Israel. Ps. 37:29 in the NRSV reads: "The righteous shall inherit the land [אֶרֶץ], and live in it forever."

105. Al-Ṭabarī, *Ta'rīkh* (de Goeje et al., *Annales*, I: 2254, 2284, 2289). See also Rubin, *Between Bible and Qur'ān*, 62–63; Ps.-Wāqidī, *Futūḥ al-Shām*, 1: 145.

106. Rubin, *Between Bible and Qur'ān*, 11–35, esp. 35. Elsewhere Rubin remarks of Sebeos that his account does not "indicate how Islam began in reality"; rather, it merely reflects "how its beginning was envisioned by Muslim historiographers. The notion that the spread of Islam into Syria represented a common Jewish-Arab messianic enterprise is only a retrospective apologetic device designed to legitimise the Islamic conquest of the Promised Land." Ibid., 49–52, esp. 52. This rather cautious position is certainly acceptable, so long as one is willing to recognize (as Rubin seems to be) that, even if this self-image is not "original," it is nevertheless extremely early, forming the earliest Islamic

self-conception that can be recovered from the sources. Furthermore, such a conclusion requires that this Islamic self-image must have been well in place already before 650, so that it could have been transmitted to Sebeos through his Palestinian Source. The issue seems to hinge partly on how one understands Sebeos's report that the Jews and Arabs joined together in Arabia. While Rubin appears to assume that Arabia here indicates the Ḥijāz, it seems more likely that Sebeos, or more precisely, the author of his Palestinian Source, had in mind Roman Arabia, that is, territory today in Jordan and northwestern Saudi Arabia. Even if Muhammad himself and many of his followers did originally hail from the Ḥijāz, it is certainly possible that his movement's interactions with Judaism began in this area, rather than in "Medina."

107. Donner, *Muhammad and the Believers*, esp. 97; see also Donner, "The Sources of Islamic Conceptions of War," 43–49; and D. Cook, "Muslim Apocalyptic and *Jihād*," esp. 66.

108. Sizgorich, however, remarks rather oddly that the connection between the Arab conquest of the Near East and the teachings of Muhammad is "anything but clear, and that the link between the two was something established only later on by the early Islamic *umma*," noting also that "if the Prophet foresaw the conquests, he never said so": Sizgorich, *Violence and Belief*, 144, 146; cf. 153. Sizgorich cites in support of his position Fred Donner, who nevertheless in the pages of *The Early Islamic Conquests* indicated by Sizgorich asserts quite to the contrary that his book "presents the thesis that Muḥammad's career and the doctrines of Islam revolutionized both the ideological bases and the political structures of Arabian society, giving rise for the first time to a state capable of organizing and executing an expansionist movement": Donner, *The Early Islamic Conquests*, 8; see also 55–82. Donner further writes, "The Islamic conquest of the Near East cannot be viewed, then, as something separate from the career of Muḥammad. . . . It must be seen as an organic outgrowth of Muḥammad's teachings": ibid., 90. Moreover, as noted above, Donner suggests that the eschatological urgency of Muhammad's preaching directly inspired these conquests. Furthermore, Donner explicitly identifies the expansion into Syria with Muhammad's leadership, and even Watt identifies such a "northern policy" as characteristic of Muhammad's final years, which aimed at expansion into Roman Syria: Donner, *The Early Islamic Conquests*, 96–111; and Watt, *Muhammad at Medina*, 105–17.

109. Donner, *Muhammad and the Believers*, 16, 97, 125. See also Alexander, *The Byzantine Apocalyptic Tradition*, esp. 151–84.

110. Donner, *Muhammad and the Believers*, 81–82, 96–97, 125, 143–44; quotations at 97 and 144.

111. Ibn al-Murajjā, *Faḍāʾil Bayt al-Maqdis*, 160; trans. Livne-Kafri, "Jerusalem in Early Islam," 384.

112. Livne-Kafri, "Some Notes on the Muslim Apocalyptic Tradition," 82; Livne-Kafri, "The Muslim Traditions 'In Praise of Jerusalem,'" 175–77. See also Elad, "The Coastal Cities of Palestine"; Gil, *A History of Palestine*, 57–60, 64.

113. Donner, *Muhammad and the Believers*, 108–10.

114. Ibid., xii.

115. Ibid., 80–82.

116. Ibid., 85.

117. See the discussion of this word and its meaning in an eschatological context in D. Cook, *Studies in Muslim Apocalyptic*, 271–72.

118. See, e.g., Meier, *A Marginal Jew*, 2: 237–508, esp. 240.

119. Regarding the religious authority of the early "caliphs," see Crone and Hinds, *God's Caliph*.

120. *Sūra* 2:142–44; trans. from Hoyland, *Seeing Islam*, 560.

121. Ibn Hishām, *Kitāb sīrat Rasūl Allāh* (Wüstenfeld, *Das Leben Muhammed's*, 1: 381); al-Ṭabarī, *Ta'rīkh* (de Goeje et al., *Annales*, I: 1280).

122. See Buhl, *Das Leben Muhammeds*, 216–18; Watt, *Muhammad at Medina*, 198–202.

123. Ibn Hishām, *Kitāb sīrat Rasūl Allāh* (Wüstenfeld, *Das Leben Muhammed's*, 1: 190). Note also the similar tradition discussed below, in which Kaʿb al-Aḥbār, the legendary early Jewish convert to Islam, tried to persuade ʿUmar to build the Jerusalem mosque on the north side of the Temple Mount so that worshippers could face both its Rock and Mecca at the same time. ʿUmar of course refused Kaʿb's request.

124. Rubin, however, suggests that such traditions were designed to hide the embarrassment that Muhammad, after originally praying toward the Kaʿba, for a time diverted his prayers toward Jerusalem: Rubin, "The Kaʿba." Neuwirth argues more persuasively that these traditions are evidence of an older Jerusalemite *qibla*: Neuwirth, "Erste Qibla—Fernstes Masǧid?," 232–38.

125. Ibn Hishām, *Kitāb sīrat Rasūl Allāh* (Wüstenfeld, *Das Leben Muhammed's*, 1: 294–95).

126. Wāsiṭī, *Faḍā'il al-Bayt al-Muqaddas*, 51; trans. Hasson, "Muslim Literature in Praise of Jerusalem," 183. Cf. Ibn al-Murajjā, *Faḍā'il Bayt al-Maqdis*, 98; trans. Livne-Kafri, "Jerusalem: The Navel of the Earth," 68–69.

127. See Rubin, "Between Arabia and the Holy Land," 352 and the sources cited there.

128. Buhl, *Das Leben Muhammeds*, 217: "sicher niemand solche erdichtet hätte, wenn die Gebetsrichtung damals wirklich dieselbe wie die spätere kanonische gewesen wäre."

129. Also much debated in this context was whether the prophets prior to Muhammad had Jerusalem's Rock or Mecca's Kaʿba as their *qibla*, a highly disputed issue: Kister, "Sanctity Joint and Divided," 52–65.

130. Bashear, "Qibla Musharriqa," 282.

131. Ibid., 269–73.

132. Andræ, *Die person Muhammeds*, 293; Andræ, "Der Ursprung des Islams," 152; Andræ, *Les origines de l'Islam*, 10–11; Buhl, *Das Leben Muhammeds*, 218. Barthold, who does not appear to engage Andrae's earlier hypothesis, supposes that the earliest Muslims believed that Muhammad's night journey took him to a heavenly sanctuary somewhere in the east, and thus they directed their prayers in this direction. Also, because the earliest mosques were entered by a western door, Barthold concludes that they must have faced east. Barthold, "Die Orientierung." Regarding the early tradition of Muhammad's night journey to a heavenly mosque, cf. Busse, "Jerusalem in the Story of Muḥammad's Night Journey," 35–37.

133. Even Bell was forced to acknowledge this problem in his rather ironically titled *The Origin of Islam in Its Christian Environment*: "there is no good evidence of any seats of Christianity in the Hijāz or in the near neighbourhood of Mecca or even of Medina." Bell, *The Origin of Islam*, 42–43. Likewise, Peters, *Muhammad and the Origins of Islam*, 1: "there were Christians at Gaza, and Christians and Jews in the Yemen, but none of either so far as we know at Mecca." See also Hawting, *The Idea of Idolatry*, 14–16.

134. Moffett, *A History of Christianity in Asia*, 1: 279–81; Gillman and Klimkeit, *Christians in Asia*, 82–86. Griffith, *The Church in the Shadow of the Mosque*, 8, notes concerning the spread of Christianity into the Ḥijāz that "while the documentation for this activity is sparse, it is not nonexistent." Nevertheless, Griffith does not here provide any references to such evidence outside of inference from the Islamic tradition.

135. Osman, "Pre-Islamic Arab Converts to Christianity."

136. Wansbrough, *The Sectarian Milieu*, 18, 22; see also 5–6, 17–20, 40, 43.

137. Sharon, "The Umayyads as *Ahl al-Bayt*."

138. Sharon, "The Birth of Islam in the Holy Land," 230–32, quotation at 232. Barthold's observation regarding the western entrance of the earliest mosques could also support this hypothesis: Barthold, "Die Orientierung," 246–48.

139. Hoyland, *Seeing Islam*, 565 n. 89 proposed the idea of a converted church, citing in support of this position Beno Rothenberg's suggestion that the structure was "a 'symbolic' early Christian church": Rothenberg, *Timna*, 221–22. Nevertheless, Hoyland seems to have overlooked that Rothenberg later adopted Sharon's position that the building was indeed a mosque: Rothenberg, "Early Islamic Copper Smelting," 3–4. Moreover, in the excavation report for the site, the excavators observe that "while one might suggest that this was a symbolic open church, it would be the only such example in the world." Sharon, Avner, and Nahlieli, "An Early Islamic Mosque," 113.

140. The main sources are cited in Sharon, "The Birth of Islam in the Holy Land," 230; see also Crone and Cook, *Hagarism*, 24–25.

141. Jacob of Edessa, *Letter 14 to John the Stylite*, British Library, Add. 12,172, fol. 124a; trans. Crone and Cook, *Hagarism*, 173 n. 30; and (slightly modified) Hoyland, *Seeing Islam*, 565–66.

142. Could Jacob's *kʿbtʾ* instead refer to the *Qubbat al-Ṣakhra*, the Dome of the Rock, on which construction had just recently begun when he wrote?

143. Al-Balādhurī, *Futūḥ al-buldān*, 276; al-Ṭabarī, *Taʾrīkh* (de Goeje et al., *Annales*, I: 2488–92). See Hoyland, *Seeing Islam*, 561–62, where the sources are discussed.

144. King, "Al-Bazdawī on the Qibla," 15–17, 36. See also Hoyland, *Seeing Islam*, 562 n. 75.

145. Hoyland, *Seeing Islam*, 567.

146. Halevi, *Muhammad's Grave*, 189.

147. Imbert, "La nécropole islamique."

148. Halevi, *Muhammad's Grave*, 190.

149. Cf. Elad, "Why Did ʿAbd al-Malik Build," 34, 54; Elad, *Medieval Jerusalem*, 54.

150. E.g., Wāsiṭī, *Faḍāʾil al-Bayt al-Muqaddas*, 45–46. Hasson, "Muslim Literature in Praise of Jerusalem," 175. See various other references signaled in Elad, *Medieval Jerusalem*, 30 n. 34.

151. See, e.g., Crone and Cook, *Hagarism*, esp. 21–26; Crone, *Meccan Trade*, esp. 186–99; Hawting, "The Origins of the Muslim Sanctuary at Mecca"; Hawting, *The Idea of Idolatry*, 10–13.

152. Crone and Cook, *Hagarism*, 173 n. 29.

153. Bashear, "Qibla Musharriqa," 268.

154. Hirschberg, "The Sources of Moslem Tradition," quotation at 321. Nevertheless, see also Goitein, "The Sanctity of Jerusalem," which combines the findings of two earlier studies on this topic.

155. Kister, "'You Shall Only Set Out,'" 173, where numerous references to various collections transmitting this *ḥadīth* are given.

156. Ibid., 174–78. For more details concerning these and other minor shrines, see Kister, "Sanctity Joint and Divided," esp. 18–49.

157. Kister, "'You Shall Only Set Out,'" 178–81, esp. 179–80.

158. Ibid., 183–84.

159. Ibid., 184–86. See also C. Robinson, *ʿAbd al-Malik*, 98.

160. Kister, "'You Shall Only Set Out,'" 181–82.

161. Ibid., 193–96.

162. Abdel Haleem, *The Qurʾān*, 14.

163. Bashear, "Qurʾān 2:114 and Jerusalem," 215–22.

164. For an example of this older view, see Sivan, "The Beginnings of the *Faḍāʾil al-Quds* Literature."

165. Kister, "A Comment on the Antiquity." See also Juynboll, *Muslim Tradition*, 74, 162–63, esp. n. 4; Elad, *Medieval Jerusalem*, 13–22, 162; Elad, "The Muslim View of Jerusalem," 365–67; Sharon, "Praises of Jerusalem"; and D. Cook, *Studies in Muslim Apocalyptic*, 54–55, 172–73, 177, all of which also argue that many of these traditions very likely date to the first Islamic century.

166. Wāsiṭī, *Faḍāʾil al-Bayt al-Muqaddas*, 22–23; Ibn al-Murajjā, *Faḍāʾil Bayt al-Maqdis*, 147; trans. Livne-Kafri, "Jerusalem: The Navel of the Earth," 47.

167. Kister, "A Comment on the Antiquity," 185. D. Cook, *Studies in Muslim Apocalyptic*, 172–73 also identifies this as an early tradition.

168. Kister, "A Comment on the Antiquity," 185–86. See also Elad, *Medieval Jerusalem*, 162; Livne-Kafri, "A Note on Some Traditions," 80–83; Livne-Kafri, "Some Notes on the Muslim Apocalyptic Tradition," 84; Livne-Kafri, "Jerusalem in Early Islam," 384–85; Sharon, "Praises of Jerusalem," 59–66; and D. Cook, *Studies in Muslim Apocalyptic*, 54–55, which similarly date these Temple traditions to the first Islamic century.

169. See, e.g., Wāsiṭī, *Faḍāʾil al-Bayt al-Muqaddas*, 59, 69, 71, 86; Ibn al-Murajjā, *Faḍāʾil Bayt al-Maqdis*, 63, 160, 231. See also Livne-Kafri, "A Note on Some Traditions," 78–80; Livne-Kafri, "Some Notes on the Muslim Apocalyptic Tradition," 81–82; Livne-Kafri, "Jerusalem in Early Islam," 384.

170. See esp. Livne-Kafri, "Jerusalem in Early Islam," as well as Livne-Kafri, "Some Notes on the Muslim Apocalyptic Tradition," and Livne-Kafri, "A Note on Some Traditions."

171. Ibn al-Murajjā, *Faḍāʾil Bayt al-Maqdis*, 88, 236. See also D. Cook, *Studies in Muslim Apocalyptic*, 172–78.

172. Al-Ṭabarī, *Jamʿī*, 16: 212; Wāsiṭī, *Faḍāʾil al-Bayt al-Muqaddas*, 70–71; Ibn al-Murajjā, *Faḍāʾil Bayt al-Maqdis*, 104.

173. Ibn al-Murajjā, *Faḍāʾil Bayt al-Maqdis*, 111, 240, 261; Wāsiṭī, *Faḍāʾil al-Bayt al-Muqaddas*, 88–89.

174. Ibn al-Murajjā, *Faḍāʾil Bayt al-Maqdis*, 254.

175. Ibid., 210, 215–17, 219; Wāsiṭī, *Faḍāʾil al-Bayt al-Muqaddas*, 62–63. See also D. Cook, *Studies in Muslim Apocalyptic*, 173–75.

176. Ibn al-Murajjā, *Faḍāʾil Bayt al-Maqdis*, 93, 211; Wāsiṭī, *Faḍāʾil al-Bayt al-Muqaddas*, 40, 92–93. See also D. Cook, *Studies in Muslim Apocalyptic*, 177.

177. Ibn al-Murajjā, *Faḍāʾil Bayt al-Maqdis*, 209; Wāsiṭī, *Faḍāʾil al-Bayt al-Muqaddas*, 54; trans. Livne-Kafri, "Jerusalem in Early Islam," 399, where other sources are indicated at n. 90.

178. Ibn al-Murajjā, *Faḍāʾil Bayt al-Maqdis*, 63–64; Wāsiṭī, *Faḍāʾil al-Bayt al-Muqaddas*, 86; trans. Livne-Kafri, "Jerusalem in Early Islam," 385.

179. Ibn Saʿd, *Ṭabaqāt* (Sachau, *Biographien Muhammeds*, 1.1: 107); trans. Livne-Kafri, "Jerusalem in Early Islam," 385–86.

180. There is some ambiguity concerning the date of Moschus's death, and while his death in 619 is a possibility, 634 seems more likely. See Di Berardino, *Patrology*, 301–3; and Louth, "Did John Moschus Really Die in Constantinople?" The passage in question is also discussed in Hoyland, *Seeing Islam*, 61–65.

181. John Moschus, *Spiritual Meadow (Georgian Version)*, Appendix, 19 (Abulaże, იოანე მოსხი, 100–102), quotation at 100. Abulaże's text is reproduced with French translation and commentary in Flusin, "L'esplanade du Temple," 19–21.

182. Regarding the date of the material in this appended collection, see Garitte, "Histoires édifiantes géorgiennes," 403–6; and Flusin, "L'esplanade du Temple," 18–19.

183. Sebeos, *History* 43 (Abgarian, Պատմութիւն Սեբէոսի, 139–40). See also Busse, "ʿOmar b. al-Ḥaṭṭāb."

184. Anastasius of Sinai, *Narrationes* C3 (Flusin, "L'esplanade du Temple," 22–31); see also Hoyland, *Seeing Islam*, 101.

185. Adomnán, *De locis sanctis* 1.I.14 (Bieler, *Itineraria*, 186).

186. Theophanes, *Chronicle* (de Boor, *Theophanis chronographia*, 1: 339); Agapius, *Chronicle* (Vasiliev, *Kitab al-ʿUnvan / Histoire universelle*, 3: 454, 475); Michael the Syrian, *Chronicle* 11.7 (Chabot, *Chronique de Michel le Syrien*, 4: 419–20); *Chronicle of 1234* (Chabot, *Chronicon ad annum Christi 1234*, 1: 255). See also Busse, "ʿOmar b. al-Ḥaṭṭāb."

187. *The Secrets of Rabbi Shimʿōn b. Yoḥai* (Jellinek, *Bet ha-midrash*, 3: 79); *Jewish Apocalypse on the Umayyads* (Lévi, "Une apocalypse judéo-arabe," 178–79).

188. See Sharon, "Praises of Jerusalem," 59–66; Elad, *Medieval Jerusalem*, 161–62; and D. Cook, *Studies in Muslim Apocalyptic*, 54–55, which all note that the traditions signaling this connection almost certainly date to the first Islamic century. See also Rubin, *Between Bible and Qurʾān*, 19–20; Hawting, *The First Dynasty of Islam*, 60–61; Crone and Cook, *Hagarism*, 10; Flusin, *Saint Anastase*, 2: 408; V. Déroche, "Polémique anti-judaïque," 158. Likewise, Busse and Oleg Grabar conclude that the Dome of the Rock was built as a successor to the Jewish Temple: Busse, "The Sanctity of Jerusalem," 454–60; Grabar, "The

Umayyad Dome of the Rock." Regarding ʿAbd al-Malik's intent, see also Soucek, "The Temple of Solomon"; Busse, "Monotheismus und islamische Christologie"; Busse, "Tempel, Grabeskirche und Ḥaram."

189. See, e.g., the sources discussed in Goldziher, *Muslim Studies*, 2: 44–46; Goitein, "The Sanctity of Jerusalem," 135–38; Elad, *Medieval Jerusalem*, 52–54.

190. See C. Robinson, *ʿAbd al-Malik*, 99; Kister, "'You Shall Only Set Out,'" 193–96.

191. Text and translation of the relevant passage from Sibṭ b. al-Jawzī's *Mirʾāt al-Zamān* with extensive analysis can be found in Elad, "Why Did ʿAbd al-Malik Build." Much of this publication is reproduced in Elad, *Medieval Jerusalem*, 51–61, which lacks the Arabic text, however.

192. Elad, *Medieval Jerusalem*, 51; Sharon, "Praises of Jerusalem," 60. See also Elad, "Pilgrims and Pilgrimage," esp. 300–302.

193. Elad, *Medieval Jerusalem*, 55.

194. Wāsiṭī, *Faḍāʾil al-Bayt al-Muqaddas*, 82–83. Wāsiṭī's account is translated in Sharon, "Praises of Jerusalem," 60.

195. Sharon, "Praises of Jerusalem," esp. 64–65.

196. Mishnah, Moed, Yoma 5:1–2 (Blackman, *Mishnayot*, 2: 293–95); cf. Jerusalem Talmud, Yoma 5:3; Babylonian Talmud, Yoma 52b, 53b, 54b.

197. *Itinerarium Burdigalense* (Geyer, *Itineraria*, 16).

198. Sharon, "Praises of Jerusalem," 64.

199. Ibid., 65.

200. Ibid., 59, 62–63.

201. Wāsiṭī, *Faḍāʾil al-Bayt al-Muqaddas*, 78; see also Kister, "'You Shall Only Set Out,'" 195.

202. Van Ess, "ʿAbd al-Malik," 93–96.

203. Rosen-Ayalon, *The Early Islamic Monuments*, 46–69.

204. Ibn Kathīr, *Al-Bidāyah*, 8: 280–81; trans. Elad, *Medieval Jerusalem*, 57. See also Elad, "Why Did ʿAbd al-Malik Build," 51–52; Donner, *Muhammad and the Believers*, 202.

205. As suggested also by Donner, *Muhammad and the Believers*, 125.

206. D. Cook, *Studies in Muslim Apocalyptic*, 172–73.

207. Wāsiṭī, *Faḍāʾil al-Bayt al-Muqaddas*, 46; Ibn al-Murajjā, *Faḍāʾil Bayt al-Maqdis*, 198–99; trans. Hasson, "Muslim Literature in Praise of Jerusalem," 181; Livne-Kafri, "Burial in the Holy Land," 421.

208. Wāsiṭī, *Faḍāʾil al-Bayt al-Muqaddas*, 77–79; Ibn al-Murajjā, *Faḍāʾil Bayt al-Maqdis*, 139–40.

209. Kister, "A Comment on the Antiquity," 185–86, citing Ibn Ḥajar al-Haythamī, *Al-Ṣawāʿiq*, 32, and an anonymous *Life of the Prophets* in MS British Museum 1510, f. 250a.

210. Wāsiṭī, *Faḍāʾil al-Bayt al-Muqaddas*, 102; trans. Hasson, "Muslim Literature in Praise of Jerusalem," 179. Suleiman Mourad interprets the *qāṣṣ*'s remarks as his interpretation of the Qurʾānic verse in question, which offers an alternative to the tradition of understanding this verse as a reference to Muhammad's Night Journey. See Mourad, "The Symbolism of Jerusalem," 96–97.

211. Hirschberg, "The Sources of Moslem Tradition," 335–42, esp. 341.

212. Ibn Saʿd, *Ṭabaqāt* (Sachau, *Biographien Muhammeds*, 1.2: 87). Concerning Kaʾb and his status in the early tradition, see, e.g., Rubin, *Between Bible and Qurʾān*, 13–19.

213. See, e.g., Humphreys, *Muʿawiya*, 3–10, 15–19; Hawting, *The First Dynasty of Islam*, 2–3, 11–18; Crone, *Slaves on Horses*, 3–8; Hodgson, *The Venture of Islam*, 247–51.

214. E.g., Goldziher, *Muslim Studies*, 2: 44–47; Caetani, *Annali dell'Islām*, 3: 773; Elad, "Why Did ʿAbd al-Malik Build," 40–48.

215. Goldziher, *Muslim Studies*, 2: 44–47. See also Besant and Palmer, *Jerusalem*, 80–86; Wellhausen, *The Arab Kingdom and Its Fall*, 212–16; Caetani, *Annali dell'Islām*, 3: 773.

216. Goitein, "The Sanctity of Palestine"; Goitein, "The Historical Background." These two articles form the basis of Goitein, "The Sanctity of Jerusalem."

217. Goitein, "The Sanctity of Jerusalem," 138.

218. Ibid., 147.

219. Elad, *Medieval Jerusalem*, 158–59.

220. E.g., Hirschberg, "The Sources of Moslem Tradition," 319–21; Grabar, "The Umayyad Dome of the Rock," 36, 45; Busse, "Der Islam und die biblischen Kultstätten," 124; Busse, "The Sanctity of Jerusalem," 454; Kessler, "ʿAbd al-Malik's Inscription," 11; Peters, *Jerusalem and Mecca*, 94–95; Rosen-Ayalon, *The Early Islamic Monuments*, 14; Gil, *A History of Palestine*, 93 n. 105.

221. Goldziher, *Muslim Studies*, 2: 45 n. 1, citing Goitein in support.

222. Elad, *Medieval Jerusalem*, 147–63.

223. Cf. Hirschberg, "The Sources of Moslem Tradition," 317.

224. Elad, *Medieval Jerusalem*, 163.

225. Elad, "Why Did ʿAbd al-Malik Build," 40–46.

226. Goitein, "The Sanctity of Jerusalem"; Kister, "'You Shall Only Set Out,'" 188–91; Kister, "Sanctity Joint and Divided," 33–35; Livne-Kafri, "The Early *Šiʿa*." The fact that Eutychius was a Christian in no way secures the neutrality of his report; undoubtedly he is dependent on an Islamic source for this information.

227. Elad, "Why Did ʿAbd al-Malik Build," 42–48.

228. Elad's most recent article, "ʿAbd al-Malik," does not actually advance the discussion much beyond his previous arguments. In the end, Elad's position still hinges on al-Yaʿqūbi's testimony from the late ninth century, which seems to be grounded more in polemic than in actual history. Elad notes a few additional sources that echo the reports of circumambulation in the Dome of the Rock (which, although attributed to earlier authorities, appear only in later sources), and he further adds the testimony of Sibṭ b. al-Jawzī's elaborate descriptions of the early rituals practiced in the Dome of the Rock. Yet these rather anomalous rituals do not reflect the practices of the *ḥajj*, which if they did might support Elad's contention. Instead, as we have noted above, these ritual practices appear to be connected with eschatological ideas of the Dome as an ersatz Temple that derive from the beliefs of the primitive community (connections that Elad does not seem to dispute) and not from any alleged effort on ʿAbd al-Malik's part to manufacture a rival to the Meccan pilgrimage. If the latter were the case, one would expect the rituals associated with the Dome to mimic more closely the rituals of *ḥajj*. But the fact that they

instead connect so strongly with the earliest beliefs of the community of the Believers indicates an entirely different basis for the Dome's construction and its religious significance. Indeed, it would seem that Elad comes to his position only by assuming that the traditional practices of the Meccan *ḥajj* are in fact primitive and thus by consequence any deviant practices that could potentially rival the *ḥajj* must be secondary and designed to challenge it. Likewise, Elad seems to accept much of the anti-Umayyad propaganda of the later historical tradition as factual. Yet as discussed below, it is not at all clear that the Meccan pilgrimage was an established practice in formative Islam prior to the beginning of the eighth century, while alternatively there is good reason to suspect that the early ritual practices observed in the Dome, as described by Sibṭ b. al-Jawzī, are in fact primitive.

229. C. Robinson, *ʿAbd al-Malik*, 96.

230. Ibid., 96, 100–104.

231. Ibid., 95–96.

232. Kister, "'You Shall Only Set Out,'" esp. 184–88; Kister, "Sanctity Joint and Divided," esp. 60–65.

233. Wansbrough, *Quranic Studies*, esp. 43–84, 122–27; Wansbrough, *The Sectarian Milieu*, esp. 15–24, 38–45, 98–129. See also Rippin, "Literary Analysis of Qurʾān," 153–63; Adams, "Reflections on the Work of John Wansbrough," 78–89; Berg, "The Methods and Theories of John Wansbrough," 4–11; Hawting, "John Wansbrough, Islam, and Monotheism," 29–36.

234. Wansbrough, *Quranic Studies*, 43–56, 122–48.

235. Ibid., 179.

236. Crone and Cook, *Hagarism*, 3–26.

237. Crone, *Meccan Trade*, 196–230. Note, however, that Crone has recently modified her position, allowing that the Arabs, including Muhammad's tribe, the Quraysh, may have traded in leather goods destined for the Roman army. While there is a possibility that these traders were based in Mecca, she concludes that this remains unlikely. See Crone, "Quraysh and the Roman Army."

238. Nevo and Koren, "The Origins of the Muslim Descriptions"; Nevo, "Towards a Prehistory"; Koren and Nevo, "Methodological Approaches," 100–106; see also the inscriptions published in Nevo, Cohen, and Heftman, *Ancient Arabic Inscriptions*. Nevertheless, see also the sharp critique of these studies in Hoyland, "The Content and Context of Early Arabic Inscriptions."

239. Crone, "How Did the Quranic Pagans Make a Living?": "All in all, the quranic passages addressed to or concerned with *mushrikūn* take us to a mixed economy in which the cultivation of grain, grapes, olives and date palms was combined with the rearing of sheep, goats, camels, cows, oxen and other animals, and also with maritime activity, at least in part for fishing. . . . The metaphors testify to a well-developed system of keeping written accounts, suggesting a community of some sophistication for all its rural setting. A high level of literacy is presupposed" (397). See also Crone, *Meccan Trade*, 198–99, n. 134.

240. Watt, *Muhammad at Mecca*, 2.

241. Hawting, "The Origins of the Muslim Sanctuary at Mecca." See also Hawting, "The Disappearance and Rediscovery"; Hawting, "'We Were Not Ordered.'" Cf. Wansbrough, *The Sectarian Milieu*, 47–48.

242. See Wensinck, *The Ideas of the Western Semites*, esp. 19, 35–37, 41; Hirschberg, "The Sources of Moslem Tradition," 333, 342; Livne-Kafri, "Jerusalem: The Navel of the Earth."

243. Hawting, *The Idea of Idolatry*, 11.

244. Ibid., 13.

245. E.g., Donner, "Review of Hawting, *The Idea of Idolatry*"; Hoyland, "Review of Hawting, *The Idea of Idolatry*"; Madelung, "Review of Hawting, *The Idea of Idolatry*." See also Rippin, "Review of Hawting, *The Idea of Idolatry*." Walid Saleh's insistence that Hawting's study is methodologically flawed because it adopts Wansbrough's perspective on the emergence of a Ḥijāzī nostalgia without simultaneously embracing his rather late dating of the Qurʾān is not persuasive. According to Wansbrough, the Qurʾān in itself lacks a distinctive historical context, and as a result the interpretive tradition invented a context in the Ḥijāz. An earlier date for the Qurʾānic text does not seem to preclude this interpretive process. Saleh, "Review of Hawting, *The Idea of Idolatry*." One should also see the response to Saleh's review by Christopher Melchert, which is illuminating on a host of issues related to the critical study of formative Islam: Melchert, "Reply to Saleh on Hawting."

246. Hawting, *The Idea of Idolatry*, 14–16. See also Wansbrough, *Quranic Studies*, 50–51; Wansbrough, *The Sectarian Milieu*, 5–6, 17–22, 39–49; Bell, *The Origin of Islam*, 42–43; Peters, *Muhammad and the Origins of Islam*, 1. On the expulsion of the Jews, see, e.g., Ibn Hishām, *Kitāb sīrat Rasūl Allāh* (Wüstenfeld, *Das Leben Muhammed's*, 1: 779–80).

247. Hawting, "John Wansbrough, Islam, and Monotheism," esp. 24–27, 36. Cf. Wansbrough, *The Sectarian Milieu*, 44–45.

248. Crone and Cook, *Hagarism*, 21–22. It is true, as Crone and Cook note, that *sūra* 44:24 refers to Mecca, followed by mention of those who had barred the Believers from worship in "the Sacred Mosque," but no shrine is specifically identified in Mecca.

249. As suggested, e.g., in Crone and Cook, *Hagarism*, 24.

250. Rubin, *Between Bible and Qurʾān*, 37; see also 61–63, 89–95, 233–39. See also Wansbrough, *Quranic Studies*, e.g., 53–58, 62, 72, 79, 122–26, 179.

251. Rubin, *Between Bible and Qurʾān*, 38–46.

252. Ibid., 46–48.

253. Van Ess, "ʿAbd al-Malik," 100. See also Busse, "Jerusalem and Mecca," which nonetheless assumes the priority of the Kaʿba seemingly from the beginning.

254. Bashear, "Abraham's Sacrifice," 265. See also Calder, "From Midrash to Scripture."

255. Bashear, "Ḥanīfiyya and Ḥajj."

256. Bashear, "Yemen in Early Islam." See also Hawting, *The First Dynasty of Islam*, 6–7; Bashear, "Qurʾān 2:114 and Jerusalem," 237; and Rubin, "Between Arabia and the Holy Land," although here Rubin seems to presume the historical accuracy of much from the traditional accounts of origins concerning a primitive Meccan *qibla*, the significance of Mecca's shrine, and the identity of the Qurʾānic *masjid al-aqṣā* with the Temple Mount.

257. See Bashear, *Arabs and Others*, esp. 112–25.

258. Bashear, "Abraham's Sacrifice," 266–77.

259. Goldziher, *Muslim Studies*, 2: 279–81.

260. E.g., Wellhausen, *The Arab Kingdom and Its Fall*, 215–16; C. Robinson, *ʿAbd al-Malik*, 103. See also Hoyland, "New Documentary Texts," 397, 409–10.

261. Hawting, "The *Ḥajj* in the Second Civil War," 36; see also Crone and Hinds, *God's Caliph*, esp. 39–42.

262. C. Robinson, *ʿAbd al-Malik*, 38; Hawting, "The *Ḥajj* in the Second Civil War," 37–39.

263. Rubin, *Between Bible and Qurʾān*, 36.

264. Hoyland, *Seeing Islam*, 552–53.

265. Madelung, "ʿAbd Allāh b. al-Zubayr," 294.

266. John bar Penkaye, *Riš Mellē* 15 (Mingana, *Sources syriaques*, 155*; S. Brock, "North Mesopotamia," 64).

267. Donner, *Muhammad and the Believers*, 205.

268. Goitein, "The Sanctity of Jerusalem," 148.

269. Rubin, *Between Bible and Qurʾān*, 36–37; C. Robinson, *ʿAbd al-Malik*, 37–38.

270. Wansbrough, *The Sectarian Milieu*, 126; referring to Bauer, *Orthodoxy and Heresy*. Somewhat surprising, however, are Wansbrough's rather negative remarks regarding related approaches in the preface to *Quranic Studies*: Wansbrough and Rippin, *Quranic Studies*, xxii.

271. Hoyland, *Seeing Islam*, 553.

272. Cf. ibid., 554–56, where Hoyland reaches similar conclusions, arguing that the resulting shift was from a "'*jihād* state,' a politico-religious entity comprising fighting men of different religious affiliations whose overriding aim was the expansion of the state in the name of God."

273. C. Robinson, *ʿAbd al-Malik*, 97–98; Hawting, *The First Dynasty of Islam*, 48–49.

274. Hawting, "The *Ḥajj* in the Second Civil War," 40.

275. C. Robinson, *ʿAbd al-Malik*, 44.

276. Creswell, *Early Muslim Architecture*, 1: 27–28, 142–49; Sauvaget, *La Mosquée omeyyade*.

277. See the traditions discussed in Hawting, "The Umayyads and the Ḥijāz."

278. E.g., Schreike, "Isrāʾ"; Schreike [and Horovitz], "Miʿrādj"; Wansbrough, *Quranic Studies*, 69; Hasson, "The Muslim View of Jerusalem," 355; van Ess, "Sūrat a-Najm." Mourad also argues, following slightly different evidence and reasoning, that the association of the Night Journey and Ascension with Jerusalem developed only later: Mourad, "The Symbolism of Jerusalem," 97–99.

279. Busse, "Jerusalem in the Story of Muḥammad's Night Journey," esp. 35–8; Hasson, "The Muslim View of Jerusalem," 355–59. See also Busse, "The Sanctity of Jerusalem," 454–60; Elad, "Why Did ʿAbd al-Malik Build," 44; van Ess, "ʿAbd al-Malik," 90–100. See also Colby, *Narrating Muḥammad's Night Journey*; regarding the absence of Jerusalem from many of the early narratives, see 44, 61, 77, 81–84, 87.

280. Rubin has recently challenged this consensus, arguing that the connection between the *masjid al-aqṣā* and Jerusalem is primitive: Rubin, "Muḥammad's Night Journey."

Rubin's argument is well made, and its focus on the primitive sanctity of Jerusalem in Islam is most welcome, but for me it is ultimately unpersuasive. In particular, it does not address the early traditions from Jewish and Islamic sources that describe the Dome of the Rock's significance in terms of the Jewish Temple. By their very nature these traditions seem to be primitive, and thus the identification of the Temple Mount's significance through Muhammad's footprint and his Ascent from the Rock would appear to be secondary. If earliest Islam was anything like what has been described above, it is hard to imagine that the early Believers would have looked past the powerful sacred history of the Rock as the location of the Holy of Holies in order to build there instead a shrine to Muhammad's heavenly ascension. Moreover, Rubin enlists the traditions of late ancient Christianity and Judaism in making his argument, which in itself is laudatory. Nevertheless, his invocation of Eusebius's concept of the earthly city of Jerusalem under Christian rule as the "New Jerusalem" is not persuasive. While it is true that Eusebius makes this equation, the New Jerusalem is much more commonly understood in Christian discourse as an eschatological, heavenly phenomenon, which thus would seem to support the scholarly consensus. It seems comparatively more likely that this more common view, rather than the political theology of Eusebius, would have affected early Islamic thinking. Likewise Rubin cites the influence of Jewish (and presumably also Christian) apocalyptic literature. But the fact of the matter is that in such apocalyptic journeys the seer almost always is brought to the heavenly Jerusalem, rather than (or in addition to) the earthly one, which again would seem to favor the consensus view. Moreover, while some early *tafsīr* may identify the *masjid al-Aqṣā* with a sanctuary in Jerusalem, Rubin neglects the fact that the earliest narratives of Muhammad's heavenly ascent make no mention of Jerusalem: see Colby, *Narrating Muḥammad's Night Journey*, 44.

281. Mourad advances a similar interpretation, although he locates this shift shortly after the Crusades: Mourad, "The Symbolism of Jerusalem," 98–99. Nevertheless, the studies cited above in n. 277 convincingly locate this new understanding of the Temple Mount's primary significance much earlier, suggesting such a shift in meaning during the eighth century.

282. Goldziher, *Muslim Studies*, 2: 279–80, citing al-Ṭabarī, *Ta'rīkh* (de Goeje et al., *Annales*, I: 1268).

283. Goldziher, *Muslim Studies*, 2: 280–81.

284. Kister, "Sanctity Joint and Divided," 39–41.

285. *Legend of Sergius Baḥīrā (East-Syrian)* 21 (Roggema, *The Legend of Sergius Baḥīrā*, 302–3).

286. It is thus somewhat peculiar that Halevi writes of the reconstruction of Muhammad's sepulcher by Walīd (Halevi, *Muhammad's Grave*, 191–96): there does not seem to be sufficient evidence that the mosque of Medina was identified as the site of Muhammad's tomb at this time.

287. Al-Ṭabarī, *Ta'rīkh* (de Goeje et al., *Annales*, II: 1192–94); al-Balādhurī, *Futūḥ al-buldān*, 6–7; Ibn Saʿd, *Ṭabaqāt* (Sachau, *Biographien Muhammeds*, 1.2: 180–82; 8: 119–20). Creswell, *Early Muslim Architecture*, 1: 143–45, signals a passage from the tenth-century *Kitāb al-Aghānī*, by Abū al-Faraj al-Iṣfahānī (897–967), which states that a man named

Wardān rebuilt Muhammad's tomb on this occasion, as well as mention of the tomb as a point of reference in passages from Ibn Rusta and Muqaddasī. Nevertheless, these tenth-century sources seem insufficient to establish a connection between the mosque and the tomb in Walīd's time.

288. Jones, "The *Maghāzī* Literature," 346; Donner, *Narratives of Islamic Origins*, 217–20.

289. Rubin, *Between Bible and Qurʾān*, 37.

290. See, e.g., Sellheim, "Prophet, Chalif und Geschichte," 39–46; C. Robinson, *Islamic Historiography*, 26–27, 122.

291. To my knowledge, the only comprehensive study of Muhammad's place in Islamic piety is Schimmel, *And Muhammad Is His Messanger.* Unfortunately, however, this work provides very little information regarding the historical development of Muhammad's tomb as a focus of Islamic piety.

292. Ibn Hishām, *Kitāb sīrat Rasūl Allāh* (Wüstenfeld, *Das Leben Muhammed's*, 1: 1019–20; Guillaume, *The Life of Muhammad*, 688).

293. Halevi would seem to suggest that in early Islam such prayers were always intercessions on behalf of the deceased, rather than reflecting any kind of veneration of the dead: Halevi, *Muhammad's Grave*, 27–31, 226–33. Nevertheless, see Goldziher's somewhat different view, which concludes that such veneration of the dead was fairly prevalent in early Islam: "On the Veneration of the Dead in Paganism and Islam," in Goldziher, *Muslim Studies*, 1: 209–38, esp. 228–38; cf. ibid., 2: 279–81. Likewise, belief in Muhammad's intercession on behalf of the faithful at the judgment, which appears already in the earliest sources, suggests that prayers at Muhammad's grave might reflect efforts to secure his final mediation: see Wensinck [and Gimaret], "Shafāʿa." See also Suliman Bashear's analysis of *zakāt* in earliest Islam, where he convincingly determines that this was originally a payment made by believers as recompense for some sin, in return for which Muhammad offered a prayer that secured forgiveness for their sins: Bashear, "On the Origns," esp. 97–99, 101, 112–13. This practice certainly suggests that such prayers at Muhammad's grave were offered in hopes of his intercessions.

294. Ibn Hishām, *Kitāb sīrat Rasūl Allāh* (Wüstenfeld, *Das Leben Muhammed's*, 1: 1021; Guillaume, *The Life of Muhammad*, 689).

295. Shoemaker, *Ancient Traditions of the Virgin Mary's Dormition*, esp. 71–76; see also Brown, *The Cult of the Saints*, esp. 1–49.

296. D. Cook, *Studies in Muslim Apocalyptic*, 172–73.

CONCLUSION

1. D. Cook, *Studies in Muslim Apocalyptic*, 302–3.

2. See, e.g., Ehrman, *Lost Christianities*, 117–20. See also Daley, *The Hope of the Early Church*, esp. 5–28, 216.

3. Bauer, *Orthodoxy and Heresy*. See the discussion of this book and its importance in Ehrman, *The Orthodox Corruption of Scripture*, 7–9, quotation at 7. See also Ehrman, *Lost Christianities*, 163–80.

4. Again citing Vincent of Lérins, *Commonitorium* 2.3 (Migne, *Patrologiae cursus completus, Series Latina*, 50: 640). Although Bauer's theory initially met with considerable controversy and resistance, it has since become fundamental to early Christian studies and has to some extent been confirmed by recent discoveries. See in particular the discussion of the book's reception by Georg Strecker and Robert A. Kraft in the English translation: Bauer, *Orthodoxy and Heresy*, 286–316. See also Ehrman, *Lost Christianities*, 173, 176–78.

5. Wansbrough, *The Sectarian Milieu*, 99, 125–26.

6. Crone, *Slaves on Horses*, 202 n. 10.

7. Peters, "The Quest of the Historical Muhammad," 301 also makes a similar comparison. More recently Peters has developed this comparison further: Peters, *Jesus and Muhammad*, 62–73. Here he seems almost as confident that Q relates actual teachings of Jesus as he is that the Qurʾān is a repository of Muhammad's *ipsissima verba*. It should be noted, however, that this relatively sanguine view of the Q traditions is out of step with most New Testament scholarship from the past century.

8. Clement of Alexandria, *Stromateis* 6.71.2 (Stählin, Früchtel, and Treu, *Clemens Alexandrinus*, 2: 467); trans from Ehrman, *Lost Christianities*, 178; cf. Roberts and Donaldson, *Ante-Nicene Christian Library*, 12: 344.

9. Origen, *Contra Celsum* II, 64–65; IV, 16; VI, 68, 77 (Borret, *Origène: Contre Celse*, 1: 434–41, 2: 220–23, 3: 348–51, 370–75). Cf. Origen, *Commentariorum series in Matthaeum*, 100 (Klostermann, Benz, and Treu, *Origenes Werke*, 11: 218–19; I thank Ronald E. Heine for his help in locating this passage). See also the *Acts of John*, where John similarly remarks, "I will tell you another glory, brethren; sometimes when I meant to touch him I encountered a material, solid body; but at other times again when I felt him, his substance was immaterial and incorporeal, and as if it did not exist at all." *Acts of John* 93 (Junod and Kaestli, *Acta Iohannis*, 1: 96–99); trans. Schneemelcher, *New Testament Apocrypha*, 2: 181. Likewise, the *Gospel According to Philip* says that Jesus appeared differently according to the capacities of different viewers, "in the manner in which [they would] be able to see him": *Gospel According to Philip* 57.28–58.11 (Layton, *Nag Hammadi Codex II, 2–7*, 1: 154–57).

10. According to Luke 3:23, Jesus began his ministry at thirty, and according to the synoptic gospels, his ministry then lasted for approximately one year. The Gospel according to John, however, ascribes three years to Jesus' ministry.

11. See Meier, *A Marginal Jew*, 1: 372–75.

12. As Crone characterizes the chronology of the *sīra* traditions in Crone, *Slaves on Horses*, 15.

13. Crossan, *Jesus*, 123–58; cf. Crossan, *Who Killed Jesus?*, 187–88.

14. Funk, *The Acts of Jesus*, 157–61.

15. E.g., R. Brown, *The Death of the Messiah*; Aus, *The Death, Burial, and Resurrection*; Ehrman, *Jesus*, 32–36.

16. See Rothschild, *Baptist Traditions and Q*. As an example of serious, respectful engagement with this hypothesis, despite strong disagreement, see Kloppenborg, "Review of Rothschild, *Baptist Traditions and Q*," which concludes: "This is an important work and well worth considering and arguing with, precisely because it proposes so radical a rereading

of Q." One certainly hopes for the day when such respectful and engaging disagreement will become more typical of reactions to "skeptical" approaches in the study of early Islam. To be sure it was not always thus in the study of Christian origins. The mid-nineteenth century in particular saw heated resistance to the emerging perspectives of higher criticism, and at the forefront of this resistance stood (among others) Nöldeke's *Doktorvater* Ewald.

17. Renan, "Mahomet et les origines de l'Islamisme," 1025; trans. Renan, "Muhammad and the Origins of Islam," 129.

18. Peters, "The Quest of the Historical Muhammad," esp. 291–95.

19. See, e.g., Perkins, *The Suffering Self*, 41–76, 124–41; Cooper, *The Virgin and the Bride*, 45–67; Jacobs, "A Family Affair."

20. See, e.g., Ehrman, *Peter, Paul, and Mary Magdalene*, xi–xv, 3–6, 65–72, 80–86, 141–52, which explains the pertinent issues well to a more general audience.

21. C. Robinson, "Reconstructing Early Islam," 123.

22. Tertullian, *De Praescriptione* 32 (Refoulé, *Tertulliani Opera*, 1: 212–13).

23. On the apocryphal *Acts of Peter*, see Schneemelcher, *New Testament Apocrypha*, 2: 271–321. See also Bremmer, *The Apocryphal Acts of Peter*; Thomas, *The Acts of Peter*.

24. T. Smith, *Petrine Controversies*, 2–3. The most compelling presentation of the case against locating Peter and the end of his life in Rome has been made by Cullmann, *Peter*, and now by Zwierlein, *Petrus in Rom*. The contrary position, that Peter was indeed martyred in Rome, has been argued by Bauckham, "The Martyrdom of Peter." Bauckham, however, is often unusually sanguine concerning the reliability of early Christian traditions, as evidenced in his recent study Bauckham, *Jesus and the Eyewitnesses*. Regarding the archaeological evidence, see O'Connor, *Peter in Rome*, which concludes rather cautiously that, despite certain problems of the literary evidence, one may conclude that the traditional association of Peter with Rome is indeed reliable. See also, however, Cullmann's discussion of the archaeological evidence in Cullmann, *Peter*, 131–56, as well as the more popular treatment in Ehrman, *Peter, Paul, and Mary Magdalene*, 80–86.

25. The tendentious and historically unreliable nature of Acts was first demonstrated by Baur, *Paul the Apostle*, initially published in 1866. For a more recent and popular presentation, see Ehrman, *Peter, Paul, and Mary Magdalene*, 106–13, 127–32, 141–44, 154–55. For a recent reconstruction of Pauline chronology, see Tatum, *New Chapters in the Life of Paul*.

26. I Clement 5.5–7 (Ehrman, *The Apostolic Fathers*, 1: 44–45). See also, e.g., the discussion in Tajra, *The Martyrdom of St. Paul*, 102–17.

27. M. Cook, *Muhammad*, 76.

28. On this methodological divide, see, e.g., Wansbrough, *Res ipsa loquitur*, reprinted in Wansbrough and Hawting, *The Sectarian Milieu*, esp. 162–63.

BIBLIOGRAPHY

ABBREVIATIONS

BSOAS	*Bulletin of the School of Oriental and African Studies*
CCSL	Corpus Christianorum Series Latina
CSCO	Corpus Scriptorum Christianorum Orientalium
EI[1]	M. Th. Houtsma, Thomas Walker Arnold, René Basset, Richard Hartmann, A. J. Wensinck, Willi Heffening, Évariste Lévi-Provençal, and H. A. R. Gibb, eds. *The Encyclopaedia of Islām*. Leiden: Brill, 1913–38.
EI[2]	P. J. Bearman, Th. Bianquis, C. E. Bosworth, E. van Donzel, and W. P. Heinrichs, eds. *The Encyclopaedia of Islam*. 2nd ed. Leiden: Brill, 1960–2004.
GCS	Die griechischen christlichen Schriftsteller der ersten Jahrhunderte
IOS	*Israel Oriental Studies*
JAOS	*Journal of the American Oriental Society*
JNES	*Journal of Near Eastern Studies*
JRAS	*Journal of the Royal Asiatic Society*
JSAI	*Jerusalem Studies in Arabic and Islam*
JSS	*Journal of Semitic Studies*
PG	J. P. Migne, ed. *Patrologiae cursus completus, Series graeca*. 161 vols. Paris: Excecudebatur et venit apud J.-P. Migne, 1857–.
SLAEI	Studies in Late Antiquity and Early Islam
TTH	Translated Texts for Historians
ZDMG	*Zeitschrift der deutschen morgenländischen Gesellschaft*

PRIMARY SOURCES

Abbott, Nabia. *Studies in Arabic Literary Papyri*. 3 vols. Chicago: University of Chicago Press, 1957.

ʿAbd al-Jabbār. *Tathbīt dalāʾil al-nubūwah*. Ed. Gabriel Said Reynolds and Samir Khalil Samir. *Critique of Christian Origins*. Provo, Utah: Brigham Young University Press, 2010.

ʿAbd al-Razzāq al-Sanʿānī. *Al-Muṣannaf.* Ed. Ḥabīburraḥmān Aʿẓamī. 11 vols. Beirut: al-Maktab al-Islāmī, 1983.

Abū Dā'ūd Sulaymān al-Sijistānī. *Sunan Abī Dāwūd.* 4 vols. [S.I.]: Dār Iḥyā' al-Sunnah al-Nabawīyah, [197–].

Abū l-Fatḥ. *Samaritan Chronicle.* Ed. Eduardus Vilmar. *Abulfathi Annales Samaritani.* Gothae: F. A. Perthes, 1865. Trans. Paul Stenhouse. *The Kitāb al-Tarīkh of Abū 'l-Fatḥ.* Studies in Judaica 1. Sydney: Mandelbaum Trust, University of Sydney, 1985.

Acts of John. Ed. Éric Junod and Jean-Daniel Kaestli. *Acta Iohannis.* 2 vols. Corpus Christianorum Series Apocryphorum, 1–2. Turnhout: Brepols, 1983.

Adomnán. *De locis sanctis.* Ed. L. Bieler. *Itineraria et alia geographica.* CCSL 175, 177–234. Turnhout: Brepols, 1965.

Agapius. *Chronicle.* Ed. Alexandre Vasiliev. *Kitab al-ʿUnvan / Histoire universelle.* 4 vols. Patrologia Orientalis 5.4, 7.4, 8.3, 11.1. Paris: Firmin-Didot, 1910–15.

Anastasius of Sinai. *Narrationes* C3. Ed. Bernard Flusin. "L'esplanade du Temple à l'arrivée des arabes d'après deux récits byzantins." In *Bayt al-Maqdis: ʿAbd al-Malik's Jerusalem,* ed. Julian Raby and Jeremy Johns, 22–31. Oxford: Oxford University Press, 1992.

al-Balādhurī, Aḥmad ibn Yaḥyā. *Ansāb al-ashrāf.* Ed. Muhammad Hamidullah. Vol. 1. Cairo: Maʿhad al-Makhṭūṭāt bi-Jāmiʿat al-Duwal al-ʿArabīyah bi-al-Ishtirāk maʿa Dār al-Maʿārif bi-Miṣr, 1959.

———. *Futūḥ al-buldān.* Ed. M. J. de Goeje. Leiden: Brill, 1866.

al-Bukhārī, Muḥammad ibn Ismāʿīl. *Al-Jāmiʿ al-ṣaḥīḥ.* Ed. M. Ludolf Krehl and Th. W. Juynboll. *Le Recueil des traditions mahométanes par Abou Abdallah Mohammed ibn Ismaîl el-Bokhâri.* 4 vols. Leiden: E. J. Brill, 1862–1908. Trans. Muhammad Muhsin Khan. *Ṣaḥīḥ al-Bukhārī: The Translation of the Meanings of Sahih al-Bukhari Arabic-English.* 9 vols. Al Nabawiya: Dar Ahya Us-Sunnah, 1976.

Byzantine-Arab Chronicle of 741. Ed. Ioannes Gil. *Corpus Scriptorum Muzarabicorum.* 2 vols. Manuales y anejos de "Emérita" 28, 1: 7–14. Madrid: Instituto Antonio de Nebrija, 1973. Ed. Theodor Mommsen. *Chronica minora saec. IV. V. VI. VII.* 3 vols. Monumenta Germaniae historica, Auctores antiquissimi 9, 11, 13, 2: 334–59. Munich: Monumenta Germaniae Historica, 1892–98.

Chronicle of 1234. Ed. J. B. Chabot. *Chronicon ad annum Christi 1234 pertinens.* CSCO 81–82, Scriptores Syri 36–37. Paris: E. Typographeo Reipublicae, 1916–20.

Chronicle of Siirt. Ed. Addai Scher. *Histoire nestorienne (Chronique de Séert).* 4 vols. Patrologia Orientalis 4, 5, 7, 13. Paris: Firmin-Didot, 1910–19.

I Clement. Ed. Bart D. Ehrman. *The Apostolic Fathers.* 2 vols. Loeb Classical Library 24–25, 1: 17–152. Cambridge, Mass.: Harvard University Press, 2003.

Clement of Alexandria. *Stromateis.* Ed. Otto Stählin, Ludwig Früchtel, and Ursula Treu. *Clemens Alexandrinus.* 3 vols. Vol. 2, *Stromata I–VI,* GCS. Berlin: Akademia-Verlag, 1960.

Continuatio of the *Samaritan Chronicle* of Abū l-Fatḥ. Ed. Milka Levy-Rubin. *The Continuatio of the Samaritan Chronicle of Abū l-Fatḥ al-Sāmirī al-Danafī.* SLAEI 10. Princeton, N.J.: Darwin Press, 2002.

Doctrina Iacobi nuper Baptizati. Ed. Gilbert Dagron and Vincent Déroche. "Juifs et Chrétiens dans l'Orient du VIIe siècle." *Travaux et mémoires* 11 (1991): 47–219.

Eulogius of Cordova. *Liber apologeticus martyrum*. Ed. Ioannes Gil. *Corpus Scriptorum Muzarabicorum*. 2 vols. Manuales y anejos de "Emérita" 28, 2: 475–95. Madrid: Instituto Antonio de Nebrija, 1973.

Gospel According to Philip. Ed. Bentley Layton. *Nag Hammadi Codex II, 2–7*. 2 vols. Nag Hammadi Studies 20, 1: 131–218. Leiden: Brill, 1989.

Hispanic Chronicle of 754. Ed. Jose Eduardo López Pereira. *Crónica mozárabe de 754: Edición crítica y traducción*. Zaragoza: Anubar Ediciones, 1980. Trans. Kenneth B. Wolf. *Conquerors and Chroniclers of Early Medieval Spain*. TTH 9, 111–58. Liverpool: Liverpool University Press, 1990.

History of the Patriarchs of Alexandria. Ed. Basil Thomas Alfred Evetts. *History of the Patriarchs of the Coptic Church of Alexandria*. 4 vols. Patrologia Orientalis 1.2, 1.4, 5.1, 10.5. Paris: Firmin-Didot, 1907–15.

Ibn Abī Shayba, ʿAbdallāh ibn Muḥammad. *Al-Kitāb al-Muṣannaf fī al-aḥādīth wa-al-āthār*. Ed. ʿAbd al-Khāliq al-Afghānī and Mukhtār Aḥmad al-Nadwī. 15 vols. Bombay: al-Dār al-Salafīya, 1979–83.

Ibn Ḥabīb, Abū Jaʿfar Muḥammad. *Kitāb al-muḥabbar*. Ed. Ilse Lichtenstädter. Beirut: Manshūrāt al-Maktab al-Tijārī lil-Ṭibāʿah wa-al-Nashr, 1942.

Ibn Ḥajar al-Haythamī. *Al-Ṣawāʿiq al-Muḥriqa*. Ed. ʿAbd al-Wahhāb ʿAbd al-Laṭīf. Cairo, 1375/1955.

Ibn Ḥanbal, Aḥmad ibn Muḥammad. *Musnad*. 6 vols. Beirut: al-Maktab al-Islāmī lil-Ṭibāʿah wa-al-Nashr, 1969.

Ibn Hishām, ʿAbd al-Malik. *Kitāb sīrat Rasūl Allāh*. Ed. Ferdinand Wüstenfeld. *Das Leben Muhammed's nach Muhammed ibn Ishâk bearbeitet von Abd el-Malik ibn Hischâm*. 2 vols. Göttingen: Dieterichsche Universitäts-Buchhandlung, 1858–60. Trans. Alfred Guillaume. *The Life of Muhammad*. London: Oxford University Press, 1955.

"Ibn Isḥāq, Muḥammad." *Kitāb al-siyar wa-al-maghāzī*. Ed. Suhayl Zakkār. Beirut: Dār al-Fikr, 1978.

Ibn Kathīr, Ismāʿīl ibn ʿUmar. *Al-Bidāyah wa-al-nihāyah fī al-tārīkh*. 14 vols. Cairo: Maṭbaʿat al-Saʿādah, 1932–39.

———. *The Life of the Prophet Muḥammad*. Trans. Trevor Le Gassick. 4 vols. Reading, U.K.: Garnet Pub., 2000.

Ibn al-Mubārak, ʿAbd Allāh. *Kitāb al-zuhd wa-al-raqāʾiq*. Beirut: Muḥammad ʿAfīf al-Zuʿbī, 1971.

Ibn al-Murajjā, Abū al-Maʿālī al-Musharraf. *Faḍāʾil Bayt al-Maqdis wa-al-Khalīl wa-faḍāʾil al-Shām*. Ed. Ofer Livne-Kafri. Shafā ʿAmr [Israel]: Dār al-Mashriq lil-Tarjamah wa-al-Ṭibāʿah wa-al-Nashr, 1995.

Ibn Saʿd, Muḥammad. *Ṭabaqāt*. Ed. E. Sachau. *Biographien Muhammeds, seiner Gefährten und der späteren Träger des Islams, bis zum Jahre 230 der Flucht*. 9 vols. Leiden: Brill, 1904–28.

Ishoʿyahb III. *Letters*. Ed. Rubens Duval. *Išoʿyahb Patriarchae III Liber epistularum*. CSCO 11–12. Paris: E Typographeo Reipublicae, 1904.

Istoria de Mahomet. Ed. Kenneth B. Wolf. "The Earliest Latin Lives of Muḥammad." In *Conversion and Continuity: Indigenous Christian Communities in Islamic Lands, Eighth to Eighteenth Centuries*, ed. Michael Gervers and Ramzi Jibran Bikhazi, 89–101. Toronto: Pontifical Institute of Mediaeval Studies, 1990.

Itinerarium Burdigalense. Ed. P. Geyer. *Itineraria et alia Geographica*. CCSL 175, 1–34. Turnhout: Brepols, 1965.

Jacob of Edessa. *Chronological Charts*. Ed. E. W. Brooks, I. Guidi, and J. B. Chabot. *Chronica minora III*. 2 vols. CSCO 5–6, Scriptores Syri 5–6, 261–330 (Syr.) and 199–258 (Lat.). Paris: E Typographeo Reipublicae, 1905.

———. *Letter 14 to John the Stylite*. MS BL Add. 12,172, ff. 122a-126b.

Jewish Apocalypse on the Umayyads. Ed. Israel Lévi. "Une apocalypse judéo-arabe." *Revue des études juives* 67 (1914): 178–82.

John bar Penkaye. *Riš Mellē*. Ed. Alphonse Mingana. *Sources syriaques*. 1:1*–171*. Leipzig: Harrassowitz, 1908. Trans. Sebastian P. Brock. "North Mesopotamia in the Late Seventh Century: Book XV of John Bar Penkāyē's *Riš Mellē* " *JSAI* 9 (1987): 51–75.

John of Damascus. *On Heresies*. PG 94: 677–780.

John Moschus. *Spiritual Meadow (Georgian Version)*. Ed. Ilia Abulaže. იოანე მოსხი: ლიმონარი *[Ioane Mosxi: Limonari]*. T'bilisi: Mec'niereba, 1960.

al-Khallāl, Abū Bakr. *Ahl al-milal wa-al-riddah wa-al-zanādiqah wa-tārik al-ṣalāh wa-al-farā'iḍ min kitāb al-Jāmiʿ lil-Khallāl*. Ed. Ibrāhīm ibn Ḥamad ibn Sulṭān. 2 vols. Riyadh: Maktabat al-Maʿārif lil-Nashr wa-al-Tawzīʿ, 1996.

Khuzistan Chronicle. Ed. Ignazio Guidi. *Chronica minora I*. 2 vols. CSCO 1–2, Scriptores Syri 1–2, 15–39 (Syr.) and 15–32 (Lat.). Paris: E Typographeo Reipublicae, 1903.

Legend of Sergius Baḥīrā. Ed. Barbara Roggema. *The Legend of Sergius Baḥīrā: Eastern Christian Apologetics and Apocalyptic in Response to Islam*. History of Christian-Muslim Relations 9. Leiden: Brill, 2009.

Ps.-Leo III. *Letter to ʿUmar II*. PG 107: 315–24. Ed. Symphorien Champier. *De triplici disciplina cujus partes sunt: Philosophia naturalis. Medicina. Theologia: Moralis philosophia integrantes quadrivuum*. Lyons: C. Davost for S. Vincentius, 1508.

Łewond. *History*. Ed. Karapet Ezeantsʿ. Պատմութիւն Ղեւոնդեայ մեծի Վարդապետի Հայոց *[Patmutʿiwn Ghewondeay Metsi Vardapeti Hayotsʿ]*. 2nd ed. St. Petersburg: I Tparani I. N. Skorokhodovi, 1887. Trans. Arthur Jeffery. "Ghevond's Text of the Correspondence between ʿUmar II and Leo III." *Harvard Theological Review* 37 (1944): 269–332. Trans. Zaven Arzoumanian. *History of Lewond, the Eminent Vardapet of the Armenians*. Wynnewood, Pa.: St. Sahag and St. Mesrob Armenian Church, 1982.

Maqrīzī, Aḥmad ibn ʿAlī. *Description historique et topographique de l'Egypte*. Trans. Paul Casanova and U. Bouriant. 4 vols. Mémoires publiés par les membres de la Mission archéologique française au Caire 17. Paris: E. Leroux, 1900.

Michael the Syrian. *Chronicle*. Ed. J. B. Chabot. *Chronique de Michel le Syrien, patriarche jacobite d'Antioche (1166–99)*. 4 vols. Paris: Ernest Leroux, 1899–1910.

Mishnah. Ed. Philip Blackman. *Mishnayot*. 2nd rev. and corr. ed. 7 vols. Gateshead: Judaica Press, 1990.

Mūsā b. ʿUqba. *Maghāzī* (fragments). Ed. E. Sachau. "Das Berliner Fragment des Musa Ibn ʿUqba." *Sitzungsberichte der Preussischen Akademie der Wissenschaften* 11 (1904): 445–70. Trans. Alfred Guillaume. *The Life of Muhammad*. London: Oxford University Press, 1955, xlvi.

Muslim b. al-Ḥajjāj. *Ṣaḥīḥ Muslim*. 5 vols. Beirut: Dār Ibn Ḥazm, 1995.

Nicephorus. *Brevarium*. Ed. Cyril Mango. *Nikephoros Patriarch of Constantinople: Short History*. Dumbarton Oaks Texts 10. Washington, D.C.: Dumbarton Oaks, 1990.

Origen of Alexandria. *Commentariorum series in Matthaeum*. Ed. Erich Klostermann, Ernst Benz, and Ursula Treu. *Origenes Werke*. 2nd ed. 12 vols. Vol. 11, *Origenes Matthäuserklärung II. Die lateinisiche Übersetzung der Commentariorum series*, GCS. Berlin: Akademie-Verlag, 1976.

———. *Contra Celsum*. Ed. Marcel Borret. *Origène: Contre Celse*. 5 vols. Sources Chrétiennes 132, 136, 147, 150, 227. Paris: Éditions du Cerf, 1967–76.

Papias. *Fragments*. Ed. Bart D. Ehrman. *The Apostolic Fathers*. 2 vols. Loeb Classical Library 24–25, 2: 85–120. Cambridge, Mass.: Harvard University Press, 2003.

The Prayer of Rabbi Shimʿōn b. Yoḥai. Ed. Adolph Jellinek. *Bet ha-midrash: Sammlung kleiner Midraschim und vermischter Abhandlungen aus der ältern jüdischen Literatur*. 6 vols., 4: 117–26. Leipzig: F. Nies, 1853–77. Trans. Bernard Lewis. "An Apocalyptic Vision of Islamic History." *BSOAS* 13 (1950): 311–20.

Sebeos. *History*. Ed. Gevorg V. Abgarian. Պատմութիւն Սեբէոսի *[Patmutʿiwn Sebeosi]*. Erevan: Haykakan SSH Gitutʿyunneri Akademiayi Hratarakchʿutʿyun, 1979.

The Secrets of Rabbi Shimʿōn b. Yoḥai. Ed. Adolph Jellinek. *Bet ha-midrash: Sammlung kleiner Midraschim und vermischter Abhandlungen aus der ältern jüdischen Literatur*. 6 vols., 3: 78–82. Leipzig: F. Nies, 1853–77. Geniza fragment: ed. Solomon Aaron Wertheimer. *Bate midrashot: Yakhilu midrashim ḳeṭanim mi-kitve yad shonim*. 4 vols. in 3 vols., 2: 25–26. Jerusalem: Bi-defus M. Lilyenṭhal, 1893; reprinted in Solomon Aaron Wertheimer and Abraham Joseph Wertheimer, eds. *Bate midrashot: ʿEśrim ṿa-ḥamishah midreshe Ḥazal ʿal pi kitve yad mi-genizat Yerushalayim u-Mitsrayim*. 2 vols., 2: 506–7. Jerusalem: Mosad ha-Rav Ḳuḳ, 1950. Munich version: Munich MS Hebr. 222, ff. 107b–111a, 107b. Partial trans. Bernard Lewis. "An Apocalyptic Vision of Islamic History." *BSOAS* 13 (1950): 321–30. Complete trans. John C. Reeves. *Trajectories in Near Eastern Apocalyptic: A Postrabbinic Jewish Apocalypse Reader*, 76–89. Leiden: Brill, 2006.

Sefer Zerubbabel. Ed. Israel Lévi. "L'Apocalypse de Zorobabel." *Revue des études Juives* 68; 69; 71 (1914; 1919; 1920): 129–60; 108–21; 57–65. Trans. Martha Himmelfarb. "Sefer Zerubbabel." In *Rabbinic Fantasies: Imaginative Narratives from Classical Hebrew Literature*. Ed. David Stern and Mark Jay Mirsky, 67–90. Philadelphia: Jewish Publication Society, 1990.

Short Syriac Chronicle of 705. Ed. J. P. N. Land. *Anecdota Syriaca*. 4 vols., 2: 10–11. Leiden: Brill, 1862–75.

Short Syriac Chronicle of 724. Ed. J. P. N. Land. *Anecdota Syriaca*. 4 vols., 1: 40–41. Leiden: Brill, 1862–75. Ed. E. W. Brooks. *Chronica minora II*. 2 vols., CSCO 3–4, Scriptores Syri 3–4, 155 (Syr) and 119 (Lat). Paris: E Typographeo Reipublicae, 1904.

Short Syriac Chronicle of 775. Ed. E. W. Brooks, I. Guidi, and J. B. Chabot. *Chronica minora III*. 2 vols. CSCO 5–6, Scriptores Syri 5–6, 337–49 (Syr.) and 267–75 (Lat.). Paris: E Typographeo Reipublicae, 1905.

Sibṭ b. al-Jawzī. *Mirʾāt al-Zamān*. Ed. Amikam Elad. "Why Did ʿAbd al-Malik Build the Dome of the Rock?: A Re-examination of the Muslim Sources." In *Bayt al-Maqdis: ʿAbd al-Malik's Jerusalem*, ed. Julian Raby and Jeremy Johns, 33–58. Oxford: Oxford University Press, 1992. (Partial edition)

Sozomen. *Ecclesiastical History*. Ed. Robert Hussey. *Sozomeni Ecclesiastica historia*. 3 vols. Oxonii: E Typographeo Academico, 1860.

al-Ṭabarī, Muḥammad ibn Jarīr. *Taʾrīkh al-rasul waʾl-mulūk*. Ed. M. J. de Goeje, J. Barth, Theodor Nöldeke, P. de Jong, Eugen Prym, Heinrich Thorbecke, Siegmund Fränkel, Ignazio Guidi, David Heinrich Müller, M. Th. Houtsma, Stanislas Guyard, and V. R. Rozen. *Annales*. 15 vols. Leiden: Brill, 1879–1901.

———. *The History of al-Ṭabarī: Volume I, General Introduction and From the Creation to the Flood*. Trans. Franz Rosenthal. Albany, N.Y.: State University of New York Press, 1988.

———. *The History of al-Ṭabarī: Volume IX, The Last Years of the Prophet*. Trans. Ismail K. Poonawala. Albany, N.Y.: State University of New York Press, 1990.

———. *The History of al-Ṭabarī: Volume X, The Conquest of Arabia*. Trans. Fred M. Donner. Albany, N.Y.: State University of New York Press, 1992.

———. *Jamʿī al-bayān fī tafsīr al-Qurʾān*. 30 vols. Cairo: Maṭbaʿat al-Maymunīyah, 1902–3.

Ten Kings Midrash. Ed. Judah David Eisenstein. *Otsar midrashim*. 2 vols., 2: 461–66. New York: J. D. Eisenstein, 1915. Partial trans. Bernard Lewis. "An Apocalyptic Vision of Islamic History." *BSOAS* 13 (1950): 321–30.

Tertullian. *De praescriptione haereticorum*. Ed. R. F. Refoulé. *Tertulliani Opera*. 2 vols. CCSL 1–2, 1: 185–224. Turnhout: Brepols, 1954.

Theophanes. *Chronicle*. Ed. Carolus de Boor. *Theophanis chronographia*. 2 vols. Leipzig: Teubner, 1883–85.

Thomas Artsruni. *History*. Ed. Kherowbe Patkanean. Պատմութիւն տանն Արծրունեաց *[Patmutʿiwn tann Artsruneatsʿ]*. St. Petersburg: Skorochodov, 1887. Trans. Robert W. Thomson. *History of the House of the Artsrunikʿ*. Detroit: Wayne State University Press, 1985.

Thomas the Presbyter. *Chronicle*. Ed. E. W. Brooks. *Chronica minora II*. 2 vols. CSCO 3–4, Scriptores Syri 3–4, 77–154 (Syr.) and 63–119 (Lat.). Paris: E Typographeo Reipublicae, 1904.

al-Tirmidhī, Muḥammad ibn ʿĪsā. *Al-Jāmiʿ al-ṣaḥīḥ*. Ed. Ibrāhīm ʿAwaḍ. 5 vols. Cairo: Muṣṭafā al-Bābī al-Ḥalabī, 1965.

al-Ṭurṭūshī, Abū Bakr Muḥammad ibn al-Walīd. *Al-Ḥawādith wa-al-bidaʿ*. Ed. Muḥammad al-Ṭālibī. Tunis: al-Maṭbaʿah al-Rasmīyah lil-Jumhūrīyah al-Tūnisīyah, 1959.

Ps.-ʿUmar II. *Letter to Leo III*. Ed. Dominique Sourdel. "Un pamphlet musulman anonyme d'époque ʿabbaside contre les chrétiens." *Revue des études islamiques* 34 (1966):

1–34. Denise Cardaillac. "La polemique anti-chrétienne du manuscrit aljamiado no. 4944 de la Bibliothèque nationale de Madrid." Ph.D. thesis, 2 vols., Université Paul Valéry Arts et lettres langues et sciences humaines, 1972. Trans. Jean-Marie Gaudeul. "The Correspondence between Leo and ʿUmar: ʿUmar's Letter Re-discovered?" *Islamochristiana* 10 (1984): 109–57.

Vincent of Lérins. *Commonitorium*. Ed. J. P. Migne. *Patrologiae cursus completus, Series Latina*. 221 vols., 50: 630–86. Paris: Apud Garnieri Fratres editores, 1844.

al-Wāqidī, Muḥammad ibn ʿUmar. *Kitāb al-maghāzī lil-Wāqidī*. Ed. Marsden Jones. 3 vols. London: Oxford University Press, 1966.

Ps.-Wāqidī. *Futūḥ al-Shām*. 2 vols. Cairo: al-Maṭbaʿah al-Sharqīyah, 1949.

Wāsiṭī, Abū Bakr Muḥammad ibn Aḥmad. *Faḍāʾil al-Bayt al-Muqaddas*. Ed. Isaac Hasson. Max Schloessinger Memorial Series 3. Jerusalem: Magnes Press, Hebrew University, 1979.

Zuqnin Chronicle. Ed. J. B. Chabot. *Incerti auctoris Chronicon anonymum Pseudo-Dionysianum vulgo dictum*. 2 vols. CSCO 91, 104, Scriptores Syri 43, 53. Paris: E Typographeo Reipublicae, 1927.

SECONDARY SOURCES

Abdel Haleem, M. A. S. *The Qurʾān*. Oxford: Oxford University Press, 2004.

Abdul-Rauf, Muhammad. "Outsiders' Interpretations of Islam: A Muslim's Point of View." In *Approaches to Islam in Religious Studies*, ed. Richard C. Martin, 179–88. Tucson: University of Arizona Press, 1985.

Adams, Charles J. "Reflections on the Work of John Wansbrough." *Method and Theory in the Study of Religion* 9 (1997): 75–90.

Afsaruddin, Asma. *The First Muslims: History and Memory*. Oxford: Oneworld, 2008.

Afzaal, Ahmed. "The Origin of Islam as a Social Movement." *Islamic Studies* 42 (2003): 203–43.

Aḥmad, ʿImad. "The Dawn Sky on Laylat al-Qadr." *Archaeoastronomy* 11 (1989–93): 97–100.

———. "Did Muḥammad Observe the Canterbury Meteor Swarm?" *Archaeoastronomy* 11 (1989–93): 95–96.

Albert, Micheline, Robert Beylot, René-G. Coquin, Bernard Outtier, and Charles Renoux. *Christianismes orientaux: Introduction à l'étude des langues et des littératures*. Paris: Éditions du Cerf, 1993.

Album, Stephen, and Tony Goodwin. *Sylloge of Islamic Coins in the Ashmolean Museum*. Vol. 1, *The Pre-reform Coinage of the Early Islamic Period*. Oxford: Ashmolean Museum, 2002.

Alexander, Paul J. *The Byzantine Apocalyptic Tradition*. Berkeley: University of California Press, 1985.

Allison, Dale C. *The New Moses: A Matthean Typology*. Minneapolis: Fortress Press, 1993.

Andræ, Tor. "Der Ursprung des Islams und das Christentum." *Kyrkohistorisk Årsskrift* 23 (1923): 149–206; 24 (1924): 213–92; 25 (1925): 45–112.

———. *Die person Muhammeds in lehre und glauben seiner gemeinde*. Archives d'études orientales Stockholm 16. Stockholm: Kungl. boktryckeriet. P. A. Norstedt & söner, 1918.

———. *Les origines de l'Islam et le Christianisme*. Trans. Jules Roche. Initiation à l'Islam 8. Paris: Adrien-Maisonneuve, 1955.

———. *Mohammed: The Man and His Faith*. Trans. Theophil William Menzel. New York: Harper and Row, 1960.

———. *Mohammed, sein Leben und sein Glaube*. Göttingen: Vandenhoeck & Ruprecht, 1932.

Anthony, Sean. "Sayf ibn 'Umar's Account of 'King' Paul and the Corruption of Ancient Christianity." *Der Islam* 85 (2009): 164–202.

Arazi, A. "Matériaux pour l'étude du conflit de préséance entre Mekke et Medine." *JSAI* 5 (1984): 177–235.

Arberry, A. J. *The Koran Interpreted*. London: Allen and Unwin, 1955.

Arkoun, Mohammed. "Bilan et perspectives des études coraniques." In *Lectures du Coran*, v–xxxiii. Paris: G. P. Maisonneuve et Larose, 1982.

Armstrong, Karen. *Muhammad: A Biography of the Prophet*. New York: HarperSanFrancisco, 1993.

Arzoumanian, Zaven, trans. *History of Lewond, the Eminent Vardapet of the Armenians*. Wynnewood, Pa.: St. Sahag and St. Mesrob Armenian Church, 1982.

Attema, D. S. *De mohammedaansche opvattingen omtrent het tijdstip van den jongsten dag en zijn voorteekenen*. Amsterdam: N.V. Noord-hollandsche uitgevers maatschappij, 1942.

Aus, Roger David. *The Death, Burial, and Resurrection of Jesus, and the Death, Burial, and Translation of Moses in Judaic Tradition*. Lanham, Md.: University Press of America, 2008.

Avner, Rina. "The Recovery of the Kathisma Church and Its Influence on Octagonal Buildings." In *One Land, Many Cultures: Archaeological Studies in Honor of Stanislao Loffreda, O.F.M.*, ed. G. C. Bottini, L. D. Segni, and D. Chrupcala, 173–88. Jerusalem: Franciscan Printing Press, 2003.

———. "ירושלים, מר אליאס—כנסיית הקתיסמה [Jerusalem, Mar Elias—Church of the Kathisma]." *Hadashot Arkheologiyot* 108 (1998): 139–42.

Ayoub, Mahmoud. *The Crisis of Muslim History: Religion and Politics in Early Islam*. Oxford: Oneworld, 2003.

B., M. [*sic*]. "Review of Paul Casanova, *Mohammed et la fin du monde: Étude critique sur l'Islam primitif*." *The Muslim World* 3, no. 2 (1913): 202–3.

Bagatti, Bellarmino. *The Church from the Circumcision: History and Archaeology of the Judaeo-Christians*. Trans. Eugene Hoade. Publications of the Studium Biblicum Franciscanum, Smaller Series 2. Jerusalem: Franciscan Printing Press, 1971.

Bagatti, Bellarmino, Michele Piccirillo, and A. Prodomo. *New Discoveries at the Tomb of Virgin Mary in Gethsemane*. Jerusalem: Franciscan Print. Press, 1975.

Baird, William. *History of New Testament Research.* 2 vols. Minneapolis: Fortress Press, 1992.

Balch, David L., ed. *Social History of the Matthean Community: Cross-disciplinary Approaches.* Minneapolis: Fortress Press, 1991.

Barkai, Ron. *Cristianos y musulmanes en la España medieval: El enemigo en el espejo.* Libros de historia 13. Madrid: Rialp, 1984.

Baron, Salo Wittmayer. *A Social and Religious History of the Jews.* 2nd ed. 18 vols. Philadelphia: Jewish Publication Society of America, 1952–83.

Barthes, Roland. "The Reality Effect." In *The Rustle of Language.* New York: Hill and Wang, 1986.

Barthold, W. "Die Orientierung der ersten muhammedanischen Moscheen." *Der Islam* 18 (1929): 245–50.

Barton, John. "Reflections on Literary Criticism." In *Method Matters: Essays on the Interpretation of the Hebrew Bible in Honor of David L. Petersen*, ed. Joel M. LeMon and Kent Harold Richards, 523–40. Atlanta: Society of Biblical Literature, 2009.

Bashear, Suliman. "Abraham's Sacrifice of His Son and Related Issues." *Der Islam* 67 (1990): 243–77.

———. "Apocalyptic and Other Materials on Early Muslim-Byzantine Wars: A Review of Arabic Sources." *JRAS* 1 (1991): 173–207.

———. *Arabs and Others in Early Islam.* SLAEI 8. Princeton, N.J.: Darwin Press, 1997.

———. "Ḥanīfiyya and Ḥajj." In *Studies in Early Islamic Tradition*, no. XIV. Jerusalem: Max Schloessinger Memorial Foundation, Hebrew University of Jerusalem, 2004.

———. "Jesus in an Early Muslim Shahāda and Related Issues: A New Perspective." In *Studies in Early Islamic Tradition*, no. XV. Jerusalem: Max Schloessinger Memorial Foundation, Hebrew University of Jerusalem, 2004.

———. "Muslim Apocalypses and the Hour: A Case-Study in Traditional Reinterpretation." *IOS* 13 (1993): 75–100.

———. "On the Origns and Development of the Meaning of *Zakāt* in Early Islam." *Arabica* 40 (1993): 84–113.

———. "Qibla Musharriqa and Early Muslim Prayer in Churches." *The Muslim World* 81 (1991): 267–82.

———. "Qurʾān 2:114 and Jerusalem." *BSOAS* 52 (1989): 215–38.

———. "Riding Beasts on Divine Missions: An Examination of the Ass and Camel Traditions." *JSS* 37 (1991): 37–75.

———. "The Title '*Fārūq*' and Its Association with ʿUmar I." *Studia Islamica* 72 (1990): 47–70.

———. "Yemen in Early Islam: An Examination of Non-Tribal Traditions." *Arabica* 36 (1989): 327–61.

Bauckham, Richard. *Jesus and the Eyewitnesses: The Gospels as Eyewitness Testimony.* Grand Rapids, Mich.: William B. Eerdmans Pub. Co., 2006.

———. "The Martyrdom of Peter in Early Christian Literature." *Aufsteig und Niedergang der römischen Welt* II.26.1 (1992): 539–95.

Bauer, Walter. *Orthodoxy and Heresy in Earliest Christianity*. Trans. Robert A. Kraft and Gerhard Krodel. Philadelphia: Fortress Press, 1971.

Baur, Ferdinand Christian. *Die tübinger Schule und ihre Stellung zur Gegenwart*. 2nd ed. Tübingen: L. Fr. Fues, 1860.

———. *Paul the Apostle of Jesus Christ, His Life and Works, His Epistles and Teachings: A Contribution to a Critical History of Primitive Christianity*. Trans. Allan Menzies. 2nd ed. 2 vols. London: Williams and Norgate, 1873.

Beck, Edmund. "Die Sura *ar-Rūm* (30)." *Orientalia* 13 (1944): 334–55.

Becker, C. H. "Zur Geschichte des islamischen Kultus." *Der Islam* 3 (1912): 374–99.

Bell, Richard. *A Commentary on the Qurʾān*. Ed. Clifford Edmund Bosworth and M. E. J. Richardson. 2 vols. Journal of Semitic Studies Monograph 14. Manchester: University of Manchester, 1991.

———. *Introduction to the Qurʾān*. Edinburgh: At the University Press, 1958.

———. *The Origin of Islam in Its Christian Environment*. London: Macmillan and Co., 1926.

———. *The Qurʾān*. 2 vols. Edinburgh: T. and T. Clark, 1937–39.

Bell, Richard, and W. Montgomery Watt. *Bell's Introduction to the Qurʾān*. Edinburgh: Edinburgh University Press, 1970.

Benkheira, Mohammad H. "L'analyse du *ḥadīṯ* en question: Á propos de A.-L. de Prémare et de G. H. A. Juynboll." *Arabica* 52 (2005): 294–303.

Bennett, Clinton. *In Search of Muhammad*. London: Cassell, 1998.

Berg, Herbert. "Context: Muḥammad." In *The Blackwell Companion to the Qurʾān*, ed. Andrew Rippin, 187–204. Oxford: Blackwell, 2006.

———. *The Development of Exegesis in Early Islam: The Authenticity of Muslim Literature from the Formative Period*. Richmond, Surrey: Curzon, 2000.

———. "The Implications of, and Opposition to, the Methods and Theories of John Wansbrough." *Method and Theory in the Study of Religion* 9 (1997): 3–22.

———, ed. "Islamic Origins Reconsidered: John Wansbrough and the Study of Early Islam." *Method and Theory in the Study of Religion* 9 (1997): 3–90.

Berg, Herbert, and Sarah Rollens. "The Historical Muḥammad and the Historical Jesus: A Comparison of Scholarly Reinventions and Reinterpretations." *Studies in Religion / Sciences Religieuses* 37 (2008): 271–92.

Bergsträsser, Gotthelf, and Otto Pretzl. *Geschichte des Qorāns III: Geschichte des Qorāntexts*. 2nd ed. Leipzig: Dieterich'sche Verlagsbuchhandlung, 1938.

Berlinerblau, Jacques. *The Secular Bible: Why Nonbelievers Must Take Religion Seriously*. New York: Cambridge University Press, 2005.

Besant, Walter, and Edward Henry Palmer. *Jerusalem, the City of Herod and Saladin*. London: R. Bentley and Son, 1871.

Birkeland, Harris. *The Lord Guideth: Studies on Primitive Islam*. Skrifter utg. av det Norske videnskaps-akademi i Oslo. II. Hist.-filos. Klasse, 1956 no. 2. Oslo: I kommisjon hos H. Aschehoug (W. Nygaard), 1956.

Blachère, Régis. *Introduction au Coran*. 2nd ed. Paris: Besson and Chantemerle, 1959.

———. *Le problème de Mahomet: Essai de biographie critique du fondateur de l'Islam.* Paris: Presses universitaires de France, 1952.

Böwering, Gerhard. "Chronology and the Qur'ān." In *Encyclopaedia of the Qur'ān*, ed. Jane Dammen McAuliffe, 316–35. Leiden: Brill, 2001–6.

Bowersock, G. W., Peter Brown, and Oleg Grabar, eds. *Late Antiquity: A Guide to the Postclassical World.* Cambridge, Mass.: Belknap Press of Harvard University Press, 1999.

Bremmer, Jan N. *The Apocryphal Acts of Peter: Magic, Miracles, and Gnosticism.* Leuven: Peeters, 1998.

Brock, Anne Graham. *Mary Magdalene, the First Apostle: The Struggle for Authority.* Harvard Theological Studies 51. Cambridge, Mass.: Harvard Divinity School, 2003.

Brock, Sebastian P. "Syriac Views of Emergent Islam." In *Studies on the First Century of Islam*, ed. G. H. A. Juynboll, 9–21, 199–203. Carbondale and Edwardsville: Southern Illinois University Press, 1982.

Brooks, E. W. "The Sources of Theophanes and the Syriac Chroniclers." *Byzantinische Zeitschrift* 15 (1906): 578–87.

Brown, Peter. *The Body and Society: Men, Women, and Sexual Renunciation in Early Christianity.* Lectures on the History of Religions, n.s., 13. New York: Columbia University Press, 1988.

———. *The Cult of the Saints: Its Rise and Function in Latin Christianity.* Haskell Lectures on History of Religions, n.s., 2. Chicago: University of Chicago Press, 1981.

———. *The World of Late Antiquity.* New York: W. W. Norton, 1971.

Brown, Raymond E. *The Birth of the Messiah: A Commentary on the Infancy Narratives in Matthew and Luke.* Garden City, N.Y.: Doubleday, 1977.

———. *The Death of the Messiah: From Gethsemane to the Grave; A Commentary on the Passion Narratives in the Four Gospels.* 2 vols. New York: Doubleday, 1994.

Buhl, Frants. *Das Leben Muhammeds.* Trans. Hans Heinrich Schaeder. Leipzig: Quelle and Meyer, 1930.

———. "Muḥammad." *EI*[1] 3: 641–57.

———. *Muhammeds liv.* 3. reviderede udgave ed. Herning: Poul Kristensen, 1998.

———. *Muhammeds liv: Med en indledning om forholdene i Arabien før Muhammeds optraeden.* Copenhagen: Gyldendalske Boghandel, 1903.

Buhl, Frants, [and A. T. Welch]. "Muḥammad: 1. The Prophet's Life and Career." *EI*[2] 7: 360–76.

Bultmann, Rudolf Karl. *The History of the Synoptic Tradition.* Trans. John Marsh. New York: Harper and Row, 1963.

Burton, John. *An Introduction to the Hadith.* Edinburgh: Edinburgh University Press, 1994.

———. "Those Are the High-Flying Cranes." *JSS* 15 (1970): 246–64.

Busse, Heribert. "Der Islam und die biblischen Kultstätten." *Der Islam* 42 (1966): 113–43.

———. "Die ʿUmar-Moschee im östlichen Atrium der Grabeskirche." *Zeitschrift des deutschen Palästina-Vereins* 109 (1993): 73–82.

———. "Jerusalem and Mecca, the Temple and the Kaaba: An Account of Their Interrelation in Islamic Times." In *Pillars of Smoke and Fire: The Holy Land in History and Thought*, ed. Moshe Sharon, 236–46. Johannesburg: Southern Book Publishers, 1988.

———. "Jerusalem in the Story of Muḥammad's Night Journey and Ascension." *JSAI* 14 (1991): 1–40.

———. "Monotheismus und islamische Christologie in der Bauinschrift des Felsendoms in Jerusalem." *Theologische Quartalschrift* 161 (1981): 168–78.

———. "'Omar's Image as the Conqueror of Jerusalem." *JSAI* 8 (1986): 149–68.

———. "'Omar b. al-Ḥaṭṭāb in Jerusalem." *JSAI* 5 (1984): 73–119.

———. "The Sanctity of Jerusalem in Islam." *Judaism* 17 (1968): 441–68.

———. "Tempel, Grabeskirche und Ḥaram aš-šarif: Drei Heiligtümer und ihre gegenseitigen Beziehungen in Legende und Wirklichkeit." In *Jerusalemer Heiligtumstraditionen in altkirchlicher und frühislamischer Zeit*, ed. Heribert Busse and G. Kretschmar, 1–27. Wiesbaden: Harrassowitz, 1987.

Buttenwieser, Moses. *Outline of the Neo-Hebraic Apocalyptic Literature*. Cincinnati: Jennings and Pye, 1901.

Caetani, Leone. *Annali dell'Islām*. 10 vols. Milano: U. Hoepli, 1905–26.

Calder, Norman. "From Midrash to Scripture: The Sacrifice of Abraham in Early Islamic Tradition." *Le Muséon* 101 (1988): 375–402.

———. *Studies in Early Muslim Jurisprudence*. Oxford: Clarendon Press, 1993.

Cameron, Averil. "Blaming the Jews: The Seventh-Century Invasions of Palestine in Context." *Travaux et Mémoires* 14 (Mélanges Gilbert Dagron) (2002): 57–78.

———. "Byzantines and Jews: Some Recent Work on Early Byzantium." *Byzantine and Modern Greek Studies* 20 (1996): 249–74.

———. "How to Read Heresiology." In *Gender, Asceticism, and Historiography*, ed. Dale B. Martin and Patricia Cox Miller, 193–212. Durham, N.C.: Duke University Press, 2005.

Cardaillac, Denise. "La polemique anti-chrétienne du manuscrit aljamiado no. 4944 de la Bibliothèque nationale de Madrid." Ph.D. thesis, 2 vols., Université Paul Valéry Arts et lettres langues et sciences humaines, 1972.

Casanova, Paul. *Mohammed et la fin du monde: Étude critique sur l'Islam primitif.* Paris: P. Gauthier, 1911–24.

Clack, Brian R. *An Introduction to Wittgenstein's Philosophy of Religion*. Edinburgh: Edinburgh University Press, 1999.

Clark, Elizabeth A. *History, Theory, Text: Historians and the Linguistic Turn*. Cambridge, Mass.: Harvard University Press, 2004.

———. "Holy Women, Holy Words: Early Christian Women, Social History, and the 'Linguistic Turn.'" *Journal of Early Christian Studies* 6 (1998): 413–30.

Colby, Frederick S. *Narrating Muḥammad's Night Journey: Tracing the Development of the Ibn 'Abbās Ascension Discourse*. Albany: State University of New York Press, 2008.

Collins, John J. *The Apocalyptic Imagination: An Introduction to the Jewish Matrix of Christianity*. New York: Crossroad, 1984.

———., ed. *Apocalypse: The Morphology of a Genre.* Semeia 14. Missoula, Mont.: Scholars Press, 1979.

———. "Response to Session on 'Islamicate Apocalypsis: Textual, Historical, and Methodological Considerations.'" Paper presented at the annual meeting of the American Academy of Religion, San Diego, 18 November 2007.

Collins, Roger. *The Arab Conquest of Spain, 710–797.* Oxford: Basil Blackwell, 1989.

Comerro, Viviane. "La nouvelle alliance dans la sourate *al-Māʾida.*" *Arabica* 48 (2001): 285–314.

Conrad, Lawrence I. "Abraha and Muḥammad: Some Observations Apropos of Chronology and Literary *Topoi* in the Early Arabic Historical Tradition." *BSOAS* 50 (1987): 225–40.

———. "The Arabs." In *The Cambridge Ancient History,* ed. Averil Cameron, Bryan Ward-Perkins, and Michael Whitby, 678–700. Cambridge: Cambridge University Press, 2000.

———. "The Conquest of Arwad: A Source-Critical Study in the Historiography of the Early Medieval Near East." In *The Byzantine and Early Islamic Near East: Papers of the First Workshop on Late Antiquity and Early Islam,* ed. Averil Cameron and Lawrence I. Conrad, 317–401. Princeton, N.J.: Darwin Press, 1992.

———. "Heraclius in Early Islamic Kerygma." In *The Reign of Heraclius (610–641): Crisis and Confrontation,* ed. Gerrit J. Reinink and Bernard H. Stolte, 113–56. Leuven: Peeters, 2002.

———. *Muhammadanea Edessensis: The Rise of Islam in Eastern Christian Historiography under the Early ʿAbbasids.* SLAEI 12. Princeton, N.J.: Darwin Press, forthcoming.

———. "Recovering Lost Texts: Some Methodological Issues." *JAOS* 113 (1993): 258–63.

———. "Seven and the *Tasbīʿ*: On the Implications of Numerical Symbolism for the Study of Medieval Islamic History." *Journal of the Economic and Social History of the Orient* 31 (1988): 42–73.

———. "Theophanes and the Arabic Historical Tradition: Some Indications of Intercultural Transmission." *Byzantinische Forschungen* 15 (1990): 1–44.

———. "Varietas Syriaca: Secular and Scientific Culture in the Christian Communities of Syria after the Arab Conquest." In *After Bardaisan: Studies on Continuity and Change in Syriac Christianity in Honour of Professor Han J. W. Drijvers,* ed. G. J. Reinink and A. C. Klugkist, 85–105. Leuven: Uitgeverij Peeters en Departement Oosterse Studies, 1999.

Cook, David. "The Beginnings of Islam as an Apocalyptic Movement." *Journal of Millennial Studies* 1 (2001). http://www.bu.edu/mille/publications/winter2001/cook.html.

———. "Messianism and Astronomical Events during the First Four Centuries of Islam." In *Mahdisme et millénarisme en Islam,* ed. Mercedes García-Arenal, 29–52. Aix-en-Provence: Édisud, 2001.

———. "Muslim Apocalyptic and *Jihād.*" *JSAI* 20 (1996): 66–105.

———. "Muslim Materials on Comets and Meteorites." *Journal for the History of Astronomy* 30 (1999): 131–60.

———. *Studies in Muslim Apocalyptic.* SLAEI 21. Princeton, N.J.: Darwin Press, 2002.

Cook, Michael. *Commanding Right and Forbidding Wrong in Islamic Thought.* Cambridge: Cambridge University Press, 2000.

———. *Early Muslim Dogma: A Source-Critical Study.* Cambridge: Cambridge University Press, 1981.

———. "Eschatology and the Dating of Traditions." *Princeton Papers in Near Eastern Studies* 1 (1992): 25–47.

———. *The Koran: A Very Short Introduction.* Oxford: Oxford University Press, 2000.

———. *Muhammad.* Oxford: Oxford University Press, 1983.

———. "The Opponents of the Writing of Tradition in Early Islam." *Arabica* 44 (1997): 437–530.

Cooper, Kate. *The Virgin and the Bride: Idealized Womanhood in Late Antiquity.* Cambridge, Mass.: Harvard University Press, 1996.

Creswell, K. A. C. *Early Muslim Architecture.* 2nd ed. 2 vols. Vol. 1, *Umayyads, A.D. 622–750.* Oxford: Clarendon Press, 1969.

Creswell, K. A. C., and James W. Allen. *A Short Account of Early Muslim Architecture.* Rev. and enl. ed. Aldershot: Scolar, 1989.

Crone, Patricia. "How Did the Quranic Pagans Make a Living?" *BSOAS* 68 (2005): 387–99.

———. *Meccan Trade and the Rise of Islam.* Princeton, N.J.: Princeton University Press, 1987.

———. "Quraysh and the Roman Army: Making Sense of the Meccan Leather Trade." *BSOAS* 70 (2007): 63–88.

———. "The Religion of the Qurʾānic Pagans: God and the Lesser Deities." *Arabica* 57 (2010): 151–200.

———. *Roman, Provincial, and Islamic Law.* Cambridge: Cambridge University Press, 1987.

———. "Serjeant and Meccan Trade." *Arabica* 39 (1992): 216–40.

———. *Slaves on Horses: The Evolution of the Islamic Polity.* Cambridge: Cambridge University Press, 1980.

———. "Two Legal Problems Bearing on the Early History of the Qurʾān." *JSAI* 18 (1994): 1–37.

———. "What Do We Actually Know about Mohammad?" *openDemocracy, 31 August 2006.* http://www.opendemocracy.net/faith-europe_islam/mohammed_3866.jsp.

Crone, Patricia, and Michael A. Cook. *Hagarism: The Making of the Islamic World.* Cambridge: Cambridge University Press, 1977.

Crone, Patricia, and Martin Hinds, *God's Caliph: Religious Authority in the First Centuries of Islam.* University of Cambridge Oriental Publications 37. Cambridge: Cambridge University Press, 1986.

Crossan, John Dominic. *Jesus: A Revolutionary Biography.* San Francisco: HarperSanFrancisco, 1994.

———. *Who Killed Jesus?: Exposing the Roots of Anti-Semitism in the Gospel Story of the Death of Jesus.* San Francisco: HarperSanFrancisco, 1995.

Cullmann, Oscar. *Peter.* 2nd rev. and exp. ed. Philadelphia: Westminster Press, 1962.

Dagron, Gilbert, and Vincent Déroche. "Juifs et Chrétiens dans l'Orient du VIIe siècle." *Travaux et mémoires* 11 (1991): 17–273.

Daley, Brian E. *The Hope of the Early Church: A Handbook of Patristic Eschatology.* Cambridge: Cambridge University Press, 1991.

Davies, T. Witton. *Heinrich Ewald, Orientalist and Theologian 1803–1903: A Centenary Appreciation.* London: T. Fisher Unwin, 1903.

de Blois, François. "Islam in Its Arabian Context." In *The Qurʾān in Context: Historical and Literary Investigations into the Qurʾānic Milieu*, ed. Angelika Neuwirth, Nicolai Sinai, and Michael Marx, 615–24. Leiden: Brill, 2010.

———. "*Naṣrānī* (Ναζωραῖος) and *Ḥanīf* (ἐθνικός): Studies on the Religious Vocabulary of Christianity and Islam." *BSOAS* 65 (2002): 1–30.

de Prémare, Alfred-Louis. "ʿAbd al-Malik b. Marwān and the Process of the Qurʾān's Composition." In *The Hidden Origins of Islam: New Research into Its Early History*, ed. Karl-Heinz Ohlig and Gerd-R. Puin, 189–221. Amherst, N.Y.: Prometheus Books, 2010.

———. "ʿAbd al-Malik b. Marwān et le Processus de Constitution du Coran." In *Die dunklen Anfänge: Neue Forschungen zur Entstehung und frühen Geschichte des Islam*, ed. Karl-Heinz Ohlig and Gerd-R. Puin, 179–210. Berlin: Verlag Hans Schiler, 2005.

———. *Aux origines du Coran: Questions d'hier, approches d'aujourd'hui.* Paris: Téraèdre, 2004.

———. "Coran et Hadîth." In *Des Alexandries*, ed. Luce Giard and Christian Jacob, 179–95. Paris: Bibliothèque nationale de France, 2001.

———. "La constitution des écritures islamiques dans l'histoire." In *Al-Kitāb: La sacralité du texte dans le monde de l'Islam ; Actes du Symposium International tenu à Leuven et Louvain-la-Neuve du 29 mai au 1 juin 2002*, ed. D. de Smet, G. de Callatay, and J. M. F. van Reeth, 175–84. Brussels: Belgian Society of Oriental Studies, 2004.

———. *Les fondations de l'islam: Entre écriture et histoire.* Paris: Éditions du Seuil, 2002.

———. "Les textes musulmans dans leur environment." *Arabica* 47 (2000): 391–408.

———. "Mise au point de A.-L. de Prémare." *Arabica* 52 (2005): 304–6.

Déroche, François. *La transmission écrite du coran dans les débuts de l'islam: Le codex parisino-petropolitanus.* Leiden and Boston: Brill, 2009.

Déroche, Vincent. "Polémique anti-judaïque et émergence de l'Islam." *Revue des Études Byzantines* 57 (1999): 141–61.

Di Berardino, Angelo, ed. *Patrology: The Eastern Fathers from the Council of Chalcedon (451) to John of Damascus (750).* Cambridge: James Clarke and Co., 2006.

Di Segni, Leah. "Christian Epigraphy in the Holy Land: New Discoveries." *Aram* 15 (2003): 247–67.

Donner, Fred M. *The Early Islamic Conquests.* Princeton, N.J.: Princeton University Press, 1981.

———. "From Believers to Muslims: Confessional Self-Identity in the Early Islamic Community." *al-Abḥāth* 50–51 (2002): 9–53.

———. "La question du messianisme dans l'islam primitif." In *Mahdisme et millénarisme en Islam*, ed. Mercedes García-Arenal, 17–27. Aix-en-Provence: Édisud, 2001.

———. *Muhammad and the Believers: At the Origins of Islam*. Cambridge, Mass.: Harvard University Press, 2010.

———. *Narratives of Islamic Origins: The Beginnings of Islamic Historical Writing*. SLAEI 14. Princeton, N.J.: Darwin Press, 1998.

———. "The Qur'ān in Recent Scholarship: Challenges and Desiderata." In *The Qur'ān in Its Historical Context*, ed. Gabriel Said Reynolds, 29–50. London: Routledge, 2008.

———. "Quranic *Furqān*. *JSS* 52 (2007): 279–300.

———. "Review of G. R. Hawting, *The Idea of Idolatry and the Emergence of Islam: From Polemic to History*." *JAOS* 121 (2001): 336–38.

———. "The Sources of Islamic Conceptions of War." In *Just War and Jihad: Historical and Theological Perspectives on War and Peace in Western and Islamic Traditions*, ed. John Kelsay and James Turner Johnson, 31–69. New York: Greenwood Press, 1991.

Dubler, César E. "Sobre la crónica arábigo-bizantina de 741 y la influencia bizantina en la Península Ibérica." *al-Andalus* 11 (1946): 283–349.

Dunn, James D. G., and Scot McKnight. *The Historical Jesus in Recent Research*. Sources for Biblical and Theological Study 10. Winona Lake, Ind.: Eisenbrauns, 2005.

Duri, Abd al-Aziz. *The Rise of Historical Writing among the Arabs*. Trans. Lawrence I. Conrad. Princeton, N.J.: Princeton University Press, 1983.

Ehrman, Bart D., ed. *The Apostolic Fathers*. 2 vols. Loeb Classical Library 24–25. Cambridge, Mass.: Harvard University Press, 2003.

———. *Jesus: Apocalyptic Prophet of the New Millennium*. New York: Oxford University Press, 1999.

———. *Lost Christianities: The Battles for Scripture and the Faiths That We Never Knew*. New York: Oxford University Press, 2003.

———. *The Orthodox Corruption of Scripture: The Effect of Early Christological Controversies on the Text of the New Testament*. New York: Oxford University Press, 1993.

———. *Peter, Paul, and Mary Magdalene: The Followers of Jesus in History and Legend*. Oxford and New York: Oxford University Press, 2006.

El Cheikh, Nadia Maria. "Sūrat al-Rūm: A Study of the Exegetical Literature." *JAOS* 118, no. 3 (1998): 356–64.

Elad, Amikam. "ʿAbd al-Malik and the Dome of the Rock: A Further Examination of the Sources." *JSAI* 35 (2008): 167–226.

———. "The Coastal Cities of Palestine during the Early Middle Ages." *Jerusalem Cathedra* 2 (1982): 146–67.

———. *Medieval Jerusalem and Islamic Worship: Holy Places, Ceremonies, Pilgrimage*. Islamic History and Civilization: Studies and Texts 8. Leiden: Brill, 1995.

———. "The Muslim View of Jerusalem—The Qur'ān and the Ḥadīth." In *The History of Jerusalem: The Early Muslim Period, 638–1099*, ed. Joshua Prawer and Haggai Ben-Shammai, 349–85. New York: New York University Press, 1996.

———. "Pilgrims and Pilgrimage to Jerusalem during the Early Muslim Period." In *Jerusalem: Its Sanctity and Centrality to Judaism, Christianity, and Islam*, ed. Lee I. Levine, 300–314. New York: Continuum, 1999.

———. "Why Did ʿAbd al-Malik Build the Dome of the Rock?: A Re-examination of the Muslim Sources." In *Bayt al-Maqdis: ʿAbd al-Malik's Jerusalem*, ed. Julian Raby and Jeremy Johns, 33–58. Oxford: Oxford University Press, 1992.

Eliot, C. W. J. "New Evidence for the Speed of the Roman Imperial Post." *Phoenix* 9, no. 2 (1955): 76–80.

Even-Shmuel, Yehuda. *Midreshe ge'ulah*. Rev. ed. Jerusalem: Mosad Byaliḳ ʿal yede "Masadah," 1953.

Fähndrich, Hartmut. "Invariable Factors Underlying the Historical Perspective in Theodor Nöldeke's Orientalische Skizzen (1892)." In *Akten des VII. Kongressesfür Arabistik und Islamwitsenschaft*, ed. Albert Dietrich, 146–54. Göttingen: Vandenhoeck & Ruprecht, 1976.

Firestone, Reuven. "Disparity and Resolution in the Qurʾānic Teachings on War: A Reevaluation of a Tradition's Problems." *JNES* 56 (1997): 1–19.

Fleischer, Ezra. "New Light on Qiliri." *Tarbiz* 50 (1980–81): 282–302 (in Hebrew) and xv–xvi (English summary).

———. "Solving the Qiliri Riddle." *Tarbiz* 54 (1984–85): 383–427 (in Hebrew) and iv–v (English summary).

Flusin, Bernard. "L'esplanade du Temple à l'arrivée des arabes d'après deux récits byzantins." In *Bayt al-Maqdis: ʿAbd al-Malik's Jerusalem*, ed. Julian Raby and Jeremy Johns, 17–31. Oxford: Oxford University Press, 1992.

———. *Saint Anastase le Perse et l'histoire de la Palestine au début du VIIe siècle*. 2 vols. Paris: Centre national de la recherche scientifique, 1992.

Fossum, Jarl, and Phillip Munoa. *Jesus and the Gospels: An Introduction to Gospel Literature and Jesus Studies*. Belmont, Calif.: Wadsworth, 2004.

Foucault, Michel. "What Is an Author?" In *The Foucault Reader*, ed. Paul Rabinow, 101–20. New York: Pantheon, 1984.

Fredriksen, Paula. *From Jesus to Christ: The Origins of the New Testament Images of Jesus*. New Haven, Conn.: Yale University Press, 1988.

Fück, Johann. *Die arabischen Studien in Europa bis in den Anfang des 20. Jahrhunderts*. Leipzig: Harrassowitz, 1955.

Funk, Robert Walter. *The Acts of Jesus: The Search for the Authentic Deeds of Jesus*. San Francisco: HarperSanFrancisco, 1998.

Funk, Robert Walter, and Roy W. Hoover. *The Five Gospels: The Search for the Authentic Words of Jesus*. New York: Macmillan, 1993.

Gager, John G. *Kingdom and Community: The Social World of Early Christianity*. Englewood Cliffs, N.J.: Prentice-Hall, 1975.

Gallez, Édouard-Marie. *Le messie et son prophète: Aux origines de l'islam*. 2 vols. Studia Arabica 1–2. Versailles: Éditions de Paris, 2005.

Garitte, Gérard. "Histoires édifiantes géorgiennes." *Byzantion* 36 (1966): 396–423.

Gaudeul, Jean-Marie. "The Correspondence between Leo and ʿUmar: ʿUmar's Letter Re-discovered?" *Islamochristiana* 10 (1984): 109–57.

———. *La correspondance de ʿUmar et Leon (vers 900).* Rome: Pontifico Instituto di Studi Arabi e d'Islamistica, 1995.

Gero, Stephen. *Byzantine Iconoclasm during the Reign of Leo III with Particular Attention to the Oriental Sources.* CSCO 346, Subsidia 41. Louvain: Secrétariat du Corpus SCO, 1973.

Gil, Moshe. *A History of Palestine, 634–1099.* Trans. Ethel Broido. New York: Cambridge University Press, 1992.

Gilliot, Claude. "Le Coran, fruit d'un travail collectif?" In *Al-Kitāb: La sacralité du texte dans le monde de l'Islam ; Actes du Symposium International tenu à Leuven et Louvain-la-Neuve du 29 mai au 1 juin 2002*, ed. D. de Smet, G. de Callatay, and J. M. F. van Reeth, 185–223. Brussels: Belgian Society of Oriental Studies, 2004.

———. "Les 'informateurs' juifs et chrétiens de Muhammad : Reprise d'un problème traité par Aloys Sprenger et Theodor Nöldeke." *JSAI* 22 (1998): 84–126.

———. "Les traditions sur la composition ou coordination du Coran (*taʾlīf al-qurʾān*)." In *Das Prophetenḥadīṯ: Dimensionen einer islamischen Literaturgattung*, ed. C. Gilliot and T. Nagel, 14–39. Göttingen: Vandenhoeck & Ruprecht, 2005.

———. "Reconsidering the Authorship of the Qurʾān: Is the Qurʾān Partly the Fruit of a Progressive and Collective Work?" In *The Qurʾān in Its Historical Context*, ed. Gabriel Said Reynolds, 88–108. London: Routledge, 2008.

———. "Review of Christoph Luxenberg, *Die syro-aramäische Lesart des Koran.*" *Arabica* 50 (2003): 381–93.

Gillman, Ian, and Hans-Joachim Klimkeit. *Christians in Asia before 1500.* Ann Arbor: University of Michigan Press, 1999.

Gnilka, Joachim. *Die Nazarener und der Koran: Eine Spurensuche.* Freiburg: Herder, 2007.

Goitein, S. D. "The Historical Background of the Erection of the Dome of the Rock." *JAOS* 70 (1950): 104–8.

———. "The Sanctity of Jerusalem and Palestine in Early Islam." In *Studies in Islamic History and Institutions*, 135–48. Leiden: Brill, 1966.

———. "The Sanctity of Palestine in Moslem Piety." *Bulletin of the Jewish Palestine Exploration Society* 12 (1945–46): 120–26 (in Hebrew).

Goldziher, Ignác. *Muslim Studies.* Trans. C. R. Barber and S. M. Stern. Ed. S. M. Stern. 2 vols. London: Allen and Unwin, 1967–71.

Görke, Andreas. "Eschatology, History, and the Common Link: A Study in Methodology." In *Method and Theory in the Study of Islamic Origins*, ed. Herbert Berg, 179–208. Leiden: Brill, 2003.

———. "The Historical Tradition about al-Ḥudaybiya: A Study of ʿUrwa b. al-Zubayr's Account." In *The Biography of Muhammad: The Issue of the Sources*, ed. Harald Motzki, 240–75. Leiden: Brill, 2000.

Görke, Andreas, and Gregor Schoeler. *Die ältesten Berichte über das Leben Muhammads: Das Korpus ʿUrwa ibn Az-Zubair.* SLAEI 24. Princeton, N.J.: Darwin Press, 2009.

———. "Reconstructing the Earliest *Sīra* Texts: The Hiğra in the Corpus of ʿUrwa b. al-Zubayr." *Der Islam* 82 (2005): 209–20.
Gottheil, Richard. "The Beginnings of Islam." *American Journal of Semitic Languages and Litteratures* 30, no. 2 (1914): 141–45.
Grabar, Oleg. *The Shape of the Holy: Early Islamic Jerusalem*. Princeton, N.J.: Princeton University Press, 1996.
———. "The Umayyad Dome of the Rock in Jerusalem." *Ars Orientalis* 3 (1959): 33–62.
Grant, Robert M. *Jesus after the Gospels: The Christ of the Second Century*. Louisville, Ky.: Westminster/John Knox Press, 1990.
Greenwood, Tim W. "Sasanian Echoes and Apocalyptic Expectations: A Re-evaluation of the Armenian History Attributed to Sebeos." *Le Muséon* 115 (2003): 323–97.
Griffith, Sidney H. *The Church in the Shadow of the Mosque: Christians and Muslims in the World of Islam*. Princeton, N.J.: Princeton University Press, 2008.
———. "Disputing with Islam in Syriac: The Case of the Monk of Bêt Hālê and a Muslim Emir." *Hugoye: Journal of Syriac Studies* 3, no. 1 (2000). http://syrcom.cua.edu/Hugoye/Vol3No1/HV3N1Griffith.html.
———. "Jews and Muslims in Christian Syriac and Arabic Texts of the Ninth Century." *Jewish History* 3 (1988): 65–94.
———. "The Prophet Muhammad: His Scripture and His Message According to the Christian Apologies in Arabic and Syriac from the First Abbasid Century." In *La vie du Prophète Mahomet: Colloque de Strasbourg, Octobre 1980*, ed. Toufic Fahd, 99–146. Paris: Presses universitaires de France, 1983.
Grimme, Hubert. *Mohammed*. Münster: Aschendorff, 1892.
Grossman, Avraham. "Jerusalem in Jewish Apocalyptic Literature." In *The History of Jerusalem: The Early Muslim Period, 638–1099*, ed. Joshua Prawer and Haggai Ben-Shammai, 295–310. New York: New York University Press, 1996.
Guillaume, Alfred. *The Life of Muhammad*. London: Oxford University Press, 1955.
———. *New Light on the Life of Muhammad*. Journal of Semitic Studies Monograph Series1. Manchester: Manchester University Press, 1960.
Haldon, John F. *Byzantium in the Seventh Century: The Transformation of a Culture*. Rev. ed. Cambridge: Cambridge University Press, 1997.
Halevi, Leor. *Muhammad's Grave: Death Rites and the Making of Islamic Society*. New York: Columbia University Press, 2007.
Hamdan, Omar. "The Second *Maṣāḥif* Project: A Step Towards the Canonization of the Qurʾānic Text." In *The Qurʾān in Context: Historical and Literary Investigations into the Qurʾānic Milieu*, ed. Angelika Neuwirth, Nicolai Sinai, and Michael Marx, 795–835. Leiden: Brill, 2010.
Harnack, Adolf von. *Dogmengeschichte*. 4. verb. und bereicherte Aufl. ed. 4 vols. Grundriss der theologischen Wissenschaften. Tübingen: Mohr, 1905.
Harrak, Amir. *The Chronicle of Zuqnīn, Parts III and IV: A.D. 488–775*. Toronto: Pontifical Institute of Mediaeval Studies, 1999.
Harris, Horton. *The Tübingen School*. Oxford: Clarendon Press, 1975.

Hasson, Isaac. "Muslim Literature in Praise of Jerusalem: Faḍā'il al-Bayt al-Muqaddas." *Jerusalem Cathedra* 1 (1981): 168–84.

———. "The Muslim View of Jerusalem: The Qur'ān and Ḥadīth." In *The History of Jerusalem: The Early Muslim Period, 638–1099*, ed. Joshua Prawer and Haggai Ben-Shammai, 349–85. New York: New York University Press, 1996.

Hawting, Gerald R. "The Disappearance and Rediscovery of Zamzam and the 'Well of Ka'ba.'" *BSOAS* 43 (1980): 44–54.

———. *The First Dynasty of Islam: The Umayyad Caliphate AD 661–750*. 2nd ed. London: Routledge, 2000.

———. "The *Ḥajj* in the Second Civil War." In *Golden Roads: Migration, Pilgrimage, and Travel in Mediaeval and Modern Islam*, ed. Ian Richard Netton, 31–42. Richmond: Curzon, 1993.

———. *The Idea of Idolatry and the Emergence of Islam: From Polemic to History*. Cambridge: Cambridge University Press, 1999.

———. "John Wansbrough, Islam, and Monotheism." *Method and Theory in the Study of Religion* 9 (1997): 23–38.

———. "The Origins of the Muslim Sanctuary at Mecca." In *Studies on the First Century of Islamic Society*, ed. G. H. A. Juynboll, 23–47. Carbondale: Southern Illinois University Press, 1982.

———. "Review of Harald Motzki, *The Origins of Islamic Jurisprudence: Meccan Fiqh before the Classical Schools*." *BSOAS* 59 (1996): 141–43.

———. "The Role of the Qur'ān and *ḥadīth* in the Legal Controversy about the Rights of a Divorced Woman during Her 'Waiting Period' (*'idda*)." *Bulletin of the Jewish Palestine Exploration Society* 52 (1989): 430–45.

———. "The Umayyads and the Ḥijāz." *Proceedings of the Seminar for Arabian Studies* 2 (1972): 39–46.

———. "'We Were Not Ordered with Entering It but Only with Circumambulating It.' *Ḥadīth* and *Fiqh* on Entering the Ka'ba." *BSOAS* 47 (1984): 228–42.

Heidemann, Stefan. "Zwischen Theologie und Philologie: Der Paradigmenwechsel in der Jenaer Orientalistik." *Der Islam* 84 (2008): 140–84.

Herrin, Judith. *The Formation of Christendom*. Princeton, N.J.: Princeton University Press, 1987.

Higgins, Andrew. "The Lost Archive." *Wall Street Journal*, 12 January 2008.

Hinds, Martin. "'Maghāzī' and 'Sīra' in Early Islamic Scholarship." In *La vie du Prophète Mahomet: Colloque de Strasbourg, Octobre 1980*, ed. Toufic Fahd, 57–66. Paris: Presses universitaires de France, 1983.

Hirschberg, J. W. "The Sources of Moslem Tradition Concerning Jerusalem." *Rocznik Orientalistyczny* 17 (1951–52): 314–50.

Hirschfeld, Hartwig. *New Researches into the Composition and Exegesis of the Qoran*. Asiatic Monographs 3. London: Royal Asiatic Society, 1902.

Hodgson, Marshall G. S. *The Venture of Islam: Conscience and History in a World Civilization*. 3 vols. Vol. 1, *The Classical Age of Islam*. Chicago: University of Chicago Press, 1974.

Horovitz, Josef. *The Earliest Biographies of the Prophet and Their Authors*. Ed. Lawrence I. Conrad. SLAEI 11. Princeton, N.J.: Darwin Press, 2002.
Hoyland, Robert G. "The Content and Context of Early Arabic Inscriptions." *JSAI* 21 (1997): 77–102.
———. "The Correspondence of Leo III (717–41) and ʿUmar II (717–20)." *Aram* 6 (1994): 165–77.
———. "The Earliest Christian Writings on Muhammad: An Appraisal." In *The Biography of Muhammad: The Issue of the Sources*, ed. Harald Motzki, 276–97. Leiden: Brill, 2000.
———. "New Documentary Texts and the Early Islamic State." *BSOAS* 69 (2006): 395–416.
———. "Review of G. R. Hawting, *The Idea of Idolatry and the Emergence of Islam: From Polemic to History*." *Islam and Christian-Muslim Relations* 13 (2002): 236–37.
———. "Sebeos, the Jews, and the Rise of Islam." *Studies in Muslim-Jewish Relations* 2 (1995): 89–102.
———. *Seeing Islam as Others Saw It: A Survey and Evaluation of Christian, Jewish, and Zoroastrian Writings on Early Islam*. SLAEI 13. Princeton, N.J.: Darwin Press, 1997.
———. "Writing the Biography of the Prophet Muhammad: Problems and Solutions." *History Compass* 5, no. 2 (2007): 581–602.
Humphreys, R. Stephen. *Islamic History: A Framework for Inquiry*. Makers of the Muslim World. Princeton, N.J.: Princeton University Press, 1991.
———. *Muʿawiya ibn Abi Sufyan: From Arabia to Empire*. Oxford: Oneworld, 2006.
Hurgronje, C. Snouck. "De Islam." *De Gids* 2 (1886): 239–73.
———. "Der Mahdi." *Revue coloniale internationale* 1 (1886): 25–59.
———. *Mohammedanism: Lectures on Its Origin, Its Religious and Political Growth, and Its Present State*. New York and London: G. P. Putnam's Sons, 1916.
———. "Theodor Nöldeke: 2. März 1836–25. Dezember 1930." *ZDMG* 85 (1931): 238–81.
———. "Une nouvelle biographie de Mohammed." *Revue de l'histoire des religions* 15, no. 30 (1894): 48–70, 149–78.
———. *Verspreide geschriften van C. Snouck Hurgronje*. Ed. A. J. Wensinck. Bonn and Leipzig: K. Schroeder, 1923–27.
Imbert, Frédéric. "La nécropole islamique de Qasṭal al-Balqāʾ en Jordanie." *Archéologie islamique* 3 (1992–93): 17–59.
Irwin, Robert. "Oriental Discourses in Orientalism." *Middle Eastern Lectures* 3 (1999): 87–110.
Jacobs, Andrew S. "A Family Affair: Marriage, Class, and Ethics in the Apocryphal Acts of the Apostles." *Journal of Early Christian Studies* 7 (1999): 105–38.
———. *Remains of the Jews: The Holy Land and Christian Empire in Late Antiquity*. Stanford, Calif.: Stanford University Press, 2004.
Jeffery, Arthur. "Ghevond's Text of the Correspondence between ʿUmar II and Leo III." *Harvard Theological Review* 37 (1944): 269–332.
Johansen, Baber. "Politics and Scholarship: The Development of Islamic Studies in the Federal Republic of Germany." In *Middle East Studies: International Perspectives on the State of the Art*, ed. Tareq Y. Ismael, 71–130. New York: Praeger, 1990.

Johnson, David W. "Further Remarks on the Arabic History of the Patriarchs of Alexandria." *Oriens Christianus* 61 (1977): 103–16.

Jones, J. M. B. "The Chronology of the Maghāzī: A Textual Survey." *BSOAS* 19 (1957): 245–80.

———. "Ibn Isḥāq and al-Wāqidī: The Dream of ʿĀtika and the Raid to Nakhla in Relation to the Charge of Plagiarism." *BSOAS* 22 (1959): 41–51.

———. "The *Maghāzī* Literature." In *Arabic Literature to the End of the Umayyad Period*, ed. A. F. L. Beeston, T. M. Johnstone, R. B. Serjeant, and G. R. Smith, 344–51. Cambridge: Cambridge University Press, 1983.

Jones, Timothy Paul. *Misquoting Truth: A Guide to the Fallacies of Bart Ehrman's Misquoting Jesus*. Downers Grove, Ill.: InterVarsity Press, 2007.

Juynboll, G. H. A. "Early Islamic Society as Reflected in Its Use of *Isnāds*." *Le Muséon* 107 (1994): 151–94.

———. *Muslim Tradition: Studies in Chronology, Provenance, and Authorship of Early Ḥadīth*. Cambridge: Cambridge University Press, 1983.

———. "On the Origins of Arabic Prose: Reflections on Authenticity." In *Studies on the First Century of Islamic Society*, ed. G. H. A. Juynboll, 161–75. Carbondale: Southern Illinois University Press, 1982.

———. "Some *Isnād*-Analytical Methods Illustrated on the Basis of Several Woman-Demeaning Sayings from *Ḥadīth* Literature." *Qantara* 10 (1989): 343–83.

Kaegi, Walter E. *Byzantium and the Early Islamic Conquests*. Cambridge: Cambridge University Press, 1992.

Kazhdan, Alexander, ed. *The Oxford Dictionary of Byzantium*. 3 vols. New York: Oxford University Press, 1991.

Kermode, Frank. *The Genesis of Secrecy: On the Interpretation of Narrative*. Cambridge, Mass.: Harvard University Press, 1979.

Kerr, Fergus. *Theology after Wittgenstein*. 2nd ed. London: SPCK, 1997.

Kessler, C. "ʿAbd al-Malik's Inscription in the Dome of the Rock: A Reconsideration." *JRAS*, n.s., 1 (1970): 2–14.

Khoury, Raif Georges. *Wahb b. Munabbih: Der Heidelberger Papyrus PSR Heid. Arab. 23*. Codices Arabici Antiqui 1. Wiesbaden: O. Harrassowitz, 1972.

King, David A. "Al-Bazdawī on the Qibla in Early Islamic Transoxania." *Journal for the History of Arabic Science* 7 (1983): 1–38.

Kister, M. J. "'A Booth like the Booth of Moses . . .': A Study of an Early *Ḥadīth*." *BSOAS* 25 (1962): 150–55.

———. "A Comment on the Antiquity of Traditions Praising Jerusalem." *Jerusalem Cathedra* 1 (1981): 185–86.

———. "'Do Not Assimilate Yourselves . . .': *Lā tashabbahū*." *JSAI* 12 (1989): 321–71.

———. "Ḥaddithū ʿan banī isrāʾīla wa-la ḥaraja: A Study of an Early Tradition." *IOS* 2 (1972): 215–39.

———. ". . . *Illā Bi-ḥaqqihi* . . . : A Study of an Early *Ḥadīth*." *JSAI* 5 (1984): 33–52.

———. "Sanctity Joint and Divided: On Holy Places in the Islamic Tradition." *JSAI* 20 (1996): 18–65.

———. "'You Shall Only Set Out for Three Mosques': A Study of an Early Tradition." *Le Muséon* 82 (1969): 173–96.

Kloppenborg, John S. "Review of Rothschild, *Baptist Traditions and Q*." *Review of Biblical Literature* (April 2007). http://www.bookreviews.org/pdf/5524_5819.pdf.

Knauf, Ernst Axel. "Aspects of Historical Topography Relating to the Battles of Mu'tah and the Yarmouk." In *Proceedings of the Second Symposium on the History of Bilad al-Sham during the Early Islamic Period up to 40 A.H./640 A.D.: The Fourth International Conference on the History of Bilad-al-Sham*, ed. A. Bakhit, 73–78. Amman: University of Jordan, 1987.

Knight, Douglas A. "Traditio-Historical Criticism: The Development of the Covanent Code." In *Method Matters: Essays on the Interpretation of the Hebrew Bible in Honor of David L. Petersen*, ed. Joel M. LeMon and Kent Harold Richards, 97–116. Atlanta: Society of Biblical Literature, 2009.

Koch, Klaus. *The Growth of the Biblical Tradition: The Form-Critical Method.* Trans. S. M. Cupitt. New York: Scribner, 1969.

Koester, Helmut. *Ancient Christian Gospels: Their History and Development.* Philadelphia: Trinity Press International, 1990.

———. *Introduction to the New Testament.* 2nd ed. 2 vols. New York: De Gruyter, 1995.

Kohlberg, Etan. "Western Accounts of the Death of the Prophet Muḥammad." In *L'Orient dans l'histoire religieuse de l'Europe: L'invention des origines*, ed. Mohammad Ali Amir-Moezzi and John Scheid, 165–95. Turnhout: Brepols, 2000.

Koren, Judith, and Yehuda D. Nevo. "Methodological Approaches to Islamic Studies." *Der Islam* 68 (1991): 97–107.

Kümmel, Werner Georg. *Introduction to the New Testament.* Trans. Howard Clark Kee. Rev. ed. Nashville, Tenn.: Abingdon Press, 1975.

———. *The New Testament: The History of the Investigation of Its Problems.* Trans. S. McLean Gilmour and Howard C. Kee. Nashville: Abingdon Press, 1972.

Lammens, Henri. "The Age of Muhammad and the Chronology of the Sira." In *The Quest for the Historical Muhammad*, ed. Ibn Warraq, 188–217. Amherst, N.Y.: Prometheus Books, 2000.

———. "Fatima and the Daughters of Muhammad." In *The Quest for the Historical Muhammad*, ed. Ibn Warraq, 218–329. Amherst, N.Y.: Prometheus Book, 2000.

———. *Fatima et les filles de Mahomet.* Rome: Sumptibus Pontificii Instituti Biblici, 1912.

———. "The Koran and Tradition: How the Life of Muhammad Was Composed." In *The Quest for the Historical Muhammad*, ed. Ibn Warraq, 169–87. Amherst, N.Y.: Prometheus Books, 2000.

———. "L'âge de Mahomet et la chronologie de la Sîra." *Journal Asiatique*, ser. 10, 17 (1911): 209–50.

———. "Qoran et tradition: Comment fut composée la vie de Mohamet?" *Recherches de Science Religieuse* 1 (1910): 25–61.

Landau-Tasseron, Ella. "Sayf ibn 'Umar in Medieval and Modern Scholarship." *Der Islam* 67 (1990): 1–26.

Lane, Edward William, and Stanley Lane-Poole. *Arabic-English Lexicon*. New York: F. Ungar Pub. Co., 1955.

Lecker, Michael. "Biographical Notes on Ibn Shihāb al-Zuhrī." *JSS* 41 (1996): 21–63.

———. *The "Constitution of Medina": Muhammad's First Legal Document*. SLAEI 23. Princeton, N.J.: Darwin Press, 2004.

Leemhuis, Fred. "From Palm Leaves to the Internet." In *The Cambridge Companion to the Qur'ān*, ed. Jane Dammen McAuliffe, 145–60. Cambridge: Cambridge University Press, 2006.

Lester, Toby. "What Is the Koran?" *Atlantic Monthly*, January 1999, 43–55. See also http://www.theatlantic.com/issues/99jan/koran.htm.

Lévi-Strauss, Claude. *Structural Anthropology*. Trans. C. Jacobson and B. Grundfest Schoepf. Harmondsworth: Peregrine, 1977.

Levin, Christoph. "Source Criticism: The Miracle at the Sea." In *Method Matters: Essays on the Interpretation of the Hebrew Bible in Honor of David L. Petersen*, ed. Joel M. LeMon and Kent Harold Richards, 39–62. Atlanta: Society of Biblical Literature, 2009.

Levy-Rubin, Milka, ed. *The Continuatio of the Samaritan Chronicle of Abū l-Fatḥ al-Sāmirī al-Danafī*. SLAEI 10. Princeton, N.J.: Darwin Press, 2002.

Lewis, Bernard. "An Apocalyptic Vision of Islamic History." *BSOAS* 13 (1950): 308–38.

Lindbeck, George A. *The Nature of Doctrine: Religion and Theology in a Postliberal Age*. Louisville, Ky.: Westminster John Knox, 1984.

Livne-Kafri, Ofer. "Burial in the Holy Land and Jerusalem According to the Muslim Tradition." *Liber Annuus* 53 (2003): 417–25.

———. "The Early *Šīʿa* and Jerusalem." *Arabica* 48 (2001): 112–20.

———. "Jerusalem: The Navel of the Earth in Muslim Tradition." *Der Islam* 84 (2008): 46–72.

———. "Jerusalem in Early Islam: The Eschatological Aspect." *Arabica* 53 (2006): 382–403.

———. "The Muslim Traditions 'in Praise of Jerusalem' (*Faḍāʾil al-Quds*): Diversity and Complexity." *Annali dell'Instituto Orientale di Napoli* 58 (1998): 165–92.

———. "A Note on Some Traditions of *Faḍāʾil al-Quds*." *JSAI* 14 (1991): 71–83.

———. "Some Notes on the Muslim Apocalyptic Tradition." *Quaderni di Studi Arabi* 17 (1999): 71–94.

Louth, Andrew. "Did John Moschus Really Die in Constantinople?" *Journal of Theological Studies*, n.s., 49 (1998): 149–54.

Luedemann, Gerd. *Early Christianity According to the Traditions in Acts: A Commentary*. Trans. John Bowden. Minneapolis: Fortress Press, 1989.

———. *Opposition to Paul in Jewish Christianity*. Trans. M. Eugene Boring. Minneapolis: Fortress Press, 1989.

Lüling, Günter. *A Challenge to Islam for Reformation: The Rediscovery and Reliable Reconstruction of a Comprehensive Pre-Islamic Christian Hymnal Hidden in the Koran under Earliest Islamic Reinterpretations*. Rev. ed. Delhi: Motilal Banarsidass Publishers, 2003.

———. "Preconditions for the Scholarly Criticism of the Koran and Islam, with Some Autobiographical Remarks." *Journal of Higher Criticism* 3 (1996): 73–109.

———. *Über den Ur-Qur'an: Ansätze z. Rekonstruktion vorislam, christl. Strophenlieder Qur'an*. Erlangen: Lüling, 1974.

Luxenberg, Christoph. *Die syro-aramäische Lesart des Koran: Ein Beitrag zur Entschlüsselung der Koransprache*. Berlin: Das Arabische Buch, 2000.

———. "Neudeutung der arabischen Inschrift im Felsendom zu Jerusalem." In *Die dunklen Anfänge: Neue Forschungen zur Entstehung und frühen Geschichte des Islam*, ed. Karl-Heinz Ohlig and Gerd-R. Puin, 124–47. Berlin: Verlag Hans Schiler, 2005.

———. "A New Interpretation of the Arabic Inscriptions in Jerusalem's Dome of the Rock." In *The Hidden Origins of Islam: New Research into Its Early History*, ed. Karl-Heinz Ohlig and Gerd-R. Puin, 125–51. Amherst, N.Y.: Prometheus Books, 2010.

———. *The Syro-Aramaic Reading of the Koran: A Contribution to the Decoding of the Language of the Koran*. Rev. ed. Berlin: Verlag Hans Schiler, 2007.

MacDonald, Dennis Ronald. *The Legend and the Apostle: The Battle for Paul in Story and Canon*. Philadelphia: Fortress Press, 1983.

Madelung, Wilferd. "'Abd Allāh b. al-Zubayr and the Mahdi." *JNES* 40 (1981): 291–305.

———. "Review of G. R. Hawting, *The Idea of Idolatry and the Emergence of Islam: From Polemic to History*." *JRAS* 11 (2001): 271–72.

———. *The Succession to Muḥammad: A Study of the Early Caliphate*. Cambridge: Cambridge University Press, 1997.

Maghen, Ze'ev. "Davidic Motifs in the Biography of Muḥammad." *JSAI* 35 (2008): 91–139.

———. "Intertwined Triangles: Remarks on the Relationship between Two Prophetic Scandals." *JSAI* 33 (2007): 17–92.

Magness, Jodi. *The Archaeology of the Early Islamic Settlement in Palestine*. Winona Lake, Ind.: Eisenbrauns, 2003.

Malcolm, Norman. *Wittgenstein: A Religious Point of View?* Ithaca, N.Y.: Cornell University Press, 1994.

Mango, Cyril. "La culture grecque et l'Occident au VIIIe siècle." *Settimane di studio del Centro italiano di studi sull'alto medioevo* 20 (1973): 683–721.

———, ed. *Nikephoros Patriarch of Constantinople: Short History*. Dumbarton Oaks Texts 10. Washington, D.C.: Dumbarton Oaks, 1990.

Martin, Dale B. *The Corinthian Body*. New Haven, Conn.: Yale University Press, 1995.

Mattock, J. N. "History and Fiction." *Occasional Papers of the School of Abbasid Studies* 1 (1986): 80–97.

McCutcheon, Russell T. *Manufacturing Religion: The Discourse on Sui Generis Religion and the Politics of Nostalgia*. New York: Oxford University Press, 1997.

McGinn, Bernard. *The Meanings of the Millennium*. Encuentros 13. Washington, D.C.: Inter-American Development Bank Cultural Center, 1996.

McNeile, R. F. "Review of Paul Casanova, *Mohammed et la fin du monde: Étude critique sur l'Islam primitif*, 2me fasc." *Muslim World* 5, no. 1 (1915): 89.

Meier, John P. *A Marginal Jew: Rethinking the Historical Jesus*. 4 vols. Vol. 1, *The Roots of the Problem and the Person*. New York: Doubleday, 1991.

———. *A Marginal Jew: Rethinking the Historical Jesus*. 4 vols. Vol. 2, *Mentor, Message, and Miracles*. New York: Doubleday, 1994.

Melchert, Christopher. "The Early History of Islamic Law." In *Method and Theory in the Study of Islamic Origins*, ed. Herbert Berg, 293–324. Leiden: Brill, 2003.

———. *The Formation of the Sunni Schools of Law, 9th–10th Centuries C.E.* Leiden: Brill, 1997.

———. "Reply to Saleh on Hawting, *The Idea of Idolatry and the Emergence of Islam*." In H-MEM http://www.h-net.org/~midmed/, 19 February 2005. Archived at http://h-net.msu.edu/cgi-bin/logbrowse.pl?trx=lx&list=H-Mideast-Medieval&user=&pw=&month=0502.

Metzger, Bruce Manning, and Bart D. Ehrman. *The Text of the New Testament: Its Transmission, Corruption, and Restoration*. 4th ed. New York: Oxford University Press, 2005.

Milbank, John. *Theology and Social Theory: Beyond Secular Reason*. Oxford: Blackwell, 1990.

Mingana, Alphonse. "The Transmission of the Kur'ān." *Journal of the Manchester Egyptian and Oriental Society* 5 (1916): 25–47.

———. "The Transmission of the Kur'ān." *Muslim World* 7 (1917): 223–32; 402–14.

Mittwoch, Eugen. "Muhammeds Geburts- und Todestag." *Islamica* 2 (1926): 397–401.

———. *Zur Entstehungsgeschichte des islamischen Gebets und Kultus*. Abhandlungen der Preussischen Akademie der Wissenschaften. Philosophisch-historische Klasse, 1913 no. 2. Berlin: Verlag der Königl. Akademie der Wissenschaften, 1913.

Modarressi, Hussein. "Early Debates on the Integrity of the Qur'ān." *Studia Islamica* 77 (1993): 5–40.

Moffett, Samuel H. *A History of Christianity in Asia*. Vol. 1, *Beginnings to 1500*. San Francisco: HarperSanFrancisco, 1992.

Mojaddedi, Jawid A. "Taking Islam Seriously: The Legacy of John Wansbrough." *JSS* 45 (2000): 103–14.

Mommsen, Theodor, ed. *Chronica minora saec. IV. V. VI. VII.* 3 vols. Monumenta Germaniae historica, Auctores antiquissimi 9, 11, 13. Munich: Monumenta Germaniae Historica, 1892–98.

Mordtmann, A. D. "Zur Pehlevi-Münzkunde." *ZDMG* 33 (1879): 82–130.

Morony, Michael G. *Iraq after the Muslim Conquest*. Princeton, N.J.: Princeton University Press, 1984.

Motzki, Harald. "Alternative Accounts of the Qur'ān's Formation." In *The Cambridge Companion to the Qur'ān*, ed. Jane Dammen McAuliffe, 59–75. Cambridge: Cambridge University Press, 2006.

———. "The Author and His Work in the Islamic Literature of the First Centuries: The Case of ʿAbd al-Razzāq's *Muṣannaf*." *JSAI* 28 (2003): 171–201.

———. "The Collection of the Qur'ān: A Reconsideration of Western Views in Light of Recent Methodological Developments." *Der Islam* 78 (2001): 1–34.

———. "The Murder of Ibn Abī l-Ḥuqayq: On the Origin and Reliability of Some *Maghāzī* Reports." In *The Biography of Muhammad: The Issue of the Sources*, ed. Harald Motzki, 170–239. Leiden: Brill, 2000.

———. "The *Muṣannaf* of ʿAbd al-Razzāq al-Ṣanʿānī as a Source of Authentic *Aḥādīth* of the First Century A.H." *JNES* 50 (1991): 1–21.

———. "The Prophet and the Cat: On Dating Mālik's *Muwaṭṭaʾ* and Legal Traditions." *JSAI* 22 (1998): 18–83.

———. "*Quo vadis, Ḥadiṯ*-Forschung?: Eine kritische Untersuchung von G. H. A. Juynboll: 'Nāfiʿ, the *Mawlā* of Ibn ʿUmar, and His Position in Muslim *Ḥadiṯ* Literature.'" *Der Islam* 73 (1996): 40–80.

———. "*Quo vadis, Ḥadiṯ*-Forschung?: Eine kritische Untersuchung von G. H. A. Juynboll: 'Nāfiʿ, the *Mawlā* of Ibn ʿUmar, and His Position in Muslim *Ḥadiṯ* Literature,' Teil 2." *Der Islam* 73 (1996): 193–231.

Motzki, Harald, Nicolet Boekhoff-van der Voort, and Sean W. Anthony. *Analysing Muslim Traditions: Studies in Legal, Exegetical, and Maghāzī Ḥadīth.* Islamic History and Civilization 78. Leiden: Brill, 2010.

Mourad, Suleiman Ali. "The Symbolism of Jerusalem in Early Islam." In *Jerusalem: Idea and Reality*, ed. Tamar Mayer and Suleiman Ali Mourad, 86–102. New York: Routledge, 2008.

Muranyi, Miklos. "Die ersten Muslime von Mekka—soziale Basis einer neuen Religion?" *JSAI* 8 (1986): 25–35.

Murphy-O'Connor, Jerome, O.P. *The Holy Land: An Oxford Archaeological Guide from Earliest Times to 1700*. 4th ed. Oxford: Oxford University Press, 1998.

Nagel, Tilman. *Mohammed: Leben und Legende*. Munich: R. Oldenbourg Verlag, 2008.

Nautin, Pierre. "L'auteur de la 'Chronique Anonyme de Guidi': Elie de Merw." *Revue de l'histoire des religions* 199 (1982): 303–14.

Neill, Stephen, and Tom Wright. *The Interpretation of the New Testament, 1861–1986*. New ed. Oxford: Oxford University Press, 1988.

Neuwirth, Angelika. "Erste Qibla—Fernstes Masǧid?: Jerusalem im Horizont des historischen Muḥammad." In *Zion, Ort der Begegnung: Festschrift für Laurentius Klein zur Vollendung des 65. Lebensjahres*, ed. Ferdinand Hahn, Frank-Lothar Hossfeld, Hans Jorissen, and Angelika Neuwirth, 227–70. Bodenheim: Athenäum, Hahn, Hanstein, 1993.

———. "Structural, Linguistic, and Literary Features." In *The Cambridge Companion to the Qurʾān*, ed. Jane Dammen McAuliffe, 97–113. Cambridge: Cambridge University Press, 2006.

———. *Studien zur Komposition der mekkanischen Suren: Die literarische Form des Koran—ein Zeugnis seiner Historizität?* 2nd ed. Berlin: De Gruyter, 2007.

Nevo, Yehuda D. "Towards a Prehistory of Islam." *JSAI* 17 (1994): 108–41.

Nevo, Yehuda D., Zemira Cohen, and Dalia Heftman. *Ancient Arabic Inscriptions from the Negev*. New Sources for the History of the Byzantine and Early Arab Periods: The Negev, Fourth to Eighth Centuries AD, 3. Midreshet Ben-Gurion: IPS Ltd., 1993.

Nevo, Yehuda D., and Judith Koren. "The Origins of the Muslim Descriptions of the Jāhilī Meccan Sanctuary." *JNES* 49 (1990): 23–44.

Newby, Gordon D. "The *Sirah* as a Source for Arabian Jewish History: Problems and Perspectives." *JSAI* 7 (1986): 121–38.

Neyrey, Jerome H., ed. *The Social World of Luke-Acts: Models for Interpretation*. Peabody, Mass.: Hendrickson, 1991.

Nöldeke, Theodor. "Epimetrum." In *Chronica minora saec. IV. V. VI. VII*, ed. Theodor Mommsen. 3 vols. Monumenta Germaniae historica, Auctores antiquissimi 9, 11, 13, 2: 368–69. Munich: Monumenta Germaniae Historica, 1892–98.

———. *Geschichte des Qorâns*. Göttingen: Dieterichschen Buchhandlung, 1860.

———. *Das Leben Muhammed's*. Hannover: Carl Rümpler, 1863.

———. *Orientalische Skizzen*. Berlin: Paetel, 1892.

Nöldeke, Theodor, and Friedrich Schwally. *Geschichte des Qorāns*. 2nd ed. 2 vols. Leipzig: Dieterich, 1909–19.

Noth, Albrecht, and Lawrence I. Conrad. *The Early Arabic Historical Tradition: A Source Critical Study*. Trans. Michael Bonner. 2nd ed. SLAEI 3. Princeton, N.J.: Darwin Press, 1994.

O'Connor, Daniel William. *Peter in Rome: The Literary, Liturgical, and Archeological Evidence*. New York: Columbia University Press, 1969.

Olster, David M. *Roman Defeat, Christian Response, and the Literary Construction of the Jew*. Philadelphia: University of Pennsylvania Press, 1994.

Orlandi, Tito, ed. *Storia della Chiesa di Alessandria*. 2 vols. Testi et documenti per lo studio dell'antichità 17, 21. Milan: Cisalpino, 1967–70.

O'Shaughnessy, Thomas J. *Muhammad's Thoughts on Death: A Thematic Study of the Qur'anic Data*. Leiden: Brill, 1969.

Osman, Ghada. "Pre-Islamic Arab Converts to Christianity in Mecca and Medina: An Investigation into the Arabic Sources." *Muslim World* 95 (2005): 67–80.

Overman, J. Andrew. *Matthew's Gospel and Formative Judaism: The Social World of the Matthean Community*. Minneapolis: Fortress Press, 1990.

Palmer, Andrew. "The Messiah and the Mahdi: History Presented as the Writing on the Wall." In *Polyphonia Byzantina: Studies in Honour of Willem J. Aerts*, ed. Hero Hokwerda, Edmé R. Smits, and Marinus M. Woesthuis, 45–84. Groningen: Egbert Forsten, 1993.

———. *The Seventh Century in West-Syrian Chronicles*. TTH 15. Liverpool: Liverpool University Press, 1993.

Paret, Rudi. "Der Koran als Geschichtsquelle." *Der Islam* 37 (1961): 24–42.

———. *Mohammed und der Koran: Geschichte und Verkündigung des arabischen Propheten*. 9th ed. Stuttgart: W. Kohlhammer, 2005.

Parrott, Douglas M. "Gnostic and Orthodox Disciples in the Second and Third Centuries." In *Nag Hammadi, Gnosticism, and Early Christianity*, ed. Charles W. Hedrick and Robert Hodgson Jr., 193–219. Peabody, Mass.: Hendrickson Publishers, 1986.

Payne Smith, R. *Thesaurus Syriacus*. 2 vols. Oxford: Clarendon Press, 1879–1901.

Penn, Michael. "Syriac Sources for Early Christian/Muslim Relations." *Islamochristiana* 29 (2003): 59–78.

Pentz, Peter. *The Invisible Conquest: The Ontogenesis of Sixth and Seventh Century Syria.* Copenhagen: National Museum of Denmark Collection of Near Eastern and Classical Antiquities, 1992.

Perkins, Judith. *The Suffering Self: Pain and Narrative Representation in the Early Christian Era*. London: Routledge, 1995.

Peters, F. E. *Jerusalem and Mecca: The Typology of the Holy City in the Near East.* New York University Studies in Near Eastern Civilization 11. New York: New York University Press, 1986.

———. *Jesus and Muhammad: Parallel Tracks, Parallel Lives.* New York: Oxford University Press, 2011.

———. *Muhammad and the Origins of Islam.* Albany: State University of New York Press, 1994.

———. "The Quest of the Historical Muhammad." *International Journal of Middle East Studies* 23 (1991): 291–315.

Phenix, Robert R., and Cornelia B. Horn. "Review of Christoph Luxenberg, *Die syro-aramäische Lesart des Koran.*" *Hugoye: Journal of Syriac Studies* 6, no. 1 (2003). http://syrcom.cua.edu/Hugoye/Vol6No1/HV6N1PRPhenixHorn.html.

Popp, Volker. "Die frühe Islamgeschichte nach inschriftlichen und numismatischen Zeugnissen." In *Die dunklen Anfänge: Neue Forschungen zur Entstehung und frühen Geschichte des Islam*, ed. Karl-Heinz Ohlig and Gerd-R. Puin, 16–123. Berlin: Verlag Hans Schiler, 2005.

———. "The Early History of Islam, Following Inscriptional and Numismatic Testimony." In *The Hidden Origins of Islam: New Research into Its Early History*, ed. Karl-Heinz Ohlig and Gerd-R. Puin, 17–124. Amherst, N.Y.: Prometheus Books, 2010.

Porter, Stanley E. *The Criteria for Authenticity in Historical-Jesus Research: Previous Discussions and New Proposals.* Journal for the Study of the New Testament Supplement Series 191. Sheffield: Sheffield Academic Press, 2000.

Powers, David S. *Muḥammad Is Not the Father of Any of Your Men: The Making of the Last Prophet.* Philadelphia: University of Pennsylvania, 2009.

Preissler, Holger. "Die Anfänge der Deutschen Morgenländischen Gesellschaft." *ZDMG* 145 (1995): 241–327.

Pritz, Ray. *Nazarene Jewish Christianity: From the End of the New Testament Period until Its Disappearance in the Fourth Century.* Jerusalem: Magnes Press; Leiden: Brill, 1988.

Rached, Hussein, Hassan Hawary, and Gaston Wiet. *Catalogue général du Musée arabe du Caire: Stèles funéraires.* 10 vols. Cairo: Imprimerie nationale, 1932.

Rada, W. S., and F. R. Stephenson. "A Catalogue of Meteor Showers in Medieval Arab Chronicles." *Quarterly Journal of the Royal Astronomical Society* 33 (1992): 5–16.

Rahman, Fazlur. "Approaches to Islam in Religious Studies: Review Essay." In *Approaches to Islam in Religious Studies*, ed. Richard C. Martin, 189–202. Tucson: University of Arizona Press, 1985.

———. *Major Themes of the Qurʾān.* Minneapolis: Bibliotheca Islamica, 1980.

Ramadan, Tariq. *In the Footsteps of the Prophet: Lessons from the Life of Muhammad.* New York: Oxford University Press, 2007.

Ramsay, A. M. "The Speed of the Roman Imperial Post." *Journal of Roman Studies* 15 (1925): 60–74.

Raven, W. "Sīra." *EI*² 9: 660–63.

Reeves, John C. *Trajectories in Near Eastern Apocalyptic: A Postrabbinic Jewish Apocalypse Reader.* Leiden: Brill, 2006.

Reimarus, Hermann Samuel. *Von dem Zwecke Jesu und seiner Jünger: Noch ein Fragment des Wolfenbüttelschen Ungenannten [H. S. Reimarus]; Herausgegeben von G. E. Lessing.* Braunschweig, 1778.

Reinink, G. J. "The Beginnings of Syriac Apologetic Literature in Response to Islam." *Oriens Christianus* 77 (1993): 165–87.

———. *Syriac Christianity under Late Sasanian and Early Islamic Rule.* Aldershot: Ashgate/Variorum, 2005.

Renan, Ernest. "Mahomet et les origines de l'Islamisme." *Revue des deux mondes* 12 (1851): 1023–60.

———. "Muhammad and the Origins of Islam." In *The Quest for the Historical Muhammad,* ed. Ibn Warraq, 127–66. Amherst, N.Y.: Prometheus Books, 2000.

Reynolds, Gabriel Said. "Introduction: Qurʾānic Studies and Its Controversies." In *The Qurʾān in Its Historical Context,* ed. Gabriel Said Reynolds, 1–25. Routledge Studies in the Qurʾān. London: Routledge, 2008.

———, ed. *The Qurʾān in Its Historical Context.* Routledge Studies in the Qurʾān. London: Routledge, 2008.

Rippin, Andrew. *The Blackwell Companion to the Qurʾān.* Oxford: Blackwell, 2006.

———. "Literary Analysis of Qurʾān, Tafsīr, and Sīra: The Methodologies of John Wansbrough." In *Approaches to Islam in Religious Studies,* ed. Richard C. Martin, 151–63, 227–32. Tuscon: University of Arizona Press, 1985.

———. "Muḥammad in the Qurʾān: Reading Scripture in the 21st Century." In *The Biography of Muhammad: The Issue of the Sources,* ed. Harald Motzki, 298–309. Leiden: Brill, 2000.

———. "*Qurʾanic Studies,* Part IV: Some Methodological Notes." *Method and Theory in the Study of Religion* 9 (1997): 39–46.

———. "Reading the Qurʾān with Richard Bell." *JAOS* 112 (1992): 639–47.

———. "Review of G. R. Hawting, *The Idea of Idolatry and the Emergence of Islam: From Polemic to History.*" *JSS* 46 (2001): 348–51.

———. "Review of *Studien zur Komposition der mekkanischen Suren.*" *BSOAS* 45 (1982): 149–50.

———. "Studying Early *Tafsir* Texts." *Der Islam* 72 (1996): 310–23.

———. "Western Scholarship and the Qurʾān." In *The Cambridge Companion to the Qurʾān,* ed. Jane Dammen McAuliffe, 235–51. Cambridge: Cambridge University Press, 2006.

Roberts, Alexander, and James Donaldson, eds. *Ante-Nicene Christian Library*. 24 vols. Edinburgh: T. and T. Clark, 1867–78.

Robinson, Chase F. *ʿAbd al-Malik*. Makers of the Muslim World. Oxford: Oneworld, 2005.

———. "The Ideological Uses of Early Islam." *Past and Present* 203, no. 1 (2009): 205–28.

———. *Islamic Historiography*. New York: Cambridge University Press, 2002.

———. "Reconstructing Early Islam: Truth and Consequences." In *Method and Theory in the Study of Islamic Origins*, ed. Herbert Berg, 101–34. Leiden: Brill, 2003.

Robinson, Neal. *Discovering the Qur'an: A Contemporary Approach to a Veiled Text*. London: SCM Press, 1996.

Rodinson, Maxime. *Mohammed*. Trans. Anne Carter. New York: Pantheon Books, 1971.

Roggema, Barbara. *The Legend of Sergius Baḥīrā: Eastern Christian Apologetics and Apocalyptic in Response to Islam*. History of Christian-Muslim Relations 9. Leiden: Brill, 2009.

Roncaglia, M. P. "Élements Ebionites et Elkésaïtes dans le Coran." *Proche-Orient Chrétien* 21 (1971): 101–25.

Rosen-Ayalon, Myriam. *The Early Islamic Monuments of al-Ḥaram al-Sharīf: An Iconographic Study*. Qedem 28. Jerusalem: Institute of Archaeology, Hebrew University of Jerusalem, 1989.

Rothenberg, Beno. "Early Islamic Copper Smelting and Worship at Beer Orah." *Institute for Archaeo-Metallurgical Studies* 12 (1988): 1–4.

———. *Timna: Valley of the Biblical Copper Mines*. New Aspects of Antiquity. London: Thames and Hudson, 1972.

Rothschild, Clare K. *Baptist Traditions and Q*. Wissenschaftliche Untersuchungen zum Neuen Testament 190. Tübingen: Mohr Siebeck, 2005.

Rubin, Uri. "Between Arabia and the Holy Land: A Mecca-Jerusalem Axis of Sanctity." *JSAI* 34 (2008): 345–62.

———. *Between Bible and Qurʾān: The Children of Israel and the Islamic Self-image*. SLAEI 17. Princeton, N.J.: Darwin Press, 1999.

———. "The 'Constitution of Medina': Some Notes." *Studia Islamica* 62 (1985): 5–23.

———. *The Eye of the Beholder: The Life of Muhammad as Viewed by the Early Muslims; A Textual Analysis*. SLAEI 5. Princeton, N.J.: Darwin Press, 1995.

———. "The Kaʿba: Aspects of Its Ritual Functions and Position in Pre-Islamic and Early Islamic Times." *JSAI* 8 (1986): 97–131.

———, ed. *The Life of Muhammad*. The Formation of the Classical Islamic World 4. Aldershot: Ashgate, 1998.

———. "The Life of Muhammad and the Qur'an: The Case of Muhammad's Hijra." *JSAI* 28 (2003): 41–64.

———. "Muḥammad's Message in Mecca: Warnings, Signs, and Miracles." In *The Cambridge Companion to Muḥammad*, ed. Jonathan E. Brockopp, 39–60. Cambridge: Cambridge University Press, 2010.

———. "Muḥammad's Night Journey (*isrāʾ*) to al-Masjid al-Aqṣā: Aspects of the Earliest Origins of the Islamic Sanctity of Jerusalem." *Al-Qanṭara* 29, no. 1 (2008): 147–64.

———. "On the Arabian Origins of the Qur'ān: The Case of *al-Furqān*." *JSS* 54 (2009): 421–33.

Rüling, Josef Bernhard. *Beiträge zur Eschatologie des Islam*. Leipzig: G. Kreysing, 1895.

Safi, Omid. *Memories of Muhammad: Why the Prophet Matters*. New York: HarperCollins, 2009.

Sahas, Daniel J. *John of Damascus on Islam: The "Heresy of the Ishmaelites."* Leiden: Brill, 1972.

Said, Edward W. *Orientalism*. New York: Pantheon Books, 1978.

Saldarini, Anthony J. "'Form Criticism' of Rabbinic Literature." *Journal of Biblical Literature* 96 (1977): 257–74.

———. *Matthew's Christian-Jewish Community*. Chicago: University of Chicago Press, 1994.

Saleh, Walid. "Review of G. R. Hawting, *The Idea of Idolatry and the Emergence of Islam: From Polemic to History*." *H-Mideast-Medieval, H-Net Reviews*, February 2005. http://www.h-net.org/reviews/showrev.php?id=10211.

al-Samuk, Sadun Mahmud. "Die historischen Überlieferungen nach Ibn Ishaq: Eine synoptische Überlieferung." Ph.D. diss., Johann Wolgang Goethe Universität, Frankfurt, 1978.

Sanders, E. P. *The Historical Figure of Jesus*. London: Allen Lane, 1993.

———. *Jesus and Judaism*. Philadelphia: Fortress Press, 1985.

Sauvaget, Jean. *La Mosquée omeyyade de Médine: Étude sur les origines architecturales de la mosquée et de la basilique*. Paris: Vanoest, 1947.

Schacht, Joseph. "On Mūsā b. ʿUqba's *Kitāb al-Maghāzī*." *Acta Orientalia* 21 (1953): 288–300.

———. *The Origins of Muhammadan Jurisprudence*. Oxford: Clarendon Press, 1950.

———. "A Revaluation of Islamic Traditions." *JRAS* 49 (1949): 143–54.

Schick, Robert. *The Christian Communities of Palestine from Byzantine to Islamic Rule: A Historical and Archaeological Study*. SLAEI 2. Princeton, N.J.: Darwin Press, 1995.

Schimmel, Annemarie. *And Muhammad Is His Messanger: The Veneration of the Prophet in Islamic Piety*. Chapel Hill: University of North Carolina Press, 1985.

Schneemelcher, Wilhelm, ed. *New Testament Apocrypha*. Trans. R. McL. Wilson. Rev. ed. 2 vols. Louisville, Ky.: Westminster/John Knox Press, 1991–92.

Schneider, Irene. "Narrativität und Authentizität: Die Geschichte vom weisen Propheten, dem dreisten Dieb und dem koranfesten Gläubiger." *Der Islam* 77 (2000): 84–115.

Schoedel, William R. "Papias." *Aufsteig und Niedergang der römischen Welt* II.27.1 (1993): 235–70.

Schoeler, Gregor. "Character and Authenticity of the Muslim Tradition on the Life of Muhammad." *Arabica* 48 (2002): 360–66.

———. *Charakter und Authentie der muslimischen Überlieferung über das Leben Mohammeds*. Studien zur Sprache, Geschichte und Kultur des islamischen Orients 14. Berlin: De Gruyter, 1996.

———. "The Codification of the Qur'an: A Comment on the Hypotheses of Burton and Wansbrough." In *The Qur'ān in Context: Historical and Literary Investigations into the Qur'ānic Milieu*, ed. Angelika Neuwirth, Nicolai Sinai, and Michael Marx, 779–94. Leiden: Brill, 2010.

———. "Die Frage der schriftlichen oder mündlichen Überlieferung der Wissenschaften im frühen Islam." *Der Islam* 62 (1985): 201–30.

———. "Foundations for a New Biography of Muḥammad: The Production and Evaluation of the Corpus of Traditions from ʿUrwa b. al-Zubayr." In *Method and Theory in the Study of Islamic Origins*, ed. Herbert Berg, 19–28. Leiden: Brill, 2003.

———. "Mündliche Thora und *Ḥadīṯ*: Überlieferung, Schreibverbot, Redaktion." *Der Islam* 66 (1989): 213–51.

———. "Mūsā b. ʿUqbas *Maghāzī*." In *The Biography of Muhammad: The Issue of the Sources*, ed. Harald Motzki, 67–97. Leiden: Brill, 2000.

———. *The Oral and the Written in Early Islam*. Trans. Uwe Vagelpohl. Ed. James E. Montgomery. Routledge Studies in Middle Eastern Literatures 13. London: Routledge, 2006.

———. "Schreiben und Veröffentlichen: Zu Verwendung und Funktion der Schrift in den ersten islamischen Jahrhunderten." *Der Islam* 69 (1992): 1–43.

———. "Wieteres zur Frage der schriftlichen oder mündlichen Überlieferung der Wissenschaften im Islam." *Der Islam* 66 (1989): 28–67.

Schoeps, Hans Joachim. *Theologie und Geschichte des Judenchristentums*. Tübingen: Mohr, 1949.

Schreike, B. "Isrāʾ." *EI*[1] 2: 553–54.

Schreike, B., [and J. Horovitz]. "Miʿrādj." *EI*[2] 7: 97–100.

Schweitzer, Albert. *The Quest of the Historical Jesus: A Critical Study of Its Progress from Reimarus to Wrede*. Trans. W. Montgomery. London: Adam and Charles Black, 1910.

———. *Von Reimarus zu Wrede: Eine Geschichte der Leben-Jesu-Forschung*. Tübingen: J. C. B. Mohr, 1906.

Sellheim, Rudolf. "Prophet, Chalif und Geschichte: Die Muhammed-Biographie des Ibn Isḥāq." *Oriens* 18–19 (1967): 32–91.

Serjeant, R. B. "Review of John Wansbrough, *Quranic Studies: Sources and Methods of Scriptural Interpretation* and Patricia Crone and Michael Cook, *Hagarism: The Making of the Islamic World*." *JRAS* (1978): 76–79.

———. "The *Sunnah, Jāmiʿah*, Pacts with the Yathrib Jews, and the *Taḥarīm* of Yathrib: Analysis and Translation of the Documents Comprised in the So-called 'Constitution of Medina.'" *BSOAS* 41 (1978): 1–42.

Seybold, Christian Friedrich, ed. *Severus ibn al Muqaffaʿ: Alexandrinische Patriarchengeschichte von S. Marcus bis Michael I, 61–767*. Veröffentlichungen aus der Hamburger Staatsbibliothek 3. Hamburg: L. Gräfe, 1912.

Sezgin, Fuat. *Geschichte des arabischen Schriftums*. 9 vols. Leiden: Brill, 1967–.

Sharon, Moshe. "The Birth of Islam in the Holy Land." In *Pillars of Smoke and Fire: The Holy Land in History and Thought*, ed. Moshe Sharon, 225–35. Johannesburg: Southern Book Publishers, 1988.

———. "Praises of Jerusalem as a Source for the Early History of Islam." *Bibliotheca orientalis* 49 (1992): 55–67.

———. "The Umayyads as *Ahl al-Bayt*." *JSAI* 14 (1991): 115–52.

Sharon, Moshe, Uzi Avner, and Dov Nahlieli. "An Early Islamic Mosque Near Beʾer Ora in the Southern Negev: Possible Evidence for an Early Eastern *Qiblah*?" *ʿAtiqot* 30 (1996): 107–14.

Shoemaker, Stephen J. *Ancient Traditions of the Virgin Mary's Dormition and Assumption*. Oxford: Oxford University Press, 2002.

———. "Christmas in the Qurʾān: The Qurʾānic Account of Jesus' Nativity and Palestinian Local Tradition." *JSAI* 28 (2003): 11–39.

———. "In Search of ʿUrwa's *Sīra*: Some Methodological Issues in the Quest for 'Authenticity' in the Life of Muḥammad." *Der Islam* 85, no. 2 (2011): 257–344.

———. "'Let Us Go and Burn Her Body': The Image of the Jews in the Early Dormition Traditions." *Church History* 68, no. 4 (1999): 775–823.

———. "Muḥammad and the Qurʾān." In *The Oxford Handbook of Late Antiquity*, ed. Scott F. Johnson, forthcoming. New York: Oxford University Press, 2011.

Ṣiddīqī, Muḥammad Zubayr. *Ḥadīth Literature: Its Origin, Development, and Special Features*. Ed. Abdal Hakim Murad. Cambridge: Islamic Texts Society, 1993.

Silvestre de Sacy, Antoine-Isaac. "Taberistanensis, id est Abu Dscaferi Mohammed ben Dsherir Ettaberi annales regum atque legatorum Dei." *Journal des Savans* (1832): 532–44.

Sinai, Nicolai. "The Qurʾān as Process." In *The Qurʾān in Context: Historical and Literary Investigations into the Qurʾānic Milieu*, ed. Angelika Neuwirth, Nicolai Sinai, and Michael Marx, 407–39. Leiden: Brill, 2010.

Sinai, Nicolai, and Angelika Neuwirth. "Introduction." In *The Qurʾān in Context: Historical and Literary Investigations into the Qurʾānic Milieu*, ed. Angelika Neuwirth, Nicolai Sinai, and Michael Marx, 1–24. Leiden: Brill, 2010.

Sivan, Emanuel. "The Beginnings of the *Faḍāʾil al-Quds* Literature." *IOS* 1 (1971): 263–72.

Sizgorich, Thomas. "'Do Prophets Come with a Sword?' Conquest, Empire, and Historical Narrative in the Early Islamic World." *American Historical Review* 112, no. 4 (2007): 993–1015.

———. "Narrative and Community in Islamic Late Antiquity." *Past and Present* 185 (November 2004): 9–42.

———. *Violence and Belief in Late Antiquity: Militant Devotion in Christianity and Islam*. Philadelphia: University of Pennsylvania Press, 2009.

Smith, Jane I. "Eschatology." In *Encyclopaedia of the Qurʾān*, ed. Jane Dammen McAuliffe, 44–54. Leiden: Brill, 2002.

Smith, Terence V. *Petrine Controversies in Early Christianity: Attitudes towards Peter in Christian Writings of the First Two Centuries*. Tübingen: J. C. B. Mohr, 1985.

Soucek, Priscilla. "The Temple of Solomon in Islamic Legend and Art." In *The Temple of Solomon*, ed. J. Guttman, 73–123, 184–93. Missoula, Mont.: Scholars Press, 1976.

Sourdel, Dominique. "Un pamphlet musulman anonyme d'époque ʿabbaside contre les chrétiens." *Revue des études islamiques* 34 (1966): 1–34.

Speight, R. Marston. "The Will of Saʿd b. a. Waqqāṣ: The Growth of a Tradition." *Der Islam* 50 (1973): 249–67.

Sprenger, Aloys. *Das Leben und die Lehre des Moḥammad*. 2nd ed. 3 vols. Berlin: Nicolai, 1869.

Spuler, Bertold. "La 'Sira' du Prophète Mahomet et les conquêtes des arabes dans le Proche-Orient d'après les sources syriaques." In *La vie du Prophète Mahomet: Colloque de Strasbourg, Octobre 1980*, ed. Toufic Fahd, 87–97. Paris: Presses universitaires de France, 1983.

Steinschneider, Moritz. "Apocalypsen mit polemischer Tendenz." *ZDMG* 28 (1874): 627–59.

Stemberger, Günter. "Jerusalem in the Early Seventh Century: Hopes and Aspirations of Christians and Jews." In *Jerusalem: Its Sanctity and Centrality to Judaism, Christianity, and Islam*, ed. Lee I. Levine, 260–72. New York: Continuum, 1999.

Stewart, Devin J. "Notes on Medieval and Modern Emendations of the Qurʾān." In *The Qurʾān in Its Historical Context*, ed. Gabriel Said Reynolds, 225–48. London: Routledge, 2008.

Stover, Dale. "Orientalism and the Otherness of Islam." *Studies in Religion / Sciences Religieuse* 17 (1988): 27–40.

Suermann, Harald. "Early Islam in the Light of Christian and Jewish Sources." In *The Qurʾān in Context: Historical and Literary Investigations into the Qurʾānic Milieu*, ed. Angelika Neuwirth, Nicolai Sinai, and Michael Marx, 135–45. Leiden: Brill, 2010.

Sweeney, Marvin A. "Form Criticism: The Question of the Endangered Matriarchs in Genesis." In *Method Matters: Essays on the Interpretation of the Hebrew Bible in Honor of David L. Petersen*, ed. Joel M. LeMon and Kent Harold Richards, 17–38. Atlanta: Society of Biblical Literature, 2009.

Szilágyi, Krisztina. "The Incorruptible and Fragrant Corpse: Muhammad's Body and Christian Hagiography." Paper presented at the Dorushe conference, Yale University, 29 March 2009. See the online abstract at http://www.yale.edu/judaicstudies/syriac_downloads/K.Szilagyi.pdf, accessed on 25 July 2009.

———. "Muḥammad and the Monk: The Making of the Christian Baḥīrā Legend." *JSAI* 34 (2008): 169–214.

Tajra, H. W. *The Martyrdom of St. Paul: Historical and Judicial Context, Traditions, and Legends*. Tübingen: J. C. B. Mohr, 1994.

Tatum, Gregory. *New Chapters in the Life of Paul: The Relative Chronology of His Career*. Washington, D.C.: Catholic Biblical Association of America, 2006.

Taylor, Joan E. *Christians and the Holy Places: The Myth of Jewish-Christian Origins*. Oxford: Clarendon Press, 1993.

Theissen, Gerd. *The Social Setting of Pauline Christianity: Essays on Corinth*. Trans. John H. Schütz. Philadelphia: Fortress Press, 1982.

———. *Studien zur Soziologie des Urchristentums*. Tübingen: Mohr, 1979.

Theissen, Gerd, and Annette Merz. *The Historical Jesus: A Comprehensive Guide.* Minneapolis: Fortress Press, 1996.

Theissen, Gerd, and Dagmar Winter. *The Quest for the Plausible Jesus: The Question of Criteria.* Louisville, Ky.: Westminster/John Knox Press, 2002.

Thomas, Christine M. *The Acts of Peter, Gospel Literature, and the Ancient Novel: Rewriting the Past.* Oxford: Oxford University Press, 2003.

Thomas, David, and Barbara Roggema, eds. *Christian Muslim Relations: A Bibliographical History.* History of Christian-Muslim Relations 11. Leiden: Brill, 2009.

Thomson, Robert W. "Muhammad and the Origin of Islam in Armenian Literary Tradition." In *Armenian Studies/Études arméniennes in Memoriam Haïg Berbérian*, ed. Dickran Kouymjian, 829–58. Lisbon: Calouste Gulbenkian Foundation, 1986.

Thomson, Robert W., and James Howard-Johnston. *The Armenian History Attributed to Sebeos.* 2 vols. TTH 31. Liverpool: Liverpool University Press, 1999.

van Bekkum, Wout Jac. "Jewish Messianic Expectations in the Age of Heraclius." In *The Reign of Heraclius (610–41): Crisis and Confrontation*, ed. Gerrit J. Reinink and Bernard H. Stolte, 95–112. Leuven: Peeters, 2002.

van der Velden, Frank. "Relations between Jews, Syriac Christians, and Early Muslim Believers in Seventh-Century Iraq." *Al-ʿUsur al-Wusta: The Bulletin of Middle East Medievalists* 19, no. 2 (2007): 27–33, 42.

van Ess, Josef. "ʿAbd al-Malik and the Dome of the Rock: An Analysis of Some Texts." In *Bayt al-Maqdis: ʿAbd al-Malik's Jerusalem*, ed. Julian Raby and Jeremy Johns, 89–104. Oxford: Oxford University Press, 1995.

———. "Sūrat a-Najm and Its Relationship with Muḥammad's *Miʿrāj*." *Journal of Qur'anic Studies* 1 (1999): 47–62.

van Reeth, Jan M. F. "Le vignoble du paradis et le chemin qui y mène: La thèse de C. Luxenberg et les sources du coran." *Arabica* 52 (2006): 511–24.

van Sivers, Peter. "The Islamic Origins Debate Goes Public." *History Compass* 1 (2003): ME 058, 1–14.

Versteegh, C. H. M. *Arabic Grammar and Quranic Exegesis in Early Islam.* Leiden: Brill, 1993.

Vilmar, Eduardus, ed. *Abulfathi Annales Samaritani.* Gothae: F. A. Perthes, 1865.

Walmsley, Alan. *Early Islamic Syria: An Archaeological Assessment.* London: Duckworth, 2007.

Wansbrough, John E. *Quranic Studies: Sources and Methods of Scriptural Interpretation.* London Oriental Series 31. Oxford: Oxford University Press, 1977.

———. *Res ipsa loquitur: History and Mimesis.* Jerusalem: Israel Academy of Sciences and Humanities, 1987.

———. "Review of Patricia Crone and Michael Cook, *Hagarism: The Making of the Islamic World.*" *BSOAS* 41 (1978): 155–56.

———. *The Sectarian Milieu: Content and Composition of Islamic Salvation History.* London Oriental Series 34. Oxford: Oxford University Press, 1978.

Wansbrough, John E., and G. R. Hawting. *The Sectarian Milieu: Content and Composition of Islamic Salvation History.* Amherst, N.Y.: Prometheus Books, 2006.

Wansbrough, John E., and Andrew Rippin. *Quranic Studies: Sources and Methods of Scriptural Interpretation*. Amherst, N.Y.: Prometheus Books, 2004.
Wasserstrom, Steven M. *Between Muslim and Jew: The Problem of Symbiosis under Early Islam*. Princeton, N.J.: Princeton University Press, 1995.
Watt, W. Montgomery. "The Dating of the Qur'ān: A Review of Richard Bell's Theories." *JRAS* (April 1957): 46–56.
———. *Islam and the Integration of Society*. London: Routledge and Paul, 1961.
———. *Muhammad: Prophet and Statesman*. London: Oxford University Press, 1961.
———. *Muhammad at Mecca*. Oxford: Clarendon Press, 1953.
———. *Muhammad at Medina*. Oxford: Clarendon Press, 1956.
———. "The Reliability of Ibn Isḥāq's Sources." In *La vie du Prophète Mahomet: Colloque de Strasbourg, Octobre 1980*, ed. Toufic Fahd, 31–43. Paris: Presses universitaires de France, 1983.
Weil, Gustav. *Geschichte der Chalifen*. 5 vols. Mannheim: F. Bassermann, 1846–51.
———. *Historisch-kritische Einleitung in den Koran*. Bielefeld: Velhagen & Klasing, 1844.
———. *Mohammed der Prophet, sein Leben und seine Lehre: Aus handschriftlichen Quellen und dem Koran geschöpft und dargestellt*. Stuttgart: J. B. Metzler'schen Buchhandlung, 1843.
Weiss, Johannes. *Die Predigt Jesu vom Reiche Gottes*. Göttingen: Vandenhoeck & Ruprecht, 1892.
Welch, A. T. "Al-Ḳur'ān." *EI*[2] 5: 400–429.
———. "Muḥammad's Understanding of Himself: The Qur'ānic Data." In *Islam's Understanding of Itself*, ed. Richard G. Hovannisian and Speros Veronis Jr., 15–52. Malibu, Calif.: Undena, 1983.
———. "Qur'ānic Studies—Problems and Prospects." *Journal of the American Academy of Religion* 47 (1980): 620–34.
———. "Review of *Studien zur Komposition der mekkanischen Suren*." *JAOS* 103 (1983): 764–67.
Wellhausen, Julius. *The Arab Kingdom and Its Fall*. Trans. Margaret Graham Weir. Calcutta: University of Calcutta, 1927.
———. "Muhammads Gemeindeordnung von Medina." In *Skizzen und Vorarbeiten*. 6 vols., 4: 65–83. Berlin: G. Reimer, 1889.
———. *Muhammed in Medina: Das ist Vakidi's Kitab al-Maghazi, in verkürzter deutscher Wiedergabe*. Berlin: G. Reimer, 1882.
———. "Prolegomena zur ältesten Geschichte des Islams." In *Skizzen und Vorarbeiten*. 6 vols., 6: 1–160. Berlin: G. Reimer, 1899.
Wensinck, A. J., ed. *Concordance et indices de la tradition musulmane: Les six livres, le Musnad d'al-Dārimī, le Muwatta' de Mālik, le Musnad de Ahmad ibn Hanbal*. 8 vols. Leiden: Brill, 1936–88.
———. *The Ideas of the Western Semites Concerning the Navel of the Earth*. Afdeeling Letterkunde. Nieuwe reeks, deel 17 no. 1. Amsterdam: J. Müller, 1916.

———. *Muhammad and the Jews of Medina*. Freiburg im Breisgau: K. Schwarz, 1975.

———. *The Muslim Creed: Its Genesis and Historical Development*. Cambridge: The University Press, 1932.

Wensinck, A. J., [and D. Gimaret]. "Shafāʿa." *EI*² 9: 177–79.

Wheatley, Paul. *The Places Where Men Pray Together: Cities in Islamic Lands, Seventh through the Tenth Centuries*. Chicago: University of Chicago Press, 2001.

Whelan, Estelle. "Forgotten Witness: Evidence for the Early Codification of the Qurʾān." *JAOS* 118 (1998): 1–14.

White, Hayden V. *Metahistory: The Historical Imagination in Nineteenth-Century Europe*. Baltimore: Johns Hopkins University Press, 1973.

Wolf, Kenneth B. *Conquerors and Chroniclers of Early Medieval Spain*. TTH 9. Liverpool: Liverpool University Press, 1990.

———. "The Earliest Latin Lives of Muḥammad." In *Conversion and Continuity: Indigenous Christian Communities in Islamic Lands, Eighth to Eighteenth Centuries*, ed. Michael Gervers and Ramzi Jibran Bikhazi, 89–101. Toronto: Pontifical Institute of Mediaeval Studies, 1990.

Wright, William. *A Short History of Syriac Literature*. London: Adam and Charles Black, 1894.

Yahalom, Joseph. "The Temple and the City in Liturgical Hebrew Poetry." In *The History of Jerusalem: The Early Muslim Period, 638–1099*, ed. Joshua Prawer and Haggai Ben-Shammai, 270–94. New York: New York University Press, 1996.

Z. [*sic*] "Review of Paul Casanova, *Mohammed et la fin du monde: Étude critique sur l'Islam primitif*." *Muslim World* 2, no. 3 (1912): 323–24.

Zaman, Muhammad Qasim. "*Maghāzī* and the *Muḥaddithūn*: Reconsidering the Treatment of 'Historical' Materials in Early Collections of Hadith." *International Journal of Middle Eastern Studies* 28 (1996): 1–18.

Zeitlin, Irving M. *The Historical Muhammad*. Cambridge: Polity Press, 2007.

Zwierlein, Otto. *Petrus in Rom: Die literarischen Zeugnisse; Mit einer kritischen Edition der Martyrien des Petrus und Paulus auf neuer handschriftlicher Grundlage*. Untersuchungen zur antiken Literatur und Geschichte 96. Berlin: De Gruyter, 2009.

INDEX

ACKNOWLEDGMENTS

The seeds of this study were sown many years ago largely through conversations that I had with John Lamoreaux concerning differences in the study of early Christianity and early Islam. It was in this context that John first introduced me to the astonishing conclusions of *Hagarism*, and from the very beginning John has been an important dialogue partner as the ideas for this study developed, answering numerous questions and providing helpful advice along the way. Although it was initially my intent to write just a brief article on the divergences regarding the end of Muhammad's life in Islamic and non-Islamic sources, the original manuscript quickly grew well beyond any reasonable size for an article. At this stage John and a number of others, including Averil Cameron, Patricia Crone, Stephen Gerö, Michael Penn, and Larry Conrad, read through the manuscript and offered comments on what was good, what not so good, and how I might advance the work further. Although each of these early readers will no doubt find much in this book that they continue to disagree with, their advice was essential for developing the project.

I also thank Elizabeth Clark, Robert Gregg, Lucas von Rompay, David Brakke, Gerald Hawting, Sidney Griffith, Annette Reed, Michael Pregill, Rina Avner, Benjamin Wold, Timothy Sailors, Ronald Heine, Scott Johnson, Andrew Jacobs, Stephen Davis, and Bert Harrill in particular for their help, advice, and criticism on specific points. I especially thank David Powers for generously sharing important chapters from his recent book, *Muḥammad Is Not the Father of Any of Your Men*, prior to its publication. Likewise, I would add thanks to my colleagues in Medieval Studies at the University of Oregon, many of whom offered helpful feedback and advice in response to a "work in progress" talk. I also thank my colleague Deborah Green, especially for her occasional assistance with Hebrew, as well as Daniel Falk, Judith Baskin, Rick Colby, and David Hollenberg for answering a variety of questions and offering helpful suggestions and encouragement. Portions of this study were presented in lectures at the Society of Biblical Literature, the North American Patristics Society, Duke University, and the University of Minnesota, and I thank those in attendance for their helpful comments and questions.

I would especially like to thank the National Endowment for the Humanities for supporting the initial work on this study through a Summer Research Award in 2004, and the John Simon Guggenheim Memorial Foundation, the American Council of Learned Societies, and the Alexander von Humboldt Foundation for their financial support of this project through research fellowships during the years 2006–8. In conjunction with the von Humboldt fellowship, I would additionally thank the Orientalisches Seminar at the Eberhard Karls Universität Tübingen and Stephen Gerö for serving as my hosts in 2006–7.

I am most grateful to the editors of the Divinations series at the University of Pennsylvania Press, Daniel Boyarin, Virginia Burrus, and especially Derek Krueger, as well as to Jerry Singerman, both for their interest in this book and for their support and encouragement through the publishing process. Thanks as well to Caroline Winschel, Erica Ginsburg, and Sandra Haviland at Penn Press for their help in shepherding this manuscript through to publication. I also express my appreciation to those who served as anonymous readers for their often helpful comments on the manuscript.

My greatest debt, however, is to Melissa, who continued to believe in this project even at times when I myself began to doubt. For her friendship and love, support and encouragement, kindness and humor, and patience and understanding I am profoundly grateful. I dedicate this book to her.

Lightning Source UK Ltd.
Milton Keynes UK
UKHW040941280619
345201UK00007B/301/P

9 780812 243567